DATA STRUCTURES & OTHER OBJECTS

Using C++

THIRD EDITION

MICHAEL MAIN
Department of Computer Science
University of Colorado at Boulder

WALTER SAVITCH
Department of Computer Science
and Engineering
University of California, San Diego

D0144753

PEARSON
Addison
Wesley

Boston   San Francisco   New York
London   Toronto   Sydney   Tokyo   Singapore   Madrid
Mexico City   Munich   Paris   Cape Town   Hong Kong   Montreal

Senior Acquisitions Editor:	Michael Hirsch	Cover Designer:	Joyce Cosentino Wells
Editorial Assistant:	Maria Campo	Cover Artwork:	© 2004 Noel Griffin
Production Supervisor:	Marilyn Lloyd	Project Management:	Argosy Publishing, Inc.
Marketing Manager:	Michelle Brown	Project Manager:	Daniel Rausch
		Prepress and Manufacturing:	Caroline Fell

Access the latest information about all Addison-Wesley titles from our World Wide Web site:
`http://www.aw-bc.com/computing`

Many of the designations used by manufacturers and sellers to distinguish their products are claimed as trademarks. Where those designations appear in this book, and Addison-Wesley was aware of a trademark claim, the designations have been printed in initial caps or all caps.

The programs and the applications presented in this book have been included for their instructional value. They have been tested with care but are not guaranteed for any particular purpose. The publisher does not offer any warranties or representations, nor does it accept any liabilities with respect to the programs or applications.

UNIX® is a registered trademark in the United States and other countries, licensed exclusively through X-Open Company, Ltd. Pez® is a registered trademark of Pez Candy, Inc.

Library of Congress Cataloging-in-Publication Data
Main, M. (Michael), 1956–
    Data structures and other objects using C++ / Michael Main, Walter Savitch.-- 3rd ed.
      p. cm.
    Includes index.
    ISBN 0-321-19716-X
    1. C++ (Computer program language) 2. Data structures (Computer science) 3. Object-oriented programming (Computer science) I. Savitch, Walter J., 1943– II. Title.

QA76.73.C153M25 2004
005.13'3—dc22

                          2004018616
                          CIP

ISBN 0-321-19716-X
1 2 3 4 5 6 7 8 9 10-PH-08 07 06 07 04

Preface

This book is written for a second course in computer science, the CS 2 course at many universities. The text's emphasis is on the *specification*, *design*, *implementation*, and *use* of the basic data types that normally are covered in a second-semester course. In addition, we cover a range of important programming techniques and provide self-contained coverage of abstraction techniques, object-oriented programming, big-O time analysis of algorithms, and sorting.

We assume that the student has already had an introductory computer science and programming class, but we do include coverage of those topics (such as recursion and pointers) that are not always covered completely in a first course. The text uses C++, but our coverage of C++ classes begins from scratch, so the text may be used by students whose introduction to programming was in C rather than C++. In our experience, such students need a brief coverage of C++ input and output techniques (such as those provided in Appendix F), and some coverage of C++ parameter types (which we provide in Chapter 2). When C programmers are over the input/output hurdle and the parameter hurdle (and perhaps a small "fear" hurdle), they can step readily into classes and other object-oriented features of C++. As this indicates, there are several pathways through the text that can be tailored to different backgrounds, including some optional features for the student who comes to the class with a stronger than usual background.

Third Edition: New Material and Additional Web Support

This third edition presents the same sequence of steps for each data type and the same outline of topics as the first edition. Instructors that are already using the earlier edition can continue to teach the course with only a few changes that are motivated by an increasing role of the C++ Standard Template Library container classes. In particular:

- New coverage of **exception handling** in Chapter 1 and Appendix L
- Expanded coverage of correct usage of **const pointers** in Chapter 5
- Expanded coverage of **STL iterators, sets,** and **multisets** in Chapter 6
- New **recursion examples** in Chapter 9
- A new project on **using vectors to implement a hash table** in Chapter 12. In addition, other projects, such as the **B-tree**, can be successfully implemented **using STL containers as the underlying data structure**.
- Expanded coverage of the **list, map,** and **multimap classes** in Chapter 12 and Appendix H

In our course, we continue to emphasize that students must understand data structures at all levels: specification, design, implementation, testing, analysis. However, in the long run, students who continue in computer science will make extensive use of the data types of the Standard Template Library (the "STL," specified as part of the 1998 Standard). We've found it particularly encouraging that with a small amount of coverage of the STL classes, students can successfully implement difficult data structures such as the B-tree.

Throughout the book, you'll also find:

- **Many new self-test exercises**
- **New programming projects**

Also keep an eye on our project web site *www.cs.colorado.edu/~main/dsoc.html* for new projects as we develop them.

The Steps for Each Data Type

Overall, the third edition remains committed to the data types: *sets, bags* (or *multisets*), *sequential lists, ordered lists* (with ordering from a "less than" operator), *stacks, queues, tables,* and *graphs.* There are also additional supplemental data types such as a priority queue. Each of these data types is introduced following a consistent pattern:

Step 1: Understand the Data Type Abstractly. At this level, a student gains an understanding of the data type and its operations at the level of concepts and pictures. For example, a student can visualize a stack and its operations of pushing and popping elements. Simple applications are understood and can be carried out by hand, such as using a stack to reverse the order of letters in a word.

Step 2: Write a Specification of the Data Type as a C++ Class. In this step, the student sees and learns how to write a specification for a C++ class that can implement the data type. The specification includes prototypes for the constructors, pubic member functions, and sometimes other public features (such as an underlying constant that determines the maximum size of a stack). The prototype of each member function is presented along with a precondition/postcondition

contract that completely specifies the behavior of the function. At this level, it's important for the students to realize that the specification is not tied to any particular choice of implementation techniques. In fact, this same specification may be used several times for several different implementations of the same data type.

Step 3: Use the Data Type. With the specification in place, students can write small applications or demonstration programs to show the data type in use. These applications are based solely on the data type's specification, as we still have not tied down the implementation.

Step 4: Select Appropriate Data Structures, and Proceed to Design and Implement the Data Type. With a good abstract understanding of the data type, we can select an appropriate data structure, such as a fixed-sized array, a dynamic array, a linked list of nodes, or a binary tree of nodes. For many of our data types, a first design and implementation will select a simple approach, such as a fixed-sized array. Later, we will redesign and reimplement the same data type with a more complicated underlying structure.

Since we are using C++ classes, an implementation of a data type will have the selected data structures (arrays, pointers, etc.) as private member variables of the class. With each implemented class, we stress the necessity for a clear understanding of the rules that relate the private member variables to an abstract notion of the data type. We require each student to write these rules in clear English sentences that we call the *invariant of the abstract data type*. Once the invariant is written, students can proceed to implementing various member functions. The invariant helps in writing correct functions because of two facts: (a) Each function (except the constructors) knows that the invariant is true when the function begins its work; and (b) each function (except the destructor) is responsible for ensuring that the invariant is again true when the function finishes.

Step 5: Analyze the Implementation. Each implementation can be analyzed for correctness, flexibility (such as a fixed size versus dynamic size), and time analysis of the operations (using big-O notation). Students have a particularly strong opportunity for these analyses when the same data type has been implemented in several different ways.

Where Will the Students Be at the End of the Course?

At the end of our course, students understand the data types inside out. They know how to use the data types, they know how to implement them several ways, and they know the practical effects of the different implementation choices. The students can reason about efficiency with a big-O analysis and argue for the correctness of their implementations by referring to the invariant of the class.

One of the important lasting effects of the course is the specification, design, and implementation experience. The improved ability to reason about programs

is also important. But perhaps most important of all is the exposure to classes that are easily used in many situations. The students no longer have to write everything from scratch. We tell our students that someday they will be thinking about a problem, and they will suddenly realize that a large chunk of the work can be done with a bag, or a stack, or a queue, or some such. And this large chunk of work is work that they won't have to do. Instead, they will pull out the bag or stack or queue or some such that they wrote this semester—using it with no modifications. Or, more likely, they will use the familiar data type from a library of standard data types, such as the C++ *Standard Template Library*. In fact, the behavior of the data types in this text is a cut-down version of the *Standard Template Library*, so when students take the step to the real STL, they will be on familiar ground. And at that point of realization, knowing that a certain data type is the exact solution he or she needs, the student becomes a real programmer.

Other Foundational Topics

Throughout the course, we also lay a foundation for other aspects of "real programming," with coverage of the following topics beyond the basic data structures material:

Object-Oriented Programming. The foundations of object-oriented programming are laid by giving students a strong understanding of C++ classes. The important aspects of classes are covered early: the notion of a member function, the separation into private and public members, the purpose of constructors, and a small exposure to operator overloading. This is enough to get students going and excited about classes.

Further major aspects of classes are introduced when the students first use dynamic memory (Chapter 4). At this point, the need for three additional items is explained: the copy constructor, the overloaded assignment operator, and the destructor. Teaching these OOP aspects with the first use of dynamic memory has the effect of giving the students a concrete picture of dynamic memory as a resource that can be taken and must later be returned.

Conceptually, the largest innovation of OOP is the software reuse that occurs via inheritance. And there are certainly opportunities for introducing inheritance right from the start of a data structures course (such as implementing a set class as a descendant of a bag class). However, an early introduction may also result in juggling too many new concepts at once, resulting in a weaker understanding of the fundamental data structures. Therefore, in our own course we introduce inheritance at the end as a vision of things to come. But the introduction to inheritance (Sections 14.1 and 14.2) could be covered as soon as copy constructors are understood. With this in mind, some instructors may wish to cover Chapter 14 earlier, just before stacks and queues.

Another alternative is to identify students who already know the basics of classes. These students can carry out an inheritance project (such as the ecosys-

tem of Section 14.2 or the game engine in Section 14.3) while the rest of the students first learn about classes.

Templates. Template functions and template classes are an important part of the proposed Standard Template Library, allowing a programmer to easily change the type of the underlying item in a container class. Template classes also allow the use of several different instantiations of a class in a single program. As such, we think it's important to learn about and use templates (Chapter 6) prior to stacks (Chapter 7), since expression evaluation is an important application that uses two kinds of stacks.

Iterators. Iterators are another important part of the proposed Standard Template Library, allowing a programmer to easily step through the items in a container object (such as the elements of a set or bag). Such iterators may be *internal* (implemented with member functions of the container class) or *external* (implemented by a separate class that is a friend of the container class). We introduce internal iterators with one of the first container classes (a sequential list in Section 3.2). An internal iterator is added to the bag class when it is needed in Chapter 6. At that point, the more complex external iterators also are discussed, and students should be aware of the advantages of an external iterator. Throughout the text, iterators provide a good opportunity for programming projects, such as implementing an external bag iterator (Chapter 6) or using a stack to implement an internal iterator of a binary search tree (Chapter 10).

Recursion. First-semester courses sometimes introduce students to recursion. But many of the first-semester examples are tail recursion, where the final act of the function is the recursive call. This may have given students a misleading impression that recursion is nothing more than a loop. Because of this, we prefer to avoid early use of tail recursion in a second-semester course. For example, list traversal and other operations on linked lists can be implemented with tail recursion, but the effect may reinforce wrong impressions about recursion (and the tail recursive list operations may need to be unlearned when the students work with lists of thousands of items, running into potential run-time stack overflow).

So, in our second-semester course, we emphasize recursive solutions that use more than tail recursion. The recursion chapter provides three examples along these lines. Two of the examples—generating random fractals and traversing a maze—are big hits with the students. In our class, we teach recursion (Chapter 9) just before trees (Chapter 10), since it is recursive tree algorithms where recursion becomes vital. However, instructors who desire more emphasis on recursion can move that topic forward, even before Chapter 2.

In a course that has time for advanced tree projects (Chapter 11), we analyze the recursive tree algorithms, explaining the importance of keeping the trees balanced—both to improve worst-case performance, and to avoid potential run-time stack overflow.

Searching and Sorting. Chapters 12 and 13 provide fundamental coverage of searching and sorting algorithms. The searching reviews binary search of an ordered array, which many students will have seen before. Hash tables also are introduced in the search chapter. The sorting chapter reviews simple quadratic sorting methods, but the majority of the chapter focuses on faster algorithms: the recursive merge sort (with worst-case time of $O(n \log n)$), Tony Hoare's recursive quicksort (with average-time $O(n \log n)$), and the tree-based heap sort (with worst-case time of $O(n \log n)$). There is also a new introduction to the C++ Standard Library sorting functions.

Advanced Projects

The text offers good opportunities for optional projects that can be undertaken by a more advanced class or by students with a stronger background in a large class. Particular advanced projects include the following:

- A polynomial class using dynamic memory (Section 4.6).

- An introduction to Standard Library iterators, culminating in an implementation of an iterator for the student's bag class (Sections 6.3 through 6.5).

- An iterator for the binary search tree (Programming Projects in Chapter 10).

- A priority queue, implemented with a linked list (Section 8.4), or implemented using a heap (Section 11.1).

- A set class, implemented with B-trees (Section 11.2). We have made a particular effort on this project to provide information that is sufficient for students to implement the class without need of another text. In our courses, we have successfully directed advanced students to do this project as independent work.

- An inheritance project, such as the ecosystem of Section 14.2.

- An inheritance project using an abstract base class such as the game base class in Section 14.3 (which allows easy implementation of two-player games such as *Othello* or *Connect 4*).

- A graph class and associated graph algorithms from Chapter 15. This is another case where advanced students may do work on their own.

C++ Language Features

C++ is a complex language with many advanced features that will not be touched in a second-semester course. But we endeavor to provide complete coverage for those features that we do touch. In the first edition of the text, we included coverage of two features that were new to C++ at the time: the new *bool* data type (Figure 2.1 on page 37) and static member constants (see page 103). The requirements for using static member constants were changed in the 1998 Standard, and we have incorporated this change into the text (the constant must now be declared both inside and outside the class definition). The other primary new feature from the 1998 Standard is the use of namespaces, which were incorporated in the second edition. In each of these cases, these features might not be supported in older compilers. We provide some assistance in dealing with this (see Appendix E, "Dealing with Older Compilers"), and some assistance in downloading and installing the GNU g++ compiler (see Appendix K).

Flexibility of Topic Ordering

This book was written to allow instructors latitude in reordering the material to meet the specific background of students or to add early emphasis to selected topics. The dependencies among the chapters are shown on page xi. A line joining two boxes indicates that the upper box should be covered before the lower box.

Here are some suggested orderings of the material:

Typical Course. Start with Chapters 1–10, skipping parts of Chapter 2 if the students have a prior background in C++ classes. Most chapters can be covered in a week, but you may want more time for Chapter 5 (linked lists), Chapter 6 (templates), Chapter 9 (recursion), or Chapter 10 (trees). Typically, we cover the material in 13 weeks, including time for exams and extra time for linked lists and trees. Remaining weeks can be spent on a tree project from Chapter 11, or on binary search (Section 12.1) and sorting (Chapter 13).

Heavy OOP Emphasis. If students cover sorting and searching elsewhere, there will be time for a heavier emphasis on object-oriented programming. The first four chapters are covered in detail, and then derived classes (Section 14.1) are introduced. At this point, students can do an interesting OOP project, based on the ecosystem of Section 14.2 or the games in Section 14.3. The basic data structures are then covered (Chapters 5–8), with the queue implemented as a derived class (Section 14.3). Finish up with recursion (Chapter 9) and trees (Chapter 10), placing special emphasis on recursive member functions.

Accelerated Course. Assign the first three chapters as independent reading in the first week, and start with Chapter 4 (pointers). This will leave two to three extra weeks at the end of the term, so that students may spend more time on searching, sorting, and the advanced topics (shaded on page xi.)

We also have taught the course with further acceleration by spending no lecture time on stacks and queues (but assigning those chapters as reading).

Early Recursion / Early Sorting. One to three weeks may be spent at the start of class on recursive thinking. The first reading will then be Chapters 1 and 9, perhaps supplemented by additional recursive projects.

If the recursion is covered early, you may also proceed to cover binary search (Section 12.1) and most of the sorting algorithms (Chapter 13) before introducing C++ classes.

Supplements via the Internet

The following supplemental materials for this text are available to all readers at www.aw-bc.com/cssupport:

- Source Code. All the C++ classes, functions, and programs that appear in the book are available to readers.
- Errata. We have tried not to make mistakes, but sometimes they are inevitable. A list of detected errors is available and updated as necessary. You are invited to contribute any errors you find.

In addition, the following supplements are available to qualified instructors. Please contact your Addison-Wesley sales representative, or send Email to aw.cse@aw.com, for information on how to access them:

- PowerPoint lecture slides
- Exam questions
- Solutions to selected programming projects
- Sample assignments and lab exercises
- Suggested syllabi

Chapter Dependencies

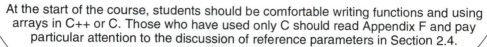

At the start of the course, students should be comfortable writing functions and using arrays in C++ or C. Those who have used only C should read Appendix F and pay particular attention to the discussion of reference parameters in Section 2.4.

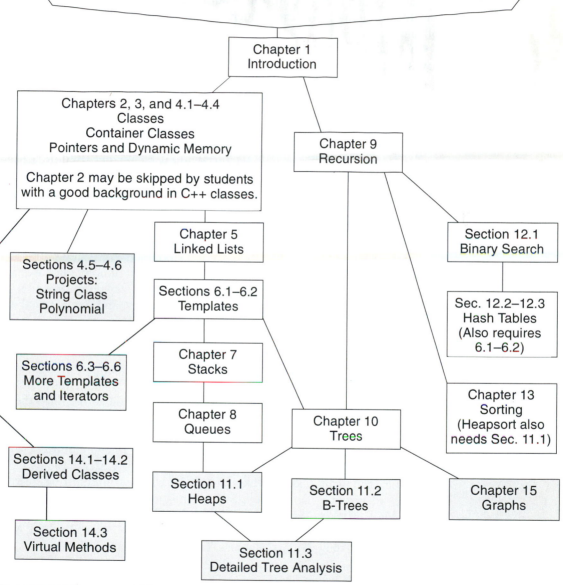

Chapter 1
Introduction

Chapters 2, 3, and 4.1–4.4
Classes
Container Classes
Pointers and Dynamic Memory

Chapter 2 may be skipped by students with a good background in C++ classes.

Chapter 9
Recursion

Sections 4.5–4.6
Projects:
String Class
Polynomial

Chapter 5
Linked Lists

Section 12.1
Binary Search

Sections 6.1–6.2
Templates

Sec. 12.2–12.3
Hash Tables
(Also requires 6.1–6.2)

Sections 6.3–6.6
More Templates
and Iterators

Chapter 7
Stacks

Chapter 13
Sorting
(Heapsort also needs Sec. 11.1)

Chapter 8
Queues

Chapter 10
Trees

Sections 14.1–14.2
Derived Classes

Section 11.1
Heaps

Section 11.2
B-Trees

Chapter 15
Graphs

Section 14.3
Virtual Methods

Section 11.3
Detailed Tree Analysis

The shaded boxes provide good opportunities for advanced work.

Acknowledgments

We started this book while Walter was visiting Michael at the Computer Science Department of the University of Colorado in Boulder. The work was completed after Walter moved back to the Department of Engineering and Computer Science at the University of California, San Diego. We are grateful to these institutions for providing facilities, wonderful students, and interaction with congenial colleagues.

Our students have been particularly helpful—nearly 4000 of our students working through the material, making suggestions, showing us how they learned. We thank the instructors who used the material in their data structures courses and provided feedback: Zachary Bergen, Cathy Bishop, Martin Burtscher, Gina Cherry, Courtney Comstock, Stephen Davies, John Gillett, Ralph Hollingsworth, Patrick Lynn, Evi Nemeth, Gary Nutt, Rick Osborne, and Karl Winklmann. During this time, the book was also extensively reviewed by Wolfgang W. Bein, Bill Hankley, Michael Milligan, Jeff Parker, Andrew L. Wright, John R. Rose, and Evan Zweifel. We thank these colleagues for their excellent critique and their encouragement.

Many thanks to Paul Nagin, who thoroughly reviewed the third edition and provided many new ideas for additional exercises and material.

Our thanks also go to the editors and staff at Addison-Wesley. Maria Campo's work has encouraged us on a daily basis and smoothed every step of the production. We thank Joyce Wells for the beautiful selection of colors and design elements on the cover. Marilyn Lloyd helped us at every stage of production, Karin Dejamaer provided friendly encouragment in Boulder, and we offer our thanks to them. Daniel Rausch and Meghan James from Argosy Publishing provided friendly daily contact, great flexibility, and continual technical support that was appreciated throughout our work on this edition. We welcome and appreciate Michael Hirsch in the role of editor where he has shown amazing energy, enthusiasm, and encouragement. Finally, our original editor Susan Hartman Sullivan has provided continual support, encouragement, and direction—the book wouldn't be here without you!

In addition to the work and support from those who put the book together, we thank those who offered us daily interest and encouragement. Our deepest thanks go to Alan Apt, David Benson, Paul Chadwick, Suzanne Church, Lynne Conklin, Andrzej Ehrenfeucht, Camille Escudaro, Mike Eisenberg, Paul Eisenbrey, Skip Ellis, Lloyd Fosdick, Rob Furey, Stace Johnson, Rich Lorentz, Rick Lowell, George Main, Mickey Main, Jim H. Martin, Jim W. Martin Jr., Tandy McKnight, Marga Powell, Grzegorz Rozenberg, Randy Salisbury, Carter Shanklin, Melanie Tem, the 2004 Young Gunns, Hannah, Timothy, and Janet.

Michael Main
main@colorado.edu
Boulder, Colorado

Walter Savitch
wsavitch@ucsd.edu
San Diego, California

Chapter List

Contents

CHAPTER 6 Software Development with Templates, Iterators, and the STL   278

CHAPTER 7 Stacks   348

CHAPTER 8 Queues   389

CHAPTER 9 Recursive Thinking   431

CHAPTER 10 Trees   469

CHAPTER 11 Tree Projects   534

CHAPTER 12 Searching 575

CHAPTER 15 Graphs   722

APPENDIXES

The Phases of Software Development

Chapter the first which explains how, why, when, and
where there was ever any problem in the first place

NOEL LANGLEY
The Land of Green Ginger

LEARNING OBJECTIVES

When you complete Chapter 1, you will be able to...

- write precondition/postcondition contracts for small functions, and use the C++ assert facility to test preconditions.
- recognize quadratic, linear, and logarithmic running time behavior in simple algorithms, and write big-*O* expressions to describe this behavior.
- create and recognize test data that is appropriate for simple problems, including testing boundary conditions and fully exercising code.

CHAPTER CONTENTS

The Phases of Software Development

This chapter illustrates the phases of software development. These phases occur in all software, including the small programs that you'll see in this first chapter. In subsequent chapters, you'll go beyond these small programs, applying the phases of software development to organized collections of data. These organized collections of data are called **data structures**, and the main topics of this book revolve around proven techniques for representing and manipulating such data structures.

Years from now you may be a software engineer writing large systems in a specialized area, perhaps computer graphics or artificial intelligence. Such futuristic applications will be exciting and stimulating, and within your work you will still see the phases of software development and fundamental data structures that you learn and practice now.

Here is a list of the phases of software development:

The Phases of Software Development

- Specification of the task
- Design of a solution
- Implementation (coding) of the solution
- Analysis of the solution
- Testing and debugging
- Maintenance and evolution of the system
- Obsolescence

---

the phases blur into each other

Do not memorize this list: Throughout the book, your practice of these phases will achieve far better familiarity than mere memorization. Also, memorizing an "official list" is misleading because it suggests that there is a single sequence of discrete steps that always occur one after another. In practice, the phases blur into each other; for instance, the analysis of a solution's efficiency may occur hand in hand with the design, before any coding. Or low-level design decisions may be postponed until the implementation phase. Also, the phases might not occur one after another. Typically there is back-and-forth travel between the phases.

Most of the work in software development does not depend on any particular programming language. Specification, design, and analysis can all be carried out with few or no ties to a particular programming language. Nevertheless, when we get down to implementation details, we do need to decide on one particular programming language. The language we use in this book is C++.

What You Should Know About C++ Before Starting This Text

The C++ language was designed by Bjarne Stroustrup at AT&T Bell Laboratories as an extension of the C language, with the purpose of supporting **object-oriented programming (OOP)**—a technique that encourages important strategies of information hiding and component reuse. Throughout this book, we introduce you to important OOP principles to use in your designs and implementations.

OOP supports information hiding and component reuse

There are many different C++ compilers that you may successfully use with this text. Ideally, the compiler should support the latest features of the ANSI/ISO C++ Standard, which we have incorporated into the text. However, there are several workarounds that can be applied to older compilers that don't fully support the standard. (See Appendix K, "Free Software Foundation's GNU C++ Compiler," and Appendix E, "Dealing with Older Compilers.")

you should already know how to write, compile, and run short C++ programs

Whichever programming environment you use, you should already be comfortable writing, compiling, and running short C++ programs built with a top-down design. You should know how to use the built-in types (the number types, char, and bool), and you should be able to use arrays.

Throughout the text, we will introduce the important roles of the C++ Standard Library, though you do not need any previous knowledge of the library. Studying the data structures of the Standard Library can help you understand trade-offs between different approaches, and can guide the design and implementation of your own data structures. When you are designing your own data structures, an approach that is compliant with the Standard Library has twofold benefits: Other programmers will understand your work more easily, and your own work will readily benefit from other pieces of the Standard Library, such as the standard searching and sorting algorithms.

C++ Standard Library

The rest of this chapter will prepare you to tackle the topic of data structures in C++, using an approach that is compliant with the Standard Library. Section 1.1 focuses on a technique for specifying program behavior, and you'll also see some hints about design and implementation. Section 1.2 illustrates a particular kind of analysis: the running time analysis of a program. Section 1.3 provides some techniques for testing and debugging programs.

1.1   SPECIFICATION, DESIGN, IMPLEMENTATION

One begins with a list of difficult design decisions which are likely to change. Each module is then designed to hide such a decision from the others.

D. L. PARNAS
On the Criteria to Be Used
in Decomposing Systems into Modules

```
CONVERSIONS FROM -50.0 to 50.0
    Celsius        Fahrenheit
     -50.0C
     -40.0C        The actual
     -30.0C        Fahrenheit
     -20.0C        temperatures
     -10.0C        will be
       0.0C        computed
      10.0C        and displayed
      20.0C        on this side of
      30.0C        the table.
      40.0C
      50.0C
```

As an example of software development in action, let's examine the specification, design, and implementation for a particular problem. The **specification** is a precise description of the problem; the **design** phase consists of formulating the steps to solve the problem; the **implementation** is the actual C++ code that carries out the design.

The problem we have in mind is to display a table for converting Celsius temperatures to Fahrenheit, similar to the table shown in the margin. For a small problem, a sample of the desired output is a sufficient specification. Such a sample is a good specification because it is *precise,* leaving no doubt about what the program must accomplish. The next step is to design a solution.

An **algorithm** is a set of instructions for solving a problem. An algorithm for the temperature problem will print the conversion table. During the design of the algorithm, the details of a particular programming language can be distracting, and can obscure the simplicity of a solution. Therefore, during the design we generally write in English. We use a rather corrupted kind of English that mixes in C++ when it's convenient. This mixture of English and a programming language is called **pseudocode**. When the C++ code for a step is obvious, then the pseudocode may use C++. When a step is clearer in English, then we will use English. Keep in mind that the reason for pseudocode is to improve *clarity*.

We'll use pseudocode to design a solution for the temperature problem, and we'll also use the important design technique of decomposing the problem.

Design Concept: Decomposing the Problem

Key Design Concept

Break down a task into a few subtasks; then decompose each subtask into smaller subtasks.

A good technique for designing an algorithm is to break down the problem at hand into a few subtasks, then decompose each subtask into smaller subtasks, then replace the smaller subtasks with even smaller subtasks, and so forth. Eventually the subtasks become so small that they are trivial to implement in C++ or whatever language you are using. When the algorithm is translated into C++, each subtask is implemented as a separate C++ function. In other programming languages, functions are called "methods" or "procedures," but it all boils down to the same thing: The large problem is decomposed into subtasks, and subtasks are implemented as separate pieces of your program.

For example, the temperature problem has at least two good subtasks: (1) converting a temperature from Celsius degrees to Fahrenheit, and (2) printing a line of the conversion table in the specified format. Using these subproblems, the first draft of our pseudocode might look like this:

1. Do preliminary work to open and set up the output device properly.
2. Display the labels at the top of the table.
3. For each line in the table (using variables `celsius` and `fahrenheit`):
   a. Set `celsius` equal to the next Celsius temperature of the table.
   b. `fahrenheit` = the `celsius` temperature converted to Fahrenheit.
   c. Print the Celsius and Fahrenheit values with labels on an output line.

what makes a good decomposition?

We have identified the major subtasks. But aren't there other ways to decompose the problem into subtasks? What are the aspects of a good decomposition? One primary guideline is that the subtasks should help you produce short pseudocode—no more than a page of succinct description to solve the entire problem, and ideally much less than a page. In your designs, you can also keep in mind two considerations for selecting good subtasks: the potential for code reuse, and the possibility of future changes to the program. Let's see how our subtasks embody these considerations.

code reuse

Step 1 opens an output device, making it ready for output in a particular form. This is a common operation that many programs must carry out. If we write a function for Step 1 with sufficient flexibility, we can probably reuse the function in other programs. This is an example of **code reuse**, in which a function is written with sufficient generality that it can be reused elsewhere. In fact, programmers often produce collections of related C++ functions that are made available in packages to be reused over and over with many different application programs. Later we will use the C++ Standard Library as this sort of package, and we will also write our own packages of this kind. For now, just keep in mind that the function for Step 1 should be written with some reuse in mind.

easily modified code

Decomposing problems also produces a good final program in the sense that the program is easy to understand, and subsequent maintenance and modifications are relatively easy. Our temperature program might be modified to convert to Kelvin degrees instead of Fahrenheit, or even to do a completely different conversion such as feet to meters. If the conversion task is performed by a separate function, much of the modification will be confined to this one function. Easily modified code is vital since real-world studies show that a large proportion of programmers' time is spent maintaining and modifying existing programs.

In order for a problem decomposition to produce easily modified code, the functions that you write need to be genuinely separated from one another. An analogy can help explain the notion of "genuinely separated." Suppose you are moving a bag of gold coins to a safe hiding place. If the bag is too heavy to carry, you might divide the coins into three smaller bags and carry the bags one by one. Unless you are a character in a comedy, you would not try to carry all three bags at once. That would defeat the purpose of dividing the coins into three groups. This strategy works only if you carry the bags one at a time. Something similar happens in problem decomposition. If you divide your programming task into three subtasks and solve these subtasks by writing three functions, then you have traded one hard problem for three easier problems. Your total job has become easier—provided that you design the functions separately. When you are working on one function, you should not worry about how the other functions perform their jobs. But the functions do interact. So when you are designing one function, you need to know something about what the other functions do. The trick is to know *only as much as you need, but no more*. This is called **information hiding**. One technique for incorporating information hiding involves specifying your functions' behavior using *preconditions* and *postconditions*.

Preconditions and Postconditions

When you write a complete function definition, you specify how the function performs its computation. However, when you are using a function, you only need to think about *what* the function does. You need not think about *how* the function does its work. For example, suppose you are writing the temperature conversion program and you are told that a function is available for you to use, as described here:

```
// Convert a Celsius temperature c to Fahrenheit degrees
double celsius_to_fahrenheit(double c);
```

Your program might have a *double* variable called celsius that contains a Celsius temperature. Knowing this description, you can confidently write the following statement to convert the temperature to Fahrenheit degrees, storing the result in a *double* variable called fahrenheit:

```
fahrenheit = celsius_to_fahrenheit(celsius);
```

When you use the celsius_to_fahrenheit function, you do not need to know the details of how the function carries out its work. You need to know *what* the function does, but you do not need to know *how* the task is accomplished.

procedural abstraction

When we pretend that we do not know how a function is implemented, we are using a form of information hiding called **procedural abstraction**. This technique simplifies your reasoning by abstracting away irrelevant details; that is, by hiding the irrelevant details. When programming in C++, it might make more sense to call it "functional abstraction," since you are abstracting away irrelevant details about how a function works. However, the term *procedure* is a more general term than *function*. Computer scientists use the term procedure for any sequence of instructions, and so they use the term *procedural abstraction*. Procedural abstraction can be a powerful tool. It simplifies your reasoning by allowing you to consider functions one at a time rather than all together.

To make procedural abstraction work for us, we need some techniques for documenting what a function does without indicating how the function works. We could just write a short comment as we did for celsius_to_fahrenheit. However, the short comment is a bit incomplete—for instance, the comment doesn't indicate what happens if the parameter c is smaller than the lowest Celsius temperature (−273.15°C, which is **absolute zero** for Celsius temperatures).

For better completeness and consistency, we will follow a fixed format that always has two pieces of information called the *precondition* and the *postcondition* of the function, described here:

precondition and postcondition

Preconditions and Postconditions

A **precondition** is a statement giving the condition that is required to be true when a function is called. The function is not guaranteed to perform as it should unless the precondition is true.

A **postcondition** is a statement describing what will be true when a function call is completed. If the function is correct and the precondition was true when the function was called, then the function will complete, and the postcondition will be true when the function call is completed.

For example, a precondition/postcondition for the `celsius_to_fahrenheit` function is shown here:

```
double celsius_to_fahrenheit(double c);
// Precondition:  c is a Celsius temperature no less than
// absolute zero (–273.15).
// Postcondition: The return value is the temperature c
// converted to Fahrenheit degrees.
```

comments in C++

This format of comments might be new to you: The characters `//` indicate the start of a comment that extends to the end of the current line. The other form of C++ comments, starting with `/*` and continuing until `*/`, is also permitted.

Preconditions and postconditions are more than a way to summarize a function's actions. Stating these conditions should be the first step in designing any function. Before you start to think about algorithms and C++ code for a function, you should write out the function's **prototype**, which consists of the function's return type, name, and parameter list, all followed by a semicolon. As you are writing the prototype, you should also write the precondition and postcondition as comments. If you later discover that your specification cannot be realized in a reasonable way, you may need to back up and rethink what the function should do.

specify the precondition and postcondition when you write the function's prototype

Preconditions and postconditions are even more important when a group of programmers work together. In team situations, one programmer often does not know how a function written by another programmer works and, in fact, sharing knowledge about how a function works can be counter-productive. Instead, the precondition and postcondition provide all the interaction that's needed. In effect, the precondition/postcondition pair forms a contract between the programmer who uses a function and the programmer who writes that function. To aid the explanation of this "contract," we'll give these two programmers names.

programming teams

Whereas Jervis Pendleton has written celsius_to_fahrenheit (henceforth known as "the function") and Judy Abbott is going to use the function, we hereby agree that:

   (i) Judy will never call the function unless she is certain that the precondition is true, and

   (ii) Whenever the function is called and the precondition is true when the function is called, then Jervis guarantees that:

      a. the function will eventually end (infinite loops are forbidden!), and

      b. when the function ends, the postcondition will be true.

             Judy Abbott

      J Pendleton

the precondition/ postcondition contract

Judy is the head of a programming team that is writing a large piece of software. Jervis is one of her programmers, who writes various functions for Judy to use in large programs. If Judy and Jarvis were lawyers, the contract might look like the scroll shown in the margin. As a programmer, the contract tells them precisely what the function does. It states that if Judy makes sure that the precondition is met when the function is called, then Jervis ensures that the function returns with the postcondition satisfied.

Using Functions Provided by Other Programmers

The programmers that you work with may or may not use the words "precondition" and "postcondition" to describe their functions, but they will provide and expect information about what a function does. For example, consider this function that sets up the standard output device (cout) to print numbers:

```
void setup_cout_fractions(int fraction_digits);
// Precondition:  fraction_digits is not negative.
// Postcondition:  All double or float numbers printed to cout will now be
// rounded to the specified number of digits on the right of the decimal point.
```

If you are curious about the setup_cout_fractions implementation, you can read Appendix F, which provides some input/output ideas for C++ programming. But even without the knowledge of how Jervis writes the function, we can write a program that uses his function. For example, the temperature program, shown in Figure 1.1, follows our pseudocode, using setup_cout_fractions and celsius_to_fahrenheit. In Chapter 2, we will see how the actual functions such as setup_cout_fractions do not need to appear in the same file as the main program, providing an even stronger separation between the use of a function and its implementation. Next, we discuss a few other implementation issues that may be new to you.

Implementation Issues for the ANSI/ISO C++ Standard

This section concludes with some implementation issues for the temperature program from Figure 1.1. Some of these issues may be new if you haven't previously used the ANSI/ISO C++ Standard.

THE STANDARD LIBRARY AND THE STANDARD NAMESPACE

During the late 1990s, the American National Standards Institute (ANSI) and the International Standards Organization (ISO) developed C++ compiler requirements called the ANSI/ISO C++ Standard. The standard aids programmers in writing portable code that can be compiled and run with many different compilers on different machines. Part of the standard is the C++ Standard Library. Each facility in the Standard Library provides a group of declared constants, data types, and functions supporting particular activities such as input/output or mathematical functions.

In 1999, C++ compilers began to provide the full C++ Standard Library. To use one of the library facilities, a program places an "include directive" at the top of the file that uses the facility. For example, for a program to use the usual C++ input/output facilities, the program should use the include directive:

```
#include <iostream>
```

This gives the program access to most of the C++ input/output facilities. Some additional input/output items require a second include directive:

```
#include <iomanip>
```

A discussion of the input/output facilities from <iostream> and <iomanip> is given in Appendix F.

FIGURE 1.1   The Temperature Conversion Program

A Program

See the C++ Feature, "The Standard Library and the Standard Namespace."

```
// File: temperature.cxx
// This conversion program illustrates some implementation techniques.
#include <cassert>      // Provides assert function
#include <cstdlib>      // Provides EXIT_SUCCESS
#include <iomanip>      // Provides setw function for setting output width
#include <iostream>     // Provides cout
using namespace std;    // Allows all Standard Library items to be used

double celsius_to_fahrenheit(double c)
// Precondition: c is a Celsius temperature no less than absolute zero (-273.15).
// Postcondition: The return value is the temperature c converted to Fahrenheit degrees.
{
    const double MINIMUM_CELSIUS = -273.15; // Absolute zero in Celsius degrees

    assert(c >= MINIMUM_CELSIUS);
    return (9.0 / 5.0) * c + 32;
}
```

(continued)

(FIGURE 1.1 continued)

```
void setup_cout_fractions(int fraction_digits)
// Precondition: fraction_digits is not negative.
// Postcondition: All double or float numbers printed to cout will now be rounded to the
// specified number of digits on the right of the decimal point.
{
    assert(fraction_digits >= 0);
    cout.precision(fraction_digits);
    cout.setf(ios::fixed, ios::floatfield);
    if (fraction_digits == 0)
        cout.unsetf(ios::showpoint);
    else
        cout.setf(ios::showpoint);
}
```

See the Programming Tip, "Use Assert to Check Preconditions," on page 12.

See the Programming Tip, "Use Declared Constants," on page 11.

```
int main( )
{
    const char   HEADING1[]  = "   Celsius"; // Heading for table's first column
    const char   HEADING2[]  = "Fahrenheit"; // Heading for table's second column
    const char   LABEL1      =        'C'; // Label for numbers in 1st column
    const char   LABEL2      =        'F'; // Label for numbers in 2nd column
    const double TABLE_BEGIN =      -50.0; // The value for the 1st line of table
    const double TABLE_END   =       50.0; // The value for the last line of table
    const double TABLE_STEP  =       10.0; // Increment between values in table
    const int    WIDTH       =          9; // Number of chars in output numbers
    const int    DIGITS      =          1; // Number of digits to right of decimal

    double value1;   // A value from the table's first column
    double value2;   // A value from the table's second column

    // Set up the output for fractions and print the table headings.
    setup_cout_fractions(DIGITS);
    cout << "CONVERSIONS from " << TABLE_BEGIN << " to " << TABLE_END << endl;
    cout << HEADING1 << "   " << HEADING2 << endl;

    // Each iteration of the loop prints one line of the table.
    for (value1 = TABLE_BEGIN; value1 <= TABLE_END; value1 += TABLE_STEP)
    {
        value2 = celsius_to_fahrenheit(value1);
        cout << setw(WIDTH) << value1 << LABEL1 << "   ";
        cout << setw(WIDTH) << value2 << LABEL2 << endl;
    }

    return EXIT_SUCCESS;
}
```

See the Programming Tip, "Use EXIT_SUCCESS in a Main Program," on page 14.

www.cs.colorado.edu/~main/chapter1/temperature.cxx   **WWW**

Older Names for the Header Files

The files `iostream` and `iomanip` are examples of C++ header files. Older C++ compilers used slightly different names for header files. For example, older compilers used `iostream.h` instead of simply `iostream`. In most cases, the new C++ header file names are the same as the old file names with the ".h" removed, and newer compilers will still allow the older names.

In addition to the C++ header files, the C++ Standard includes a collection of header files from the original C language. Two examples are the C Standard Library `<stdlib.h>` and the assert facility `<assert.h>`. These original names can still be used in a C++ program, or you can use the new C++ header file names, which are constructed by removing the ".h" and putting the letter "c" at the front of the name (such as `<cstdlib>` and `<cassert>`).

A discussion of `<cstdlib>` and `<cassert>` is given as part of Appendix G, "Selected Library Functions."

The Standard Namespace

There is one difference between using old header file names (such as `<iostream.h>` or `<stdlib.h>`) and the new names (such as `<iostream>` or `<cstdlib>`). All of the items in the new header files are part of a feature called the **standard namespace**, also called **std**. For now, when you use one of the new header files, your program should also have this statement after the include directives:

```
using namespace std;
```

This statement is a global namespace directive, which allows your program to use all items from the standard namespace. Chapter 2 discusses alternatives to the global namespace directive, and also shows how to create your own namespaces to avoid conflicts between the names that occur in different pieces of a program.

PROGRAMMING TIP

USE DECLARED CONSTANTS

Throughout the temperature program, there are several declarations of the form:

```
const double TABLE_BEGIN = -50.0;
```

This is a declaration of a *double* number called TABLE_BEGIN, which is given an initial value of −50.0. The keyword *const*, appearing before the declaration, makes TABLE_BEGIN more than just an ordinary declaration. It is a **declared constant**, which means that its value will never be changed while the program is running. A common programming style is to use all capital letters for any declared constant. This makes it easy to identify such values within a program.

There are several advantages to defining TABLE_BEGIN as a declared constant, rather than using the number −50.0 directly in the program. Using the name TABLE_BEGIN makes it easy to understand the purpose of the constant. Moreover, once a constant has been declared, it can be used throughout the program. For example, our program uses TABLE_BEGIN twice (once when printing the heading at the top, and once to determine a beginning value used in the for-loop).

Using declared constants also makes it easier to alter a program. For example, we may decide to alter the program so that the table starts at −100.0 instead of −50.0. This change is accomplished by finding the declared constant (TABLE_BEGIN), changing its initial value to −100.0, then recompiling the program. By changing the initial value, all occurrences of TABLE_BEGIN will have the new value.

To increase clarity and to ease alterations, some programmers use declared constants for *all* fixed values in a program. As rules go, this is a reasonable one. However, there is another side to the issue. Well-known formulas may be more easily recognized in their original form (using numbers directly rather than artificially introduced names). For example, the conversion from Celsius to Fahrenheit is recognizable as $F = \frac{9}{5}C + 32$. Thus, Figure 1.1 uses the return statement shown here:

```
return (9.0/5.0) * c + 32;
```

This return statement is clearer and less error-prone than a version that uses declared constants for the values $\frac{9}{5}$ and 32.

CLARIFYING THE CONST KEYWORD
<u>Part 1: Declared Constants</u>

1. DECLARED CONSTANTS
2. CONSTANT MEMBER FUNCTIONS: PAGE 38
3. CONST REFERENCE PARAMETERS: PAGE 72
4. STATIC MEMBER CONSTANTS: PAGE 103
5. CONST PARAMETERS THAT ARE POINTERS OR ARRAYS: PAGE 162
6. THE CONST KEYWORD WITH A POINTER TO A NODE, AND THE NEED FOR TWO VERSIONS OF SOME MEMBER FUNCTIONS: PAGE 218
7. CONST ITERATORS: PAGE 308

For programmers who implement data structures, the C++ keyword *const* has several uses that must be coordinated with each other. Because of potential confusion between the different uses, we'll clarify each use when we first use it in an example.

You can use the keyword *const* in front of any variable declaration. This indicates that the program is not allowed to change the variable's value.

Syntax:
    const   \<Data type\>   \<Variable name\> = \<Value\> ;

Examples:
```
const double TABLE_BEGIN = 50.0;
const char LABEL1 = 'C';
```

🛈 PROGRAMMING TIP

USE ASSERT TO CHECK A PRECONDITION

Consider the function celsius_to_fahrenheit from the temperature program. The function has a precondition, requiring its parameter to be no less than absolute zero (because lower temperatures have no physical meaning). The programmer who uses the function is always responsible for ensuring that the precondition is valid. But, what if a programmer uses the function and the precondition is not valid? This is a programming error, similar to other errors, such as accidentally dividing by zero or attempting to use an array element beyond the array's bounds.

In a perfect world, such programming errors would never occur: No program would ever attempt to divide by zero, or access an array beyond its bounds, or call a function with an invalid precondition. Of course, programmers aren't perfect; both novice and experienced programmers make errors. During program development, functions should be designed to help programmers find errors as easily as possible. As part of this effort, the first action of a function should be to check that its precondition is valid. If the precondition fails, then the function prints a message and either halts the entire program, or performs some other error actions before returning.

At first glance, this approach may seem harsh. Why stop the whole program? It's just a little invalid data! But think back to programs you have written. Did you ever make an error such as accessing an array beyond its bounds, perhaps writing `x[42]` when the last valid location was `x[41]`? When this happens, a program won't always stop immediately; instead the program can continue computing with corrupted data, eventually producing a crash long after the actual error, or just silently producing a wrong answer. Difficult debugging work is sometimes needed to track down the actual location of the error. Testing and debugging is easier if a program produces an error message at the earliest detection of invalid data.

The `assert` facility is a good approach to detecting invalid data at an early point. To use `assert`, the program includes this directive:

```
#include <cassert>
```

(Older compilers may use `<assert.h>` instead.) The primary item in the `cassert` facility is called `assert`, which is used like a function with one argument. The argument is usually a true/false expression. The expression is evaluated. If the result is true, then no action is taken. But if the result is false, then an error message is printed, and the program is halted. These checks are called **assertions**. For example, the `celsius_to_fahrenheit` function uses this assertion:

```
assert(c >= MINIMUM_CELSIUS);
```

If the expression `(c >= MINIMUM_CELSIUS)` is true, then `c` is valid and the assertion takes no action. On the other hand, if the expression is false, then the precondition has been violated, so a message is printed and the program is halted.

After testing and debugging is complete, the programmer has the option of turning off all assertion checks to speed up the program. Assertions can be turned off by placing this statement immediately before the program's include directives:

```
#define NDEBUG
```

🕐 PROGRAMMING TIP

USE **EXIT_SUCCESS** IN A MAIN PROGRAM

When the temperature program finishes, it executes the statement:

> *return* EXIT_SUCCESS;

This return statement ends the main program and also sends the value of the constant EXIT_SUCCESS back to your computer's operating system. The operating system is the software that is responsible for running all programs on your computer. Although you may not realize it, the operating system is able to take further actions based on the return value from a main program. For example, the return value of EXIT_SUCCESS tells the operating system that the program ended normally, and the operating system can then proceed with its next task. Other return values tell the operating system about abnormal terminations such as problems opening files or running out of memory. The EXIT_SUCCESS constant is defined in cstdlib (or stdlib.h). For most operating systems, this constant is defined as zero (which is why you may have used *return* 0 in other programming).

By the way, a program can also return another constant, EXIT_FAILURE, as a simple way of indicating non-normal completion.

⁂ C++ FEATURE

EXCEPTION HANDLING

The C++ language provides built-in support for handling unusual situations, known as "exceptions," which may occur during the execution of your program. Exception handling is commonly used to handle run-time errors. It is a very good alternative to traditional techniques of error handling, which are often inadequate, error-prone, and ad hoc. Once you have a program working for the core situation where things always go as planned, you can use the C++ exception handling facilities to add code for unusual cases. Please refer to Appendix L for more information about these facilities. In order to focus on data structures, formal exception handling is not incorporated into the examples in this book.

Self-Test Exercises for Section 1.1

Each section of this book finishes with a few self-test exercises. Answers to these exercises are given at the end of each chapter.

1. What are two considerations for selecting good subtasks?
2. What are the elements of a C++ function prototype?
3. This exercise refers to a function that Jervis has written for *you* to use. The prototype and precondition/postcondition contract are shown at the top of the next page.

```
int date_check(int year, int month, int day);
// Precondition: The three parameters are a legal year, month, and
// day of the month.
// Postcondition: If the given date has been reached on or before today,
// then the function returns 0. Otherwise, the value returned is the number
// of days until the given date will occur.
```

Suppose you call the function `date_check(2009, 7, 29)`. What is the return value if today is July 22, 2009? What if today is July 30, 2009? What about February 1, 2010?

4. Write an assert statement that checks whether the month variable in the function date_check is a valid integer.

5. One of the libraries is the `<cmath>` facility, which contains a function with this prototype:

```
double sqrt(double x);
```

The function returns the square root of x. Write a reasonable precondition and postcondition for this function, and compare your answer to the solution at the end of the chapter.

6. Write the include directive that must appear before using the `sqrt` function from Self-Test Exercise 5.

7. Write the *using* statement that must appear before using any of the items from the C++ Standard Library.

8. Write a program to print a conversion table from feet to meters. Use the temperature conversion program as the starting point (available online at http://www.cs.colorado.edu/~main/chapter1/temperature.cxx).

9. Why is it a good idea to stop a program at the earliest point when invalid data is detected?

10. What is the easiest way to turn off all assertion checking in a program?

1.2 RUNNING TIME ANALYSIS

Time analysis consists of reasoning about an algorithm's speed. *Does the algorithm work fast enough for my needs? How much longer does the method take when the input gets larger? Which of several different methods is fastest?* We'll discuss these issues in this section. An example will help start the discussion.

The Stair-Counting Problem

Suppose that you and your friend Judy are standing at the top of the Eiffel Tower. As you gaze out over the French landscape, Judy turns to you and says, "I wonder how many steps there are to the bottom?" You, of course, are the ever-accommodating host, so you reply, "I'm not sure . . . but I'll find out." We'll look at three different methods that you could use and analyze the time requirements of each.

Method 1: Walk down and keep a tally. In the first method, Judy gives you a pen and a sheet of paper. "I'll be back in a minute," you say as you dash down the stairs. Each time you take a step down, you make a mark on the sheet of paper. When you reach the bottom, you run back up, show Judy the piece of paper, and say "There are this many steps."

Method 2: Walk down, but let Judy keep the tally. In the second method, Judy is unwilling to let her pen or paper out of her sight. But you are undaunted. Once more you say, "I'll be back in a minute," and you set off down the stairs. But this time you stop after one step, lay your hat on the step, and run back to Judy. "Make a mark on the paper!" you exclaim. Then you run back to your hat, pick it up, take one more step, and lay the hat down on the second step. Then back up to Judy: "Make another mark on the paper!" you say. You run back down the two stairs, pick up your hat, move to the third step, and lay down the hat. Then back up the stairs to Judy: "Make another mark!" you tell her. This continues until your hat reaches the bottom, and you speed back up the steps one more time. "One more mark, please." At this point, you grab Judy's piece of paper and say, "There are this many steps."

Method 3: Jervis to the rescue. In the third method, you don't walk down the stairs at all. Instead, you spot your friend Jervis by the staircase, holding the sign drawn here:

The translation is *There are 2689 steps in this stairway (really!).* So, you take the paper and pen from Judy, write the number 2689, and hand the paper back to her, saying, "There are this many steps."

This is a silly example, but even so, it does illustrate the issues that arise when performing a time analysis for an algorithm or program. The first issue is deciding exactly how you will measure the time spent carrying out the method or executing the program. At first glance the answer seems easy: For each of the three stair-counting methods, just measure the actual time it takes to carry out the method. You could do this with a stopwatch. But, there are some drawbacks to measuring actual time. Actual time can depend on various irrelevant details, such as whether you or somebody else carried out the method. The actual elapsed time may vary from person to person, depending on how fast each person can run the stairs. Even if we decide that *you* are the runner, the time may vary depending on other factors such as the weather, what you had for breakfast, and what other things are on your mind.

So, instead of measuring the actual elapsed time during each method, we count certain operations that occur while carrying out the methods. In this example, we will count just two kinds of operations:

1. Each time you walk up or down one step, that is one operation.
2. Each time you or Judy marks a symbol on the paper, that is one operation.

Of course, each of these operations takes a certain amount of time, and making a mark may take a different amount of time than taking a step. But this doesn't concern us because we won't measure the actual time taken by the operations. Instead, we ask: *How many operations are needed for each of the three methods?* We could consider additional operations, such as operations to convert the list of marks to a printed number (would would be convenient for Methods 1 and 2), but these limited operations will be adequate for our example.

decide what operations to count

In the first method, you take 2689 steps down, another 2689 steps up, and you also make 2689 marks on the paper, for a total of 3×2689 operations—that is 8067 total operations.

In the second method, there are also 2689 marks made on Judy's paper, but the total number of operations is considerably more. You start by going down one step and back up one step. Then down two and up two. Then down three and up three, and so forth. The total number of operations taken is:

Downward steps	$= 3,616,705$ (which is $1 + 2 + \ldots + 2689$)
Upward steps	$= 3,616,705$
Marks made	$= 2689$
Total operations	$=$ Downward steps
	$+$ Upward steps
	$+$ Marks made
$=$	$7,236,099$

The third method is the quickest of all: Only four marks are made on the paper (that is, we're counting one "mark" for each digit of 2689), and there is no going up and down stairs. The number of operations used by each of the methods is summarized here:

Method 1	8067 operations
Method 2	7,236,099 operations
Method 3	4 operations

Doing a time analysis for a program is similar to the analysis of the stair-counting methods. For a time analysis of a program, we do not usually measure the actual time taken to run the program because the number of seconds can depend on too many extraneous factors—such as the speed of the processor, and whether the processor is busy with other tasks. Instead, the analysis counts the

typical operations for program time analysis

number of operations required. There is no precise definition of what constitutes an **operation**, although an operation should satisfy your intuition of a "small step." An operation can be as simple as the execution of a single program statement. Or we could use a finer notion of operation that counts each arithmetic operation (addition, multiplication, etc.) and each assignment to a variable as a separate operation.

dependence on input size

For most programs, the number of operations depends on the program's input. For example, a program that sorts a list of numbers is quicker with a short list than with a long list. In the stairway example, we can view the Eiffel Tower as the input to the problem. In other words, the three different methods all work on the Eiffel Tower, but the methods also work on Toronto's CN Tower, or the stairway to the top of the Statue of Liberty, or any other stairway.

When a method's time depends on the size of the input, then the time can be given as an expression, where part of the expression is the input's size. The time expressions for our three methods are given here:

Method 1 $3n$

Method 2 $n + 2 \, (1 + 2 + \ldots + n)$

Method 3   The number of digits in the number n

The expressions on the right give the number of operations performed by each method when the stairway has n steps.

The expression for the second method is not easy to interpret. It needs to be simplified in order to become a formula that we can easily compare to other formulas. So, let's simplify it. We start with the subexpression:

$$(1 + 2 + \ldots + n)$$

simplification of the Method 2 time analysis

There is a trick that will enable us to find a simplified form for this expression. The trick is to *compute twice the amount of the expression and then divide the result by 2*. Unless you've seen this trick before, it sounds crazy. But it works fine. The trick is illustrated in Figure 1.2. Let's go through the computation of that figure step-by-step.

We write the expression $(1 + 2 + \ldots + n)$ twice and add the two expressions. But as you can see in Figure 1.2, we also use another trick: When we write the expression twice, *we write the second expression backwards*. After we write down the expression twice, we see the following:

$$(1 + 2 + \ldots + n)$$
$$+(n + \ldots + 2 + 1)$$

We want the sum of the numbers on these two lines. That will give us twice the value of $(1 + 2 + \ldots + n)$, and we can then divide by 2 to get the correct value of the subexpression $(1 + 2 + \ldots + n)$.

FIGURE 1.2   Deriving a Handy Formula

$(1 + 2 + \ldots + n)$ can be computed by first computing the sum of twice $(1 + 2 + \ldots + n)$, as shown here:

$$
\begin{array}{ccccccccc}
1 & + & 2 & + \ldots + & (n-1) & + & n & \\
+ \quad n & + & (n-1) & + \ldots + & 2 & + & 1 & \\
\hline
(n+1) & + & (n+1) & + \ldots + & (n+1) & + & (n+1) &
\end{array}
$$

The sum is $n(n+1)$, so $(1 + 2 + \ldots + n)$ is half this amount:

$$(1 + 2 + \ldots + n) = \frac{n(n+1)}{2}$$

Now, rather than proceed in the most obvious way, we instead add pairs of numbers from the first and second lines. We add the 1 and the n to get $n + 1$. Then we add the 2 and the $n - 1$ to again get $n + 1$. We continue until we reach the last pair consisting of an n from the top line and a 1 from the bottom line. All the pairs add up to the same amount, namely $n + 1$. Now that is handy! We get n numbers, and all the numbers are the same, namely $n + 1$. So the total of all the numbers on the preceding two lines is:

$n(n+1)$

The value of twice the expression is n multiplied by $n + 1$. We are now essentially done. The number we computed is twice the quantity we want. So, to obtain our simplified formula, we only need to divide by 2. The final simplification is thus:

$$(1 + 2 + \ldots + n) = \frac{n(n+1)}{2}$$

We will use this formula to simplify the Method 2 expression, but you'll also find that the formula occurs in many other situations. The simplification for the Method 2 expression is as shown at the top of the next page.

Number of operations for Method 2

$$= n + 2\,(1 + 2 + \ldots + n)$$

$$= n + 2\,\left(\frac{n(n+1)}{2}\right) \qquad \text{\textit{Plug in the formula for }} (1 + 2 + \ldots + n)$$

$$= n + n(n+1) \qquad \text{\textit{Cancel the 2s}}$$

$$= n + n^2 + n \qquad \text{\textit{Multiply out}}$$

$$= n^2 + 2n \qquad \text{\textit{Combine terms}}$$

simplification of the Method 3 time analysis

So, Method 2 requires $n^2 + 2n$ operations.

The number of operations for Method 3 is just the number of digits in the integer n when written in the usual way. The usual way of writing numbers is called **base 10 notation**. As it turns out, the number of digits in a number n, when written in base 10 notation, is approximately equal to another mathematical quantity known as the **base 10 logarithm** of n. The notation for the base 10 logarithm of n is written:

$$\log_{10} n$$

base 10 notation and base 10 logarithms

The base 10 logarithm does not always give a whole number. For example, the actual base 10 logarithm of 2689 is about 3.43 rather than 4. If we want the actual number of digits in an integer n, we need to carry out some rounding. In particular, the exact number of digits in a positive integer n is obtained by rounding $\log_{10} n$ downward to the next whole number, and then adding 1. The notation for rounding down and adding 1 is obtained by adding some marks to the logarithm notation as follows:

$$\lfloor \log_{10} n \rfloor + 1$$

This is all fine if you already know about logarithms, but what if some of this is new to you? For now, you can simply define the above notation to mean *the number of digits in the base 10 numeral for n*. You can do this because if others use any of the other accepted definitions for this formula, they will get the same answers that you do. You will be right! (And they will also be right.) In Section 11.3 of this book, we will show that the various definitions of the logarithm function are all equivalent. For now, we will not worry about all that detail. We have larger issues to discuss first. The table of the number of operations for each method can now be expressed more concisely, as shown here:

Method 1 $3n$

Method 2 $n^2 + 2n$

Method 3 $\lfloor \log_{10} n \rfloor + 1$

Big-*O* Notation

The time analyses we gave for the three stair-counting methods were very precise. They computed the exact number of operations for each method. But such precision is sometimes not needed. Often it is enough to know in a rough manner how the number of operations is affected by the input size. In the stair example, we developed the methods thinking about a particular tower, the Eiffel Tower, with a particular number of steps. We expressed our formulas for the operations in terms of n, which stood for the number of steps in the tower. Now suppose that we apply our various stair-counting methods to a tower with ten times as many steps as the Eiffel Tower. If n is the number of steps in the Eiffel Tower, then this taller tower will have $10n$ steps. The number of operations needed for Method 1 on the taller tower increases tenfold (from $3n$ to $3 \times (10n) = 30n$); the time for Method 2 increases approximately 100-fold (from about n^2 to about $(10n)^2 = 100n^2$); and Method 3 increases by only one operation (from the number of digits in n to the number of digits in $10n$, or to be very concrete, from the 4 digits in 2689 to the 5 digits in 26,890). We can express this kind of information in a format called **big-*O* notation**. The symbol *O* in this notation is the letter O, so big-*O* is pronounced "big Oh."

We will describe three common examples of the big-*O* notation. In these examples, we use the notion of "the largest term in a formula." Intuitively, this is the term with the largest exponent on n, or the term that grows the fastest as n itself becomes larger. For now, this intuitive notion of "largest term" is enough. Here are the examples:

Quadratic time. If the largest term in a formula is no more than a constant times n^2, then the algorithm is said to be "**big-*O* of** n^2," written $O(n^2)$, and the algorithm is called **quadratic**. In a quadratic algorithm, doubling the input size makes the number of operations increase by approximately fourfold (or less). For a concrete example, consider Method 2, requiring $n^2 + 2n$ operations. A 100-step tower requires 10,200 operations (that is, $100^2 + 2 \times 100$). Doubling the tower to 200 steps increases the time by approximately fourfold, to 40,400 operations (that is, $200^2 + 2 \times 200$). *quadratic time $O(n^2)$*

Linear time. If the largest term in a formula is a constant times n, then the algorithm is said to be "**big-*O* of** n," written $O(n)$, and the algorithm is called **linear**. In a linear algorithm, doubling the input size makes the time increase by *linear time $O(n)$*

approximately twofold (or less). For example, a formula of $3n + 7$ is linear, so that $3 \times 200 + 7$ is about twice $3 \times 100 + 7$.

logarithmic time
O(log n)

Logarithmic time.   If the largest term in a formula is a constant times a logarithm of n, then the algorithm is "**big-O of the logarithm of** n," written $O(\log n)$, and the algorithm is called **logarithmic**. (The base of the logarithm may be base 10, or possibly another base. We'll talk about the other bases in Section 11.3.) In a logarithmic algorithm, doubling the input size will make the time increase by no more than a fixed number of new operations, such as one more operation, or two more operations—or in general by c more operations, where c is a fixed constant. For example, Method 3 for stair-counting has a logarithmic time formula. And doubling the size of a tower (perhaps from 500 stairs to 1000 stairs) never requires more than one extra operation.

Using big-O notation, we can express the time requirements of our three stair-counting methods as follows:

Method 1 $O(n)$

Method 2 $O(n^2)$

Method 3 $O(\log n)$

order of an
algorithm

When a time analysis is expressed with big-O, the result is called the **order** of the algorithm. We want to reinforce one important point: Multiplicative constants are ignored in the big-O notation. For example, both $2n$ and $42n$ are linear formulas, so both are expressed as $O(n)$, ignoring the multiplicative constants 2 and 42. As you can see, this means that a big-O analysis loses some information about relative times. Nevertheless, a big-O analysis does provide some useful information for comparing algorithms. The stair example illustrates the most important kind of information provided by the order of an algorithm:

The order of an algorithm generally is more important than the speed of the processor.

For example, using the quadratic method (Method 2) the fastest stair climber in the world is still unlikely to do better than a slowpoke—provided that the slowpoke uses one of the faster methods. In an application such as sorting a list, a quadratic algorithm can be impractically slow on even moderately sized lists, regardless of the processor speed. To see this, notice the comparisons showing actual numbers for our three stair-counting methods, which are shown in Figure 1.3.

FIGURE 1.3   Number of Operations for Three Methods

Number of stairs (n)	Logarithmic $O(\log n)$ Method 3, with $\lfloor \log_{10} n \rfloor + 1$ operations	Linear $O(n)$ Method 1, with $3n$ operations	Quadratic $O(n^2)$ Method 2, with $n^2 + 2n$ operations
10	2	30	120
100	3	300	10,200
1000	4	3000	1,002,000
10,000	5	30,000	100,020,000

Time Analysis of C++ Functions

The principles of the stairway example can be applied to counting the number of operations required by a function written in a high-level language such as C++. As an example, consider the function implemented in Figure 1.4. When the function is called, the user is asked to think of a number, and then the function asks a series of questions until the number is found. An example is shown at the bottom of the figure, where the user is asked to "think of a whole number from 1 to 100."

As with the stairway example, the first step of the time-analysis is to decide precisely what we will count as a single operation. For C++ functions, a good choice is to count the total number of C++ operations (such as an assignment, the < operation, or the << operation) plus the number of function calls (such as the call to assert). If the function calls did complex work themselves, then we would also need to count the operations that are carried out there.

With this in mind, let's analyze the guess_game function for the case where the parameter is a positive integer *n,* and (just to be difficult) the user is thinking of the number 1. How many operations does the function carry out in all? Our analysis has three parts:

1. Prior to the for-loop, there are seven operations (one >= comparison, one call to assert, four output operations, and an assignment to answer). Then there is the loop initialization (guess = n). Thus, before the loop body occurs, there are eight operations.

2. We then execute the body of the loop, and because our user is thinking of the number 1, we execute this body *n* times. How many operations occur during each execution of the loop body? We could count this number, but let's just say that each execution of the loop body requires *k* operations, where *k* is some number around 10 or 20. If necessary, we'll figure out *k* later, but for now it is enough to know that we execute the loop body *n* times, and each execution takes *k* operations, for a total of *kn* operations.

3. After the loop finishes, there are five more operations (three in the test of the if-statement, plus two << operations).

FIGURE 1.4   Guessing Game Function for the Time Analysis Example

A Function Implementation

```
void guess_game(int n)
// Precondition: n > 0.
// Postcondition: The user has been asked to think of a number between 1 and n. The function
// asks a series of questions until the number is found.
// Library facilities used: cassert, iostream
{
    int guess;
    char answer;

    assert(n >= 1);

    cout << "Think of a whole number from 1 to " << n << "." << endl;
    answer = 'N';
    for (guess = n; (guess > 0) && (answer != 'Y') && (answer != 'y'); --guess)
    {
        cout << "Is your number " << guess << "?" << endl;
        cout << "Please answer Y or N, and press return: ";
        cin >> answer;
    }

    if ((answer == 'Y') || (answer == 'y'))
        cout << "I knew it all along." << endl;
    else
        cout << "I think you are cheating!" << endl;
}
```

A Sample Dialogue from Calling guess_game(100):

```
Think of a whole number from 1 to 100.
Is your number 100?
Please answer Y or N, and press return: N
Is your number 99?
Please answer Y or N, and press return: N
Is your number 98?
Please answer Y or N, and press return: Y
I knew it all along.
```

www.cs.colorado.edu/~main/chapter1/guess.cxx   **WWW**

The total number of operations is now $kn + 12$. Regardless of how big k is, this formula is always linear time. So, in the case where the user thinks of the number 1, the guess_game function takes linear time. In fact, this is a frequent pattern that we summarize here:

Linear Pattern

A loop that does a fixed amount of operations n times requires $O(n)$ time.

Later you will see additional patterns, resulting in quadratic, logarithmic, and other times. In fact, in Chapter 12 you will rewrite the guess_game function in a better way that requires only logarithmic time.

Worst-Case, Average-Case, and Best-Case Analyses

The guess_game function has another important feature: For any particular value of n, the number of required operations can differ depending on the user's input. For example, with n equal to 100, the user might think of the number 100, and the loop body executes just one time. On the other hand, when the user is thinking of the number 1, the loop body executes the maximum number of times (n times). In other words, for any given n, different possible inputs from the user result in a different number of operations. When this occurs, then we usually count the *maximum* number of required operations for inputs of a given size. Counting the maximum number of operations is called the **worst-case** analysis.

worst-case analysis

During a time analysis, you may sometimes find yourself unable to provide an exact count of the number of operations. If the analysis is a worst-case analysis, you may estimate the number of operations, always making sure that your estimate is on the high side. In other words, the actual number of operations must be guaranteed to be always less than the estimate that you use in the analysis.

In Chapter 12, when we begin the study of searching and sorting, you'll see two other kinds of time-analysis: **average-case** analysis, which determines the average number of operations required for a given n, and **best-case** analysis, which determines the fewest number of operations required for a given n.

Self-Test Exercises for Section 1.2

11. Each of the following are formulas for the number of operations in some algorithm. Express each formula in big-O notation.

    a. $n^2 + 5n$

    b. $3n^2 + 5n$

    c. $(n + 7)(n - 2)$

    d. $100n + 5$

    e. $5n + 3n^2$

    f. The number of digits in $2n$

    g. The number of times that n can be divided by 10 before dropping below 1.0

12. Determine which of the following formulas is $O(n)$:
    a. $16n^3$ c. $\lfloor n^2/2 \rfloor$
    b. $n^2 + n + 2$ d. $10n + 25$

13. What is meant by *worst-case analysis*?

14. What is the worst-case big-O analysis of the following code fragment?
```
for (i = 0; i < n; ++i) {
    for (j = i; j < n; ++j) {
        j += n;
    }
}
```

15. List the following formulas in order of running time analysis, from least to greatest time requirements, assuming that n is very large:
    $n^2 + 1$; $50 \log n$; $1,000,000$; $10n + 10,000$.

16. Write code for a function that uses a loop to compute the sum of all integers from 1 to n. Do a time analysis, counting each basic operation (such as assignment and ++) as one operation.

1.3 TESTING AND DEBUGGING

Always do right. This will gratify some people, and astonish the rest.

MARK TWAIN
To the Young People's Society, February 16, 1901

program testing **Program testing** occurs when you run a program and observe its behavior. Each time you execute a program on some input, you are testing to see how the program works for that particular input, and you are also testing to see how long the program takes to complete. Part of the science of *software engineering* is the systematic construction of a set of test inputs that is likely to discover errors, and such test inputs are the topic of this section.

Choosing Test Data

To serve as good test data, your test inputs need two properties:

Properties of Good Test Data

1. You must know what output a correct program should produce for each test input.

2. The test inputs should include those inputs that are most likely to cause errors.

Do not take the first property lightly—you must choose test data for which you know the correct output. Just because a program compiles, runs, and produces output that looks about right does not mean the program is correct. If the correct answer is 3278 and the program outputs 3277, then something is wrong. How do you know the correct answer is 3278? The most obvious way to find the correct output value is to work it out with pencil and paper using some method other than that used by the program. To aid you in doing this, you might choose test data for which it is easy to calculate the correct answer, perhaps by using smaller input values or by using input values for which the answer is well known.

Boundary Values

We focus on two methods for finding test data that is most likely to cause errors. The first method is based on identifying and testing inputs called *boundary values*, which are particularly apt to cause errors. A **boundary value** of a problem is an input that is one step away from a different kind of behavior. For example, consider a function called `time_check`, with this precondition:

```
int time_check(int hour);
// Precondition: hour lies in the range 0 <= hour <= 23.
```

Two boundary values for `time_check` are `hour` equal to 0 (the lowest legal value) and `hour` equal to 23 (the highest legal value). If we expect the function to behave differently for morning hours (0 to 11) than for afternoon hours (12 through 23), then 11 and 12 are also boundary values. If we expect a different behavior for `hour` equal to 0, then 1 is a boundary value. In fact, 0 and 1 have special behavior in so many situations that it is a good idea to consider 0, 1, and even –1 to be boundary values whenever they are legal input.

In general, there is no precise definition of a boundary value, but you should develop an intuitive feel for finding inputs that are "one step away from different behavior."

Test Boundary Values

If you cannot test all possible inputs, at least test the boundary values. For example, if legal inputs range from zero to one million, then be sure to test input 0 and input 1000000. It is a good idea also to consider 0, 1, and –1 to be boundary values whenever they are legal input.

Fully Exercising Code

The second widely used testing technique requires intimate knowledge of how a program has been implemented. The technique, called **fully exercising code**, is simple, with two rules:

1. Make sure that each line of your code is executed at least once by some of your test data. For example, there might be a portion of your code that is only handling a rare situation. Make sure that this rare situation is included among your set of test data.

2. If there is some part of your code that is sometimes skipped altogether, then make sure that there is at least one test input that actually does skip this part of your code. For example, there might be a loop where the body sometimes is executed zero times. Make sure that there is a test input that causes the loop body to be executed zero times.

profiler

Many compilers have a software tool called a **profiler** to help fully exercise code. A typical profiler will generate a listing indicating how often each statement of your program was executed. This can help you spot parts of your program that were not tested.

Fully Exercising Code

1. Make sure that each line of your code is executed at least once by some of your test data.

2. If there is some part of your code that is sometimes skipped altogether, then make sure that there is at least one test input that actually does skip this part of your code.

Use a software tool called a *profiler* to ensure that you are fully exercising your code.

---

online debugging suggestions

Debugging

Fixing the errors in your programming—debugging—is an important skill that you've had to practice since your first days as a programmer. Some of our debugging suggestions are available online at http://www.cs.colorado.edu/~main/debugging.html. For this textbook, we'll emphasize just one tip that we've found most important.

🛈 PROGRAMMING TIP

HOW TO DEBUG

Finding a test input that causes an error is only half the problem of testing and debugging. After an erroneous test input is found, you still must determine exactly why the "bug" occurs, and then "debug the program." When you have found an error, there is an impulse to dive right in and start changing code. It is tempting to look for suspicious parts of your code and change these suspects to something "that might work better."

Avoid the temptation.

An impulsive change to suspicious code almost always makes matters worse. Instead, you must discover *exactly* why a test case is failing and limit your changes to *corrections of known errors*. Once you have corrected a known error, all test cases should be rerun.

Tracking down the exact reason why a test case is failing can be difficult. For large programs, tracking down errors is nearly impossible without the help of a software tool called a **debugger**. A debugger executes your code one line at a time, or it may execute your code until a certain condition arises. Using a debugger, you can specify what conditions should cause the program execution to pause. You can also keep a continuous watch on the location of the program execution and on the values of specified variables.

debugger

Debugging Tip

1. Never start changing suspicious code on the hope that the change "might work better."

2. Instead, you should discover *exactly* why a test case is failing and limit your changes to *corrections of known errors*.

3. Once you have corrected a known error, all test cases should be rerun.

Use a software tool called a *debugger* to help track down exactly why an error occurs.

Self-Test Exercises for Section 1.3

17. List two properties of good test data.

18. What boundary values should you use as test inputs for the day variable in the function `date_check` from page 15?

19. Suppose you write a program that accepts as input any integer in the range –20 through 20, and outputs the number of digits in the input integer. What boundary values should you use as test inputs?

20. What are two rules for fully exercising code?

21. Suppose you write a program that accepts a single line as input, and outputs a message telling whether or not the line contains the letter A, and whether or not it contained more than three A's. What is a good set of test inputs?

22. Describe how a profiler and a debugger typically aid in testing and debugging programs.

CHAPTER SUMMARY

- The first step in producing a program is to write a precise description of what the program is supposed to do.

- One good method for specifying what a function is supposed to do is to provide a *precondition* and *postcondition* for the function. These form a contract between the programmer who uses the function and the programmer who writes the function. Using the `assert` function to check preconditions can significantly reduce debugging time, and the assertion-checking can later be turned off if program speed is a consideration.

- *Pseudocode* is a mixture of C++ (or some other programming language) and English (or some other natural language). Pseudocode is used to express algorithms so that you are not distracted by details of C++ syntax.

- Understanding and using the *C++ Standard Library* can make program development easier. In addition, studying the data structures of the Standard Library can help you understand trade-offs between different approaches, and can guide the design and implementation of your own data structures. When you are designing your own data structures, an approach that is compliant with the Standard Library allows others to more easily understand your work, and your own work will readily benefit from other pieces of the Standard Library.

- *Time analysis* is an analysis of how many operations an algorithm requires. Often, it is sufficient to express a time analysis in big-O notation, which is the *order* of an algorithm. The order analysis is often enough to compare algorithms and estimate how running time is affected by changing input size.

- Three important examples of big-O analyses are *linear* ($O(n)$), *quadratic* ($O(n^2)$), and *logarithmic* ($O(\log n)$).

- An important testing technique is to identify and test *boundary values*. These are values that lie on a boundary between different kinds of behavior for your program.

- A second important testing technique is to ensure that your test cases are *fully exercising* the code. A software tool called a *profiler* can aid in fully exercising code.

- During debugging, you should discover exactly why a test case is failing and limit your changes to corrections of known errors. Once you have corrected a known error, all test cases should be rerun. Use a software tool called a *debugger* to help track down exactly why an error occurs.

1. a) The potential for code reuse. b) The possibility of future changes to the program.

2. A function prototype consists of the return type, name, and parameter list, which are all followed by a semicolon.

3. The function returns 7 on July 22, 2009. On both July 30, 2009 and February 1, 2010 the function returns 0 (since July 29, 2009 has already passed).

4. `assert (month > 0 && month <=12);`

5. Precondition: x >= 0. Postcondition: The return value is the positive square root of x.

6. `#include <cmath>`
Older compilers may require `<math.h>` instead.

7. `using namespace std;`

8. The modification should change only the constants at the top of the program, the function `celsius_to_fahrenheit` and the call to this function.

9. Stopping early with an error message makes debugging easier.

10. `#define NDEBUG` should appear before any include directives.

11. Part d is linear (i.e., $O(n)$); parts f and g are logarithmic (i.e., $O(\log n)$); all of the others are quadratic (i.e., $O(n^2)$).

12. The only $O(n)$ formula is (d).

13. Worst-case analysis counts the maximum required number of operations for a function. If the exact count of the number of operations cannot be determined, the number of operations may be estimated, providing that the estimate is guaranteed to be higher than the actual number of operations.

14. This is a nested loop in which the number of times the inner loop executes is one more than the value of the outer loop index. The inner loop statements execute $n + (n - 1) + \ldots + 2 + 1$ times. This sum is $n(n + 1)/2$ and gives $O(n^2)$.

15. $n^2 + 1$; $10n + 10000$; $50 \log n$; 1,000,000.

16. Here is one implementation of the function:
```
int sum(int n)
// Precondition: n >= 1.
// Postcondition: The value returned is the
// sum of all integers from 1 to n.
{
    int answer, i;

    answer = 0;
    for (i = 1; i <= n; ++i)
        answer += i;
    return answer;
}
```

Our solution uses `answer += i`, which causes the current value of `i` to be added to what's already in `answer`.

For a time analysis, there are two assignment operations (`answer = 0` and `i = 1`). The `<=` test is executed `n + 1` times (the first `n` times it is true, and the final time, with `i` equal to `n + 1`, it is false). The `++` and `+=` operations are each executed `n` times. The entire code is $O(n)$.

17. Choose test data for which you know the correct output. Test inputs should include those that are most likely to cause errors.

18. 28, 29, 30, and 31 should be boundary values to account for the number of days in any month. 1 should also be tested as a lower boundary value, and 27 as the biggest number that cannot be the number of days in a month. To some extent, though, this is a trick question: Any time that the number of possible inputs to a function is relatively small, we'd suggest that a test program test all possible input values.

19. As always, 0, 1, and –1 are boundary values. In this problem, –20 (smallest value) and 20 (largest value) are also boundary values, as are 9 and 10 (since the number changes from a single digit to two digits) and –9 and –10. (By the way, this particular problem is small enough that it would be reasonable to test *all* legal inputs, rather than testing just the boundary values.)

20. Make sure that each line of your code is executed at least once by some of your test data. If part of your code is sometimes skipped during execution, make sure that at least one test input that skips this part of your code.

21. You should include an empty line (with no characters before the carriage return) and lines with 0, 1, 2, and 3 A's. Also include a line with 4 A's (the smallest case with more than three) and a line with more than 4 A's. For the lines with 1 or more A's, include lines that have only the A's, and also include lines that have A's together with other characters. Also test the case where all the A's appear at the front or the back of the line.

22. A profiler can ensure that your code is being fully exercised (by printing the count of how many times each line of your code has been executed). Once an error has been noticed, a debugger can help track down the cause of the error by displaying the values of variables while the code executes one line at a time.

CHAPTER **2**

Abstract Data Types and C++ Classes

The happiest way to deal with a man is never to tell him anything he does not need to know.

ROBERT A. HEINLEIN
Time Enough for Love

LEARNING OBJECTIVES

When you complete Chapter 2, you will be able to...

- specify and design new classes using a pattern of information hiding with private member variables, const member functions, and modification member functions.
- write a header file and a separate implementation file for any new class.
- create and use namespaces to organize new classes.
- use your new classes in small test programs.
- use the automatic assignment operator and the automatic copy constructor for your new classes.
- identify situations in which member functions and constructors can benefit from using default arguments.
- correctly identify and use value parameters, reference parameters, and const reference parameters.
- overload certain binary operators and input/output operators for new classes.
- identify the need for friend functions of a new class and correctly implement such nonmember functions (which are sometimes overloaded operators).

CHAPTER CONTENTS

Abstract Data Types and C++ Classes

Object-oriented programming (**OOP**) is an approach to programming in which data occurs in tidy packages called *objects*. Manipulation of an object happens with functions called *member functions,* which are part and parcel of their objects.

In C++, the mechanism to create objects and member functions is called a **class**. Classes can support information hiding, which was presented as a cornerstone of program design in Chapter 1. Typically one programming team designs and implements a class, while other programmers use the class. The programmers that *use* the class have no knowledge of *how* the class is implemented. In fact, the implementor of a C++ class can completely hide the knowledge of how the class is implemented—resulting in ideal information hiding.

emphasize what work is done rather than how the work is done

Such a strong emphasis on information hiding is motivated partly by mathematical research about how programmers can improve their reasoning about data types that are used in programs. These mathematical data types are called **abstract data types**, or ADTs—and therefore, programmers sometimes use the term **ADT** to refer to a class that is presented to other programmers with information hiding. This chapter presents two examples of such classes. The examples illustrate the features of C++ classes, with emphasis on information hiding. By the end of the chapter you will be able to implement your own classes in C++. Other programmers could *use* one of your classes without knowing the details of *how* you implemented the class.

2.1 CLASSES AND MEMBERS

A class is a new kind of data type. Each class that you define is a collection of data, such as integers, characters, and so on. In addition, a class has the ability to include special functions, called *member functions.* Member functions are incorporated into the class's definition and are designed specifically to manipulate the class. A programmer who designs a class can even mandate that the *only* way of manipulating the class is through its member functions. But this abstract discussion does not really tell you what a class is. We need some examples. As you read through the first example, concentrate on learning the techniques for implementing a class. Also notice features that allow you to use a class written by another programmer, without knowing details of the class's implementation.

PROGRAMMING EXAMPLE: The Throttle Class

the throttle class

Our first example of a class is a new data type to store and manipulate the status of a simple throttle. Classes such as our throttle class appear in programs that simulate real-world objects. For instance, a flight simulator might include classes for the plane and various parts of the plane such as the engines, the rudder, the altimeter, and even the throttle.

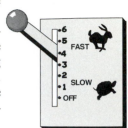

The simple throttle that we have in mind is a lever that can be moved to control fuel flow. The throttle we have in mind has a single shutoff point (where there is no fuel flow) and a sequence of six on positions where the fuel is flowing at progressively higher rates. At the topmost position, the fuel flow is fully on. At the intermediate positions, the fuel flow is proportional to the location of the lever. For example, with six possible positions, and the lever in the fourth position, the fuel flows at $\frac{4}{6}$ of its maximum rate.

One function provided with the class permits a program to initialize a throttle to its shutoff position. Once the throttle has been initialized, there is another function to shift the throttle lever by a given amount.

We also have two functions to examine the status of a throttle. The first of these functions returns the amount of fuel currently flowing, expressed as a proportion of the maximum flow. For example, this function will return approximately 0.667 when the six-position throttle is in its fourth position. The other function returns a true-or-false value, telling whether the throttle is currently on (that is, whether the lever is above the zero position). Thus, the throttle has a total of four functions:

1. A function to set a throttle to its shutoff position.
2. A function to shift a throttle's position by a given amount.
3. A function that returns the fuel flow, expressed as a proportion of the maximum flow.
4. A function to tell us whether the throttle is currently on.

four throttle functions

We can define this new data type as a "class" called throttle that includes data (to store the throttle's current position) and the four functions to modify and examine the throttle. Once the new class is defined, a programmer can declare objects of type throttle and manipulate those objects with the functions. Here is the class definition:

```
class throttle
{
public:
    // MODIFICATION MEMBER FUNCTIONS
    void shut_off( );
    void shift(int amount);
    // CONSTANT MEMBER FUNCTIONS
    double flow( ) const;
    bool is_on( ) const;
private:
    int position;
};
```

declaring the throttle class

This class definition defines a new data type called throttle. The new data type is a *class*, meaning that it may have some components that are data and other components that are functions. Let's examine the definition piece by piece.

The class head. The *head* of the definition consists of the C++ keyword *class*, followed by the name of the new class. You may use any legal identifier for the class's name. We chose the name throttle. We use nouns for the names of new classes—this isn't required by C++, but it's a part of our documentation standard (Appendix J).

The member list. The rest of the definition, from the opening bracket to the closing semicolon, is the *member list* of the definition.

The public section. The first part of the member list is called the *public section*. It begins with the C++ keyword *public* followed by a colon and a list of items. These items are available to anyone who uses the new data type. For the throttle, the list contains the four functions. Such functions are called **member functions** to distinguish them from ordinary functions. Another term is **method**, which means the same as "member function." When a member function is listed in a class body, we list only the function's prototype (that is, the head followed by a semicolon). For example, one of the throttle function prototypes is:

```
void shift(int amount);
```

The prototype indicates that the function has one parameter (an integer called amount). We will use this function to shift a throttle's lever up or down by a given amount. The implementation of the shift function does not appear in the class definition; it will appear elsewhere with other function implementations.

One of the other throttle functions has the following prototype:

```
bool is_on( );
```

the bool type

This function can be used to determine whether a throttle is currently on. The return value of the function has the data type *bool*, which is a built-in data type provided in the ANSI/ISO C++ Standard. The *bool* data type is intended solely for true-or-false values (also called **boolean values** or **logical values**). The important properties of the *bool* type are shown in Figure 2.1. If your compiler does not support the *bool* type, then see Appendix E, "Dealing with Older Compilers," for alternatives.

public member functions

Anyone who declares a variable of type throttle can manipulate that throttle with the four public member functions. In fact, these four functions are the *only* way that a throttle may be manipulated, since there is nothing else available in the public section of the definition.

modification member functions

You should notice that we have classified the public member functions into two groups. The first two functions, shut_off and shift, are **modification member functions**. A modification member function can change the value of an object. For the throttle, the modification functions can change the position of the throttle's lever.

FIGURE 2.1 The Boolean Data Type

C++ Has a Boolean Data Type

The results of true-or-false tests play an important role in programming. For example, we might test whether two variables are equal (x == y), or compare the relative ordering of two integer variables (i < j). In these cases, and others, the result of the test is either *true* or *false*.

In early versions of C and C++, *false* was represented by the integer 0, and *true* was represented by any nonzero integer. But the 1996 C++ Standard provided a new built-in data type called *bool*. The data type is intended to store true-or-false values that are generated from various tests. Along with the data type are two new keywords, *true* and *false*, which are *bool* constants.

Here is a summary of the important features of the *bool* type:

- A *bool* value may be *true* or *false*; no other values are permitted.
- The built-in relational operators (==, !=, <, <=, >, >=) produce a *bool* value.
- The binary "and" operator (&&) combines two *bool* arguments, producing a *true* result only if both arguments are *true*. The binary "or" operator (||) combines two *bool* arguments, producing a *true* result if either of its arguments is *true*. The "not" operator (!) is applied to a single *bool* argument, producing a *false* result from a *true* argument, and vice versa.
- User-defined functions may also compute and return *bool* values.
- A *bool* value may be used as the controlling expression of an if-statement or a loop.

For example, suppose we write a function with the following specification:

```
bool is_even(int i);
// Postcondition: The return value is true if and only if i is an even number.
```

We could use the is_even function in code that prints a message about a number:

```
if (is_even(j))
    cout << j << " is even." << endl;
else
    cout << j << " is odd." << endl;
```

If your compiler does not support the bool type, see Appendix E.

The name "bool" is derived from the name of George Boole, a 19th-century mathematician who developed the foundations for a formal calculus of logical values. Boole was a self-educated scholar with limited formal training. He began his teaching career at the age of 16 as an elementary school teacher and eventually became a professor at Queen's College in Cork. As a dedicated teacher, he died at the early age of 49—the result of pneumonia brought on by a two-mile trek through the rain to lecture to his students.

*constant
member
functions*

On the other hand, the functions flow and is_on are classified as **constant member functions.** A constant member function may examine the status of an object, but changing the object is forbidden. In our example, the two constant member functions can examine but not change a throttle. The prototypes of the constant member functions have the keyword *const* at the end (just after the parameter list). Using the *const* keyword tells the compiler and other programmers that the function cannot change the object.

CLARIFYING THE CONST KEYWORD
Part 2: Constant Member Functions

1. DECLARED CONSTANTS: PAGE 12
2. CONSTANT MEMBER FUNCTIONS
3. CONST REFERENCE PARAMETERS: PAGE 72
4. STATIC MEMBER CONSTANTS: PAGE 103
5. CONST PARAMETERS THAT ARE POINTERS OR ARRAYS: PAGE 162
6. THE CONST KEYWORD WITH A POINTER TO A NODE, AND THE NEED FOR TWO VERSIONS OF SOME MEMBER FUNCTIONS: PAGE 218
7. CONST ITERATORS: PAGE 308

The keyword *const* can be placed after the parameter list of a member function. This use of *const* indicates that the function is a constant member function.

A **constant member function** may examine the status of its object, but it is forbidden from changing the object.

Examples:
  double flow( ) *const*;
  bool is_on( ) *const*;

The private section. The second part of the member list is called the **private section**. It begins with the C++ keyword *private* followed by a colon. After the colon is a list of items that are part of the class but are not directly available to programmers who use the class. In our example, the private section contains one integer called position. This component is a **member variable** of the class, in contrast to the other four members, which are member *functions*. Member variables may be of any data type, such as *int*, *char*, *double*, and so on.

*private member
variables*

Our intention is to use the private member variable to store the *current position* of a throttle, ranging from 0 to 6. The member variable is private, which means that the programmer who *implements* the throttle class can access this member. But programmers who *use* the new class have no way to read or assign values directly to the private member variable.

A Common Pattern for Classes

Public member functions permit programmers to modify and examine objects of the new class. Use the keyword *const* (after the function's parameter list) when a member function examines data without making modifications.

Private member variables of the class store the information about the status of an object of the class.

To summarize, we have declared two public member functions that examine our new class without alterations, and these two functions are declared as *const* functions. Two other public member functions actually allow data to be modified. The data itself is declared as a private member of the new class. This follows a pattern that we will generally use for classes. Later you will see examples that include private member functions (i.e., member functions that are available to the implementor of the new class but forbidden to other programmers), and occasionally public member variables (that may be used by any programmer).

As you have seen, the class body contains prototypes for the member functions but not the full definitions of these functions. The full definitions for the member functions occur after the class definition, in the same place as any other function definition. There are a few peculiarities about the definition of a member function, but before we look at the definitions, we'll tackle another question: How does a programmer use a class such as throttle?

Using a Class

As with any other data type, you may declare throttle variables. These variables are called throttle **objects,** or sometimes throttle **instances.** They are declared in the same way as variables of any other type. Here are two sample declarations of throttle objects:

programs can declare objects of a class

```
throttle my_throttle;
throttle control;
```

Every throttle object contains the private member variable position, but there is no way for a program to access this component directly, because it is a *private* member. The only way that a program can use its throttle objects is by using the four *public* member functions. For example, suppose we have declared the variables shown above, and we want to set control to its third notch. We do this by calling the member functions, as shown here:

```
control.shut_off( );
control.shift(3);
```

Calling a member function always involves the following four steps:

1. Start with the name of the object that you are manipulating. In the examples, we are manipulating control, so we begin with control. If instead, we wanted to manipulate my_throttle, then we would begin with my_throttle. Remember that you cannot just call a member function—you must always indicate which object is being manipulated.

2. After the object name, place a single period.

how to use a member function

3. Next, write the name of the member function. For example, to call control's **shut_off** function, we write control.shut_off—which you can pronounce "control dot shut off."

4. Finally, list the arguments for the function call. In our example, `shut_off` has no arguments, so we have an empty list ( ). The second function call, to the function `shift`, requires one argument, which is the amount (3) that we are shifting the throttle.

```
control.shut_off( );
control.shift(3);
```

Our example made function calls to the `shut_off` and `shift` member functions of `control`. An OOP programmer usually would use slightly different terminology, saying that we **activated** the `shut_off` and `shift` member functions. "Activating a member function" is nothing more than OOP jargon for *making a function call* to a member function.

As another example, here is a sequence of several activations to set a throttle according to user input, and then print the throttle's flow:

```
throttle control;
int user_input;

control.shut_off( );
cout << "Please type a number from 0 to 6: ";
cin >> user_input;
control.shift(user_input);
if (control.is_on( ))
    cout << "The flow is " << control.flow( ) << endl;
else
    cout << "The flow is now off" << endl;
```

Notice how the return value of `control.flow` is used directly in the output statement. As with any other function, the return value of a member function can be used as part of an output statement or other expression.

Using a `throttle` is easy because we don't worry about how the member functions accomplish their work. We simply activate each member function and wait for it to return, just like any other function. This is information hiding at its best.

A Small Demonstration Program for the Throttle Class

An example of a program using the `throttle` class is shown in Figure 2.2. The program declares a throttle called `sample` and shifts the throttle upward according to the user's input. The throttle is then moved down one notch at a time, with the flow printed at each notch. A typical dialogue with the program would look like this (with the user's input printed in bold):

dialogue with the demo program

```
I have a throttle with 6 positions.
Where would you like to set the throttle?
Please type a number from 0 to 6: 3
The flow is now 0.5
The flow is now 0.333333
The flow is now 0.166667
The flow is now off
```

FIGURE 2.2   Sample Program for the Throttle Class

A Program

```
// FILE: demo1.cxx
// This small demonstration shows how the throttle class is used.
#include <iostream>          // Provides cout and cin
#include <cstdlib>           // Provides EXIT_SUCCESS
using namespace std;         // Allows all Standard Library items to be used

class throttle
{
public:
    // MODIFICATION MEMBER FUNCTIONS
    void shut_off( );
    void shift(int amount);
    // CONSTANT MEMBER FUNCTIONS
    double flow( ) const;
    bool is_on( ) const;
private:
    int position;
};

int main( )
{
    throttle sample;
    int user_input;

    // Set the sample throttle to a position indicated by the user.
    cout << "I have a throttle with 6 positions." << endl;
    cout << "Where would you like to set the throttle? " << endl;
    cout << "Please type a number from 0 to 6: ";
    cin >> user_input;
    sample.shut_off( );
    sample.shift(user_input);

    // Shift the throttle down to zero, printing the flow along the way.
    while (sample.is_on( ))
    {
        cout << "The flow is now " << sample.flow( ) << endl;
        sample.shift(-1);
    }
    cout << "The flow is now off" << endl;
    return EXIT_SUCCESS;
}
```

These lines are the definition of the throttle class.

This is the declaration of a throttle object called sample.

In the actual program, you would place the implementations of the throttle's four member functions here, but we haven't yet written these implementations!

www.cs.colorado.edu/~main/chapter2/demo1.cxx   **WWW**

Implementing Member Functions

using the class name with two colons : :

The demonstration program in Figure 2.2 includes everything except the complete definitions of the member functions. Writing definitions for member functions is just like writing any other function, with one small difference: In the head of the function definition, the class name must appear before the function name, separated by two colons. In our example, throttle:: appears in the head, before the function name. This requirement, called the **scope resolution operator**, tells the compiler that the function is a member function of a particular class. For example, the definition of our first member function must include the full name throttle::shut_off, as shown here:

implementation of shut_off

```
void throttle::shut_off( )
// Precondition: None.
// Postcondition: The throttle has been turned off.
{
    position = 0;
}
```

The reason for the scope resolution operator is that a function name might be used as the name of another class's member function, or as the name of another ordinary function. By specifying the full name, throttle::shut_off, we indicate that this is the implementation of the throttle member function, and not some other shut_off function.

We use the term **function implementation** to describe a full function definition such as this. The function implementation provides all the details of how the function works, as opposed to the mere prototype that appears in the class definition and gives no indication of how the function accomplishes its work.

Our implementation of shut_off simply sets the private member variable position to zero. But just whose position is being used here? Are we assigning to my_throttle.position? Or to control.position? Or even to some other throttle's position member? The answer depends on just which object activates shut_off. If my_throttle.shut_off is activated, then position refers to my_throttle.position. If we activate control.shut_off, then position in the implementation refers to control.position.

The Key to Member Variables

Each object keeps its own copies of all member variables.

When a member function's implementation refers to a member variable, then the actual member variable used always comes from the object that activated the member function.

Because each object of a class keeps its own copies of the member variables, it is possible to have several different objects of the same class in a single program. For example, we might have these statements in a program:

```
throttle big;
throttle low;

big.shut_off( );
low.shut_off( );
big.shift(6);
low.shift(1);

cout << "The big flow is: " << big.flow( ) << endl;
cout << "The low flow is: " << low.flow( ) << endl;
```

Declare two throttles.

Set the positions of the throttle's levers.

Print the flows.

The first output statement prints 1.0 (which is big's flow). The second output statement prints 0.166667 (which is low's flow).

By now you know enough about member functions to implement the other three member functions of a throttle. For example, the shift function changes the position member variable by the amount specified in the parameter. In the implementation, we make sure that the shift doesn't go below 0 or above 6, as shown here:

implementing shift

```
void throttle::shift(int amount)
// Precondition: shut_off has been called at least once to initialize the throttle.
// Postcondition: The throttle's position has been moved by amount (but
// not below 0 or above 6).
{
    position += amount;

    if (position < 0)
        position = 0;
    else if (position > 6)
        position = 6;
}
```

using +=

This might be the first time you've seen the += operator. Its effect is to take the amount on the right side (such as amount) and add it to what's already in the variable on the left (such as position). This sum is then stored back in the variable on the left side of +=.

Notice that the shift function has a precondition indicating that "shut_off has been called at least once to initialize the throttle." Without this precondition, the member variable position would contain garbage—although this is an example of a precondition that we cannot actually verify. Later we will use a feature called *constructors* to guarantee that every object is properly initialized.

implementing flow

The flow function simply returns the current flow as determined by the position member variable, as shown here:

```
double throttle::flow( ) const
// Precondition: shut_off has been called at least once to initialize the throttle.
// Postcondition: The value returned is the current flow as a proportion of
// the maximum flow.
{
    return position / 6.0;
}
```

Divide by 6.0, since the throttle has six positions.

Since flow is a constant member function, we must include the keyword *const* at the end of the function's head.

implementing is_on

The final throttle function is called is_on. The function returns a boolean true-or-false value, indicating whether the fuel flow is on. Here is one way to implement is_on so that it returns the correct boolean value:

```
bool throttle::is_on( ) const
// Precondition: shut_off has been called at least once to initialize the throttle.
// Postcondition: If the throttle's flow is above 0, then the function
// returns true; otherwise, it returns false.
{
    return (flow( ) > 0);
}
```

Member Functions May Activate Other Members

The implementation of is_on illustrates a final important feature of member functions: The implementation of a member function may activate other member functions. For example, our implementation of is_on activates the flow member function. When flow is used within the body of is_on, it is used without an object name such as my_throttle or control. No object name is needed in front of it—we just write flow( ); the actual instance of flow that will be used is determined by the activation of is_on. So when my_throttle.is_on is activated, it uses my_throttle.flow. On the other hand, when control.is_on is activated, it uses control.flow.

⊕ PROGRAMMING TIP

STYLE FOR BOOLEAN VARIABLES

In the return statement of is_on, we wrote: *return* (flow( ) > 0);. The test in the parentheses is evaluated, and the true-or-false value of this test is returned by the function. Whenever possible, use a true-or-false test (such as >) to return a boolean value. This tip is one of several style issues concerning boolean values.

A second issue for boolean values is that the value can be used to directly control an if-statement or a loop. For example, in Figure 2.2 on page 41 we have the following while-loop:

```
while (sample.is_on( ))
{
    cout << "The flow is now " << sample.flow( ) << endl;
    sample.shift(-1);
}
```

If the return value of the is_on function is true, then the loop continues. When is_on returns false, the loop will end.

As a final tip, we generally use the word "is" for the first part of the name of a function that returns a boolean value. This increases the readability of statements such as the statement written above that reads "while sample is on ...".

Self-Test Exercises for Section 2.1

1. What kind of member of a class supports information hiding?
2. When should a member of a class be declared public?
3. What values can a bool variable hold?
4. What is the difference between a class and an object?
5. Describe the difference between a modification member function and a constant member function.
6. Describe the one common place where the scope resolution operator throttle:: is used.
7. Write a C++ program that declares a throttle, shifts the throttle halfway up (to the third position), and prints the current flow.
8. Add a new throttle member function that will return true if the current flow is more than half. The body of your implementation should activate flow and use the guidelines for boolean values listed above.

2.2 CONSTRUCTORS

The throttle class is complete. It can be used in a program, as we did in Figure 2.2 on page 41. In that program we started with the throttle class definition, followed by the program that uses the new class, and finally the implementations of the four member functions. This works fine; all of Figure 2.2 can be placed in a single file that is compiled and run like any other program. But there are some improvements to make before leaving the throttle example.

The first improvement deals with initializing a throttle. Three of the member functions have a precondition indicating that "shut_off has been called at least once to initialize the throttle." Without this precondition, the member variable `position` would contain garbage, and anything might happen. Unfortunately, there is no way to test the precondition to ensure that a throttle has been initialized.

Constructors are a way to solve this problem by providing an initialization function that is *guaranteed* to be called. A **constructor** is a member function with these special properties:

- If a class has a constructor, then a constructor is called automatically whenever a variable of the class is declared. If a constructor has any parameters, then the arguments for the constructor call must be given after the variable name (at the point where the variable is declared).

- The name of a constructor must be the same as the name of the class. In our example, the name of the constructor is `throttle`. This seems strange: Normally we *avoid* using the same name for two different things. But it is a requirement of C++ that the constructor use the same name as the class.

- A constructor does not have *any* return value. Because of this, you must *not* write *void* (or any other return type) at the front of the constructor's head. The compiler knows that every constructor has no return value, but a compiler error occurs if you actually write *void* at the front of the constructor's head.

The Throttle's Constructor

Let's make these features concrete by implementing a throttle constructor. The constructor we have in mind will actually make the throttle more flexible by allowing the total number of throttle positions to vary from one throttle to another. We will no longer be restricted to throttles with only six positions. For example, a lawn mower throttle might need only four positions, whereas a forty-position throttle could be used for a rocket that needs finer control.

adding a constructor to the throttle class

Our throttle constructor has one parameter, which tells the total number of positions that the throttle contains. We do not need a second parameter for the "current throttle position" because our constructor will always initialize the current position to zero. Here is the prototype for the new constructor, along with its precondition/postcondition contract:

```
throttle(int size);
// Precondition: 0 < size.
// Postcondition: The throttle has size positions above the shutoff position,
//   and its current position is off.
```

It does look strange, seeing the word `throttle` used in this way, but we have no choice: The name of the constructor must be the same as the name of the class.

Also notice that the word *void* does not appear at the front of the prototype, nor is there any other return type for the function. The constructor's prototype is placed in the throttle class definition along with the other member functions' prototypes, as indicated here:

```
class throttle
{                           This is the prototype for the
public:                     throttle constructor.
    // CONSTRUCTOR
    throttle(int size);
    // MODIFICATION MEMBER FUNCTIONS
    void shut_off( );       Prototypes for other member
    . . .                   functions appear as usual.
```

We'll look at the implementation of the constructor in a moment, but first let's see some examples of using the constructor in declarations of throttle objects. For example, here are the declarations of two throttles:

```
throttle mower_control(4);
throttle apollo(40);
```

After these declarations, each throttle is shut off. The mower_control has four positions, and the apollo throttle has forty.

Often it is useful to provide several different constructors, each of which does a different kind of initialization. For instance, suppose many of our throttles require just one on position—a kind of all-or-nothing throttle. Then we could provide a second constructor with no parameters. The second constructor gives the throttle just one on position, and sets the current position to zero. The prototype for this constructor is shown here:

```
throttle( );
// Precondition: None.
// Postcondition: The throttle has one position above the shutoff position,
// and its current position is off.
```

A constructor with no parameters is called a **default constructor**. Here is a declaration of two throttles, with the first using the default constructor and the second using the other constructor:

```
throttle toggle;
throttle complicated(100);
```

When toggle uses the default constructor, there is no argument list—not even a pair of parentheses. In other words, to use the default constructor, just declare an object with no argument list. The default constructor will be called.

You may declare as many constructors as you like—one for each different way of initializing an object. Each constructor must have a distinct parameter list so that the compiler can tell them apart. Only one default constructor is allowed.

To implement our new constructors, we need a new private member variable called `top_position`, which keeps track of the maximum position of the throttle. The default constructor sets `top_position` to 1, and the other constructor sets `top_position` according to the constructor's `size` parameter. The complete new class definition, along with the implementations of the new constructors, is given in Figure 2.3.

FIGURE 2.3   Constructors for the Throttle

A Class Definition

```
class throttle
{
public:
    // CONSTRUCTORS
    throttle( );
    throttle(int size);
    // MODIFICATION MEMBER FUNCTIONS
    void shut_off( );
    void shift(int amount);
    // CONSTANT MEMBER FUNCTIONS
    double flow( ) const;
    bool is_on( ) const;
private:
    int top_position;
    int position;
};
```

prototype for the default constructor

prototype for the other constructor

A new private member variable keeps track of how many positions the throttle has.

Implementations of the Constructors

```
throttle::throttle( )
{
    top_position = 1;
    position = 0;
}
```

```
throttle::throttle(int size)
// Library facilities used: cassert
{
    assert(0 < size);
    top_position = size;
    position = 0;
}
```

What Happens If You Write a Class with No Constructors?

If you write a class with no constructors, then the compiler automatically creates a simple default constructor. This **automatic default constructor** doesn't do much work. It just calls the default constructor for the member variables that are objects of some other class. Generally, you should write your own constructors, including your own default constructor, rather than depending on the automatic default constructor.

PROGRAMMING TIP

ALWAYS PROVIDE CONSTRUCTORS

When you write a class, and you define the constructors, each variable of the class will have one of your constructors called when the variable is declared. This increases the reliability of programs by reducing the chance of using uninitialized variables. We also recommend that you define a default constructor for each of your classes. This allows programmers to declare a variable of your class, without having to provide any arguments for a constructor.

Revising the Throttle's Member Functions

Because we added a new member variable, `top_position`, we must revise the member functions to use `top_position` rather than the number 6 for the number of throttle positions. For example, here is the revised implementation of `shift`:

```
void throttle::shift(int amount)
// Postcondition: The throttle's position has been moved by amount (but
// not below 0 or above the top position).
{
    position += amount;

    if (position < 0)
        position = 0;
    else if (position > top_position)
        position = top_position;
}
```

Use the member variable top_position instead of the number 6.

Notice that we no longer need a precondition, because we are guaranteed to have one of the constructors called. When there is no precondition you may omit it, as we have done here, or you may list the precondition as "None."

when there is no precondition

Inline Member Functions

We'll use a new technique to revise the other three member functions. The technique is to place the complete definitions of `shut_off`, `flow`, and `is_on` inside the class definition, as shown in the three highlighted lines of Figure 2.4.

The use of *double* in the definition of `flow` changes `top_position` from an integer to a *double* number (otherwise the division will perform an integer division, throwing away any remainder). This change of data types is called a **type cast**. It is needed whenever you compute the ordinary division of two integers (and you want to include the fractional part in the result).

The other change we made in the implementations is to have is_on merely examine position. This seems simpler than our original implementation (which activated the flow function).

Placing a function definition inside the class definition is called an **inline member function**. It has two effects:

- You don't have to write the implementation later.
- Each time the inline function is used in your program, the compiler will recompile the short function definition and place a copy of this compiled short definition in your code. This saves some execution time (there is no actual function call and function return), but it may be inefficient in space (you end up with many copies of the same compiled code).

Notice that when you declare an inline member function, there is no semicolon before the opening curly bracket or after the closing curly bracket.

⬆ PROGRAMMING TIP

WHEN TO USE AN INLINE MEMBER FUNCTION

Inline functions cause some inefficiency—your compiled code might be longer than it needs to be. Inline functions also result in a messier class definition, which is harder to read and harder to debug. Because of these problems, we recommend using an inline member function only for the simple situation when the function definition consists of a single short statement.

FIGURE 2.4   Inline Member Functions

A Class Definition

```
class throttle
{
public:
    // CONSTRUCTORS
    throttle( );                              The highlighted code shows
    throttle(int size);                       three inline member functions.
    // MODIFICATION MEMBER FUNCTIONS
    void shut_off( ) { position = 0; }
    void shift(int amount);
    // CONSTANT MEMBER FUNCTIONS
    double flow( ) const { return position / double(top_position); }
    bool is_on( ) const { return (position > 0); }
private:
    int top_position;
    int position;
};
```

The type name "double" changes top_position from an integer to a double number. The change is called a "type cast," and it prevents an unintended integer division.

Self-Test Exercises for Section 2.2

   9. Use an inline function to rewrite the "halfway on" function from Self-Test Exercise 8 on page 45.

10. When an object variable is declared, what happens if the programmer did not write a constructor for the class?

11. Find the error with the following constructor prototype:

```
void throttle(int size);
```

12. Write a new throttle constructor with two parameters: the total number of positions for the throttle, and its initial position.

2.3   USING A NAMESPACE, HEADER FILE, AND IMPLEMENTATION FILE

It makes sense to make our new `throttle` class easily available to any program that needs it. (After all, you never know when you might need a throttle.) We'd like to do so without revealing all the details of the new class's implementation. In addition, we don't want other programmers to worry about whether their own selection of names for variables and such will conflict with the names that we happen to use.

These goals are accomplished by three steps:

1. Creating a namespace

2. Writing the header file

3. Writing the implementation file

The purposes and techniques for each of these steps are discussed next. We also discuss how another programmer can use the items that you have written with these techniques.

Creating a Namespace

When a program uses different classes written by several different programmers, there is a possibility of a name conflict. We have written a throttle class, but perhaps NASA also writes a throttle and a program needs to use both throttles. This isn't too likely with demonstration classes such as the throttle, but common realistic names often have conflicts.

The solution is to use an organizational technique called a *namespace*. A **namespace** is a name that a programmer selects to identify a portion of his or her work. The name should be descriptive, but it should also include part of your real name or email address so that it is unlikely to cause conflicts. Our first namespace in Chapter 2 will be `main_savitch_2A`; later in the chapter we will have `main_savitch_2B`, and we will use similar names for other chapters.

namespace grouping

All work that is part of our namespace must be in a **namespace grouping**, in the following form:

```
namespace main_savitch_2A
{
    ‖ Any item that belongs to the namespace is written here.
}
```

The word *namespace* is a C++ keyword. The word `main_savitch_2A` is the name that we chose for our namespace; it may be any legal C++ identifier. All our other code appears inside the curly brackets. For example, the throttle class declaration and the implementation of the throttle member functions will all be placed in the namespace.

A single namespace, such as `main_savitch_2A`, may have several different namespace groupings. For example, the throttle class definition can appear in a namespace grouping for `main_savitch_2A` at one point in the program. Later, when we are ready to implement the throttle member functions, we can open a second namespace grouping for `main_savitch_2A`, and place the function definitions in that second grouping. These two namespace groupings are both for the `main_savitch_2A` namespace, although surprisingly, they don't need to be in the same file. Typically, they appear in two separate files:

- The class definition appears in a **header file** that provides all the information that a programmer needs in order to use the class.
- The member function definitions appear in a separate **implementation file**.

The rest of this section illustrates our format of the header and implementation files for our throttle class, along with an example of how a program can use the items in a namespace.

The Header File

a comment in the header file tells how to use the class

The **header file** for a class provides all the information that a programmer needs to use the class. In fact, all the information needed to use the class should appear in a **header file comment** at the top of the header file. To use the class, a programmer need only read this informative comment. The comment should include a list of all the public member functions, along with a precondition/postcondition contract for each function. (If a function has no precondition, then we will usually omit it, listing the postcondition on its own.) The comment does not list any private members, because a programmer who *uses* the new class is not concerned with private members.

The class definition for the new class appears in a namespace grouping after the header file comment. But only the class definition appears—the implementations of the member functions do not appear here (except for inline functions).

There are some problems with putting the class definition in the header file. One problem is that programmers who use the class might think that they have to read this definition to use the class. They don't. All the information needed to use the class is in the header file comment. But C++ requires the class definition to appear here, so we have no way around this problem.

A second problem arises from the way that header files are sometimes used. As you will see in later chapters, a program sometimes includes a header file more than once. As a result, the class definition appears more than once, and compilation fails because of "duplicate class definition." We can avoid duplicate class definition by placing all the header file's definitions inside a compiler directive called a **macro guard**. The total form of the throttle class declaration in our namespace with a macro guard is shown here:

avoid duplicate definition by using a macro guard

```
#ifndef MAIN_SAVITCH_THROTTLE_H
#define MAIN_SAVITCH_THROTTLE_H
namespace main_savitch_2A
{
    class throttle
    {
        ‖  The usual class definition appears here.
    };
}
#endif
```

The first line, `#ifndef MAIN_SAVITCH_THROTTLE_H`, indicates the start of the macro guard. All the statements that appear between here and the `#endif` are under the power of the macro guard. These statements will be compiled only if the compiler has not yet seen a definition of the rather long word `MAIN_SAVITCH_THROTTLE_H`.

So how does this avoid a duplicate definition? At the first appearance of the code:

- The class definition is compiled.

- The word `MAIN_SAVITCH_THROTTLE_H` is also defined (by the definition `#define MAIN_SAVITCH_THROTTLE_H`).

Now, if the code should appear a second time, the class definition is skipped (since `MAIN_SAVITCH_THROTTLE_H` is already defined). Our throttle header file, called `throttle.h`, is shown in Figure 2.5. In the past, most programmers used `.h` as the end of the header file name (such as `throttle.h`), although this practice has become less common because the standard header files (such as `iostream`) no longer use the `.h`. However, we'll continue to use the `.h` because some text editing programs or compilers provide special modes based on the `.h` file type.

<hr>

Header File for a Class

When you design and implement a class, you should provide a separate header file.

At the top of the header file, place all of the documentation that a programmer needs to use the class.

The class definition for the class appears after the documentation. But only the class definition appears and not the implementations of member functions (except inline functions).

Place the class definition inside a namespace, and place a "macro guard" around the entire thing. The macro guard prevents accidental duplicate definition.

<hr>

FIGURE 2.5   Header File for the Throttle Class

A Header File

```
// FILE: throttle.h
// CLASS PROVIDED: throttle (part of the namespace main_savitch_2A)
//
// CONSTRUCTORS for the throttle class:
//    throttle( )
//      Postcondition: The throttle has one position above the shut_off position, and it is
//      currently shut off.
//
//    throttle(int size)
//      Precondition:  size > 0.
//      Postcondition: The throttle has size positions above the shut_off position, and it is
//      currently shut off.
//
// MODIFICATION MEMBER FUNCTIONS for the throttle class:
//    void shut_off( )
//      Postcondition: The throttle has been turned off.
//
//    void shift(int amount)
//      Postcondition: The throttle's position has been moved by
//      amount (but not below 0 or above the top position).
```

Member functions often have no precondition.

(continued)

(FIGURE 2.5 continued)

```
//
// CONSTANT MEMBER FUNCTIONS for the throttle class:
//    double flow( ) const
//       Postcondition: The value returned is the current flow as a
//       proportion of the maximum flow.
//
//    bool is_on( ) const
//       Postcondition: If the throttle's flow is above 0 then
//       the function returns true; otherwise it returns false.
//
// VALUE SEMANTICS for the throttle class (see the discussion on page 57):
//       Assignments and the copy constructor may be used with throttle objects.
```

```
#ifndef MAIN_SAVITCH_THROTTLE
#define MAIN_SAVITCH_THROTTLE                       start of the macro guard

namespace main_savitch_2A
{                                      start of the namespace grouping
    class throttle
    {
    public:
        // CONSTRUCTORS
        throttle( );
        throttle(int size);
        // MODIFICATION MEMBER FUNCTIONS
        void shut_off( ) { position = 0; }
        void shift(int amount);
        // CONSTANT MEMBER FUNCTIONS
        double flow( ) const { return position / double(top_position); }
        bool is_on( ) const { return (position > 0); }
    private:
        int top_position;
        int position;
    };
                              end of the namespace grouping
}


                              end of the macro guard
#endif
```

www.cs.colorado.edu/~main/chapter2/throttle.h   **W W W**

Describing the Value Semantics of a Class Within the Header File

The **value semantics** of a class determines how values are copied from one object to another. In C++, the value semantics consists of two operations: the assignment operator and the copy constructor.

The assignment operator. For two objects x and y, an assignment y = x copies the value of x to y. Assignments such as this are permitted for any new class that we define. For a new class, C++ normally carries out assignments by simply copying each member variable from the object on the right of the assignment to the object on the left of the assignment. This method of copying is called the **automatic assignment operator**. Later we will see examples where the automatic assignment operator does not work. But for now, our new classes can use the automatic assignment operator.

The copy constructor. A **copy constructor** is a constructor with exactly one argument, and the data type of the argument is the same as the constructor's class. For example, a copy constructor for the throttle has one argument, and that argument is itself a throttle. The usual purpose of a copy constructor is to initialize a new object as an exact copy of an existing object. For example, here is a bit of code that creates a 100-position throttle called x, shifts x to its middle position, and then declares a second throttle that is initialized as an exact copy of x:

```
throttle x(100);        The throttle y is initialized as a
x.shift(50);            copy of x, so that both throttles
throttle y(x);          are at position 50 out of 100.
```

The highlighted statement activates the throttle's copy constructor to initialize y as an exact copy of x. After the initialization, x and y may take different actions, ending up with different fuel flows, but at this point, both throttles are set to position 50 out of 100.

There is an alternative syntax for calling the copy constructor. Instead of writing `throttle y(x);`, you may write `throttle y = x;`. This alternative syntax looks like an assignment statement, but keep in mind that the actual effect is a bit different. The assignment `y = x;` merely copies x to the already existing object, y. On the other hand, the declaration `throttle y = x;` both declares a new object, y, and calls the copy constructor to initialize y as a copy of x. We will always use the original form `throttle y(x);`, because this form is less likely to be confused with an ordinary assignment statement.

As the implementor of a class, you may write a copy constructor much like any other constructor—and you will do so for classes in future chapters. But for now we can take advantage of a C++ feature: C++ provides an **automatic copy constructor**. The automatic copy constructor initializes a new object by merely copying all the member variables from the existing object. For example, in the declaration `throttle y(x);`, the automatic copy constructor will copy the two member variables from the existing throttle x to the new throttle y.

For many classes, the automatic assignment operator and the automatic copy constructor work fine. But as we have warned, we will later see classes where the automatic versions fail. Merely copying member variables is not always sufficient. Because of this, programmers are wary of assignments and the copy constructor. To address this problem, we suggest that your documentation include a comment indicating that the value semantics is safe to use.

<hr>

PROGRAMMING TIP

DOCUMENT THE VALUE SEMANTICS

When you implement a class, the documentation should include a comment indicating that the value semantics is safe to use. For example, in our throttle header file we wrote:

```
//  VALUE SEMANTICS  for the throttle class:
//      Assignments and the copy constructor may be used with throttle
//      objects.
```

The Implementation File

An **implementation file** for a new class has several items: First, a small comment appears, indicating that the documentation is available in the header file. Second, an include directive appears, causing the compiler to grab the class definition from the header file. In our throttle example, the include directive is:

1. comment

2. include directives

```
#include "throttle.h"
```

When we list the name of the header file, "throttle.h", we use quotation marks rather than angle brackets. The angle brackets (such as the include directive #include <iostream>) are used only to include a Standard Library facility, but we use quotation marks for our own header files.

After the include directive, the program reopens the namespace and gives the implementations of the class's member functions. The namespace is reopened by the same syntax we saw in the header file:

3. reopen the namespace and define the implementations

```
namespace main_savitch_2A
{
    ‖ The definitions of the member functions are written here.
}
```

Most compilers require specific endings for the name of an implementation file, such as .cpp or .C. We will use .cxx for the endings of our implementation file names, such as the complete implementation file throttle.cxx shown in Figure 2.6.

Implementation File for a Class

Each class has a separate implementation file that contains the implementations of the class's member functions. For more coverage of implementation and header files, please see www.cs.colorado.edu/~main/separation.html

FIGURE 2.6 Implementation File for the Throttle Class

An Implementation File

```
// FILE: throttle.cxx
// CLASS IMPLEMENTED: throttle (see throttle.h for documentation)

#include <cassert>     // Provides assert
#include "throttle.h"  // Provides the throttle class definition

namespace main_savitch_2A
{
    throttle::throttle( )
    {   // A simple on-off throttle
        top_position = 1;
        position = 0;
    }

    throttle::throttle(int size)
    // Library facilities used: cassert
    {
        assert(size > 0);
        top_position = size;
        position = 0;
    }

    void throttle::shift(int amount)
    {
        position += amount;

        if (position < 0)
            position = 0;
        else if (position > top_position)
            position = top_position;
    }
}
```

www.cs.colorado.edu/~main/chapter2/throttle.cxx **WWW**

Using the Items in a Namespace

Once the header and implementation files are in place, any program can use our new class. At the top of the program, you place an include directive to include the header file, as shown here for our example:

```
#include "throttle.h"
```

Notice that we include only the header file, and not the implementation file.

After the include directive, the program can use the items that are defined in the namespace in one of three ways:

1. Place a using statement that makes all of the namespace available. The format for the statement is:

   using namespace main_savitch_2A;

   This using statement makes all items available from the specified name-space (main_savitch_2A). This is the same technique that we've been using to pick up all the available items from the Standard Library (with the statement *using namespace* std;).

2. If we need to use only a specific item from the namespace, then we put a using statement consisting of the keyword *using* followed by the name of the namespace, two colons, and the item we want to use. For example:

   using main_savitch_2A::throttle;

   This allows us to use throttle from the namespace; if there are other items in the namespace, however, they are not available.

3. With no using statement, we can still use any item by prefixing the item name with the namespace and "::" at the point where the item is used. For example, we could declare a throttle variable with the statement:

   main_savitch_2A::throttle apollo;

   This use of "::" is an example of the scope resolution operator that we saw on page 42. It clarifies which particular throttle we are asking to use.

A summary for creating and using namespaces is shown in Figure 2.7, including a warning never to place a using statement in a header file.

Our complete demonstration program using the revised throttle appears in Figure 2.8 on page 61. When the complete program actually is compiled, you may need to provide extra information about where to find a compiled version of the implementation file, throttle.cxx. This process, called *linking*, varies from compiler to compiler (see Appendix D).

FIGURE 2.7 Summary for Creating and Using a Namespace

1. **The Global Namespace:** Any items that are not explicitly placed in a namespace become part of the so-called **global namespace**. These items can be used at any point without any need for a using statement or a scope resolution operator.

2. **C++ Standard Library:** If you use the *new C++ header file names* (such as `<iostream>` or `<cstdlib>`), then all of the items in the C++ Standard Library are automatically part of the `std` namespace. The simplest way to use these items is to place a using directive after the include statements: `using namespace std;`. On the other hand, if you use the *old C++ header file names* (such as `<iostream.h>` or `<stdlib.h>`), then the items are part of the global namespace, so that no using statement or scope resolution operator is needed.

3. **Creating Your Own Namespace:** To create a new namespace, the items are placed in a **namespace grouping**, in the following form:

   `namespace` <The name for the namespace>
   {
   ‖ Any item that belongs to the namespace is written here.
   }

   The word `namespace` is a C++ keyword. The name of the namespace may be any C++ identifier, but it should be chosen to avoid likely conflicts with others' namespaces (by using part of your real name or email address). A single namespace may have several different namespace groupings, possibly in different files. For example, a class definition can appear in a namespace grouping in a header file, whereas the member function definitions appear in a second grouping of the same namespace in the implementation file.

4. **Using a Namespace:**
   - To use all items from a namespace, put a using directive after all include statements, in the form:
     `using namespace` < The name for the namespace> `;`
   - To use one item from a namespace, put a specific using directive after all include statements, in the form:
     `using` < The name for the namespace>`::`<The name of the item> `;`
   - With no using directive, you can still use an item directly in a program by preceding the item with the name of the namespace and "`::`".

PITFALL

NEVER PUT A USING STATEMENT ACTUALLY IN A HEADER FILE

Sometimes a header file itself needs to use something from a namespace. In this case, always use the third form shown above; never put a using statement in a header file (since doing so can have unexpected results in other programs that include the header file).

FIGURE 2.8 Sample Program for the Revised Throttle Class

A Program

```
// FILE: demo2.cxx
// This small demonstration shows how the revised throttle class is used.
#include <iostream>      // Provides cout and cin
#include <cstdlib>       // Provides EXIT_SUCCESS
#include "throttle.h"    // Provides the throttle class
using namespace std;     // Allows all Standard Library items to be used
using main_savitch_2A::throttle;

const int DEMO_SIZE = 5;   // Number of positions in a demonstration throttle

int main( )
{
    throttle sample(DEMO_SIZE);   // A throttle to use for our demonstration
    int user_input;               // The position to which we set the throttle

    // Set the sample throttle to a position indicated by the user.
    cout << "I have a throttle with " << DEMO_SIZE << " positions." << endl;
    cout << "Where would you like to set the throttle?" << endl;
    cout << "Please type a number from 0 to " << DEMO_SIZE << ": ";
    cin >> user_input;
    sample.shift(user_input);

    // Shift the throttle down to zero, printing the flow along the way.
    while (sample.is_on( ))
    {
        cout << "The flow is now " << sample.flow( ) << endl;
        sample.shift(-1);
    }
    cout << "The flow is now off" << endl;
    return EXIT_SUCCESS;
}
```

A Sample Dialogue

```
I have a throttle with 5 positions.
Where would you like to set the throttle?
Please type a number from 0 to 5: 3
The flow is now 0.6
The flow is now 0.4
The flow is now 0.2
The flow is now off
```

Self-Test Exercises for Section 2.3

13. What would a programmer read to learn how to use a new class?

14. What is the purpose of a macro guard?

15. What is the normal action of an assignment `y = x`, if x and y are objects?

16. Suppose that x is a throttle. What is the effect of the declaration `throttle y(x)`?

17. Write the `#include` directive and a *using* statement that must be present for a main program to use the `throttle` class.

18. Design and implement a class called `circle_location` to keep track of the position of a single point that travels around a circle. An object of this class records the position of the point as an angle, measured in a clockwise direction from the top of the circle. Include these public member functions:

    • A default constructor to place the point at the top of the circle

    • Another constructor to place the point at a specified position

    • A function to move the point a specified number of degrees around the circle. Use a positive argument to move clockwise, and a negative argument to move counterclockwise.

    • A function to return the current position of the point, in degrees, measured clockwise from the top of the circle.

    Your solution should include a separate header file, implementation file, and an example of a main program using the new class.

19. Design and implement a class called `clock`. A `clock` object holds one instance of a time value such as 9:48 P.M. Have at least these public member functions:

    • A default constructor that sets the time to midnight

    • A function to explicitly assign a given time (you will have to give some thought to appropriate parameters for this function)

    • Functions to retrieve information: the current hour, the current minute, and a boolean function to determine whether the time is at or before noon

    • A function to advance the time forward by a given number of minutes

20. What is the global namespace?

21. Which of the three forms from page 59 should be used when part of a namespace needs to be used within an actual header file?

2.4 CLASSES AND PARAMETERS

Every programmer requires an unshakable understanding of functions and parameters. The realm of OOP requires extra understanding because classes can be used as the type of a function's parameter, or as the type of the return value from a function. This section illustrates several such functions, including a review of different kinds of parameters. The examples use a new class called `point`.

PROGRAMMING EXAMPLE: **The Point Class**

The new class is a data type to store and manipulate the location of a single point on a plane, as shown in Figure 2.9. The example point in Figure 2.9(a) lies at a location with coordinates $x = -1.0$ and $y = 0.8$. The `point` class has the member functions listed here:

- There is a constructor to initialize a point. The constructor's parameters use default arguments that we'll discuss in a moment.
- There is a member function to shift a point by given amounts along the x and y axes, as shown in Figure 2.9(b).
- There is a member function to rotate a point by 90° in a clockwise direction around the origin, as shown in Figure 2.9(c).
- There are two constant member functions that allow us to retrieve the current x and y coordinates of a point.

These functions are simple, yet they form the basis for an actual data type that is used in drawing programs and other graphics applications. All the member functions, including the constructor, are listed in the header file of Figure 2.10 on page 64, with an implementation in Figure 2.11 on page 65. After you've looked through the figures, we'll review the implementations, starting with *default arguments*, which are used in an interesting way in the point's constructor.

FIGURE 2.9 Three Points in a Plane

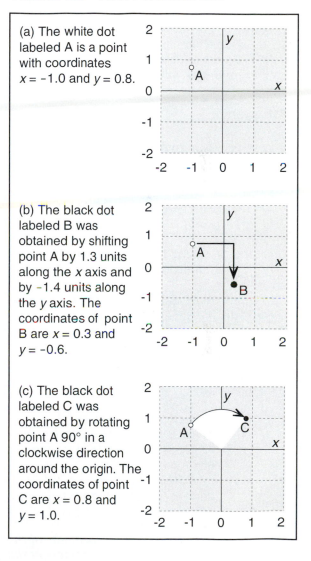

(a) The white dot labeled A is a point with coordinates $x = -1.0$ and $y = 0.8$.

(b) The black dot labeled B was obtained by shifting point A by 1.3 units along the x axis and by -1.4 units along the y axis. The coordinates of point B are $x = 0.3$ and $y = -0.6$.

(c) The black dot labeled C was obtained by rotating point A 90° in a clockwise direction around the origin. The coordinates of point C are $x = 0.8$ and $y = 1.0$.

FIGURE 2.10   Header File for the Point Class

A Header File

```
// FILE: point.h
// CLASS PROVIDED: point (part of the namespace main_savitch_2A)
//
// CONSTRUCTOR for the point class:
//    point(double initial_x = 0.0, double initial_y = 0.0)
//    Postcondition: The point has been set to (initial_x, initial_y).
//
// MODIFICATION MEMBER FUNCTIONS for the point class:
//    void shift(double x_amount, double y_amount)
//    Postcondition: The point has been moved by x_amount along the x axis
//     and by y_amount along the y axis.
//
//    void rotate90( )
//    Postcondition: The point has been rotated clockwise 90 degrees around the origin.
//
// CONSTANT MEMBER FUNCTIONS for the point class:
//    double get_x( ) const
//    Postcondition: The value returned is the x coordinate of the point.
//
//    double get_y( ) const
//    Postcondition: The value returned is the y coordinate of the point.
//
// VALUE SEMANTICS for the point class:
//    Assignments and the copy constructor may be used with point objects.

#ifndef MAIN_SAVITCH_POINT_H
#define MAIN_SAVITCH_POINT_H
namespace main_savitch_2A
{
    class point
    {
    public:
        // CONSTRUCTOR
        point(double initial_x = 0.0, double initial_y = 0.0);
        // MODIFICATION MEMBER FUNCTIONS
        void shift(double x_amount, double y_amount);
        void rotate90( );
        // CONSTANT MEMBER FUNCTIONS
        double get_x( ) const { return x; }
        double get_y( ) const { return y; }
    private:
        double x;  // x coordinate of this point
        double y;  // y coordinate of this point
    };
}
#endif
```

| **FIGURE 2.11** | Implementation File for the Point Class |

An Implementation File

```
// FILE: point.cxx
// CLASS IMPLEMENTED: point (see point.h for documentation)

#include "point.h"

namespace main_savitch_2A
{
    point::point(double initial_x, double initial_y)
    {   // Constructor sets the point to a given position.
        x = initial_x;
        y = initial_y;
    }

    void point::shift(double x_amount, double y_amount)
    {
        x += x_amount;
        y += y_amount;
    }

    void point::rotate90( )
    {
        double new_x;
        double new_y;

        new_x = y;   // For a 90-degree clockwise rotation, the new x is the original y,
        new_y = -x;  // and the new y is -1 times the original x.
        x = new_x;
        y = new_y;
    }
}
```

www.cs.colorado.edu/~main/chapter2/point.cxx   **W W W**

Default Arguments

A **default argument** is a value that will be used for an argument when a programmer does not provide an actual argument. Default arguments may be listed in the prototype of any function. For example, here is a modified version of a function prototype that we used on page 15:

```
int date_check(int year, int month = 1, int day = 1);
```

The exact behavior of date_check is not important. The important thing is that we have added default arguments for the month and day parameters. As shown in the shaded part of the example, the default argument appears with an equals sign after the parameter name. Once a default argument is available, the function can be called with or without certain arguments.

For example, a program can call `date_check` with just the `year` argument:

```
date_check(2000);
```

Since the last two arguments were omitted in this function call, the default arguments (`month = 1` and `day = 1`) will be used. The function call is identical to calling `date_check(2000, 1, 1)`.

The function can also be called with a year and a month, omitting the day, as in this example:

```
date_check(2000, 7);
```

In this example, the default argument will be used for the day, so the function call is identical to calling `date_check(2000, 7, 1)`.

default arguments are especially convenient for constructors

The general rules for providing and using default arguments are summarized in Figure 2.12 on page 67. Default arguments are especially convenient for constructors, such as the point's constructor in Figure 2.10 on page 64. The constructor's prototype has these two default arguments:

```
point(double initial_x = 0.0, double initial_y = 0.0);
```

Both arguments of the constructor have a default of the double number 0.0, as shown in these three declarations of point objects:

```
point a(-1, 0.8);  ← Uses the usual constructor with two arguments
point b(-1);  ← Uses -1 for the first argument and uses the default
point c;  ←        argument, initial_y = 0.0, for the second argument
                   Uses default arguments for both initial_x = 0.0
                   and initial_y = 0.0
```

The third use of our constructor—simply `point c;`—is interesting because defaults are used for both arguments. In effect, we have a constructor with no arguments. A constructor with no arguments is a **default constructor**. As we saw with the throttle, it's important always to provide a default constructor. One way to provide a default constructor is to have a constructor with a complete set of default arguments.

⬆ PROGRAMMING TIP

A DEFAULT CONSTRUCTOR CAN BE PROVIDED BY USING DEFAULT ARGUMENTS

A good way to provide a default constructor is to have one constructor with default arguments for all of its arguments. Don't forget that default constructors are always used with no argument list; not even the parentheses are present. So to use the point's default constructor, we write `point c;` .

FIGURE 2.12 Default Arguments

Default Arguments

A default argument is a value that will be used for an argument when no actual argument is provided. The usage follows the format and rules listed here.

Syntax in a prototype's parameter list:

    <type name> <variable name> = <default value>

Example:

    int date_check(*int* year, *int* month = 1, *int* date = 1);

1. The default argument is specified only once—in the prototype—and not in the function's implementation.

2. A function with several arguments does not need to specify default arguments for every argument. But if only some of the arguments have defaults, then those arguments must be rightmost in the parameter list.

3. In a function call, arguments with default values may be omitted from the right end of the actual argument list. For example:

    date_check(2000);   — *Uses default arguments for month = 1 and date = 1*
    date_check(2000, 7);   — *Uses default argument for date = 1*
    date_check(2000, 7, 22);   — *Does not use the default arguments at all*

Parameters

Classes can be used as the type of a function's parameter, just like any other data type. We'll review three different kinds of parameters, with examples that use the new point class.

review of function parameters

FIGURE 2.13 A Rotating Point

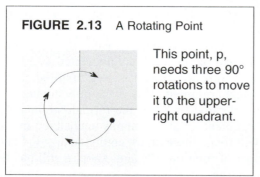

This point, p, needs three 90° rotations to move it to the upper-right quadrant.

Value parameters. The simplest parameters are *value parameters*. To illustrate a value parameter, we'll write a simple function. The function we have in mind has one value parameter, a point that we'll call p. The integer returned by the function is the number of 90° rotations that would be needed to move p into the upper-right quadrant, as shown in Figure 2.13.

Here is the function's implementation:

```
int rotations_needed(point p)
// Postcondition: The value returned is the number of 90-degree
// clockwise rotations needed to move p into the upper-right
// quadrant (where x >= 0 and y >= 0).
{
    int answer;

    answer = 0;
    while ((p.get_x( ) < 0) || (p.get_y( ) < 0))
    {
        p.rotate90( );
        ++answer;
    }
    return answer;
}
```

In C++, a value parameter is declared by placing the type name followed by the parameter name. So, we have written `point p` in the parameter list. The effect of a value parameter is that any change made to the parameter within the body of the function does not change the actual argument from the calling program. Let's look at an example in a program:

```
point sample(6, -4); // Constructor places the point at x = 6, y = -4.
cout << "  x coordinate is " << sample.get_x( )
     << "  y coordinate is " << sample.get_y( ) << endl;
cout << "  Rotations: " << rotations_needed(sample) << endl;
cout << "  x coordinate is " << sample.get_x( )
     << "  y coordinate is " << sample.get_y( ) << endl;
```

formal parameters and arguments

After the constructor, the code prints a message with the point's coordinates. Then, in the second output statement, `rotations_needed` is called. The function's parameter (p in this case) is referred to as the **formal parameter** to distinguish it from the value that is passed in during the function call. The passed value (`sample` in this case) is the **argument** (sometimes called the **actual argument** or the **actual parameter**).

the effect of a value parameter

With a value parameter, the argument provides the initial value for the formal parameter. To be more precise, the formal parameter is implemented as a local variable of the function, and the class's copy constructor is used to initialize the formal parameter as a copy of the actual argument. This is the only connection between the argument and the formal parameter. So, if the formal parameter p changes in our function body, the argument `sample` remains unchanged in the calling program. In our example, p will rotate three times, ending up at $x = 4$ and $y = 6$. The function returns the number of rotations (3), and `sample` still has its original value in the calling program. Therefore, the complete output from the code is:

```
x coordinate is 6   y coordinate is -4
Rotations: 3
x coordinate is 6   y coordinate is -4
```

The value of the argument, `sample`, did not change.

Value Parameters

A **value parameter** is declared by writing the type name followed by the parameter name. With a value parameter, the argument provides the initial value for the formal parameter. The value parameter is implemented as a local variable of the function, so that any changes made to the parameter in the body of the function will leave the argument unaltered.

Example:
```
int rotations_needed(point p);
```

Reference parameters. *Reference parameters* are important types of parameters in C++. Our example of a reference parameter is similar to the `rotations_needed` function. But this time the point p will be a reference parameter. The new function does not return a value; it merely rotates p into the upper-right quadrant, as shown here:

```
void rotate_to_upper_right(point& p)
// Postcondition: The point p has been rotated in 90-degree
// increments until p has been moved into the upper-right
// quadrant (where x >= 0 and y >= 0).
{
    while ((p.get_x( ) < 0) || (p.get_y( ) < 0))
        p.rotate90( );
}
```

In C++, a reference parameter is declared by placing the type name followed by the symbol & and the parameter name. So, we have written `point& p` in the parameter list.

Here is the key to reference parameters: Any use of the parameter within the body of the function will access the argument in the calling program. Let's look at an example in a program:

the effect of a reference parameter

```
point sample(6, -4); // Constructor places point at x = 6, y = -4.
cout << "  x coordinate is " << sample.get_x( )
     << "  y coordinate is " << sample.get_y( ) << endl;
rotate_to_upper_right(sample);
cout << "  x coordinate is " << sample.get_x( )
     << "  y coordinate is " << sample.get_y( ) << endl;
```

As we did before, the code prints the point's coordinates and then calls the function. The formal parameter is still called p and the argument is still `sample`—but p is now a reference parameter.

Because p is a reference parameter, any use of p within the body of the function will actually access `sample`. Thus, it is the argument `sample` that is rotated into the upper-right quadrant. When the function returns, `sample` has a new value. The complete output from the code is:

```
x coordinate is 6   y coordinate is -4
x coordinate is 4   y coordinate is 6
```

The value of the argument `sample` was changed by the function.

Reference Parameters

A **reference parameter** is declared by writing the type name followed by the character & and the parameter name. With a reference parameter, any use of the parameter within the body of the function will access the argument from the calling program. Changes made to the formal parameter in the body of the function will alter the argument.

Example:
```
    void rotate_to_upper_right(point& p);
```

⚓ **PITFALL**

USING A WRONG ARGUMENT TYPE FOR A REFERENCE PARAMETER

In order for a reference parameter to work correctly, the data type of an argument must match exactly with the data type of the formal parameter. For example, suppose we have this reference parameter:

```
void make_int_42(int& i)
// Postcondition: i has been set to 42.
{
    i = 42;
}
```

Suppose we have an integer variable j, and we make the call make_int_42(j).

After the function returns, j will have the value 42. But you might be surprised at the output from this code:

```
double d;
d = 0;                              does not change d
make_int_42(d);
cout << d;         prints 0
```

This example compiles, but because d is the wrong data type, a separate *integer* copy of d is created to use as the argument. The *double* variable d is never changed to 42.

If the argument's data type does not exactly match the data type of the formal parameter, then the compiler will try to convert the argument to the correct type. If the conversion is possible, then the compiler treats the argument like a value parameter, passing a *copy* of the argument to the function. Fortunately, most compilers provide a warning message such as "Temporary used for parameter 'i' in call to 'make_int_42'"—just make sure that you pay attention to the compiler's warnings!

Const reference parameters. For large data types, value parameters are less efficient than reference parameters. This is because a value parameter must make an extra copy of the argument to use within the body of the function. Hence, we generally prefer to use reference parameters. But often a reference parameter is unattractive because we don't want a programmer to worry about whether the function changes the actual argument. Changes are a definite possibility with a reference parameter, but they cannot occur with a value parameter.

Sometimes there is a solution that provides the efficiency of a reference parameter along with the security of a value parameter. The new parameter type is called a *const reference parameter*, and it may be used whenever a function does not attempt to make any changes to the parameter. For example, we can write a function that computes the distance between two points. The function has two point parameters, and neither parameter is changed by the function. Therefore we can use const reference parameters, as shown in Figure 2.14. The figure shows a function that computes the distance between two points, using this prototype:

the effect of a const reference parameter

```
double distance( const point& p1, const point& p2 );
```

The const reference parameter uses the keyword *const* before the parameter's type, and it also uses the symbol & after the type. A const reference parameter is efficient (since it is a reference parameter), but a programmer is guaranteed that the actual argument will not be altered by the function. For example, in our implementation of distance we use only get_x and get_y, both of which are *const* member functions and therefore cannot change p1 and p2. It is important that get_x and get_y are actually declared as *const* member functions, otherwise the compiler would not permit us to use them with the *const* reference parameters p1 and p2.

FIGURE 2.14   A Function with Const Reference Parameters

A Function Implementation

```
double distance(const point& p1, const point& p2)
// Postcondition: The value returned is the distance between p1 and p2.
// Library facilities used: cmath
{
    double a, b, c_squared;

    // Calculate differences in x and y coordinates.
    a = p1.get_x( ) - p2.get_x( ); // Difference in x coordinates
    b = p1.get_y( ) - p2.get_y( ); // Difference in y coordinates

    // Use Pythagorean Theorem to calculate the square of the distance between the points.
    c_squared = a*a + b*b;

    return sqrt(c_squared);

}
```

$a^2 + b^2 = c^2$

Pythagorean
Theorem

www.cs.colorado.edu/~main/chapter2/newpoint.cxx   **WWW**

CLARIFYING THE CONST KEYWORD
Part 3: Const Reference Parameters

A **const reference parameter** is declared by writing the keyword *const* before a reference parameter and placing & after the parameter's type. The parameter is efficient, but unlike an ordinary reference parameter, the function cannot attempt to make any changes to the value of the parameter.

1. DECLARED CONSTANTS: PAGE 12
2. CONSTANT MEMBER FUNCTIONS: PAGE 38
3. CONST REFERENCE PARAMETERS
4. STATIC MEMBER CONSTANTS: PAGE 103
5. CONST PARAMETERS THAT ARE POINTERS OR ARRAYS: PAGE 162
6. THE CONST KEYWORD WITH A POINTER TO A NODE, AND THE NEED FOR TWO VERSIONS OF SOME MEMBER FUNCTIONS: PAGE 218
7. CONST ITERATORS: PAGE 308

Example:
```
double distance(const point& p1, ...
```

If you use const reference parameters, be sure to follow the consistency requirements in the Programming Tip on page 73.

USE CONST CONSISTENTLY

When you define a new class along with functions and member functions to manipulate the class, you should make a consistent use of *const*. In particular:

1. Any member functions that do not change the value of the object should be declared constant member functions. This is accomplished by placing the keyword *const* after the parameter list in both the prototype and the head of the function's definition (see page 38). For example, the prototype of the throttle's *flow* function is:

```
double flow( ) const;
```

2. Whenever you use the class as the type of a parameter, and the function does not alter the parameter, use a const reference parameter. This is accomplished by placing the keyword *const* before the parameter's type in the parameter list, and placing the symbol & after the type name (see page 72); for example, the prototype:

```
double distance(const point& p1, const point& p2);
```

You should not use *const* unless you intend to use it at every location that meets these requirements.

When the Type of a Function's Return Value Is a Class

The type of a function's return value may be a class. Here is a typical example:

```
point middle(const point& p1, const point& p2)
// Postcondition: The value returned is the point that
// is halfway between p1 and p2.
{
    double x_midpoint, y_midpoint;

    // Compute the x and y midpoints.
    x_midpoint = (p1.get_x( ) + p2.get_x( )) / 2;
    y_midpoint = (p1.get_y( ) + p2.get_y( )) / 2;

    // Construct a new point and return it.
    point midpoint(x_midpoint, y_midpoint);
    return midpoint;
}
```

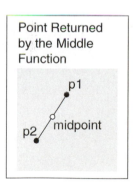

Point Returned by the Middle Function

The function computes a new point in the local variable midpoint and then returns a copy of this point. Often the return value of a function is stored in a local variable such as `midpoint`, but not always. Here's another example, in which one of the parameters is the return value:

```
throttle slower(const throttle& t1, const throttle& t2)
// Postcondition: The value returned is a copy of t1 or t2, whichever
//  has the slower flow. If the flows are equal, then t1 is returned.
{
    if (t1.flow( ) <= t2.flow( ))
        return t1;
    else
        return t2;
}
```

By the way, the C++ return statement uses the copy constructor to copy the function's return value to a temporary location before returning the value to the calling program.

Self-Test Exercises for Section 2.4

22. Add default arguments to your throttle constructor from Self-Test Exercise 12 on page 51. Once you have done this, are the other two constructors still needed?

23. Which of these function calls could change the value of a point p:
    ```
    cout << rotations_needed(p);
    rotate_to_upper_right(p);
    ```

24. What is the difference between a formal parameter and an argument?

25. Suppose a function has a parameter named x, and the body of the function changes the value of x. When should x be a value parameter? When should it be a reference parameter? With this function, could x ever be a const reference parameter?

26. Suppose the data type of a parameter is a class. The parameter cannot be modified inside the function. What kind of parameter is most efficient and secure for this purpose?

2.5   OPERATOR OVERLOADING

A **binary function** is a function with two arguments. Often, when you design a new class, there are binary functions to manipulate objects in the class. Sometimes the new binary functions are naturally described using symbols such as `==` and `+`, which are symbols that C++ already uses to describe its own operations on numbers and other data types. For example, we might want to test whether two points are equal, and it seems natural to write this code:

```
point p1, p2;
if (p1 == p2 )
    cout << "Those points are equal." << endl;
```

Unfortunately, the == operator cannot be used with a new class—unless you define a binary function that tells exactly what == means. In fact, C++ lets you define the meaning of many operators for a new class. Defining a new meaning for an operator is called **overloading** the operator. We'll look at several common overloading examples.

Overloading Binary Comparison Operators

The == operator that "compares for equality" can be overloaded for any new class by defining a function with a rather peculiar name. The name of the new function is "*operator* ==" as shown in this example:

```
bool operator == (const point& p1, const point& p2)
// Postcondition: The value returned is true if p1 and p2
// are identical; otherwise false is returned.
{
    return
        (p1.get_x( ) == p2.get_x( ))
        &&
        (p1.get_y( ) == p2.get_y( ));
}
```

In order for this function to return true, both parts of the && expression must be true—in other words, both *x* and *y* coordinates of p1 must be equal to the corresponding coordinate in p2.

Apart from the peculiar name *operator* ==, the function is just like any other function. It returns a boolean value that can be used as a true-or-false value, such as in an if-statement:

operator ==

```
if (p1 == p2 )...
```

The overloaded operator is used in a program just like any other use of ==, by putting the first argument before == and the second argument after ==.

When you overload an operator, the common usages of that operator are still available. For example, we can still use == to test the equality of two integers or two doubles. In fact, in the body of our *operator* ==, we *do* use the ordinary == to compare the doubles p1.get_x( ) and p2.get_x( ). This is fine. For each use of ==, the compiler determines the data type of the objects being compared and uses the appropriate comparison function.

common usages of == are still available

Once you have overloaded one operator, you can sometimes use the overloaded operator to make an easy implementation of another operator. For example, suppose we have defined *operator* == for the point class. Then we can quickly overload != to be the "not equal" operator:

operator !=

```
bool operator !=(const point& p1, const point& p2)
// Postcondition: The value returned is true if p1 and p2
// are not identical; otherwise false is returned.
{
    return !(p1 == p2) ;
}
```

The expression !(p1 == p2) deserves some examination. The == operator that we use is the overloaded == that we just defined for points. It returns true if the two points are equal, and false otherwise. We take the result of (p1 == p2) and reverse it with the usual not operator, "!". So, if (p1 == p2) is true, then !(p1 == p2) is false, and the != function returns false. On the other hand, if (p1 == p2) is false, then !(p1 == p2) is true, and the != function returns true.

The *operator* == and *operator* != functions can also be defined as member functions rather than existing on their own. In this case, the p1 in an expression (p1 == p2) is the object that actually activates the member function, and p2 is an argument. In fact, p2 will be the *only* argument if we implement == as a member function (since the object that activates a member function is never actually listed in the parameter list). The choice between member function and nonmember function is partly an issue of programming style. We prefer the use of the nonmember function since a nonmember function places the two arguments (p1 and p2) on equal footing. There really is no reason to say that p1 activates the operator any more than p2 does. (Later, you will find that nonmember functions also provide more flexibility for classes with a feature called *conversions*.)

other binary comparison operators

Figure 2.15 shows the six binary operators from C++ that are often overloaded as binary comparison operators for new classes.

FIGURE 2.15

Binary Operators that Are Often Overloaded as Comparison Functions

==	!=
<	>
<=	>=

Overloading Binary Arithmetic Operators

In addition to the comparison operators, most of the other binary operators of C++ also can be overloaded for a new class. For example, the operators +, -, *, and /, which we normally think of as arithmetic operators, can all be overloaded for a new class. As a natural example, physicists often use points as objects that can be added by adding their *x* and *y* coordinates. If we could add two of our points, then we might write this program:

```
point speed1(5, 7);
point speed2(1, 2);
point total;                              sets total to
                                          the sum of speed1
                                          and speed2
total = speed1 + speed2;
cout << total.get_x( ) << endl;    prints 6
cout << total.get_y( ) << endl;    prints 9
```

In fact, we can define the meaning of + for points by overloading the + operator. *operator +*
The overloaded operator has two parameters, which are the two points being
added. And the function returns the sum of these two points, as shown here:

```
point operator +(const point& p1, const point& p2)
// Postcondition: The sum of p1 and p2 is returned.
{
    double x_sum, y_sum;

    // Compute the x and y of the sum.
    x_sum = (p1.get_x( ) + p2.get_x( ));
    y_sum = (p1.get_y( ) + p2.get_y( ));
    point sum(x_sum, y_sum);
    return sum;
}
```

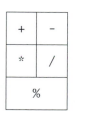

FIGURE 2.16

Binary Operators that
Are Often Overloaded
as Arithmetic Functions

As with the binary comparison operators, a
binary arithmetic operator can also be defined as a
member function rather than a function that stands
on its own. The member function would have just
one parameter, which is the right-hand argument in
an expression such as (p1 + p2). The left-hand argument is the object that activates the member function. Our programming style prefers implementing
the binary operators as nonmember functions.

Figure 2.16 shows the five binary operators from
C++ that are most often overloaded to perform arith- *other arithmetic*
metic operations. *operators*

Overloading Output and Input Operators

The standard C++ data types can be written and read using the output operator
<< and the input operator >>. For example, we can read and write an integer:

```
int i;
cin >> i;         reads the value of i from the
                  standard input
cout << i;
                  writes the value of i to
                  the standard output
```

No doubt you would like to do the same with your impressive new `point` class:

```
point p;              reads the x and y coordinates
cin >> p;             of p from the standard input

cout << p;            writes the x and y coordinates
                      of p to the standard output
```

You can provide input/output power to the `point` class by overloading the `<<` and `>>` operators. We start by overloading the output operator, which has the mysterious prototype shown here:

```
ostream& operator <<(ostream& outs, const point& source);
```

Let's demystify this problematic prototype. The function has two parameters: `outs` (which is an `ostream`) and `source` (which is a `point`). We use the function by listing the two arguments like this:

```
               The first argument, cout, is an ostream.
cout << p;     The second argument, p, is a point.
```

As shown, the data type of `cout` is `ostream`, which means "output stream." The `ostream` class is part of the `iostream` library facility. The facility also defines `cout` (the **console output device** or "standard output") and provides the ability for programmers to define other output streams (such as output streams connected to a disk file or a printer). In any case, our intention is for the `<<` function to print the `point` named `source` to the `ostream` named `outs`. We can now write most of our postcondition:

```
ostream& operator <<(ostream& outs, const point& source);
// Postcondition: The x and y coordinates of source have been
// written to outs.
```

The `outs` parameter is a reference parameter, meaning that the function can change the output stream (by writing to it), and the change will affect the actual argument (such as the standard output stream, `cout`). The `source` parameter is a const reference parameter, meaning that the function will not alter the point that it is writing.

One last mystery remains: The return type of the function is `ostream&`:

```
ostream& operator <<(ostream& outs, const point& source);
```

For the most part, this return type means that the function returns an `ostream`. In fact, the function returns the `ostream` that it has just written. There is additional meaning of the `&` symbol (called a **reference return type**). But we won't use that additional meaning until Chapter 6, so it is enough to know that the output and input operators both require a reference return type.

With this in mind, we can now write the complete postcondition:

```
ostream& operator <<(ostream& outs, const point& source);
// Postcondition: The x and y coordinates of source have been
// written to outs. The return value is the ostream outs.
```

The reason that the function returns an `ostream` is that C++ will then permit the "chaining" of output statements such as the following:

```
cout << "The points are " << p << " and " << q << endl;
```

This example calls five `<<` functions, with each function changing the `ostream` and passing the result on to the next function call.

The complete implementation of the point's output operator is shown at the top of Figure 2.17. Most of the work is done in this statement:

operator <<

```
outs << source.get_x( ) <<  " "  << source.get_y( );
```

The statement uses the ordinary `<<` operator to print the coordinates of the point, with a single blank character in between.

FIGURE 2.17   Output and Input Operations for the Point

Function Implementations

```
ostream& operator <<(ostream& outs, const point& source)
// Postcondition: The x and y coordinates of source have been
// written to outs. The return value is the ostream outs.
// Library facilities used: iostream
{
    outs << source.get_x( ) <<  " "  << source.get_y( );
    return outs;
}
```

This prints the point's coordinates with a blank in between.

```
istream& operator >>(istream& ins, point& target)
// Postcondition: The x and y coordinates of target have been
// read from ins. The return value is the istream ins.
// Library facilities used: iostream
// Friend of: point class
{
    ins >> target.x >> target.y;
    return ins;
}
```

This function must be a friend function since it requires direct access to the private members of the point class.

www.cs.colorado.edu/~main/chapter2/newpoint.cxx   **W W W**

The prototype for the point's input function is similar to the output function, but it uses an istream (input stream) instead of an ostream, as shown here:

```
istream& operator >>(istream& ins, point& target);
// Postcondition: The x and y coordinates of target have been
// read from ins. The return value is the istream ins.
```

operator >>

The implementation of the input function is shown at the bottom of Figure 2.17. The key work is accomplished with the usual >> operator reading two double numbers in the statement shown here:

```
ins >> target.x >> target.y;
```

But hold on! The statement sends input directly to the *private* member variables x and y of the point. Only *member* functions can access private member variables, and the input function is not a point member function. There are two possible solutions to the problem:

1. We could write new member functions to set a point's coordinates and use these member functions within the input function's implementation.
2. Because we are the implementor of the point class, and we are also writing the input function ourselves, we can grant special permission for the input function to access the private members of the point class.

The second approach is called using a *friend function*, which we'll explain now.

Friend Functions

*friend functions
can access
private members*

A **friend function** is a function that is *not* a member function, but that still has access to the private members of the objects of a class. To declare a friend function, the function's prototype is placed in a class definition, preceded by the keyword *friend*.

For example, to declare the point's input function as a friend, we must insert the friend prototype in the class definition, as shown here:

```
class point
{
public:                              The point class with a new friend
    ...
    // FRIEND FUNCTIONS
    friend istream& operator >>(istream& ins, point& target);

private:
    ...
};
```

Once the friend prototype has been placed in the class definition, the body of the function may access private members of its `point` parameter, as shown here:

```
istream& operator >>(istream& ins, point& target)
// Postcondition: The x and y coordinates of target have been
// read from ins. The return value is the istream ins.
// Library facilities used: iostream
// Friend of: point class
{
    ins >> target.x >> target.y;
    return ins;
}
```

Notice that a friend function is not a member function, so it is not activated by a particular object of a class. All of the information that the friend function manipulates must be present in its parameters. It would be illegal to simply write x or y in the body of our function; we must write `target.x` and `target.y`. In our case, the *friend operator >>* has one point parameter, and it is the private member variables of this parameter that the function may access.

Friendship may be provided to any function, not just to operator functions. But friendship should be limited to functions that are written by the programmer who implements the class—after all, this programmer is the only one who really knows about the private members. In this way, information hiding about a new class remains intact.

friendship and information hiding

Friend Functions

A **friend function** is a function that is not a member function, but that still needs access to private members of some of its parameters. To declare a friend function, the function's prototype is placed in a class definition, preceded by the keyword *friend*.

Friendship should be limited to functions that are written by the programmer who implements the class.

PROGRAMMING TIP

WHEN TO USE A FRIEND FUNCTION

When you are implementing a class, you often implement additional functions to manipulate objects of the class. If a function needs access to private members of the class, then you should first consider providing the access via a member function. However, if a member function is inconvenient or unacceptable for other reasons, then you may grant friendship to a function, giving it access to the class's private members.

The Point Class—Putting Things Together

We have defined quite a few new functions to manipulate points. In all, we now have:

- The constructor
- The two original modification functions (`shift` and `rotate90`), and the two original constant functions (`get_x` and `get_y`)
- Overloaded comparison operators == and !=
- Overloaded arithmetic operator + to add two points
- Overloaded output and input operators
- Functions `middle`, `rotations_needed`, `rotate_to_upper_right`, and `distance` from Section 2.4

We could continue with more point functions, but there is a definite danger of never finishing Chapter 2. So we'll stop here, collecting most of the items into a new, improved point class. The header file for the new class is `newpoint.h`, shown in Figure 2.18. Notice that the header file needs to use `ostream` and `istream` from the `std` namespace. But, a *using* statement should never appear in a header file (see page 60), so we use the full names `std::ostream` and `std::istream`.

The implementation should go in a separate file named `newpoint.cxx`. What should be present in `newpoint.cxx`? (See Self-Test Exercise 32 on page 86.)

When you provide functions or operators to manipulate a class, you should follow these lists for good information hiding:

In the Header File:

- Documentation, including a precondition/postcondition contract for each function
- Class definitions for any new classes
- Prototypes for any other functions that are neither member functions nor friend functions

In the Implementation File:

- An include directive to include the header file
- Implementations for each member function (except for the inline functions)
- Implementations for each friend function and other functions that are not member functions

FIGURE 2.18   Header File for the New Point Class

A Header File

```
//  FILE: newpoint.h (revised from point.h in Figure 2.10 on page 64)
//  CLASS PROVIDED: point (a class for a point on a two-dimensional plane)
//
//  CONSTRUCTOR for the point class:
//     point(double initial_x = 0.0, double initial_y = 0.0)
//        Postcondition: The point has been set to (initial_x, initial_y).
//
//  MODIFICATION MEMBER FUNCTIONS for the point class:
//     void shift(double x_amount, double y_amount)
//        Postcondition: The point has been moved by x_amount along the x axis
//        and by y_amount along the y axis.
//
//     void rotate90( )
//        Postcondition: The point has been rotated clockwise 90 degrees.
//
//  CONSTANT MEMBER FUNCTIONS for the point class:
//     double get_x( ) const
//        Postcondition: The value returned is the x coordinate of the point.
//
//     double get_y( ) const
//        Postcondition: The value returned is the y coordinate of the point.
//
//  NONMEMBER FUNCTIONS for the point class:
//     double distance(const point& p1, const point& p2)
//        Postcondition: The value returned is the distance between p1 and p2.
//
//     point middle(const point& p1, const point& p2)
//        Postcondition: The point returned is halfway between p1 and p2.
//
//     point operator +(const point& p1, const point& p2)
//        Postcondition: The sum of p1 and p2 is returned.
//
//     bool operator ==(const point& p1, const point& p2)
//        Postcondition: The return value is true if p1 and p2 are identical.
//
//     bool operator !=(const point& p1, const point& p2)
//        Postcondition: The return value is true if p1 and p2 are not identical.
//
//     ostream& operator <<(ostream& outs, const point& source)
//        Postcondition: The x and y coordinates of source have been
//        written to outs. The return value is the ostream outs.
```

(continued)

(FIGURE 2.18 continued)

```
//
//     istream& operator >>(istream& ins, point& target)
//        Postcondition: The x and y coordinates of target have been
//        read from ins. The return value is the istream ins.
//
// VALUE SEMANTICS  for the point class:
//     Assignments and the copy constructor may be used with point objects.

#ifndef MAIN_SAVITCH_NEWPOINT_H
#define MAIN_SAVITCH_NEWPOINT_H
#include <iostream> // Provides ostream and istream

namespace main_savitch_2B
{
    class point
    {
    public:
        // CONSTRUCTOR
        point(double initial_x = 0.0, double initial_y = 0.0);
        // MODIFICATION MEMBER FUNCTIONS
        void shift(double x_amount, double y_amount);
        void rotate90( );
        // CONSTANT MEMBER FUNCTIONS
        double get_x( ) const { return x; }
        double get_y( ) const { return y; }
        // FRIEND FUNCTION
        friend std::istream& operator >>(std::istream& ins, point& target);
    private:
        double x, y;  // x and y coordinates of this point
    };

    // NONMEMBER FUNCTIONS for the point class
    double distance(const point& p1, const point& p2);
    point middle(const point& p1, const point& p2);
    point operator +(const point& p1, const point& p2);
    bool operator ==(const point& p1, const point& p2);
    bool operator !=(const point& p1, const point& p2);
    std::ostream& operator <<(std::ostream & outs, const point& source);
}

#endif
```

Using a new namespace avoids conflict with the other point class from Section 2.4.

prototype for a friend function

prototypes for nonmember functions

www.cs.colorado.edu/~main/chapter2/newpoint.h   **W W W**

FIGURE 2.19 Guidelines for Operator Overloading

Binary comparison operators `==` `!=` `<=` `>=` `<` `>`	Overload as a nonmember function with two parameters, returning a boolean value	See point example on page 75
Binary arithmetic operators `+` `-` `*` `/` `%`	Overload as a nonmember function with two parameters	See point example on page 76
Input and output `>>` `<<`	Overload as a nonmember function, returning an istream or ostream	See point example on page 77
Auxiliary assignment operators `+=` `-=` etc.	When the `+` operator is overloaded, then we will usually also overload `+=` as a member function so that x `+=` y has the same effect as x `=` x `+` y	See bag example on page 101
Assignment operator `=`	Must be overloaded as a member function if we want x `=` y to do more than copy member variables from the object y to the object x	See bag example on page 179

Summary of Operator Overloading

We have mentioned more than a dozen C++ operators that may be overloaded for your own classes. In all, there are 44 such operators, although we shall use only the ones you have seen in this chapter plus two assignment operators that you'll meet in the next two chapters.

Programming style varies widely for overloading operators. The eventual style you adopt should be clear and consistent. Our own guidelines for operator overloading within this book are listed in Figure 2.19.

Self-Test Exercises for Section 2.5

27. Overload the `<` operator for the throttle. The function should return true if the flow of the first throttle is less than the flow of the second.
28. Overload the `-` operator for the point, as a binary arithmetic operator.
29. Why should friend functions be written only by the programmer who implements a class?

30. What is incorrect in the following implementation of a friend input function of the point class?
```
istream& operator >> (istream& ins, point& target)
// target has x and y data members
// friend of : point class
{
    ins >> x >> y;
    return ins;
}
```

31. Overload the output operator for the throttle so that it prints 100 times the current flow, followed by a % sign.

32. What should be present in the implementation file `newpoint.cxx`?

CHAPTER SUMMARY

- Object-oriented programming (OOP) supports information hiding by placing data in packages called *objects*, which are implemented via *classes* in C++. Objects are manipulated through functions called *member functions*, which are defined along with their classes.

- A new data type, together with the functions to manipulate the type, is called an *abstract data type* or *class*. The term abstract refers to the fact that we emphasize the abstract specification of *what* has been provided, disassociated from any actual implementation.

- *Private member variables* support information hiding by forbidding data components of a class to be accessed outside of the class's member functions. If the implementor of a new class needs other functions to have access to the member variables, then the other functions may be declared as *friend* functions.

- A *constructor* is a member function that is automatically called to initialize a variable when the variable is declared. Defining constructors increases the reliability of your classes by reducing the chance of using an uninitialized variable.

- To avoid conflicts between different items with the same name, your work should be placed in a namespace. When choosing a name for the namespace, use part of your real name or email address to avoid conflicts with other namespaces.

- Place the documentation and class definition for a new class in a separate *header file*. Place the implementations of the member functions in a separate *implementation file*.

- C++ provides three common kinds of parameters: With a *value parameter*, the argument provides only the initial value for the formal parameter. With a *reference parameter*, any use of the parameter within the body of the function will access the argument from the calling program. A *const reference parameter* has the efficiency of an ordinary reference parameter, but there is a guarantee that the argument will not be changed by the function.

- C++ permits you to define the meaning of *operators* such as + and == for your new classes.

Solutions to Self-Test Exercises ?

1. The *private* members.

2. Public members of a class are available to anyone using the class. Member functions are often declared public so that users can call them in order to manipulate an instance of the class.

3. `true` and `false`

4. A class is a kind of data type that defines data members and member functions that operate on the data. An object is an instance of a class, and is declared as a variable. Once a class is defined, a programmer can declare many objects of that class and manipulate the objects with its functions.

5. A constant member function cannot make any changes to the object's member variables.

6. The scope resolution operator is used at the head of each member function implementation. See the example use of the scope resolution operator on page 42.

7. The program should include the following statements:
```
throttle exercise;
exercise.shut_off( );
exercise.shift(3);
cout << exercise.flow( ) << endl;
```

8. The prototype for the new member function is placed in the class definition. The function implementation is:
```
bool throttle::is_above_half( ) const
// Precondition: shut_off has been called at
// least once to initialize the throttle.
// Postcondition: The return value is true if
// the current flow is above 0.5.
{
    return (flow( ) > 0.5);
}
```

9. In the public section of the class definition:
```
bool is_above_half( ) const
    { return (flow( ) > 0.5); }
```

10. The compiler automatically creates a simple default constructor.

11. The keyword `void` should be removed. Constructors do not have a return type.

12. The prototype for the new constructor is placed in the class definition. The constructor implementation is:
```
throttle::throttle
(int size, int initial)
// Precondition: (0 < size) and
// (0 <= initial <= size).
// Postcondition: The throttle has size
// positions above the shutoff position, and
// it is currently in the position given by the
// parameter initial.
// Libraries used: cassert
```

```
    {
        assert(size > 0);
        assert(initial >= 0);
        assert(initial <= size);
        top_position = size;
        position = initial;
    }
```

13. All the information needed to use the class is in the comment at the front of the header file.

14. A macro guard prevents accidental duplication of a class definition. Normally, if a program includes a header file more than once, compilation will fail. A macro guard directs the compiler to skip duplicate class definitions.

15. The automatic assignment operator will copy the member variables of x to y.

16. The automatic copy constructor will initialize y as a copy of x (by copying the member variables).

17. `#include "throttle.h"`
    `using namespace main_savitch_2A;`

18. Hint: Keep track of the current angle in a private member variable. If the variable goes below zero, or becomes >= 360, then readjust it so that it lies between 0 and 360.

19. You'll find part of a solution in Figure 14.1 on page 675.

20. Any items that are not explicitly placed in a namespace become part of a global namespace, and can be used without a using statement or a scope resolution operator.

21. Never put a *using* statement in a header file; the third form should be used.

22. Change the constructor's prototype to this:
    `throttle(int size = 1, int initial = 0)`
    The other two constructors are no longer needed.

23. `rotate_to_upper_right` can change `p` because the parameter is a reference parameter. But the call to `rotations_needed` cannot change p because it uses a value parameter.

24. A function's parameter is referred to as the *formal* parameter to distinguish it from the value that is passed in during the function call. The argument is the passed value.

25. x should be a value parameter if you want the actual argument to remain unchanged. It should be a reference parameter if you want changes to x to affect the actual argument. It can never be a const reference parameter because the function's body alters the parameter.

26. Value parameters are less efficient for large data types because their values are copied. However, reference types are less secure because they are modifiable. A *const reference* parameter provides the best solution by providing a reference parameter that cannot be modified.

27. Here is the implementation:
    ```
    int operator < (
        const throttle& t1,
        const throttle& t2
    )
    // Postcondition: The return value is true if
    // the flow of t1 is less than the flow of t2.
    {
        return (t1.flow( ) < t2.flow( ));
    }
    ```

28. The solution is the same as the + operator on page 77, but replace each plus sign with a minus sign.

29. This advice supports information hiding, because the programmer who implements the class is the only one who knows about the private members.

30. Friend functions are not activated by a particular object of a class. Therefore, the name of the object variable must precede the member variables accessed by the friend function, as follows:
    `ins >> target.x >> target.y;`

31. Here is the implementation (you fill in the postcondition):

```
ostream& operator << (
    ostream& outs,
    const throttle& source
)
{
    outs << 100*source.flow( ) << '%';
    return outs;
}
```

32. The top of `newpoint.cxx` contains a short comment indicating that the documentation for how to use the `point` class is in the header file. The function implementations appear after the comment, including all the functions listed in Figure 2.18 on page 83, except for `get_x` and `get_y` (which are inline functions). These implementations must be in a namespace grouping. In the header file, we used `main_savitch_2B` for the namespace to avoid conflict with the earlier point (which was in the namespace `main_savitch_2A`).

PROGRAMMING PROJECTS

For more in-depth projects, please see www.cs.colorado.edu/~main/projects/

1 Specify, design, and implement a class that can be used in a program that simulates a combination lock. The lock has a circular knob, with the numbers 0 through 39 marked on the edge, and it has a three-number combination, which we'll call *x, y, z*. To open the lock, you must turn the knob clockwise at least one entire revolution, stopping with *x* at the top; then turn the knob counter-clockwise, stopping the *second* time that *y* appears at the top; finally turn the knob clockwise again, stopping the next time that *z* appears at the top. At this point, you may open the lock.

Your `lock` class should have a constructor that initializes the three-number combination (use 0, 0, 0 for default arguments). Also provide member functions:

(a) to alter the lock's combination to a new three-number combination

(b) to turn the knob in a given direction until a specified number appears at the top

(c) to close the lock

(d) to attempt to open the lock

(e) to inquire the status of the lock (open or shut)

(f) to tell you what number is currently at the top

2 Specify, design, and implement a class called `statistician`. After a statistician is initialized, it can be given a sequence of double numbers. Each number in the sequence is given to the statistician by activating a member function called `next_number`. For example, we can declare a statistician called `s`, and then give it the sequence of numbers 1.1, –2.4, 0.8 as shown here:

```
statistician s;
s.next_number(1.1);
s.next_number(-2.4);
s.next_number(0.8);
```

After a sequence has been given to a statistician, there are various member functions to obtain information about the sequence. Include member functions that will provide the length of the sequence, the last number of the sequence, the sum of all the numbers in the sequence, the arithmetic mean of the numbers (i.e., the sum of the numbers divided by the length of the sequence), the smallest number in the sequence, and the largest number in the sequence. Notice that the length and sum functions can be called at any time, even if there are no numbers in the sequence. In this case of an "empty" sequence, both length and sum will be zero. But the other member functions all have a precondition requiring that the sequence is non-empty.

You should also provide a member function that erases the sequence (so that the statistician can start afresh with a new sequence).

Notes: Do not try to store the entire sequence (because you don't know how long this sequence will be). Instead, just store the necessary information about the sequence: What is the sequence length, what is the sum of the numbers in the sequence, what are the last, smallest, and largest numbers? Each of these pieces of information can be stored in a private member variable that is updated whenever next_number is activated.

3 Overload the + operator to allow you to add two statisticians from the previous project. If s1 and s2 are two statisticians, then the result of s1 + s2 should be a new statistician that behaves as if it had all of the numbers of s1 followed by all of the numbers of s2.

4 Specify, design, and implement a class for a card in a deck of playing cards. The object should contain methods for setting and retrieving the suit and rank of a card.

5 Specify, design, and implement a class that can be used to keep track of the position of a point in three-dimensional space. For example consider the point drawn at the top of the next column. The point shown there has three coordinates:

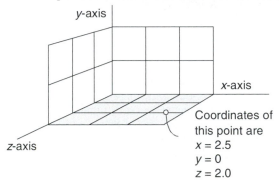

Coordinates of this point are
$x = 2.5$
$y = 0$
$z = 2.0$

$x = 2.5$, $y = 0$, and $z = 2.0$. Include member functions to set a point to a specified location, to shift a point a given amount along one of the axes, and to retrieve the coordinates of a point. Also provide member functions that will rotate the point by a specified angle around a specified axis.

To compute these rotations, you will need a bit of trigonometry. Suppose you have a point with coordinates x, y, and z. After rotating this point (counterclockwise) by an angle θ, the point will have new coordinates, which we'll call x', y', and z'. The

equations for the new coordinates use the cmath library functions sin and cos, as shown here:

After a θ rotation around the x-axis:
$$x' = x$$
$$y' = y \cos(\theta) - z \sin(\theta)$$
$$z' = y \sin(\theta) + z \cos(\theta)$$

After a θ rotation around the y-axis:
$$x' = x \cos(\theta) + z \sin(\theta)$$
$$y' = y$$
$$z' = -x \sin(\theta) + z \cos(\theta)$$

After a θ rotation around the z-axis:
$$x' = x \cos(\theta) - y \sin(\theta)$$
$$y' = x \sin(\theta) + y \cos(\theta)$$
$$z' = z$$

6 In three-dimensional space, a line segment is defined by its two endpoints. Specify, design, and implement a class for a line segment. The class should have two private member variables that are points from the previous project.

7 Specify, design, and implement a class that can be used to hold information about a musical note. A programmer should be able to set and retrieve the length of the note and the value of the note. The length of a note may be a sixteenth note, eighth note, quarter note, half note, or whole note. A value is specified by indicating how far the note lies above or below the A note that orchestras use in tuning. In counting "how far," you should include both the white and black notes on a piano. For example, the note numbers for the octave beginning at middle C are shown here:

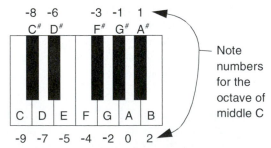

Note numbers for the octave of middle C

The default constructor should set a note to a middle C quarter note. Include member functions to set a note to a specified length and value. Write member functions to retrieve information about a note, including functions to tell you the letter of the note (A, B, C, etc.), whether the note is natural or sharp (i.e., white or black on the piano), and the frequency of a note in hertz. To calculate the frequency, use the formula $440 \times 2^{n/12}$, where n is the note number. Feel free to include other useful member functions.

8 A one-variable **quadratic expression** is an arithmetic expression of the form $ax^2 + bx + c$, where a, b, and c are some fixed numbers (called the **coefficients**) and x is a variable that can take on different values. Specify, design, and implement a class that can store information about a quadratic expression. The default constructor should set all three coefficients to zero, and another member function should allow you to change these coefficients. There should be constant member functions to retrieve the current values of the coefficients. There should also be a member function to allow you to "evaluate" the quadratic expression at a particular value of x (i.e., the function has one parameter x, and returns the value of the expression $ax^2 + bx + c$).

Also overload the following operators (as nonmember functions) to perform these indicated operations:

```
quadratic operator +(
    const quadratic& q1,
    const quadratic& q2
);
// Postcondition: The return value is the
// quadratic expression obtained by adding
// q1 and q2. For example, the c coefficient
// of the return value is the sum of q1's c
// coefficient and q2's c coefficient.

quadratic operator *(
    double r,
    const quadratic& q
);
// Postcondition: The return value is the
// quadratic expression obtained by
// multiplying each of q's
// coefficients by the number r.
```

Notice that the left argument of the overloaded *operator* * is a double number (rather than a quadratic expression). This allows expressions such as 3.14 * q, where q is a quadratic expression.

9 This project is a continuation of the previous project. For a quadratic expression such as $ax^2 + bx + c$, a **real root** is any double number x such that $ax^2 + bx + c = 0$. For example, the quadratic expression $2x^2 + 8x + 6$ has one of its real roots at $x = -3$, because substituting $x = -3$ in the formula $2x^2 + 8x + 6$ yields the value:

$$2 \times (-3^2) + 8 \times (-3) + 6 = 0$$

There are six rules for finding the real roots of a quadratic expression:

(1) If a, b, and c are all zero, then every value of x is a real root.

(2) If a and b are zero, but c is nonzero, then there are no real roots.

(3) If a is zero, and b is nonzero, then the only real root is $x = -c/b$.

(4) If a is nonzero and $b^2 < 4ac$, then there are no real roots.

(5) If a is nonzero and $b^2 = 4ac$, then there is one real root $x = -b/2a$.

(6) If a is nonzero, and $b^2 > 4ac$, then there are two real roots:

$$x = \frac{-b - \sqrt{b^2 - 4ac}}{2a}$$

$$x = \frac{-b + \sqrt{b^2 - 4ac}}{2a}$$

Write a new member function that returns the number of real roots of a quadratic expression. This answer could be 0, or 1, or 2, or infinity. In the case of an infinite number of real roots, have the member function return 3. (Yes, we know that 3 is not infinity, but for this purpose it is close enough!) Write two other member functions that calculate and return the real roots of a quadratic expression. The precondition for both functions is that the expression has at least one real root. If there are two real roots, then one of the functions returns the smaller of the two roots, and the other function returns the larger of the two roots. If every value of x is a real root, then both functions should return zero.

10 Specify, design, and implement a class that can be used to simulate a lunar lander, which is a small spaceship that transports astronauts from lunar orbit to the surface of the moon. When a lunar lander is constructed, the following items should be specified, with default values as indicated:

(1) Current fuel flow rate as a fraction of the maximum fuel flow (default zero)
(2) Vertical speed of the lander (default zero meters/sec)
(3) Altitude of the lander (default 1000 meters)
(4) Amount of fuel (default 1700 kg)
(5) Mass of the lander when it has no fuel (default 900 kg)
(6) Maximum fuel consumption rate (default 10 kg/sec)
(7) Maximum thrust of the lander's engine (default 5000 newtons)

Don't worry about other properties (such as horizontal speed).

The lander has constant member functions that allow a program to retrieve the current values of any of these seven items. There are only two modification member functions, described next.

The first modification function changes the current fuel flow rate to a new value ranging from 0.0 to 1.0. This value is expressed as a fraction of the maximum fuel flow.

The second modification function simulates the passage of a small amount of time. This time, called *t*, is expressed in seconds and will typically be a small value such as 0.1 seconds. The function will update the first four values in the previous list, to reflect the passage of *t* seconds. To implement this function, you will require a few physics formulas, listed next. These formulas are only approximate, because some of the lander's values are changing during the simulated time period. But if the time span is kept short, these formulas will suffice.

Fuel flow rate: Normally, the fuel flow rate does not change during the passage of a small amount of time. But there is one exception: If the fuel flow rate is greater than zero, and the amount of fuel left is zero, then you should reset the fuel flow rate to zero (because there is no fuel to flow).

Velocity change: During *t* seconds, the velocity of the lander changes by approximately this amount (measured in meters/sec):

$$t \times \left(\frac{f}{m} - 1.62 \right)$$

The value *m* is the total mass of the lander, measured in kilograms (i.e., the mass of a lander with no fuel, plus the mass of any remaining fuel). The value *f* is the thrust of the lander's engine, measured in newtons. You can calculate *f* as the current fuel flow rate times the maximum thrust of the lander. The number −1.62 is the downward acceleration from gravity on the moon.

Altitude change: During *t* seconds, the altitude of the lander changes by $t \times v$ meters, where *v* is the vertical velocity of the lander (measured in meters/sec, with negative values downward).

Change in remaining fuel: During *t* seconds, the amount of remaining fuel is reduced by $t \times r \times c$ kilograms. The value of *r* is the current fuel flow rate, and *c* is the maximum fuel consumption (measured in kilograms per second).

We suggest that you calculate the changes to the four items in the order listed here. After all the changes have been made, there are two further adjustments. First, if the altitude has dropped below zero, then reset both altitude and velocity to zero (indicating that the ship has landed). Second, if the total amount of remaining fuel drops below zero, then reset this amount to zero (indicating that we have run out of fuel).

11 In this project you will design and implement a class that can generate a sequence of **pseudorandom** integers, which is a sequence that appears random in many ways. The approach uses the **linear congruence method**, explained here.

The linear congruence method starts with a number called the **seed**. In addition to the seed, three other numbers are used in the linear congruence method, called the **multiplier**, the **increment**, and the **modulus**. The formula for generating a sequence of pseudorandom numbers is quite simple. The first number is:

```
(multiplier * seed + increment) % modulus
```

This formula uses the C++ % operator, which computes the remainder from an integer division.

Each time a new random number is computed, the value of the seed is changed to that new number. For example, we could implement a pseudorandom number generator with `multiplier` = 40, `incre-ment` = 725, and `modulus` = 729. If we choose the seed to be 1, then the sequence of numbers will proceed as shown here:

First number
= (multiplier * seed + increment) % modulus
= (40 * 1 + 725) % 729
= 36
and 36 becomes the new seed.

Next number
= (multiplier * seed + increment) % modulus
= (40 * 36 + 725) % 729
= 707
and 707 becomes the new seed.

Next number
= (multiplier * seed + increment) % modulus
= (40 * 707 + 725) % 729
= 574
and 574 becomes the new seed, and so on.

These particular values for multiplier, increment, and modulus happen to be good choices. The pattern generated will not repeat until 729 different numbers have been produced. Other choices for the constants might not be so good.

For this project, design and implement a class that can generate a pseudorandom sequence in the manner described. The initial seed, multiplier, increment, and modulus should all be parameters of the constructor. There should also be a member function to permit the seed to be changed, and a member function to generate and return the next number in the pseudorandom sequence.

12 Add a new member function to the random number class of the previous project. The new member function generates the next pseudorandom number but does not return the number directly. Instead, the function returns this number divided by the modulus. (You will have to cast the modulus to a double number before carrying out the division; otherwise, the division will be an integer division, throwing away the remainder.)

The return value from this new member function is a pseudorandom double number in the range [0...1). (The square bracket, '[', indicates that the range does include 0, but the rounded parenthesis, ')', indicates that the range goes up to 1, without actually including 1.)

13 Run some experiments to determine the distribution of numbers returned by the new pseudorandom function from the previous project. Recall that this function returns a *double* number in the range [0...1). Divide this range into ten intervals, and call the function one million times, producing a table such as this:

Range	Number of Occurrences
[0.0 ... 0.1)	99889
[0.1 ... 0.2)	100309
[0.2 ... 0.3)	100070
[0.3 ... 0.4)	99940
[0.4 ... 0.5)	99584
[0.5 ... 0.6)	100028
[0.6 ... 0.7)	99669
[0.7 ... 0.8)	100100
[0.8 ... 0.9)	100107
[0.9 ... 1.0)	100304

Run your experiment for different values of the multiplier, increment, and modulus. With good choices of the constants, you will end up with about 10% of the numbers in each interval. A pseudorandom number generator with this equal-interval behavior is called **uniformly distributed**.

14 This project is a continuation of the previous project. Many applications require pseudorandom number sequences that are *not* uniformly distributed. For example, a program that simulates the birth of babies can use random numbers for the birth weights of the newborns. But these birth weights should have a **Gaussian distribution**. In a Gaussian distribution, numbers are more likely to fall in intervals near the center of the overall distribution. The exact probabilities of falling in a particular interval can be computed from knowing two numbers: (1) the center of the overall distribution (called the *median*), and (2) a number called the *standard deviation*, which indicates how widely spread the distribution appears.

Generating a pseudorandom number sequence with an exact Gaussian distribution can be difficult, but there is a good way to approximate a Gaussian distribution using uniformly distributed random numbers in the range [0...1). The approach is to generate 12 uniformly distributed pseudorandom numbers, each in the range [0...1). These numbers are then combined to produce the next number in the Gaussian sequence. The formula to combine the numbers is given here, where sum is the sum of the 12 numbers and sd is the desired standard deviation:

Next number in the Gaussian sequence
$$= \text{median} + (\text{sum} - 6) \times \text{sd}$$

Add a new member function to the random number class, which produces a sequence of pseudorandom numbers with approximate Gaussian distribution.

15 Write a class for rational numbers. Each object in the class should have two integer values that define the rational number: the numerator and the denominator. For example, the fraction 5/6 would have a denominator of 5 and a numerator of 6. Include a constructor with two arguments that can be used to set the numerator and denominator (forbidding zero in the denominator). Provide default values of zero for the numerator and one for the denominator.

Overload the input and output operators. Numbers are to be read and written in the form 1/2, 32/15, 300/401, and so forth. Note that the numerator, the denominator, or both may contain a minus sign, so -1/2, 32/-15, and -300/-401 are possible.

Include a function to normalize the values stored so that, after normalization, the denominator is positive and as small as possible. For example, after normalization, 4/-8 would be represented the same as -1/2.

Overload the usual arithmetic operators to provide addition, subtraction, multiplication, and division of two rational numbers. Overload the usual comparison operations to allow comparison of two rational numbers.

Hints: Two rational numbers *a/b* and *c/d* are equal if *a*d* equals *c*b*. For positive rational numbers, *a/b* is less than *c/d*, provided *a*d* is less than *c*b*.

16 Write a class to keep track of a balance in a bank account with a varying annual interest rate. The constructor will set both the balance and the annual interest rate to some initial values (with defaults of zero).

The class should have member functions to change or retreive the current balance or interest rate. There should also be functions to make a deposit (add to the balance) or a withdrawal (subtract from the balance). Finally, there should be a function that adds interest to the balance at the current interest rate. This function should have a parameter indicating how many years worth of interest are to be added (for example, 0.5 years indicates that the account should have six months' interest added).

Use the class as part of an interactive program that allows the user to determine how long an initial balance will take to grow to a given value. The program should allow the user to specify the initial balance, the interest rate, and whether there are additional yearly deposits.

17 Specify, design, and implement a class called date. Use integers to represent a date's month, day, and year. Write a member function to increment the date to the next day.

Include friend functions to display a date in both number and word format.

18 Specify, design, and implement a class called employee. The class has data members for the employee's name, ID number, and salary based on an hourly wage. Member functions include computing the yearly salary and increasing the salary by a certain percentage. Add additional data members to store biweekly paycheck information and calculate overtime (for over 40 hours per week) for each paycheck.

19 Write a class for complex numbers. A complex number has the form $a + bi$, where a and b are real numbers and i is the square root of -1. We refer to a as the real part and b as the imaginary part of the number. The class should have two data members to represent the real and imaginary numbers; the constructor takes two arguments to set these members. Discuss and implement other appropriate operators for this class.

3

Container Classes

(I am large. I contain multitudes.)

WALT WHITMAN
"Song of Myself"

LEARNING OBJECTIVES

When you complete Chapter 3, you will be able to...

- design and implement collection classes that use partially filled arrays to store a collection of elements, generally using linear-time algorithms to access, insert, and remove elements.

- use typedef statements within a container class definition to specify the data type of the container's elements.

- use static const members within a class definition to define fixed integer information such as the size of an array.

- use the C++ Standard Library copy function to copy part of an array from one location to another.

- write and maintain an accurate invariant for each class that you implement.

- write simple interactive test programs to test any newly implemented container class.

CHAPTER CONTENTS

Container Classes

a class in which
each object
contains a
collection of
items

The throttle and point classes in Chapter 2 are good examples of abstract data types. But their applicability is limited to a few specialized programs. This chapter begins the presentation of several classes with broad applicability in programs large and small. The two particular classes in this chapter—bags and sequences—are examples of **container classes**. Intuitively, a container class is a class where each object contains a collection of items. For example, one program might keep track of a collection of integers, perhaps the ages of all the people in your family. Another program, perhaps a cryptography program, can use a collection of characters.

The bag and sequence classes are both simple versions of more complex classes from the C++ Standard Library. The goal is for you to understand and use the bag and sequence classes as a bridge to understanding and using the Standard container classes. Over the next few chapters, variations of the bag and sequence classes will teach you how to write your own container classes that are compliant with the C++ Standard Library, and therefore your own classes can take advantage of standard algorithms for such tasks as searching and sorting.

A key feature of a good container class is that it should be easy to change the type of item in the container so that a new application can use the container. With this kind of "easy reuse," many different applications can use the same container class. The same container class can be used by one program for a collection of integers, and by another program for a collection of characters or some other data type. In this chapter we use **typedef statements** to provide the ability to easily change the type of item in a container class. In Chapter 6, which focuses explicitly on software reusability, we'll use a different feature called **templates**, which is also used by the Standard Library container classes.

3.1 THE BAG CLASS

This section provides an example of a container class, called a *bag of integers*. To define the new bag data type, think about an actual bag—a grocery bag or a garbage bag—and imagine writing integers on slips of paper and putting them in the bag. A **bag of integers** is similar to this imaginary bag: a container that can hold a collection of integers that we place into it. A bag of integers can be used by any program that needs to store a collection of integers for later use. For example, later we will write a program that keeps track of the ages of your family's members. If you have a large family with ten people, the program keeps track of ten ages—and these ages are kept in a bag of integers.

The Bag Class—Specification

We've given an intuitive description of a bag of integers, but for a more precise specification of the bag class, we must describe the collection of functions to manipulate a bag object. We'll do this by providing a prototype for each of the functions, most of which are member functions. With each prototype we also specify the precise action that the function will perform. These specifications will later become our precondition/postcondition contracts. Let's look at the functions one at a time.

The constructor. The bag class has a default constructor to initialize a bag to be empty. The name of the constructor must be the same as the name of the class itself, so the prototype for our constructor is the following:

```
bag( );
```

The value semantics. As part of our specification, we require that bag objects can be copied with an assignment statement. Also, a newly declared bag can be initialized as a copy of another bag, using the copy constructor such as:

```
bag b;
b.insert(42);
bag c(b);
```

b now contains a 42.

c is initialized with the copy constructor to be a copy of b.

At this point, because we are only specifying which operations can manipulate a bag, we don't need to say anything more about the value semantics.

A typedef for the value_type. So far we have considered only bags of integers. But to be more flexible, we won't actually use the name *int* when we refer to the types of the items in the bag. Instead, we will use the name `value_type` for the data type of the items in a bag. Some programs might need a bag of integers, and those programs will set the `value_type` to an *int*. Other programs might use a different `value_type`. In order for the bag to have this flexible `value_type`, we will place the following statement at the top of the public section of the bag's class definition:

```
class bag
{
public:
    typedef int value_type;
    ...
```

This statement is a **typedef** statement. It consists of the keyword *typedef* followed by a data type (such as *int*) and then a new identifier, such as `value_type`. We are not required to use the specific name `value_type`; we could have used any meaningful name. But the Standard Library container classes use the name `value_type`, so we have done so for consistency.

The effect of the typedef statement is that bag functions can use the name value_type as a synonym for the data type *int*. Wherever a bag member function uses the name value_type, the compiler will recognize it as simply another name for *int*. Other functions, which are not bag member functions, can use the name bag::value_type as the type of the items in a bag. Moreover, if we want a new kind of bag, we can simply change the word *int* to a new data type and recompile. No other changes will be needed anywhere in our program. For example, to declare a bag of double numbers we change the typedef statement to the following:

```
class bag
{
public:
    typedef  double  value_type;
    ...
```

In Chapter 6, we will use an alternative way to define value_type. The alternative, called a *template class*, is more cumbersome, but it overcomes some drawbacks of the typedef statement. Meanwhile, the top next C++ Feature shows how we used the C++ typedef statement.

⭐ C++ Feature

Typedef Statements Within a Class Definition

Within a class definition, we can place a typedef statement of the following form:

```
class  < Name of the class >
{
public:
    typedef   < A data type such as int or double >   < A new name >
    ...
```

This statement is a **typedef** statement. It consists of the keyword *typedef* followed by a data type (such as *int*) and then a new identifier (such as value_type). The effect of this typedef statement is that member functions can use the new name value_type as a synonym for the data type. Functions that are not member functions can also use the name, but its use must be preceded by the class name and "::" (for example bag::value_type).

The size_type. In addition to the value_type, our bag defines another data type that can be used for variables that keep track of how many items are in a bag. This type will be called size_type, with its definition near the top of the bag class definition:

```
class bag
{
public:
    typedef  int  value_type;
    typedef  <an integer type of some kind>  size_type;
    ...
```

Once we have provided the size_type definition, we can use size_type for any variable that's counting how many items are in a bag. This is another programming idea that we got from the Standard Library containers—they all have a built-in size_type as part of the class.

Of course, we still must decide which data type to use for "an integer type of some kind" in the typedef statement. We could use an ordinary *int*, but C++ provides a better alternative: the size_t data type, described next.

C++ FEATURE

THE STD::SIZE_T DATA TYPE

The data type size_t is an integer data type that can hold only non-negative numbers. Each C++ implementation guarantees that the values of the size_t type are sufficient to hold the size of any variable that can be declared on your machine. Therefore, when you want to describe the size of some array or other variable, the best choice is the size_t data type. The size_t type is part of the std namespace from the Standard Library facility, cstdlib. To use size_t in a header file, we must include cstdlib and use the full name std::size_t.

Our bag definition uses size_t as shown here:

```
class bag
{
public:
    typedef  int value_type;
    typedef  std::size_t   size_type;
    ...
```

With the bag definition, or within an implementation of a bag member function, we can use the type size_type. Other programmers can also use this data type, but they must write the full name—bag::size_type.

The size member function. The bag has a constant member function called size. The prototype uses the bag's size_type:

```
size_type size( ) const;
```

As you might guess, the return value of the size function tells how many items are currently in the bag. To illustrate the use of the function, suppose first_bag contains one copy of the number 4 and two copies of the number 8. Then first_bag.size( ) returns 3.

The insert member function. This is a member function that places a new integer, called entry, into a bag. Here is the prototype:

```
void insert(const value_type& entry);
```

As an example, here is a sequence of function calls for a bag called `first_bag`:

```
bag first_bag;
first_bag.insert(8);
first_bag.insert(4);
first_bag.insert(8);
```

After these statements, first_bag contains two 8s and a 4.

After these statements are executed, `first_bag` contains three integers: the number 4 and two copies of the number 8. It is important to realize that a bag can contain many copies of the same integer, such as this example with two copies of 8.

Notice that the `entry` parameter is a const reference parameter. This may seem strange since the usual purpose of a const reference parameter is to improve efficiency when a parameter is a large object. Integers are not large, but we may later change the `value_type` to something that is large. With this in mind, we will use const reference parameters for `value_type` parameters, whenever this is possible (i.e., whenever the function's implementation does not change the value of the parameter).

The count member function. This is a constant member function that determines how many copies of a *particular* number are in a bag. The prototype uses `size_type`:

```
size_type count(const value_type& target) const;
```

The activation of `count(n)` returns the number of occurrences of n in a bag. For example, if `first_bag` contains the number 4 and two copies of the number 8, then we will have these values:

```
cout << first_bag.count(1) << endl;    Prints 0
cout << first_bag.count(4) << endl;    Prints 1
cout << first_bag.count(8) << endl;    Prints 2
```

The erase_one and erase member functions. These two member functions have the following prototypes:

```
bool erase_one(const value_type& target);
size_type erase(const value_type& target);
```

Provided that the `target` is actually in the bag, the `erase_one` function removes one copy of `target` and returns true. If `target` is not in the bag, attempting to erase one copy has no effect on the bag, and the function returns false. The `erase` function removes all copies of the target; its return value tells how many copies were removed (which could be zero).

Union operator. The **union** of two bags is a new larger bag that contains all the numbers in the first bag plus all the numbers in the second bag, as shown here:

In the drawing we wrote "+" for "union." To implement the union, we will overload the + operator as a nonmember function with this prototype:

```
bag operator +(const bag& b1, const bag& b2);
```

The function is not a member function because of our guidelines about overloading binary operators (see page 85).

Overloading the += operator. The + operator is defined for bags, so it is sensible to also overload +=. The overloaded += will allow us to add the contents of one bag to the existing contents of another bag in much the same way that += works for integers or real numbers. We intend to use += as shown here:

```
bag first_bag, second_bag;
first_bag.insert(8);
second_bag.insert(4);
second_bag.insert(8);
first_bag += second_bag;
```

This adds the contents of second_bag to what's already in first_bag.

After these statements `first_bag` contains one 4 and two 8s.

Our style preference is to overload += as a member function. The reason is that the first argument (to the left of the +=) has special significance: It is the argument that actually has its value changed. The second argument (to the right of the +=) never has its value changed. By making the operator += into a member function, we place special emphasis on the left argument in a statement such as:

overload += as a member function

```
first_bag += second_bag;
```

This statement means "activate the += member function of `first_bag`, and use `second_bag` as the argument." Here is the prototype of the member function:

```
void operator +=(const bag& addend);
```

There are several points to notice:

- This is a *void* function. It does not return a value. It only alters the contents of the bag that activates the function.

- The function has only one parameter, `addend`. This is the right-hand bag in an expression such as `first_bag += second_bag`. The left-hand bag is the bag that activates `+=` and that has its contents altered.
- We use the name `addend` for the parameter, meaning "something to be added," but you may use whatever name you like.

The bag's CAPACITY. That's the end of our list of functions, and we're almost ready to write the header file. But first, we describe one more handy C++ feature that is related to how we will store the items in a bag.

Our plan is for bounded bags that can hold 30 items each. (Later we will remove this restriction, providing an unbounded bag class.) There is nothing magic about the number 30—we just picked it as a conveniently small size for our first bags. Later, we might want to change the size 30, allowing bags that hold 42 or 5000 or some other number of items. To make it easy to change the bag's size, and also to make our programs more readable, we will use a name such as CAPACITY rather than simply using the number 30.

The best way to define CAPACITY is as a **static member constant**, as shown in the example here:.

```
class bag
{
public:
    typedef int value_type;
    typedef std::size_t size_type;
    static const size_type CAPACITY = 30;
    ...
```

The keyword *const* has the same meaning that we have seen with other constant declarations, so that the value of CAPACITY is defined once and cannot be changed while the program is running.

The keyword *static* modifies the definition in a useful way. Usually each object has its own copy of each member variable. But when the keyword *static* is used with a class member, it means that *all* of the class's objects use the *same* value. This is different! For example, with the bag's static member constant, every bag has the same CAPACITY of 30. In fact, the only reason that we can set the CAPACITY to 30 *within* the class definition is because every bag has the same value for CAPACITY. When a program declares a bag b, the program can refer to the capacity with the usual notation for selecting a member: b.CAPACITY. Because every bag has the same capacity, a program can also refer to a bag's capacity using the bag:: "scope resolution operator," as shown in this example:

```
bag b;
cout << "The capacity of b is " << b.CAPACITY << endl;
cout << "Every bag has capacity " << bag::CAPACITY << endl;
```

As shown in this example, we recommend all uppercase letters for the name of any constant. This makes it easy to recognize which values are constant.

In addition to declaring the static member constant within the class definition, the program must also repeat the declaration of the constant in the implementation file. In our example, the following single line must appear in the implementation file: `const bag::size_type bag::CAPACITY;`

We have described the general format of a static member constant, but there are a few pitfalls to beware of:

- The keyword `static` is not repeated in the implementation file because `static` has a different meaning outside of the class definition.

- When the constant is declared in the implementation file, we must use the full type name (such as `bag::size_type`), rather than the short version (such as `size_type`) because the short version may be used only in the class definition or within an implementation of a member function.

- In the implementation file, we must also use the full name of the constant (such as `bag::CAPACITY`) rather than the short version (such as `CAPACITY`); otherwise the compiler won't know that this is a member of a class.

For future reference, here is a summary of static member constants, including a note about where the initial value must appear for different types of constants.

CLARIFYING THE CONST KEYWORD
Part 4: Static Member Constants

A **static member constant** has the two keywords `static` and `const` before its declaration in a class. For example, in our bag class definition:

```
static const size_type CAPACITY = 30;
```

The keyword `static` indicates that the entire class has only one copy of this member, and the keyword `const` indicates that a program cannot change the value (which is just like ordinary declared constants).

In addition to declaring the static member constant within the class definition, the constant must be redeclared in the implementation file without the keyword `static`. For example:

```
const bag::size_type bag::CAPACITY;
```

Notice that the initial value (such as 30), is given only in the header file, not the implementation file. However, this technique of defining the value in the header file is allowed only for integer types such as `int` and `size_t`. Non-integer types must be done the other way around, leaving the value out of the header file and defining this value in the implementation file. The reason for this difference is that integral values are often used within the class definition to define something such as an array size.

Older Compilers Do Not Support Initialization of Static Member Constants

The ability to initialize and use a static member constant within the class definition is a relatively new feature. If you have an older compiler that does not support static constant members, then Appendix E, "Dealing with Older Compilers," provides an alternative for your programming.

The Bag Class—Documentation

We now know enough about the bag class to write the documentation of the header file, as shown in Figure 3.1. We've used the name `bag1.h` for this header file because it is the first of several different kinds of bags that we plan to implement.

The documentation includes information about the two typedef statements (`value_type` and `size_type`) and the static member constant (`CAPACITY`). In particular, notice that we have been very specific about what sort of data type is required for the `value_type`. The `value_type` may be any of the C++ built-in data types (such as *int* or *char*), or it may be a class with a default constructor, an assignment operator, and operators to test for equality (x == y) and non-equality (x != y).

Take a moment to read and understand all of the preconditions in Figure 3.1, such as this precondition for the += operator:

Precondition: size( ) + addend.size( ) <= CAPACITY.

In this precondition, `size( )` refers to the size of the bag that activates the function, and `CAPACITY` refers to the capacity of the bag that activates the function. On the other hand, `addend.size( )` refers to the size of the `addend`, which is a parameter of the function.

FIGURE 3.1   Documentation for the Bag Header File

Documentation for a Header File

```
//  FILE: bag1.h
//  CLASS PROVIDED: bag (part of the namespace main_savitch_3)
//
//  TYPEDEFS and MEMBER CONSTANTS for the bag class:
//     typedef _____ value_type
//        bag::value_type is the data type of the items in the bag. It may be any of the C++
//        built-in types (int, char, etc.), or a class with a default constructor, an assignment
//        operator, and operators to test for equality (x == y) and  non-equality (x != y).
```

(continued)

(FIGURE 3.1 continued)

```
//    typedef ____ size_type
//       bag::size_type is the data type of any variable that keeps track of how many items
//       are in a bag.
//
//    static const size_type CAPACITY = _____
//       bag::CAPACITY is the maximum number of items that a bag can hold.
//
// CONSTRUCTOR for the bag class:
//    bag( )
//       Postcondition: The bag has been initialized as an empty bag.
//
// MODIFICATION MEMBER FUNCTIONS for the bag class:
//    size_type erase(const value_type& target)
//       Postcondition: All copies of target have been removed from the bag.
//       The return value is the number of copies removed (which could be zero).
//
//    bool erase_one(const value_type& target)
//       Postcondition: If target was in the bag, then one copy has been removed;
//       otherwise the bag is unchanged. A true return value indicates that one
//       copy was removed; false indicates that nothing was removed.
//
//    void insert(const value_type& entry)
//       Precondition:  size( ) < CAPACITY.
//       Postcondition: A new copy of entry has been added to the bag.
//
//    void operator +=(const bag& addend)
//       Precondition:  size( ) + addend.size( ) <= CAPACITY.
//       Postcondition: Each item in addend has been added to this bag.
//
// CONSTANT MEMBER FUNCTIONS for the bag class:
//    size_type size( ) const
//       Postcondition: The return value is the total number of items in the bag.
//
//    size_type count(const value_type& target) const
//       Postcondition: The return value is number of times target is in the bag.
//
// NONMEMBER FUNCTIONS for the bag class:
//    bag operator +(const bag& b1, const bag& b2)
//       Precondition:  b1.size( ) + b2.size( ) <= bag::CAPACITY.
//       Postcondition: The bag returned is the union of b1 and b2.
//
// VALUE SEMANTICS  for the bag class:
//       Assignments and the copy constructor may be used with bag objects.
```

Documenting the Value Semantics

One of the requirements for the value_type may seem peculiar—why do we require that value_type "must have an assignment operator"? Doesn't every data type permit assignments such as x = y? Won't there always be an automatic assignment operator? No! For example, x = y is forbidden when x and y are arrays. Later we will see other data types that require care in defining what the assignment operator actually means.

The Bag Class—Demonstration Program

With the documentation in hand, we can write a program that uses a bag. We don't need to know how the functions are implemented. As an example, a demonstration program appears in Figure 3.2. The program asks a user about the ages of family members. The user enters the ages followed by a negative number to indicate the end of the input, and these ages are put into a bag. The program then asks the user to type the ages again, as a simple test.

FIGURE 3.2   Demonstration Program for the Bag Class

A Program

```
// FILE: bag_demo.cxx
// This is a small demonstration program showing how the bag class is used.
#include <iostream>      // Provides cout and cin
#include <cstdlib>       // Provides EXIT_SUCCESS
#include "bag1.h"        // With value_type defined as an int
using namespace std;
using namespace main_savitch_3;

// PROTOTYPES for functions used by this demonstration program:
void get_ages(bag& ages);
// Postcondition: The user has been prompted to type in the ages of family members. These
// ages have been read and placed in the ages bag, stopping when the bag is full or when the
// user types a negative number.

void check_ages(bag& ages);
// Postcondition: The user has been prompted to type in the ages of family members again.
// Each age is removed from the ages bag when it is typed, stopping when the bag is empty.

int main( )
{
    bag ages;

    get_ages(ages);
    check_ages(ages);
    cout << "May your family live long and prosper." << endl;
    return EXIT_SUCCESS;
}
```
(continued)

(FIGURE 3.2 continued)

```cpp
void get_ages(bag& ages)
{
    int user_input;

    cout << "Type the ages in your family." << endl;
    cout << "Type a negative number when you are done:" << endl;
    cin >> user_input;
    while (user_input >= 0)
    {
        if (ages.size( ) < ages.CAPACITY)
            ages.insert(user_input);
        else
            cout << "I have run out of room and can't add that age." << endl;
        cin >> user_input;
    }
}

void check_ages(bag& ages)
{
    int user_input;

    cout << "Type those ages again. Press return after each age:" << endl;
    while (ages.size( ) > 0)
    {
        cin >> user_input;
        if (ages.erase_one(user_input))
            cout << "Yes, I've found that age and removed it." << endl;
        else
            cout << "No, that age does not occur!" << endl;
    }
}
```

Sample Dialogue with the Program

```
Type the ages in your family.
Type a negative number when you are done:
5 19 47 -1
Type those ages again. Press return after each age:
19
Yes, I've found that age and removed it.
36
No, that age does not occur!
5
Yes, I've found that age and removed it.
47
Yes, I've found that age and removed it.
May your family live long and prosper.
```

www.cs.colorado.edu/~main/chapter3/bag_demo.cxx   **WWW**

The Bag Class—Design

There are several ways to design the bag class. For now, we'll keep things simple and design a somewhat inefficient data structure using an array. The data structure will be redesigned several times to allow more efficient functions.

use the beginning part of an array

We start the design by thinking about the data structure—the actual configuration of private member variables used to implement the class. The primary structure for our design is an array that stores the items of a bag. Or, to be more precise, we use *the beginning* part of a large array. Such an array is called a **partially filled array**. For example, if the bag contains the integer 4 and two copies of 8, then the first part of the array could look this way:

Components of
the partially filled
array contain the
items of the bag.

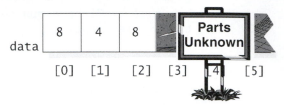

This array will be one of the private member variables of the bag class. The length of the array will be determined by the constant CAPACITY, but as the picture indicates, when we are using the array to store a bag with just three items, we don't care what appears beyond the first three components. Starting at index 3, the array might contain all zeros, or it might contain garbage, or our favorite number—it really doesn't matter.

Because part of the array can contain garbage, the bag class must keep track of one other item: *How much of the array is currently being used?* For example, in the picture above, we are using only the first three components of the array because the bag contains three items. The amount of the array being used can be as small as zero (an empty bag) or as large as CAPACITY (a full bag). The amount increases as items are added to the bag, and it decreases as items are removed. In any case, we will keep track of the amount in a private member variable called used. With this approach, there are two private members for a bag. Notice that the total size of the array is determined by the CAPACITY constant.

the bag's member variables

```
class bag
{
public:
    // TYPEDEFS and MEMBER CONSTANTS
    typedef int value_type;
    typedef std::size_t size_type;
    static const size_type CAPACITY = 30;
    || The rest of the public members will be listed later.
private:
    value_type data[CAPACITY];   // An array to store items
    size_type used;              // How much of the array is used
};
```

two private member variables for the bag

THE value_type MUST HAVE A DEFAULT CONSTRUCTOR

The value_type is used as the component type of an array in the private member variable shown here:

```
class bag
{
...
private:
    value_type data[CAPACITY];   // An array to store items
...
```

If the value_type is a class with constructors (rather than one of the C++ built-in types), then the compiler must initialize each component of the data array using the item's default constructor. This is why our bag documentation includes the statement that the value_type type must be "a class with a default constructor...."

The point to remember is that when an array has a component type that is a class, the compiler uses the default constructor to initialize the array components.

The Invariant of a Class

We've defined the bag data structure, and we have a good intuitive idea of how the structure will be used to represent a bag of items. But as an aid in implementing the class we should also write down an explicit statement of how the data structure is used to represent a bag. In the case of the bag, we need to state how the member variables of the bag class are used to represent a bag of items. There are two rules for our bag implementation:

1. The number of items in the bag is stored in the member variable used.

2. For an empty bag, we do not care what is stored in any of data; for a non-empty bag, the items in the bag are stored in data[0] through data[used-1], and we don't care what is stored in the rest of data.

rules that dictate how the member variables are used to represent a value

The rules that dictate how the member variables of a class represent a value (such as a bag of items) are called the **invariant of the class**. The knowledge of these rules is essential to the correct implementation of the class's functions. With the exception of the constructors, each function depends on the invariant being valid when the function is called. And each function, including the constructors, has a responsibility of ensuring that the invariant is valid when the function finishes. In some sense, the invariant of a class is a condition that is an *implicit* part of every function's postcondition. And (except for the constructors) it is also an implicit part of every function's precondition. The invariant is not usually written as an *explicit* part of the preconditions and postconditions because the programmer who uses the class does not need to know about these conditions. But to the implementor of the class, the invariant is indispensable. In other words, the invariant is a critical part of the implementation of a class, but it has no effect on the way the class is used.

Key Design Concept

The invariant is a critical part of a class's implementation.

The Invariant of a Class

Always make an explicit statement of the rules that dictate how the member variables of a class are used. These rules are called the **invariant of the class**. All of the functions (except the constructors) can count on the invariant being valid when the function is called. Each function also has the responsibility of ensuring that the invariant is valid when the function finishes.

The Bag Class—Implementation

Once the invariant of the bag is stated, the implementation of the functions is relatively simple because there is no interaction between the functions—except for their cooperation at keeping the invariant valid. Let's discuss each function along with its implementation.

The constructor. The default constructor initializes a bag as an empty bag, and does no other work. The only task involved is to set the member `used` to zero, which can be accomplished with an inline member function:

*implementing
the constructor*

```
bag( ) { used = 0; }
```

The value semantics. Our documentation indicates that assignments and the copy constructor may be used with a bag. Our plan is to use the automatic assignment operator and the automatic copy constructor, each of which simply copies the member variables from one bag to another. This is fine because the copying process will copy both the `data` array and the member variable `used`.

For example, if a programmer has two bags x and y, then the statement `y = x` will invoke the automatic assignment operator to copy all of `x.data` to `y.data`, and to copy `x.used` to `y.used`. This is exactly what we want the assignment operator to do, and the automatic copy constructor is also correct.

So, our only "work" for the value semantics is confirming that the automatic operations are correct. Don't you wish all implementations were that easy?

The count member function. To count the number of occurrences of a particular item in a bag, we step through the used portion of the partially filled array. Remember that we are using locations `data[0]` through `data[used-1]`, so the correct loop is shown in this implementation:

*implementing
the count
function*

```
bag::size_type bag::count(const value_type& target) const
{
    size_type answer;
    size_type i;
    answer = 0;
    for (i = 0; i < used; ++i)
        if (target == data[i])
            ++answer;
    return answer;
}
```

NEEDING TO USE THE FULL TYPE NAME BAG::SIZE_TYPE

When we implement the `count` function, we must take care to write the return type as shown here:

```
bag::size_type  bag::count(const value_type& target)
```

We have used the completely specified type `bag::size_type` rather than just `size_type`. This is because many compilers do not recognize that you are implementing a bag member function until after seeing `bag::count`. In the implementation, after `bag::count`, we may use simpler names such as `size_type` and `value_type`, but before `bag::count`, we should use the full type name `bag::size_type`.

The insert member function. The insert function checks that there is room to insert a new item. If so, then the item is placed in the next available location of the array. What is the index of the next available location? For example, if `used` is 3, then `data[0]`, `data[1]`, and `data[2]` are already occupied, and the next location is `data[3]`. In general, the next available location is `data[used]`. We can place the new item in `data[used]`, as shown in this implementation:

```
void bag::insert(const value_type& entry)
// Library facilities used: cassert
{
    assert(size( ) < CAPACITY);
    data[used] = entry;
    ++used;
}
```

See Self-Test Exercise 13 for an alternative approach to these steps.

implementing insert

Within a member function we can refer to the static member constant `CAPACITY` with no extra notation. This refers to the `CAPACITY` member constant of the bag that activates the insert function.

MAKE ASSERTIONS MEANINGFUL

At the start of the insert member function, we wrote the assertion:

```
assert(size( ) < CAPACITY);
```

Of course, we could have written "used < CAPACITY" instead, but it is better to write assertions with public members (such as the size function). The public member is better because it has meaning to the programmer who uses our class. If the assertion fails, that programmer will understand the message "Assertion failed: size( ) < CAPACITY."

The erase_one member function. The `erase_one` function takes several steps to remove an item named `target` from a bag. In the first step, we find the index of `target` in the bag's array, and store this index in a local variable named `index`. For example, suppose that `target` is the number 6 in the five-item bag drawn at the top of the next page.

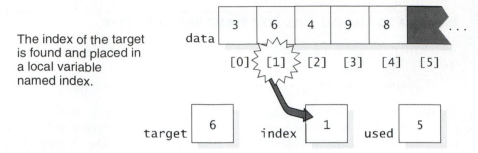

The index of the target is found and placed in a local variable named index.

In this example, `target` is a parameter to the `erase_one` member function, `index` is a local variable in the `erase_one` member function, and `used` is the familiar bag member variable. As you can see in the drawing, the first step of `erase_one` was to locate the target (6) and place the index of the target in the local variable named `index`.

Once the index of the target is found, the second step is to take the *final* item in the bag and copy it to `data[index]`. The reason for this copying is so that all the bag's items stay together at the front of the partially filled array, with no holes. In our example, the number 8 is copied to `data[index]` as shown here:

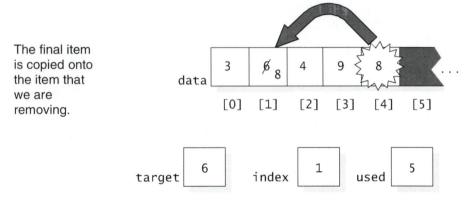

The final item is copied onto the item that we are removing.

The third step is to reduce the value of `used` by one—in effect reducing the used part of the array by one. In our example, `used` is reduced from 5 to 4:

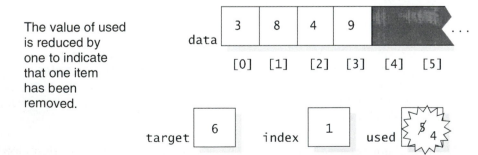

The value of used is reduced by one to indicate that one item has been removed.

The code for the `erase_one` function, shown in Figure 3.3, follows these three steps. The only item added is a check that the target is actually in the bag. If we discover that the target is not in the bag, then we do not need to remove anything (and the function returns false). Also note that our function works correctly for the boundary values of removing the first or last item in the array.

Before we continue, we want to point out some programming techniques. Look at the following while-loop from Figure 3.3:

implementing
erase_one

```
index = 0;
while ((index < used) && (data[index] != target))
      ++index;
```

To begin, the `index` is set to zero. The boolean expression indicates that the loop continues as long as `index` is still a location in the used part of the array (i.e., `index < used`) and we have not yet found the target (i.e., `data[index] != target`). Each time through the loop, the `index` is incremented by one

---

FIGURE 3.3   Implementation of the Member Function to Remove an Item

---

A Member Function Implementation

```
bool bag::erase_one(const value_type& target)
// Postcondition: If target was in the bag, then one copy has been removed;
// otherwise the bag is unchanged. A true return value indicates that one
// copy was removed; false indicates that nothing was removed.
{
    size_type index; // The location of target in the data array

    // First, set index to the location of target in the data array, which could be as small as
    // 0 or as large as used-1. If target is not in the array, then index will be set equal to
    // used.
    index = 0;
    while ((index < used) && (data[index] != target))
        ++index;

    if (index == used)
        return false; // target isn't in the bag, so no work to do.

    // When execution reaches here, target is in the bag at data[index].
    // So, reduce used by 1 and copy the last item onto data[index].
    --used;
    data[index] = data[used];  ⟵——  See Self-Test Exercise 13 for an
    return true;                      alternative approach to this step.
}
```

www.cs.colorado.edu/~main/chapter3/bag1.cxx   **WWW**

(++index). No other work is needed in the loop, so the body of the loop has no other statements.

An important programming technique concerns the boolean expression shown here:

```
index = 0;
while ((index < used) && (data[index] != target))
    ++index;
```

Look at the expression data[index] in the second part of the test. The valid indexes for data range from 0 to used-1. But, if the target is not in the array, then index will eventually reach used, which could be an invalid index. At that point, with index equal to used, we must not evaluate the expression data[index]. In some situations, trying to evaluate data[index] with an invalid index can even cause your program to crash. The general rule: *Never use an invalid index with an array.*

short-circuit evaluation of logical operations

Avoiding the invalid index is the reason for the first part of the logical test (i.e., index < used). Moreover, the test for (index < used) must appear *before* the other part of the test. Placing (index < used) first ensures that only valid indexes are used. The insurance comes from a technique called *short-circuit evaluation,* which C++ uses to evaluate boolean expressions. In **short-circuit evaluation** a boolean expression is evaluated from left to right, and the evaluation stops as soon as there is enough information to determine the value of the expression. In our example, if index equals used, then the first part of the logical expression (index < used) is false, so the entire && expression *must* be false. It doesn't matter whether the second part of the && expression is true or false. Therefore, C++ doesn't bother to evaluate the second part of the expression, and the potential error of an invalid index is avoided.

The operator +=. The operator += is a member function. Most of the work of this function is accomplished by a loop that copies each of the items from addend.data to the data array of the object that activates +=. One possible implementation uses a loop, something like this:

```
void bag::operator +=(const bag& addend)
{
    ...
    for (i = 0; i < number of items to copy; ++i)
    {
        data[used] = addend.data[i];
        ++used;
    }
}
```

implementing operator +=

The key assignment statement in the loop is highlighted. On the left of the assignment we have written data[used], which is the next available location of the data array for the object that activated the function. On the right of the assignment we have written addend.data[i], which is item number i from the data array that we are copying.

There's nothing wrong with the loop-based implementation, but an alternative that avoids an explicit loop is shown in Figure 3.4. The implementation uses the copy function from the <algorithm> Standard Library. This function can copy items from one array to another, as described in the following C++ Feature.

C++ FEATURE ▄▀

THE COPY FUNCTION FROM THE C++ STANDARD LIBRARY

The Standard Library contains a `copy` function for easy copying of items from one location to another. The function is part of the `std` namespace in the `<algorithm>` facility, and is used as follows:

    copy(<beginning location>, <ending location>, <destination>);

The function starts at the specified beginning location and copies an item to the destination. It continues beyond the beginning location, copying more and more items to the next spot of the destination, until we are about to copy the ending location. The ending location is **not** copied. All three parameters are often locations within arrays. For example, suppose that b and c are arrays. To copy the items b[0]...b[9] into locations c[40]...c[49], we could write:

    copy(b, b + 10, c + 40);

This call to `copy` starts copying items from b[0], b[1], b[2], ... It stops when it reaches b[10] (and b[10] is not copied). The copied items go into array c, at locations c[40], c[41], c[42], ... The destination must not overlap the source.

As shown in this example, to specify a location that is at the start of an array, just use the array name (such as b). To specify a location at index i of an array, write the array name followed by "+ i" (such as b + 10 or c + 40).

The statement `copy(addend.data, addend.data + addend.used, data + used)` is used in Figure 3.4 to copy items from `addend.data` into the `data` array. The copied items come from the start of `addend.data`, continuing up to but not including `addend.data[addend.used]`. The copied items are placed in the `data` array starting at location `data[used]`.

FIGURE 3.4   Implementation of the Operator += Member Function

A Member Function Implementation

```
void bag::operator +=(const bag& addend)
// Precondition: size( ) + addend.size( ) <= CAPACITY.
// Postcondition: Each item in addend has been added to this bag.
// Library facilities used: algorithm, cassert
{
    assert(size( ) + addend.size( ) <= CAPACITY);

    copy(addend.data, addend.data + addend.used, data + used);
    used += addend.used;
}
```

The copy function is from the <algorithm> part of the C++ Standard Library

www.cs.colorado.edu/~main/chapter3/bag1.cxx   **WWW**

The operator +. The operator + is different from our other functions. It is an ordinary function rather than a member function. The function must take two bags, add them together into a third bag, and return this third bag. The "third bag" is declared as a local variable called answer in this implementation:

```
bag operator +(const bag& b1, const bag& b2)
// Library facilities used: cassert
{
    bag answer;

    assert(b1.size( ) + b2.size( ) <= bag::CAPACITY);

    answer += b1;  ←————————— Add in the items of b1.
    answer += b2;  ←
    return answer;
}                        ←———— Add in the items of b2.
```

Notice that this function does not need to be a friend function. Why not? (See the answer to Self-Test Exercise 11.) Also, the function implementation can access the static member constant with the notation bag::CAPACITY.

The Bag Class—Putting the Pieces Together

Only the erase and size functions remain to be implemented. We'll leave erase as an exercise (it is similar to erase_one), and size will be an inline function of the class definition shown in the completed header file of Figure 3.5 on page 117. Notice that in the header file we also list the prototype of the bag's *operator +* function. This is not a member function, so the prototype appears *after* the end of the bag class definition.

All the function implementations are collected in the implementation file of Figure 3.6 on page 118.

⬆ PROGRAMMING TIP

DOCUMENT THE CLASS INVARIANT IN THE IMPLEMENTATION FILE

We wrote the invariant for the bag class at the top of the implementation file in Figure 3.6. This is the best place to document the class's invariant. In particular, do not write the invariant in the header file, because a programmer who uses the class does not need to know about how the invariant dictates the use of private fields. But the programmer who implements the class does need to know about the invariant.

FIGURE 3.5 Header File for the Bag Class

A Header File

```
// FILE: bag1.h
// CLASS PROVIDED: bag (part of the namespace main_savitch_3)
```

║ See Figure 3.1 on page 104 for the other documentation that goes here.

```
#ifndef MAIN_SAVITCH_BAG1_H
#define MAIN_SAVITCH_BAG1_H
#include <cstdlib>   // Provides size_t

namespace main_savitch_3
{
    class bag
    {
    public:
        // TYPEDEFS and MEMBER CONSTANTS
        typedef int value_type;
        typedef std::size_t size_type;
        static const size_type CAPACITY = 30;
        // CONSTRUCTOR
        bag( ) { used = 0; }
        // MODIFICATION MEMBER FUNCTIONS
        size_type erase(const value_type& target);
        bool erase_one(const value_type& target);
        void insert(const value_type& entry);
        void operator +=(const bag& addend);
        // CONSTANT MEMBER FUNCTIONS
        size_type size( ) const { return used; }
        size_type count(const value_type& target) const;
    private:
        value_type data[CAPACITY];   // The array to store items
        size_type used;              // How much of array is used
    };

    // NONMEMBER FUNCTIONS for the bag class
    bag operator +(const bag& b1, const bag& b2);
}

#endif
```

If your compiler does not permit initialization of static constants, see Appendix E.

FIGURE 3.6   Implementation File for the Bag Class

An Implementation File

```
//  FILE: bag1.cxx
//  CLASS IMPLEMENTED: bag (see bag1.h for documentation)
//  INVARIANT for the bag class:
//     1. The number of items in the bag is in the member variable used.
//     2. For an empty bag, we do not care what is stored in any of data; for a non-empty bag,
//        the items in the bag are stored in data[0] through data[used-1], and we don't care
//        what's in the rest of data.

#include <algorithm> // Provides copy function
#include <cassert>   // Provides assert function
#include "bag1.h"
using namespace std;

namespace main_savitch_3
{
    const bag::size_type bag::CAPACITY;
```

See "Static Member Constants" on page 103 for an explanation of this line.

```
    bag::size_type bag::erase(const value_type& target)
    {
```
        ‖ See the solution to Self-Test Exercise 12 on page 139.
```
    }

    bool bag::erase_one(const value_type& target)
    {
        size_type index; // The location of target in the data array

        // First, set index to the location of target in the data array,
        // which could be as small as 0 or as large as used-1.
        // If target is not in the array, then index will be set equal to used.
        index = 0;
        while ((index < used) && (data[index] != target))
            ++index;

        if (index == used) // target isn't in the bag, so no work to do
            return false;

        // When execution reaches here, target is in the bag at data[index].
        // So, reduce used by 1 and copy the last item onto data[index].
        --used;
        data[index] = data[used];
        return true;
    }
```

See Self-Test Exercise 13 for an alternative approach to this step.

(continued)

(FIGURE 3.6 continued)

```
void bag::insert(const value_type& entry)
// Library facilities used: cassert
{
    assert(size( ) < CAPACITY);

    data[used] = entry;
    ++used;
}
```

See Self-Test Exercise 13
for an alternative approach
to these steps.

```
void bag::operator +=(const bag& addend)
// Library facilities used: algorithm, cassert
{
    assert(size( ) + addend.size( ) <= CAPACITY);

    copy(addend.data, addend.data + addend.used, data + used);
    used += addend.used;
}
```

The copy function is
from the <algorithm>
part of the C++
Standard Library.

```
bag::size_type bag::count(const value_type& target) const
{
    size_type answer;
    size_type i;

    answer = 0;
    for (i = 0; i < used; ++i)
        if (target == data[i])
            ++answer;
    return answer;
}
```

```
bag operator +(const bag& b1, const bag& b2)
// Library facilities used: cassert
{
    bag answer;

    assert(b1.size( ) + b2.size( ) <= bag::CAPACITY);

    answer += b1;
    answer += b2;
    return answer;
}
}
```

The Bag Class—Testing

Thus far, we have focused on the design and implementation of new classes, including new member functions and operator overloading. But it's also important to continue practicing the other aspects of software development, particularly testing. Each of the bag's new functions must be tested, including the overloaded operators. As shown in Chapter 1, it is important to concentrate the testing on boundary values. At this point, we will alert you to only one potential pitfall, leaving the complete testing to Programming Project 1 on page 140.

◐ PITFALL

AN OBJECT CAN BE AN ARGUMENT TO ITS OWN MEMBER FUNCTION

The same variable is sometimes used on both sides of an assignment or other operator. For example, the value of an integer d is doubled by the highlighted statement here:

```
int d = 5;            Add the current value of d
d += d;          ←    to d, giving it a value of 10.
```

A similar technique can be used with a bag, as shown here:

```
bag b;
b.insert(5);          b now contains a 5 and a 2.
b.insert(2);  ←
b += b;  ←            Now b contains two 5s and two 2s.
```

The highlighted statement takes all the items in b (the 5 and the 2) and adds them to what's already in b, so b ends up with two copies of each number.

In the += statement, the bag b is activating the += operator, but this same bag b is the actual argument to the operator. This is a situation that must be carefully tested. As an example of the danger, consider the incorrect implementation of += in Figure 3.7. Do you see what goes wrong with b += b? (See the answer to Self-Test Exercise 14.)

The situation: A member function has a parameter type that is the same as the member function's class. For example, the bag's += operator has a parameter that is itself a bag.

The danger: The member function might fail when an object activates the member function, and the same object is used as the actual argument. For example, a bag b could be used in the statement: b += b.

Always test this special situation.

FIGURE 3.7   Wrong Implementation of the Bag's += Operator

A Wrong Member Function Implementation

```
void bag::operator +=(const bag& addend)
// Library facilities used: cassert
{
    size_type i; // An array index

    assert(size( ) + addend.size( ) <= CAPACITY);

    for (i = 0; i < addend.used; ++i)
    {
        data[used] = addend.data[i];
        ++used;
    }
}
```

WARNING!

There is a bug in this implementation. See Self-Test Exercise 14.

The Bag Class—Analysis

We finish this section with a time analysis of the bag's functions. We'll use the number of items in a bag as the input size. For example, if b is a bag containing n integers, then the number of operations required by b.count is a formula involving n. To count the operations, we'll count the number of statements executed by the function, although we won't need an exact count since our answer will use big-O notation. Except for the return statement, all of the work in count happens in this loop:

```
for (i = 0; i < used; ++i)
    if (target == data[i])
        ++answer;
```

We can see that the body of the loop will be executed exactly n times—once for each item in the bag. The body of the loop also has another important property: The body contains no other loops or calls to functions that contain loops. This is enough to conclude that the total number of statements executed by count is no more than:

$n \times$ (number of statements in the loop) + 3

The "+3" at the end is for the initialization of i, the final test of (i < used), and the return statement. Regardless of how many statements are actually in the loop, the time expression is *always* $O(n)$—so the count function is linear.

FIGURE 3.8   Time Analysis for the Bag Functions (First Version)

Operation	Time Analysis	
Default constructor	$O(1)$	Constant time
count	$O(n)$	n is the size of the bag
erase_one	$O(n)$	Linear time
erase	$O(n)$	Linear time

Operation	Time Analysis	
+= another bag	$O(n)$	n is the size of the other bag
b1 + b2	$O(n_1 + n_2)$	n_1 and n_2 are the sizes of the bags
insert	$O(1)$	Constant time
size	$O(1)$	Constant time

constant time
O(1)

A similar analysis shows that `erase_one` is also linear, although its loop sometimes executes fewer than n times. However, the fact that `erase_one` *sometimes* requires fewer than $n \times$ (number of statements in the loop) does not change the fact that the function is $O(n)$. In the worst case, the loop does execute a full n iterations, therefore the correct time analysis is no better than $O(n)$.

Several of the other bag functions do not contain any loops at all, and do not call any functions with loops. This is a pleasant situation because the time required for any of these functions does not depend on the number of items in the bag. For example, when an item is added to a bag, the new item is always placed at the end of the array, and the `insert` function never looks at the items that were already in the bag. When the time required by a function does not depend on the size of the input, the procedure is called **constant time**, which is written $O(1)$. But be careful in analyzing the `+=` operator. Its call to the copy function requires time that is proportional to the size of the addend bag, so it is not constant time.

The time analyses of all the functions are summarized in Figure 3.8.

Self-Test Exercises for Section 3.1

1. When are typedef statements useful?

2. What is the `size_t` data type, and where is it defined?

3. The bag's documentation in Figure 3.1 on page 104 says that the `value_type` may be a class, but only if it has a default constructor and several operators. Why?

4. In the bag class, why is the `entry` parameter in the `insert` member function a const reference parameter?

5. Draw a picture of `mybag.data` after these statements:
   ```
   bag mybag;
   mybag.insert(1);
   mybag.insert(2);
   mybag.insert(3);
   mybag.erase_one(1);
   ```

6. Suppose the following statement is added to the statements in the previous exercise: `cout << mybag.count(1) << endl;` What output is produced?

7. Why is the static member constant, `CAPACITY`, given a value in the header file, and not in the implementation file?

8. Write the invariant of the bag class.

9. What is short-circuit evaluation?

10. Use the `copy` function to copy six elements from the start of an array `x` into an array `y` starting at `y[42]`.

11. Why isn't the bag's *operator* + function a friend function?

12. Implement the bag's `erase` member function.

13. Rewrite the last two statements of `erase_one` (Figure 3.3 on page 113) as a single statement, using the expression `--used` as the index. (If you are unsure of the meaning of `--used` as an index, then go ahead and peek at our answer at the back of the chapter.) Use `used++` as the index to make a similar alteration to the `insert` function member.

14. Suppose we implement the `+=` operator as shown in Figure 3.7 on page 121. What goes wrong with `b += b`?

15. What is the meaning of $O(1)$?

3.2 PROGRAMMING PROJECT: THE SEQUENCE CLASS

You are ready to tackle a container class implementation on your own. The class is a container class called a **sequence**. A sequence is similar to a bag—both contain a bunch of items. But unlike a bag, the items in a sequence are arranged in an order, one after another.

How does this differ from a bag? After all, aren't the bag items arranged one after another in the partially filled array that implements the bag? Yes, but that's a quirk of our particular bag implementation, and the order is just haphazard.

how a sequence differs from a bag

In contrast, the items of a sequence are kept one after another, and member functions will allow a program to step through the sequence one item at a time. Member functions also permit a program to control precisely where items are inserted and removed within the sequence. The technique of using member functions to access items is called an **internal iterator**, which differs from **external iterators** of the Standard Library containers. Later, in Chapter 6, we will examine external iterators in detail and add them to both the bag and the sequence.

internal iterators versus external iterators

The Sequence Class—Specification

Our sequence is a class that depends on an underlying `value_type`, and the class also provides a `size_type`. It's a good habit to use these particular names for all our classes since you'll find the same names for the Standard Library container classes. At the moment, a sequence will be limited to no more than 30 items. As with our bag, the `value_type`, `size_type`, and sequence capacity will be defined in the public section of the class definition. Throughout the discussion, we will use examples in which the items are *double* numbers, and the sequence has no more than 30 items. So the header file has these definitions:

```
class sequence
{
public:
    //  TYPEDEF and MEMBER CONSTANTS
    typedef double value_type;
    typedef std::size_t size_type;
    static const size_type CAPACITY = 30;
    ...
```

Keep in mind that the capacity and item type can easily be changed and recompiled if we need other kinds of sequences. Also, remember the alternatives if your compiler does not support this way of initializing a static constant in a class definition (see Appendix E).

The class that we implement will be called `sequence`. We'll now specify the member functions of this new class.

Default constructor. The sequence class has just one constructor—a default constructor that creates an empty sequence.

The size member function. The `size` member function returns the number of items in the sequence. The prototype is given here along with the postcondition:

```
size_type size( ) const;
// Postcondition: The return value is the number of items in the sequence.
```

For example, if `scores` is a sequence containing the values 10.1, 40.2, and 1.1, then `scores.size( )` returns 3. Throughout our examples, we will draw sequences vertically, with the first item on top, as shown in the picture in the margin (where the first item is 10.1).

| 10.1 |
| 40.2 |
| 1.1 |

Member functions to examine a sequence. We will have member functions to build a sequence, but it will be easier to first explain the member functions that examine a sequence which has already been built. Now, with the bag class, all that we can do is inquire how many copies of a particular item are in the bag. A sequence is more flexible, allowing us to examine the items one after another. The items must be examined in order, from the front to the back of the sequence. Three member functions work together to enforce the in-order retrieval rule. The functions' prototypes are given here:

```
void start( );
value_type current( ) const;
void advance( );
```

When we want to retrieve the items in a sequence, we begin by activating `start`. After activating `start`, the `current` function returns the first item in the sequence. Each time we call `advance`, the `current` function changes so that it returns the next item in the sequence. For example, if a sequence named `numbers` contains the four numbers 37, 10, 83, and 42, then we can write the following code to print the first three numbers:

```
numbers.start( );
cout << numbers.current( ) << endl;        Prints 37
numbers.advance( );
cout << numbers.current( ) << endl;        Prints 10
numbers.advance( );
cout << numbers.current( ) << endl;        Prints 83
```

*start,
current,
advance*

One other member function cooperates with `current`. The function, called `is_item`, returns a boolean value to indicate whether there actually is another item for `current` to provide, or whether `current` has advanced right off the end. The `is_item` prototype is given here with a postcondition:

```
bool is_item( ) const;
// Postcondition: A true return value indicates that there is a valid
// "current" item that can be obtained from the current member function.
// A false return value indicates that there is no valid current item.
```

Using all four of the member functions in a for-loop, we can print an entire sequence, as shown here for the `numbers` sequence:

```
for (numbers.start( ); numbers.is_item( ); numbers.advance( ))
    cout << numbers.current( ) << endl;
```

The insert and attach member functions.   There are two member functions to add new items to a sequence. One of the functions, called `insert`, places a new item before the current item. For example, suppose that we have created the sequence shown to the right with three items, and that the current item is 8.8. In this example, we want to add 10.0, immediately before the current item. When 10.0 is inserted before the current item, other items—such as 8.8 and 99.0—will move down to make room for the new item. After the insertion, the sequence has the four items shown in the lower box.

If there is no current item, then `insert` places the new item at the front of the sequence. In any case, after the `insert` function returns, the newly inserted item will be the current item, as specified in this precondition/postcondition contract:

```
void insert(const value_type& entry);
// Precondition: size( ) < CAPACITY.
// Postcondition: A new copy of entry has been inserted in the sequence
// before the current item. If there was no current item, then the new entry
// has been inserted at the front. In either case, the new item is now the
// current item of the sequence.
```

| 42.1 |
| 8.8 |
| 99.0 |

The sequence grows by inserting 10.0 before the current item.

| 42.1 |
| 10.0 |
| 8.8 |
| 99.0 |

A second member function, called `attach`, also adds a new item to a sequence, but the new item is added *after* the current item, as specified here:

```
void attach(const value_type& entry);
// Precondition: size( ) < CAPACITY.
// Postcondition: A new copy of entry has been inserted in the sequence
// after the current item. If there was no current item, then the new entry
// has been attached to the end. In either case, the new item is now the
// current item of the sequence.
```

If there is no current item, then the `attach` function places the new item at the end of the sequence (rather than the front). Either `insert` or `attach` can be used to place the first item on a sequence.

The remove_current member function. The current item can be removed from a sequence. The member function for a removal has no parameters:

```
void remove_current( );
// Precondition: is_item returns true.
// Postcondition: The current item has been removed from the sequence,
// and the item after this (if there is one) is now the new current item.
```

The function's precondition requires that there is a current item; it is this current item that is removed. For example, suppose `scores` is the four-item sequence shown at the top of the box in the margin, and the highlighted 8.3 is the current item. After activating `scores.remove_current( )`, the 8.3 has been deleted, and the 4.1 is now the current item.

3.7	Before
8.3	the
4.1	removal
3.1	

After	3.7
the	4.1
removal	3.1

The Sequence Class—Documentation

The header file for this first version of our `sequence` class is shown in Figure 3.9 on page 128. The header file includes the class definition with our suggestion for three member variables. We discuss these member variables next.

The Sequence Class—Design

Our suggested design for the sequence class has three private member variables. The first variable, `data`, is an array that stores the items of the sequence. Just like the bag, `data` is a partially filled array. A second member variable, called `used`, keeps track of how much of the `data` array is currently being used. Therefore, the used part of the array extends from `data[0]` to `data[used-1]`. The third member variable, `current_index`, gives the index of the "current" item in the array (if there is one). If there is no valid current item in the sequence, then `current_index` will be the same number as `used` (since this is larger than any valid index). Here is the complete invariant of our class, stated as three rules:

1. The number of items in the sequence is stored in the member variable `used`.

2. For an empty sequence, we do not care what is stored in any of `data`; for a non-empty sequence, the items are stored in their sequence order from

data[0] to data[used-1], and we don't care what is stored in the rest of data.

3. If there is a current item, then it lies in data[current_index]; if there is no current item, then current_index equals used.

As an example, suppose that a sequence contains four numbers, with the current item at data[2]. The member variables of the object might appear as shown here:

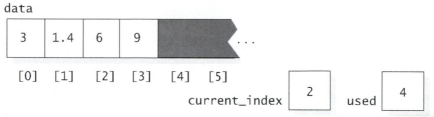

In this example, the current item is at data[2], so the current( ) function would return the number 6. At this point, if we called advance( ), then current_index would increase to 3, and current( ) would then return 9.

Normally, a sequence has a "current" item, and the member variable current_index contains the location of that current item. But if there is no current item, then current_index contains the same value as used. In our example, if current_index was 4, then that would indicate that there is no current item. Notice that this value (4) is beyond the used part of the array (which stretches from data[0] to data[3]).

The stated requirements for the member variables form the invariant of the sequence class. You should place this invariant at the top of your implementation file (sequence1.cxx). We will leave most of this implementation file up to you, but we will offer some hints and a bit of pseudocode.

invariant of the class

The Sequence Class—Pseudocode for the Implementation

The remove_current function. This function removes the current item from the sequence. First check that the precondition is valid (use is_item( ) in an assertion). Then remove the current item by shifting each of the subsequent items leftward one position. For example, suppose we are removing the current item from the sequence drawn here:

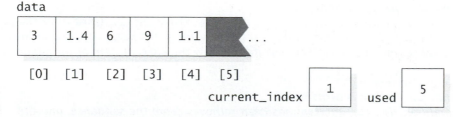

What is the current item in this picture? It is the 1.4 since current_index is 1, and data[1] contains the 1.4.

(text continues on page 130)

FIGURE 3.9   Header File for the Sequence Class

A Header File

```
//  FILE: sequence1.h
//  CLASS PROVIDED: sequence (part of the namespace main_savitch_3)
//
//  TYPEDEF and MEMBER CONSTANTS for the sequence class:
//     typedef _____ value_type
//        sequence::value_type is the data type of the items in the sequence. It may be any of the
//        C++ built-in types (int, char, etc.), or a class with a default constructor, an assignment
//        operator, and a copy constructor
//
//     typedef _____ size_type
//        sequence::size_type is the data type of any variable that keeps track of how many
//        items are in a sequence.
//
//     static const size_type CAPACITY = _____
//        sequence::CAPACITY is the maximum number of items that a sequence can hold.
//
//  CONSTRUCTOR for the sequence class:
//     sequence( )
//        Postcondition: The sequence has been initialized as an empty sequence.
//
//  MODIFICATION MEMBER FUNCTIONS for the sequence class:
//     void start( )
//        Postcondition: The first item in the sequence becomes the current item (but if the
//        sequence is empty, then there is no current item).
//
//     void advance( )
//        Precondition: is_item returns true.
//        Postcondition: If the current item was already the last item in the sequence, then there
//        is no longer any current item. Otherwise, the new item is the item immediately after
//        the original current item.
//
//     void insert(const value_type& entry)
//        Precondition: size( ) < CAPACITY.
//        Postcondition: A new copy of entry has been inserted in the sequence before the
//        current item. If there was no current item, then the new entry has been inserted at the
//        front. In either case, the new item is now the current item of the sequence.
//
//     void attach(const value_type& entry)
//        Precondition: size( ) < CAPACITY.
//        Postcondition: A new copy of entry has been inserted in the sequence after the current
//        item. If there was no current item, then the new entry has been attached to the end of
//        the sequence. In either case, the new item is now the current item of the sequence.
//
//     void remove_current( )
//        Precondition: is_item returns true.
//        Postcondition: The current item has been removed from the sequence, and the
//        item after this (if there is one) is now the new current item.              (continued)
```

(FIGURE 3.9 continued)

```
//  CONSTANT MEMBER FUNCTIONS for the sequence class:
//    size_type size( ) const
//      Postcondition: The return value is the number of items in the sequence.
//
//    bool is_item( ) const
//      Postcondition: A true return value indicates that there is a valid "current" item that
//      may be retrieved by the current member function (listed below). A false return value
//      indicates that there is no valid current item.
//
//    value_type current( ) const
//      Precondition: is_item( ) returns true.
//      Postcondition: The item returned is the current item in the sequence.
//
// VALUE SEMANTICS  for the sequence class:
//      Assignments and the copy constructor may be used with sequence objects.

#ifndef MAIN_SAVITCH_SEQUENCE_H
#define MAIN_SAVITCH_SEQUENCE_H
#include <cstdlib>  // Provides size_t

namespace main_savitch_3
{
    class sequence
    {
    public:
        // TYPEDEFS and MEMBER CONSTANTS
        typedef double value_type;
        typedef std::size_t size_type;
        static const size_type CAPACITY = 30;
        // CONSTRUCTOR
        sequence( );
        // MODIFICATION MEMBER FUNCTIONS
        void start( );
        void advance( );
        void insert(const value_type& entry);
        void attach(const value_type& entry);
        void remove_current( );
        // CONSTANT MEMBER FUNCTIONS
        size_type size( ) const;
        bool is_item( ) const;
        value_type current( ) const;
    private:
        value_type data[CAPACITY];
        size_type used;
        size_type current_index;
    };
}

#endif
```

If your compiler does not permit initialization of static constants, see Appendix E.

The three private member variables are discussed in the section "The Sequence Class—Design" on page 126.

In the case of the bag, we could remove an element such as 1.4 by copying the final item (1.1) onto the 1.4. But this approach won't work for the *sequence* because the items would lose their sequence order. Instead, each item after the 1.4 must be moved leftward one position. The 6 moves from data[2] to data[1]; the 9 moves from data[3] to data[2]; the 1.1 moves from data[4] to data[3]. This is a lot of movement, but a simple for-loop suffices to carry out all the work. This is the pseudocode:

> *for* (i = the index after the current item; i < used; ++i)
>   Move an item from data[i] back to data[i-1];

do not use the copy function

You should not use the copy function from <algorithm> since that function forbids the overlap of the source with the destination.

When the loop completes, you should reduce used by one. The final result for our example is shown here:

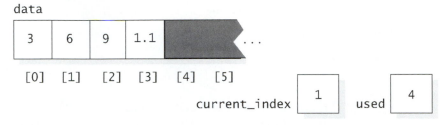

After the removal, the current_index is unchanged. In effect, this means that the item that was just after the removed item is now the current item. You should check that the function works correctly for boundary values—removing the first item and removing the final item. In fact, both these cases do work fine. When the final item is removed, current_index will end up with the same value as used, indicating that there is no longer a current item.

The insert function. If there is a current item, then the insert function must take care to insert the new item just before the current position. Items that are already at or after the current position must be shifted rightward to make room for the new item. We suggest that you start by checking the precondition. Then shift items at the end of the array rightward one position each until you reach the position for the new item.

For example, suppose you are inserting 1.4 at the location data[1] in this sequence:

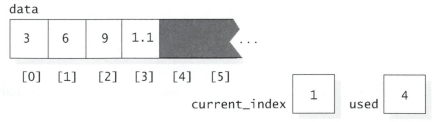

You would begin by shifting the 1.1 rightward from data[3] to data[4]; then move the 9 from data[2] to data[3]; then the 6 moves from data[1] right- ward to data[2]. At this point, the array looks like this:

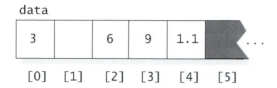

data

3		6	9	1.1	
[0]	[1]	[2]	[3]	[4]	[5]

Of course, data[1] actually still contains a 6 since we just copied the 6 from data[1] to data[2]. But we have drawn data[1] as an empty box to indicate that data[1] is now available to hold the new item (that is, the 1.4 that we are inserting). At this point we can place the 1.4 in data[1] and add one to used, as shown here:

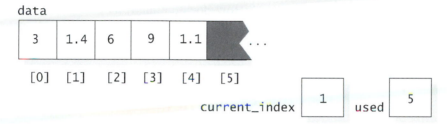

data

3	1.4	6	9	1.1	
[0]	[1]	[2]	[3]	[4]	[5]

current_index | 1 | used | 5 |

The pseudocode for shifting the items rightward uses a for-loop. Each itera- tion of the loop shifts one item, as shown here:

```
for (i = used;  data[i] is the wrong spot for entry ;  --i)
    data[i] = data[i-1];
```

The key to the loop is the test data[i] is the wrong spot for entry. How do we test whether a position is the wrong spot for the new item? A position is wrong if (i > current_index). Can you now write the entire member function in C++? (See the solution to Self-Test Exercise 17, and don't forget to handle the special case when there is no current item.)

Other member functions. The other member functions are straightforward; for example, the attach function is similar to insert. You'll need to watch out for the pitfall about using full names (see page 111). Some additional useful member functions are described in Programming Projects 3 and 4 on pages 140 and 141, respectively.

Self-Test Exercises for Section 3.2

16. What is the difference between a sequence and a bag? What additional operations does a sequence require?

17. What is the difference between internal and external iterators?

18. Write the `insert` function for the sequence. Why should this implementation avoid using the `copy` function from `<algorithm>`?

19. Suppose that a sequence has 24 items, and there is no current item. According to the invariant of the class, what is `current_index`?

20. Suppose g is a sequence with 10 items. You activate g.`start( )`, then activate g.`advance( )` three times. What value is then in g.`current_index`?

21. What are good boundary values to test the `remove_current` function?

22. Write a demonstration program that asks the user for a list of family member ages, then prints the list in the same order that it was given.

23. Write a new member function to remove a specified item from a sequence. The function has one parameter (the item to remove).

24. For a sequence of numbers, suppose that you attach 1, then 2, then 3, and so on up to *n*. What is the big-*O* time analysis for the combined time of attaching all *n* numbers? How does the analysis change if you insert *n* first, then *n*-1, and so on down to 1—always using `insert` instead of `attach`?

3.3   INTERACTIVE TEST PROGRAMS

Your sequence class is a good candidate for an interactive test program that follows a standard format. The format, illustrated by the program of Figure 3.10, can be used with any class. The start of the main program declares an object—in this case, a `sequence` object. The rest of the main program is an interactive loop that continues as long as the user wants. Three things occur inside the loop:

1. A small menu of choices is written for the user. Each choice is printed along with a letter or other meaningful character to allow the user to select the choice.

2. The user's selection from the menu is read.

3. Based on the user's selection, some action is taken on the `sequence` object.

Our example interactive test program for the sequence is shown in Figure 3.10, with part of a sample dialogue in Figure 3.11 on page 136. Some of the techniques used in the test program are familiar. For example, subtasks, such as printing the menu, are accomplished with functions. Two techniques in the test program may be new to you: converting input to uppercase letters, and acting on the input via a *switch* statement. We'll discuss these two techniques after you've looked through the program.

CONVERTING INPUT TO UPPERCASE LETTERS

Even small test programs should have some flexibility regarding user input. For example, the program should accept either upper- or lowercase letters for each menu choice. We accomplish this by reading the user's input and then, if necessary, converting a lowercase letter to the corresponding uppercase letter. The conversion is carried out by a function `toupper` with this specification:

```
char toupper(char c);
// Postcondition: If c is a lowercase letter, then the return value is the
// uppercase equivalent of c. Otherwise the return value is just c itself.
```

The `toupper` function is part of the `<cctype>` facility. In our main program, we use `toupper` to convert the result of the `get_user_command` function, as shown here:

```
choice = toupper(get_user_command( ));
```

FIGURE 3.10 Interactive Test Program for the Sequence Class

A Program

```
// FILE: sequence_test.cxx
// An interactive test program for the new sequence class
#include <cctype>          // Provides toupper
#include <iostream>        // Provides cout and cin
#include <cstdlib>         // Provides EXIT_SUCCESS
#include "sequence1.h"     // With value_type defined as double
using namespace std;
using namespace main_savitch_3;

// PROTOTYPES for functions used by this test program:
void print_menu( );
// Postcondition: A menu of choices for this program has been written to cout.

char get_user_command( );
// Postcondition: The user has been prompted to enter a one-character command.
// The next character has been read (skipping blanks and newline characters),
// and this character has been returned.

void show_sequence(sequence display);
// Postcondition: The items on display have been printed to cout (one per line).

double get_number( );
// Postcondition: The user has been prompted to enter a real number. The
// number has been read, echoed to the screen, and returned by the function.
```

(continued)

(FIGURE 3.10 continued)

```
int main( )
{
    sequence test;  // A sequence that we'll perform tests on
    char choice;    // A command character entered by the user

    cout << "I have initialized an empty sequence of real numbers." << endl;

    do
    {
        print_menu( );
        choice = toupper(get_user_command( ));
        switch (choice)
        {
            case '!': test.start( );
                      break;
            case '+': test.advance( );
                      break;
            case '?': if (test.is_item( ))
                          cout << "There is an item." << endl;
                      else
                          cout << "There is no current item." << endl;
                      break;
            case 'C': if (test.is_item( ))
                          cout << "Current item is: " << test.current( ) << endl;
                      else
                          cout << "There is no current item." << endl;
                      break;
            case 'P': show_sequence(test);
                      break;
            case 'S': cout << "Size is " << test.size( ) << '.' << endl;
                      break;
            case 'I': test.insert(get_number( ));
                      break;
            case 'A': test.attach(get_number( ));
                      break;
            case 'R': test.remove_current( );
                      cout << "The current item has been removed." << endl;
                      break;
            case 'Q': cout << "Ridicule is the best test of truth." << endl;
                      break;
            default:  cout << choice << " is invalid." << endl;
        }
    }
    while ((choice != 'Q'));

    return EXIT_SUCCESS;
}
```

(continued)

(FIGURE 3.10 continued)

```
void print_menu( )
// Library facilities used: iostream
{
    cout << endl; // Print blank line before the menu
    cout << "The following choices are available: " << endl;
    cout << " !   Activate the start( ) function" << endl;
    cout << " +   Activate the advance( ) function" << endl;
    cout << " ?   Print the result from the is_item( ) function" << endl;
    cout << " C   Print the result from the current( ) function" << endl;
    cout << " P   Print a copy of the entire sequence" << endl;
    cout << " S   Print the result from the size( ) function" << endl;
    cout << " I   Insert a new number with the insert(...) function" << endl;
    cout << " A   Attach a new number with the attach(...) function" << endl;
    cout << " R   Activate the remove_current( ) function" << endl;
    cout << " Q   Quit this test program" << endl;
}


char get_user_command( )
// Library facilities used: iostream
{
    char command;

    cout << "Enter choice: ";
    cin >> command; // Input of characters skips blanks and newline character

    return command;
}


void show_sequence(sequence display)
// Library facilities used: iostream
{
    for (display.start( ); display.is_item( ); display.advance( ))
        cout << display.current( ) << endl;
}


double get_number( )
// Library facilities used: iostream
{
    double result;

    cout << "Please enter a real number for the sequence: ";
    cin  >> result;
    cout << result << " has been read." << endl;
    return result;
}
```

www.cs.colorado.edu/~main/chapter3/sequence_test.cxx   **WWW**

FIGURE 3.11   Part of a Sample Dialogue from the Program of Figure 3.10

A Sample Dialogue

```
I have initialized an empty sequence of real numbers.

The following choices are available:
 !  Activate the start( ) function
 +  Activate the advance( ) function
 ?  Print the result from the is_item( ) function
 C  Print the result from the current( ) function
 P  Print a copy of the entire sequence
 S  Print the result from the size( ) function
 I  Insert a new number with the insert(...) function
 A  Attach a new number with the attach(...) function
 R  Activate the remove_current( ) function
 Q  Quit this test program
Enter choice: A
Please enter a real number for the sequence: 3.14
3.14 has been read.

The following choices are available:
 !  Activate the start( ) function
 +  Activate the advance( ) function
 ?  Print the result from the is_item( ) function
 C  Print the result from the current( ) function
 P  Print a copy of the entire sequence
 S  Print the result from the size( ) function
 I  Insert a new number with the insert(...) function
 A  Attach a new number with the attach(...) function
 R  Activate the remove_current( ) function
 Q  Quit this test program
Enter choice: S
Size is 1.
```

|| The dialogue continues until the user types **Q** to stop the program.

THE SWITCH STATEMENT

After the user's choice is read, the main program takes an action. The action depends on the single character that the user typed from the menu. An effective statement to select among many possible actions is the *switch* statement, with the general form:

```
switch (<Control value>)
{
    <Body of the switch statement>
}
```

When the switch statement is reached, the control value is evaluated. The program then looks through the body of the switch statement for a matching case label. For example, if the control value is the character 'A', then the program looks for a case label of the form `case 'A':`. If a matching case label is found, then the program goes to that label and begins executing statements. Statements are executed one after another—but if a **break** statement (of the form `break;`) occurs, then the program skips to the end of the body of the switch statement.

If the control value has no matching case label, then the program will look for a **default label** of the form `default:`. This label handles any control values that don't have their own case label.

If there is no matching case label and no default label, then the whole body of the switch statement is skipped.

For an interactive test program, the switch statement has one case label for each of the menu choices. For example, one of the menu choices is the character 'A', which allows the user to attach a new number to the sequence. In the switch statement, the 'A' command is handled as shown here:

```
switch (choice)
{
    ...
    case 'A': test.attach(get_number( ));
              break;
    ...
}
```

Self-Test Exercises for Section 3.3

25. Name the library facilities that provide `toupper`, `EXIT_SUCCESS`, `cout`, and `cin`.

26. What are values of `toupper('a')`, `toupper('A')`, and `toupper('+')`?

27. What situation calls for a switch statement?

28. The `show_sequence` function on page 135 uses a *value* parameter rather than a *reference* parameter. Why?

CHAPTER SUMMARY

- A *container class* is a class where each object contains a collection of items. Bags and sequences are two examples of container classes; the C++ Standard Library also provides a variety of flexible container classes.

- A container class should be implemented in a way that makes it easy to alter the data type of the underlying items. In C++, the simple approach to this problem uses a typedef statement to define the type of the container's item.

- The simplest implementations of container classes use a *partially filled array*. Using a partially filled array requires each object to have at least two member variables: the array itself and another variable to keep track of how much of the array is being used.

- When you design a class, always make an explicit statement of the rules that dictate how the member variables are used. These rules are called the *invariant of the class*, and should be written at the top of the implementation file for easy reference.

- Small classes can be tested effectively with an *interactive test program* that follows the standard format of our sequence test program.

? Solutions to Self-Test Exercises

1. A typedef statement allows for flexibility when the data type for an item needs to be modified for a program depending on the application. The data type may simply be modified in the typedef statement rather than in the entire program.

2. The `size_t` data type is an integer that can hold only non-negative numbers. It is part of the of the C++ Standard Library facility, `cstdlib`.

3. The default constructor is required because `value_type` is used as the component type of an array. Each of the required operators (=, ==, and !=) is used with the `value_type` in at least one of the bag's member functions.

4. The `entry` parameter is an item of type `value_type`. It is more efficient to make the parameter a const reference parameter for those cases in which `value_type` is a large object.

5.

3	2
[0]	[1]

We don't care what appears beyond data[1].

6. 0

7. Static member constants that are integer types can be given a value in the header file because integral values are often used within the class definition to define other objects, such as the size of an array.

8. See the two rules on page 109.

9. A short-circuit evaluation of a boolean expression evaluates the expression from left to right, stopping as soon as there is enough

information to determine the value of the expression. If two logical operations in an expression must be true for the entire expression to be true, the second operation is not evaluated if the first operation is false.

10. `copy(x, x+6, y+42);`

11. It does not need to be a friend function because it does not directly access any private members of the bag.

12.
```
bag::size_type
bag::erase(const value_type& target)
{
    size_type index = 0;
    size_type many_removed = 0;

    while (index < used)
    {
        if (data[index] == target)
        {
            --used;
            data[index] = data[used];
            ++many_removed;
        }
        else
            ++index;
    }

    return many_removed;
}
```

13. The two statements can be replaced by one statement: `data[index] = data[--used];` When `--used` appears as an expression, the variable `used` is decremented by one, and the resulting value is the value of the expression. (On the other hand, if `used--` appears as an expression, the value of the expression is the value of `used` prior to subtracting one.) Similarly, the last two statements of `insert` can be combined to `data[used++] = entry;`. In this case, we have the expression `used++` as the index because we want to use the old value of `used` (before adding one) as the index.

14. If we activate `b += b`, then the private member variable `used` is the same variable as `addend.used`. Each iteration of the loop adds 1 to `used`, and hence `addend.used` is also in-

creasing, and the loop never ends. To correct the problem, you could store the initial value of `addend.used` in a local variable, and use this local variable to determine when the loop ends.

15. A running time of $O(1)$ means that a function does not depend on the size of the input and runs in constant time.

16. Both contain a collection of items, but the items in a sequence are arranged in order, one after another. The `start`, `advance`, `current`, `remove_current`, `attach`, and `is_item` functions are required to manipulate items at a precise location.

17. Internal iterators use the member functions of a container to access the items of a container. External iterators have their own member functions to access items of a sequence.

18.
```
void sequence::insert
(const value_type& entry)
{
    size_type i;

    assert(size( ) < CAPACITY);

    if (!is_item( ))
        current_index = 0;
    for (i = used; i > current_index; --i)
        data[i] = data[i-1];
    data[current_index] = entry;
    ++used;
}
```

19. 24

20. `g.current_index` will be 3 (since the fourth item occurs at `data[3]`).

21. The `remove_current` function should be tested when the sequence size is just 1, and when the sequence is at its full capacity. At full capacity, you should try removing the first item and the last item in the sequence.

22. Your program can be similar to Figure 3.2 on page 106.

23. Here is our function's prototype, with a post-condition:

```
void
remove(const value_type& target);
// Postcondition: If target was in the
// sequence, then the first copy of target has
// been removed, and the item after
// the removed item (if there is one)
// becomes the new current item; otherwise
// the sequence remains unchanged.
```

The easiest implementation searches for the index of the target. If this index is found, then set current_index to this index, and activate the ordinary remove_current function.

24. The total time to attach 1, 2, ... , *n* is $O(n)$. The total time to insert *n*, *n*–1, ... , 1 is $O(n^2)$. The larger time for the insert is because an insertion at the front of the sequence requires all of the existing items to be shifted right to make room for the new item. Hence, on the second insertion, one item is shifted. On the third insertion, two items are shifted. And so on to the *n*th item, which needs *n*–1 shifts. The total number of shifts is 1+2+...+(*n*–1), which is $O(n^2)$. (To show that this sum is $O(n^2)$, use a technique similar to that used in Figure 1.2 on page 19.)

25. `toupper` is in `cctype`; `EXIT_SUCCESS` is in `cstdlib`; `cout` and `cin` are in `iostream`.

26. The first two calls return `'A'`. The function call `toupper('+')` returns `'+'`.

27. Use a switch statement when a single control value determines which of several possible actions is to be taken.

28. With a reference parameter, the advancing of the current element through the sequence would alter the actual argument.

PROGRAMMING PROJECTS
For more in-depth projects, please see www.cs.colorado.edu/~main/projects/

1 A **black box** test of a class is a program that tests the correctness of the class's member functions without directly examining the private members of the class. You can imagine that the private members are inside an opaque black box where they cannot be seen, so all testing must occur only through activating the public member functions.

Write a black box test program for the bag class. Make sure that you test the boundary values, such as an empty bag, a bag with one item, and a full bag.

2 Implement operators for - and -= for the bag class from Section 3.1. For two bags x and y, the bag x-y contains all the items of x, with any items from y removed. For example, suppose that x has seven copies of the number 3, and y has two copies of the number 3. Then x-y will have five copies of the number 3 (i.e., 7 - 2 copies of number 3). In the case where y has more copies of an item than x does, the bag x-y will have no copies of that item. For example, suppose that x has nine copies of the number 8, and y has ten copies of the number 8. Then x-y will have no 8s. The statement x -= y should have the same effect as the assignment x = x-y;

3 Implement the sequence class from Section 3.2. You may wish to provide some additional useful member functions, such as: (1) a function to add a new item at the front of the sequence; (2) a function to remove the item from the front of the sequence; (3) a function to add a new item at the end of the sequence; (4) a function that makes the last item of the sequence become the current item; (5) operators for + and +=. For the + operator, x + y contains all the items of x, followed by all the items of y. The statement x += y appends all of the items of y to the end of what's already in x.

4 For a sequence x, we would like to be able to refer to the individual items using the usual C++ notation for arrays. For example, if x has three items, then we want to be able to write x[0], x[1], and x[2] to access these three items. This use of the square brackets is called the **subscript operator**. The subscript operator may be overloaded as a member function, with the prototype shown here as part of the sequence class:

```
class sequence
{
public:
    ...
    value_type operator [ ] (size_type index)
    const;
    ...
```

As you can see, the *operator* [ ] is a member function with one parameter. The parameter is the index of the item that we want to retrieve. The implementation of this member function should check that the index is a valid index (i.e., index is less than the sequence size), and then return the specified item.

For this project, specify, design, and implement this new subscript operator for the sequence.

5 A bag can contain more than one copy of an item. For example, the chapter describes a bag that contains the number 4 and two copies of the number 8. This bag behavior is different from a **set**, which can contain only a single copy of any given item. Write a new container class called set, which is similar to a bag, except that a set can contain only one copy of any given item. You'll need to change the interface a bit. For example, instead of the bag's count function, you'll want a constant member function such as this:

```
bool set::contains
(const value_type& target) const;
// Postcondition: The return value is true if
// target is in the set; otherwise the return
// value is false.
```

Make an explicit statement of the invariant of the set class. Do a time analysis for each operation. At this point, an efficient implementation is not needed. For example, just adding a new item to a set will take linear time because you'll need to check that the new item isn't already present. Later we'll explore more efficient implementations (including the implementation of set in the C++ Standard Library).

You may also want to add additional operations to your set class, such as an operator for subtraction.

6 Suppose that you implement a sequence where the value_type has a comparison operator < to determine when one item is "less than" another item. For example, integers, double numbers, and characters all have such a comparison operator (and classes that you implement yourself may also be given such a comparison). Rewrite the sequence class using a new class name, sorted_sequence. In a sorted sequence, the insert function always inserts a new item so that all the items stay in order from smallest to largest. There is no attach function. All the other functions are the same as the original sequence class.

7 In this project, you will implement a new class called a **bag with receipts**. This new class is similar to an ordinary bag, but the way that items are added and removed is different. Each time an item is added to a bag with receipts, the insert function returns a unique integer called the **receipt**. Later, when you want to remove an item, you must provide a copy of the receipt as a parameter to the remove function. The remove function removes the item whose receipt has been presented, and also returns a copy of that item through a reference parameter.

Here's an implementation idea: A bag with receipts can have *two* private arrays, like this:

```
class bag_with_receipts
{
...
private:
    value_type data[CAPACITY];
    bool in_use[CAPACITY];
};
```

Arrays such as these, which have the same size, are called **parallel arrays**. The idea is to keep track of which parts of the data array are being used by placing boolean values in the second array. When in_use[i] is true, then data[i] is currently being used; when in_use[i] is false, then data[i] is currently unused. When a new item is added, we will find the first spot that is currently unused and store the new item there. The receipt for the item is the index of the location where the new item is stored.

8 Another way to store a collection of items is called a **keyed bag**. In this type of bag, whenever an item is added, the programmer using the bag also provides an integer called the **key**. Each item added to the keyed bag must have a unique key; two items cannot have the same key. So, the insertion function has the specification shown here:

```
void keyed_bag::insert
(const value_type& entry, int key);
// Precondition: size( ) < CAPACITY, and the
// bag does not yet contain any item with
// the given key.
// Postcondition: A new copy of entry has
// been added to the bag, with the given key.
```

When the programmer wants to remove an item from a keyed bag, the key of the item must be specified, rather than the item itself. The keyed bag should also have a boolean member function that can be used to determine whether the bag has an item with a specified key.

A keyed bag differs from the bag with receipts (in the previous project). In a keyed bag, the programmer using the class specifies a particular key when an item is inserted. In contrast, for a bag with receipts, the insert function returns a receipt, and the programmer using the class has no control over what that receipt might be.

For this project, do a complete specification, design, and implementation of a keyed bag.

9 This is a simple version of a longer project that will be developed in Chapter 4. The project starts with the definition of a one-

variable **polynomial**, which is an arithmetic expression of the form:

$$a_0 + a_1x + a_2x^2 + \ldots + a_kx^k$$

The highest exponent, k, is called the **degree** of the polynomial, and the constants $a_0, a_1, \ldots$ are the **coefficients**. For example, here are two polynomials with degree three:

$$2.1 + 4.8x + 0.1x^2 + (-7.1)x^3$$

$$2.9 + 0.8x + 10.1x^2 + 1.7x^3$$

Specify, design, and implement a class for polynomials. The class may contain a static member constant, MAXDEGREE, which indicates the maximum degree of any polynomial. (This allows you to store the coefficients in an array with a fixed size.) Spend some time thinking about operations that make sense on polynomials. For example, you can write an operation that adds two polynomials. Another operation should evaluate the polynomial for a given value of x.

10 Specify, design, and implement a class that can be one player in a game of tic-tac-toe. The constructor should specify whether the object is to be the first player (X's) or the second player (O's). There should be a member function to ask the object to make its next move, and a member function that tells the object what the opponent's next move is. Also include other useful member functions, such as a function to ask whether a given spot of the tic-tac-toe board is occupied, and if so, whether the occupation is with an X or an O. Also, include a member function to determine when the game is over, and whether it was a draw, an X win, or an O win.

Use the class in two programs: a program that plays tic-tac-toe against the program's user, and a program that has two tic-tac-toe objects that play against each other.

11 Specify, design, and implement a container class that can hold up to five playing cards. Call the class pokerhand, and overload the boolean comparison operators to allow you to compare two poker hands. For two hands x and y, the relation x > y means that x is a better hand than y. If you do not play in a weekly poker game yourself, then you may need to consult a card rule book for the rules on the ranking of poker hands.

12 Specify, design, and implement a class that keeps track of rings stacked on a peg, rather like phonograph records on a spindle. An example with five rings is shown here:

Rings stacked
on a peg

The peg may hold up to 64 rings, with each ring having its own diameter. Also, there is a rule that requires each ring to be smaller than any ring underneath it, as shown in our example. The class's member functions should include: (a) a constructor that places *n* rings on the peg (where *n* may be as large as 64); use 64 for a default argument. These *n* rings have diameters from *n* inches (on the bottom) to one-inch (on the top). (b) a constant member function that returns the number of rings on the peg. (c) a constant member function that returns the diameter of the topmost ring. (d) a member function that adds a new ring to the top (with the diameter of the ring as a parameter to the function). (e) a member function that removes the topmost ring. (f) an overloaded output function that prints some clever representation of the peg and its rings. Make sure that all functions have appropriate preconditions to guarantee that the rule about ring sizes is enforced. Also spend time designing appropriate private data fields.

13 In this project, you will design and implement a class called towers, which is part of a program that lets a child play a game called Towers of Hanoi. The game consists of three pegs and a collection of rings that stack on the pegs. The rings are different sizes. The initial configuration for a five-ring game is shown here, with the first tower having rings ranging in size from one inch (on the top) to five inches (on the bottom).

The rings are stacked in decreasing order of their

Initial configuration for
a five-ring game of
Towers of Hanoi

size, and the second and third towers are initially empty. During the game, the child may transfer rings one at a time from the top of one peg to the top of another. The object of the game is to move all the rings from the first peg to the second peg. The difficulty is that the child may not place a ring on top of one with a smaller diameter. There is the one extra peg to hold rings temporarily, but the prohibition against a larger ring on a smaller ring applies to it as well as to the other two pegs. A solution for a three-ring game is shown here:

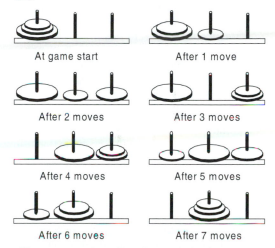

At game start	After 1 move
After 2 moves	After 3 moves
After 4 moves	After 5 moves
After 6 moves	After 7 moves

The towers class must keep track of the status of all three pegs. You might use an array of three pegs, where each peg is an object from the previous project. The towers functions are specified here:

```
towers::towers(size_t n = 64);
// Precondition: 1 <= n <= 64.
// Postcondition: The towers have been initialized
// with n rings on the first peg and no rings on
// the other two pegs. The diameters of the first
// peg's rings are from one inch (on the top) to n
// inches (on the bottom).
```

```
size_t towers::many_rings
(int peg_number) const;
// Precondition: peg_number is 1, 2, or 3.
// Postcondition: The return value is the number
// of rings on the specified peg.

size_t towers::top_diameter
(int peg_number) const;
// Precondition: peg_number is 1, 2, or 3.
// Postcondition: If many_rings(peg_number) > 0,
// then the return value is the diameter of the top
// ring on the specified peg; otherwise the return
// value is zero.

void towers::move
(int start_peg; int end_peg);
// Precondition: start_peg is a peg number
// (1, 2, or 3), and many_rings(start_peg) > 0;
// end_peg is a different peg number (not equal
// to start_peg), and top_diameter(end_peg) is
// either 0 or more than top_diameter(start_peg).
// Postcondition: The top ring has been moved
// from start_peg to end_peg.
```

Also overload the output operator so that a `towers` object may be displayed easily.

Use the `towers` object in a program that allows a child to play Towers of Hanoi. Make sure that you don't allow the child to make any illegal moves.

14 Specify, design, and implement a class where each object keeps track of a large integer with up to 100 digits in base 10. The digits can be stored in an array of 100 elements and the sign of the number can be stored in a separate member variable, which is +1 for a positive number and –1 for a negative number.

The class should include several convenient constructors, such as a constructor to initialize an object from an ordinary `int`. Also overload the usual arithmetic operators and comparison operators (to carry out arithmetic and comparisons on these big numbers) and overload the input and output operators.

15 Use the card class developed in Chapter 2 (Programming Project 4) to create a new class for a deck of cards. The deck class has a sequence with a capacity of 52 to hold the cards.

The constructor assigns 52 cards in order of suit and rank to the sequence. A friend function should display the entire deck using words (*i.e.*, "the ace of spades"). More functions will be added to this class in Chapter 5 (Project 16).

16 Specify, design, and implement a program that stores the birthdays of your friends. Create a person class, which stores a name and a date object. The name can be a string (see Appendix H) and the date object can be from Project 17 of Chapter 2. The person class can use the automatic assignment operator and copy constructor, but it will need an overloaded equality comparison operator and an overloaded output operator. Store the person objects in a sequence. Provide member functions to find and display a person, as well as to display the entire sequence. Write an interactive test program that gives the user options to insert, find, and display the contents of the sequence.

17 In this project, you will design and implement a class that contains a container of employees, using the employee class from Project 18 in Chapter 2. Modify the employee class to include equality and comparison operators.

Provide functions that calculate statistics on the employees, such as average age, average salary, number of hours worked, number of overtime hours, ratio of male/females, etc. Feel free to add data members and modify the constructor to the employee class to store any necessary information.

Write an interactive test program. The program should give the user a menu of choices to add, remove, or modify an employee, and to print any available statistics.

CHAPTER **4**

Pointers and Dynamic Arrays

And bade his messengers ride forth
East and west and south and north
To summon his array–

THOMAS BABINGTON
"Horatius"

LEARNING OBJECTIVES

When you complete Chapter 4, you will be able to...

- trace through code with simple pointers that contain the addresses of individual variables.
- use pointer variables along with the C++ new operator to allocate single dynamic variables and dynamic arrays.
- use the C++ delete operator to release dynamic variables and dynamic arrays when they are no longer needed.
- follow the behavior of pointers and arrays as parameters to functions.
- implement container classes so that the elements are stored in a dynamic array with a capacity that is adjusted by the class's member functions as needed.

CHAPTER CONTENTS

Pointers and Dynamic Arrays

The container classes from Chapter 3 still have a vexing limitation. Their capacity is declared as a constant in the class definition. For example, the `bag::CAPACITY` constant determines the capacity of every bag. If we need bigger bags, then we can increase the constant and recompile, but doing so increases the size of *every* bag. This is wasteful for a program that needs one large bag and many small bags. Even the small bags have the capacity of the largest bag.

the size of each bag will be independent of the other bags

The solution is to provide control over the size of each bag, independent of each of the other bags. This control can come from *dynamic arrays*, which are arrays whose size is determined only after a program is actually running. Dynamic arrays require an understanding of pointers and dynamic memory, which are introduced and developed in the first two sections of this chapter. The dynamic arrays are then used for a new implementation of the bag class in Section 4.3, and for two projects. The understanding of pointers that you gain in this chapter also forms the foundation for many classes in subsequent chapters.

4.1 POINTERS AND DYNAMIC MEMORY

In order to improve our container class implementations, we need to know about pointers. A **pointer** is the memory address of a variable. To understand this definition, you need a mental picture of the computer's memory as consisting of numbered memory locations (called *bytes*). Each variable in a program is stored in a sequence of adjacent bytes. For example, on some machines each integer variable requires four bytes. On such a machine, an integer declaration such as `int i;` provides four adjacent bytes of memory to store the value of the integer i. The example drawn here provides bytes numbered 990 through 993 for an integer variable i.

An integer variable might require four bytes of memory.

A program might provide these four bytes for an integer i.

998	
997	
996	
995	
994	
993	
992	
991	
990	
989	
988	

The numbers labeling each byte are called the **memory addresses**. When a variable occupies several adjacent bytes, then the memory address of the first byte is also called the memory address of the variable. So in our example, the address of the integer i is 990. The address of a variable is called a **pointer**. These addresses are called pointers because they can be thought of as "pointing" to a variable. The address "points" to the variable because it identifies the variable by telling *where* the variable is, rather than telling what the variable's name is. Our integer i can be pointed out by saying, "It's over there at location 990."

Pointer Variables

Pointers are much more useful than mere indications of variable locations. To begin to see the utility of pointers, we must look at variables that are designed to store pointers. A variable to store a pointer must be declared as a special *pointer variable* by placing an asterisk before the pointer variable's name. The complete declaration of a pointer variable must contain three items, as shown here:

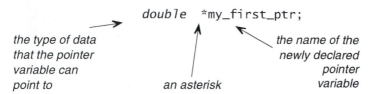

double   *my_first_ptr;

the type of data
that the pointer
variable can
point to

an asterisk

the name of the
newly declared
pointer
variable

declaring pointer variables

In our example, `my_first_ptr` is a pointer variable that is capable of pointing to any double variable. In other words, `my_first_ptr` can hold the memory address of a double variable. The pointer variable `my_first_ptr` does not actually contain a double number itself—it merely contains the address of a double variable. Also, since we used the double data type in our declaration, `my_first_ptr` cannot contain a pointer to a variable of some other type, such as *int* or *char*. It may contain only a pointer to a double variable.

If you declare several pointer variables on a single line, then an asterisk must appear before each variable name. For example, to declare two pointers to characters:

```
char *c1_ptr, *c2_ptr;
```
⟵ *declaring two char pointers*

If you omit the asterisk before `c2_ptr`, then `c2_ptr` will be an ordinary character variable rather than a pointer to a character. For additional clarity we often use "_ptr" as the end of a pointer variable's name, or we use "cursor" as part of a pointer variable's name because a "cursor" means a pointer that "runs through a structure."

Pointer Variable Declarations

A variable that is a pointer to other variables of type *Type_Name* is declared in the same way that you declare a variable of type *Type_Name*, except that you place an asterisk at the beginning of the variable name.

Syntax:
```
Type_Name *var_name1;
```

Examples:
```
int *cursor;
char *c1_ptr, *c2_ptr;
```

Of course, a pointer variable is of no use unless there is something for it to point to. For example, consider these two declarations:

```
int *example_ptr;
int i;
```

We can make `example_ptr` contain the address of `i` by using the & operator shown here:

```
example_ptr = &i;
```
This statement puts the address of i into the pointer variable example_ptr.

the & operator

The & operator, called the **address** operator, provides the address of a variable; for instance, `&i` is "the address of the integer variable `i`." So the assignment statement places "the address of `i`" into `example_ptr`. Or we could simply say that `example_ptr` now "points to" `i`.

*the * operator*

After the assignment, you have two ways to refer to `i`: You can call it `i`, or you can call it "the variable pointed to by `example_ptr`." In C++ "the variable pointed to by `example_ptr`" is written `*example_ptr`. This is the same asterisk notation that we used to declare `*example_ptr`, but now it has yet another meaning. When the asterisk is used in this way, it is called the **dereferencing operator**, and the pointer variable is said to be **dereferenced**. For example:

```
i = 42;
example_ptr = &i;
cout << i << endl;
cout << *example_ptr << endl;
```
Both statements print 42.

This dereferences example_ptr.

The dereferencing operator can produce some surprising results. Consider the following code:

```
i = 42;
example_ptr = &i;
*example_ptr = 0;
cout << *example_ptr << endl;
cout << i << endl;
```
This prints 0.

This also prints 0.

As long as `example_ptr` contains a pointer to `i`, then `i` and `*example_ptr` refer to the same variable. So when you set `*example_ptr` equal to 0, you are really setting `i` equal to 0.

The symbol & that is used as the address operator is the same symbol that is used in a function's parameter list to specify a reference parameter (see page 69). This is more than a coincidence. The implementation of a reference parameter is accomplished by using the *address* of the actual argument, rather than making a completely separate copy (as a value parameter does). These two usages of the symbol & are much the same, but since they are slightly different, we will consider them to be two different (but closely related) usages of the symbol &.

Using the Assignment Operator with Pointers

You can copy the value of one pointer variable to another with the usual assignment operator. For example:

```
int i = 42;
int *p1;
int *p2;                      p1 now points to i.
p1 = &i;                      Now p2 also points to i.
p2 = p1;
cout << *p1 << endl;          So, both statements
cout << *p2 << endl;          will print 42.
```

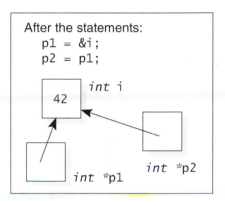

After the statements:
```
p1 = &i;
p2 = p1;
```

The highlighted assignment statement says "make p2 point to the same variable that p1 is already pointing to."

A pointer variable is usually drawn as a box containing an arrow. The arrow points to the variable whose address is stored in the pointer. For example, after the assignment p2 = p1, we would draw the picture shown in the margin. There are now three names for the variable i: You can call it i, or you can call it *p1, or you can call it *p2.

When dealing with pointer variables, there is a critical distinction between a pointer variable (such as p1) and the thing it points to (such as *p1). Do not confuse the meaning of these two assignment statements:

$$p2 = p1; \quad \textbf{versus} \quad *p2 = *p1;$$

As we have seen, p2 = p1 means "make p2 point to the same variable that p1 is already pointing to." On the other hand, the inclusion of the dereferencing asterisks in *p2 = *p1 gives the statement quite a different meaning. The new meaning is to "copy the value from the variable that p1 points to, to the variable that p2 points to." Here is an example, which starts by declaring two integers and two pointers to integers:

```
int i = 42;
int j = 80;
int *p1;
int *p2;
p1 = &i;
p2 = &j;
```

After the statements, the pointer variables are as shown to the right.

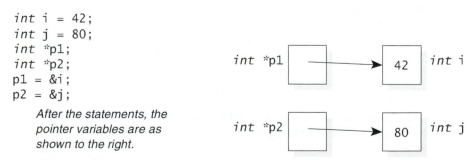

Once the two pointers are initialized, we can see the effect of an assignment statement:

```
*p2 = *p1;
```

After this assignment statement, the pointer variables still point to different locations, but the contents of one of those locations has changed.

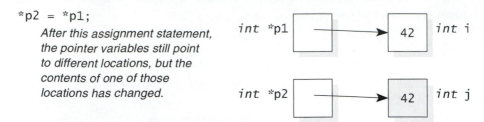

The assignment statement has copied the value 42 from the variable that `p1` points to, to the variable that `p2` points to. In effect, `j` has changed its contents, but the pointers themselves still point to separate memory locations.

Pointer Variables Used with =

If `p1` and `p2` are pointer variables, then the assignment `p2 = p1` changes `p2` so that it points to the same variable that `p1` already points to.

On the other hand, the assignment `*p2 = *p1` copies the value from the variable that `p1` points to, to the variable that `p2` points to—but the pointers `p1` and `p2` still point to the memory locations that they pointed to before the assignment statement.

Dynamic Variables and the new Operator

Pointers may point to ordinary variables, such as `i` in our previous example. But the real power of pointers arises when pointers are used with special kinds of variables called *dynamically allocated variables*, or more simply, *dynamic variables*. **Dynamic variables** are like ordinary variables, with two important differences:

1. Dynamic variables are not declared. A program may use many dynamic variables, but the dynamic variables never appear in any declaration the way an ordinary variable does. Moreover, a dynamic variable has no identifier (such as the identifiers `i` and `j` that are used in our examples).

2. Dynamic variables are created during the execution of a program. Only at that time does a dynamic variable come into existence.

To create a dynamic variable while a program is running, C++ programs use an operator called *new*, as shown here:

```
double *d_ptr;
d_ptr = new double;
```

In this example, the *new* operator creates a new dynamic variable of type *double* and returns a pointer to this new dynamic variable. The pointer is assigned to the pointer variable d_ptr. The creation of new dynamic variables is called memory **allocation** and the memory is **dynamic memory**, so we may say that "d_ptr points to a newly *allocated* double variable from *dynamic memory*." Here is another example, which allocates a new *int* variable:

```
int *p1;
```
At this point, p1 is declared, but it has nothing to point to.

```
p1 = new int;
```
Now p1 is pointing to a newly allocated integer variable.

A new integer is allocated by the new operator.

```
*p1 = 42;
```
The new integer variable now contains our favorite number, 42.

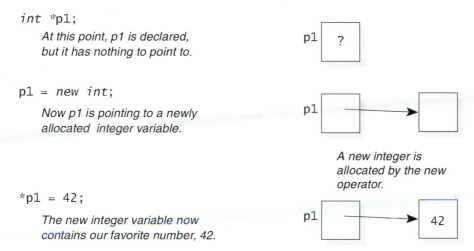

The assignment statement at the end of this example places 42 in the dynamic variable that p1 points to.

Using new to Allocate Dynamic Arrays

We have seen the *new* operator allocate one dynamic variable at a time. But in fact, *new* can allocate an entire array at once. The number of array components is listed in square brackets, immediately after the component data type, as shown here:

```
double *d_ptr;
d_ptr = new double[10];
```
The new operator allocates an array of 10 double components and points d_ptr to the first component.

When *new* allocates an entire array, it actually returns a pointer to the *first* component of the array. In our example, the *new* operator allocates an array of 10 *double* components and returns a pointer to the first component of the array. The pointer is assigned to the pointer variable d_ptr. After the allocation, the array can be accessed by *using array notation* with the pointer variable d_ptr.

For example, the following statement will place 3.14 in the [9] component of the new array:

d_ptr[9] = 3.14;   *Because d_ptr points to an array with 10 components, we can use array notation to access component [9].*

Here is another example, which allocates a new *int* array:

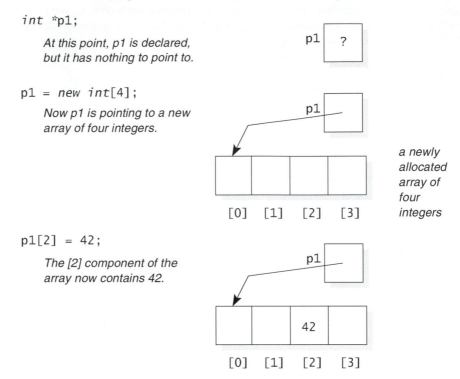

```
int *p1;
```
At this point, p1 is declared, but it has nothing to point to.

p1 | ?

```
p1 = new int[4];
```
Now p1 is pointing to a new array of four integers.

p1

a newly allocated array of four integers

[0] [1] [2] [3]

```
p1[2] = 42;
```
The [2] component of the array now contains 42.

p1

| | | 42 | |

[0] [1] [2] [3]

The assignment statement at the end of this example places 42 in the [2] component of the array that p1 points to.

All the versions of *new* are summarized in Figure 4.1, including information about which constructor gets called when *new* allocates a new *object* of a class. The array version of *new* is particularly useful because the number of array components can be calculated while the program is running. Therefore, the number of components can depend on factors such as user input. This is **dynamic** behavior—behavior that is determined when a program is *running*—and the arrays allocated by *new* are called **dynamic arrays**.

dynamic behavior is determined while a program is running

As an example of dynamic behavior, consider a program that reads a list of numbers and computes the average of the numbers. After computing the average, the program prints the list with an indication of which numbers are below the average and which are above. We would like this program to work for ten numbers, or a hundred numbers, or however many numbers we happen to have. The size of the array can be determined by user input, as shown here:

```
size_t array_size;
int *numbers;

cout << "How many numbers do you have? ";
cin >> array_size;
numbers = new int[array_size];
```

We'll fully develop this example in a moment, but first we need a closer look at memory allocation.

FIGURE 4.1 The new Operator

The new Operator

The *new* operator allocates memory for a dynamic variable of a specified type and returns a pointer to the newly allocated memory. For example, the following code allocates a new dynamic integer variable and sets p to point to this new variable:

```
int *p;
p = new int;
```

If the dynamic variable is an object of a class, then the default constructor will be called to initialize the new class instance. A different constructor will be called if you place the constructor's arguments after the type name in the new statement. For example:

```
throttle *t_ptr;
t_ptr = new throttle(50);
```
← *This calls the constructor with an integer argument.*

The *new* operator can also allocate a dynamic array of components, returning a pointer to the first element. The size of the array is specified in square brackets after the data type of the components:

```
double *d_ptr;
d_ptr = new double[50];
```
← *This allocates a dynamic array of 50 doubles.*

```
d_ptr[3] = 3.14;
```
← *This assigns 3.14 to the [3] component of the array that d_ptr points to.*

If the data type of the array component is a class, then the default constructor is used to initialize all components of the dynamic array. There is no mechanism to use a different constructor on the array components.

The Heap and the bad_alloc Exception

the heap

When *new* allocates a dynamic variable or dynamic array, the memory comes from a location called the program's **heap** (also called the **free store**). Some computers provide huge heaps, more than a billion bytes. But even the largest heap can be exhausted by allocating too many dynamic variables. When the heap runs out of room, the *new* operator fails.

the bad_alloc exception

The *new* operator indicates its failure by a mechanism called the **bad_alloc exception**. Normally, an exception causes an error message to be printed and the program halts. Alternately, a programmer can "catch" an exception and try to fix the problem, but we won't discuss catching exceptions here.

Some older versions of C++ deal with *new* failure in a different way, by returning a special pointer value called the *null pointer*. This older behavior can still be obtained if the programmer writes the *new* operator in the form *new*(nothrow) rather than simply *new*. The word nothrow is a constant in the header file <new>.

For us, the normal failure—resulting in an error message and halting—will be sufficient. We will, however, clearly document which functions use *new* so that more experienced programmers can deal with a bad_alloc in their own manner.

Failure of the new Operator

The *new* operator usually indicates failure by throwing an exception called the **bad_alloc exception**. Normally, an exception causes an error message to be printed and the program halts. (Older C++ implementations use a different mechanism for new failure.)

We clearly document which functions use *new* so that experienced programmers can deal with the failure in their own manner.

The delete Operator

The size of the heap varies from one computer to another. It could be just a few thousand bytes or more than a billion. Small programs are not likely to use all of the heap. However, even with small programs, it is an efficient practice to release any heap memory that is no longer needed. If your program no longer needs a dynamic variable, the memory used by that dynamic variable can be returned to the heap where it can be reused for more dynamic variables. In C++, the *delete* operator is used to return the memory of a dynamic variable back to the heap. The *delete* operator is called by writing the word *delete*, followed by the pointer variable. An example appears at the top of the next page.

```
int *example_ptr;
example_ptr = new int;

// Various statements that use *example_ptr appear here. When the
// program no longer needs the dynamic variable that example_ptr
// points to, the memory for that dynamic variable is returned to
// the heap with the following statement:

delete example_ptr;
```

After the *delete* statement, the memory that example_ptr was pointing to has been returned to the heap for reuse. Using the *delete* operation is called **freeing** or **releasing** memory.

A slightly different version of *delete* is used to release a dynamic array. In this case, the square brackets [ ] appear between the word *delete* and the pointer variable's name, as shown here:

```
int *example_ptr;
example_ptr = new int[50];

// Various statements that use the array example_ptr[...] appear
// here. When the program no longer needs the dynamic array, the
// memory for that dynamic array is returned to the heap with
// the following statement:

delete [ ] example_ptr;
```

When *delete* [ ] releases a dynamic array, there is no need for the array's size inside the square brackets. The software that controls the heap automatically keeps track of the array's size. Figure 4.2 on page 156 summarizes the *delete* operator.

PROGRAMMING TIP

DEFINE POINTER TYPES

You can define a name for a pointer type so that pointer variables can be declared like other variables, without placing an asterisk in front of each pointer variable. For example, the following defines a data type called int_pointer, which is the type for pointer variables that point to *int* variables:

```
typedef int* int_pointer;
```

A type definition such as this usually appears in a header file or with the collection of function prototypes that precede a main program. After this type definition, the declaration int_pointer i_ptr; is equivalent to *int* *i_ptr; .

FIGURE 4.2   The delete Operator

The delete Operator

The *delete* operator frees memory that has been used for dynamic variables. The memory is returned to the heap, where it can be reused at a later time. For example, the following code allocates an integer dynamic variable, and frees the memory when it is no longer needed:

```
int *p;
p = new int;
```

```
// Various statements that use *p appear here. When the program no longer
// needs the dynamic variable that p points to, the memory for that
// dynamic variable is returned to the heap with the following statement:
```

```
delete p;
```

The *delete* operator can also free a dynamic array of components. All of the array's memory is returned to the heap, where it can be reused. To free an entire array, the array brackets [ ] are placed after the word delete, as shown here:

```
int *p;
p = new int[50];
```

```
// Various statements that use the array p[...] appear here. When the program no
// longer needs the dynamic array, the memory for that dynamic array is returned
// to the heap with the following statement:
```

```
delete [ ] p;
```

The array size does not need to be specified with the *delete* operator.

Self-Test Exercises for Section 4.1

1. Describe two different uses of & in a C++ program.

2. Write two different statements that print the value of i after the following code has been executed:
    ```
    int *int_ptr, i;
    i = 30;
    int_ptr = &i;
    ```

3. Write code that (1) allocates a new array of 1000 integers; (2) places the numbers 1 through 1000 in the components of the new array; and (3) returns the array to the heap.

4. How are dynamic variables different than ordinary variables?

5. What happens if the *new* operator fails to allocate memory from the heap?

6. What output is produced by the following?

```
int *p1;
int *p2;

p1 = new int;
p2 = new int;
*p1 = 100;
*p2 = 200;
cout << *p1 << " and " << *p2 << endl;
delete p1;
p1 = p2;
cout << *p1 << " and " << *p2 << endl;
*p1 = 300;
cout << *p1 << " and " << *p2 << endl;
*p2 = 400;
cout << *p1 << " and " << *p2 << endl;
delete p1;
```

7. The previous exercise calls *delete*. Why is this a good idea?

4.2 POINTERS AND ARRAYS AS PARAMETERS

A function parameter may be a pointer or an array—but some care is needed to ensure that the connection between the argument and the formal parameter is the intended connection. We'll look at several common situations.

Value parameters that are pointers. Figure 4.3 shows a silly function to illustrate a value parameter that is a pointer. The function's prototype is:

```
void make_it_42(int* i_ptr);
```

The prototype indicates that the parameter i_ptr has type *int**; that is, a pointer to an integer. The parameter is a value parameter because the reference symbol & does not appear. Within the parameter list, most programmers place

most programmers place the * with the data type

FIGURE 4.3   A Value Parameter That Is a Pointer

A Function Implementation

```
void make_it_42(int* i_ptr)
// Precondition: i_ptr is pointing to an integer variable.
// Postcondition: The integer that i_ptr is pointing at has been changed to 42.
{
    *i_ptr = 42;
}
```

the asterisk with the data type (*int*) rather than with the parameter name (i_ptr)—although the compiler will accept the asterisk in either position. The reason for the placement with the data type is to emphasize that the "complete type" of the parameter is "an integer pointer."

The only purpose of make_it_42 is to show what happens when a value parameter is a pointer. Notice that the body of the function does not actually change i_ptr, it changes only the integer that i_ptr points to. Let's examine a program that calls make_it_42. The program declares a pointer to an integer, allocating memory for the pointer to point to and calls make_it_42:

```
int *main_ptr;
main_ptr = new int;
```
*Now main_ptr is pointing
to a newly allocated integer.
Next, we call make_it_42, with
main_ptr as the actual parameter.*

main_ptr [ ] ⟶ [ ]
a new integer

```
make_it_42(main_ptr);
```

As with any value parameter, the *actual* argument provides the initial value for the *formal* parameter. In the example, main_ptr provides the initial value for the formal parameter i_ptr of the make_it_42 function. This means that the parameter i_ptr will point to the same place that main_ptr is already pointing to. At the start of the function's execution, we have this situation:

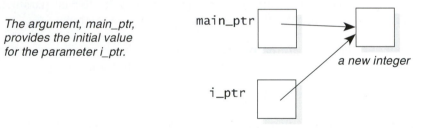

*The argument, main_ptr,
provides the initial value
for the parameter i_ptr.*

Within the make_it_42 function, we have the assignment *i_ptr = 42. The assignment places 42 in the location that i_ptr points to, as shown here:

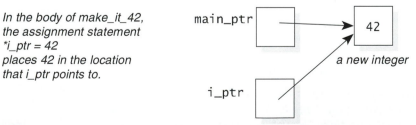

*In the body of make_it_42,
the assignment statement
*i_ptr = 42
places 42 in the location
that i_ptr points to.*

Finally, the function returns and the formal parameter i_ptr is no longer available. However, the pointer variable main_ptr is still around, and it is still pointing to the same location. But the location has a new value of 42, as shown here:

The original argument, main_ptr, is pointing to the same location, but the location has a new value.

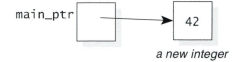

a new integer

Value Parameters That Are Pointers

When a value parameter is a pointer, the function may change the value in the location that the pointer points to. The actual argument in the calling program will still point to the same location, but that location will have a new value.

Syntax in the parameter list:
    Type_Name* var_name

Example from Figure 4.3 on page 157:
    void make_it_42(*int** i_ptr);

In ordinary C programming (rather than C++), pointers are frequently used as value parameters. This is because C did not originally have reference parameters, so the only convenient way for a function to affect its actual arguments is with a value parameter that is a pointer.

Array parameters. There is a surprising twist when a parameter is an array. *The parameter is automatically treated as a pointer that points to the first element of the array.* Within the body of the function, the pointer can be used with array notation, which is just like any other pointer that points to the first element of an array. For example, Figure 4.4 shows a function to set the first n elements of an array to the number 42.

Notice that the array parameter is indicated by placing brackets after the parameter name so the function's prototype is:

    void make_it_all_42(*double* data[ ], size_t n);

a surprising twist for array parameters

The size of the array is not needed inside the brackets, but usually there is another parameter (such as size_t n) that indicates the size of the array.

If the body of the function changes the components of the array, the changes *do* affect the actual argument. The reason that the argument is affected is that an array parameter is actually a pointer to the first element of the array. Here is an example that calls the function from Figure 4.4:

```
double main_array[10];                    Set all 10 array components to 42.
make_it_all_42(main_array, 10);
cout << main_array[5];                     This prints 42.
```

The actual argument of make_it_all_42 may be a dynamic array, as shown here:

```
double *numbers;                          Allocate a dynamic array.
numbers = new double[10];
make_it_all_42(numbers, 10);              Set all elements to 42.
```

Array Parameters

A parameter that is an array is indicated by placing [ ] after the parameter name, as shown here:

Syntax in the parameter list:
    Type_Name var_name[ ]

Example from Figure 4.4:
    void make_it_all_42(*double* data[ ], size_t n);

There is usually a separate size_t parameter to indicate the size of the array. Any changes that the function makes to the components of the array *do* affect the actual argument.

FIGURE 4.4   An Array Parameter

A Function Implementation

```
void make_it_all_42(double data[ ], size_t n)
// Precondition:  data is an array with at least n components.
// Postcondition: The first n elements of the array data have been set to 42.
// Library facilities used: cstdlib
{
    size_t i;

    for (i = 0; i < n; ++i)
        data[i] = 42;
}
```

Const parameters that are pointers or arrays. A parameter that is a pointer or an array may also include the *const* keyword, as in these two prototypes:

```
bool is_42(const int* i_ptr);
double average(const double data[ ], size_t n);
```

The *const* keyword in the first prototype indicates that i_ptr is a pointer to a constant integer. In other words, the implementation of is_42 may examine *i_ptr, but may not change the value of *i_ptr. The complete body of is_42 is shown in Figure 4.5, where *i_ptr is compared to the number 42.

The second prototype indicates that data is an array and, because of the *const* keyword, the function cannot change the array entries. The average function may examine all the array entries, but it may not change them. Our intention is for average to return the arithmetic average of all the entries in the data array, as shown in the second half of Figure 4.5.

FIGURE 4.5   A Const Parameter That Is a Pointer or Array

A Function Implementation

```
bool is_42(const int* i_ptr)
// Precondition: i_ptr is pointing to an integer variable.
// Postcondition: The return value is true if *i_ptr is 42.
{
    return (*i_ptr == 42);

}

double average(const double data[ ], size_t n)
// Library facilities used: cassert, cstdlib
{
    size_t i;    // An array index
    double sum;  // The sum of data[0] through data[n - 1]

    assert(n > 0);

    // Add up the n numbers and return the average.
    sum = 0;
    for (i = 0; i < n; ++i)
        sum += data[i];
    return (sum/n);
}
```

CLARIFYING THE CONST KEYWORD
Part 5: Const Parameters That Are Pointers or Arrays

A parameter that is a pointer or array may include the *const* keyword, as shown here:

1. DECLARED CONSTANTS: PAGE 12
2. CONSTANT MEMBER FUNCTIONS: PAGE 38
3. CONST REFERENCE PARAMETERS: PAGE 72
4. STATIC MEMBER CONSTANTS: PAGE 103
5. CONST PARAMETERS THAT ARE POINTERS OR ARRAYS
6. THE CONST KEYWORD WITH A POINTER TO A NODE, AND THE NEED FOR TWO VERSIONS OF SOME MEMBER FUNCTIONS: PAGE 218
7. CONST ITERATORS: PAGE 308

Syntax in the parameter list:

```
const Type_Name* var_name
const Type_Name var_name[ ]
```

Examples from Figure 4.5:

```
bool is_42(const int* i_ptr);
double average(const double data[ ], ...
```

The functions may examine the item that is pointed to (or the array), but changing the item (or array) is forbidden.

Reference parameters that are pointers.   Sometimes a function will actually *change a pointer parameter so that the pointer points to a new location*, and the programmer needs the change to affect the actual argument. This is the only situation where a reference parameter will be a pointer. For example, Figure 4.6 shows a function named `allocate_doubles` that allocates memory for a new dynamic array. Here is the function's prototype:

```
void allocate_doubles(double*& p, size_t& n);
```

The parameter p is a pointer to a *double* (that is, *double**) and it is a reference parameter (indicated by the symbol &). The complete parameter type is thus *double*&*.

   In the implementation of `allocate_doubles`, the parameter p is changed so that it points to a newly allocated array. In a program, we can use `allocate_doubles` to allocate an array of double values, with the size of the array determined by interacting with the user. Here is an example that calls `allocate_doubles`:

```
double *numbers;
size_t array_size;
allocate_doubles(numbers, array_size);
```

In this example, the `allocate_doubles` function asks the user how many *double* numbers should be allocated. The user's answer is used to set the

---

FIGURE 4.6   A Reference Parameter That Is a Pointer

A Function Implementation

```
void allocate_doubles(double*& p, size_t& n)
//  Postcondition: The user has been prompted for a size n, and this size has been read.
// The pointer p has been set to point to a new dynamic array containing n doubles.
// NOTE: If there is insufficient dynamic memory, then bad_alloc is thrown.
// Library facilities used: iostream, cstdlib
{
    cout << "How many doubles should I allocate?" << endl;
    cout << "Please type a positive integer answer: ";
    cin  >> n;
    p = new double[n];  ←——— Allocate the array of n doubles.
}
```

---

argument, `array_size`. The function then allocates an array of the requested size, and the argument called `numbers` is set to point to the first component of the array. Because the function makes its formal parameter p point to a newly allocated array of double numbers, and we want the actual argument `numbers` to point to the newly allocated memory, we are required to use a *reference* parameter.

If you have defined a type definition for a pointer type, then you can avoid the cumbersome syntax of *&. For example, if `double_ptr` has been defined to be a pointer to a double number, then we could write this prototype:

```
void allocate_doubles(double_ptr& p , size_t& n);
```

Reference Parameters That Are Pointers

Sometimes a function will actually *change a pointer parameter so that the pointer points to a new location*, and the programmer needs the change to affect the actual parameter. This is the only situation in which a reference parameter will be a pointer.

Syntax in the parameter list:
    `Type_Name*&` `var_name`

Example from Figure 4.5:
    `void allocate_doubles(`*double*`*& p,` `size_t& n);`

Self-Test Exercises for Section 4.2

8. Suppose that p is a value parameter of type int*. What happens when a function does an assignment to *p?

9. When should a pointer parameter be a reference parameter?

10. Suppose that an array is passed as a parameter. How does this differ from the usual use of a value parameter?

11. Write the prototype for a function called make_intarray. The function takes two reference parameters: a pointer that will be used to point to the array, and a size_t data type to indicate the size of the array.

12. Write a function with one reference parameter that is a pointer to an integer. The function allocates a dynamic array of n integers, making the pointer point to this new array. It then fills the array with 0 through n - 1.

13. Why do average and compare on page 166 use the keyword *const* with the data array, but fill_array does not?

14. Write a function that copies n elements from the front of one integer array to the front of another. One of the arrays should be a const parameter, and the other should be an ordinary array parameter.

15. Describe in English the behavior of the program in Figure 4.7.

FIGURE 4.7 Demonstration Program for Dynamic Arrays

A Program

```
// FILE: dynademo.cxx
// This is a small demonstration program showing how a dynamic array is used.
#include <iostream>      // Provides cout and cin
#include <cstdlib>       // Provides EXIT_SUCCESS and size_t
#include <cassert>       // Provides assert
using namespace std;

// PROTOTYPES for functions used by this demonstration program
void allocate_doubles(double*& p, size_t& n);
// Postcondition: The user has been prompted for a size n, and this size has been read.
// The pointer p has been set to point to a new dynamic array containing n doubles.
// NOTE: If there is insufficient dynamic memory, then bad_alloc is thrown.

void fill_array(double data[ ], size_t n);
// Precondition:  data is an array with at least n components.
// Postcondition: The user has been prompted to type n doubles, and these
// numbers have been read and placed in the first n components of the array.
```

(continued)

(FIGURE 4.7 continued)

```
double average(const double data[ ], size_t n);
// Precondition: data is an array with at least n components, and n > 0.
// Postcondition: The value returned is the average of data[0]..data[n - 1].

void compare(const double data[ ], size_t n, double value);
// Precondition: data is an array with at least n components.
// Postcondition: The values data[0] through data[n - 1] have been printed with a
//   message saying whether they are above, below, or equal to value.

int main( )
{
    double *numbers;     // Will point to the first component of an array
    size_t array_size;
    double mean_value;

    // Allocate an array of doubles to hold the user's input.
    cout << "This program will compute the average of some numbers. The\n";
    cout << "numbers will be stored in an array of doubles that I allocate.\n";
    allocate_doubles(numbers, array_size);

    // Read the user's input and compute the average.
    fill_array(numbers, array_size);
    mean_value = average(numbers, array_size);

    // Print the output.
    cout << "The average is: " << mean_value << endl;
    compare(numbers, array_size, mean_value);
    cout << "This was a mean program.";

    return EXIT_SUCCESS;
}

void allocate_doubles(double*& p, size_t& n)
║ See Figure 4.6 on page 163 for the body of this function.

void fill_array(double data[ ], size_t n)
// Library facilities used: cstdlib
{
    size_t i;
    cout << "Please type " << n << " double numbers: " << endl;

    // Read the n numbers one at a time.
    for (i = 0; i < n; ++i)
        cin >> data[i];
}
```

(continued)

(FIGURE 4.7 continued)

```
void compare(const double data[ ], size_t n, double value)
{
    size_t i;

    for (i = 0; i < n; ++i)
    {
        cout << data[i];
        if (data[i] < value)
            cout << " is less than ";
        else if (data[i] > value)
            cout << " is more than ";
        else
            cout << " is equal to  ";
        cout << value << endl;
    }
}

double average(const double data[ ], size_t n)
// Library facilities used: cassert, cstdlib
{
    size_t i;    // An array index
    double sum;  // The sum of data[0] through data[n - 1]

    assert(n > 0);

    // Add up the n numbers and return the average.
    sum = 0;
    for (i = 0; i < n; ++i)
        sum += data[i];
    return (sum/n);
}
```

A Sample Dialogue

```
This program will compute the average of some numbers. The
numbers will be stored in an array of doubles that I allocate.
How many doubles should I allocate?
Please type an integer answer: 3
Please type 3 double numbers:
15.1    24.6    86.3
The average is: 42
15.1 is less than 42
24.6 is less than 42
86.3 is more than 42
This was a mean program.
```

www.cs.colorado.edu/~main/chapter4/dynademo.cxx   **WWW**

4.3 THE BAG CLASS WITH A DYNAMIC ARRAY

Pointers enable us to define data structures whose size is determined when a program is actually *running* rather than at *compilation time*. Such data structures are called **dynamic data structures**. This is in contrast to **static data structures**, which have their size determined when a program is compiled.

A class may be a dynamic data structure—in other words, it may use dynamic memory. When a class uses dynamic memory, several new factors come into play. In this section, we'll illustrate these factors by implementing a new bag class that contains its items in a *dynamic* array rather than an array of fixed size. Apart from the use of a dynamic array, the new bag is much the same as the original bag class from Section 3.1.

Pointer Member Variables

The original bag class in Section 3.1 has a member variable that is a static array containing the bag's items. Our new, dynamic bag has a member variable that is a pointer to a dynamic array. In both cases, the array is a *partially filled* array, containing the bag's items at the front of the array. Here is a comparison of the member variables of the two class definitions:

The Static Bag:

```
// From bag1.h in Section 3.1:
class bag
{
    ...
private:
    value_type data[CAPACITY];
    size_type used;
};
```

The Dynamic Bag:

```
// From bag2.h in this section:
class bag
{
    ...
private:
    value_type *data;
    size_type used;
    ...
};
```

A static bag has a private member variable, data, which is an array that can hold up to CAPACITY items. The static bag can never hold more than CAPACITY items. That's the limit.

On the other hand, a dynamic bag has a private member variable, also called data, which is a *pointer* to a value_type item. The constructor for the dynamic bag will allocate a dynamic array, and point data at the newly allocated array. As a program runs, a new larger dynamic array can be allocated when we need more capacity. Because the size of the dynamic array can change, the dynamic bag actually needs one more private member variable to keep track of how much memory is currently allocated. At the top of the next page, we show the complete private section of the new bag class, including the extra member variable.

```
class bag
{
public:
    ...
private:
    value_type *data;      // Pointer to dynamic array
    size_type used;        // How much of array is being used
    size_type capacity;    // Current capacity of the bag
};
```

With this much of the class definition in hand, we can now state the invariant of the dynamic bag class:

Invariant for the Revised Bag Class

1. The number of items in the bag is in the member variable used.

2. The actual items of the bag are stored in a partially filled array. The array is a dynamic array, pointed to by the member variable data.

3. The total size of the dynamic array is in the member variable capacity.

Member Functions Allocate Dynamic Memory as Needed

When a class uses dynamic memory, *the class's member functions allocate dynamic memory as needed.* For example, the constructor of the dynamic bag allocates the dynamic array that the member variable data points to. But how big should this array be? Our plan is to have the constructor allocate a dynamic array whose initial size is determined by a parameter to the constructor. As a bag is used in a program, the size of its dynamic array may, in effect, increase to whatever capacity is needed.

In other words, the parameter to the constructor determines the *initial capacity of the bag,* but even after this initial capacity is reached, more items can be inserted. Whenever items are inserted into a bag—through the insert member function or the += operator—the bag's current capacity is examined. If the current capacity is too small, then the member function allocates a new, larger dynamic array. The user of a bag does not need to do anything special to obtain the increased capacity. The insert and += functions increase the capacity as needed.

the importance of the initial capacity

You might wonder why a programmer needs to be concerned about the initial capacity of a bag. Can't a programmer just start with a small initial capacity and insert items one after another? The insert function will take care of increasing the capacity as needed. Yes, this approach will always work correctly. But if there are many items, then many of the activations of insert would need to increase the capacity. This could be inefficient. Each time the capacity is increased, new memory is allocated, the items are copied into the new memory, and the old memory is released. To avoid this repeated allocation of memory, a programmer can request a large initial capacity. With this in mind, here is the documentation for the new bag constructor:

```
bag(size_type initial_capacity = DEFAULT_CAPACITY);
// Postcondition: The bag is empty with a capacity given by the parameter.
// The insert function will work efficiently (without allocating new
// memory) until this capacity is reached.
```

For example, suppose that a programmer is going to place 1000 items into a bag named kilosack. When the bag is declared, the programmer can specify a capacity of 1000, as shown here:

```
bag kilosack(1000);  ◄──── 1000 items can be efficiently added to kilosack.
```

After the initial capacity is reached, the insert function continues to work *correctly*, but it might be slowed down by memory allocations.

Notice that the parameter of the constructor has a default argument, DEFAULT_CAPACITY, which will be a constant in our class definition. Because of the default argument, the single constructor actually serves two purposes: It can be used with an argument to construct a bag with a specific capacity, or it can be used as a default constructor (with no argument list). When the constructor is used with no argument list, DEFAULT_CAPACITY is used for the initial capacity. Here are two examples, using the default constructor and using the constructor with an argument:

the constructor serves as a default constructor

```
bag ordinary;  ◄──────── The initial capacity is DEFAULT_CAPACITY.
bag super(9000);  ◄──── The initial capacity is 9000.
```

Here is one more example to show how the new constructor works with the other members. The example declares a bag with an initial capacity of 6 and places three items in the bag:

```
bag sixpack(6);  ◄──────── The constructor creates a bag
sixpack.insert(10);        with an initial capacity of 6.
sixpack.insert(20);
sixpack.insert(30);
```

After these declarations, the bag's private member variables look like this:

The private member variables of the bag include a pointer to a dynamically allocated array of six elements. The first three elements are now being used.

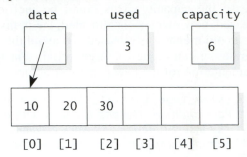

Later, the program could insert more items into this bag, maybe even more than six. If there are more than six items, then the bag's member functions will increase the bag's capacity as needed.

After a bag has been declared and is already in use, a programmer can make an explicit adjustment to the bag's capacity via a new member function called `reserve`. Here is the specification of the member function:

```
void reserve(size_type new_capacity);
// Postcondition: The bag's current capacity is changed to the
// new_capacity (but not less than the number of items already in the bag).
// The insert function will work efficiently (without allocating new memory) until
// the new capacity is reached.
```

To some extent, the `reserve` function is a luxury. Programmers can avoid `reserve` altogether, allowing the other member functions to adjust the size of a bag as needed. But by using the `reserve` member function, the bag's efficiency is improved.

use names from the Standard Library container classes when possible

Using the name `reserve` for this function may seem like a strange choice. We choose the name to match the Standard Library container classes that have a `reserve` member function to change the container's capacity.

All told, five of the member functions that we have seen so far can allocate new dynamic memory: the constructor, `reserve`, `insert`, and the two operators (`+=` and `+`). As with any function that allocates dynamic memory, these functions are subject to possible failure—the heap might run out of room. In this case, the function calls the *new* operator, and the *new* operator will fail, throwing the `bad_alloc` exception. This prints an error message and halts the program. For our programs, the error-message-and-halt will suffice. But part of our class documentation will indicate which member functions allocate dynamic memory so that more experienced programmers can deal with the exception in their own way. You can see this documentation at the bottom of Figure 4.8, which provides the complete documentation for the header file (`bag2.h`) of our new bag class.

FIGURE 4.8   Documentation for the Dynamic Bag Header File

Documentation for a Header File

```
//  TYPEDEFS and MEMBER CONSTANTS for the bag class:
//     typedef _____ value_type
//        bag::value_type is the data type of the items in the bag. It may be any of the C++
//        built-in types (int, char, etc.), or a class with a default constructor, an assignment
//        operator, and operators to test for equality (x == y) and non-equality (x != y).
//
//     typedef _____ size_type
//        bag::size_type is the data type of any variable that keeps track of how many items
//        are in a bag.
//
//     static const size_type DEFAULT_CAPACITY = _____
//        bag::DEFAULT_CAPACITY is the initial capacity of a bag that is created by the default
//        constructor.
//
//  CONSTRUCTOR for the bag class:
//     bag(size_type initial_capacity = DEFAULT_CAPACITY)
//        Postcondition: The bag is empty with an initial capacity given by the parameter. The
//        insert function will work efficiently (without allocating new memory) until this capacity
//        is reached.
//
//  MODIFICATION MEMBER FUNCTIONS for the bag class:
//     size_type erase(const value_type& target)
//        Postcondition: All copies of target have been removed from the bag.
//        The return value is the number of copies removed (which could be zero).
//
//     bool erase_one(const value_type& target)
//        Postcondition: If target was in the bag, then one copy has been removed;
//        otherwise the bag is unchanged. A true return value indicates that one
//        copy was removed; false indicates that nothing was removed.
//
//     void insert(const value_type& entry)
//        Postcondition: A new copy of entry has been inserted into the bag.
//
//     void reserve(size_type new_capacity)   ← The reserve member function provides efficiency.
//        Postcondition: The bag's current capacity is changed to the
//        new_capacity (but not less than the number of items already in
//        the bag). The insert function will work efficiently (without allocating
//        new memory) until the new capacity is reached.
//
//     void operator +=(const bag& addend)
//        Postcondition: Each item in addend has been added to this bag.
//
```

(continued)

(FIGURE 4.8 continued)
```
//  CONSTANT MEMBER FUNCTIONS for the bag class:
//    size_type size( ) const
//        Postcondition: The return value is the total number of items in the bag.
//
//    size_type count(const value_type& target) const
//        Postcondition: The return value is the number of times target is in the bag.
//
//  NONMEMBER FUNCTIONS for the bag class:
//    bag operator +(const bag& b1, const bag& b2)
//    Postcondition: The bag returned is the union of b1 and b2.
//
//  VALUE SEMANTICS for the bag class:
//    Assignments and the copy constructor may be used with bag objects.
//
//  DYNAMIC MEMORY USAGE by the bag:
//    If there is insufficient dynamic memory, then the following functions throw bad_alloc:
//    The constructors, reserve, insert, operator += , operator +, and the assignment operator.
```

www.cs.colorado.edu/~main/chapter4/bag2.h   **WWW**

PROGRAMMING TIP

PROVIDE DOCUMENTATION ABOUT POSSIBLE DYNAMIC MEMORY FAILURE

When a class uses dynamic memory, you should include documentation to indicate which member functions allocate dynamic memory. This will allow experienced programmers to deal with potential failure.

The documentation in Figure 4.8 provides adequate information for a programmer to use our new bag class. But before we implement the class there are two extra factors that play an important role whenever a class uses dynamic memory. The first factor is the *value semantics* (i.e., the assignment operator and the copy constructor). The second factor is a requirement for a special member function called a *destructor*. We'll discuss these two factors before completing the implementation.

Value Semantics

the value semantics determines how values are copied

The value semantics of the bag class determines how values are copied from one bag to another—in assignment statements and when one bag is initialized as a copy of another. Until now, we have not worried much about value semantics. With all our other classes, it was sufficient to use the automatic assignment operator and the automatic copy constructor. So, in the past, when we wrote y = x, we were content to let the automatic assignment operator copy all the member variables from the object x to the object y.

Our days of easy contentment are done. The automatic assignment operator fails for the dynamic bag (or for any other class that uses dynamic memory).

Here is an example to show what goes wrong. Suppose we set up a bag called x with an initial capacity of 5, containing the integers 10, 20, and 30—then we copy the private member variables of x to another bag y. The result is that the two pointers, x.data and y.data, both point to the same dynamic array, like this:

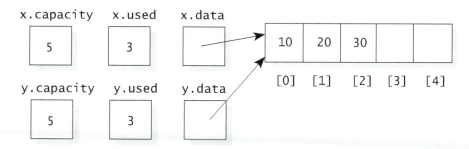

The problem with this arrangement is that a subsequent change to x's array will also change y's array. Normally, this is not what we want; after an assignment y = x, we do not want further changes to one object to directly affect the other.

Instead, when we assign y = x, we want y to have its own dynamic array, completely separate from x's dynamic array. Of course, the dynamic array of y will contain the same values as the x array, but these two arrays will not share the same dynamic memory. The desired situation after the assignment looks like this:

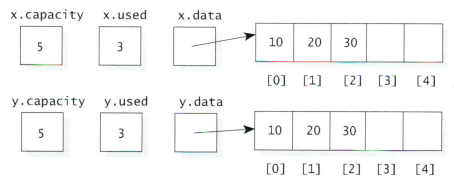

To achieve this situation, we must provide our own assignment operator rather than relying on the automatic assignment operator. We can do this by overloading the assignment operator for the bag class, in roughly the same way that we have overloaded other operators for the bag. The operator will be overloaded as a bag member function with the prototype given here:

```
void bag::operator =(const bag& source);
// Postcondition: The bag that activated this function has the same items
// and capacity as source.
```

When you overload the assignment operator, C++ requires it to be a member function. In an assignment statement `y = x`, the bag y is activating the function, and the bag x is the argument for the parameter named `source`. In a moment we will implement this member function, and you will see how it correctly makes a new dynamic array rather than merely copying the pointer.

The second part of the value semantics is the copy constructor, which is activated when a new object is initialized as a copy of an existing object, such as the declaration:

```
bag y(x);  // Initialize y as a copy of the bag x.
```

Unless you indicate otherwise, y is initialized using the automatic copy constructor, which merely copies the member variables from x to y. If you want to avoid the simple copying of member variables, then you must provide a copy constructor with the prototype:

```
bag::bag(const bag& source);
// Postcondition: The bag that is being constructed has been initialized
// with the same items and capacity as source.
```

The parameter of the copy constructor is usually a const reference parameter (although it is seldom used, C++ also permits an ordinary reference parameter, but does not allow a value parameter). If a copy constructor is present, then it is used instead of the automatic copy constructor. The copy constructor also has several other uses that we'll discuss on page 186.

Our documentation of the bag in Figure 4.8 on page 171 indicates that the assignment operator and copy constructor are safe to use with the bag class:

```
// VALUE SEMANTICS for the bag class:
//    Assignments and the copy constructor may be used with bag objects.
```

Value Semantics and Dynamic Memory

If a class uses dynamic memory, the automatic assignment operator and the automatic copy constructor fail. The implementor of the class must provide member functions for the assignment operator and the copy constructor. For example:

```
class bag
{
public:
    bag(const bag& source);
    void operator =(const bag& source);
    . . .
```

The documentation of the class should indicate that the value semantics may be used.

One final point about the value semantics: The programmer who uses the bag does not need to know whether the implementor has overridden the automatic value semantics. This programmer needs to know only that there is a valid value semantics. Therefore, the bag documentation indicates that there is a valid value semantics, but does not indicate whether the automatic value semantics was overridden.

The Destructor

The final new factor for a class that uses dynamic memory is a special member function called the **destructor**. The primary purpose of the destructor is to return an object's dynamic memory to the heap when the object is no longer in use. The destructor has three unique features:

- The name of the destructor is always the tilde character ~ followed by the class name. In our example the name of the destructor is ~bag.

- The destructor has no parameters and no return value. As with the constructor, you must *not* write *void* (or any other return type) at the front of the destructor's prototype. However, you must list the empty parameter list, as shown in this prototype: `~bag( );`.

- Programmers who *use* a class should not need to know about the destructor. This is because programs rarely activate the destructor *explicitly.* What good is a destructor that is never activated? The answer is that destructors *are* activated, but the activation is usually *automatic* whenever an object becomes inaccessible.

Several common situations cause automatic destructor activation:

1. Suppose a function has a *local* variable that is an object, like this:
   ```
   void example1( )
   {
       bag sample1;
       . . .
   ```
   When the function `example1` returns, the destructor `sample1.~bag( )` is automatically activated. The general situation: When a local variable is an object with a destructor, the destructor is automatically activated when the function returns.

2. Suppose a function has a *value* parameter that is an object, like this:
   ```
   void example2(bag sample2)
   // Does some calculation using a bag
   ```
   As with the previous example, when the function `example2` returns, the destructor `sample2.~bag( )` is automatically activated. On the other hand, if `sample2` was a reference parameter, then the destructor would not be activated because a reference parameter is actually an object in the calling program, and that object is still accessible.

destructors are automatically activated when an object becomes inaccessible

3. Suppose that a dynamic variable is an object, as shown here:
```
bag *b_ptr;
b_ptr = new bag;
...
delete b_ptr;
```

When *delete* b_ptr is executed, the destructor for *b_ptr is automatically activated. The destructor ensures that the dynamic array used by
*b_ptr is released.

There are several other situations where a destructor is automatically called,
but the three examples you have seen provide the general idea. Because destructors are not directly activated by a program, we omitted the destructor from the
how-to-use-a-bag documentation of Figure 4.8 on page 171.

The Destructor

The **destructor** of a class is a member function that is automatically activated when an object becomes inaccessible.
The destructor has no arguments and its name must be the
character ~ followed by the class name (e.g., ~bag for the
bag class).

Because the destructor is automatically called, programs
rarely make explicit calls to the destructor, and we generally
omit the destructor from the documentation that tells how to
use the class.

The primary responsibility of the destructor is simply
releasing dynamic memory.

The Revised Bag Class—Class Definition

We can now write the complete class definition for the dynamic bag. As usual,
the class definition appears in the header file, surrounded by a macro guard.
This definition is shown in Figure 4.9 (where the file is called bag2.h).
Notice that the bag's *operator* + function is not a member function.

FIGURE 4.9   Header File for the Bag Class with a Dynamic Array

A Header File

```
// FILE: bag2.h (part of the namespace main_savitch_4)
// CLASS PROVIDED: bag
```

See Figure 4.8 on page 171 for the other documentation that goes here.

```
#ifndef MAIN_SAVITCH_BAG2_H
#define MAIN_SAVITCH_BAG2_H
#include <cstdlib>  // Provides size_t

namespace main_savitch_4
{
    class bag
    {
    public:
        // TYPEDEFS and MEMBER CONSTANTS
        typedef int value_type;
        typedef std::size_t size_type;
        static const size_type DEFAULT_CAPACITY = 30;
        // CONSTRUCTORS and DESTRUCTOR
        bag(size_type initial_capacity = DEFAULT_CAPACITY);
        bag(const bag& source);
        ~bag( );
        // MODIFICATION MEMBER FUNCTIONS
        void reserve(size_type new_capacity);
        bool erase_one(const value_type& target);
        size_type erase(const value_type& target);
        void insert(const value_type& entry);
        void operator +=(const bag& addend);
        void operator =(const bag& source);
        // CONSTANT MEMBER FUNCTIONS
        size_type size( ) const { return used; }
        size_type count(const value_type& target) const;
    private:
        value_type *data;      // Pointer to partially filled dynamic array
        size_type used;        // How much of array is being used
        size_type capacity;    // Current capacity of the bag
    };

    // NONMEMBER FUNCTIONS for the bag class
    bag operator +(const bag& b1, const bag& b2);
}
#endif
```

If your compiler does not permit initialization of static constants, see Appendix E.

Prototype for the copy constructor is discussed on page 174.

Prototype for the destructor is discussed on page 175.

Prototype for the overloaded operator = is discussed on page 173.

The Revised Bag Class—Implementation

We'll look at the implementation of the new bag member functions. Three functions are particularly important: the copy constructor, the destructor, and the assignment operator. These three member functions are always needed when a class uses dynamic memory.

The constructors. Each of the constructors is responsible for setting up the three private member variables in a way that satisfies the invariant of the dynamic bag class. For example, here is the implementation of the first constructor. Notice how all three private member variables are assigned values:

```
bag::bag(size_type initial_capacity)
{
    data = new value_type[initial_capacity];
    capacity = initial_capacity;
    used = 0;
}
```

The parameter, initial_capacity, tells how many items to allocate for the dynamic array.

the copy constructor

The bag's copy constructor is similar, also allocating memory for a dynamic array. In the case of the copy constructor, the capacity of the dynamic array is the same as the capacity of the bag that is being copied. After the dynamic array has been allocated, the items may be copied into the newly allocated array, as shown here:

```
bag::bag(const bag& source)
{
    data = new value_type[source.capacity];
    capacity = source.capacity;
    used = source.used;
    copy(source.data, source.data + used, data);
}
```

The amount of memory allocated for source determines how much memory to allocate for the new dynamic array.

Notice that we used the Standard Library copy function (described in the C++ Feature on page 115).

The destructor. The primary responsibility of the destructor is releasing dynamic memory. Sometimes there is other "cleanup" work needed, but not for the bag's destructor, which has only one statement:

the destructor

```
bag::~bag( )
{
    delete [ ] data;
}
```

The private member variable called data points to the dynamic array.

The most formidable aspect of the destructor is getting used to the ~ in the name.

The assignment operator. The implementation of the assignment operator is nearly identical to the copy constructor. There are only small differences:

- The copy constructor is constructing a bag from scratch. It allocates the initial memory for the partially filled array.

- The assignment operator is not constructing a new bag, meaning that there is already a partially filled array allocated. The size of this array might need to be changed, or we might be satisfied with the array that already exists. If we do end up allocating a new array, then the original array must be returned to the heap.

- In the assignment operator, it is possible that the source parameter (which is being copied) is the same object that activates the operator. With a bag b, this would occur if a programmer writes b = b (called a **self-assignment**). Perhaps you think that self-assignments are pointless, but nevertheless the assignment operator should work correctly, assigning b to be equal to its current value—that is, leave the bag unchanged.

The solution for the self-assignment is to provide a special check at the start of the operator. If we find that an assignment such as b = b is occurring, then we will return immediately. We can check for this condition by determining whether source is the same object as the object that activated the operator. This is done with a special boolean test that can be used at the start of any assignment operator:

```
// Check for possible self-assignment:
if (this == &source)
    return;
```

The test uses the keyword *this*, which can be used inside any member function to provide a pointer to the object that activated the function. The expression &source is a common use of the & operator, which provides the address of the source object. If the *this* pointer is the same as the address of the source object, we have a self-assignment and we can return immediately, with no work.

the keyword "this"

HOW TO CHECK FOR SELF-ASSIGNMENT

At the start of any assignment operator, always check for a possible self-assignment with the pattern:

```
if (this == &source)
    return;
```

After checking for a possible self-assignment, our bag assignment operator handles potential new memory allocation, using a local variable, new_data, which is a pointer to a new dynamic array: `value_type *new_data;` . The code for this potential memory allocation is given at the top of the next page.

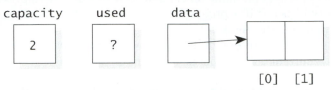

```
if (capacity != source.capacity)
{
    new_data = new value_type[source.capacity];
    delete [ ] data;
    data = new_data;
    capacity = source.capacity;
}
```

Allocate memory for the new array.

Return the old array to the heap.

The pointer, data, now points to the newly allocated array.

Let's trace through the statements of this memory allocation. To trace the statements we assume that source is a bag with a capacity of 5. We will execute the statements assuming that the bag that activated the function has a mere capacity of 2. When the assignment begins, we have this situation:

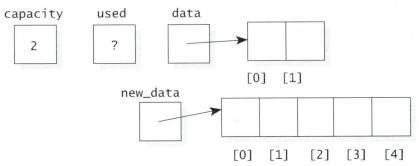

Since the current capacity (2) is not equal to the amount needed (5), the code enters the body of the if-statement. In the body, we have a local variable, new_data, which is set to point to a newly allocated array of five items, as shown here:

Once the new array has been allocated, we return the old array to the heap and assign data = new_data, so that the data pointer points to the new array:

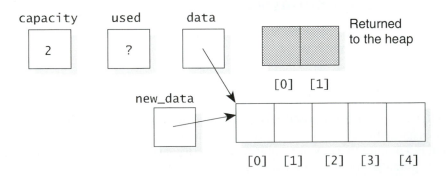

Finally, capacity is changed to 5, and we no longer need the local variable new_data, as shown here:

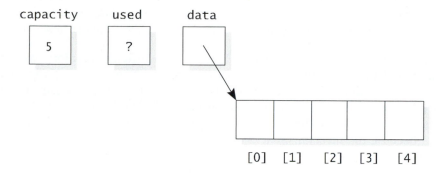

At this point, all that remains is to copy the items from source's array into the newly allocated array, and to correctly set the value of used. You can see how this is accomplished with the copy function in the complete function implementation in Figure 4.10.

FIGURE 4.10   Implementation of the Bag's = Operator

A Member Function Implementation

```
void bag::operator =(const bag& source)
// Library facility used: algorithm
{
    value_type *new_data;

    // Check for possible self-assignment:
    if (this == &source)
        return;

    if (capacity != source.capacity)
    {
        new_data = new value_type[source.capacity];
        delete [ ] data;
        data = new_data;
        capacity = source.capacity;
    }

    used = source.used;
    copy(source.data, source.data + used, data);
}
```

If necessary, allocate a dynamic array of a different size.

Use the copy function to copy data from the source.

It is tempting to implement the new memory allocation without the local variable `new_data`, using just two statements:

```
delete [ ] data;                           // Release old array
data = new value_type[source.capacity];    // Allocate new array
```

This shortcut could cause a headache. If there is insufficient memory, the *new* operator will throw a `bad_alloc` exception—but with the shortcut approach, the bag is not valid when the exception is thrown (since the array has already been released). With an invalid bag, the usual exception handling mechanism can fail before it has a chance to print a sensible error message. The failure occurs because the mechanism activates the destructor for any object that was previously constructed. When the destructor is given an invalid object—such as our invalid bag—the destructor may cause an error message that will be more confusing than the usual message from `bad_alloc`. As a result, your programs will be harder to debug. The invalid bag also makes it harder for experienced programmers to deal with the `bad_alloc` exception in a way that tries to recover without halting the program.

Because of these problems, we suggest that member functions always ensure that all objects are valid prior to calling *new*. Also, your documentation should indicate which functions allocate dynamic memory. For the bag, we have already taken care of this documentation in the header file with this comment (from the bottom of Figure 4.8 on page 172):

```
// DYNAMIC MEMORY USAGE by the bag:
//     If there is insufficient dynamic memory then the following functions
//     throw bad_alloc: The constructors, reserve, insert, operator +=,
//     operator +, and the assignment operator.
```

ⓘ Programming Tip

How to Allocate Memory in a Member Function

When a member function allocates memory, it is a good idea to have the invariant of the class valid when the call to the *new* operator is made. Also, the documentation should indicate which functions allocate dynamic memory. This approach aids debugging and allows experienced programmers to deal with `bad_alloc` exceptions in a sensible way.

This tip is not necessary (and often not possible) for constructors that allocate dynamic memory. But it is critical for easy debugging of other member functions.

The reserve member function.   Our design includes a member function called `reserve`, which is called to explicitly increase the capacity of a bag. Here is the function's prototype with a precondition/postcondition contract:

```
void reserve(size_type new_capacity);
// Postcondition: The bag's current capacity is changed to the
// new_capacity (but not less than the number of items already in the bag).
// The insert function will work efficiently (without allocating new memory)
// until the new capacity is reached.
```

Our implementation of `reserve` is one of the functions implemented in the complete implementation file of Figure 4.11. The function first carries out a couple of checks. After the checks, the new array is allocated with a new size, the items are copied into the new array, and the original array is released. The private member variable `data` is then made to point at the new array, and `capacity` is set to indicate how much memory is now allocated.

The Revised Bag Class—Putting the Pieces Together

Several of the other bag member functions need small changes to work correctly with the dynamic array. The most obvious change is that member functions such as `insert` must ensure that there is sufficient capacity before a new item is inserted. If more room is needed, then the function increases the bag's capacity by activating `reserve`. The necessary changes to the bag functions are marked in the new implementation file of Figure 4.11.

FIGURE 4.11   Implementation File for the Bag Class with a Dynamic Array

An Implementation File

```
// FILE: bag2.cxx (part of namespace main_savitch_4)
// CLASS implemented: bag (see bag2.h for documentation)
// INVARIANT for the bag class:
//    1. The number of items in the bag is in the member variable used.
//    2. The actual items of the bag are stored in a partially filled array.
//       The array is a dynamic array, pointed to by the member variable data.
//    3. The size of the dynamic array is in the member variable capacity.

#include <algorithm>      // Provides copy function
#include <cassert>        // Provides assert function
#include "bag2.h"
using namespace std;

namespace main_savitch_4
{
    const bag::size_type bag::DEFAULT_CAPACITY;
```

(continued)

(FIGURE 4.11 continued)

```
bag::bag(size_type initial_capacity)
{
    data = new value_type[initial_capacity];
    capacity = initial_capacity;
    used = 0;
}

bag::bag(const bag& source)
// Library facilities used: algorithm
{
    data = new value_type[source.capacity];
    capacity = source.capacity;
    used = source.used;
    copy(source.data, source.data + used, data);
}


bag::~bag( )
{
    delete [ ] data;
}


void bag::reserve(size_type new_capacity)
// Library facilities used: algorithm
{
    value_type *larger_array;

    if (new_capacity == capacity)
        return; // The allocated memory is already the right size.

    if (new_capacity < used)
        new_capacity = used; // Can't allocate less than we are using.

    larger_array = new value_type[new_capacity];
    copy(data, data + used, larger_array);
    delete [ ] data;
    data = larger_array;
    capacity = new_capacity;
}
```

The revised bag has two constructors. The first constructor serves as a default constructor since the parameter has a default argument. The second constructor is a copy constructor, which you can read about on page 178.

Read about the destructor on page 178.

```
bag::size_type bag::erase(const value_type& target)
```
|| No change from the original bag: See the solution to Self-Test Exercise 12 on page 139.

```
bool bag::erase_one(const value_type& target)
```
|| No change from the original bag: See the implementation in Figure 3.3 on page 113.

(continued)

(FIGURE 4.11 continued)

```
void bag::insert(const value_type& entry)
{
    if (used == capacity)
        reserve(used+1);
    data[used] = entry;
    ++used;
}
```

The first action of the insert function is to ensure that there is room for a new item.

```
void bag::operator +=(const bag& addend)
// Library facilities used: algorithm
{
    if (used + addend.used > capacity)
        reserve(used + addend.used);

    copy(addend.data, addend.data + addend.used, data + used);
    used += addend.used;
}
```

The += operator starts by ensuring that there is enough room for the new items.

```
void bag::operator =(const bag& source)
```
‖ See the implementation in Figure 4.10 on page 181.

```
bag::size_type bag::count(const value_type& target) const
```
‖ No change from the original bag: See the implementation in Figure 3.6 on page 118.

```
bag operator +(const bag& b1, const bag& b2)
{
    bag answer(b1.size( ) + b2.size( ));

    answer += b1;
    answer += b2;
    return answer;
}
}
```

The function declares a bag of sufficient size.

www.cs.colorado.edu/~main/chapter4/bag2.cxx **WWW**

Self-Test Exercises for Section 4.3

16. Describe the difference between a dynamic data structure and a static data structure.

17. Why does a programmer need to be concerned with the initial capacity of a container if dynamic memory can be allocated as needed?

18. Suppose that you declare a bag like this: `bag exercise;`. What is the initial capacity? What will happen if you try to put 31 items in the bag?

19. If a bag is full, then the `insert` function increases the bag's capacity by only one. This could be inefficient if we are inserting a sequence of items to a full bag, since each insertion calls `reserve`. Rewrite the bag's `insert` function so that it increases the capacity by at least 10%.

20. What is the primary responsibility of the destructor? When is the destructor of an object activated?

21. Write a prototype for the destructor of the `sequence` class described in Chapter 3.

22. What does the keyword `this` refer to?

23. Why does the bag's assignment operator need to be overloaded? Does our implementation work correctly for self-assignment (`x = x`)?

4.4 PRESCRIPTION FOR A DYNAMIC CLASS

This section summarizes the important factors for a class that uses dynamic memory. We also point out the additional importance of the copy constructor.

Four Rules

When a class uses dynamic memory, you will generally follow these four rules:

1. Some of the member variables of the class are pointers.

2. Member functions allocate and release dynamic memory as needed.

3. The automatic value semantics of the class is overridden (otherwise two different objects end up with pointers to the same dynamic memory). This means that the implementor must write an assignment operator and a copy constructor for the class.

4. The class has a destructor. The primary purpose of the destructor is to return all dynamic memory to the heap.

Special Importance of the Copy Constructor

When a class uses dynamic memory, the programmer who implements the class writes a copy constructor. The copy constructor is used when one object is to be initialized as a copy of another, as in the declaration:

    bag y(x); // *Initialize y as a copy of x.*

There are three other common situations where the copy constructor is used. These situations reinforce the need for special value semantics when an object uses dynamic memory.

Alternative syntax. The first situation is really just an alternative syntax for using the copy constructor to initialize a newly declared object. The alternative syntax is:

    bag y = x; // *Initialize y as a copy of x.*

This syntax is an alternative to `bag y(x);`. Both versions merely activate the copy constructor to initialize y as a copy of x.

Returning an object from a function. The second situation that uses the copy constructor is when a return value of a function is an object. For example, the bag's *operator* + returns a bag object. The function computes its answer in a local variable, and then has a return statement. When the return statement is executed, here's what actually happens: The value from the local variable is copied to a temporary location called the **return location**. The local variable itself is then destroyed (along with any other local variables), and the function returns to the place where it was called.

Unless you indicate otherwise, the copying into the return location occurs by using the automatic copy constructor, which copies all the member variables from the local variable to the return location. If you want to avoid the simple copying of member variables, then you must provide a copy constructor. If a copy constructor is present, then it is used to copy the return value from a function's local variable to the return location.

When a value parameter is an object. A third situation arises when a value parameter is an object. For example, on page 68 we declared a function to do a calculation on a `point`, with this prototype:

```
int rotations_needed(point p);
```

When the function is called, the actual argument is copied to the formal parameter p. The copying occurs by using the copy constructor.

PITFALL ⏻

USING DYNAMIC MEMORY REQUIRES A DESTRUCTOR, A COPY CONSTRUCTOR, AND AN OVERLOADED ASSIGNMENT OPERATOR

When a member variable of a class is a pointer to dynamic memory, the class should always be given a destructor, and the value semantics should always be defined (that is, a copy constructor and an overloaded assignment operator should be provided).

- The destructor is responsible for returning an object's dynamic memory to the heap. If you forget the destructor, then dynamic memory that is allocated to the object will continue to occupy heap memory, even when the object is no longer needed.

- The copy constructor and the overloaded assignment operator are responsible for correctly copying one object to another. Make sure that the copying process allocates new memory for the new copy, rather than just copying the pointers from one object to another. If you forget the copy constructor, then value parameters and return values from functions will perform incorrectly.

Self-Test Exercises for Section 4.4

24. Name the three situations where a copy constructor is activated.

25. Suppose a function returns an object. What value does the function return if the class did not provide a new copy constructor?

4.5 PROGRAMMING PROJECT: THE STRING CLASS

C programs abound with oversize arrays to hold character sequences of worst-case length. Or they contain ornate logic to allocate and free storage, copy strings about, and get those terminating null characters where they belong.

Little wonder, then, that writing string classes is one of the more popular indoor sports among C++ programmers.

P. J. PLAUGER
The Draft Standard C++ Library

As P.J. Plauger notes, writing classes for string manipulation has been a popular pastime. Or at least that was the case in olden days (prior to the ANSI/ISO C++ Standard). The new standard includes a string class itself, so the string-writing sport has recently declined in popularity. Nevertheless, designing and implementing part of a dynamic string class is still an instructive exercise. In this section, we'll outline such a string project, consistent with the Standard Library string class. If you actually undertake the project, you'll find more details in the Chapter 4 section of www.cs.colorado.edu/~main/projects/.

Null-Terminated Strings

In C or C++, an array of characters can be used to hold a simple kind of string. This is natural since a string is a sequence of characters, and an array of characters is just what's needed to store a sequence of characters. Thus, the following array declaration provides us with a string variable capable of storing a string with 9 or fewer characters:

```
char s[10];
```

the null character marks the end of the string

That is not a mistake. We said that s can hold a string with 9 or fewer characters. The string variable s cannot hold a full 10 characters even though the array does contain 10 components. That is because the characters of the string are placed in the array followed by the special symbol '\0', which is placed in the array immediately after the last character of the string. Thus, if s contains the string "Hi Mom!" then the array components are filled as shown here:

the longest possible string is one less than the size of the array

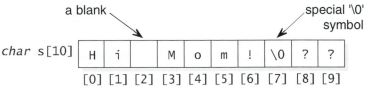

The character '\0' marks the end of the string. If you read the characters in the string starting at s[0], and proceed to s[1], and then to s[2], and so on, you know that when you encounter the symbol '\0', then you have reached the end of the string. Since the symbol '\0' always occupies one component of the array, the length of the longest possible string is one less than the size of the array.

The character '\0' is called the **null character**, and the string itself is called a **null-terminated string**. In a program, the null character is written '\0'—the single quote marks are used with all C++ characters such as 'a', 'b', 'c'. The \0 (a backslash followed by a zero) indicates the null character. It looks like two characters, but it is officially a single character, and it occupies just one location in a character array.

The only distinction between a string variable and an array of characters is the fact that a string variable must use the null character to mark the end of the string. This is a distinction in how the array is used rather than a distinction about what the array is. *A string variable is a character array, but it is used in a different way.*

string variables versus arrays of characters

Initializing a String Variable

You can initialize a string variable when you declare it, as shown here:

```
char proclaim[20] = "Make it so.";
```

Notice that the string assigned to the string variable need not fill the entire array.

When you initialize a string variable, you can omit the array size and C++ will automatically calculate the size to be exactly long enough to hold the string plus the null terminating character. For example:

```
char thought[ ] = "Peace";
```
← *This allocates an array of six characters.*

The Empty String

Sometimes a program needs a string that has no characters at all, not even a single blank. This string with no characters is called the **empty string**, and it is specified by two double quotes with nothing in between. For example:

```
char quiet[20] = "";
```

There is not even a space between the two double quote marks. The initialization of quiet will put the null terminator at location quiet[0], so there are no characters before the termination. This is a very quiet quip indeed.

Reading and Writing String Variables

C++ supports reading and writing string variables with the usual >> and << operators. For example:

```
char message[20] = "Noise";          This prints Noise.
cout << message;                     This reads a string from
cin >> message;                      standard input device.
```

The string-reading mechanism begins by skipping any *white space* in the input stream. **White space** consists of any blank, tab, or the return key. The operation then reads characters until some more white space is encountered, placing these characters in the string variable. The white space character itself is not read, but a null terminating character is placed at the end of the string, making it a valid null-terminated string.

ⓘ PITFALL

USING = AND == WITH STRINGS

Strings are not like other data types. Many of the usual operations simply do not work for strings. You cannot use a string variable in an assignment statement using =. If you use == to test strings for equality, you will not get the result you expect. The reason for these problems is that strings are implemented as arrays rather than simple values.

An attempt to assign a value to a string variable will quickly show the problem, as in this example:

```
char greeting[10];                   Illegal!
greeting = "Hello";
```

This example results in a compilation error. Although you can use the equals sign to assign a value to a string variable when the variable is declared, you cannot do it any place else in your program.

You also cannot use the operator == in an expression to compare two strings for equality. Things are actually worse than that. You can use == to test two string variables, but it does not test for the strings being equal. A good compiler will warn you that == actually tests to see whether the starting addresses of the arrays are the same. But you will get incorrect results if you think you are testing for string equality.

There are ways around the string problems, which we will discuss next.

The strcpy Function

The easiest way to assign a value to a string variable is with the library function strcpy, as shown here:

```
                                     This is legal, using
strcpy(greeting, "Hello");           strcpy from cstring.
```

This function call will set the value of `greeting` to `"Hello"`, using the `strcpy` function from the `cstring` library. The precise function prototype is:

```
char* strcpy(char target[ ], const char source[ ]);
// Precondition: source is a null-terminated string, and target is an array
// that is long enough to hold a copy of source.
// Postcondition: source has been copied to target, and the return value is
// a pointer to the first character of target.
```

Notice that the return value is a pointer to a character, indicated by *char** in the prototype. This pointer points to the first character of the `target` array.

The strcat Function

Another `cstring` library function is `strcat`, which serves to add one string onto the end of another. The "cat" in "strcat" comes from **catenate** (or *concatenate*), meaning to connect in a series. The `strcat` function copies its second argument onto the end of its first argument, as shown here:

```
char greeting[20] = "Hello ";
strcat(greeting, "Good-bye");
```
"Good-bye" is added to the end of what's already in greeting.

After the function call, `greeting` contains `"Hello Good-bye"`. The precise prototype of `strcat` is:

```
char* strcat(char target[ ], const char source[ ]);
// Precondition: target and source are null-terminated strings,
// and target is long enough to catenate source on the end.
// Postcondition: source has been catenated to target, and the
// return value is a pointer to the first character of target.
```

PITFALL

DANGERS OF STRCPY, STRCAT, AND READING STRINGS

Be careful using the `strcpy` and `strcat` functions, and also reading strings. None of these operations check that the string variable actually has sufficient room to hold the copied string. If you try to copy a string with 100 characters into an array of size 50, the result will be the same disaster that occurs whenever you try to access an array beyond its declared bounds. Such behavior usually results in writing to memory locations that are not part of the array, often changing values of other declared variables.

During debugging, if you notice that a variable seems to be changing its value for no apparent reason, then think about the string variables and other arrays that your program uses. Have you accessed a string variable or array beyond its declared size?

The strlen Function

A `cstring` library function named `strlen` returns the number of characters in a null-terminated string, as shown here:

```
size_t strlen(const char s[ ]);
// Precondition: s is a null-terminated string.
// Postcondition: The return value is the number of characters in s,
// up to (but not including) the null character.
```

For example, `strlen("Hello Good-bye")` is 14. The `strlen` function returns 0 for the length of the empty string.

The strcmp Function

You can use the library function `strcmp` to compare two strings. The function is part of `cstring`, with the prototype given here:

```
int strcmp(const char s1[ ], const char s2[ ]);
// Precondition: s1 and s2 are null-terminated strings.
// Postcondition: The return value indicates the following:
//     The return value is 0 -- s1 is equal to s2;
//     The return value < 0 -- s1 is lexicographically before s2;
//     The return value > 0 -- s1 is lexicographically after s2.
```

As you can see, `strcmp` returns zero if its two string arguments are equal to each other. If the strings are not equal, then they are compared in the **lexicographic order**, which is the normal alphabetical order for ordinary words of all lowercase letters. For example, `strcmp("chaos", "order")` will return some negative number, since `"chaos"` is alphabetically before `"order"`. On the other hand, `strcmp("order", "chaos")` will return some positive integer.

comparing strings with strcmp

Strings of all uppercase letters are also handled alphabetically, but strings that mix upper- and lowercase letters have unspecified results. For example, most compilers use a lexicographic order that places all uppercase letters before any lowercase letters, so that `"Order"` (with a capital O) is actually before `"chaos"`, although some compilers might reverse this order.

The complete `cstring` library facility has more than a dozen functions for manipulating null-terminated strings. But the four functions, `strcpy`, `strcat`, `strlen`, and `strcmp`, are enough to start us on our own string project.

The String Class—Specification

We'd like a `string` class that avoids the pitfalls of null-terminated strings. In particular, we want our strings to have a proper *value semantics*, allowing assignment statements and other copying of values without problems.

We'd also like to be able to compare strings using the usual six operators to test for equality (==), and various inequalities (!=, >=, <=, >, <). The inequalities should use the familiar lexicographic ordering that we just talked about. For example, "chaos" < "order" will be true because "chaos" is lexicographically before "order".

The specification for a simple version of a string class is shown in Figure 4.12, including comparison operations using the lexicographic order. The specification has a few new features that we'll discuss starting on page 194.

FIGURE 4.12   Documentation for the Simple String Class

Documentation for a Header File

```
// FILE: mystring.h
// CLASS PROVIDED: string (a simple version of the Standard Library string class)
//
// CONSTRUCTOR for the string class:
//     string(const char str[ ] = "") -- default argument is the empty string.
//         Precondition: str is an ordinary null-terminated string.
//         Postcondition: The string contains the sequence of chars from str.
//
// CONSTANT MEMBER FUNCTIONS for the string class:
//     size_t length( ) const
//         Postcondition: The return value is the number of characters in the string.
//
//     char operator [ ](size_t position) const
//         Precondition: position < length( ).
//         Postcondition: The value returned is the character at the specified position of the
//         string. A string's positions start from 0 at the start of the sequence and go up to
//         length( ) – 1  at the right end.
//
// MODIFICATION MEMBER FUNCTIONS for the string class:
//     void operator +=(const string& addend)
//         Postcondition: addend has been catenated to the end of the string.
//
//     void operator +=(const char addend[ ])
//         Precondition: addend is an ordinary null-terminated string.
//         Postcondition: addend has been catenated to the end of the string.
//
//     void operator +=(char addend)
//         Postcondition: The single character addend has been catenated to the end of the string.
//
//     void reserve(size_t n)
//         Postcondition: All functions will now work efficiently (without allocating new memory)
//         until n characters are in the string.
```

(continued)

(FIGURE 4.12 continued)

```
// NONMEMBER FUNCTIONS for the string class:
//     string operator +(const string& s1, const string& s2)
//        Postcondition: The string returned is the catenation of s1 and s2.
//
//     istream& operator >>(istream& ins, string& target)
//        Postcondition: A string has been read from the istream ins, and the istream ins is then
//        returned by the function. The reading operation skips white space (i.e., blanks, tabs,
//        newlines) at the start of ins. Then the string is read up to the next white space or the end
//        of the file. The white space character that terminates the string has not been read.
//
//     ostream& operator <<(ostream& outs, const string& source)
//        Postcondition: The sequence of characters in source has been written to outs.
//        The return value is the ostream outs.
//
//     istream& getline(istream& ins, string& target, char delimiter = '\n')
//        Postcondition: A string has been read from the istream ins. The reading operation reads
//        all characters (including white space) until the delimiter is read and discarded (but not
//        added to the end of the string). The return value is the istream ins.
//
// VALUE SEMANTICS for the string class:
//     Assignments and the copy constructor may be used with string objects.
//
// COMPARISONS for the string class:
//     The six comparison operators (==, !=, >=, <=, >, and <) are implemented for the string
//     class, using the usual lexicographic order on strings.
//
// DYNAMIC MEMORY usage by the string class:
//     If there is insufficient dynamic memory, the following functions throw bad_alloc:
//     the constructors, reserve, operator +=, operator +, and the assignment operator.
```

www.cs.colorado.edu/~main/chapter4/mystring.h   **WWW**

Constructor for the String Class

The string class has a constructor with one argument, shown in this prototype:

```
string(const char str[ ] = "");
```

The constructor initializes the string to contain the sequence of characters that is in the ordinary null-terminated string called str. For example, if we want to create one of our strings that contains the sequence "Peace", then we may write:

```
char sequence[6] = "Peace";
string greeting(sequence);
```

Without the variable sequence, we could also declare greeting as shown here:

```
string greeting("Peace");
```

Both approaches declare `greeting` to be one of our string objects that contains the sequence of characters `"Peace"`.

The string constructor can also be used with no arguments (that is, as a default constructor). In this case, the `str` argument uses the default argument, which is the empty string. For example, the following declares `jack` to be a `string` object with no characters:

```
string jack;
```

Overloading the operator [ ]

One of the string's member functions is an overloaded operator with this specification:

```
char operator [ ](size_t position) const;
// Precondition: position < length( ).
// Postcondition: The value returned is the character at the specified
// position of the string. Note: A string's positions start from 0 at the start
// of the sequence and go up to length( ) − 1 at the right end.
```

This member function allows you to use the syntax of square brackets to examine the individual characters of a `string` object. For example:

```
string greeting("Peace");
cout << greeting[0]; // Prints the P from greeting.
```

The name of this member function, *operator* [ ], is rather peculiar, but other than that it is just like any other overloaded operator.

Some Further Overloading

The string specification introduces another important feature of classes. Often, a class has several different functions with the same name. In our `string` class, there are three different += member functions with these prototypes:

```
void string::operator +=(const string& addend);
void string::operator +=(const char addend[ ]);
void string::operator +=(char addend);
```

All three of these functions are called "operator +=" and all three can be used in a program. This is an example of overloading a single function name to carry out several related tasks.

When one of the functions is used, the compiler looks at the type of the argument to determine which of the three functions to call. For example:

```
string jack;
string adjective("nimble");

jack += adjective;
jack += '&';
jack += "quick";
```

When the compiler sees the first += in the statement `jack += adjective`, the argument `adjective` is seen to be a `string`, so the compiler will call the member function with this prototype:

```
void string::operator +=(const string& addend);
```

On the other hand, in the statement `jack += '&'`, the argument `'&'` is a character, so the compiler will call the member function with this prototype:

```
void string::operator +=(char addend);
```

Finally, with the third statement `jack += "quick"`, the compiler sees the string constant "quick" as a character array and calls the member function with this prototype:

```
void string::operator +=(const char addend [ ]);
```

At the end of the three statements, the string `jack` contains the phrase "nimble&quick". The three different += functions are easily handled by the compiler. As the implementor of the class, you write all three functions just like any other function.

Other Operations for the String Class

In addition to the features that we have already mentioned, our specification indicates that assignments and the copy constructor may be used with `string` objects (that is, a valid *value semantics*). Since the string uses dynamic memory, you cannot rely on the automatic assignment operator and copy constructor. Instead, you must implement your own assignment operator and copy constructor. There are also functions for reading, writing, and comparing strings.

The String Class—Design

With our design, a programmer can use strings with no worries about how long a string becomes. That programmer does not need to think about how a string is stored or what happens when the length of a string increases.

The plan is to have a private member variable that is a dynamic array to hold the null-terminated string. Each member function ensures that the array has sufficient room, increasing the size of the array whenever necessary. A programmer can also explicitly set the size of the dynamic array that holds the null-terminated string, by calling the `reserve` function. But, similar to the dynamic bag class, explicit resizing is not required—it is just a convenience for efficiency. Let's examine the design considerations that our plan entails. We suggest three private member variables, shown here:

```
class string
{
    ...
private:
    char *characters;
    std::size_t allocated;
    std::size_t current_length;
};
```

The use of the member variables is controlled by the invariant of the class:

Invariant for the String Class

1. The string is stored as a null-terminated string in the dynamic array that `characters` points to.
2. The total length of the dynamic array is stored in the member variable `allocated`.
3. The total number of characters prior to the null character is stored in `current_length`, which is always less than `allocated`.

Notice that there is a requirement for the current length of the string to always be *less than* the amount of memory allocated for the dynamic array. This allows room for the extra null terminator at the end of the sequence.

The String Class—Implementation

We'll leave most of the string implementation up to you, but we will discuss a few points including the constructors, the destructor, and some of the operators.

Before the discussion, we should point out a small extravagance in our three member variables. We could manage without `current_length` by using the library function `strlen`, but keeping track of the length ourselves is likely to be more efficient than continually asking `strlen` to recompute the length.

Constructors. The constructor is responsible for initializing the three private member variables. The initialization occurs by copying a character sequence from an ordinary null-terminated string, as shown in the first part of Figure 4.13. Notice that the constructor makes use of the library function `strcpy` to copy the null-terminated string from the parameter `str` to the dynamic array `characters`. Within your string implementation, you should make use of the library functions whenever they are needed.

The destructor. We did not list a destructor in the documentation of the `string` class, since programmers typically do not activate a destructor directly. But, since the class uses dynamic memory, you must implement a destructor. Your destructor will return the string's dynamic array to the heap.

Comparison operators. The string class has six comparison operators. For example, the prototype for the equality comparison is:

```
bool operator ==(const string& s1, const string& s2);
```

use friend functions when necessary

Each comparison function can be implemented with an appropriate call to the library function `strcmp`. For example, an implementation of == is shown in the second part of Figure 4.13. Notice that our implementation must be a friend since it accesses `characters`, which is a private member variable.

FIGURE 4.13   Implementation of a String Constructor and an Operator

---

Implementations of a Constructor and an Operator

```
string::string(const char str[ ])
// Library facilities used: cstring
{
    current_length = strlen(str);
    allocated = current_length + 1;
    characters = new char[allocated];
    strcpy(characters, str);
}
```
The constructor must provide initial values for the three member variables.

```
bool operator ==(const string& s1, const string& s2)
// Postcondition: The return value is true if s1 is identical to s2.
// Library facilities used: cstring
{
    return (strcmp(s1.characters, s2.characters) == 0);
}
```
The boolean operator == must be a friend of the string class.

The reserve function. Our design includes a member function called reserve, similar to the dynamic bag's reserve function. Here is the precondition/postcondition contract:

```
void reserve(size_t n);
// Postcondition: All functions will now work efficiently (without allocating
// new memory) until n characters are in the string.
```

Programmers who use our string class never need to activate reserve, but they may wish to, for better efficiency.

Our own implementations of other member functions can also activate reserve whenever a larger array is needed. When a member function activates reserve, the activation should occur before any other changes are made to the string. This follows our usual programming guideline of allocating new memory before changing an object. (See "How to Allocate Memory in a Member Function" on page 182.)

The operator >>. Our input operator begins by skipping any *white space* in the input stream. (All the standard >> operators in C++ start by skipping white space.) After skipping the initial white space, our string input operator reads a string—reading up to but not including the next white space character (or until the input stream fails, which might occur from several causes, such as reaching the end of the file). The function isspace from the <cctype> library facility can help. This function has one argument (a character); it returns true if its argument is one of the white space characters. With this in mind, we can skip any initial white space with this loop:

```
while (ins && isspace(ins.peek( )))
    ins.ignore( );
```

The loop also uses three `istream` features:

isspace, eof, peek, ignore

1. In a boolean expression, the name of the `istream` (which is `ins`) acts as a test of whether the input stream is bad. If `ins` results in a true value, then the stream is okay; a false value indicates a bad input stream.
2. The `peek` member function returns the next character to be read (without actually reading it).
3. The `ignore` member function reads and discards the next character.

After skipping the initial white space, your implementation should set the string to the empty string, and then read the input characters one at a time, adding each character to the end of the string. The reading stops when you reach more white space (or the end of file).

Once the target string reaches its current capacity, our approach continues to work correctly, although it is inefficient because `target` is probably resized by the `+=` operator each time that we add another character. Your documentation should warn programmers of this inefficiency so that a programmer can explicitly resize the target before calling the input operator.

An alternative method of reading input is provided by the `getline` function.

Demonstration Program for the String Class

Figure 4.14 shows a short demonstration program for the `string` class. The program asks the user for his or her first and last name, and then prints some messages. A sample dialogue would go something like this:

```
What is your first name? Timothy
My first name is Demo.
What is your last name? Program
That is the same as my last name!
I am happy to meet you, Timothy Program.
```

The program uses several C++ object features such as an automatic conversion from ordinary strings to our new class. We'll discuss these features on page 201, and you can try them out with your own `string` class.

FIGURE 4.14   Demonstration Program for the String Class

A Program

```
// FILE: str_demo.cxx (a small demonstration program showing how the string class is used)
#include <iostream>      // Provides cout and cin
#include <cstdlib>       // Provides EXIT_SUCCESS
#include "mystring.h"    // Provides our new string class
using namespace std;

// PROTOTYPES for functions used by this demonstration program:
void match(const main_savitch_4::string& variety,
           const main_savitch_4::string& mine,
           const main_savitch_4::string& yours);
// The two strings, mine and yours, are compared. If they are the same, then a
//  message is printed saying they are the same; otherwise mine is printed
//  in a message. In either case, the string variety is part of the message.

int main( )
{
    const main_savitch_4::string BLANK(" ");
    main_savitch_4::string me_first("Demo");
    main_savitch_4::me_last("Program");
    main_savitch_4::string you_first, you_last, you;

    cout << "What is your first name? ";
    cin >> you_first;
    match("first name", me_first, you_first);
    cout << "What is your last name? ";
    cin >> you_last;
    match("last name", me_last, you_last);

    you = you_first + BLANK + you_last;
    cout << "I am happy to meet you, " << you << "." << endl;
    return EXIT_SUCCESS;
}

void match(const main_savitch_4::string& variety,
           const main_savitch_4::string& mine,
           const main_savitch_4::string& yours)
{
    if (mine == yours)
        cout << "That is the same as my " << variety << '!' << endl;
    else
        cout << "My " << variety << " is " << mine << '.' << endl;
}
```

Constants of type string may be declared. (See page 201.)

See "Constructor-Generated Conversions" on page 201 to read about the use of an ordinary string for the first argument of the match function.

Overloaded operators, such as the + operator, may be used in complex expressions. (See page 202.)

www.cs.colorado.edu/~main/chapter4/str_demo.cxx   **WWW**

Chaining the Output Operator

Look at the function `match` at the bottom of Figure 4.14. The function has three constant string parameters. Two of the parameters (`mine` and `yours`) are compared using the string's `==` operator. If the strings are equal, then the third parameter (`variety`) is printed as part of a message:

```
cout << "That is the same as my " << variety << '!' << endl;
```

For example, if `variety` is the string `"first name"`, then the output statement prints `"That is the same as my first name!"` The actual output involves a sequence, or "chaining," of four occurrences of the output operator `<<`.

1. The first `<<` prints the string constant: `"That is the same as my "`. This is an ordinary C++ string constant, not a `string` object.
2. The second `<<` prints the `string` object, `variety`, using the `<<` operator of the new `string` class.
3. The third `<<` prints an exclamation point as an ordinary character.
4. The final `<<` prints the end-of-line.

The key point is that the `<<` operator of the `string` class may be chained in combination with other objects to print a series of objects—some `string` objects, some not.

Declaring Constant Objects

The top of the main program in Figure 4.14 declares several strings. The first declaration is:

```
const string BLANK(" ");
```
A single blank is written here between two quote marks.

This declares a *constant* string named `BLANK`, which is initialized as a sequence that contains just a single blank. Using the name `BLANK` in this way makes it easier to read statements that use a blank. The use of the keyword *const* forbids the program from actually changing `BLANK` to a different string. As part of our documentation standard (Appendix J), we use all uppercase letters for the names of declared constants.

Constructor-Generated Conversions

In the main program of Figure 4.14, we have two calls to the `match` function. For example:

```
match("first name", me_first, you_first);
```

Look at the first argument, `"first name"`, which is an ordinary string constant.

But the first parameter of match is not an ordinary string; it is a string object from our new string class:

```
void match(const string& variety, ...
```

How can this be? Isn't this an error because the argument is a different type than the formal parameter? The answer is no, because of a special conversion operation that is automatically applied by C++. Here is how the conversion works: When a type mismatch is detected, the compiler attempts to convert the given value into a value of the needed type. In our example, the compiler tries to convert the string constant "first name" into a string object. One of the conversion mechanisms is to find a constructor for the needed type, with a single parameter. In our example, the compiler uses this constructor:

```
string(const char str[ ]);
```

to convert the ordinary string constant to a string object. The constructed string object is then used for the first argument of match.

Using Overloaded Operations in Expressions

The string class has overloaded binary + to perform string catenation. The way that + is used in the main program of Figure 4.14 may seem unusual:

```
you = you_first + BLANK + you_last;
```

The compiler treats the expression using ordinary associativity rules for the + operator in an expression. As usual for a series of + operations, the leftmost + is applied first, equivalent to this parenthesized expression, where the highlighted part is evaluated first:

```
you = (you_first + BLANK) + you_last;
```

Our String Class versus the C++ Library String Class

The new string class is implemented with a header file (mystring.h) and an implementation file (mystring.cxx) that you write. The class has only a handful of operations—enough for us to write some sample programs. With these sample programs, and programs that you write, you may use mystring.h. However, if you have a newer compiler that provides a Standard Library string class, then you may wish to use the library's class instead of our simple class. The library string class has all of our operations and more.

Self-Test Exercises for Section 4.5

26. Write C++ code that declares a regular C++ null-terminated string that holds up to 20 characters, reads user-input into the string, appends an exclamation point to the end of the string, and prints the result.

27. Suppose that `strlen` was not part of the `cstring` library. Implement `strlen` yourself, using the prototype on page 192.

28. Describe the major motivation for implementing a `string` class instead of using ordinary string variables.

29. What are the three private member variables for our `string` class?

30. Why does the `string` class need a destructor?

31. Which of the `string` member functions are likely to activate `reserve`?

32. Which of the nonmember functions should be friends of the `string` class?

33. What modifications would be needed in the demonstration program of Figure 4.14 if the Standard Library `string` class were used instead of the `mystring` class?

4.6   PROGRAMMING PROJECT: THE POLYNOMIAL

A one-variable **polynomial** is an arithmetic expression of the form:

$$a_k x^k + \ldots + a_2 x^2 + a_1 x^1 + a_0 x^0$$

The highest exponent, k, is called the **degree** of the polynomial, and the constants $a_0, a_1, \ldots$ are the **coefficients**. For example, here is a polynomial with degree three:

$$0.3x^3 + 0.5x^2 + (-0.9)x^1 + 1.0x^0$$

Each individual **term** of a polynomial consists of a real number as a coefficient (such as 0.3), the variable x, and a non-negative integer as an **exponent**. The x^1 term is usually written with just an x rather than x^1; the x^0 term is usually written with just the coefficient (since x^0 is always defined to be 1); and a negative coefficient may also be written with a subtraction sign, so another way to write the same polynomial is:

$$0.3x^3 + 0.5x^2 - 0.9x + 1.0$$

For any specific value of x, a polynomial can be evaluated by plugging the value of x into the expression. For example, the value of the sample polynomial at $x = 2$ is:

$$0.3(2)^3 + 0.5(2)^2 - 0.9(2) + 1.0 = 3.6$$

A typical algebra exercise is to plot the graph of a polynomial for each value of x in a given range. For example, Figure 4.15 plots the value of a polynomial for each x in the range of –2 to +2.

FIGURE 4.15   A Polynomial

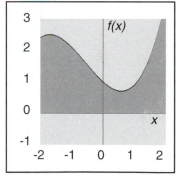

*The graph of the function f(x)
defined by the polynomial*

$$0.3x^3 + 0.5x^2 - 0.9x + 1.0$$

For this project, you should specify, design, and implement a class for polynomials. The coefficients are double numbers, and the exponents are nonnegative integers. The coefficients should be stored in a dynamic array of double numbers, with the exponent for the x^k term stored in location [k] of the array. The maximum index of the array needs to be at least as big as the degree of the polynomial, so that the largest nonzero coefficient can be stored. For the example polynomial $0.3x^3 + 0.5x^2 - 0.9x + 1.0$, the start of the coefficient array contains these numbers:

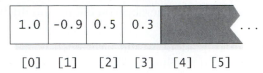

$$\boxed{1.0} \quad \boxed{-0.9} \quad \boxed{0.5} \quad \boxed{0.3} \quad \ldots$$

[0] [1] [2] [3] [4] [5]

In addition, the class should have a member variable to keep track of the current size of the dynamic array and another member variable to keep track of the current degree of the polynomial. (You could manage without the degree variable, but having it around makes certain operations more efficient.)

The rest of this section lists some member functions and nonmember functions that you could provide to the `polynomial` class.

A. Constructors and destructor.

```
polynomial( );                           // Default constructor
polynomial(double a0);                   // Set the x⁰ coefficient only
polynomial(const polynomial& source);    // Copy constructor
~polynomial( );
```

The default constructor creates a polynomial with all zero coefficients. The second constructor creates a polynomial with the specified parameter as the coefficient of the x^0 term, and all other coefficients are zero. For example:

```
polynomial p(4.2); // p has only one nonzero term, 4.2x⁰, which is the
                   // same as the number 4.2 (since x⁰ is defined as
                   // equal to 1).
```

B. Assignment operator.

```
polynomial& operator = (const polynomial& source);
```

This is the usual overloaded assignment operator, with one change: The return type is `polynomial&` rather than *void*. This return type is similar to an ordinary polynomial, but the extra symbol & makes it a reference return type, similar to the return type `ostream&` of our output operators. The complete details of a reference return type are beyond this project. For your implementation, you should know two facts:

1. The function implementation should return the object that activated the assignment. This is accomplished with the keyword *this* (which we also saw on page 179). The syntax is: *return *this;* , which means "return

the object that *this* points to." Since *this* always points to the object that activates the function, the return statement has the effect that we need.

2. Using polynomial& as the return type permits a sequence of chained assignments. For example, if a, b, and c are three polynomials, we can write a = b = c, which copies the value of c to b, and then copies the new value of b to a (chained assignments work from right to left). *chained assignment a = b = c*

Remember to have your implementation check for a possible self-assignment.

C. A second assignment operator.

```
polynomial& operator =(double a0);
```

For a polynomial b, this assignment can be activated in a statement such as b = 4.2. The double number, 4.2, becomes the argument a0 for this assignment. The implementation will use this number as the coefficient for the x^0 term, and all other coefficients are set to zero.

If you read the information on constructor-generated conversions (page 201), then you might notice that this second version of the assignment operator isn't entirely needed. Even without this assignment operator, we could write an assignment b = 4.2; in this case, the compiler would apply the polynomial constructor to the number 4.2 (creating the polynomial $4.2x^0$), and then this polynomial would be assigned to b. However, writing an explicit assignment operator to allow b = 4.2 is generally more efficient because we avoid the overhead of the constructor-generated conversion.

D. Modification member functions.

```
void add_to_coef(double amount, unsigned int k);
void assign_coef(double new_coefficient, unsigned int k);
void clear( );
void reserve(size_t number);
```

The add_to_coef function adds the specified amount to the coefficient of the x^k term. The assign_coef function sets the x^k coefficient to new_coefficient. In both cases, the parameter k is an *unsigned int*, which is the C++ data type that is like an *int*, but may never have a negative value.

The clear function sets all coefficients to zero. The reserve function works like reserve for the bag class, making sure that the underlying array has at least the requested size.

E. Constant member functions.

```
double coefficient(unsigned int k) const;
unsigned int degree( ) const;
unsigned int next_term(unsigned int k) const;
```

The coefficient function returns the coefficient of the x^k term.

The degree function returns the degree of the polynomial. For a polynomial where all coefficients are zero, our degree function returns 0 (although mathematicians usually use −1 for the degree of such a polynomial).

The `next_term` function returns the exponent of the next term with a nonzero coefficient after x^k. For example, if the x^3 term of p is zero and the x^4 term of p is $6x^4$, then `p.next_term(2)` returns the exponent 4 (since 4 is the next exponent after 2 with a nonzero coefficient). If there are no nonzero terms after x^k, then `next_term(k)` should return the constant `UINT_MAX` from the library facility `<climits>`. (This constant is the largest `unsigned int`.)

F. Evaluation functions.

    double eval(*double* x) *const*;
    double operator ( )(*double* x) *const*;

The `eval` function evaluates a polynomial at the given value of x. For example, if p is $0.3x^3 + 0.5x^2 - 0.9x + 1.0$, then `p.eval(2)` is $0.3(2)^3 + 0.5(2)^2 - 0.9(2) + 1.0$, which is 3.6.

The second function also evaluates the polynomial, but it does so with some strange syntax. The name of this second function is "operator ( )," and it has one parameter (the *double* number x). To activate the operator ( ) for a polynomial p, you write the name p followed by the parameter in parentheses. For example: `p(2)`. The implementation of the operator ( ) does the same work as the `eval` function; the two separate implementations just give the programmer a choice of syntax. You can write `p.eval(2)`, or you can write `p(2)` in a program.

G. Arithmetic operators.
You can overload the binary arithmetic operators of addition, subtraction, and multiplication to add, subtract, and multiply two polynomials in the usual manner. (Division is not possible, because it can result in fractional exponents.) For example:

Suppose $q = 2x^3 + 4x^2 + 3x + 1$ and $r = 7x^2 + 6x + 5$.

Then: $q + r = 2x^3 + 11x^2 + 9x + 6$

$$q - r = 2x^3 - 3x^2 - 3x - 4$$

$$q \times r = 14x^5 + 40x^4 + 55x^3 + 45x^2 + 21x + 5$$

The product, $q \times r$, is obtained by multiplying each separate term of q times each separate term of r and adding the results together.

Other operations.
You might consider other member functions, which are described in the Chapter 4 part of the online projects at www.cs.colorado.edu/~main/projects. Among other things, this online description includes operations that first-semester calculus students can connect to their calculus studies of derivatives, integeration, and finding a root of a polynomial.

CHAPTER SUMMARY

- A *pointer* stores an address of another variable. Pointers are most useful when they are used to point to *dynamically allocated memory*, such as a *dynamic array*. The size of a dynamic array does not need to be determined until a program is running. Such behavior, determined at run time, is called *dynamic behavior*. Dynamic behavior is more flexible than decisions that are made at compile time (i.e., *static behavior*).

- The member variables of classes are frequently arrays or dynamic arrays. Ordinary arrays are simple to program, and are often sufficient. Dynamic arrays provide better flexibility since their size can vary according to need. However, dynamic arrays also involve more complex programming since the necessary memory must be allocated correctly, and freed when it is no longer needed.

- In C++, the *new* operator is used to allocate dynamic memory. The *delete* operator is used to free dynamic memory.

- The *new* operator usually indicates failure by throwing a special function exception bad_alloc. Normally the exception halts the program with an error message. You should clearly document which functions use *new*, so that experienced programmers can deal with the exception in their own way.

- Strings and bags are two examples of classes that can be implemented with dynamic arrays.

- Classes that use dynamic memory should always include a copy constructor, an overloaded assignment operator, and a destructor. The copy constructor and assignment operator must each copy an object by making a new copy of the dynamic memory (rather than just copying a pointer). The destructor is responsible for freeing dynamic memory.

Solutions to Self-Test Exercises   ?

1. One use of & indicates a reference parameter. A second use of & provides the address of a variable.

2.
```
cout << *int_ptr << endl;
cout << i << endl;
```

3.
```
int *exercise;
size_t i;

exercise = new int[1000];
for (i = 1; i <= 1000; ++i)
    exercise[i-1] = i;
delete [ ] exercise;
```

4. Dynamic variables are not declared, but are created during the execution of a program.

5. If the new operator is unable to allocate memory because of a full heap, the bad_alloc exception is thrown. If the exception is not caught, an error message is printed and the program halts.

6.
```
100  and  200
200  and  200
300  and  300
400  and  400
```

7. We no longer need the memory that p1 points to.

8. The function changes the value in the location that the pointer points to. The actual argument in the calling program will still point to the same location, but that location will have a new value.

9. A parameter that is a pointer must be a reference parameter if the function makes the pointer point to a new location and you want the actual argument to point to this new location also.

10. When an array is passed as a parameter, changes to the array affect the actual argument. This is because the parameter is treated as a pointer that points to the first component of the array. This is different from a value parameter (where changes to the parameter do not affect the actual argument).

11. *void* make_intarray
    (*double**& array_ptr, size_t& n);

12. The critical point is that the pointer parameter must be a reference parameter, as shown here:
    void exercise(*int**& p, size_t n);

13. Neither average nor compare changes the contents of the array, so the keyword *const* may be used. The fill_array function does change the array's contents, so *const* must not be used.

14. Here is the function:
```
void copyints(
    int target[ ],
    const int source[ ],
    size_t n
)
// Postcondition: source[0] through
// source[n –1] have been copied to
// target[0] through target[n –1].
{
    size_t i;

    for (i = 0; i < n; ++i)
        target[i] = source[i];
}
```

15. The program reads a list of numbers, storing the values in a dynamic array. The program then calculates the average and prints the list of the numbers with each number compared to the average.

16. Typically, the size of a dynamic data structure is not determined until a program is running. But the size of a static data structure is determined at the time of compilation.

17. If the initial capacity is too small, numerous calls to reallocate memory, copy items into new memory, and release old memory will be needed. To avoid this inefficiency, programmers should attempt to make the initial capacity sufficiently large.

18. The initial capacity is DEFAULT_CAPACITY (which is 30). If 31 items are placed in the bag, then the insert function will increase the capacity to 31.

19. In the insert implementation, the call to reserve becomes :
    reserve(int(used*1.1 + 1));
    The extra "+1" causes fractions to round up.

20. The primary responsibility of a destructor is to free the dynamic memory used by an object. See the list on page 175 for situations when the destructor is automatically called.

21. ~sequence();

22. The keyword this can be used inside any member function to provide a pointer to the object that activated the member function.

23. Ordinarily, the assignment operator merely copies member variables from one object to another. But since the new bag uses dynamic memory, the assignment operator must make a copy of the dynamic memory rather than just copying the pointer, which is a member variable. The way to get the assignment operator to do the extra work is by overloading the assignment operator.
    Our implementation of the assignment operator does work correctly for a self-assignment.

24. The copy constructor can be called to construct a new object, just like any other constructor. It is also called when a value parameter is an object or when a function returns an object.

25. If no copy constructor is provided, the automatic copy constructor simply copies all the member variables from the local variable to the return location.

26.
```
char s[21];
cin >> s;
strcat(s, "!");
cout << s;
```

27. Here is the function:
```
size_t strlen(const char s[ ])
{
    size_t len = 0;

    while s[len] != '\0')
        ++len;
    return len;
}
```

28. Ordinary string variables do not support operations such as assignment and comparisons.

29. Private member variables of the `string` class are `characters`, `current_length`, and `allocated` (see the definition on page 196).

30. Any class that uses dynamic memory needs a destructor to return its dynamic memory to the heap.

31. The operators =, +, +=, and >> and the copy constructor.

32. Any nonmember function that accesses a private member variable must be a friend function. In our implementation, the output operator and the six boolean functions were friends, but your implementation might need different friends (depending on where you access private member variables).

33. The header file `"mystring.h"` would be replaced with `<string>`.

PROGRAMMING PROJECTS

For more in-depth projects, please see www.cs.colorado.edu/~main/projects/

1 Add more operations to the `string` class from Section 4.5. Some possibilities are listed here:

(a) A new constructor that has one parameter (a character). The constructor initializes the string to have just this one character.

(b) An insert function that allows you to insert a string at a given position in another string.

(c) A deletion function that allows you to delete a portion of a string.

(d) A replacement function that allows you to replace a single character in a string with a new character.

(e) A replacement function that allows you to replace a portion of a string with another string.

(f) A search function that searches a string for the first occurrence of a specified character.

(g) A search function that counts the number of occurrences of a specified character in a string.

(h) A more complex search function that searches through a string for an occurrence of some smaller string.

2 Revise one of the container classes from Chapter 3, so that it uses a dynamic array. Some choices are: (a) the sequence from Section 3.2; (b) the set (Project 5 on page 141); (c) the sorted sequence (Project 6 on page 141); (d) the bag with receipts (Project 7 on page 141); (e) the keyed bag (Project 8 on page 142).

3 Implement the polynomial class from Section 4.6 using a dynamic array so that there is no maximum degree. If you have studied calculus, then include the optional member functions from the Chapter 4 section of the project page at www.cs.colorado.edu/~main/projects/

4 Write a checkbook balancing program. The program will read in the following for all checks that were not cashed as of the last time you balanced your checkbook: the number of each check, the amount of the check, and whether it has been cashed yet. Use a dynamic array of "checks," where each check is an object of a data type called `check` that you design and implement yourself. In addition to the checks, the program also reads all the deposits as well as the old and new account balance. You may want a second dynamic array to hold the list of deposits. The new account balance should equal the old balance plus all deposits, minus all checks that have been cashed.

The program also prints several items: the total of the checks cashed, the total of the deposits, what the new balance should be, and how much this figure differs from what the bank says the new account balance is. Also print two lists of checks: the checks cashed since the last time you balanced your checkbook, and a list of checks still not cashed.

5 Write a program that uses a dynamic list of strings to keep track of a list of chores that you have to accomplish today. The user of the program can request several services: (1) Add an item to the list of chores; (2) Ask how many chores are in the list; (3) Have the list of chores printed to the screen; (4) Delete an item from the list; (5) Exit the program.

If you know how to read and write strings from a file, then have the program obtain its initial list of chores from a file. When the program ends, it should write all unfinished chores back to this file.

6 A common operation for input strings is to tokenize, or separate, strings with a delimiter of the user's choice. Write a string tokenizer function for a string class (either the one developed in this class, or the STL string). The function takes three parameters: A const string that contains the original input; a const string that designates the delimiter (for example, " "); and a container to store each token as it is found. Write a test program that prints out the tokens.

7 In this project, you will use the STL string class to manipulate an input string. Refer to Appendix H for various string functions that might be useful.

Write an interactive program that prompts a user to input text of up to 10 lines. The input can be terminated with a special symbol(s), such as an asterisk, at the beginning of the final line. Give a second prompt to the user to enter a string of the form sub:replace, where sub is a substring of the original sentence and replace is a replacement string. The program should find each occurrence of sub and prompt the user for confirmation to replace the original text with the replacement string. Print the modified text after completion and prompt the user to exit or to enter another replacement string.

CHAPTER 5

Linked Lists

The simplest way to interrelate or link a set of elements is to line them up in a single list... For, in this case, only a single link is needed for each element to refer to its successor.

NIKLAUS WIRTH
Algorithms + Data Structures = Programs

LEARNING OBJECTIVES

When you complete Chapter 5, you will be able to...

- design, implement, and test functions to manipulate nodes in a linked list, including inserting new nodes, removing nodes, searching for nodes, and processing (such as copying) that involves all the nodes of a list.
- design, implement, and test collection classes that use linked lists to store a collection of elements, generally using a node class to create and manipulate the linked lists.
- analyze problems that can be solved with linked lists and, when appropriate, propose alternatives to simple linked lists, such as doubly linked lists and lists with dummy nodes.

CHAPTER CONTENTS

Linked Lists

We begin this chapter with a concrete discussion of a new data structure, the *linked list*, which is used to implement a list of items arranged in some kind of order. The linked-list structure uses dynamic memory that shrinks and grows as needed, but in a different manner than dynamic arrays. The discussion of linked lists includes the necessary class definition in C++, together with fundamental functions to manipulate linked lists.

Once you understand the fundamentals, linked lists can be used as part of your container classes, similar to the way that arrays have been used in previous classes. For example, linked lists can be used to reimplement the bag and sequence classes from Chapter 3.

By the end of the chapter you will understand linked lists well enough to use them in various programming projects (such as the revised bag and sequence classes), and in the projects of future chapters. You will also know the advantages and drawbacks of using linked lists versus dynamic arrays for these projects.

linked lists are used to implement a list of items arranged in some kind of order

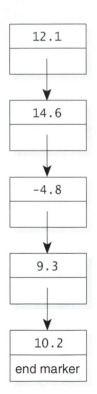

FIGURE 5.1
Linked List
Made of Nodes
Connected with
Links

5.1 A FUNDAMENTAL NODE CLASS FOR LINKED LISTS

A **linked list** is a sequence of items arranged one after another, with each item connected to the next by a link. A common programming technique is to place each item together with the link to the next item, resulting in a simple component called a **node**. A node is represented pictorially as a box with the item written inside the box and the link drawn as an arrow pointing out of the box.

Several typical nodes are drawn in Figure 5.1. For example, the topmost node has the number 12.1 as its data. Most of the nodes in the figure also have an arrow pointing out of the node. These arrows, or *links*, are used to connect one node to another. The links are represented as arrows because they do more than simply connect two nodes. The links also place the nodes in a sequence. In Figure 5.1, the five nodes form a sequence from top to bottom. The first node is linked to the second node, the second node is linked to the third node, and so on until we reach the last node. We must do something special when we reach the last node, since the last node is not linked to another node. In this special case, we replace the link in this node with a note saying "end marker."

Declaring a Class for Nodes

As you might guess from our pictures, the links between nodes are implemented using pointers. But pointers to *what*? Remember that we cannot simply declare a pointer; each pointer must be declared as a pointer to a particular type of data. For example, we have pointers to integers, pointers to characters, pointers to throttles. In the case of a linked list, each link is a pointer to a *node*.

But what exactly is a *node*? To answer this question, look once more at our pictures. Each node is a combination of two things: a piece of data (a double number in our example) and a link to the next node. In C++, we can define a new class for a node that contains these as two member variables shown here:

```
class node
{
...
private:
    double data_field;
    node *link_field;
};
```

We'll look at the member functions shortly, but first let's examine some other issues.

Using a Typedef Statement with Linked-List Nodes

Until now we have considered only nodes where the data consists of a double number. But, in general, other kinds of data are just as useful. Linked lists of integers, or characters, or even strings, are all useful. In other words, the node class depends on an underlying data type—the type of data in each node. To allow for easy changing of the item type, we generally use a typedef statement to define the name value_type to be a synonym for the type of data in each node. The value_type is then used within the node class, as shown here:

```
class node
{
public:
    typedef double value_type ;
    ...
private:
    value_type data_field;
    node *link_field;
};
```

This is the same technique that we've used before to define the type of elements in a bag or sequence. If we need to change the type of items in the nodes, then we will change only the value_type in the typedef statement. Whenever a program needs to refer to the item type, we can use the expression node::value_type.

Head Pointers, Tail Pointers

Usually, programs do not actually declare node variables. Instead, when we build and manipulate a linked list, the list is accessed through one or more *pointers* to nodes. The most common access to a linked list is through the list's first node, which is called the **head** of the list. A pointer to the first node is called the **head pointer**. Sometimes we maintain a pointer to the last node in a linked list. The last node is the **tail** of the list, and a pointer to the last node is the **tail pointer**. We could also maintain pointers to other nodes in a linked list.

Each pointer to a node must be declared as a pointer variable. For example, if we are maintaining a linked list with a head and tail pointer, then we would declare two pointer variables:

```
node *head_ptr;
node *tail_ptr;
```

The program could now proceed to create a linked list, always keeping head_ptr pointing to the first node and tail_ptr pointing to the last node, as shown in Figure 5.2.

Building and Manipulating Linked Lists

Whenever a program builds and manipulates a linked list, the access to the nodes in the list is through one or more pointers to nodes. Typically, a program includes a pointer to the first node (the **head pointer**) and a pointer to the last node (the **tail pointer**).

FIGURE 5.2   Node Class Declaration in a Program with a Linked List

Class Declaration for a Node

```
class node
{
public:
    typedef double value_type;
    ...
private:
    value_type data_field;
    node *link_field;
};
```

Declarations of Two Pointers to Nodes

```
node *head_ptr;
node *tail_ptr;
```

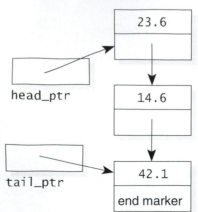

A computation might create a small linked list with three nodes, as shown here. The head_ptr and tail_ptr variables provide access to two nodes inside the list.

The Null Pointer

Figure 5.3 illustrates a linked list with a head pointer and one new feature. Look at the link of the final node. Instead of a pointer, we have written the word NULL. The word NULL indicates the **null pointer**, which is a special C++ constant. You can use the null pointer for any pointer value that has no place to point. There are two common situations where the null pointer is used:

- Use the null pointer for the link field of the final node of a linked list.
- When a linked list does not yet have any nodes, use the null pointer for the value of the head pointer and tail pointer. Such a list is called the **empty list**.

In a program, the null pointer may be written as NULL, which is defined in the Standard Library facility <cstdlib>. (Though surprisingly, it's not part of the std namespace. You can simply write NULL without std::.)

The null pointer can be assigned to a pointer variable with an ordinary assignment statement. For example:

```
node *head_ptr;
head_ptr = NULL; // Uses the constant NULL from cstdlib
```

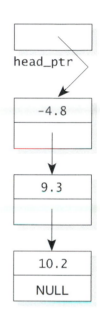

FIGURE 5.3
Linked List with the Null Pointer at the Final Link

The Null Pointer

The NULL pointer is a special C++ pointer value that can be used for any pointer that does not point anywhere. It is defined as NULL in <cstdlib>. NULL is not part of the std namespace, so you write NULL without std::.

The Meaning of a Null Head Pointer or Tail Pointer

Keep in mind that the head pointer and tail pointer of a linked list may be NULL, which indicates that the list is empty (has no nodes). In fact, this is the way that most linked lists start out. Any functions that you write to manipulate linked lists *must* be able to handle a null head pointer and tail pointer.

The Node Constructor

The node constructor has parameters to initialize both the data and link fields, as shown in this prototype:

```
node(
    const value_type& init_data = value_type( ),
    const node* init_link = NULL
);
```

The default value for the data is listed as `init_data = value_type( )`. This notation means "the parameter named `init_data` has a default argument that is created by the `value_type` default constructor." This syntax was not allowed in older versions of C++, since the built-in types (such as *int* and *double*) did not have default constructors. But the new ANSI/ISO C++ Standard does permit the notation with the built-in types. Each of the built-in types has a default constructor that returns zero (for numbers) or false (for the *bool* type).

In our case, `value_type` is defined as *double*, so the `init_data` parameter will be zero if a default argument is needed. And the `init_link` parameter will be NULL if a default argument is needed.

The constructor's implementation merely copies the two parameters (`init_data` and `init_link`) to the node's two member variables (`data_field` and `link_field`).

As an example, consider three activations of the *new* operator for three variables (p, q, and r) that are pointers to nodes. The three activations of the *new* operator will call the constructor in three different ways, as shown next.

```
// With no arguments, we will use both default values, so p's data will be
// set to zero and p's link will be set to NULL:
p = new node;
// We can explicitly set the data part of q's node to 4.9, and use the
// default argument of NULL for q's link field, like this:
q = new node(4.9);
// We can create a new node for r to point to with data of 1.6 and a
// link field that points to the same node as p:
r = new node(1.6, p);
```

After these three assignments, the three nodes are set up like this:

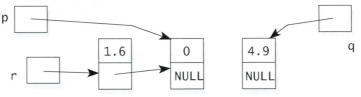

The Node Member Functions

The node has five public member functions for setting and retrieving the data and link fields. The prototypes and inline implementations are shown in the complete node definition in Figure 5.4. The first two functions, `set_data` and `set_link`, simply store a new value in the data or link field of the node. The `data` member function returns a copy of the node's current data field. And when you look at the `link` function, you might think that you have double vision because the `link` function appears in two slightly different forms. We'll explain that duplication in a moment. But first, let's examine a new notation for activating member functions.

FIGURE 5.4 The Complete Node Class Definition

A Class Definition

```
class node
{
public:
    // TYPEDEF
    typedef double value_type;

    // CONSTRUCTOR
    node(
        const value_type& init_data = value_type( ),
        node* init_link = NULL
    )
    { data_field = init_data; link_field = init_link; }

    // Member functions to set the data and link fields:
    void set_data(const value_type& new_data) { data_field = new_data; }
    void set_link(node* new_link)             { link_field = new_link; }

    // Constant member function to retrieve the current data:
    value_type data( ) const { return data_field; }

    // Two slightly different member functions to retreive the current link:
    const node* link( ) const { return link_field; }
    node* link( )             { return link_field; }
private:
    value_type data_field;
    node* link_field;
};
```

www.cs.colorado.edu/~main/chapter5/node1.h   **WWW**

The Member Selection Operator

Suppose that a program has built the linked list shown in the margin. Now, head_ptr is a pointer to a node, so here is a small quiz: Using the dereferencing asterisk, what is the data type of *head_ptr? Remember that *head_ptr means "the thing that head_ptr points to." Looking at the picture you can see that the data type of *head_ptr is a node.

As with any object, you can access the public member functions of *head_ptr. For example, the following writes the data (12.1) from the head node:

```
cout << (*head_ptr).data( );
```

The expression (*head_ptr).data( ) means "activate the data member function of the node pointed to by head_ptr." The parentheses are necessary around the first part of the expression, (*head_ptr), because the operation of accessing a member (such as the data member function) has higher precedence than the dereferencing asterisk. Without the parentheses, the

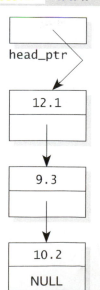

meaning of `*head_ptr.data( )` will cause a syntax error, trying to activate `head_ptr.data( )` before dereferencing.

Because of the parentheses problem, C++ offers an alternative way to select a member of a class, shown here:

The `->` Operator

If `p` is a pointer to a class, and `m` is a member of the class, then `p->m` means the same as `(*p).m`.

Example: `head_ptr->data( )` is the syntax for activating the `data` function of the node pointed to by `head_ptr`.

---

the -> operator

The symbol "`->`" is considered a single operator (rather than two separate symbols "`-`" and "`>`"). It is called the **member selection operator** or **component selection operator**. Visually, the `p->m` operator reminds you of an arrow, leading from the pointer p to the object that contains the member m. Using the member selection operator, we can print the data from the first node of the list in Figure 5.3, as shown here: `cout << head_ptr->data( );`.

CLARIFYING THE CONST KEYWORD

Part 6: The Const Keyword with a Pointer to a Node, and the Need for Two Versions of Some Member Functions

Consider this pointer to a node:

```
node *p;
```

After this declaration, we can allocate a node for p to point to (`p = new node;`) and then activate any of the member functions (such as `p->set_data( )` or `p->data( )`).

1. DECLARED CONSTANTS: PAGE 12
2. CONSTANT MEMBER FUNCTIONS: PAGE 38
3. CONST REFERENCE PARAMETERS: PAGE 72
4. STATIC MEMBER CONSTANTS: PAGE 103
5. CONST PARAMETERS THAT ARE POINTERS OR ARRAYS: PAGE 162
6. THE CONST KEYWORD WITH A POINTER TO A NODE, AND THE NEED FOR TWO VERSIONS OF SOME MEMBER FUNCTIONS
7. CONST ITERATORS: PAGE 308

In constrast, consider the situation in Chapter 4 (page 161), where we saw the use of the keyword *const* with a pointer. A simple example using the *const* keyword is a parameter declared this way:

```
const node *c;
```

This parameter is a pointer to a node. The *const* keyword means that the pointer c cannot be used to change the node. To be precise, for the declaration `const node *c` :

1. You might think that the *const* keyword prevents c from moving around and pointing to different nodes. That is wrong. The pointer c can move and point to many different nodes, but we are forbidden from using c to change any of those nodes that c points to. (If you should wish to create a pointer that can be set once during its definition and never changed to point to a new object, then put the word const after the *. For example: `node *const c = &first;`.)

2. Because of the *const* keyword, you might think that the node which c points to can never be changed by any means. That's not quite right either. Why not? The reason is that we might have another ordinary pointer that points to the same node which c points to. In that case, the node could be changed by accessing it through the ordinary pointer. The *const* keyword only prevents changing the node by accessing it through c.

3. To enforce the *const* rule, the C++ compiler permits a pointer such as c to activate only constant member functions. For example, with our declaration of c as `const node *c` , we can activate `c->data( )`, but `c->set_data( )` is forbidden.

The third rule is a good one, but for applications such as linked lists, the rule of the C++ compiler doesn't go quite far enough. We recommend an additional programming tip that increases reliability:

PROGRAMMING TIP

A RULE FOR A NODE'S CONSTANT MEMBER FUNCTIONS

A node's constant member functions should never provide a result that could later be used to change any part of the linked list. This increases reliability because we can clearly see which functions have the possibility of causing an alteration to the underlying data structure.

Our programming tip has a surprising effect: We must sometimes write two similar versions of the same member function. For example, the purpose of the link member function is to obtain a copy of a node's link field. At first glance, this sounds like a constant member function, since retrieving a member variable does not change an object. We might write this:

providing a const version and a non-const version of a function

```
node* link( ) const { return link_field; }
```

This implementation does compile, but it violates our programming tip about constant member functions. For example, suppose we have this list set up:

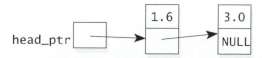

WARNING! This link implementation has a bug!

Using the constant member function, link, we can execute two statements that change the data in one of the nodes:

```
node *second = head_ptr->link( );
```

After this first statement, we have the following situation:

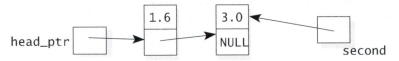

The variable second is just an ordinary pointer to a node. It is not a pointer to a constant node, so we can activate any of its member functions, such as:

```
second->set_data(9.2);
```

After this statement, the data in the second node is now 9.2:

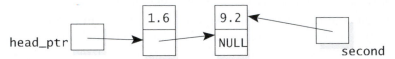

This is a bad situation because the node's constant member functions should never provide a result that we can later use to change any part of the linked list. With this in mind, it makes sense to implement link as a non-constant member function. Making the function non-constant provides better accuracy about how the function's results might be used. So, we will implement link as a non-constant member function, like this:

```
node* link( ) { return link_field; }
```

Unfortunately, this solution has another problem. Suppose that c is a parameter *const* node *c* . We are allowed to activate only the constant member functions. So, with the non-constant link implementation, we could never activate c->link( ). The final solution is to provide a second version of the link member function, implemented this way:

```
const node* link( ) const { return link_field; }
```

This second version is a constant member function, so c->link( ) can be used, even if c is declared with the *const* keyword. Even though the implementations of both functions are the same (they both return the link_field), the compiler converts the link_field to the type *const* node* for the const version of the function. Therefore, the return value from the const version of the function cannot later be used to change any part of the linked list.

When both a const and a non-const version of a function are present, the compiler automatically chooses the correct version, depending on whether the function was activated by a constant node (such as `const node *c`) or by an ordinary node.

When to Provide Both Const and Non-Const Versions of a Member Function

When the return value of a member function is a pointer to a node, you should generally have two versions: A const version that returns a `const node*`, and an ordinary version that returns an ordinary pointer to a node.

PITFALL

DEREFERENCING THE NULL POINTER

One of the most common pointer errors is writing the expression *p or p-> when the value of the pointer p is the null pointer. This must always be avoided because the null pointer does not point to anything. Therefore, when p is the null pointer, *p (which means "the thing that p points to") is meaningless. In this case, p-> is also meaningless. Because the asterisk in *p is called the *dereferencing operator*, we can state this rule: *Never dereference the null pointer*.

Accidental dereferencing of the null pointer is sometimes a hard error to track down. The error does not cause a syntax error. Instead, when the program is running, there will be an attempt to interpret the null pointer as if it were a valid address. Sometimes this causes an immediate run-time error with a message such as "Address protection violation" or "Bus error, core dumped." But on other machines, the null address might be a valid address, causing your program to read or write an unintended memory location. Often this memory location is part of the machine's operating system, resulting in part of the operating system being corrupted. At some later point, perhaps after your program has completed, the corrupted operating system can cause an error. Fortunately, restarting your machine usually writes a fresh copy of the operating system into memory—but even so, *never dereference the null pointer*!

Self-Test Exercises for Section 5.1

1. Write the class definition needed for a node in a linked list. Use the name `value_type` for the type of the data.

2. What is the meaning of the C++ constant NULL? What additional code is needed in a program in order to use NULL?

3. Describe two common uses for the null pointer.

4. What value does the default constructor of `value_type` give if the `value_type` is one of the built-in number or bool types?

5. What is the data type of `head_ptr` in Figure 5.3 on page 215? What is the data type of `*head_ptr`? What is the data type of `head_ptr->data( )`?

6. Suppose that `head_ptr` points to the first node of a non-empty linked list. Write code to print the word "zero" if the data in the first node is 0.

7. Consider this statement: `cout << (*head_ptr).data( );` What would happen if the parentheses around `head_ptr` were omitted? Write the alternative syntax to activate the `data( )` class member.

8. Suppose that `b_ptr` is a pointer to a bag (from Chapter 3). One of the bag's member functions is `size`, which returns the number of elements in a bag. Write a statement that prints the number of elements in the bag pointed to by `b_ptr`. Use the member selection operator.

9. Describe a problem that can occur if you dereference the null pointer.

10. Why is this `link` implementation wrong?
    ```
    node* link( ) const { return link_field; }
    ```

11. What is the solution for the problem in the previous exercise?

12. Why is it okay to have just a single const version of the node's `data` member function (without a second non-const version)?

5.2   A LINKED-LIST TOOLKIT

We're now in a position to design container classes that use linked lists to store their items. The member functions of the container class will put things into the linked list and take them out. This use of a linked list is similar to our previous use of an array in a container class. However, you may find that storing and retrieving items from a linked list is more work than using an array because we don't have the handy indexing mechanism (such as `data[i]`) to read or write elements. Instead, the class requires extra functions just to build and manipulate the lists—parts that are not central to the container's main objectives.

a collection of linked-list functions

In fact, many container classes might need these same extra functions, which suggests that we write a collection of linked-list functions once and for all, allowing any programmer to use the functions in the implementation of a container class. This is what we will do, creating a small toolkit of fundamental linked-list functions. The primary purpose of the toolkit is to allow a container class to store elements in a linked list with a simplicity and clarity that is similar to using an array. In addition, having the functions written and thoroughly tested once will allow us to use the functions to implement many different container classes with high confidence in their reliability.

The toolkit comes in two parts: a header file and an implementation file. The contents of the two files are discussed in this section.

Linked-List Toolkit—Header File

For functions that manipulate linked lists of double numbers, the header file contains the node class definition and prototypes for the functions. For example, one function prototype is as shown here:

```
size_t list_length(const node* head_ptr);
```

The `list_length` function computes the number of nodes in a linked list. The parameter, `head_ptr`, is a pointer to the first node of the linked list. An empty list is indicated by setting `head_ptr` to the null pointer. Since we are not going to change the list, this parameter is a `const node*`.

The functions, including `list_length`, are implemented in a separate implementation file. Each of the functions has one or more parameters that are pointers to nodes in a linked list.

Functions That Manipulate Linked Lists

A function that manipulates linked lists has one or more parameters that are pointers to nodes in the list. If the function does not plan to change the list, then the parameter should be a `const node*`.

The functions should generally be capable of handling an empty list (which is indicated by a head pointer that is null). In fact, the ability to handle an empty list is one of the reasons why list manipulation functions are generally not node member functions (since each node member function must be activated by a specific node, and the empty list has no nodes!).

Computing the Length of a Linked List

Our first toolkit function computes the **length of a linked list**, which is simply the number of nodes. Here is the prototype:

```
size_t list_length(const node* head_ptr);
// Precondition: head_ptr is the head pointer of a linked list.
// Postcondition: The value returned is the number of nodes in
// the linked list.
```

list_length

The parameter, `head_ptr`, is a pointer to a head node of a list. If the list is not empty, then `head_ptr` points to the first node of the list. If the list is empty, then head_ptr is the null pointer (and the function returns zero, since there are no nodes).

Our implementation uses a pointer variable to step through the list, counting the nodes one at a time. Here are the three steps of the pseudocode, using a pointer variable named cursor to step through the nodes of the list one at a time. (We often use the name cursor for such a pointer, since "cursor" means a "pointer that runs through a structure.")

1. Initialize a variable named answer to zero (this variable will keep track of how many nodes we have seen so far).

2. Make cursor point to each node of the list, starting at the head node. Each time cursor points to a new node, add one to answer.

3. *return* answer.

Both cursor and answer are local variables in the function.

The first step initializes answer to zero, because we have not yet seen any nodes.

how to traverse all the nodes of a linked list

The implementation of Step 2 is a for-loop, following a pattern that you should use whenever *all of the nodes of a linked list must be traversed*. The general pattern looks like this:

```
for (cursor = head_ptr; cursor != NULL; cursor = cursor->link( ))
{                     Inside the body of the loop, you may
     ...              carry out whatever computation is
}                     needed for a node in the list.
```

In our function, the computation inside the loop is simple because we are just counting the nodes. Therefore, in our body we will just add one to answer, as shown in this code:

```
for (cursor = head_ptr; cursor != NULL; cursor = cursor->link( ))
     ++answer;
```

Let's examine the loop on an example. Suppose that the linked list has three nodes containing the numbers 10, 20, and 30. After the loop initializes (with cursor = head_ptr), we have the situation shown next.

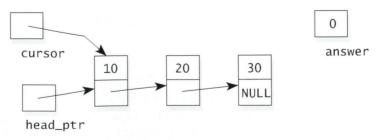

Notice that cursor points to the same node that head_ptr is pointing to.

Since cursor is not NULL, we enter the body of the loop. Each iteration increments answer and then executes cursor = cursor->link( ). The effect of cursor = cursor->link( ) is to copy the link field of the first node into cursor itself, so that cursor ends up pointing to the second node. In general, the statement cursor = cursor->link( ) moves cursor to the next node. So, at the completion of the loop's first iteration, the situation is this:

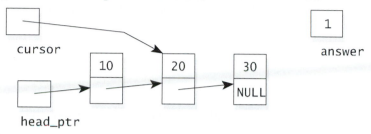

The loop continues. After the second iteration, answer is 2, and cursor points to the third node of the list, as shown here:

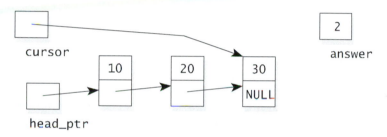

Each time we complete an iteration of the loop, cursor points to some location in the list, and answer is the number of nodes *before* this location. In our example, we are about to enter the loop's body for the third and last time. During the last iteration, answer is incremented to 3, and cursor becomes NULL, as shown here:

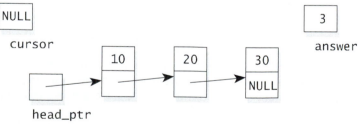

The pointer variable cursor has become NULL because the loop control statement cursor = cursor->link( ) copied the link field of the third node into cursor. Since this link is NULL, the value in cursor is now NULL. At this point, the loop's control test cursor != NULL is false. The loop ends, and the function returns the answer 3.

FIGURE 5.5   A Function to Compute the Length of a Linked List

A Function Implementation

```
size_t list_length(const node* head_ptr)
// Precondition: head_ptr is the head pointer of a linked list.
// Postcondition: The value returned is the number of nodes in the linked list.
// Library facilities used: cstdlib
{
    const node *cursor;
    size_t answer;

    answer = 0;
    for (cursor = head_ptr; cursor != NULL; cursor = cursor->link( ))
        ++answer;
    return answer;
}
```

Step 2 of the pseudocode

www.cs.colorado.edu/~main/chapter5/node1.cxx   **WWW**

The complete implementation of the `list_length` function is shown in Figure 5.5. Notice that the local variable, `cursor`, is declared using the const keyword: `const node *cursor;`. This is required because the head_ptr param-eter is const, so that if `cursor` was not const, then the compiler would not permit the assignment `cursor = head_ptr`. In general: If a pointer is declared using the *const* keyword, then that pointer can be assigned only to another pointer that is also declared with the *const* keyword.

⬆ PROGRAMMING TIP

HOW TO TRAVERSE A LINKED LIST

You should learn the important pattern for traversing a linked list, as used in the `list_length` function (Figure 5.5). The same pattern can be used whenever you need to step through the nodes of a linked list one at a time.

The first part of the pattern concerns moving from one node to another. Whenever we have a pointer that points to some node, and we want the pointer to point to the next node, we must use the link of the node. Here is the reasoning that we follow:

1. Suppose `cursor` points to some node;
2. Then `cursor->link( )` points to the next node (if there is one), as shown here:

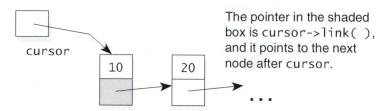

The pointer in the shaded box is cursor->link( ), and it points to the next node after cursor.

3. To move cursor to the next node, we use the assignment statement:

cursor = cursor->link( );

If there is no next node, then cursor->link( ) will be NULL, and therefore our assignment statement will set cursor to NULL.

The key is to know that the assignment statement cursor = cursor->link( ) moves cursor so that it points to the next node. If there is no next node, then the assignment statement sets cursor to NULL.

The second part of the pattern shows how to traverse all of the nodes of a linked list, starting at the head node. The pattern of the loop looks like this:

```
for (cursor = head_ptr; cursor != NULL; cursor = cursor->link( ))
{
    . . .       Inside the body of the loop, you may
                carry out whatever computation is
}               needed for a node in the list.
```

You'll find yourself using this pattern continually in functions that manipulate linked lists.

PITFALL 🔱

FORGETTING TO TEST THE EMPTY LIST

Functions that manipulate linked lists should always be tested to ensure that they have the right behavior for the empty list. For example, when head_ptr is NULL (indicating the empty list), our list_length function should return 0.

Parameters for Linked Lists

When a function manipulates a linked list, one of the parameters must be a pointer to a node in the list—often the head pointer, but sometimes another pointer is used. These pointers to nodes are generally used as parameters in just three ways, requiring a bit of discussion before we can proceed with our toolkit. (And you thought you *already* knew everything there is to know about parameters!)

how to use a node pointer as a parameter

Parameters that are pointers with the const keyword. We have already examined this case in some detail. For example, the list_length function has such a parameter:

```
size_t list_length(const node* head_ptr);
```

The function uses the head pointer to access the list's nodes, but the function does not change any part of the list. In general, this is the situation when you should use *const* node*: *A pointer to a constant node should be used when the function needs access to the linked list and the function will not make any changes to any of the list's nodes.*

Value parameters that are pointers to a node. The second sort of node pointer parameter is a value parameter without the *const* keyword. For example, one of the toolkit's functions will add a new node after a specified node in the list. The function has this prototype with a node*:

```
void list_insert(node* p, const node::value_type& entry)
// Precondition: previous_ptr points to a node in a linked list.
// Postcondition: A new node containing the given entry has been added
// after the node that p points to.
```

The function uses the pointer p to access the list's nodes, and a new node is added after the p node. The pointer p will not change; it will stay pointing at the same node. But that node's link field will change and a new node will be added to the list. In general, this is the situation when you should use a value parameter: *A node pointer should be a value parameter when the function needs access to the linked list, and the function might change the linked list, but the function does not need to make the pointer point to a new node.*

Reference parameters that are pointers to a node. Sometimes a function must make a pointer point to a new node. For example, one of the toolkit functions will adds a new node at the front of a linked list, with this prototype and precondition/postcondition contract:

```
void list_head_insert
(node*& head_ptr, const node::value_type& entry);
// Precondition: head_ptr is the head pointer of a linked list.
// Postcondition: A new node containing the given entry has been added at
// the head of the list; head_ptr now points to the head of the new, longer
// linked list.
```

The head_ptr is a reference parameter, since the function creates a new head node and makes the head pointer point to this new node. *A node pointer should be a reference parameter when the function needs access to the linked list and the function makes the pointer point to a new node. This change to the pointer will make the actual argument point to a new node.*

Parameters for Linked Lists

When a function needs access to a linked list, use a node*
parameter and follow these guidelines:

1. Use a pointer to a constant node, *const* node*, when
   the function needs access to the linked list and the function will not make any changes to any of the list's nodes.

2. Use a value parameter, node*, when the function may
   change the list in some way, but it does not need to
   make the pointer point to a new node.

3. Use a reference parameter, node*&, when the function
   needs access to the linked list and the function may
   make the pointer point to a new node.

Inserting a New Node at the Head of a Linked List

The next function in our toolkit is the `list_head_insert` function that we
mentioned earlier, with a reference parameter that is a pointer. The function
adds a new node at the head of a linked list. This is the easiest place to add a
new node. The function prototype with complete documentation is given here:

```
void list_head_insert
(node*& head_ptr, const node::value_type& entry);
// Precondition: head_ptr is the head pointer of a linked list.
// Postcondition: A new node containing the given entry has been added at
// the head of the list; head_ptr now points to the head of the new, longer
// linked list.
// NOTE: If there is insufficient dynamic memory for a new
// node, then bad_alloc is thrown.
```

list_head_insert

As we saw a moment ago, the head pointer is a reference parameter, since the
function makes the head pointer point to a new node. Also, the documentation
indicates what happens if there is insufficient dynamic memory for a new node.

Inserting a new node at the head of the linked list requires just a single statement:

```
head_ptr = new node(entry, head_ptr);
```

Let's step through the execution of this statement to see how the new node is
added at the front of the list. For the example, suppose that `head_ptr` points to
the short list shown here, and that the new `entry` is the number 5:

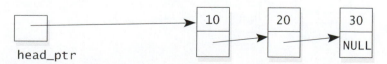

When the *new* operator is called, it activates the constructor and a new node is created with the entry as the data and with the link pointing to the same node that `head_ptr` points to. Here's what the picture looks like, with the link of the new node shaded (and the new `entry` equal to 5):

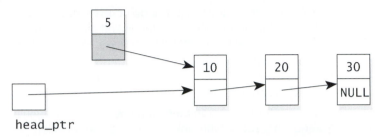

The *new* operator returns a pointer to the newly created node, and in the statement we wrote, `head_ptr = new node(entry, head_ptr)`. You can read this statement as saying "make `head_ptr` point to the newly created node." Therefore, we end up with this situation:

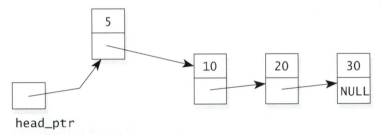

The technique works correctly even if we start with an empty list (in which the `head_ptr` is null). In this case, the *new* operator correctly creates the first node of the list. To see this, suppose we start with a null `head_ptr` and execute the statement with `entry` equal to 5. The constructor creates a new node with 5 as the data and with `head_ptr` as the link. Since `head_ptr` is null, the new node looks like this (with the link of the new node shaded):

After the constructor returns, `head_ptr` is assigned to refer to the new node, so the final situation looks like this:

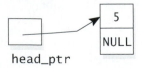

FIGURE 5.6   A Function to Insert at the Head of a Linked List

A Function Implementation

```
void list_head_insert(node*& head_ptr, const node::value_type& entry)
// Precondition: head_ptr is the head pointer of a linked list.
// Postcondition: A new node containing the given entry has been added at the head of the linked
// list; head_ptr now points to the head of the new, longer linked list. NOTE: If there is insufficient
// dynamic memory for a new node, then bad_alloc is thrown before changing the list.
{
    head_ptr = new node(entry, head_ptr);
}
```

www.cs.colorado.edu/~main/chapter5/node1.cxx   **WWW**

As you can see, the statement `head_ptr = new node(entry, head_ptr)` has correctly added the first node to a list. If we are maintaining a pointer to the tail node, then we would also set the tail to point to this one node.

> **Adding a New Node at the Head of a Linked List**
>
> Suppose that `head_ptr` is the head pointer of a linked list. Then this statement adds a new node at the front of the list with the specified new entry:
>
>   head_ptr = new node(entry, head_ptr);
>
> This statement works correctly even if we start with an empty list (in which case the head pointer is null).

The complete implementation of `list_head_insert` is shown in Figure 5.6.

Inserting a New Node That Is Not at the Head

New nodes are not always inserted at the head of a linked list. They may be inserted in the middle or at the tail of a list. For example, suppose you want to insert the number 42 after the 20 in this list:

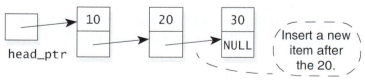

After the insertion, the new, longer list has these four nodes:

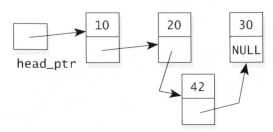

Whenever an insertion is not at the head, the insertion process requires a pointer to the node that is just *before* the intended location of the new node. In our example, we would require a pointer to the node that contains 20, since we want to insert the new node after this node. We use the name `previous_ptr` for the pointer to the node that is just before the location of the new node. So to insert an item after the 20, we would first have to set up `previous_ptr` as shown here:

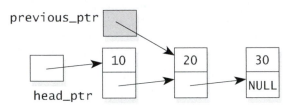

Once a program has calculated `previous_ptr`, the insertion can proceed. Our third toolkit function carries out the insertion, as indicated by this prototype:

list_insert

```
void list_insert
(node* previous_ptr, const node::value_type& entry);
// Precondition: previous_ptr points to a node in a linked list.
// Postcondition: A new node containing the given entry
//   has been added after the node that previous_ptr points to.
// NOTE: If there is insufficient dynamic memory for a new
//   node, then bad_alloc is thrown before changing the list.
```

Notice that `previous_ptr` is a value parameter that is a pointer to a node. This allows us to change the list (by inserting a new node), but we will not make `previous_ptr` point to a new node.

The `list_insert` could be implemented with a single line, similar to `list_head_insert`. But the implementation is more clear if we break it into four steps:

1. Allocate a new node pointed to by a local variable called `insert_ptr`.
2. Place the new entry in the `data` field of the new node.
3. Make the `link_field` of the new node point to the node after the new node's location (or `NULL` if there are no nodes after the new location).
4. Make `previous_ptr->link_field` point to the new node that we just created.

Let's follow the four steps for the example of inserting 42 after the second node of a small list. After the first two steps, the new node has been created, containing the number 42, as shown here:

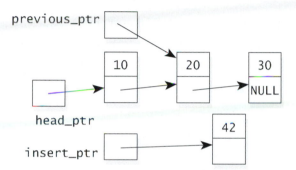

We have drawn the head pointer in this picture, though the function does not actually use the head pointer. Steps 3 and 4 make use of only `previous_ptr`. For example, Step 3 sets the link field of the new node to point to the node that's after the new node's location. What is the node after the new location? It is not `previous_ptr`, since `previous_ptr` points to the node *before* the new location. But the pointer named `previous_ptr->link( )` does point to the node that's after the location of the new node. The pointer `previous_ptr->link( )` is shaded in this picture, to show you that it points to the spot that's after the new node's location:

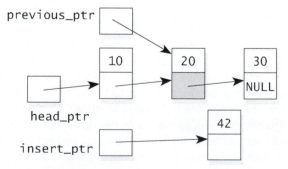

Here is the function activation that carries out Step 3:

```
insert_ptr->set_link( previous_ptr->link( ) );
```

After setting this link, we have this situation:

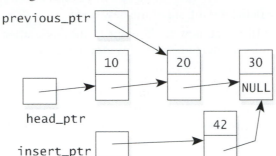

Another statement, `previous_ptr->set_link(insert_ptr);`, does Step 4, as shown here:

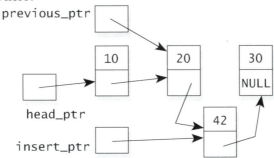

After inserting the new node containing 42, you can step through the complete linked list, starting at the head node 10, then 20, then 42, and finally 30. The `list_insert` function implementation is shown in Figure 5.7 on page 235. Notice that `previous_ptr` is not a reference parameter, since we are not making `previous_ptr` point to a new node.

☹ PITFALL

UNINTENDED CALLS TO DELETE AND NEW

The `list_insert` function uses a local variable, `insert_ptr`, that is a pointer. When the function finishes, `insert_ptr` is no longer needed, and it will go away, just like any other local variable. But watch out! A common error is to think "`insert_ptr` is no longer needed, so I should write the statement *delete* `insert_ptr` at the end of the `list_insert` function." *Don't!*

The effect of *delete* `insert_ptr` is to get rid of *the node* that `insert_ptr` points to. In other words, you will get rid of the very node that you worked so hard to insert. The general rule is this: *Never call delete unless you are actually reducing the number of nodes.*

A similar error might occur with the local variable `cursor` in the `list_length` function. You might be tempted to write `cursor = new node` to try to initialize this pointer variable. *Don't!* The effect of `cursor = new node` is to create a new node that was not previously part of the linked list. But `cursor` does not need to point

FIGURE 5.7 Implementations of Three Linked-List Functions

Three Function Implementations

```
void list_insert(node* previous_ptr, const node::value_type& entry)
// Precondition: previous_ptr points to a node in a linked list.
// Postcondition: A new node containing the given entry has been added after the node that
// previous_ptr points to. NOTE: If there is insufficient dynamic memory for a new
// node, then bad_alloc is thrown before changing the list.
{
    node *insert_ptr;

    insert_ptr = new node;
    insert_ptr->set_data(entry);
    insert_ptr->set_link( previous_ptr->link( ) );
    previous_ptr->set_link(insert_ptr);
}


node* list_search(node* head_ptr, const node::value_type& target)
// Precondition: head_ptr is the head pointer of a linked list.
// Postcondition: The return value is a pointer to the first node containing the specified target in its
// data field. If there is no such node, the null pointer is returned.
// Library facilities used: cstdlib
{
    node *cursor;

    for (cursor = head_ptr; cursor != NULL; cursor = cursor->link( ))
        if (target == cursor->data( ))
            return cursor;
    return NULL;
}


const node* list_search(const node* head_ptr, const node::value_type& target)
// Precondition: head_ptr is the head pointer of a linked list.
// Postcondition: The return value is a pointer to the first node containing the specified target in its
// data field. If there is no such node, the null pointer is returned.
// Library facilities used: cstdlib
{
    const node *cursor;

    for (cursor = head_ptr; cursor != NULL; cursor = cursor->link( ))
        if (target == cursor->data( ))
            return cursor;
    return NULL;
}
```

www.cs.colorado.edu/~main/chapter5/node1.cxx   **WWW**

to a new node; it merely steps through the existing nodes of the linked list. The general rule is this: *Never call new unless you are actually increasing the number of nodes.*

Searching for an Item in a Linked List. When the job of a subtask is to find a single node, it makes sense to implement the subtask as a function that returns a pointer to that node. Our next toolkit operation is such a function, returning a pointer to a node that contains a specified item. We will actually implement two versions of the search function, with these slightly different prototypes:

```
node* list_search
(node* head_ptr, const node::value_type& target);
// Precondition: head_ptr is the head pointer of a linked list.
// Postcondition: The return value is a pointer to the first node containing
//   the specified target in its data field. If there is no such node,
//   the null pointer is returned.
```

```
const node* list_search
(const node* head_ptr, const node::value_type& target);
// Precondition: head_ptr is the head pointer of a linked list.
// Postcondition: The return value is a pointer to the first node containing
//   the specified target in its data field. If there is no such node,
//   the null pointer is returned.
```

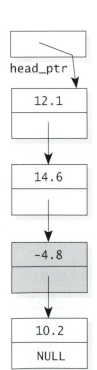
head_ptr

The first version of `list_search` has a `node*` parameter, and the return value is also a `node*`. This means that the return value of the first function could be used to change the list. For example, with the linked list shown in the margin, we could execute these statements to find a pointer to the shaded node (containing –4.8) and change its data to 6.8:

```
node* p;
p = list_search(head_ptr, -4.8); // p now points to the –4.8 node.
p->set_data(6.8);                 // Change p's data to 6.8.
```

On the other hand, the return value from the second version of the function is `const node*`. So the second function can find a specified node, but the compiler will prevent us from using the returned pointer to change the list.

For any use of `list_search`, the compiler looks at the type of the first argument to determine which version to use. If the first argument is a pointer that is declared as `node*`, then the compiler will use the `list_search` that returns `node*`. But if the first argument is `const node*`, then the compiler will use the second version of `list_search`, whose return value is also `const node*`.

The implementations of `list_search` are shown in Figure 5.7. Most of the work is carried out with the usual traversal pattern, using a local pointer variable called `cursor` to step through the nodes one at a time:

```
for (cursor = head_ptr; cursor != NULL; cursor = cursor->link( ))
{
    if (target == the data in the node that cursor points to)
        return cursor;
}
```

As the loop executes, cursor points to the nodes of the list, one after another. The test inside the loop determines whether we have found the sought-after node, and if so, then a pointer to the node is immediately returned with the return statement *return* cursor. When a return statement occurs like this, inside a loop, the function returns without ado—the loop is not run to completion.

On the other hand, should the loop actually complete by eventually setting cursor to NULL, then the sought-after node is not on the list. According to the function's postcondition, the function returns NULL when the node is not on the list. This is accomplished with one more return statement— *return* NULL—at the end of the function's implementation.

When to Provide Two Versions for a Function

When a nonmember function has a parameter that is a pointer to a node, and the return value is also a pointer to a node, you should often have two versions: one version where the parameter and return value are both node*, and a second version where the parameter and return values are both *const* node*.

Finding a Node by Its Position in a Linked List

Our toolkit has another function that returns a pointer to a node in a linked list. Here is the prototype:

```
node* list_locate(node* head_ptr, size_t position);
// Precondition: head_ptr is the head pointer of a linked list, and position > 0.
// Postcondition: The pointer returned points to the node at the specified
// position in the list. (The head node is position 1, the next node is position
// 2, and so on.) If there is no such position, then the null pointer is
// returned.
```

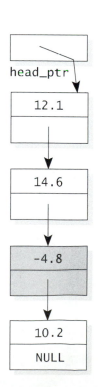

In this function, a node is specified by giving its position in the list, with the head node at position 1, the next node at position 2, and so on. For example, with the list shown in the margin, the function list_locate(head_ptr, 3) will return a pointer to the shaded node. Notice that the first node is number 1, not number 0 as in an array. The specified position might also be larger than the length of the list. In this case, the function returns the null pointer.

The implementation of list_locate is left as Self-Test Exercise 25, where you will implement two versions: one where the head pointer and return value are node* and a second version using *const* node*. You can use a variation of the list traversal technique that we have already seen. The variation is useful when we want to move to a particular node in a linked list and we know the ordinal position of the node (such as position number 1, position number 2, and so on). Start by pointing a pointer variable, `cursor`, to the head node of the list. A loop then moves the `cursor` forward the correct number of spots, as shown here:

```
cursor = head_ptr;
for (i = 1; (i < position) && (cursor != NULL); ++i)
    cursor = cursor->link( );
```

Each iteration of the loop executes `cursor = cursor->link( )` to move the cursor forward one node. Normally, the loop stops when i reaches `position`, and `cursor` points at the correct node. The loop can also stop if `cursor` becomes `NULL`, indicating that `position` was larger than the number of nodes on the list.

Copying a Linked List

Our next linked-list function makes a copy of a linked list, providing both head and tail pointers for the newly created copy. Here is the prototype:

```
void list_copy
(const node* source_ptr, node*& head_ptr, node*& tail_ptr);
// Precondition: source_ptr is the head pointer of a linked list.
// Postcondition: head_ptr and tail_ptr are the head and tail pointers for
//   a new list that contains the same items as the list pointed to by
//   source_ptr. NOTE: If there is insufficient dynamic memory to create the
//   new list, then bad_alloc is thrown.
```

For example, suppose that `source_ptr` points to the following list:

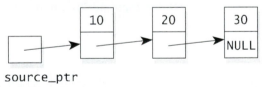

source_ptr

The `list_copy` function creates a completely separate copy of the three-node list. The copy of the list has its own three nodes, which also contain the numbers 10, 20, and 30. Through the parameter list, the `list_copy` function returns pointers to the head and tail of the newly created list. The original list remains unchanged and there are no pointers connecting the new list to the original list (therefore the `source_ptr` parameter can be declared as *const* node*).

The pseudocode begins by setting the new head and tail pointers to `NULL`, then handling one special case—the case where the original list is empty (so that `source_ptr` is the null pointer). In this case the function simply returns (since the head and tail pointers have already been set to `NULL`). The complete pseudocode is given here:

1. Set `head_ptr` and tail_ptr to NULL.
2. *if* (source_ptr == NULL), then return with no further work.
3. Allocate a new node for the head node of the new list that we are creating. Make both `head_ptr` and `tail_ptr` point to this new node, and copy data from the head node of the original list to our new node.
4. Make `source_ptr` point to the second node of the original list, then the third node, then the fourth node, and so on until we have traversed all of the original list. At each node that `source_ptr` points to, add one new node to the tail of the new list, and move the tail pointer forward to the newly added node, as follows:

   4.1 `list_insert(tail_ptr, source_ptr->data( ));`
   4.2 `tail_ptr = tail_ptr->link( );`

The fourth step of the pseudocode is implemented by this code:

```
source_ptr = source_ptr->link( );
while (source_ptr != NULL)
{
    list_insert(tail_ptr, source_ptr->data( ));
    tail_ptr = tail_ptr->link( );
    source_ptr = source_ptr->link( );
}
```

Prior to the loop, we set `source_ptr` to the second node of the original list with the assignment statement `source_ptr = source_ptr->link( )`. If there is no second node of the original list, then this assignment will set `source_ptr` to the null pointer, which is fine since we require the test `source_ptr != NULL` in order for the loop to continue.

The first two statements in the body of the loop are Steps 4.1 and 4.2 in our pseudocode. Step 4.1 inserts a new node at the tail end of the newly created list. Step 4.2 moves the tail pointer of the new list forward, to the new end of the list.

At the end of each loop iteration, we move `source_ptr` to the next node in the original list with the assignment `source_ptr = source_ptr->link( )`.

As an example, consider again the three-node list with data 10, 20, and 30. The first two steps of the pseudocode are carried out and then the `source_ptr` is initialized with the statement `source_ptr = source_ptr->link( )`. At this point, the function's pointers look like this:

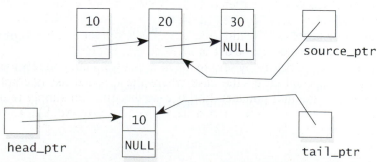

Notice that we have already copied the first node of the linked list. During the first iteration of the loop, we copy the second node of the linked list—the node that is pointed to by source_ptr. The first part of copying the node is a call to one of our other tools, list_insert, as shown here:

```
list_insert(tail_ptr, source_ptr->data( ));
```

This function call adds a new node to the end of the list that we are creating (i.e., *after* the node pointed to by tail_ptr), and the data in the new node is the number 20 (i.e., the data from source_ptr->data( )). Immediately after the insertion, the function's pointers look like this:

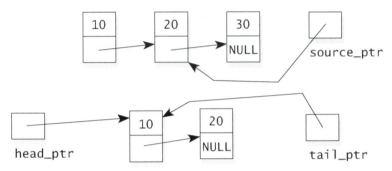

The second statement in the loop body moves tail_ptr forward to the new tail of the new list, as shown here:

```
tail_ptr = tail_ptr->link( );
```

This is the usual way that we make a pointer "move to the next node," as we have seen in other functions such as list_search. After moving the tail pointer, the function's pointers are configured as shown next.

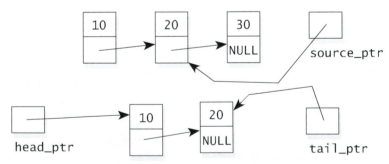

In this example, source_ptr will move to the third node, and the body of the loop will execute one more time to copy the third node to the new list. Then the loop will end. The full implementation of list_copy is shown in Figure 5.8.

FIGURE 5.8	Function for Copying a Linked List

Function Implementation

```
void list_copy(const node* source_ptr, node*& head_ptr, node*& tail_ptr)
// Precondition: source_ptr is the head pointer of a linked list.
// Postcondition: head_ptr and tail_ptr are the head and tail pointers for a new list that contains
// the same items as the list pointed to by source_ptr. NOTE: If there is insufficient
// dynamic memory to create the new list, then bad_alloc is thrown.
// Library facilities used: cstdlib
{
    head_ptr = NULL;
    tail_ptr = NULL;

    // Handle the case of the empty list.
    if (source_ptr == NULL)
        return;

    // Make the head node for the newly created list, and put data in it.
    list_head_insert(head_ptr, source_ptr->data( ));
    tail_ptr = head_ptr;

    // Copy the rest of the nodes one at a time, adding at the tail of new list.
    source_ptr = source_ptr->link( );
    while (source_ptr != NULL)
    {
        list_insert(tail_ptr, source_ptr->data( ));      Loop for Step 4
        tail_ptr = tail_ptr->link( );
        source_ptr = source_ptr->link( );
    }
}
```

www.cs.colorado.edu/~main/chapter5/node1.cxx	**WWW**

Removing a Node at the Head of a Linked List

Our toolkit has three more functions, all of which remove nodes from a linked list. The first removal function removes the head node, as specified here:

```
void list_head_remove(node*& head_ptr);
// Precondition: head_ptr is the head pointer of a linked list,
// with at least one node.
// Postcondition: The head node has been removed and returned to the
// heap; head_ptr is now the head pointer of the new, shorter linked list.
```
*list_head
_remove*

As with `list_head_insert`, the head pointer is a reference parameter, since the function makes the head pointer point to a different node.

At first glance, it seems that the head node can be removed with just two steps: (1) Move the head pointer to the next node of the list; and (2) return the original head node to the heap. There is a small flaw with these steps: After we move the head pointer in Step 1, we no longer have any contact with the original head node. So, our complete pseudocode requires three steps:

1. Set a pointer named `remove_ptr` to point to the head node. (This is how we maintain contact with the original head node.)
2. Move the head pointer so that it points to the second node (or it becomes `NULL` if there is no second node).
3. *delete* `remove_ptr`. (This returns the original head node to the heap.)

These three steps are implemented in the top of Figure 5.9 on page 244.

Removing a Node That Is Not at the Head

Our second removal function removes a node that is not at the head of a linked list. The approach is similar to inserting a node in the middle of a linked list. To remove a midlist node, we must set up a pointer to the node that is just *before* the node that we are removing. For example, to remove the 42 from the following list, we would need to set up `previous_ptr` as shown here:

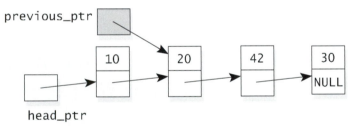

As you can see, `previous_ptr` does not actually point to the node that we are deleting (the 42); instead it points to the node that is just before the condemned node. This is because the link field of the previous node must be reassigned, hence we need a pointer to this previous node. The removal function's prototype, using `previous_ptr`, is shown next.

list_remove

```
void list_remove(node* previous_ptr);
// Precondition: previous_ptr points to a node in a linked list,
//   and this is not the tail node of the list.
// Postcondition: The node after previous_ptr has been removed
//   from the linked list.
```

The steps required by `list_remove` are similar to removing at the head of a list. Here is the pseudocode:

1. Set a pointer named `remove_ptr` to point to the condemned node. (This is the node after the one pointed to by `previous_ptr`.)

2. Reset the link field of `previous_ptr` so that it points to the node after the condemned node (or NULL if the condemned node is the tail node).

3. *delete* `remove_ptr`. (This returns the condemned node to the heap.)

As an example, let's remove the node 42 from the list that we just saw. The `previous_ptr` is set to point to the previous node, and then Step 1 of the removal pseudocode is executed. After Step 1, the pointers look like this:

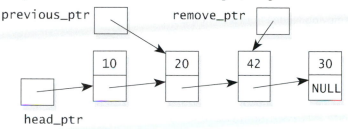

Step 2 of the pseudocode needs to make the previous node's link point to the node that's after the node we are removing. This step changes the shaded pointer in the drawing shown here:

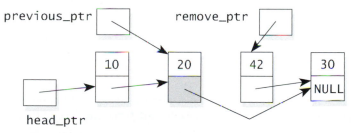

At this point, the node containing 42 is no longer part of the linked list. The list's first node contains 10, the next node has 20, and following the pointers we arrive at the third and last node containing 30. All that remains is Step 3, *delete* `remove_ptr`, which returns the deleted node to the heap.

The complete implementation is shown in the middle part of Figure 5.9. You should check that the function works properly, even if the removed node is the last node of the list. In this case, the link of the previous node should be set to NULL, which occurs with no need for special code.

Clearing a Linked List

Our final function removes all the nodes from a linked list, returning them to the heap. The implementation (`list_clear` in Figure 5.9) is a loop that repeatedly calls `list_head_remove` until all the nodes are gone. Notice that when the final node of the list is removed, the head pointer will be null, and this stops the loop. Also, the head pointer is a reference parameter, so that when the function returns, the actual head pointer in the calling program will be null.

list_clear

Linked-List Toolkit—Putting the Pieces Together

The functions of the toolkit are complete. Figure 5.10 on page 245 shows a header file for the toolkit, called `node1.h`. In addition to the documentation, the header file provides the class definition for the `node`, plus prototypes for the functions. In the file, we have defined the `value_type` to be a *double*, but as the documentation indicates, `value_type` may be changed to another data type.

| **FIGURE 5.9** | Functions for Removing Nodes from a Linked List |

Three Function Implementations

```
void list_head_remove(node*& head_ptr)
// Precondition: head_ptr is the head pointer of a linked list, with at least one node.
// Postcondition: The head node has been removed and returned to the heap;
// head_ptr is now the head pointer of the new, shorter linked list.
{
    node *remove_ptr;

    remove_ptr = head_ptr;
    head_ptr = head_ptr->link( );
    delete remove_ptr;
}
```

This statement causes head_ptr to point to the second node (or it becomes NULL if there is no second node).

```
void list_remove(node* previous_ptr)
// Precondition: previous_ptr points to a node in a linked list, and this is not the tail node of the list.
// Postcondition: The node after previous_ptr has been removed from the linked list.
{
    node *remove_ptr;

    remove_ptr = previous_ptr->link( );
    previous_ptr->set_link( remove_ptr->link( ) );
    delete remove_ptr;
}
```

```
void list_clear(node*& head_ptr)
// Precondition: head_ptr is the head pointer of a linked list.
// Postcondition: All nodes of the list have been deleted, and head_ptr is now NULL.
// Library facilities used: cstdlib
{
    while (head_ptr != NULL)
        list_head_remove(head_ptr);
}
```

www.cs.colorado.edu/~main/chapter5/node1.cxx   **WWW**

The implementations of the functions should be placed in a separate implementation file called `node1.cxx`. We do not provide a listing of this file, but you can build it with the implementations from Figures 5.5 through 5.9.

Using the Linked-List Toolkit

The purpose of the node class and its functions is to allow a container class to store elements on a basic linked list with the simplicity and clarity of using an array. In addition, having the functions written and thoroughly tested once will allow us to use the functions to implement many different container classes with high confidence in their reliability.

So, any programmer can use our node and the toolkit. The programmer defines the `value_type` according to his or her need and places the include directive in the program:

```
#include "node1.h"
```

The node class and all the functions (which are in the namespace `main_savitch_5`) can then be used to build and manipulate linked lists. This is what we will do in the rest of the chapter, providing two classes that use the linked-list toolkit.

Finally, keep in mind that the programmer who uses a class that was built with the linked-list toolkit does not need to know about the underlying linked lists.

FIGURE 5.10   Header File for the Node Class and the Linked-List Toolkit

A Header File

```
// FILE: node1.h (part of the namespace main_savitch_5)
// PROVIDES: A class for a node in a linked list and a collection of functions for
// manipulating linked lists
//
// TYPEDEF for the node class:
//    Each node of the list contains a piece of data and a pointer to the next node. The
//    type of the data is defined as node::value_type in a typedef statement. The value_type
//    may be any of the C++ built-in types (int, char, etc.), or a class with a default constructor,
//    a copy constructor, an assignment operator, and a test for equality.
//
// CONSTRUCTOR for the node class:
//    node(const value_type& init_data, node* init_link)
//       Postcondition: The node contains the specified data and link.
//       NOTE: The init_data parameter has a default value that is obtained from the default
//       constructor of the value_type. In the ANSI/ISO standard, this notation is also allowed
//       for the built-in types, providing a default value of zero. The init_link has a default
//       value of NULL.
```
(continued)

(FIGURE 5.10 continued)

```
// NOTE:
//    Some of the functions have a return value that is a pointer to a node. Each of these
//    functions comes in two versions: a non-const version (where the return value is node* )
//    and a const version (where the return value is const node* ).
// EXAMPLES:
//    const node *c;
//    c->link( ) activates the const version of link
//    list_search(c, ... calls the const version of list_search
//    node *p;
//    p->link( ) activates the non-const version of link
//    list_search(p, ... calls the non-const version of list_search
//
// MEMBER FUNCTIONS for the node class:
//    void set_data(const value_type& new_data)
//       Postcondition: The node now contains the specified new data.
//
//    void set_link(node* new_link)
//       Postcondition: The node now contains the specified new link.
//
//    value_type data( ) const
//       Postcondition: The return value is the data from this node.
//
//    const node* link( ) const   <----- const version
//    and
//    node* link( )               <----- non-const version
//    See the previous note about the const version and non-const versions.
//       Postcondition: The return value is the link from this node.
//
// FUNCTIONS in the linked-list toolkit:
//    size_t list_length(const node* head_ptr)
//       Precondition: head_ptr is the head pointer of a linked list.
//       Postcondition: The value returned is the number of nodes in the linked list.
//
//    void list_head_insert(node*& head_ptr, const node::value_type& entry)
//       Precondition: head_ptr is the head pointer of a linked list.
//       Postcondition: A new node containing the given entry has been added at the head of
//       the linked list; head_ptr now points to the head of the new, longer linked list.
//
//    void list_insert(node* previous_ptr, const node::value_type& entry)
//       Precondition: previous_ptr points to a node in a linked list.
//       Postcondition: A new node containing the given entry has been added after the node
//       that previous_ptr points to.
//
```

(continued)

(FIGURE 5.10 continued)

```
//    const node* list_search
//        (const node* head_ptr, const node::value_type& target)
//    and
//    node* list_search(node* head_ptr, const node::value_type& target)
//    See the previous note about the const version and non-const versions.
//        Precondition: head_ptr is the head pointer of a linked list.
//        Postcondition: The pointer returned points to the first node containing the specified
//        target in its data field. If there is no such node, the null pointer is returned.
//
//    const node* list_locate(const node* head_ptr, size_t position)
//    and
//    node* list_locate(node* head_ptr, size_t position)
//    See the previous note about the const version and non-const versions.
//        Precondition: head_ptr is the head pointer of a linked list, and position > 0.
//        Postcondition: The pointer returned points to the node at the specified position in the
//        list. (The head node is position 1, the next node is position 2, and so on.) If there is no
//        such position, then the null pointer is returned.
//
//    void list_head_remove(node*& head_ptr)
//        Precondition: head_ptr is the head pointer of a linked list, with at least one node.
//        Postcondition: The head node has been removed and returned to the heap;
//        head_ptr is now the head pointer of the new, shorter linked list.
//
//    void list_remove(node* previous_ptr)
//        Precondition: previous_ptr points to a node in a linked list, and this is not the tail node of
//        the list.
//        Postcondition: The node after previous_ptr has been removed from the linked list.
//
//    void list_clear(node*& head_ptr)
//        Precondition: head_ptr is the head pointer of a linked list.
//        Postcondition: All nodes of the list have been returned to the heap, and the head_ptr is
//        now NULL.
//
//    void list_copy(const node* source_ptr, node*& head_ptr, node*& tail_ptr)
//        Precondition: source_ptr is the head pointer of a linked list.
//        Postcondition: head_ptr and tail_ptr are the head and tail pointers for a new list that
//        contains the same items as the list pointed to by source_ptr.
//
// DYNAMIC MEMORY usage by the functions:
//    If there is insufficient dynamic memory, then the following functions throw bad_alloc:
//    the node constructor, list_head_insert, list_insert, list_copy
```

(continued)

(FIGURE 5.10 continued)

```
#ifndef MAIN_SAVITCH_NODE1_H
#define MAIN_SAVITCH_NODE1_H
#include <cstdlib> // Provides size_t and NULL

namespace main_savitch_5
{
    class node
    {
    public:
        // TYPEDEF
        typedef double value_type;
        // CONSTRUCTOR
        node(const value_type& init_data=value_type( ), node* init_link=NULL)
            { data_field = init_data; link_field = init_link; }
        // MODIFICATION MEMBER FUNCTIONS
        node* link( ) { return link_field; }
        void set_data(const value_type& new_data) { data_field = new_data; }
        void set_link(node* new_link) { link_field = new_link; }
        // CONST MEMBER FUNCTIONS
        value_type data( ) const { return data_field; }
        const node* link( ) const { return link_field; }
    private:
        value_type data_field;
        node *link_field;
    };

    // FUNCTIONS for the linked-list toolkit
    std::size_t list_length(const node* head_ptr);
    void list_head_insert(node*& head_ptr, const node::value_type& entry);
    void list_insert(node* previous_ptr, const node::value_type& entry);
    node* list_search(node* head_ptr, const node::value_type& target);
    const node* list_search
        (const node* head_ptr, const node::value_type& target);
    node* list_locate(node* head_ptr, std::size_t position);
    const node* list_locate(const node* head_ptr, std::size_t position);
    void list_head_remove(node*& head_ptr);
    void list_remove(node* previous_ptr);
    void list_clear(node*& head_ptr);
    void list_copy(const node* source_ptr, node*& head_ptr, node*& tail_ptr);
}
#endif
```

Self-Test Exercises for Section 5.2

13. Suppose you want to use a linked list where the items are strings from the Standard Library string class. How would you need to change the node1.h header file?

14. Write the general pattern for a loop statement that traverses all the nodes of a linked list.

15. When should a node pointer be a value parameter in a function's parameter list?

16. Suppose that locate_ptr is a pointer to a node in a linked list (and it is not the null pointer). Write a statement that will make locate_ptr move to the next node in the list. What does your statement do if locate_ptr was already pointing to the last node in the list?

17. Suppose that head_ptr is a head pointer for a linked list of numbers. Write a few lines of code that will insert the number 42 as the second item of the list. (If the list was originally empty, then 42 should be added as the first node instead of the second.)

18. Write a statement to correctly set the tail pointer of a list when a new first node has been added to the list. Assume that head_ptr points to the new first node.

19. Which of the toolkit functions use *new* to allocate a new node? Which use *delete* to return a node to the heap?

20. What is the general rule to follow when using the delete operator with node pointers?

21. Suppose that head_ptr is a head pointer for a linked list of numbers. Write a few lines of code that will remove the second item of the list. (If the list originally had only one item, then remove that item instead; if it had no items, then leave the list empty.)

22. Suppose that head_ptr is a head pointer for a linked list with just one node. What will head_ptr be after list_head_remove(head_ptr)?

23. Rewrite the list_insert with just one line of code in the implementation.

24. Implement this function:
    ```
    void list_piece(
          const node* start_ptr, const node* end_ptr,
          node*& head_ptr, node*& tail_ptr
          )
    ```
    // Precondition: start_ptr and end_ptr are pointers to nodes on the same
    // linked list, with the start_ptr node at or before the end_ptr node.
    // Postcondition: head_ptr and tail_ptr are the head and tail pointers
    // for a new list that contains the items from start_ptr up to but not
    // including end_ptr. The end_ptr may also be NULL, in which case the
    // new list contains elements from start_ptr to the end of the list.

25. Implement two versions of the list_locate function (one where the parameter is node* and a second version using const node*).

5.3 THE BAG CLASS WITH A LINKED LIST

We're ready to write a container class that is implemented with a linked list. We'll start with the familiar bag class, which we have previously implemented with an array (Section 3.1) and a dynamic array (Section 4.3). So this is our third bag implementation. At the end of this chapter we'll compare the advantages and disadvantages of these different implementations. But first, let's see how a linked list is used in our third bag implementation.

Our Third Bag—Specification

The advantage of using a familiar class is that you already know the specification. The documentation for the header file is nearly identical to our previous bag. The major difference is that our new bag has no worries about capacity: There is no default capacity and no need for a "reserve" function that reserves a specified capacity. This is because our planned implementation—storing the bag's items in a linked list—can easily grow and shrink by adding and removing nodes from the linked list. Of course, the programmer who uses the new bag class does not need to know about linked lists, and the documentation of our new header file will make no mention of linked lists.

The new bag will also have one other minor change. Just for fun, we'll add a new member function called grab, which returns a randomly selected item from a bag. In Programming Project 1 on page 275 we'll use the grab function in a program that generates some silly sentences.

Our Third Bag—Class Definition

Our plan has been laid. We will implement the new bag by storing the items in a linked list. The class will have two private member variables: (1) a head pointer that points to the head of a linked list that contains the items of the bag; and (2) a variable that keeps track of the length of the list. The second member variable isn't really needed since we could call list_length to determine the length of the list. But when we keep the length in a member variable, then the length can be quickly determined by examining the variable (a constant time operation). This is in contrast to actually counting the length by traversing the list (a linear time operation). In any case, the private members of our class are shown here:

```
class bag
{
public:
    typedef std::size_t size_type;
    ...
private:
    node *head_ptr;           // List head pointer
    size_type many_nodes;     // Number of nodes on the list
};
```

Keep in mind that our design is not the only way to implement a bag. In fact, we have already seen two other implementations. To avoid confusion over how we are using our linked list, we now make an explicit statement of the invariant for our third design of the bag class:

Invariant for the Third Bag Class

1. The items in the bag are stored in a linked list.
2. The head pointer of the list is stored in the member variable `head_ptr`.
3. The total number of items in the list is stored in the member variable `many_nodes`.

Having decided on our class definition, we can write the header file for the third bag. (See Figure 5.11.) In this header file, we use the node data type from the previous section. Therefore, before the bag's class definition we need the include directive `#include "node1.h"`. This allows us to use the node type within our bag class definition. When we use this node class, we may use the name `node` by itself (since the bag and node are both in the same `main_savitch_5` namespace). But if the bag were not in this same namespace, then the full name, `main_savitch_5::node`, would be required.

How to Make the Bag value_type Match the Node value_type

The bag's class definition also depends on the data type of the items in the bag. This data type, called `node::value_type`, is already defined in `node1.h`, so there is no absolute need for a second definition of `value_type` in the bag's class definition. However, the programmers who use our bag don't know about nodes, so for their benefit it's reasonable to go ahead and define `value_type` as part of the bag, too. The beginning of the bag's definition looks this way:

```
#include "node1.h" // Provides node class
...
class bag
{
public:
    typedef node::value_type value_type;
    ...
```

The definition makes `bag::value_type` the same as `node::value_type`, so that a programmer who uses the bag can write `bag::value_type` without having to know about the implementation details of nodes and linked lists.

FIGURE 5.11   Header File for Our Third Bag Class

A Header File

```
//  FILE: bag3.h (part of the namespace main_savitch_5)
//  CLASS PROVIDED: bag (a collection of items, where each item may appear multiple times)
//
//  TYPEDEFS for the bag class:
//     typedef _____ value_type
//        bag::value_type is the data type of the items in the bag. It may be any of the C++
//        built-in types (int, char, etc.), or a class with a default constructor, a copy constructor,
//        an assignment operator, and a test for equality (x == y).
//
//     typedef _____ size_type
//        bag::size_type is the data type of any variable that keeps track of how many items are
//        in a bag.
//
//  CONSTRUCTOR for the bag class:
//     bag( )
//        Postcondition: The bag is empty.
//
//  MODIFICATION MEMBER FUNCTIONS for the bag class:
//     size_type erase(const value_type& target)
//        Postcondition: All copies of target have been removed from the bag. The return value
//        is the number of copies removed (which could be zero).
//
//     bool erase_one(const value_type& target)
//        Postcondition: If target was in the bag, then one copy of target has been removed from
//        the bag; otherwise the bag is unchanged. A true return value indicates that one copy
//        was removed; false indicates that nothing was removed.
//
//     void insert(const value_type& entry)
//        Postcondition: A new copy of entry has been inserted into the bag.
//
//     void operator +=(const bag& addend)
//        Postcondition: Each item in addend has been added to the bag.
//
//  CONSTANT MEMBER FUNCTIONS for the bag class:
//     size_type size( ) const
//        Postcondition: The return value is the total number of items in the bag.
//
//     size_type count(const value_type& target) const
//        Postcondition: The return value is the number of times target is in the bag.
//
//     value_type grab( ) const
//        Precondition: size( ) > 0.
//        Postcondition: The return value is a randomly selected item from the bag.     (continued)
```

(FIGURE 5.11 continued)

```
// NONMEMBER FUNCTIONS for the bag class:
//    bag operator +(const bag& b1, const bag& b2)
//        Postcondition: The bag returned is the union of b1 and b2.
// VALUE SEMANTICS for the bag class:
//    Assignments and the copy constructor may be used with bag objects.
// DYNAMIC MEMORY USAGE by the bag:
//    If there is insufficient dynamic memory, then the following functions throw bad_alloc:
//    The constructors, insert, operator +=, operator +, and the assignment operator.

#ifndef MAIN_SAVITCH_BAG3_H
#define MAIN_SAVITCH_BAG3_H
#include <cstdlib>    // Provides size_t and NULL
#include "node1.h"    // Provides node class
namespace main_savitch_5
{
    class bag
    {
    public:
        // TYPEDEFS
        typedef std::size_t size_type;
        typedef node::value_type value_type;
        // CONSTRUCTORS and DESTRUCTOR
        bag( );
        bag(const bag& source);
        ~bag( );
        // MODIFICATION MEMBER FUNCTIONS
        size_type erase(const value_type& target);
        bool erase_one(const value_type& target);
        void insert(const value_type& entry);
        void operator +=(const bag& addend);
        void operator =(const bag& source);
        // CONSTANT MEMBER FUNCTIONS
        size_type size( ) const { return many_nodes; }
        size_type count(const value_type& target) const;
        value_type grab( ) const;
    private:
        node *head_ptr;        // List head pointer
        size_type many_nodes;  // Number of nodes on the list
    };

    // NONMEMBER FUNCTIONS for the bag class:
    bag operator +(const bag& b1, const bag& b2);
}
#endif
```

Prototype for the copy constructor

Prototype for the destructor

Prototype for the overloaded operator =

www.cs.colorado.edu/~main/chapter5/bag3.h   **WWW**

If we need a different type of item, we can change `node::value_type` to the required new type and recompile. The `bag::value_type` will then match the new `node::value_type`. For example, suppose we want a bag of strings using the Standard Library string class (from `<string>`). In order to obtain the bag of strings, the start of our node definition will be:

```
#include <string>
class node
{
public:
    typedef std::string value_type;
    ...
```

In this case, the `node::value_type` is defined as the string class, so that `bag::value_type` will also be a string. By the way, when we get to the implementation details, we will use examples where the items are strings; keep in mind, however, that the underlying item type could easily be changed.

Following the Rules for Dynamic Memory Usage in a Class

Our new bag is a class that uses dynamic memory, therefore it must follow the four rules that we outlined in "Prescription for a Dynamic Class" on page 186. Let's review these rules:

1. Some of the member variables of the class are pointers. In particular, our new bag has a member variable, `head_ptr`, which is a head pointer of a linked list.

2. Member functions allocate and release dynamic memory as needed. We will see this when the bag's member functions are implemented. For example, the bag's `insert` function will allocate a new node.

3. The automatic value semantics of the class is overridden. In other words, the class must implement a copy constructor and an assignment operator that correctly copy one bag to another. You can see that the bag's class definition in Figure 5.11 on page 253 accounts for this by including the prototypes for the copy constructor and the assignment operator.

4. The class has a destructor. Again, the bag's class definition in Figure 5.11 provides for this with the destructor's prototype.

Also notice that the bag's documentation does not list a destructor, since the programmer who uses the class does not normally make explicit calls to the destructor. But our planned implementation uses dynamic memory, so a destructor will be part of the class.

The Third Bag Class—Implementation

With our design in mind, we can implement each of the member functions, starting with the constructors. The key to simple implementations is to use the linked-list functions whenever possible.

Constructors. The default constructor sets `head_ptr` to be the null pointer (indicating the empty list) and sets `many_nodes` to zero. The copy constructor uses `list_copy` to make a separate copy of the source list, and `many_nodes` is then copied from the source to the newly constructed bag. Only a few statements are needed for the copy constructor, as shown here:

```
bag::bag(const bag& source)
// Library facilities used: node1.h
{
    node *tail_ptr; // Needed for argument to list_copy

    list_copy(source.head_ptr, head_ptr, tail_ptr);
    many_nodes = source.many_nodes;
}
```

constructors

Overloading the assignment operator. The overloaded assignment operator needs to change an existing bag so that it is the same as some other bag. The main difference between this and the copy constructor is that we must remember that when the assignment operator begins, the bag already has a linked list, and this linked list must be returned to the heap. With this in mind, you might write the implementation shown here, with the highlighted statement returning the existing linked list to the heap:

```
void bag::operator =(const bag& source)
// Library facilities used: node1.h
{
    node *tail_ptr; // Needed for argument to list_copy

    list_clear(head_ptr);
    many_nodes = 0;
    list_copy(source.head_ptr, head_ptr, tail_ptr);
    many_nodes = source.many_nodes;
}
```

WARNING!
Can you find the bug?

In fact, we actually did write this implementation for our first attempt on the assignment operator. Then we remembered the programming tip from Chapter 4: "How to Check for Self-Assignment" on page 179. For a bag b, it is possible for a programmer to write `b = b`. Perhaps you think this is a pointless assignment statement, but nevertheless the operator should work correctly, assigning b to be equal to its current value—that is, leave the bag unchanged. But instead, when the buggy assignment operator is activated with `b = b`, the first thing that happens is that the bag b (which activated the operator) is cleared. Once that list is cleared, there is no hope of leaving the bag unchanged.

The solution is to check for this special "self-assignment" at the start of the operator. If we find that an assignment such as b = b is occurring, then we will return immediately. We can check for this condition with the test `this == &source`, described on page 179. This is done in the highlighted statement in this correct implementation:

the correct
assignment
operator

```
void bag::operator =(const bag& source)
// Library facilities used: node1.h
{
        node *tail_ptr; // Needed for argument to list_copy

        if (this == &source)
            return;

        list_clear(head_ptr);
        many_nodes = 0;

        list_copy(source.head_ptr, head_ptr, tail_ptr);
        many_nodes = source.many_nodes;
}
```

One other point about the implementation: After we clear the linked list, we also set many_nodes to zero. The reason for this is that we want the bag to be valid before calling list_copy. In general, we will ensure that the bag is valid before calling any function that allocates dynamic memory; otherwise debugging is difficult (see "How to Allocate Memory in a Member Function" on page 182).

PITFALL

THE ASSIGNMENT OPERATOR CAUSES TROUBLE WITH LINKED LISTS

When a class uses a linked list, you must take care with the assignment operator. Part of the care is checking for the special situation of "self-assignment" such as b = b. The easiest way to handle self-assignment is to check for it at the start of the assignment operator and simply return with no work if self-assignment is discovered.

Care is also needed before allocating dynamic memory. Before calling a function that allocates dynamic memory, make sure that the invariant of your class is valid.

The destructor. Our documentation, which is meant for other programmers, never mentioned a destructor, but a destructor is needed because our particular implementation uses dynamic memory. The destructor is responsible for returning all dynamic memory to the heap. The job is accomplished by list_clear, shown next.

```
bag::~bag( )
// Library facilities used: node1.h
{
    list_clear(head_ptr);
    many_nodes = 0;
}
```

This returns all nodes to the heap and sets head_ptr to NULL.

destructor

There is no absolute need for the second statement, `many_nodes = 0`, since the bag is not supposed to be used after the destructor has been called. But setting `many_nodes` to zero does no harm and in some ways makes it clear that we are "zeroing out the list."

The erase_one member function.   There are two approaches to implementing the `erase_one` function. The first approach uses the toolkit's removal functions—using `list_head_remove` if the removed item is at the head of the list, and using the ordinary `list_remove` to remove an item that is farther down the line. This first approach is fine, although it does require a bit of thought because `list_remove` requires a pointer to the node that is just *before* the item that you want to remove. We could certainly find this "before" node, but not by using the toolkit's `list_search` function.

The second approach actually uses `list_search` to obtain a pointer to the node that contains the item to be deleted. For example, suppose our target is the string mynie in the bag shown here:

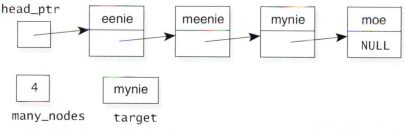

Our approach begins by setting a local variable named `target_ptr` to point to the node that contains our target. This is accomplished with the function call `target_ptr = list_search(head_ptr, target)`. After the function call, the `target_ptr` is set this way:

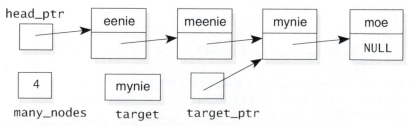

Now we can remove the target from the list with two more steps: (1) Copy the data from the head node to the target node, as shown here:

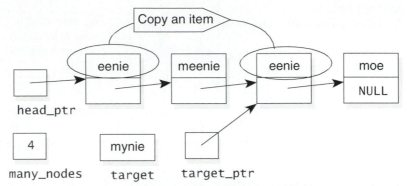

After this step, we have certainly removed the target, but we are left with two eenies. So, we proceed to a second step: (2) Use list_head_remove to remove the head node (that is, one of the copies of eenie). These steps are all implemented in the erase_one function shown in Figure 5.12. The only other steps in the implementation are performing a test to ensure that the target is actually in the bag and subtracting one from many_nodes.

🖐 PROGRAMMING TIP
HOW TO CHOOSE BETWEEN APPROACHES

We had two possible approaches for the erase_one function. How do we select the best approach? Normally, when two approaches have equal efficiency, we will choose the approach that makes the best use of the toolkit. This saves us work and also reduces the chance of new errors from writing new code to do an old job. In the case of erase_one we choose the second approach because it made better use of list_search.

FIGURE 5.12　　A Function to Remove an Item from a Bag

A Function Implementation

```
bool bag::erase_one(const value_type& target)
// Library facilities used: cstdlib, node1.h
{
    node *target_ptr;
    target_ptr = list_search(head_ptr, target);
    if (target_ptr == NULL)
        return false; // target isn't in the bag, so no work to do
    target_ptr->set_data( head_ptr->data( ) );
    list_head_remove(head_ptr);
    --many_nodes;
    return true;
}
```

www.cs.colorado.edu/~main/chapter5/bag3.cxx　　**WWW**

The count member function.   Two possible approaches come to mind for the count member function. One of the approaches simply steps through the linked list one node at a time, checking each piece of data to see whether it is the sought-after target. We count the occurrences of the target and return the answer. The second approach uses list_search to find the first occurrence of the target, then uses list_search again to find the next occurrence, and so on until we have found all occurrences of the target. Our second approach for count makes better use of the toolkit, so that is the approach we will take.

As an example of the second approach to the count function, suppose we want to count the number of occurrences of meenie in this bag:

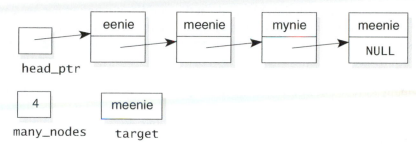

We'll use two local variables: answer, which keeps track of the number of occurrences that we have seen so far, and cursor, which is a pointer to a node in the list. We initialize answer to zero, and we use list_search to make cursor point to the first occurrence of the target (or to be NULL if there are no occurrences). After this initialization, we have this situation:

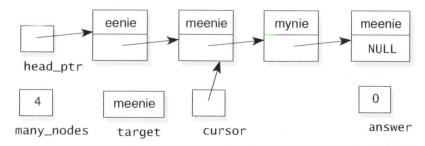

Next, we enter a loop. The loop stops when cursor becomes NULL, indicating that there are no more occurrences of the target. Each time through the loop we do two steps: (1) Add one to answer, and (2) move cursor to point to the next occurrence of the target (or to be NULL if there are no more occurrences). Can we use the toolkit to execute Step 2? At first, it might seem that the toolkit is of no use, since list_search finds the *first* occurrence of a given target. But there is an approach that will use list_search together with the cursor to find the *next* occurrence of the target. The approach begins by moving cursor to the next node in the list, using the statement cursor = cursor->link( ). In our example, this results in the following situation:

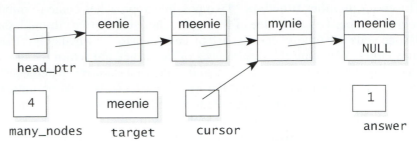

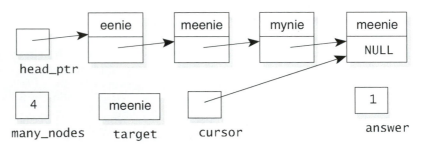

As you can see, `cursor` now points to a node in the middle of a linked list. But any time that a pointer points to a node in the middle of a linked list, we can pretend that the pointer is a head pointer for a smaller linked list. In our example, `cursor` is a head pointer for a two-item list containing the strings mynie and meenie. Therefore, we can use `cursor` as an argument to `list_search` in the assignment statement `cursor = list_search(cursor, target)`. This assignment moves `cursor` to the next occurrence of the target. This occurrence could be at the cursor's current spot, or it could be farther down the line. In our example, the next occurrence of meenie is farther down the line, so `cursor` is moved as shown here:

Eventually there will be no more occurrences of the target and `cursor` becomes NULL, ending the loop. At that point the function returns `answer`. The complete implementation of `count` is shown at the top of Figure 5.13 on page 261.

Finding the Next Occurrence of an Item

The situation: A pointer named `cursor` points to a node in a linked list that contains a particular item called `target`.

The task: Make `cursor` point to the next occurrence of `target` (or NULL if there are no more occurrences).

The solution:
```
cursor = cursor->link( );
cursor = list_search(cursor, target);
```

FIGURE 5.13   Implementations of Two Bag Member Functions

Two Function Implementations

```
bag::size_type bag::count(const value_type& target) const
// Library facilities used: cstdlib, node1.h
{
    size_type answer;
    const node *cursor; // This is const node* because it won't change the list's nodes.

    answer = 0;
    cursor = list_search(head_ptr, target);
    while (cursor != NULL)
    {
        // Each time that cursor is not NULL, we have another occurrence of target, so we
        // add one to answer and then move cursor to the next occurrence of the target.
        ++answer;
        cursor = cursor->link( );
        cursor = list_search(cursor, target);
    }
    return answer;
}

bag::value_type bag::grab( ) const
// Library facilities used: cassert, cstdlib, node1.h
{
    size_type i;
    const node *cursor; // This is const node* because it won't change the list's nodes.

    assert(size( ) > 0);
    i = (rand( ) % size( )) + 1;
    cursor = list_locate(head_ptr, i);
    return cursor->data( );
}
```

www.cs.colorado.edu/~main/chapter5/bag3.cxx   **WWW**

The grab member function.   The bag has a new grab function, specified here:

```
value_type grab( ) const;
//   Precondition: size( ) > 0.
//   Postcondition: The return value is a randomly selected item from the bag.
```

The implementation starts by generating a random integer between 1 and the size of the bag. The random integer can then be used to select a node from the bag, and we'll return the data from the selected node. So, the body of the function will look something like this:

```
i = some random integer between 1 and the size of the bag;
cursor = list_locate(head_ptr, i);
return cursor->data( );
```

Of course the trick is to generate "some random integer between 1 and the size of the bag." The rand function from the C++ Standard Library can help:

```
int rand( );
// Postcondition: The return value is a non-negative pseudorandom integer.
```

the rand function   The values returned by rand are not truly random. They are generated by a simple rule (which is discussed in Chapter 2 Programming Project 11 on page 92). But the numbers *appear* random and so the function is referred to as a **pseudo-random number generator**. For most applications, a pseudorandom number generator is a close enough approximation to a true random number generator. In fact, a pseudorandom number generator has one advantage over a true random number generator: The sequence of numbers it produces is repeatable. If run twice with the same initial conditions, a pseudorandom number generator will produce exactly the same sequence of numbers. This is handy when you are debugging programs that use these sequences. When an error is discovered, the corrected program can be tested with the *same* sequence of pseudorandom numbers that produced the original error.

But at this point we don't need a complete memoir on pseudorandom numbers. All we need is a way to use the rand function to generate a number between 1 and the size of the bag. The following assignment statement does the trick:

```
i = (rand( ) % size( )) + 1; // Set i to a random number from
                              // 1 to the size of the bag.
```

the % operator   Let's look at how the expression works. When x >= 0 and y > 0 are integers, then x % y is the remainder when x is divided by y. The remainder could be as small as 0 or as large as y - 1. Therefore, the expression rand( ) % size( ) lies somewhere in the range from 0 to size( ) - 1. Since we want a number from 1 to size( ), we add one, resulting in i = (rand( ) % size( )) + 1. This assignment statement is used in the complete grab implementation shown at the bottom part of Figure 5.13.

The Third Bag Class—Putting the Pieces Together

The remaining member functions are straightforward. For example, the size function just returns many_nodes; this is implemented as an inline member function in the header file of Figure 5.11 on page 252. The other bag functions all are implemented in the complete implementation file of Figure 5.14.

Take particular notice of how the bag's += operator is implemented. The implementation makes a copy of the linked list of the addend. This copy is then attached at the front of the linked list for the bag that's being added to. The bag's + operator is implemented by way of the += operator.

Self-Test Exercises for Section 5.3

26. In a linked-list implementation of a bag, why is it a good idea to typedef node::value_type as value_type in the bag's definition?

27. Suppose you want to use a bag where the items are strings from the Standard Library `string` class. How would you do this?

28. Write a few lines of code to declare a bag of strings and place the strings squash and handball in the bag. Then grab and print a random string from the bag. Finally, print the number of items in the bag.

29. Which is preferable: an implementation that uses previously defined linked-list functions, or manipulating a linked list directly?

30. Suppose that p is a pointer to a node in a linked list and that p->data( ) has a copy of an item called d. Write two lines of code that will move p to the next node that contains a copy of d (or set p to NULL if there is no such node). How can you combine your two statements into just one?

31. Describe the steps taken by count if the target is not in the bag.

32. Examine our erase function on page 264. What goes wrong if we move the list_head_remove function call two lines earlier?

33. What C++ function generates a pseudorandom integer? How might this be advantageous to a true random number generator?

34. Write an expression that will give a random integer between –10 and 10.

35. Do big-O time analyses of the bag's functions.

FIGURE 5.14	Implementation File for Our Third Bag Class

An Implementation File

```
// FILE: bag3.cxx
// CLASS implemented: bag (See bag3.h for documentation.)
// INVARIANT for the bag class:
//    1. The items in the bag are stored in a linked list.
//    2. The head pointer of the list is stored in the member variable head_ptr.
//    3. The total number of items in the list is stored in the member variable many_nodes.

#include <cassert>    // Provides assert
#include <cstdlib>    // Provides NULL, rand, size_t
#include "node1.h"    // Provides node and the linked-list functions
#include "bag3.h"
using namespace std;

namespace main_savitch_5
{
```

(continued)

(FIGURE 5.14 continued)

```
bag::bag( )
// Library facilities used: cstdlib
{
    head_ptr = NULL;
    many_nodes = 0;
}

bag::bag(const bag& source)
// Library facilities used: node1.h
{
    node *tail_ptr;   // Needed for argument of list_copy
    list_copy(source.head_ptr, head_ptr, tail_ptr);
    many_nodes = source.many_nodes;
}

bag::~bag( )
// Library facilities used: node1.h
{
    list_clear(head_ptr);
    many_nodes = 0;
}
```

`bag::size_type bag::count(const value_type& target) const`
|| See the implementation in Figure 5.13 on page 261.

`bag::size_type bag::erase(const value_type& target)`
```
// Library facilities used: cstdlib, node1.h
{
    size_type answer = 0;
    node *target_ptr;

    target_ptr = list_search(head_ptr, target);
    while (target_ptr != NULL)
    {
        // Each time that target_ptr is not NULL, we have another occurrence of target.
        // We remove this target using the same technique that was used in erase_one.
        target_ptr->set_data( head_ptr->data( ) );
        target_ptr = target_ptr->link( );
        target_ptr = list_search(target_ptr, target);
        list_head_remove(head_ptr);
        --many_nodes;
        ++answer;
    }
    return answer;
}
```

`bool bag::erase_one(const value_type& target)`
|| See the implementation in Figure 5.12 on page 258.   *(continued)*

(FIGURE 5.14 continued)

```
bag::value_type bag::grab( ) const
|| See the implementation in Figure 5.13 on page 261.

void bag::insert(const value_type& entry)
// Library facilities used: node1.h
{
    list_head_insert(head_ptr, entry);
    ++many_nodes;
}

void bag::operator +=(const bag& addend)
// Library facilities used: cstdlib, node1.h
{
    node *copy_head_ptr;
    node *copy_tail_ptr;

    if (addend.many_nodes > 0)
    {
        list_copy(addend.head_ptr, copy_head_ptr, copy_tail_ptr);
        copy_tail_ptr->set_link(head_ptr);
        head_ptr = copy_head_ptr;
        many_nodes += addend.many_nodes;
    }
}

void bag::operator =(const bag& source)
// Library facilities used: node1.h
{
    node *tail_ptr; // Needed for argument to list_copy

    if (this == &source)
        return;

    list_clear(head_ptr);
    many_nodes = 0;
    list_copy(source.head_ptr, head_ptr, tail_ptr);
    many_nodes = source.many_nodes;
}

bag operator +(const bag& b1, const bag& b2)
{
    bag answer;

    answer += b1;
    answer += b2;
    return answer;
}
}
```

5.4   PROGRAMMING PROJECT: THE SEQUENCE CLASS WITH A LINKED LIST

In Section 3.2 on page 123 we gave a specification for a sequence class that was implemented using an array. Now you can reimplement this class using a *linked list* as the data structure rather than an array. Start by rereading the class's specification on page 123, then return here for some implementation suggestions.

The Revised Sequence Class—Design Suggestions

Using a linked list to implement the sequence class seems natural. We'll keep the items stored in a linked list, in their sequence order. The "current" item on the list can be maintained by a member variable that points to the node that contains the current item. When the start function is activated, we set this "current pointer" to point to the first node of the linked list. When advance is activated, we move the "current pointer" to the next node on the linked list.

With this in mind, we propose five private member variables for the new sequence class. The first variable, many_nodes, keeps track of the number of nodes in the list. The other four member variables are node pointers:

- head_ptr and tail_ptr—the head and tail pointers of the linked list. If the sequence has no items, then these pointers are both NULL. The reason for the tail pointer is the attach function. Normally this function adds a new item immediately after the current node. But if there is no current node, then attach places its new item at the tail of the list, so it makes sense to keep a tail pointer around.

- cursor—points to the node with the current item (or NULL if there is no current item).

- precursor—points to the node before current item (or NULL if there is no current item, or the current item is the first node). Can you figure out why we propose a *pre*cursor? The answer is the insert function, which normally adds a new item immediately *before* the current node. But the linked-list functions have no way of inserting a new node before a specified node. We can only add new nodes after a specified node. Therefore, the insert function will work by adding the new item *after* the precursor node—which is also just *before* the cursor node.

For example, suppose that a list contains four strings, with the current item at the third location. The member variables of the object might appear as shown in the following drawing.

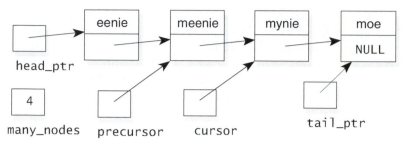

Notice that `cursor` and `precursor` are pointers to nodes rather than actual nodes.

Start your implementation by writing the header file and the invariant for the new sequence class. You might even write the invariant in large letters on a sheet of paper and pin it up in front of you as you work. Each of the member functions count on that invariant being true when the function begins. And each function is responsible for ensuring that the invariant is true when the function finishes.

what is the invariant of the new sequence class?

Keep in mind the four rules for a class that uses dynamic memory:

1. Some of your member variables are pointers. In fact, for your `sequence` class, four member variables are pointers.

2. Member functions allocate and release memory as needed. Don't forget to write documentation indicating which member functions allocate dynamic memory so that experienced programmers can deal with failures.

3. You must override the automatic copy constructor and the automatic assignment operator. Otherwise two different sequences end up with pointers to the same linked list. Some hints on these implementations are given in the following "value semantics" section.

4. The class requires a destructor, which is responsible for returning all dynamic memory to the heap.

The Revised Sequence Class—Value Semantics

The value semantics of your new sequence class consists of a copy constructor and an assignment operator. The primary job of both these functions is to make one sequence equal to a new copy of another. The sequence that you are copying is called the "source," and we suggest that you handle the copying in these cases:

1. If the source sequence has no current item, then simply copy the source's linked list with `list_copy`. Then set both `precursor` and `cursor` to the null pointer.

2. If the current item of the source sequence is its first item, then copy the source's linked list with `list_copy`. Then set `precursor` to null, and set `cursor` to point to the head node of the newly created linked list.

3. If the current item of the source sequence is after its first item, then copy the source's linked list in two pieces using `list_piece` from Self-Test Exercise 24 on page 249. The first piece that you copy goes from the head pointer to the precursor; the second piece goes from the cursor to the tail pointer. Put these two pieces together by making the link field of the precursor node point to the cursor node. The reason for copying in two separate pieces is to easily set the precursor and cursor.

After copying the linked list, be sure to set `many_nodes` to equal the number of nodes in the source. Also, beware of the potential pitfalls that accompany the implementation of your assignment operator (see "The Assignment Operator Causes Trouble with Linked Lists" on page 256).

To test the new sequence class, you can use the same interactive test program that you used to test your original sequence (see "Interactive Test Programs" on page 132).

Self-Test Exercises for Section 5.4

36. Why is a precursor node pointer necessary in the linked-list implementation of a sequence class?

37. Suppose a sequence contains your three favorite strings, and the current item is the first item in the sequence. Draw the member variables of this sequence using our suggested implementation.

38. Write a new member function to remove a specified item from a sequence. The function has one parameter (the item to remove). After the removal, the current item is the item after the removed item (if there is one). You may assume that `value_type` has `==` and `!=` operators defined.

39. Which of the sequence member functions allocate dynamic memory?

40. Which of the sequence functions might use `list_piece` from Self-Test Exercise 24?

5.5 DYNAMIC ARRAYS VS LINKED LISTS VS DOUBLY LINKED LISTS

Many classes can be implemented with either dynamic arrays or linked lists. Certainly the bag, the string, and the sequence classes could each be implemented with either approach.

Which approach is better?

There is no absolute answer. But there are certain operations that are better performed by dynamic arrays and others where linked lists are preferable. Here are some guidelines:

Arrays are better at random access. The term **random access** refers to examining or changing an arbitrary element that is specified by its position in a list. For example: *What is the 42nd item in the list?* Or another example: *Change the item at position 1066 to a 7.* These are constant time operations for an array (or dynamic array). But, in a linked list, a search for item *i* must begin at the head and will take $O(i)$ time. Sometimes there are ways to speed up the process, but even improvements remain linear time.

If a class makes significant use of random access operations, then a dynamic array is better than a linked list.

Linked lists are better at insertions/deletions at a cursor. Our sequence class maintains a *cursor* that points to a "current element." Typically, a cursor moves through a list one item at a time without jumping around to random locations. If all operations occur at the cursor, then a linked list is preferable to an array. In particular, insertions and deletions at a cursor are generally linear time for an array (since items that are after the cursor must *all* be shifted up or back to a new index in the array). But these operations are constant time operations for a linked list. Also remember that effective insertions and deletions in a linked list generally require maintaining both a cursor and a *precursor* (which points to the node before the cursor).

If class operations take place at a cursor, then a linked list is better than a dynamic array.

Doubly linked lists are better for a two-way cursor. Sometimes list operations require a cursor that can move forward and backward through a list—a kind of **two-way cursor**. This situation calls for a **doubly linked list**, which is like a simple linked list, except that each node contains two pointers: one pointing to the next node and one pointing to the previous node. An example of a doubly linked list of integers is shown in Figure 5.15. A possible set of definitions for a doubly linked list of items is the following:

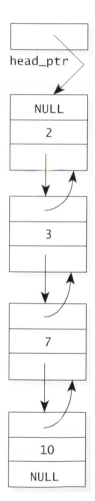

```
class dnode
{
public:
    typedef _____ value_type;      ← Fill in the value_type
    ...                              however you like.
private:
    value_type data_field;
    dnode *link_fore;
    dnode *link_back;
};
```

The `link_back` field points to the previous node, and the `link_fore` points to the next node in the list.

If class operations take place at a two-way cursor, then a doubly linked list is the best implementation.

FIGURE 5.15
Doubly Linked List

Resizing can be inefficient for a dynamic array. A container class that uses a dynamic array generally provides a resize function to allow a programmer to adjust the capacity as needed. But resizing an array can be inefficient. The new memory must be allocated; the items are then copied from the old memory to the new memory, and then the old memory is deleted. If a program can predict the necessary capacity ahead of time, then resizing is not a big problem, since the object can be given sufficient capacity from the outset. But sometimes the eventual capacity is unknown and a program must continually adjust the capacity. In this situation, a linked list has advantages. When a linked list grows, it grows one node at a time, and there is no need to copy items from old memory to new larger memory.

If a class is frequently adjusting its size, then a linked list may be better than a dynamic array.

Making the Decision

Your decision on what kind of implementation to use is based on your knowledge of which operations occur in the class, which operations you expect to be performed most often, and whether you expect your containers to require frequent resizing. Figure 5.16 summarizes these considerations.

Self-Test Exercises for Section 5.5

41. What underlying data structure is quickest for random access?
42. What underlying data structure is quickest for insertions/deletions at a cursor?
43. What underlying data structure is best if a cursor must move both forward and backward?
44. What is the typical worst-case time analysis for a resizing operation on a container class that is implemented with a dynamic array?
45. Implement a complete class for nodes of a doubly linked list. All member functions should be inline functions.
46. For your dnode class in the previous exercise, write a function that adds a new item at the head of a doubly linked list.

FIGURE 5.16 Guidelines for Choosing Between a Dynamic Array and a Linked List

Frequent random access operations	Use a dynamic array
Operations occur at a cursor	Use a linked list
Operations occur at a two-way cursor	Use a doubly linked list
Frequent resizing may be needed	A linked list avoids resizing inefficiency

CHAPTER SUMMARY

- A *linked list* consists of nodes; each *node* contains some data and a pointer to the next node in the list. The pointer field of the final node contains the null pointer.

- Typically, a linked list is accessed through a *head pointer* that points to the *head node* (i.e., the first node). Sometimes a linked list is accessed elsewhere, such as through the *tail pointer* that points to the last node.

- You should be familiar with our functions to manipulate a linked list. These functions follow basic patterns that every programmer uses. Such functions are not node member functions (so that they can handle empty lists with no nodes).

- Linked lists can be used to implement a class. Such a class has one or more private member variables that are pointers to nodes in a linked list. The member functions of the class use the linked-list functions to manipulate the linked list, which is accessed through private member variables.

- You have seen two classes implemented with the linked-list toolkit: a bag and a list. You will see more in the chapters that follow.

- Classes can often be implemented in many different ways, such as by using a dynamic array or using a linked list. In general, arrays are better at *random access*; linked lists are better at insertions/removals at a *cursor*.

- A *doubly linked list* has nodes with two pointers: one to the next node and one to the previous node. Doubly linked lists are a good choice for supporting a cursor that moves forward and backward.

Solutions to Self-Test Exercises ?

1. See the class definition on page 217.

2. The NULL pointer is a special value that can be used for any pointer that does not point anywhere. The `cstdlib` library should be included to use NULL, but because NULL is not part of the `std` namespace, it can be written without a preceding `std::`.

3. The null pointer is used for the link field of the final node of a linked list; it is also used for the head and tail pointers of a list that doesn't yet have any nodes.

4. Numbers are given a default value of 0, and bools are given a default value of false.

5. `head_ptr` is a pointer to a node. On the other hand, `*head_ptr` is a `node`, and the type of `head_ptr->data( )` is `node::value_type`.

6. `if (head_ptr->data( ) == 0)`
   `    cout << "zero";`

7. The operation of accessing a data member has higher precedence than the dereferencing asterisk. Therefore, `head_ptr.data( )` will cause a syntax error because the call to `data( )` is attempted before deferencing head. The alternative syntax is `head_ptr->data( );`

8. `cout << b_ptr->size( );`

9. The portions of the operating system that are currently in memory can be overwritten.

10. The implementation will compile correctly. But since the return value is a pointer to a node in the list, a programmer could use the return value to change the linked list. In general, the return value from a constant member function should never allow the underlying linked list to be changed.

11. Change the return type to *const* node*, and provide a second non-const function that returns the link as an ordinary node*.

12. We need only one function to access the data field because this function returns a copy of the data (and it is not possible to change the underlying linked list by having merely a copy of the data from a node).

13. The #include <string> directive must be added to the other include directives in the toolkit's header file. Then we can change the typedef statement to:

    typedef string value_type;

14. ```
    for (
          cursor = head_ptr;
          cursor != NULL;
          cursor = cursor -> link( )
       )
     {...}
    ```

15. A node pointer should be a value parameter when the function accesses and possibly modifies a linked list, but does not need to make the pointer point to a new node.

16. locate_ptr = locate_ptr->link( );
    If locate_ptr is already pointing to the last node before this assignment statement, then the assignment will set locate_ptr to the null pointer.

17. Using functions from Section 5.2:
    ```
    if (head_ptr == NULL)
        list_head_insert(head_ptr, 42);
    else
        list_insert(head_ptr, 42);
    ```

18. ```
    if (head_ptr->link( )==NULL)
        tail_ptr = head_ptr;
    ```

19. The *new* operator is used in the functions: list_insert, list_copy, list_piece (if you implement it from Exercise 18), and list_head_insert. The *delete* operator is used in the functions list_head_remove, list_remove, and list_clear.

20. Never call *delete* unless you are actually reducing the number of nodes.

21. Using functions from Section 5.2:
    ```
    if (head_ptr != NULL)
    {
        if (head_ptr->link() == NULL)
            list_head_remove(head_ptr);
        else
            list_remove(head_ptr);
    }
    ```

22. It will be the null pointer.

23. The one line will be:
    ```
    previous_ptr->set_link
        (new node
            (entry, previous_ptr->link())
    );
    ```

24. The implementation is nearly the same as list_copy, but the copying must stop when the end node has been copied.

25. Here is the const version:
    ```
    const node* list_locate(
        const node* head_ptr,
        size_t position
    )
    // Library facilities used: cassert, cstdlib
    {
        const node *cursor;
        size_t i;
        assert(0 < position);
        cursor = head_ptr;
        for (
              i = 1;
              (i < position)
              &&
              (cursor != NULL);
              ++i
           )
            cursor = cursor->link();
        return cursor;
    }
    ```

26. The definition makes bag::value_type the same as node::value_type, so that a programmer can use bag::value_type without having to know the details of the linked-list implementation.

27. The value_type in the node class would need to be changed to string (as in the answer to Self-Test Exercise 13).

28. Assuming that we have set the bag's value_type to a string, we would write this code:

```
bag exercise;
exercise.insert("squash");
exercise.insert("handball");
cout << exercise.grab( ) << endl;
cout << exercise.size( ) << endl;
```

29. Generally we will choose the approach that makes the best use of the previously written functions. This saves us work and also reduces the chance of new errors from writing new code to do an old job. The preference would change if writing new functions offered better efficiency.

30. The two lines of code that we have in mind:

```
p = p->link( );
p = list_search(p, d);
```

These two lines are the same as the single line:

```
p = list_search(p->link( ), d);
```

31. When the target is not in the bag, the first assignment statement to cursor will set it to the null pointer. This means that the body of the loop will not execute at all, and the function returns the answer zero.

32. The problem occurs when the target is the first item on the linked list. In this case, the target pointer is at the head of the list, so it would be a mistake to remove the head node before moving the target pointer forward.

33. The rand function from csdtlib generates a non-negative pseudorandom integer. A pseudorandom generator is advantageous for debugging a program because if the program is run again with the same initial conditions, the generator will produce exactly the same sequence of numbers.

34. (rand( ) % 21) - 10;

35. All the functions are constant time except for remove, grab, and count (which all are linear); the copy constructor and operator = (which are $O(n)$, where n is the size of the bag being copied); the operator += (which is $O(n)$, where n is the size of the addend); and the operator + (which is $O(m+n)$, where m and n are the sizes of the two bags).

36. A precursor node pointer is necessary in the sequence class because its insert function adds a new item immediately before the current node. Because the linked-list toolkit's insert function adds an item after a specified node, the precursor node is designated as that node.

37. many_nodes is 3, and these are the other member variables:

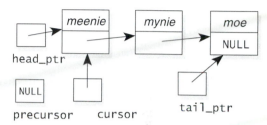

38. First check that the item occurs somewhere in the list. If it doesn't, then return with no work. If the item is in the list, then set the current item to be equal to this item, and call the ordinary erase_one function.

39. The insert and attach functions both allocate dynamic memory, as do the copy constructor and assignment operator.

40. The copy constructor and assignment operator might use list_piece.

41. Arrays are quickest for random access.

42. Linked lists are quickest for insertions/deletions at a cursor.

43. A doubly linked list is best.

44. $O(n)$, where n is the size of the array prior to resizing

45. See Figure 5.17 on page 274.

46. Here is one solution:

```
void dlist_head_insert(
    dnode*& head_ptr,
    const dnode::value_type& entry
)
{
    dnode *insert_ptr;
    insert_ptr =
        new dnode(entry, head_ptr);
    if (head_ptr != NULL)
        head_ptr->set_back(insert_ptr);
    head_ptr = insert_ptr;
}
```

FIGURE 5.17   Class Definition for a Node of Doubly Linked List

A Class Definition

```
class dnode
{
public:
    // TYPEDEF
    typedef double value_type;

    // CONSTRUCTOR
    dnode(
        const value_type& init_data = value_type( ),
        dnode* init_fore = NULL,
        dnode* init_back = NULL
    )
    { data_field = init_data; link_fore = init_fore; link_back = init_back;}

    // Member functions to set the data and link fields:
    void set_data(const value_type& new_data) { data_field = new_data; }
    void set_fore(dnode* new_fore)            { link_fore = new_fore; }
    void set_back(dnode* new_back)            { link_back = new_back; }

    // Const member function to retrieve the current data:
    value_type data( ) const { return data_field; }

    // Two slightly different member functions to retrieve each current link:
    const dnode* fore( ) const { return link_fore; }
    dnode* fore( )             { return link_fore; }
    const dnode* back( ) const { return link_back; }
    dnode* back( )             { return link_back; }
private:
    value_type data_field;
    dnode *link_fore;
    dnode *link_back;
};
```

www.cs.colorado.edu/~main/chapter5/dnode.cxx   **WWW**

PROGRAMMING PROJECTS
For more in-depth projects, please see www.cs.colorado.edu/~main/projects/

1 For this project, you will use the bag class with the value_type being a string from the <string> facility. The bag class should include the grab function from Figure 5.13 on page 261. Use this class in a program that does the following:

1. Asks the user for a list of ten nouns.
2. Asks the user for a list of ten verbs.
3. Prints some random sentences using the provided nouns and verbs.

For example, if two of the nouns were "monkey" and "piano," and two of the verbs were "eats" and "plays," then we can expect any of these sentences:

```
The monkey eats the piano.
The monkey plays the piano.
The piano eats the monkey.
The piano plays the monkey.
```

Needless to say, the sentences are not entirely sensible. Your program will need to declare two bag variables: one to store the nouns and one to store the verbs. Use an appropriate top-down design.

2 Write a function that takes a linked list of items and deletes all repetitions from the list. In your implementation, assume that items can be compared for equality using ==.

3 Write a function with three parameters. The first parameter is a head pointer for a linked list of items, and the next two parameters are items x and y. The function should write to the screen all items in the list that are between the first occurrence of x and the first occurrence of y. You may assume that items can be compared for equality using ==.

4 Write a function with one parameter that is a head pointer for a linked list of items. The function reverses the order of the nodes so that the last node is first, the first node is last, and so forth. The head pointer is a reference parameter, so that after the function completes, this same pointer variable is pointing to the head of the reversed list.

5 Write a function that has two linked-list head pointers as parameters. Assume that the linked list's items are ordered by the < operator. On each list, every item is less than the next item on the same list. The function should create a new linked list that contains all the items on both lists, and the new linked list should also be ordered (so that every item is less than the next item on the list). The new linked list should also eliminate duplicate items (i.e., if the same item appears on both input lists, then only one copy is placed in the newly constructed linked list). To eliminate duplicate items, you may assume that two items can be compared for equality using ==. The function should return a head pointer for the newly constructed linked list.

6 Write a function that starts with a single linked list of items and a special value called the *splitting value*. Two item values can be compared using the < operator—but the items of the original linked list are in no particular order. The procedure divides the nodes into two linked lists: one containing all the nodes that contain an item less than the splitting value, and one that contains all the other nodes. If the original linked list had any repeated integers (i.e., any two or more nodes with the same item in them) then the new linked list that has this item should have the same number of nodes that repeat this item. It does not matter whether you preserve the original linked list or destroy it in the process of building the two new lists, but your comments should document what happens to the original linked list.

7 Write a function that takes a linked list of integers and rearranges the nodes so that the integers stored are sorted into the order smallest to largest, with the smallest integer in the node at the head of the list. If the original list had any integers occurring more than once, then the changed list will have the same number of each integer. For concreteness you will use lists of integers, but your function should still work if you replace the integer type with any other type for which the less than operation is part of a total order semantics. Use the following function prototype and specification:

```
void sort_list(node*& head_ptr);
// Precondition: head_ptr is a head pointer of
// a linked list of items, and these items can be
// compared with a less-than operator.
// Postcondition: head_ptr points to the head
// of a linked list with exactly the same entries
// (including repetitions if any), but the entries
// in this list are sorted from smallest to
// largest. The original linked list is no longer
// available.
```

Your procedure will implement the following algorithm (which is often called **selection sort**): The algorithm removes nodes one at a time from the original list and adds the nodes to a second list until all the nodes have been moved to the second list. The second list will then be sorted.

```
// Pseudocode for selection sort
while (the first list still has some nodes)
{
        1. Find the node with the largest item of all
           the nodes in the first list.
        2. Remove this node from the first list.
        3. Insert this node at the head of the second
           list.
}
```

After all the nodes are moved to the second list, the pointer, head_ptr, can be moved to point to the head of the second list. Note that your function will move entire nodes, not just items, to the second list. Thus, the first list will get shorter and shorter until it is an empty list. Your function should not need to call the *new* operator since it is just moving nodes from one list to another (not creating new nodes).

8 Write a program for keeping a course list for each student in a college. The information about each student should be kept in an object that contains the student's name and a list of courses completed by the student. The courses taken by a student are stored as a linked list in which each node contains the name of a course, the number of units for the course, and the course grade. The program gives a menu with choices that include adding a student's record, deleting a student's record, adding a single course record to a student's record, deleting a single course record from a student's record, and printing a student's record to the screen. The program input should accept the student's name in any combination of upper- and lowercase letters. A student's record should include the student's GPA (grade point average) when displayed on the screen. When the user is through with the program, the program should store the records in a file. The next time the program is run, the records should be read back out of the file and the list should be reconstructed. (Ask your instructor if there are any rules about what type of file you should use.)

9 Implement operators for - and -= for the bag class from Section 5.3. See Chapter 3, Programming Project 2 on page 140 for details about how the operations work with a bag.

10 Implement operators for + and += for your sequence class from Section 5.4. For two lists x and y, the list x+y contains all the items of x, followed by all the items of y. The statement x += y appends all of the items of y to the end of what's already in x.

11 You can represent an integer with any number of digits by storing the integer as a linked list of digits. A more efficient representation will store a larger integer in each node. Design and implement a class for whole number arithmetic in which a number is implemented as a linked list of integers. Each node will hold an integer less than or equal to 999. The number represented is the concatenation of the numbers in the nodes. For example, if there are four nodes with the four integers 23, 7, 999, and 0, then this represents the number 23,007,999,000. Note that the number in a node is always considered to be three digits long. If it is not three digits long, then leading zeros are added to make it three digits long. Overload all the usual integer operators to work with your new class.

12 Revise one of the container classes from Chapter 3 or 4 so that it uses a linked list. Some choices are (a) the string from Section 4.5; (b) the set (Project 5 on page 141); (c) the sorted list (Project 6 on page 141); (d) the bag with receipts (Project 7 on page 141); (e) the keyed bag (Project 8 on page 142).

13 Revise the polynomial class from Section 4.6, so that the coefficients are stored in a linked list. The nodes should be stored in order from smallest to largest exponent. Also, there should never be two separate nodes with the same exponent.

Include an operation to allow you to multiply two polynomials in the usual way. For example:

$$(3x^2 + 7) * (2x + 4) = (6x^3 + 12x^2 + 14x + 28)$$

With this approach, many operations will be inefficient because each time a coefficient is needed, the search for that coefficient begins at the start of the linked list. A solution for this problem is discussed at www.cs.colorado.edu/~main/polynomial.html.

14 Implement the sequence class from Section 5.4 without a precursor. One problem caused by the missing precursor is the insert function is difficult to implement efficiently. One idea to overcome this problem is, when inserting a new item, to create a new node after the current node, copy the current data into the new node, and put the new entry into the current node.

15 Use a doubly linked list to implement the sequence class from Section 5.4. With a doubly linked list, there is no need to maintain a precursor. Your implementation should include a retreat member function that moves the cursor backward to the previous element.

16 Modify the card and deck classes from Chapter 2 (Project 4) and Chapter 3 (Project 15), so that they well be useful in a program to shuffle a deck of cards, deal all the cards to four players, and display each player's hand. For the shuffle function, generate a random number k for each card index whose value is from 0 to index. Then define a swap function to exchange the values for card[index] and card[k], using a swap function that you define.

17 In this project, you will implement a variation of the linked list called a *circular linked list*. The link field of the final node of a circular linked list is not NULL; instead the link member of the tail pointer points back to the first node. In this project, an external pointer is used to point to the beginning of the list; this pointer will be NULL if the list is empty (see Programming Project 9 in Chapter 8 for another variation of a circular linked list). Revise the third bag class developed in this chapter to use a circular linked-list implementation.

18 Use a circular linked list to run a simple simulation of a card game. Use the card and deck classes, and shuffle and deal functions from previous Programming Projects. Create a player class to hold a hand of dealt cards. During each turn, a player will discard a card. Use rand( ) to determine who gets the first turn in each hand, and make sure each person has a turn during every hand. The program ends when all cards have been played.

CHAPTER **6**

Software Development with Templates, Iterators, and the STL

*The goal of software reuse is to build systems of systems by
putting together independently developed software components.*
JEANNETTE WING
Address to the 12th MFPS Workshop, June 1996

LEARNING OBJECTIVES

When you complete Chapter 6, you will be able to...

- recognize situations in which template functions and template classes are appropriate.
- design and implement template functions and template classes.
- use the standard template classes for sets, multisets, and lists.
- use iterators to step through all the elements of an object for any of the standard template classes.
- manipulate objects of the standard template classes using functions from the algorithms library facility.
- implement simple forward iterators for our own classes, such as the bag class.

CHAPTER CONTENTS

Software Development with Templates, Iterators, and the STL

Professional programmers try to write functions and classes that have general applicability in many settings. To some extent, our classes do this already. Certainly, the bag, sequence, and node classes can be used in many different settings. However, these classes suffer from the fact that they require the underlying value_type to be fixed. A program cannot easily use both a bag of integers and a bag of strings.

This chapter provides a better approach to writing code that is meant to be reused in a variety of settings. The approach, called **templates**, is applicable to individual functions and to classes. By the end of the chapter you will know how to write **template functions** and **template classes** that can easily be used in a variety of settings. You will also learn how to provide a container class with a new kind of object—an **iterator**, which is an object that can step through all the items of a container in a standard manner. By following a standard approach that uses both templates and iterators, you will write classes that are easier for others to use and you yourself will be able to take advantage of certain components of the C++ Standard Template Library (STL).

6.1   TEMPLATE FUNCTIONS

Sometimes it seems that programmers intentionally make extra work for themselves. For example, suppose we write this function:

```
int maximal(int a, int b)
// Postcondition: The return value is the larger of a and b.
{
    if (a > b)
        return a;
    else
        return b;
}
```

This is a fine function, reliably returning the larger of two integers. But suppose that tomorrow you have another program that needs to compute the larger of two double numbers. Then you'll write a new function:

```
double maximal(double a, double b)
// Postcondition: The return value is the larger of a and b.
{
    if (a > b)
        return a;
    else
        return b;
}
```

The next day, you need a third function that returns the larger of two strings, (using the > relationship from the Standard Library `string` class). You'll write a third function:

```
string maximal(string a, string b)
// Postcondition: The return value is the larger of a and b.
{
    if (a > b)
        return a;
    else
        return b;
}
```

In fact, a single program can use all three of the `maximal` functions. When one of the functions is used, the compiler looks at the type of the arguments and selects the appropriate version of the `maximal` function. But with this approach, you do need to write a new function for each type of values that you want to compare.

Of course, you could write just one function, along with a typedef statement, like this:

```
typedef _____ item;
item maximal(item a, item b)
// Postcondition: The return value is the larger of a and b.
{
    if (a > b)
        return a;
    else
        return b;
}
```

Now, a programmer can fill in the typedef statement with any data type that has the > operator defined and that has a copy constructor. The copy constructor is needed because the function has two value parameters and returns an `item`, both of which use the copy constructor (see "Returning an Object from a Function" on page 187).

But the typedef approach has a problem. Suppose that a single program needs to use several different versions of the `maximal` function. The typedef approach does not allow this, since the program can define only one data type for the `item`.

The solution is a more flexible mechanism called a **template function**, which is similar to an ordinary function with one important difference: The definition of a template function can depend on an underlying data type. The underlying data type is given a name—such as `Item`—but `Item` is not pinned down to a specific type anywhere in the function's implementation. When a template function is used, the compiler examines the types of the arguments and at that point the compiler automatically determines the data type of `Item`. Moreover, in a single program, several different usages of a template function can result in several different underlying data types.

We avoided introducing template functions right away because the typedef has a simpler syntax. Also, extra pitfalls and cryptic compilation errors can arise from templates. Nevertheless, the advantages of templates make it worthwhile to use them. So, let's dive into the cumbersome syntax that we've been avoiding.

Syntax for a Template Function

As an example of a template function, we will alter the `maximal` function. The template function requires one change from the typedef approach, as shown next.

Using a Typedef Statement:	Defining a Template Function:

```
typedef int item;
item maximal(item a, item b)
{
    if (a > b)
        return a;
    else
        return b;
}
```

```
template <class Item>
Item maximal(Item a, Item b)
{
    if (a > b)
        return a;
    else
        return b;
}
```

With the typedef approach on the left, the `maximal` function compares two integers. Of course, we can change the underlying type of the compared elements by changing the typedef statement. On the other hand, the single definition of the template function allows a program to use the `maximal` function with two integers, or with two doubles, or with two strings—with any data type that has the > operator and a copy constructor.

The expression `template <class Item>` is called the **template prefix**. It warns the compiler that the following definition will use an unspecified data type called `Item`. The template prefix always precedes the template function's definition. In effect, the template prefix says, "`Item` is a data type that will be filled in later; don't worry about it for now, just use it inside the function definition!" The "unspecified type" is called the **template parameter**.

PROGRAMMING TIP

CAPITALIZE THE NAME OF A TEMPLATE PARAMETER

A common programming style capitalizes the name of template parameters to make it easy to recognize that these names are not specific types. Thus, the template function uses the name `Item` rather than `item`.

Notice that the template parameter is preceded by the keyword `class` and is surrounded by *angle brackets* (which are the same as the less-than and greater-than signs). An alternative is to use the keyword `typename` instead of `class`, but older compilers do not support this alternative.

Using a Template Function

A program can use a template function with any Item type that has the necessary features. In the case of the maximal function, the Item type can be any of the C++ built-in types (such as *int* or *char*), or it may be a class with the > operator and a copy constructor. For example, a program with the maximal template function can have the statement:

```
cout << maximal(1000, 2000);
```
⟵ *Print the larger integer.*

When the compiler sees this function call, it determines that the type of Item must be *int*, and it automatically uses the maximal function with Item defined as *int*. A C++ programmer says, "The maximal function has been **instantiated** with Item equal to *int*." The same program can use the template function to compare two strings, as shown here:

```
string s1("frijoles");
string s2("beans");
cout << maximal(s1, s2);
```
Print the string that is lexicographically larger.

A demonstration program using the maximal template function is shown in Figure 6.1. This program begins with the maximal template function. We placed the function at the start of the file because some compilers require that the entire template function appears before its use (rather than just a prototype). The maximal function itself is used twice in the main program—once to compare two strings and once to compare two integers.

Keep in mind that the compiler does not actually compile anything when it sees the implementation of the template function. It is only when the function is instantiated by using it in the main program (or elsewhere), that the compiler takes action to compile a certain version of the template function, using the specified type for the template parameter. In the case of our maximal function, the program in Figure 6.1 has one implementation of the maximal template function, and the one implementation is *instantiated* in two different ways (that is, with string class as the item type and with *int* as the item type).

 PITFALL

FAILED UNIFICATION ERRORS

There is a rule for template functions: *The template parameter must appear in the parameter list of the template function.* For example, Item appears twice in the parameter list maximal(Item a, Item b). Without this rule, the compiler cannot figure out how to instantiate the template function when it is used. Violating this rule will likely result in cryptic error messages such as "Failed unification." **Unification** is the compiler's term for determining how to instantiate a template function.

FIGURE 6.1	Demonstration Program for Template Functions

A Program

```
// FILE: maximal.cxx
// A demonstration program for a template function called maximal.

#include <cstdlib>    // Provides EXIT_SUCCESS
#include <iostream>   // Provides cout
#include <string>     // Provides string class
using namespace std;

// TEMPLATE FUNCTION used in this demonstration program:
// Note that some compilers require the entire function definition to appear before its use
// (rather than a mere prototype). This maximal function is similar to max from <algorithm>.
template <class Item>
Item maximal(Item a, Item b)
// Postcondition: Returns the larger of a and b.
// Note: Item may be any of the C++ built-in types (int, char, etc.), or a class with
// the > operator and a copy constructor.
{
    if (a > b)
        return a;
    else
        return b;
}

int main( )
{
    string s1("frijoles");
    string s2("beans");

    cout << "Larger of frijoles and beans: " << maximal(s1, s2) << endl;
    cout << "Larger of 10 and 20 : " << maximal(10, 20) << endl;
    cout << "It's a large world." << endl;

    return EXIT_SUCCESS;
}
```

The main program has two different uses of the maximal template function.

A Sample Dialogue

```
Larger of frijoles and beans: frijoles
Larger of 10 and 20: 20
It's a large world.
```

www.cs.colorado.edu/~main/chapter6/maximal.cxx   **WWW**

A Template Function to Swap Two Values

Here is a definition of another template function. The function swaps the values of two variables, as shown here:

```
template <class Item>
void swap(Item& x, Item& y);
// Postcondition: The values of x and y have been interchanged, so that y
//   now has the original value of x and vice versa. NOTE: Item may be any
//   of the C++ built-in types (int, char, etc.), or a class with an assignment
//   operator and a copy constructor.
{
    Item temp = x;
    x = y;
    y = temp;
}
```

In this example, the values of x and y are interchanged by the usual three assignment statements that use an intermediary temporary variable (`temp`). The example shows two new features. First, notice that the function uses a local variable, `temp`, whose type is `Item`. This is fine, so long as the `Item` type has the necessary constructor (we have indicated this requirement in the documentation).

The second feature of the function is that the underlying data type, `Item`, is used as a *reference* parameter. Thus, when swap is called, the actual parameters will have their values interchanged, as shown in this string example:

```
string name1("Castor");
string name2("Pollux");
swap(name1, name2);
cout << name1;
```

The two values are interchanged so that "Pollux" is printed.

★ C++ FEATURE

SWAP, MAX, AND MIN FUNCTIONS

The `<algorithm>` facility in the C++ Standard Library contains the swap function, a max function that is similar to our `maximal`, and a min function that returns the smaller of two items.

Parameter Matching for Template Functions

Our next template function searches an array for the biggest item and returns the index of that item. For example, the array could be an array of six integers, shown here:

10	20	30	1	2	3
[0]	[1]	[2]	[3]	[4]	[5]

The biggest value, 30, appears at location [2], so with this array as the argument, our function returns 2. Here is the template function's complete specification:

```
template <class Item>
size_t index_of_maximal(const Item data[ ], size_t n);
// Precondition: data is an array with at least n items, and n > 0.
// Postcondition: The return value is the index of a maximal item from
// data[0] ... data[n - 1]. Note: Item may be any of the C++ built-in types
// (int, char, etc.), or any class with the > operator defined.
```

Actually, this specification is not exactly what we want. To explain the problem, we need to know a bit more about how the compiler uses template functions.

When a template function is instantiated, the compiler tries to select the underlying data type so that the type of each argument results in an *exact match* with the type of the corresponding formal parameter. For example, suppose that d is a *double* variable. You cannot write `maximal(d, 1)`, since there is no way for the compiler to have `Item` be an exact match with the type of the first argument (*double*) and also be an exact match with the type of the second argument (*int*). The compiler does not convert arguments for a template function. The arguments must have an exact match, with no type conversion.

The requirement of an exact match applies to *all* parameters of a template function. For example, consider the `index_of_maximal` prototype:

```
template <class Item>
size_t index_of_maximal(const Item data[ ], size_t n);
```

When we call the function, the second argument must be a `size_t` value. Many compilers won't accept any deviation: not an *int*, not a *const* `size_t`, only a `size_t` value. On such a strict compiler, the following will fail:

```
const size_t SIZE = 5;
double data[SIZE];
...
cout << index_of_maximal(data, SIZE);
cout << index_of_maximal(data, 5);
```

These won't work with many compilers.

The first function call, with `SIZE` as the second argument, fails on many compilers because `SIZE` is declared as *const* `size_t` rather than a mere `size_t`. The second function call, with 5 as the second argument, fails because the compiler takes 5 to be an *int* rather than a `size_t` value.

A Template Function to Find the Biggest Item in an Array

For the `index_of_maximal` function, we can deal with the problem by slightly changing the specification. The new specification uses two template parameters, one for the data type of the array's components, and a second for the data type of the size of the array, as shown here:

```
template <class Item, class SizeType>
size_t index_of_maximal(const Item data[ ], SizeType n);
// Precondition: data is an array with at least n items, and n > 0.
// Postcondition: The return value is the index of a maximal item from
// data[0] ... data[n - 1]. Note: Item may be any of the C++ built-in types
// (int, char, etc.), or any class with the > operator defined.
// SizeType may be any of the integer or const integer types.
```

With this template function, we have more flexibility. Both of these are okay:

```
const size_t SIZE = 5;
double data[SIZE];
...
cout << index_of_maximal(data, SIZE);
cout << index_of_maximal(data, 5);
```

SizeType will be const size_t.

SizeType will be int.

Now we can implement the template function. The function uses a local variable, answer, to keep track of the index of the biggest item that has been seen so far. Initially, answer is set to zero, meaning that the biggest item seen so far is at data[0]. Then we step through the rest of the array: data[1], data[2], and so on. If we spot an item that is bigger than data[answer], then we change answer to the index of that bigger item. Notice that it's okay to use size_t for the return type or for a local variable (or, to be more complete, we have used std::size_t in case this function is not under the control of a directive to use the namespace std):

```
template <class Item, class SizeType>
std::size_t index_of_maximal(const Item data[ ], SizeType n)
// Library facilities used: cassert, cstdlib
{
    std::size_t answer;
    std::size_t i;

    assert(n > 0);
    answer = 0;

    for (i = 1; i < n; ++i)
    {
        if (data[answer] < data[i])
            answer = i;
        // data[answer] is now biggest from data[0]...data[i]
    }

    return answer;
}
```

PITFALL

MISMATCHES FOR TEMPLATE FUNCTION ARGUMENTS

Each argument to a template function must be an exact match to the data type of the formal parameter, with no type conversions. C++ compilers provide a little leeway on the meaning of "exact match." For example, with an *int* argument the formal parameter may be any of the following:

> *int* (a value parameter)
> *int&* (a reference parameter)
> *const int&* (a const reference parameter)

But for many compilers, an *int* argument does *not* provide an exact match to size_t. With this in mind, we generally will use an extra template parameter for the data type of an integer or size_t argument. For example:

```
template <class Item, class SizeType>
std::size_t index_of_maximal(const Item data[ ], SizeType n);
```

A Template Function to Insert an Item into a Sorted Array

Our next example defines a template function to insert a new entry into an array that is already sorted from small to large. The insertion must keep all the items in order from small to large. Here is the function's specification:

```
template <class Item, class SizeType>
void ordered_insert(Item data[ ], SizeType n, Item entry);
// Precondition: data is a partially filled array containing n items sorted from
// small to large. The array is large enough to hold at least one more item.
// Postcondition: data is a partially filled array containing the n original items
// plus the new entry. These items are still sorted from small to large.
// NOTE: Item may be any of the C++ built-in types (int, char, etc.), or a
// class with the < operator, an assignment operator, and a copy
// constructor. SizeType may be any of the integer or const integer types.
```

For example, suppose that data is this partially filled array of integers, sorted from small to large:

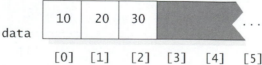

We can use the ordered_insert function to insert a new number, as shown here:

```
ordered_insert(data, 3, 15);
```

The compiler will call `ordered_insert`, with both `Item` and `SizeType` instantiated as *int*. After the insertion, the partially filled array contains four items, which are still sorted from small to large:

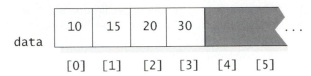

The function must take care to insert the new entry at the correct position so that everything stays sorted. We suggest that you shift items at the end of the array rightward one position each until you find the correct position for the new entry.

For example, suppose you are inserting 3 in this partially filled, sorted array:

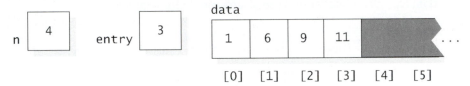

You would begin by shifting the 11 rightward from `data[3]` to `data[4]`; then move the 9 from `data[2]` to `data[3]`; then the 6 moves from `data[1]` to `data[2]`. At this point, the array looks like this:

Of course, `data[1]` actually still contains a 6 since we just copied the 6 from `data[1]` to `data[2]`. But we have drawn `data[1]` as an empty box to indicate that `data[1]` is now available to hold the new entry (i.e., the 3 that we're inserting). At this point we can place the 3 in `data[1]`, as shown here:

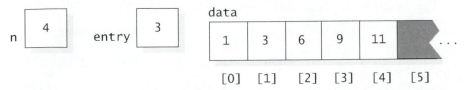

The pseudocode for shifting the items rightward uses a for-loop. Each iteration of the loop shifts one item, as shown here:

```
for (i = n;  data[i] is the wrong spot for entry ;  --i)
    data[i] = data[i-1];
```

The key to the loop is the test "`data[i]` is the wrong spot for `entry`." A position is wrong if (`i > 0`) and the item at `data[i-1]` is greater than the new entry. We know that such a position must be wrong because placing the new entry at this position would end up with `data[i-1] > data[i]`. Can you now write the loop's test in C++? (See the answer to Self-Test Exercise 7.)

Self-Test Exercises for Section 6.1

1. Describe the main purpose of a template function.
2. What is the disadvantage of the typedef approach of generalizing a data type compared to the template approach? Is there any advantage to the typedef approach?
3. What is the template prefix, and where is it used in a template function?
4. What is meant by unification?
5. Which data types are allowed for the template `Item` parameter in the maximal function?
6. Write a template function that compares two items. If the items are equal, then the message "Those are the same" is printed. Otherwise the message "Those are different" is printed. The function has two parameters. The parameter type may be any type that has a copy constructor and has the `==` operator defined.
7. Write an implementation of the `ordered_insert` template function.
8. Why is it a bad idea to have a `size_t` parameter for a template function?

6.2 TEMPLATE CLASSES

A template function is a function that depends on an underlying data type. In a similar way, when a class depends on an underlying data type, the class can be implemented as a **template class**, resulting in the same advantages that you have seen for template functions. For example, with the bag as a template class, a single program can use a bag of integers, and a bag of characters, and a bag of strings, and so on. Our first example will implement a bag as a template class.

Syntax for a Template Class

Our original approach to the bag used a typedef statement to define the underlying data type. Implementing a bag as a template class requires three changes from this original approach. The changes are outlined below.

1. The template class definition. The first change is to the class definition. We put the template prefix *template <class Item>* immediately before the bag's class definition, and define the bag's `value_type` to be equal to this unspecified `Item`. This template syntax is compared to the typedef approach here:

Using a Typedef Statement:	**Using a Template Class:**

```
class bag
{
public:
    typedef int value_type;
    . . .
```

```
template <class Item>
class bag
{
public:
    typedef Item value_type;
    . . .
```

The expression `template <class Item>` is the **template prefix**. It warns the compiler that the following definition will use an unspecified data type called `Item`. We are telling the compiler "`Item` is a data type that will be filled in later; don't worry about it now, just use it inside the bag class!"

2. Implementing functions for the template class. The bag's `value_type` is now dependent on the `Item` type. If `Item` is *int*, then we have a bag of integers; if `Item` is *double*, then we have a bag of doubles; if `Item` is a frijole (whatever that is!), then we have bags of frijoles.

Within the template class definition, the compiler already knows about the dependency on the `Item` data type, so that we may write the name of the data type bag, just as we always have. But, *outside of the template class definition* (that is, after the closing semicolon of the definition), some rules are required to tell the compiler about the dependency on the `Item` data type:

- The template prefix `template <class Item>` is placed immediately before each function prototype and definition. This occurs for member defintions and other functions that manipulate bags. In other words, each of these functions is now a template function, dependent on the data type of the items.

- Outside of the template class definition, each use of the class name (such as bag) is changed to the template class name (such as bag<Item>). This tells the compiler that the class is a template class, rather than an ordinary class. One warning: The name `bag` is changed to `bag<Item>` *only* when it is used as a class name. In particular, the name bag is also used as the name of the bag's constructor, and that usage remains simply bag.

use Item instead of value_type

- Within a class definition or within a member function, we can still use the bag's type names such as `size_type` or `value_type`. However, we will typically use `Item` instead of `value_type` because it reminds us that the class is a template class.

the need for the typename keyword

- Outside of a member function, to use a type such as bag<Item>:: `size_type`, we must add a new keyword, *typename*, writing the expression *typename* bag<Item>::`size_type`. This uses the new *typename* keyword to tell the compiler that the expression is the name of a data type.

- Some compilers require that any default argument is placed in both the prototype and the function implementation (though we followed the more usual standard of listing it only in the prototype).

Some examples can illustrate how these rules are applied. As a first example, recall that the bag has overloaded the + operator as a nonmember function. For our original bag class, the function's implementation began this way:

```
bag operator +(const bag& b1, const bag& b2)...
```

For the template class, the start of the implementation is shown here:

```
template <class Item>
bag<Item> operator +(const bag<Item>& b1, const bag<Item>& b2)...
```

As another example of these rules, consider the beginning of the count function in the original bag:

```
bag::size_type bag::count(const value_type& target) const ...
```

The function's return type is specified as `bag::size_type`. But this return type is specified before the compiler realizes that this is a bag member function. So we must put the keyword *typename* before bag<Item>::size_type. We also use Item instead of `value_type`:

```
template <class Item>
typename bag<Item>::size_type  bag<Item>::count
     (const Item & target) const ...
```

USE THE NAME ITEM AND THE TYPENAME KEYWORD

To us, it is clear that an expression such as bag<Item>::value_type is the name of a data type. But many compilers will not recognize that it is a data type. To help the compiler, use Item instead of value_type. Also, outside of a member function, you must put the keyword *typename* in front of any member of a template class that is the name of a data type (for example *typename* bag<Item>:: size_type). This is required only when the Item is still unspecified; for example it is not needed if a program uses a particular item such as bag<*int*>::size_type.

Examples:

In the Original Bag	In the Template Bag Class
value_type	Item
size_type (inside a member function)	size_type
size_type (outside a member function)	*typename* bag<Item>::size_type

3. Make the implementation visible. The third change to create a template class is an annoying requirement: In the header file, you place the documentation and the prototypes of the functions—*then you must include the actual implementations of all the functions.* This is annoying because we try to *avoid* revealing our implementations, and suddenly all is revealed! The reason for the requirement is to make the compiler's job simpler. We recommend that you meet the requirement in a backdoor manner: Keep the implementations in a separate implementation file, but place an include directive at the bottom of the header file to pick up these implementations, as shown at the bottom of our new bag's header file (`bag4.h`) shown in Figure 6.2. Near the end of the header file, on page 294, we have the following line, which causes the inclusion of the implementation file:

```
#include "bag4.template"    // Include the implementation.
```

 **PITFALL**

DO NOT PLACE USING DIRECTIVES IN A TEMPLATE IMPLEMENTATION

Because a template class has its implementation included in the header file, we must not place any using directives in the implementation (otherwise, every program that uses our template class will inadvertently pick up our using directives).

More About the Template Implementation File

Figure 6.2 shows the new bag header file (`bag4.h`) and implementation file (`bag4.template`). The name of the implementation file is `bag4.template` (rather than `bag4.cxx`) reminding us that the implementations cannot be compiled on their own. In the implementation, we could have used any of the previous bag techniques: a *static array*, a *dynamic array*, or a *linked list*. The actual approach that we used in the new template class is an implementation with a dynamic array.

Summary
How to Convert a Container Class to a Template

1. The template prefix precedes each function prototype or implementation.

2. Outside the class defintion, place the word `<Item>` with the class name, such as `bag<Item>`.

3. Use the name `Item` instead of `value_type`.

4. Outside of member functions and the class defintion itself, add the keyword *typename* before any use of one of the class's type names. For example:
   typename `bag<Item>::size_type`

5. The implementation file name now ends with `.template` (instead of `.cxx`), and it is included in the header by an include directive.

6. Eliminate any using directives in the implementation file. Therefore, we must then write `std::` in front of any Standard Library function such as `std::copy`.

7. Some compilers require any default argument to be in both the prototype and the function implementation.

A Header File

```
// FILE: bag4.h (part of the namespace main_savitch_6A)
// TEMPLATE CLASS PROVIDED:  bag<Item>
//
// TEMPLATE PARAMETER, TYPEDEFS, and MEMBER CONSTANTS for the bag<Item> class:
//     The template parameter, Item, is the data type of the items in the bag, also defined as
//     bag::value_type. It may be any of the C++ built-in types (int, char, etc.), or a class with a
//     default constructor, a copy constructor,  an assignment operator, and operators to test
//     for equality (x == y) and non-equality (x != y). The definition bag::size_type is the data
//     type of any variable that keeps track of how many items are in a bag. The static const
//     DEFAULT_CAPACITY is the initial capacity of a bag created by the default constructor.
//
// CONSTRUCTOR for the bag<Item> template class:
//     bag(size_type initial_capacity = DEFAULT_CAPACITY)
//         Postcondition: The bag is empty with the specified initial capacity. The insert
//         function works efficiently (without allocating new memory) until this capacity is reached.
//
// MODIFICATION MEMBER FUNCTIONS for the bag<Item> template class:
//     size_type erase(const Item& target)
//         Postcondition: All copies of target have been removed from the bag.
//         The return value is the number of copies removed (which could be zero).
//
//     bool erase_one(const Item& target)
//         Postcondition: If target was in the bag, then one copy has been removed;
//         otherwise the bag is unchanged. A true return value indicates that one
//         copy was removed; false indicates that nothing was removed.
//
//     void insert(const Item& entry)
//         Postcondition: A new copy of entry has been inserted into the bag.
//
//     void operator +=(const bag& addend)
//         Postcondition: Each item in addend has been added to this bag.
//
//     void reserve(size_type new_capacity)
//         Postcondition: The bag's current capacity is changed to the new_capacity (but not less
//         than the number of items already in the bag). The insert function will work efficiently
//         (without allocating new memory) until the new capacity is reached.
//
// CONSTANT MEMBER FUNCTIONS for the bag<Item> template class:
//     size_type count(const Item& target) const
//         Postcondition: Return value is the number of times target is in the bag.
//
//     Item grab( ) const
//         Precondition: size( ) > 0.
//         Postcondition: The return value is a randomly selected item from the bag.
//
//     size_type size( ) const
//         Postcondition: The return value is the total number of items in the bag.    (continued)
```

(FIGURE 6.2 continued)

```
// NONMEMBER FUNCTIONS for the bag<Item> template class:
//     bag<Item> operator +(const bag<Item>& b1, const bag<Item>& b2)
//     Postcondition: The bag returned is the union of b1 and b2.
// VALUE SEMANTICS: Assignments and the copy constructor may be used with bag objects.
// DYNAMIC MEMORY USAGE by the bag<Item> template class:
//     If there is insufficient dynamic memory, then the following functions throw bad_alloc:
//     the constructors, reserve, insert, operator += , operator +, and the assignment operator.

#ifndef MAIN_SAVITCH_BAG4_H
#define MAIN_SAVITCH_BAG4_H
#include <cstdlib> // Provides size_t

namespace main_savitch_6A
{
    template <class Item>  ←————————— the template prefix
    class bag
    {
    public:
        // TYPEDEFS and MEMBER CONSTANTS
        typedef Item value_type;
        typedef std::size_t size_type;
        static const size_type DEFAULT_CAPACITY = 30;
        // CONSTRUCTORS and DESTRUCTOR
        bag(size_type initial_capacity = DEFAULT_CAPACITY);
        bag(const bag& source);
        ~bag( );
        // MODIFICATION MEMBER FUNCTIONS
        size_type erase(const Item& target);
        bool erase_one(const Item& target);
        void insert(const Item& entry);
        void operator =(const bag& source);
        void operator +=(const bag& addend);
        void reserve(size_type capacity);
        // CONSTANT MEMBER FUNCTIONS
        size_type count(const Item& target) const;
        Item grab( ) const;
        size_type size( ) const { return used; }
    private:
        Item *data;             // Pointer to partially filled dynamic array
        size_type used;         // How much of array is being used
        size_type capacity;     // Current capacity of the bag
    };

    // NONMEMBER FUNCTION
    template <class Item>
    bag<Item> operator +(const bag<Item>& b1, const bag<Item>& b2);
}

#include "bag4.template"   // Include the implementation.
#endif
```

(continued)

(FIGURE 6.2 continued)

An Implementation File

```
// FILE: bag4.template
// TEMPLATE CLASS IMPLEMENTED: bag<Item> (see bag4.h for documentation)
// This file should be included in the header file and not compiled separately.
// Because of this, we must not have any using directives in the implementation.
//
// INVARIANT for the bag class:
//   1. The number of items in the bag is in the member variable used.
//   2. The actual items of the bag are stored in a partially filled array.
//      The array is a dynamic array, pointed to by the member variable data.
//   3. The size of the dynamic array is in the member variable capacity.
#include <algorithm> // Provides copy
#include <cassert>   // Provides assert
#include <cstdlib>   // Provides rand
```

Outside of the class definition, each definition is preceded by the template prefix.

```
namespace main_savitch_6A
{
    template <class Item>
    const typename bag<Item>::size_type bag<Item>::DEFAULT_CAPACITY;

    template <class Item>
    bag<Item>::bag(size_type initial_capacity)
    {
        data = new Item[initial_capacity];
        capacity = initial_capacity;
        used = 0;
    }
```

Outside of the class definition, the use of bag as a type name is changed to bag<Item>. Also, the keyword typename must precede any use of bag<Item>::size_type and the value_type is written as Item.

```
    template <class Item>
    bag<Item>::bag(const bag<Item>& source)
    // Library facilities used: algorithm
    {
        data = new Item[source.capacity];
        capacity = source.capacity;
        used = source.used;
        std::copy(source.data, source.data + used, data);
    }
```

```
    template <class Item>
    bag<Item>::~bag( )
    {
        delete [ ] data;
    }
```

Within the implementation file, we don't put any using directives, so we must write std::copy rather than simply copy.

(continued)

(FIGURE 6.2 continued)

```
template <class Item>
typename bag<Item>::size_type bag<Item>::erase(const Item& target)
```
‖ No change from the original bag: See the solution to Self-Test Exercise 12 on page 139.

```
template <class Item>
bool bag<Item>::erase_one(const Item& target)
```
‖ No change from the original bag: See the implementation in Figure 3.3 on page 113.

```
template <class Item>
void bag<Item>::insert(const Item& entry)
```
‖ No change from the Chapter 4 bag: See the implementation in Figure 4.11 on page 183.

```
template <class Item>
void bag<Item>::operator =(const bag<Item>& source)
```
‖ This uses std::copy (instead of copy); otherwise the same as Figure 4.10 on page 181.

```
template <class Item>
void bag<Item>::operator +=(const bag<Item>& addend).
```
‖ This uses std::copy (instead of copy); otherwise the same as Figure 4.11 on page 183.

```
template <class Item>
void bag<Item>::reserve(size_type new_capacity)
```
‖ This uses std::copy (instead of copy); otherwise the same as Figure 4.11 on page 183.

```
template <class Item>
typename bag<Item>::size_type bag<Item>::count(const Item& target) const
```
‖ No change from the original bag: See the implementation in Figure 3.6 on page 118.

```
template <class Item>
Item bag<Item>::grab( ) const
{
    size_type i;

    assert(size( ) > 0);
    i = (std::rand( ) % size( )); // i is in the range of 0 to size( ) - 1.
    return data[i];
}
```

```
template <class Item>
bag<Item> operator +(const bag<Item>& b1, const bag<Item>& b2)
```
‖ This uses bag<Item> (for the answer); otherwise the same as Figure 4.11 on page 183.

```
}
```

www.cs.colorado.edu/~main/chapter6/bag4.h and bag4.template　　**WWW**

Parameter Matching for Member Functions of Template Classes

In the implementation of a template function, we are careful to help the compiler by providing a template parameter for each of the function's parameters. (See "Mismatches for Template Function Arguments" on page 287.) However, this help is not needed for *member* functions of a template class. For example, we can use a simple `size_type` parameter for the bag's `reserve` function. Unlike an ordinary template function, the compiler is able to match a `size_type` parameter of a member function with any of the usual integer arguments (such as *int* or *const int*). If b is a bag object of our new template class, then we may call `b.reserve(42)`, with the actual argument being the integer 42. The compiler will convert this integer to the equivalent `size_type` value.

Using the Template Class

Using the `bag` template class is easy. A program includes the `bag4.h` header file, and then any kind of bag can be declared. To declare a bag, you write the class name, bag, followed by the name of the data type for the template parameter (in angle brackets). For example, if a program needs one bag of characters and one bag of double numbers, then the program uses these two declarations:

```
bag<char> letters;
bag<double> scores;
```

When an actual bag is declared, as in these examples, the template parameter is said to be **instantiated**. In the `letters` bag, the template parameter is instantiated as a character; in the `scores` bag, the template parameter is instantiated as a double number. A program that includes the `<string>` header file can even create a bag of strings, as shown here:

```
bag<string> verbs;
```

Figure 6.3 on page 298 shows a program that uses a bag of integers and two bags of strings. The program asks the user to type several adjectives, numbers, and names. These items are placed in the bags, and then items are grabbed out of the bags in order for the program to write a silly story called "Life."

The bags are declared in the demonstration program as you would expect:

```
bag<string> adjectives;  // Contains adjectives typed by user
bag<int>    ages;        // Contains ages in the teens
bag<string> names;       // Contains names typed by user
```

After these declarations, the program can use the bags `adjectives` and `names` just like any other bag of strings, whereas `ages` can be used just like any other bag of integers. Let's discuss the details of the story-writing program.

FIGURE 6.3   Demonstration Program for the Bag Template Class

A Program

```
// FILE: author.cxx
// The program reads some words into bags of strings, and some numbers into
// a bag of integers. Then a silly story is written using these words.

#include <cstdlib>       // Provides EXIT_SUCCESS
#include <iostream>      // Provides cout and cin
#include <string>        // Provides string class
#include "bag4.h"        // Provides the bag template class
using namespace std;
using namespace main_savitch_6A;

const int ITEMS_PER_BAG = 4;   // Number of items to put into each bag
const int MANY_SENTENCES = 3;  // Number of sentences in the silly story

template <class Item, class SizeType, class MessageType>
void get_items(bag<Item>& collection, SizeType n, MessageType description)
// Postcondition: The description has been written as a prompt to the
// screen. Then n items have been read from cin and added to the collection.
// Library facilities used: bag4.h, iostream
{
    Item user_input; // An item typed by the program's user
    SizeType i;

    cout << "Please type " << n << " " << description;
    cout << ", separated by spaces.\n";
    cout << "Press the <return> key after the final entry:\n";
    for (i = 1; i <= n; ++i)
    {
        cin >> user_input;
        collection.insert(user_input);
    }
    cout << endl;
}
```

(continued)

(FIGURE 6.3 continued)

```
int main( )
{
    bag<string> adjectives;    // Contains adjectives typed by user
    bag<int>    ages;          // Contains ages in the teens typed by user
    bag<string> names;         // Contains names typed by user
    int line_number;           // Number of the output line

    // Fill the three bags with items typed by the program's user.
    cout << "Help me write a story.\n";
    get_items(adjectives, ITEMS_PER_BAG, "adjectives that describe a mood");
    get_items(ages,       ITEMS_PER_BAG, "integers in the teens");
    get_items(names,      ITEMS_PER_BAG, "first names");
    cout << "Thank you for your kind assistance.\n\n";

    // Use the items to write a silly story.
    cout << "LIFE\n";
    cout << "by A. Computer\n";
    for (line_number = 1; line_number <= MANY_SENTENCES; ++line_number)
        cout << names.grab( )         << " was only "
             << ages.grab( )          << " years old, but he/she was "
             << adjectives.grab( ) << ".\n";
    cout << "Life is " << adjectives.grab( ) << ".\n";
    cout << "The (" << adjectives.grab( ) << ") end\n";

    return EXIT_SUCCESS;
}
```

A Sample Dialogue

```
Help me write a story.
Please type 4 adjectives that describe a mood, separated by spaces.
Press the <return> key after the final entry:
joyous  happy  sad  glum

Please type 4 integers in the teens, separated by spaces.
Press the <return> key after the final entry:
19  16  13  16

Please type 4 first names, separated by spaces.
Press the <return> key after the final entry:
Mike  Walt  Cathy  Harry

Thank you for your kind assistance.

LIFE
by A. Computer
Cathy was only 13 years old, but he/she was happy.
Walt was only 19 years old, but he/she was happy.
Mike was only 16 years old, but he/she was joyous.
Life is glum.
The (sad) end
```

www.cs.colorado.edu/~main/chapter6/author.cxx   **W W W**

.

Details of the Story-Writing Program

The story-writing program uses a function, get_items, which is actually a template function with this specification:

```
template <class Item, class SizeType, class MessageType>
void get_items(bag<Item>& collection, SizeType n, MessageType description);
// Postcondition: The description has been written as a prompt to the
// screen. Then n items have been read from cin and added to the collection.
```

The function uses the third parameter, description, as part of a prompt that asks the user to type n items. For example, if description is the string constant "first names" and n is 4, then the get_items function writes this prompt:

```
Please type 4 first names, separated by spaces.
Press the <return> key after the final entry:
```

The function then reads n items and places them in the bag with the insert member function. Because the function is a template function that depends on the Item data type, we can use the function with any kind of bag—with a bag of strings, or a bag of integers, or even some other kind of bag. In fact, the template prefix indicates that the function depends on *three* classes:

- *class* Item: This is the type of the item in the bag.
- *class* SizeType: This is the type of the second parameter, n. It may be any integer data type such as *int* or size_t.
- *class* MessageType: This may be any printable data type such as a string constant or even a string variable.

The literary merit of the program's story is debatable, but the ability to use several different kinds of bags in the same program is clearly important.

Self-Test Exercises for Section 6.2

9. When you implement a template class, the entire implementation file is included in the header file. Why is this needed?
10. When you write a template class, where does the template prefix occur?
11. Why should the using directive be avoided in an implementation file of a template class?
12. When does instantiation of a template parameter occur?
13. Name two places in the bag template class where the name bag is not changed to bag<Item>.
14. Describe the purpose of the C++ keyword *typename* as used in this section.

15. The bag implementation uses the `copy` function from the `<algorithm>` facility. Why do we need to write the full name `std::copy` in the implementation of the bag template, but we write the shorter version, `copy`, in the implementation of the ordinary class?

16. Write declarations for three bags with three different item types. Can you use all three bags in a single program?

6.3   STANDARD TEMPLATE CLASSES AND THEIR ITERATORS

The ANSI/ISO C++ Standard provides a variety of container classes called the **Standard Template Library** (STL). The STL classes are summarized in Appendix H. This section provides a first introduction to one of the classes—the multiset—including a feature called the *iterator*, which permits a programmer to easily step through all the elements of an STL container class.

The Multiset Template Class

A multiset is an STL class similar to our bag. Just like the bag, it permits a collection of items to be stored, where each item may occur multiple times in the multiset. Another STL class, the set class, has the same interface as the multiset class, except that it stores elements without repetition. Additional insertions of an element that is already in a set will have no effect.

A program that uses multisets or sets must include the header file `<set>`. Here's a small example that creates a multiset of integers, called `first`:

```
multiset<int> first;
first.insert(8);
first.insert(4);            After these statements, first
first.insert(8);            contains two 8s and a 4.
```

In the example, `first` is a multiset of integers, as indicated by `<int>`, which instantiates the type of the container's items as integers. The type of the item in a multiset has one restriction that is not required for our own bag: it must be possible to compare two items using a "less than" operator. Usually, this comparison operator is simply the "<" operator that is provided for a built-in data type (such as integers) or provided as a function for a class (such as strings). There are several other ways to provide a comparison function, but however it is defined, it must satisfy the rules of a strict weak ordering, as shown in Figure 6.4. The reason for the restriction is to allow a more efficient implementation that we will examine in Chapter 10. But before we get to that implementation, let's examine some of the multiset member functions.

Some Multiset Members

Constructors. A default constructor creates an empty multiset; a copy constructor makes a copy of another multiset. There are also other constructors that we won't use.

Members that are similar to the bag. These members are similar to our bag:

A type definition for the `value_type`
A type definition for the `size_type`
`size_type count(`*const* `value_type& target)` *const*;
`size_type erase(`*const* `value_type& target)`;
`size_type size( )` *const*;

The insert member function. The multiset's `insert` function can be used exactly like the bag's `insert` function to add an item to a multiset. However, the actual prototype for the multiset's `insert` function specifies a return value called an iterator, as shown here:

`iterator insert(`*const* `value_type& entry);`

Let's examine the multiset's iterator in some detail.

Iterators and the [...] Pattern

An **iterator** is an object that permits a programmer to easily step through all the items in a container, examining the items and (perhaps) changing them. Any STL container has a standard member function called `begin`. The return value of the `begin` function is an iterator that provides access to the first item in the container.

For a multiset, this "first" element is the smallest item according to the "less than" ordering that must be provided for the item type of any multiset. For other kinds of container classes, the "first" element might be implemented in some other way, and the exact mechanism used by `begin` isn't usually important.

FIGURE 6.4   Strict Weak Ordering

A **strict weak ordering** for a class is a comparison operator (<) that meets these requirements:

1. **Irreflexivity:** If x and y are equal, then neither (x < y) nor (y < x) is true. Among other things, this means that (x < x) is never true.

2. **Antisymmetry:** If x and y are not equal, then either (x < y) or (y < x) is true, but not both.

3. **Transitivity:** Whenever there are three values (x, y, and z) with (x < y) and (y < z), then (x < z) is also true.

The important concept is a general pattern whereby a programmer can use the begin function and related operations to step through all the items in a container. In all, there are four operations required for the pattern:

- **begin:** A container has a begin member function that we have already discussed. Its return value is an iterator that provides access to the first item in the container. For example, suppose that actors is a multiset of strings, then we can write this code to obtain the beginning iterator:

  ```
  multiset<string>::iterator role;
  role = actors.begin( );
  ```

  The iterator in this example is a variable called role, and its data type is multiset<string>::iterator. The multiset<string>::iterator data type is part of the multiset class, similar to the way that value_type and size_type are part of the class.

- **The * operator:** Once a program has created an iterator, the * (asterisk) operator can be used to access the current element of the iterator. In the role example, we could print the current string of the role iterator with this statement:

  ```
  cout << *role << endl;
  ```

  The asterisk can be applied to any iterator, causing the iterator to return its current item. The notation *role was intentionally designed to make the iterator look as if it were a pointer to an item. If it actually was a pointer, then *role would mean "the item that role points to." Of course, role is an iterator, not a pointer, but *role can still be thought of as "getting the iterator's current item."

  In general, the *role notation can be used for both accessing and changing the iterator's current item. For example, an item might be changed with an assignment: *role = "shemp";. However, some iterators forbid the item from being changed. This is the case for the multiset's iterator, where the * operator can be used to access an item in the multiset, but not to change an item. *the multiset iterator cannot be used to change an item directly*

- **The ++ operator:** The ++ operator can be used to move an iterator forward to the next item in its collection. Here's an example statement:

  ```
  ++role;
  ```

  The ++ operator can be used before the iterator (as in ++role) or after the iterator (as in role++). In addition to moving the iterator forward, both versions of the ++ operator are actually functions that return an iterator. In particular: the return value of ++role is the iterator *after* it has already moved forward, whereas the return value of role++ is a copy of the iterator *before* it has moved forward. For most iterators, the ++role version is more efficient because it does not need to keep a copy of the old iterator before it moved forward. Therefore, we prefer to use the ++role version.

- **end:** A container has an end member function that returns an iterator to mark the end of its items. If an iterator moves forward through the container, it will eventually reach the end. Once it reaches the end, it has already gone *beyond* the last item of the container and the * operator must not be used any more because there are no more items.

example of using an iterator

It's time to see the whole pattern for using an iterator in a small example. The example creates a multiset of strings, then uses an iterator to step through those strings one at a time.

```
multiset<string> actors;
multiset<string>::iterator role;
actors.insert("moe");
actors.insert("curly");
actors.insert("larry");
actors.insert("curly");

for (role = actors.begin( ); role != actors.end( ); ++role)
{
    cout << *role << endl;
}
```

The for-loop steps through the items of the multiset, printing the four strings, in order from smallest to largest (using the lexicographic order that strings have). Notice that the multiset has two copies of curly (perhaps he is our favorite):

```
curly
curly
larry
moe
```

Notice what happens when role is at the moe string. At this point, it has not yet reached actors.end( ). In effect, you can imagine that actors.end( ) is "one item beyond the last item." So, the body of the loop is entered, and we print *role (which is the string moe). After this, the loop moves role forward with the statement ++role. This moves role beyond the last item, so now role is equal to actors.end( ), and the loop finishes. Once role reaches the end, we must not access *role because role has gone beyond the last item.

⊘ PITFALL

DO NOT ACCESS AN ITERATOR'S ITEM AFTER REACHING END( )

When an iterator i is equal to the end( ) iterator of its container, you must not try to access the item *i. Remember that end( ) is one location past the last item of the container.

Here is the general pattern that you can use for any iterator i and container object c:

```
for (i = c.begin( );  i != c.end( );  ++i)
{
    ...statements to access the item *i
}
```

This pattern is called the [...) pattern, or the **left-inclusive pattern**. The notation comes from the way that mathematicians write [0...100) to indicate the set of numbers starting at zero and going up to (but not including) 100. In the same way, our for-loop iterates through the set of values starting at begin( ) and going up to (but not including) the end( ) value.

the [...) pattern

The [. . .) Pattern

Iterators are often used with the **[. . .)** pattern (called the **left-inclusive pattern**). For an iterator i and a container c, the pattern is:

```
for (i = c.begin( );  i != c.end( );  ++i)
{
    ...statements to access the item *i
}
```

The for-loop iterates through the set of values starting at begin( ) and going up to (but not including) the end( ) value.

By the way, we can now explain the return value of the multiset's insert function:

```
iterator insert(const value_type& entry);
```

The return value of this member function is an iterator where the current item is the item that was just inserted.

Testing Iterators for Equality

The [...) pattern uses one operation on iterators that you might not have noticed: It uses the != operation to test whether two iterators of the same container are not equal. Iterators can also be compared to see whether they are equal (using the == operation). For a container object, two of its iterators are equal if they are at the same location, or if they have both gone to the end( ) of the container. (It is an error to compare two iterators from different containers.)

Other Multiset Operations

Multisets have other operations, some of which use iterators. Here are two example multiset member functions:

```
iterator find(const value_type& target);
void erase(iterator i);
```

The find function searches for the first item in the multiset that is equal to the specified target. If it finds such an item, then it returns an iterator whose current element is equal to that item. If there is no such item, then find returns an iterator that is equal to end( ). The erase function is an alternative to the usual erase function. Its parameter is an iterator, and the function removes the iterator's current item.

erasing one
occurrence
of an item

Using find and erase together, we can write code that will erase the first occurrence of a given target. For example, this code will erase the first occurrence of 42 in the multiset m:

```
multiset<int> m;
multiset<int>::iterator position;

position = m.find(42);
if (position != m.end( ))
    m.erase(position);
```

Further multiset functions are listed in Appendix H.

Set Algorithms

The STL contains a group of functions in the <algorithm> library facility that can manipulate containers that store their elements in a sorted order. These containers include the set, multiset, map, and multimap classes (the STL map is discussed in Chapter 12). The reason for requiring sorted containers is so that the algorithms can be more efficient. One example set operation is the set_union function:

```
iterator set_union (iterator1 first1, iterator1 last1,
                    iterator2 first2, iterator2 last2,
                    iterator3 result);
```

This function can be used to create a union of two containers. In other words, it can create a new container that includes copies of all the elements from two other containers. The five parameters need some explanation.

The first two parameters, first1 and last1, are iterators in a container such as a set. All the elements in the range [first1...last1) will be copied to the result. Notice that this range is a left-inclusive pattern, so that the current element of the first1 iterator is included, but the range ends just before the last1 iterator. The `first2` and `last2` parameters define a second left-inclusive range [`first2...last2`) which is also copied to the result.

The location for the result is determined by the fifth parameter. This parameter, called `result`, must be an **output iterator**, which is a kind of iterator that provides an alternative way to insert new elements into a container. Programmers don't usually use output iterators directly, but they often them as an argument to one of the STL algorithms. One way to create an output iterator for a container class called c is with the expression `inserter(c, c.begin( ))`.

some of the STL algorithms use output iterators to add new items to a container

The following code creates two sets, uses the STL `set_union` function to create a union of the sets, and iterates through the result.

```
set<string> actors1;
set<string> actors2;
set<string> result;
set<string>::iterator role;

actors1.insert("moe");
actors1.insert("curly");
actors2.insert("larry");
actors2.insert("curly");

// Notice how we create the output iterator for the fifth argument:
set_union(actors1.begin( ), actors1.end( ),
        actors2.begin( ), actors2.end( ),
        inserter(result,result.begin( )));

for (role = result.begin( ); role != result.end( ); ++role)
{
    cout << *role << " ";
}
cout<< endl;
```

The output shows all three actors in the union, with only one copy of the duplicate curly:

```
curly larry moe
```

A list of more set operations is given in Appendix H.

Invalid Iterators

After an iterator has been set, it can easily move through its container. However, changes to the container—either insertions or removals—can cause all of the container's iterators to become invalid. The precise operations that invalidate iterators vary from one container to another. Some examples are obvious; for example, the position iterator in the code just shown is invalid after its item is erased. Other examples are not so obvious, such as containers where insertions can invalidate all iterators (perhaps because the items are stored in a dynamic array and the insertion caused the array to be resized).

When an iterator becomes invalid because of a change to its container, that iterator can no longer be used until it is assigned a new value.

 **PITFALL**

CHANGING A CONTAINER OBJECT CAN INVALIDATE ITS ITERATORS

When an iterator's underlying container changes (by an insertion or a deletion), the iterator generally becomes invalid. Unless the class documentation says otherwise, that iterator should no longer be used until it is reassigned a new value from the changed container.

CLARIFYING THE CONST KEYWORD Part 7: Const Iterators

1. DECLARED CONSTANTS: PAGE 12
2. CONSTANT MEMBER FUNCTIONS: PAGE 38
3. CONST REFERENCE PARAMETERS: PAGE 72
4. STATIC MEMBER CONSTANTS: PAGE 103
5. CONST PARAMETERS THAT ARE POINTERS OR ARRAYS: PAGE 162
6. THE CONST KEYWORD WITH A POINTER TO A NODE, AND THE NEED FOR TWO VERSIONS OF SOME MEMBER FUNCTIONS: PAGE 218
7. CONST ITERATORS

A **const iterator** is an iterator that is forbidden from changing its underlying container in any way. For example, a const iterator cannot be used with the multiset `erase` function. Const iterators can be obtained from the `begin` and `end` functions of any constant container, such as a parameter that is declared as a *const* `multiset`. Here's an example of a small function that counts how many integers in a multiset are less than a specified target:

```
// Counts number of integers less than a given target:
multiset<int>::size_type count_less_than_target
    (const multiset<int>& m, int target)
{
    multiset<int>::size_type answer = 0;
    multiset<int>::const_iterator cursor;

    for (cursor = m.begin( ); cursor != m.end( ); ++cursor)
    {
        if (*cursor < target)
            ++answer;
    }
    return answer;
}
```

The iterator (cursor) is declared as `multiset<int>::const_iterator` rather than `multiset<int>::iterator`. The const_iterator data type is part of the multiset class, just like `value_type`, `size_type`, and the ordinary `iterator`. It is written as a single word (`const_iterator`) and does not use the keyword *const*, but its purpose is related to the keyword *const*, as explained here:

1. Consider a multiset that is declared with the keyword *const*, such as the multiset m in the `count_less_than_target` function. In this case, the return value of m.begin( ) and m.end( ) are `const_iterator` rather than `iterator`.

2. A const iterator can move through its container of items, but it is forbidden from adding, removing, or changing any items. For example, if `cursor` is a const iterator for the multiset m, then we may not activate `m.erase(cursor)`.

a const iterator is forbidden from changing any items in its container

From the second rule, we would say that the words "const iterator" are a bit misleading because the iterator itself isn't constant, it can move through the collection. It is the objects in the collection that cannot be changed by a const iterator. This is similar to the way that a const pointer works (see page 218). In any case, each of the STL container classes provides both an `iterator` and a `const_iterator` type.

Standard Categories of Iterators

The C++ Standard specifies five significant categories of iterators, based on their abilities. In order to use some of built-in algorithms provided by the C++ Standard, a programmer must know which category is provided by a container class. The first two categories—an *input iterator* and an *output iterator*—are specialized iterators for retrieving and inserting elements. The other three categories are the *forward iterator*, the *bidirectional iterator*, and the *random access iterator*. Each of these categories has increasingly stronger abilities.

We'll finish this section with a list of each category's abilities.

Output iterator.   We've already seen one example of an output iterator as the final parameter for the `set_union` function on page 306. The current element of an output iterator can be assigned to, such as *p = "shemp"; for an output operator called p. The ++ increment operator moves the iterator forward to another item. The intention is that an algorithm that uses an output iterator will do an assignment followed by an increment (++), over and over again. However, the output operator itself cannot be used to retrieve those elements, so the output iterator's usefulness is limited to the situation where some algorithm needs to put a sequence of elements in a container or other object with an output iterator.

Input iterator.   An input iterator is designed to provide a sequence of values. The current element of an input operator can be retrieved by using the dereferencing * operator such as x = *p; for an input operator called p. The ++ increment operator moves the iterator forward to another item. The intention is that an algorithm that uses an input iterator will retrieve an element (with the dereferencing *) followed by an increment (++), over and over again. The end of an input iterator's elements is usually detected by comparing the input iterator with another iterator that is known to be just beyond the end of the input range.

Forward iterator.   A forward iterator p is an object that provides these items:

- Iterators have a default constructor (to create an iterator that is not yet initialized), a copy constructor, and an assignment operator.

- The * operator accesses the iterator's current item. In some cases, the item is assignable (meaning it can be directly changed with an assignment such as `*p = "shemp";`); in other cases, direct changes of the item are forbidden.

- The ++ operator moves the iterator forward to the next item. The operator can be used in prefix notation (such as ++p) or postfix notation (such as p++). Both versions move the iterator forward, and both versions are actually function calls that return an iterator (which can be used as part of a larger expression). In particular, ++p returns the iterator after it has moved forward, whereas p++ returns a copy of the iterator before it moved.

- Iterators can be tested for equality (p == q) and inequality (p != q). Two iterators over the same container are equal if their current items are in the same position, or if they are both past the end of the container. Iterators from different containers should not be compared with each other.

Bidirectional iterator.   A bidirectional iterator has all the abilities of a forward iterator, plus it can move backward with the -- operator. The --p operator moves the iterator p backward one position (and returns the iterator after it has moved backward). The p-- operator also moves the iterator backward one position (and returns a copy of the iterator before it moved).

The STL multiset, which we have used, has a bidirectional iterator with const items (`*p = "shemp";` is forbidden).

Random access iterator.   The term *random access* refers to the ability to quickly access any randomly selected location in a container. A random access iterator allows this quick access by providing six new operations in addition to those of the bidirectional iterator. Appendix H covers these six operations in detail. For now, you should know that a random access iterator p can use the notation p[n] to provides access to the item that is n steps in front of the current item. For example, p[0] is the current item, p[1] is the next item, and so on. In addition, a random access iterator can always be used as if it were any of the other types of iterators because it has all of the same operations.

Iterators for Arrays

A random access iterator looks a lot like an array. In fact, the opposite is also true: C++ will allow any pointer to an element in an array to be used as if it were a random access iterator. The "current item" of such a pointer is the array element that it points to. The ++ and -- operators move the pointer forward or backward one spot. And for a pointer p, the notation p[i] refers to the item that is i steps ahead of the current item.

Since a pointer to an array is a random access iterator, we can use these pointers in Standard Library functions that expect an iterator. For example, the copy function from `<algorithm>` is a template function with this prototype:

```
template <class SourceIterator, class DestinationIterator>
DestinationIterator copy(
    SourceIterator source_begin,
    SourceIterator source_end,
    DestinationIterator destination_begin
);
```

Both `source_begin` and `source_end` are iterators over the same object. The function copies elements from the source to the destination. The first element that is copied comes from `source_begin`, and the copying continues up to (but not including) `source_end`. Notice that this is another example of the left-inclusive pattern [...) that we have seen before. The return value is an iterator that is one position beyond the last copied element in the destination.

the [...) pattern occurs again

Anyway, we wanted to show you how an array can be used as an iterator in the arguments of the copy function. Here are some typical examples:

```
int numbers[7] = { 0, 10, 20, 30, 40, 50, 60 };
int small[3];
int *p = numbers + 2;       // An iterator that starts at numbers[2]
int *mid = numbers + 5;     // An iterator that starts at numbers[5]
int *small_front = small;   // An iterator that starts at small[0]

// p, mid, and small can all be used as iterators in the copy function.
// This will copy numbers[2]...numbers[4] into small:
copy(p, mid, small_front);

// The name of an array itself can also be used as the argument for an
// iterator (either by itself or with an offset such as numbers + 6).
// This statement copies the last three elements of numbers into small.
// Notice that numbers + 7 is one step beyond the end of the numbers ///
// array.
copy(numbers + 4, numbers + 7, small);
```

The Standard Template Library List Class

The C++ Standard Template Library (STL) has a `list` class, part of which is completely specified in Appendix H. For now, we'll provide just a quick introduction. The STL `list` is a doubly linked list, such as the one described in Section 5.5, with a bidirectional iterator. The functions `size`, `clear`, and `count` are similar to the analogous list operations in Section 5.2.

The STL list differs from the linked-list implementation in this book in several ways. Some key differences include: 1) the `erase` and `insert` functions of the STL list operate on items based on a specified iterator, and return an iterator as well; 2) the STL list's remove function removes all items with a specified value; and 3) the begin and end functions of the STL list return a bidirectional iterator.

The STL list also provides several additional functions, including the push_back and push_front operations to insert items to the front and back of a list. The generic search functions for STL containers can be used to locate an item in the list. These will be discussed in Chapter 12.

The following code creates a list, inserts items into the list with the push_back method, and prints out its contents with an iterator.

```
int i;
list<int> int_list;
list<int>::iterator iter;

for (i = 1; i <= 10; i++)
    int_list.push_back(i);

for (iter = int_list.begin(); iter != int_list.end(); ++iter)
    cout << *iter << " ";
```

Self-Test Exercises for Section 6.3

17. What is the difference between the set and multiset STL classes?

18. Which of the iterator categories is provided by a multiset?

19. Write some code that allows the user to type 10 strings. Each string is put in a multiset. When the user is finished, the strings are printed in lexicographic order.

20. Suppose m is a multiset. In what situation would m.begin( ) equal m.end( )?

21. Write the left-inclusive pattern for an iterator i and a container c.

22. In general, how does an iterator become invalid?

23. How does a random access iterator provide access to an item that is n steps in front of the current item?

24. Write a function that has one parameter: a non-empty const multiset of strings. The return value is a copy of the longest string in the multiset. If there are several strings of equally long length, then return the one that is found earliest by an iterator.

6.4 THE NODE TEMPLATE CLASS

In Sections 5.1 and 5.2, we implemented a node class for manipulating linked lists. As you might guess, the node will be more useful if we implement the node as a template class that depends on the underlying item data type. Each of the node's functions can then be implemented as a template function that also depends on the item.

Here is a comparison of the original toolkit's node definition to our new plan:

Original Node Class:

```
class node
{
public:
    typedef double value_type;
    ...
```

New Template Node Class:

```
template <class Item>
class node
{
public:
    typedef Item value_type;
    ...
```

With the new definition, the node is now a template class. Each of the node functions can be changed to a template function by making the same changes that we saw in Section 6.2.

For example, here is the original prototype for the list_insert function:

```
void list_insert(node* previous_ptr, const node::value_type& entry);
```

The new prototype for the list_insert template function is preceded by the template prefix and uses Item within its parameter list, as shown here:

```
template <class Item>
void list_insert(node<Item>* previous_ptr, const Item& entry);
```

One of the toolkit's functions, list_locate, needs some extra care. Our original node had a const and a non-const version, both of which have a size_t parameter, as shown here:

```
node* list_locate(node* head_ptr, size_t position);
const node* list_locate(const node* head_ptr, size_t position);
```

As we explained in the pitfall "Mismatches for Template Function Arguments" on page 287, the presence of the size_t parameter can cause mismatches for an argument type. The solution is the same approach that we used before: Add a second template parameter. In addition, we can actually combine the two functions into a single function by using a template parameter called NodePtr, as shown in this new prototype:

```
template <class NodePtr, class SizeType>
NodePtr list_locate(NodePtr head_ptr, SizeType position);
```

When a program calls list_locate, the head pointer may be either an ordinary pointer to a node or it may be a pointer declared with the *const* keyword. The return type will always match the type of the head pointer.

Functions That Return a Reference Type

We have one other change that will simplify later usages of the node. The change involves the `data` member function, which retrieves a copy of the node's data field. A reasonable thought for the implementation is shown here:

```
Item data( ) const { return data_field; }
```

This is a const member function, so it cannot be used to actually change a node (it returns only a *copy* of the data field).

The change that we have planned is to add the symbol & to the return type, and alter the function so that it is no longer a const function, as shown here:

```
Item& data( ) { return data_field; }
```

The & symbol changes the return value to a *reference type*. Reference types have several uses in C++, but we have only a narrow use in mind: the use of a reference type as a return value of a function, as described here.

Reference Type as a Return Value

A function can use a reference type as a return value by placing the symbol & after the return type name. The use of a reference type has these effects:

1. The return value must be a variable or object that will still exist after the function returns. In particular, the return value must not be a local variable.

2. The function returns this actual variable or object (not a copy of the object).

Let's look at an example to see how the new `data` function can be used to change the data field of a node. Suppose that `cursor` is pointing to the second node of this linked list of strings:

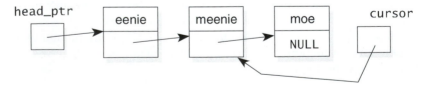

Let's examine some statements to see how `cursor->data( )` can be used to directly manipulate the data field of the second node:

```
cursor->data( ) = "mynie";
```

This is simply an assignment statement, but the left side of the assignment is a reference to the actual data field of the cursor's node, so this data will change to the string "mynie," as shown here:

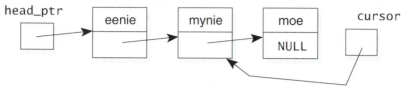

An assignment to a node's data field is not too exciting; we could have accomplished the same thing with `cursor->set_data("mynie")`. A better example shows how we can change a node's data by activating one of its member functions. For example, consider this statement for the preceding linked list:

```
head_ptr->data( ).erase(0,2);
```

The string's `erase(0,2)` member function erases two characters starting at the front of the string, changing "eenie" to "nie" and resulting in the linked list shown here:

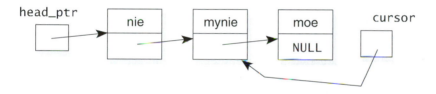

The data( ) Function with a Reference Return Type

Any use of the data( ) function will now refer directly to the node's data field. When data( ) is used in an expression, changes can be made directly to the node's data field.

What Happens When a Reference Return Value Is Copied Elsewhere

It's easy to be confused about what happens when a reference return value is copied to another variable. For example, consider the final linked list shown earlier, where the cursor's data is "mynie". Can you figure out what will happen with these two statements?

```
string exclamation = cursor->data( );
exclamation = "drat!";
```

The `exclamation` variable is completely separate from the `cursor`'s data. The first statement puts a copy of the `cursor`'s data into `exclamation`. The second statement changes `exclamation` to "drat!" but does not alter the `cursor`'s data.

In general, `cursor->data( )` can be used to change the cursor's data only by an assignment to `cursor->data( )` or by activating one of `cursor->data( )`'s member functions.

The Data Member Function Now Requires Two Versions

Changing the `data` return value to a reference type has one drawback: This version of the data function can no longer be used as a constant member function. The solution is similar to the idea that we have already used for the `link` member function: Provide a second constant version of the data function, as shown here:

```
const Item& data( ) const { return data_field; }
```

This version has two changes from our other version:

- The return value is a reference to a const value. Since it is a reference type, it will still refer directly to the node's data field. But because of the keyword *const*, it cannot be used to change that data field.
- Since the return value cannot be used to change the node, the function can be declared as a constant member function of the node class.

The approach of having two `data` member functions has the same motivation that we used on page 219 to provide two separate `link` member functions. Also, the compiler is able to determine which function to call in any situation. If a pointer `p` is a pointer to a const node, then `p->data( )` will activate the const version of `data`; otherwise the non-const version is used.

Header and Implementation Files for the New Node

The header file (`node2.h`) and implementation file (`node2.template`) for the new node are given in Figure 6.5. We have also updated the documentation to indicate the effect of the two versions of the `data` member function. For your reference, you might want to flip back to the complete list of changes that are needed to convert a container class to a template class (page 292).

Self-Test Exercises for Section 6.4

25. Suppose that a function from Chapter 5 has a local variable called `insert_ptr`, which is a pointer to a `node`. How will you declare this variable in a template version of the function?

26. Write the implementation of the template version of `list_head_remove`.

27. Suppose that p is a pointer to a node in a linked list of strings, and the data of that node is the string "help". What is the value of that data after these two statements: `p->data( ).erase(3,1);`
                                                `p->data( ).append("lo");`

28. Suppose that p is a pointer to a const node in the previous exercise. Would those two statements be allowed?

29. In the node template class, how does the compiler determine which `data( )` member function to call in any situation?

FIGURE 6.5   Header File and Implementation for the Node Template Class

A Header File

```
// FILE: node2.h (part of the namespace main_savitch_6B)
// PROVIDES: A template class for a node in a linked list and functions for
// manipulating linked lists. The template parameter is the type of data in each node.
//
// TYPEDEF for the node<Item> template class:
//     Each node of the list contains a piece of data and a pointer to the next node. The
//     type of the data (node<Item>::value_type) is the Item type from the template parameter.
//     The type may be any of the C++ built-in types (int, char, etc.), or a class with a default
//     constructor, an assignment operator, and a test for equality.
//
// CONSTRUCTOR for the node<Item> class:
//     node(const Item& init_data, node* init_link)
//         Postcondition: The node contains the specified data and link.
//         NOTE: The init_data parameter has a default value that is obtained from the default
//         constructor of the Item type. In the ANSI/ISO standard, this notation is also allowed
//         for the built-in types, providing a default value of zero. The init_link has a default
//         value of NULL.
//
// NOTE about const and non-const versions of the data and link member functions:
//     The data function returns a reference to the data field of a node and the link function
//     returns a copy of the link field of a node. Each of these functions comes in two versions: a
//     const version and a non-const version. If the function is activated by a const node, then
//     the compiler chooses the const version (and the return value is const). If the function is
//     activated by a non-const node, then the compiler chooses the non-const version (and the
//     return value will be non-const).
// EXAMPLES:
//     const node<int> *c;
//     c->link( )  activates the const version of link returning const node<int>*
//     c->data( )  activates the const version of data returning const Item&
//     c->data( ) = 42; ... is forbidden
//     node<int> *p;
//     p->link( )  activates the non-const version of link returning node<int>*
//     p->data( )  activates the non-const version of data returning Item&
//     p->data( ) = 42; ... actually changes the data in p's node          (continued)
```

(FIGURE 6.5 continued)

```
//   MEMBER FUNCTIONS for the node<Item> class:
//      const Item& data( ) const          <----- const version
//      and
//      Item& data( )                      <----- non-const version
//      See the note (above) about the const version and non-const version.
//         Postcondition: The return value is a reference to the data from this node.
//
//      const node* link( ) const  <----- const version
//      and
//      node* link( )              <----- non-const version
//      See the note (above) about the const version and non-const version.
//         Postcondition: The return value is the link from this node.
//
//      void set_data(const Item& new_data)
//         Postcondition: The node now contains the specified new data.
//
//      void set_link(node* new_link)
//         Postcondition: The node now contains the specified new link.
//
//   NONMEMBER FUNCTIONS to manipulate nodes:
//      template <class Item>
//      void list_clear(node<Item>*& head_ptr)
//         Precondition: head_ptr is the head pointer of a linked list.
//         Postcondition: All nodes of the list have been returned to the heap, and the head_ptr is
//         now NULL.
//
//      template <class Item>
//      void list_copy
//      (const node<Item>* source_ptr, node<Item>*& head_ptr, node<Item>*& tail_ptr)
//         Precondition: source_ptr is the head pointer of a linked list.
//         Postcondition: head_ptr and tail_ptr are the head and tail pointers for a new list that
//         contains the same items as the list pointed to by source_ptr.
//
//      template <class Item>
//      void list_head_insert(node<Item>*& head_ptr, const Item& entry)
//         Precondition: head_ptr is the head pointer of a linked list.
//         Postcondition: A new node containing the given entry has been added at the head of
//         the linked list; head_ptr now points to the head of the new, longer linked list.
//
//      template <class Item>
//      void list_head_remove(node<Item>*& head_ptr)
//         Precondition: head_ptr is the head pointer of a linked list, with at least one node.
//         Postcondition: The head node has been removed and returned to the heap;
//         head_ptr is now the head pointer of the new, shorter linked list.
```

(continued)

(FIGURE 6.5 continued)

```
//      template <class Item>
//      void list_insert(node<Item>* previous_ptr, const Item& entry)
//        Precondition: previous_ptr points to a node in a linked list.
//        Postcondition: A new node containing the given entry has been added after the node
//        that previous_ptr points to.
//
//      template <class Item>
//      size_t list_length(const node<Item>* head_ptr)
//        Precondition: head_ptr is the head pointer of a linked list.
//        Postcondition: The value returned is the number of nodes in the linked list. The list
//        itself is unaltered.
//
//      template <class NodePtr, class SizeType>
//      NodePtr list_locate(NodePtr head_ptr, SizeType position)
//        NOTE: NodePtr may be either node<Item>* or const node<Item>*
//        Precondition: head_ptr is the head pointer of a linked list, and position > 0.
//        Postcondition: The return value is a pointer that points to the node at the specified
//        position in the list. (The head node is position 1, the next node is position 2, and so on.)
//        If there is no such position, then the null pointer is returned. The list itself is unaltered.
//
//      template <class Item>
//      void list_remove(node<Item>* previous_ptr)
//        Precondition: previous_ptr points to a node in a linked list, and this is not the tail node of
//        the list.
//        Postcondition: The node after previous_ptr has been removed from the linked list.
//
//      template <class NodePtr, class Item>
//      NodePtr list_search(NodePtr head_ptr, const Item& target)
//        NOTE: NodePtr may be either node<Item>* or const node<Item>*
//        Precondition: head_ptr is the head pointer of a linked list.
//        Postcondition: The return value is a pointer that points to the first node containing the
//        specified target in its data field. If there is no such node, the null pointer is returned.
//
//  DYNAMIC MEMORY usage by the toolkit:
//    If there is insufficient dynamic memory, then the following functions throw bad_alloc:
//    the node constructor, list_copy, list_head_insert, list_insert.

#ifndef MAIN_SAVITCH_NODE2_H
#define MAIN_SAVITCH_NODE2_H
#include <cstdlib>    // Provides NULL and size_t
#include <iterator>   // Will be used for the node_iterator in Section 6.5
```

(continued)

(FIGURE 6.5 continued)

```
namespace main_savitch_6B
{
    template <class Item>
    class node
    {
    public:
        // TYPEDEF
        typedef Item value_type;
        // CONSTRUCTOR
        node(const Item& init_data=Item( ), node* init_link=NULL)
            { data_field = init_data; link_field = init_link; }
        // MODIFICATION MEMBER FUNCTIONS
        Item& data( ) { return data_field; }
        node* link( ) { return link_field; }
        void set_data(const Item& new_data) { data_field = new_data; }
        void set_link(node* new_link) { link_field = new_link; }
        // CONST MEMBER FUNCTIONS
        const Item& data( ) const { return data_field; }
        const node* link( ) const { return link_field; }
    private:
        Item data_field;
        node *link_field;
    };

    // FUNCTIONS to manipulate a linked list:
    template <class Item>
    void list_clear(node<Item>*& head_ptr);

    template <class Item>
    void list_copy
        (const node<Item>* source_ptr, node<Item>*& head_ptr, node<Item>*& tail_ptr);

    template <class Item>
    void list_head_insert(node<Item>*& head_ptr, const Item& entry);

    template <class Item>
    void list_head_remove(node<Item>*& head_ptr);

    template <class Item>
    void list_insert(node<Item>* previous_ptr, const Item& entry);

    template <class Item>
    std::size_t list_length(const node<Item>* head_ptr);
```

(continued)

(FIGURE 6.5 continued)

```
template <class NodePtr, class SizeType>
NodePtr list_locate(NodePtr head_ptr, SizeType position);

template <class Item>
void list_remove(node<Item>* previous_ptr);

template <class NodePtr, class Item>
NodePtr list_search(NodePtr head_ptr, const Item& target);
```

|| A definition for a node iterator class will be placed here in Section 6.5.

```
}

#include "node2.template"
#endif
```

An Implementation File

```
// FILE: node2.template
// IMPLEMENTS: The functions of the node template class (see node2.h for documentation)
//
// NOTE:
//     Since node is a template class, this file is included in node2.h.
//     Therefore, we should not put any using directives in this file.
//
// INVARIANT for the node class:
//     The data of a node is stored in data_field, and the link in link_field.

#include <cassert>      // Provides assert
#include <cstdlib>      // Provides NULL and size_t

namespace main_savitch_6B
{
    template <class Item>
    void list_clear(node<Item>*& head_ptr)
    // Library facilities used: cstdlib
    {
        while (head_ptr != NULL)
            list_head_remove(head_ptr);
    }
```

(continued)

(FIGURE 6.5 continued)

```
template <class Item>
void list_copy
   (const node<Item>* source_ptr, node<Item>*& head_ptr, node<Item>*& tail_ptr)
// Library facilities used: cstdlib
{
    head_ptr = NULL;
    tail_ptr = NULL;

    // Handle the case of the empty list.
    if (source_ptr == NULL)
        return;

    // Make the head node for the newly created list, and put data in it.
    list_head_insert(head_ptr, source_ptr->data( ));
    tail_ptr = head_ptr;

    // Copy the rest of the nodes one at a time, adding at the tail of new list.
    source_ptr = source_ptr->link( );
    while (source_ptr != NULL)
    {
        list_insert(tail_ptr, source_ptr->data( ));
        tail_ptr = tail_ptr->link( );
        source_ptr = source_ptr->link( );
    }
}


template <class Item>
void list_head_insert(node<Item>*& head_ptr, const Item& entry)
{
    head_ptr = new node<Item>(entry, head_ptr);
}


template <class Item>
void list_head_remove(node<Item>*& head_ptr)
{
    node<Item> *remove_ptr;

    remove_ptr = head_ptr;
    head_ptr = head_ptr->link( );
    delete remove_ptr;
}
```

(continued)

(FIGURE 6.5 continued)

```
template <class Item>
void list_insert(node<Item>* previous_ptr, const Item& entry)
{
    node<Item> *insert_ptr;

    insert_ptr = new node<Item>(entry, previous_ptr->link( ));
    previous_ptr->set_link(insert_ptr);
}


template <class Item>
std::size_t list_length(const node<Item>* head_ptr)
// Library facilities used: cstdlib
{
    const node<Item> *cursor;
    std::size_t answer;

    answer = 0;
    for (cursor = head_ptr; cursor != NULL; cursor = cursor->link( ))
        ++answer;
    return answer;
}


template <class NodePtr, class SizeType>
NodePtr list_locate(NodePtr head_ptr, SizeType position)
// Library facilities used: cassert, cstdlib
{
    NodePtr cursor;
    std::size_t i;

    assert(0 < position);
    cursor = head_ptr;
    for (i = 1; (i < position) && (cursor != NULL); ++i)
        cursor = cursor->link( );
    return cursor;
}


template <class Item>
void list_remove(node<Item>* previous_ptr)
{
    node<Item> *remove_ptr;

    remove_ptr = previous_ptr->link( );
    previous_ptr->set_link(remove_ptr->link( ));
    delete remove_ptr;
}
```

(continued)

(FIGURE 6.5 continued)

```
template <class NodePtr, class Item>
NodePtr list_search(NodePtr head_ptr, const Item& target)
// Library facilities used: cstdlib
{
    NodePtr cursor;

    for (cursor = head_ptr; cursor != NULL; cursor = cursor->link( ))
        if (target == cursor->data( ))
            return cursor;
    return NULL;
}

}
```

www.cs.colorado.edu/~main/chapter6/node2.h and node2.template   **WWW**

6.5   AN ITERATOR FOR LINKED LISTS

We'll use the node template class to build various container classes. It will be useful if we have a simple way for each of these containers to build its own iterators. The best approach is to start by defining iterators that can step through the nodes of a linked list. We can put this node iterator into node2.h, so that any container class that uses a node can also use the node iterator.

The Node Iterator

The node iterator will have two constructors: (1) a constructor that attaches the iterator to a specified node in a linked list, and (2) a default constructor that creates a special iterator that marks the position that is beyond the end of a linked list.

We'll be able to use our iterator to step through a linked list following the usual [...) left-inclusive pattern. For example, suppose that head_ptr is the head pointer for a list of integers. The following loop will step through the list, changing to zero any number that is odd:

```
node_iterator<int> start(head_ptr); // start is at the first node
node_iterator<int> finish;          // finish is beyond the end
node_iterator<int> position;        // position moves through list

for (position = start; position != finish; ++position)
{
    if (((*position % 2) == 1) // The number is odd.
        *position = 0;          // Change the odd number to zero.
}
```

In this code, suppose that the list contains the three numbers 42, 13, 67. After the statement `position = start`, the `position` iterator will be at the first element of the list, which we can draw in this way:

```
position
```

```
42   13   67
```

This drawing indicates that the `position` iterator is currently at the number 42 in the list. We enter the loop body and the test `((*position % 2) == 1)` checks whether `*position` is an odd number. Since 42 is not odd, we skip the if-statement and proceed to `++position`. The `++position` statement moves the iterator forward one spot, like this:

```
position
```

```
42   13   67
```

Now we enter the loop and 13 is odd, so the assignment `*position = 0` is executed, changing the 13 to 0, as shown here:

```
position
```

```
42   0   67
```

Next, `position` is moved forward again, and the body of the loop is entered, looking like this:

```
position
```

```
42   0   67
```

Since 67 is odd, it is changed to 0 and `position` is advanced right off the end of the list:

```
position
```

```
42   0   0
```

At this point, `position` is equal to the `finish` iterator, so the loop stops.

The `node_iterator` class definition we have in mind is given in Figure 6.6. This definition can be placed at the end of `node2.h`. The definition is short, but it does have several features that need explanation.

FIGURE 6.6 Definition of the Iterator for the Node Template Class

Definition of a Template Class

```
template <class Item>
class node_iterator
: public std::iterator<std::forward_iterator_tag, Item>
{
public:
    node_iterator(node<Item>* initial = NULL)
        { current = initial; }
    Item& operator *( ) const
        { return current->data( ); }
    node_iterator& operator ++( ) // Prefix ++
        {
            current = current->link( );
            return *this;
        }
    node_iterator operator ++(int) // Postfix ++
        {
            node_iterator original(current);
            current = current->link( );
            return original;
        }
    bool operator ==(const node_iterator other) const
        { return current == other.current; }
    bool operator !=(const node_iterator other) const
        { return current != other.current; }
private:
    node<Item>* current;
};
```

Part of www.cs.colorado.edu/~main/chapter6/node2.h   **WWW**

The Node Iterator Is Derived from std::iterator

At the front of our iterator definition, before the opening bracket, we have the
line:

```
    : public std::iterator<std::forward_iterator_tag, Item>
```

We will see the full meaning of this line when we study inheritance in Chapter
14. For now, it is enough to know that this line should be placed with any iterator that we create. It allows our iterator to pick up some features of the Standard
Library iterators. In the angle brackets, we place one of three Standard Library

"iterator tags." In our case, we plan to create a forward iterator (as described on page 310), so we use the tag `std::forward_iterator_tag`. This will allow Standard Library algorithms (such as `copy`) to determine which operations our iterator has. Also, inside the angle brackets, we indicate the data type of the items that our iterator will refer to. This is the name `Item` (from the template parameter).

PITFALL ⊍

STD::ITERATOR MIGHT NOT EXIST

The iterator class is defined in the `<iterator>` facility, but it was one of the last items to be added. Therefore, many compilers don't support the line:
```
    : public std::iterator<std::forward_iterator_tag, Item>
```
Some alternatives are discussed in Appendix E.

The Node Iterator's Private Member Variable

Our iterator has one private member variable, `current`, which is a pointer to the node that contains its current item. If the iterator has moved beyond the end of a list, then `current` will be null.

Node Iterator—Constructor

The node iterator has one constructor with one parameter. The parameter is a pointer to a node where the iterator will start. The parameter might also be null, indicating that the iterator will be off the end of the list. It's useful to have a way to create an iterator that is off the list so that other iterators can be tested to see whether they have moved off the list.

The constructor's parameter has a default argument, which is null. Therefore, the constructor can be called with no arguments (a default constructor) and the result will be an iterator that's off the end of the list.

Node Iterator—The * Operator

The node iterator implements the * operation in this way:

```
Item& operator *( )
    { return current->data( ); }
```

For a node iterator p, this operator allows us to use the notation *p to access p's current item. The return value comes from activating `current->data( )`, and the `data` function returns a *reference* to the actual item in the node. The return type of the * operator is also a reference to the item (indicated by the symbol & in the return type of `Item&`). Having a return value that is a reference was fully discussed on page 314, but in this case, all we need to know is that the return value from *p allows us to both access and change p's current item. For example, when the item type is an *int*:

```
cout << *p << endl;  // Prints the value of p's item
*p = 42;             // Changes the value of p's item to 42
```

Node Iterator—Two Versions of the ++ Operator

The node iterator has two versions of the ++ operator. These versions allow us to write either ++p or p++. Let's examine the versions to see their differences.

The prefix version.   The prefix version begins this way:

```
node_iterator& operator ++( ) // Prefix ++
...
```

For a node iterator, p, this function allows us to write ++p, with the ++ in front of p. Most often, we write the expression ++p on its own. In this case, the ++ function is activated by the iterator p, and p moves forward to the next item.

The expression ++p can also be used as part of a larger expression. When ++p is used as part of a larger expression, it is important to know that the return value of ++p is a the iterator p itself *after* it has already been moved forward. As an example, suppose that p is currently at the first item in this list:

p

42   13   67

We can write the statement `cout << *(++p);`. In this statement, the expression ++p moves p forward to the second item and returns the iterator p to be used in the cout statement. The * operator is applied to p after it has moved forward, so the result of the cout statement is to print the second item (13) of the list.

You may have noticed that the return type of this operator is a reference type (`node_iterator&` rather than merely `node_iterator`). This means that the return value of ++p is actually p itself (after the move), rather than a copy of p. Let's see how this is done in the complete implementation, shown here:

```
node_iterator& operator ++( ) // Prefix ++
{
    current = current->link( );
    return *this;
}
```

When ++p is activated, the first statement moves p's current pointer forward one node. The second statement is: `return *this;`. The statement uses the keyword *this*, which is always a pointer to the object that activated the function (see page 179). Therefore, *this* is always the object that activated the member function, and `return *this;` is the common way to cause the function to return the object that actually activated the function in the first place.

The postfix version.   The postfix version begins this way:

```
node_iterator operator ++(int) // Postfix ++
...
```

the meaning of (int)

This notation does seem strange! It looks as if this version of the ++ operator has an *int* parameter. But, in fact that's not the case. Instead, using the keyword *int* (where the parameters usually go) serves to say "this is the postfix version of the ++ operator." It would make more sense to use a more meaningful keyword, or perhaps two keywords "prefix" and "postfix." But we're stuck with the original C++ requirement of (*int*) to indicate that we're implementing the postfix version.

In any case, this function allows us to write p++, with the ++ following p. When written on its own (not part of a larger expression), p++ has the same meaning as ++p, moving p forward to the next item. However, in a larger expression, the return value of p++ differs from ++p. In particular, the return value of p++ is a copy of p before it was changed. For example, suppose that p is currently at the first item in this list:

p

42   13   67

We can write the statement cout << *(p++);. In this statement, the expression p++ moves p forward to the second item, but the return value is a copy of p before the move. The * operator is applied to this copy, so the result of the cout statement is to print the first item (42) of the list.

Since the return value of the postfix operator is a copy of the original value of p, the return type is not a reference type (it is node_iterator rather than node_iterator&). In general, do not use a reference return type if you want to return a copy of an object. Let's see how the copy is made in the complete implementation, shown here:

```
node_iterator operator ++(int) // Postfix ++
{
    node_iterator original(current);
    current = current->link( );
    return original;
}
```

The copy is made at the start of the function, and stored in the local variable original. The current pointer is then moved forward, and the return statement returns a copy of the original iterator.

ⓘ Programming Tip

++p Is More Efficient Than p++

When you are moving p forward on its own (not part of a larger expression), it is more efficient to write ++p rather than p++. The reason is that each activation of p++ makes a copy of p before the change, even if the return value is never used.

Node iterator—comparisons for equality and inequality. The last two member functions of the node iterator are comparison functions to allow us to write tests for equality and inequality. The functions simply compare the iterator's current pointers to see whether they are pointing to the same location.

Iterators for Constant Collections

As we've seen before, we must take care when a pointer is declared with the const keyword, because we must forbid any change to the associated linked list. For example, consider this function, which is supposed to traverse a linked list of integers, adding up the value of all the integers:

```
int add_values(const node<int>* head_ptr)
{
```

> *WARNING!*
>
> *This add_values implementation has a bug!*

```
    node_iterator<int> start(head_ptr);  // start is at the first node
    node_iterator<int> finish;           // finish is beyond the end
    node_iterator<int> position;         // position moves through list
    int sum = 0;

    for (position = start; position != finish; ++position)
    {
        sum += *position;
    }

    return sum;
}
```

The problem is that head_ptr is declared as *const* node<int>* , and therefore it cannot be used as the argument to the constructor of the node iterator. That constructor has the following prototype, which requires an ordinary pointer to a node:

```
node_iterator(node<Item>* initial);
```

The solution is to provide another iterator—a const_node_iterator—that can be used with a const node. We have seen this kind of const iterator for the multiset (page 308); it can move through the container, but it cannot change the container in any way.

Figure 6.7 shows our implementation of a const iterator for the node class. The name of our iterator is `const_node_iterator` (which is just one name, not two or more separate words). In addition to the name change, the `const_node_iterator` also differs from the ordinary `node_iterator` in one other way: Each use of the data type `Item` or `node<Item>*` is now written as `const Item` or `const node<Item>*`.

FIGURE 6.7   Definition of a Const Iterator for the Node Template Class

Definition of a Template Class

```
template <class Item>
class const_node_iterator
: public std::iterator<std::forward_iterator_tag, const Item>
{
public:
    const_node_iterator(const node<Item>* initial = NULL)
        { current = initial; }
    const Item& operator *( ) const
        { return current->data( ); }
    const_node_iterator& operator ++( ) // Prefix ++
        {
            current = current->link( );
            return *this;
        }
    const_node_iterator operator ++(int) // Postfix ++
    {
        const_node_iterator original(current);
        current = current->link( );
        return original;
    }
    bool operator ==(const const_node_iterator other) const
        { return current == other.current; }
    bool operator !=(const const_node_iterator other) const
        { return current != other.current; }
private:
    const node<Item>* current;
};
```

Part of www.cs.colorado.edu/~main/chapter6/node2.h   **WWW**

Using the `const_node_iterator`, we can write a correct `add_values` function, as shown here:

```
int add_values(const node<int>* head_ptr)
{

    const_node_iterator<int> start(head_ptr);
    const_node_iterator<int> finish;
    const_node_iterator<int> position;
    int sum = 0;

    for (position = start; position != finish; ++position)
    {
        sum += *position;
    }

    return sum;
}
```

ⓘ PROGRAMMING TIP

WHEN TO USE A CONST ITERATOR

Use a const iterator to move through a container of constant items. The iterator itself is not constant; it can move through the container, but it cannot change any of the container in any way.

Self-Test Exercises for Section 6.5

30. Write a function that steps through a linked list of nodes with integer values, changing every other item to zero. The function's parameter should be a pointer to a node, and it should have a local variable that is a node iterator.

31. Why is the `node_iterator` class in this chapter derived from an STL iterator?

32. Write a function that steps through a linked list of nodes with integer values, counting the number of occurrences of zero. The function's parameter should be a pointer to a const node, and it should have a local variable that is a `const_node_iterator`.

33. How does the node iterator's implementation differentiate between the prefix and postfix versions of the ++ operator?

34. Which version of ++ is generally more efficient? Why?

6.6 LINKED-LIST VERSION OF THE BAG TEMPLATE CLASS WITH AN ITERATOR

We can use the template version of the node class to implement another bag template class. This new version of the bag template class will store the items on a linked list, just like the bag class in Section 5.3. But our new version will be a *template* class, making use of the template version of the linked-list toolkit. Here is part of the declaration of the new bag template class, which stores its items on a linked list:

```
template <class Item>
class bag
{
public:
    ...
private:
    node<Item> *head_ptr;    // Head pointer for the list
    size_type many_nodes;    // Number of nodes on the list
};
```

Within the bag's class definition we can refer to the class bag on its own, with no need to specify bag<Item>. However, when we use the node class in the definition node<Item> *head_ptr, we must use the full name node<Item>. This indicates that we are using a node, and that the data in the node is the same data type as the bag's items. For example, consider this declaration:

```
bag<char> vowels;
```

This declares a bag with the item instantiated as a *char*. This bag has a private member variable, head_ptr, which is a pointer to a node<char>.

Most of the implementation of this new bag will be a straightforward translation of the Chapter 5 bag that used an ordinary linked list. However, we will add one new feature: Our new bag will have an iterator, similar to the multiset's iterator from Section 6.3. The bag's iterator will be easy to implement because we can use the node_iterator and const_node_iterator from Section 6.5.

How to Provide an Iterator for a Container Class That You Write

To provide an iterator for a class that you write, you must generally provide these items in the public section of the class definition:

- There is a definition for a small class, usually called iterator. This class has a few member functions such as the * operator and ++, which all iterators must have. In the case of the bag, the iterator will be defined as a node_iterator from Section 6.5.

- The container also needs a definition for a second small class, usually called `const_iterator` (written as one word with an underscore between "const" and "iterator"). This is the same as an ordinary iterator, except its member functions must not change the container in any way. Our bag will use a `const_node_iterator` for its `const_iterator`.

- The container needs a `begin` member function, which creates and returns an iterator that refers to the container's first item. For the bag, this iterator will be positioned at the head element of the linked list. Actually, we'll need two versions of the `begin` function: an ordinary version that returns a bag `iterator`, and a constant member function that returns a bag `const_iterator`.

- The container needs two `end` member functions (one of which is a constant member function), which return an `iterator` (or a `const_iterator`), indicating a position that is beyond the end of the container.

The Bag Iterator

For our bag, the `begin` and `end` functions are simple enough that they can go inside the bag's class definition, like this:

```
template <class Item>
class bag
{
public:
    // TYPEDEFS
    typedef node_iterator<Item> iterator;
    typedef const_node_iterator<Item> const_iterator;
    ...

    // FUNCTIONS TO PROVIDE ITERATORS
    iterator begin( )
        { return iterator(head_ptr); }
    const_iterator begin( ) const
        { return const_iterator(head_ptr); }
    iterator end( ) // Using the iterator's default constructor
        { return iterator( ); }
    const_iterator end( ) const // Using the default constructor
        { return const_iterator( ); }

private:
    node<Item> *head_ptr;       // Head pointer for the list
    size_type many_nodes;       // Number of nodes on the list
};
```

The return statements in the `begin` and `end` functions may be new to you. When the name of a data type is used as part of an expression, the programmer is requesting a type conversion. For example:

```
return iterator(head_ptr);
```

This expression requests a type conversion from the type of `head_ptr` (which is a pointer to a node) to an `iterator`. The conversion is carried out by selecting the appropriate `iterator` constructor (the one that has an argument that is a pointer to a node). The return statement will create a temporary `iterator` object, using the `head_ptr` as the argument to the `iterator` constructor. A copy of this temporary object is returned by the `begin` member function. In a similar manner, the `end` function returns a copy of the `iterator` that is created with the `iterator`'s default function, by using this return statement:

```
return iterator( ); // Uses the iterator's default constructor
```

Why the Iterator Is Defined Inside the Bag

By putting the `iterator` class definition inside the definition of the `bag` template class, the iterator becomes a member of the bag class. To use this iterator, a program specifies the bag, followed by `::iterator`. For example:

```
bag<int>::iterator position; // Declare an iterator for a bag<int>
```

This is our fifth approach to the bag, so we'll use the names `bag5.h` and `bag5.template` for the files. These two files are shown in Figures 6.8 and 6.9.

Self-Test Exercises for Section 6.6

35. Within the definition of the `bag` template class, can we write `bag` on its own, or do we need `bag<Item>`? Can we write `node` on its own, or do we need `node<Item>`?

36. What is the primary difference between the `bag` template class suggested in this section, and the `bag` template class from Section 6.2?

37. What is the primary difference between the `bag` template class suggested in this section, and the `bag` class from Chapter 5?

38. Write a function with one parameter, a const bag of integers. The function steps through the bag, counting how many items are less than a specified target.

FIGURE 6.8   Header File for the Fifth Bag Template Class

A Header File

```
// FILE: bag5.h (part of the namespace main_savitch_6B)
// CLASS PROVIDED: bag<Item> (a collection of items; each item may appear multiple times)
//
// TYPEDEFS for the bag<Item> class:
//    bag<Item>::value_type
//       bag<Item>::value_type is the data type of the items in the bag. It may be any of the
//       C++ built-in types (int, char, etc.), or a class with a default constructor, a copy
//       constructor, an assignment operator, and a test for equality (x == y).
//
//    bag<Item>::size_type
//       bag<Item>::size_type is the data type of any variable that keeps track of how many
//       items are in a bag.
//
//    bag<Item>::iterator  and bag<Item>::const_iterator
//       Forward iterators for a bag and a const bag.
//
// CONSTRUCTOR for the bag<Item> class:
//    bag( )
//       Postcondition: The bag is empty.
//
// MODIFICATION MEMBER FUNCTIONS for the bag<Item> class:
//    size_type erase(const Item& target)
//       Postcondition: All copies of target have been removed from the bag. The return value
//       is the number of copies removed (which could be zero).
//
//    bool erase_one(const Item& target)
//       Postcondition: If target was in the bag, then one copy of target has been removed from
//       the bag; otherwise the bag is unchanged. A true return value indicates that one copy
//       was removed; false indicates that nothing was removed.
//
//    void insert(const Item& entry)
//       Postcondition: A new copy of entry has been inserted into the bag.
//
//    void operator +=(const bag& addend)
//       Postcondition: Each item in addend has been added to this bag.
//
```

(continued)

(FIGURE 6.8 continued)

```
// CONSTANT MEMBER FUNCTIONS for the bag<Item> class:
//    size_type count(const Item& target) const
//       Postcondition: Return value is the number of times target is in the bag.
//
//    Item grab( ) const
//       Precondition: size( ) > 0.
//       Postcondition: The return value is a randomly selected item from the bag.
//
//    size_type size( ) const
//       Postcondition: Return value is the total number of items in the bag.
//
// STANDARD ITERATOR MEMBER FUNCTIONS (provide a forward iterator):
//    iterator begin( )
//    const_iterator begin( ) const
//    iterator end( )
//    const iterator end( ) const
//
// NONMEMBER FUNCTIONS for the bag<Item> class:
//    template <class Item>
//    bag<Item> operator +(const bag<Item>& b1, const bag<Item>& b2)
//       Postcondition: The bag returned is the union of b1 and b2.
//
// VALUE SEMANTICS for the bag<Item> class:
//    Assignments and the copy constructor may be used with bag objects.
//
// DYNAMIC MEMORY USAGE by the bag<Item>:
//    If there is insufficient dynamic memory, then the following functions throw bad_alloc:
//    The constructors, insert, operator +=, operator +, and the assignment operator.

#ifndef MAIN_SAVITCH_BAG5_H
#define MAIN_SAVITCH_BAG5_H
#include <cstdlib>    // Provides NULL and size_t and NULL
#include "node2.h"    // Provides node class

namespace main_savitch_6B
{
    template <class Item>
    class bag
    {
    public:
        // TYPEDEFS
        typedef std::size_t size_type;
        typedef Item value_type;
        typedef node_iterator<Item> iterator;
        typedef const_node_iterator<Item> const_iterator;
```
                                                                        (continued)

(FIGURE 6.8 continued)

```
            // CONSTRUCTORS and DESTRUCTOR
            bag( );
            bag(const bag& source);
            ~bag( );

            // MODIFICATION MEMBER FUNCTIONS
            size_type erase(const Item& target);
            bool erase_one(const Item& target);
            void insert(const Item& entry);
            void operator +=(const bag& addend);
            void operator =(const bag& source);

            // CONST MEMBER FUNCTIONS
            size_type count(const Item& target) const;
            Item grab( ) const;
            size_type size( ) const { return many_nodes; }

            // FUNCTIONS TO PROVIDE ITERATORS
            iterator begin( )
                { return iterator(head_ptr); }
            const_iterator begin( ) const
                { return const_iterator(head_ptr); }
            iterator end( )
                { return iterator( ); } // Uses default constructor
            const_iterator end( ) const
                { return const_iterator( ); } // Uses default constructor

    private:
            node<Item> *head_ptr;       // Head pointer for the list of items
            size_type many_nodes;       // Number of nodes on the list
        };

        // NONMEMBER FUNCTIONS for the bag<Item> template class
        template <class Item>
        bag<Item> operator +(const bag<Item>& b1, const bag<Item>& b2);
}

// The implementation of a template class must be included in its header file:
#include "bag5.template"

#endif
```

FIGURE 6.9   Implementation File for the Fifth Bag Template Class

An Implementation File

```
// FILE: bag5.template
// CLASS implemented: bag (see bag5.h for documentation)
// NOTE:
//    Since bag is a template class, this file is included in node2.h.
// INVARIANT for the bag class:
//    1.  The items in the bag are stored on a linked list;
//    2.  The head pointer of the list is stored in the member variable head_ptr;
//    3.  The total number of items in the list is stored in the member variable many_nodes.

#include <cassert>   // Provides assert
#include <cstdlib>   // Provides NULL, rand
#include "node2.h"   // Provides node

namespace main_savitch_6B
{
    template <class Item>
    bag<Item>::bag( )
    // Library facilities used: cstdlib
    {
        head_ptr = NULL;
        many_nodes = 0;
    }

    template <class Item>
    bag<Item>::bag(const bag<Item>& source)
    // Library facilities used: node2.h
    {
        node<Item> *tail_ptr;   // Needed for argument of list_copy

        list_copy(source.head_ptr, head_ptr, tail_ptr);
        many_nodes = source.many_nodes;
    }

    template <class Item>
    bag<Item>::~bag( )
    // Library facilities used: node2.h
    {
        list_clear(head_ptr);
        many_nodes = 0;
    }
```

(continued)

(FIGURE 6.9 continued)

```
template <class Item>
typename bag<Item>::size_type bag<Item>::count(const Item& target) const
// Library facilities used: cstdlib, node2.h
{
    size_type answer;
    const node<Item> *cursor;

    answer = 0;
    cursor = list_search(head_ptr, target);
    while (cursor != NULL)
    {   // Each time that cursor is not NULL, we have another occurrence of target, so
        // we add one to answer, and move cursor to the next occurrence of the target.
        ++answer;
        cursor = cursor->link( );
        cursor = list_search(cursor, target);
    }

    return answer;
}

template <class Item>
typename bag<Item>::size_type bag<Item>::erase(const Item& target)
// Library facilities used: cstdlib, node2.h
{
    size_type answer = 0;
    node<Item> *target_ptr;

    target_ptr = list_search(head_ptr, target);
    while (target_ptr != NULL)
    {
        // Each time that target_ptr is not NULL, we have another occurrence of target.
        // We remove this target using the same technique that was used in erase_one.
        ++answer;
        target_ptr->set_data( head_ptr->data( ) );
        target_ptr = target_ptr->link( );
        target_ptr = list_search(target_ptr, target);
        list_head_remove(head_ptr);
    }

    return answer;
}
```

(continued)

(FIGURE 6.9 continued)

```cpp
template <class Item>
bool bag<Item>::erase_one(const Item& target)
// Library facilities used: cstdlib, node2.h
{
    node<Item> *target_ptr;

    target_ptr = list_search(head_ptr, target);
    if (target_ptr == NULL)
        return false;  // target isn't in the bag, so no work to do
    target_ptr->set_data( head_ptr->data( ) );
    list_head_remove(head_ptr);
    --many_nodes;
    return true;
}

template <class Item>
Item bag<Item>::grab( ) const
// Library facilities used: cassert, cstdlib, node2.h
{
    size_type i;
    const node<Item> *cursor;

    assert(size( ) > 0);
    i = (std::rand( ) % size( )) + 1;
    cursor = list_locate(head_ptr, i);
    return cursor->data( );
}

template <class Item>
void bag<Item>::insert(const Item& entry)
// Library facilities used: node2.h
{
    list_head_insert(head_ptr, entry);
    ++many_nodes;
}
```

(continued)

(FIGURE 6.9 continued)

```
template <class Item>
void bag<Item>::operator +=(const bag& addend)
// Library facilities used: node2.h
{
    node<Item> *copy_head_ptr;
    node<Item> *copy_tail_ptr;

    if (addend.many_nodes > 0)
    {
        list_copy(addend.head_ptr, copy_head_ptr, copy_tail_ptr);
        copy_tail_ptr->set_link( head_ptr );
        head_ptr = copy_head_ptr;
        many_nodes += addend.many_nodes;
    }
}

template <class Item>
void bag<Item>::operator =(const bag& source)
// Library facilities used: node2.h
{
    node<Item> *tail_ptr; // Needed for argument to list_copy

    if (this == &source)
        return;

    list_clear(head_ptr);
    many_nodes = 0;
    list_copy(source.head_ptr, head_ptr, tail_ptr);
    many_nodes = source.many_nodes;
}

template <class Item>
bag<Item> operator +(const bag<Item>& b1, const bag<Item>& b2)
{
    bag<Item> answer;

    answer += b1;
    answer += b2;
    return answer;
}
}
```

FIGURE 6.10   Our Five Bag Classes (with Template Classes Shaded)

Approach	Define item with...	Files
Store the items in an array with a fixed size.	typedef	bag1.h and bag1.cxx in Section 3.1
Store the items in a dynamic array.	typedef	bag2.h and bag2.cxx in Section 4.3
Store the items in a linked list, using the node class.	typedef	bag3.h and bag3.cxx in Section 5.3
Store items in a dynamic array.	template parameter	bag4.h and bag4.template in Section 6.3
Store items in a linked list, using the template version of the node class. This implementation also has an iterator.	template parameter	bag5.h and bag5.template in Section 6.6

CHAPTER SUMMARY AND SUMMARY OF THE FIVE BAGS

- **Summary of the Five Bag Implementations.** If nothing else, you should now know how to program your way out of a paper bag, using one of the five bag classes of Figure 6.10. The bag class is a good example, showing different approaches to implementing a simple container class, but keep in mind that the same approaches can be used for any container class.

- A **template function** is similar to an ordinary function with one important difference: The definition of a template function can depend on an underlying data type. The underlying data type is given a name—such as `Item`—but `Item` is not pinned down to a specific type anywhere in the function's implementation.

- When a template function is used, the compiler examines the types of the arguments. At that point, the compiler determines the data type of `Item`. This is called the **instantiation** of the template.

- In a single program, several different usages of a template function can result in several different instantiations.

- When a class depends on an underlying data type, the class can be implemented as a **template class**.

- Our node class can be implemented as a template class, providing more flexibility to implement other container classes (such as our bag).

- An **iterator** allows a programmer to easily step through the items of a container class. The C++ Standard Library container classes are all provided with iterators. We can also implement iterators for our own classes in a way that matches the STL iterators.

Solutions to Self-Test Exercises

1. A single template function serves to implement many functions that are identical except for a different underlying data type.

2. A typedef approach allows only one data type to be defined for the data item within a program, whereas a template function allows several different usages in a single program because the compiler determines the data type when the template function is used. The typedef approach has a simpler syntax, which makes for easier debugging.

3. The template prefix defines the list of underlying data types that a template function depends upon, for example:
   `template <class Item>`

   It appears immediately before the prototype and immediately before the implementation of the template function.

4. Unification is the compiler's term for determining how to instantiate a template function through the template parameter. If a template parameter does not appear in the parameter list of a template function, the compiler will generate the message "Failed unification."

5. `Item` may be any of the C++ built-in types, or a class with an assignment operator and a copy constructor.

6. Here is one implementation:
   ```
   template <class Item>
   void compare
   (const Item& a, const Item& b)
   // Postcondition: A message has
   // been printed indicating whether
   // a and b are different or the same.
   // Note: The Item type must have the
   // == operator defined.
   // Library facilities used: iostream
   ```
   ```
   {
     if (a == b)
       cout << "Those are the same";
     else
       cout << "Those are different";
   }
   ```

7. Here is one solution:
   ```
   template <class Item, class SizeType>
   void ordered_insert(
       Item data[ ],
       SizeType n,
       Item entry
   )
   {
     size_t i;
     i = n;

     while (i > 0 && data[i-1] > entry)
     {
       data[i] = data[i-1];
       --i;
     }
     data[i] = entry;
   }
   ```

8. See "Mismatches for Template Function Arguments" on page 287.

9. In a header file for a template class, there is an include statement to include the implementation file. This makes the compiler's job simpler.

10. For a template class, the template prefix occurs before the template class definition and before each member function implementation. It also must appear before the prototype and implementation of any other template functions that manipulate the template class.

11. A program using the template class will inadvertently pick up using directives in the template header file, because a template class has its implementation included in the header file.

12. Instantiation of a template parameter occurs when an actual variable of the template class is declared.

13. Within the class definition, bag is not changed to bag<Item>. Also, the name of the constructor is simply bag (not bag<Item>), and the name of the destructor is simply ~bag.

14. See the discussion on page 290.

15. The implementation file is included in the header file, and you should never put a using directive in a header file. Therefore, our new bag implementation file does not have a using directive for std, and we must write the full name std::copy.

16. All three of these definitions can appear in the same program:
```
bag<char> vowel;
bag<int> ages;
bag<double> weights;
```

17. The multiset class allows duplicate values in the container, whereas the set class requires unique values.

18. A bidirectional iterator

19. This code uses the std namespace, the string class from <string> and the multiset<string> class from <set>:
```
string response;
multiset<string> s;
multiset<string>::iterator p;
int i;

cout << "Please type 10 strings:";
for (i = 0; i < 10; ++i)
{
  getline(cin, response);
  s.insert(response);
}

cout << "Your strings: " << endl;
for (p=s.begin(); p!=s.end(); ++p)
{
  cout << *p << endl;
}
```

20. When m contains no items

21. `for (i = c.begin(); i != c.end(); ++i) {...}`

22. An iterator can become invalid whenever a change is made to the underlying container.

23. A random access iterator p can use the notation p[n] to provide access to the item n steps in front of the current item.

24. Here is one solution. We assume that <set> and <string> have been included, and that we are using the std namespace. Our solution is simplified because of an item that you might not have seen: When *p is an object (such as a string), we can use the member selector operator (such as p->length( )).
```
string
longest(const multiset<string>& m)
{
  multiset<string>::const_iterator
    p, long_spot;
  string::size_type
    p_length, long_length;

  assert(m.size( ) > 0);
  long_spot = m.begin( );
  long_length = long_spot->length( );

  p = ++(m.begin( ));
  while (p != m.end( ))
  {
    if (p->length( ) > long_length)
    {
      long_spot = p;
      long_length = p->length( );
    }
    ++p;
  }
  return *long_spot;
}
```

25. In a template function the declaration is:
`node<Item> *insert_ptr;`

26. See the solution on page 322.

27. hello

28. If p is a pointer to a const node, then the activation of p->data( ) will use the const version of data, and the erase or append functions will not be allowed.

29. If a pointer p is a pointer to a const node, then p->data() will activate the const version of data(); otherwise the non-const version is used.

30. The body looks like this (with parameter ptr):
```
node_iterator spot(ptr);
node_iterator done; // Default const.
while (spot != done)
{
    *spot = 0;
    if (++spot != done)
        ++spot;
}
```

31. Deriving the node_iterator from an STL iterator allows the node_iterator to use features of the STL iterators.

32. Only a hint here: The local variable must be a const_node_iterator rather than an ordinary node_iterator.

33. The postfix version puts the keyword *int* in its parameter list, whereas the prefix version leaves its parameter list empty. This is an artificial use of *int*; there is no actual *int* parameter.

34. The prefix version is more efficient because it doesn't have to make a copy of the iterator.

35. Within the bag's template class, bag is correct on its own, but the type node cannot be used on its own: node<Item> is required.

36. In Section 6.2 we used a dynamic array; now we are using a linked list. Also, the latest version includes an iterator.

37. In Chapter 5, we used a typedef to define the item; now we are using a template parameter.

38. Here is one solution:
```
template <class Item>
typename bag<Item>::size_type
less_than(
    const bag<Item>& b,
    const Item& target
)
{
    bag<Item>::const_iterator spot;
    bag<Item>::size_type count = 0;

    p = b.begin( );
    while (p != b.end( ))
    {
        if (*p < target)
            ++count;
        ++p;
    }
}
```

PROGRAMMING PROJECTS
For more in-depth projects, please see www.cs.colorado.edu/~main/projects/

1 Rewrite the selection sort (Programming Project 7 on page 275) so that it is a template function, with the template parameter specifying the type of data in each node. Your new selection sort function will use the template version of the node.

2 Revise one of the container classes from Chapter 3, 4, or 5, so that it becomes a template class. Some choices are (a) the set (Project 5 on page 141); (b) one of the sequence classes (Section 3.2 or Section 5.4); (c) the sorted list (Project 6 on page 141); (d) the bag with receipts (Project 7 on page 141); (e) the keyed bag (Project 8 on page 142).

3 Add begin and end member functions to the bag from Section 6.2. This project is easier than it sounds—you just have to think of the right kind of iterator to use. Hint: Read the section about "Iterators for Arrays" on page 310.

4 This project starts with the keyed bag (Project 8 on page 142). Implement this class using a dynamic array of pairs. These pairs are from the C++ pair template class which is part of <utility>.

For example, pair<string, *int*> is a data type, where the first component is a string and the second component is an integer. The pair class has a default constructor (which uses the default constructors of each component) and it also has a constructor that creates a pair from two explicit values. Once a pair p is created, a program can access the two components directly with the two public member variables p.first and p.second.

Your implementation of this new keyed bag should be a template class that depends on the data types of the keys and the data type of the underlying data.

Your class should include begin and end functions for a const iterator (which can be used to examine items in the keyed bag, but not to change them). The return type of the * operator of the const iterator should be a pair consisting of a key and its associated data value.

5 Write a program that uses a multiset of strings to keep track of a list of chores that you have to accomplish today. The user of the program can request several services: 1) Add an item to the list of chores; 2) ask how many chores are in the list; 3) use the iterator to print the list of chores to the screen; 4) delete an item from the list; 5) exit the program.

If you know how to read and write strings from a file, then have the program obtain its initial list of chores from a file. When the program ends, it should write all unfinished chores back to this file.

6 Rewrite the polynomial class of Section 4.6 so that the data type of the coefficients is a template parameter. This data type can be any type that has operators for addition, subtraction, multiplication, and assignment. The class should also have a default constructor, which results in a zero value. For example, our template class would allow us to build polynomials where coefficients are complex numbers (using the complex<*double*> type from <complex>).

7 Revise the shuffle function (Programming Project 16 from Chapter 5) as a template function, so that it shuffles the contents of a sequence, regardless of the type of item the sequence holds. Note that the copy constructor and assignment operators must be defined for the item.

8 Design and implement a class that stores a gift list for your friends and relatives. You will need a container of containers to hold a list of persons, each of which has a list of possible gift ideas. Choose the optimal container for this project, noting that no duplicates should be permitted. Feel free to use STL classes. Develop a test program, which allows options to add, remove, and list persons and their gift list.

9 Revise the doubly linked-list implementation developed in Programming Project 15 in Chapter 5 to be a template class and use a bidirectional iterator. You will need to provide the decrement (--) operator to move backward through the list.

CHAPTER **7**

Stacks

The pushdown store is a "first in-last out" list. That is, symbols may be entered or removed only at the top of the list.

JOHN E. HOPCROFT AND JEFFREY D. ULLMAN
Formal Languages and Their Relation to Automata

LEARNING OBJECTIVES

When you complete Chapter 7, you will be able to...

- follow and explain stack-based algorithms using the usual computer science terminology of *push*, *pop*, *top*, and *peek*.
- use the STL stack class to implement stack-based algorithms such as the evaluation of arithmetic expressions.
- implement a stack class of your own using either an array or a linked-list data structure.

CHAPTER CONTENTS

Stacks

This chapter introduces a data structure known as a *stack*, or as
it is sometimes called, a *pushdown store*. It is a simple structure, even simpler
than a list. Yet it turns out to be one of the most useful data structures known to
computer science.

7.1 INTRODUCTION TO STACKS AND THE STL STACK

The drawings in the margin depict some stacks. There is a stack of pancakes,
some stacks of coins, and a stack of books. A **stack** is an ordered collection of
entries that can be accessed at only one end. That may not sound like what you
see in these drawings, but think for a moment. Each of the stacks is ordered
from top to bottom; you can identify any item in a stack by saying it is the top
item, second from the top, third from the top, and so on. Unless you mess up one
of the neat stacks, you can access only the top item. To remove the bottom book
from the stack, you must first remove the two books that are on top of it. The
abstract definition of a stack reflects this intuition.

Stack Definition

A **stack** is a data structure of ordered entries such that
entries can be inserted and removed at only one end (called
the **top**).

When we say that the entries in a stack are *ordered*, all we mean is that there is
one that can be accessed first (the one on top), one that can be accessed second
(just below the top), a third one, and so forth. We do not require that the entries
can be compared using the < operator. The entries may be of any type.

Stack entries must be removed in the reverse order to that in which they are
placed on the stack. For example, you can create a stack of books by first placing
a dictionary, placing a thesaurus on top of the dictionary, and placing a novel on
top of those, so the stack has the novel on top. When the books are removed, the
novel must come off first (since it is on top), and then the thesaurus, and finally
the dictionary. Because of this property, a stack is called a *Last-In/First-Out* data
structure (abbreviated **LIFO**).

LIFO

A stack is a Last-In/First-Out data structure. Entries are taken
out of the stack in the reverse order of their insertion.

pushing

popping

Of course, in a program a stack stores information rather than physical entries, such as books or pancakes. Therefore, it may help to visualize a stack as a pile of papers on which information is written. In order to place some information on the stack, you write the information on a new sheet of paper and place this sheet of paper on top of the stack. Getting information out of the stack is also accomplished by a simple operation, since the top sheet of paper can be removed and read. There is just one restriction: Only the top sheet of paper is accessible. In order to read the third sheet from the top, for example, the top two sheets must be removed from the stack.

A stack is analogous to a mechanism that is used in a popular candy holder called a *Pez*® *dispenser*, shown in the margin. The dispenser stores candy in a slot underneath an animal head figurine. Candy is loaded into the dispenser by pushing each piece into the hole. There is a spring under the candy with the tension adjusted so that when the animal head is tipped backward, one piece of candy pops out. If this sort of mechanism were used as a stack data structure, then the data would be written on the candy (which may violate some health laws, but it still makes a good analogy). Using this analogy, you can understand why adding an entry to a stack is called a **push** operation, and removing an entry from a stack is called a **pop** operation.

The Standard Library Stack Class

The C++ Standard Template Library (STL) has a stack class, part of which is specified in in Figure 7.1. As usual for a container class, the stack is specified as

---

FIGURE 7.1   The Standard Library Stack Class

Partial List of Members for the stack<Item> Class from <stack>

```
// TYPEDEFS
//    value_type:  The data type of the items in the stack from the Item parameter
//    size_type:   The data type for a variable that keeps track of how many items in a stack
//
// CONSTRUCTOR
//    Default constructor: Creates an empty stack
//
// VOID FUNCTIONS TO INSERT AND REMOVE ITEMS:
//    pop( ): Pop is a void function that pops (removes) the top item of the stack
//    push(const Item& entry): Pushes the item onto the top of the stack
//
// FUNCTIONS TO EXAMINE THE STACK AND ITS ITEMS:
//    empty( ) const: Returns true if the stack is empty (otherwise returns false)
//    size( ) const:   Returns the number of items in the stack
//    top( ):      Returns a reference to the top item on the stack (without removing it)
//
// VALUE SEMANTICS:
//    Assignments and the copy constructor may be used with stack<Item> objects.
```

a *template class*, allowing us to have stacks of integers, or stacks of strings, or stacks of whatever. As a learning experience, we will later implement this template class ourselves in several different ways, first using a fixed-size array to hold the items of the stack, and later using dynamic memory instead.

The stack specification lists a stack constructor and five member functions. The most important member functions are push (to add an entry at the top of the stack), pop (to remove the top entry), and top (to get the item at the top of the stack without removing it). There are no functions that allow a program to access entries other than the top entry. To access any entry other than the top one, the program must remove entries one at a time from the top until the desired entry is reached.

If a program attempts to pop an item off an empty stack, then it is asking for the impossible; this error is called **stack underflow**. To help you avoid a stack underflow, the class provides a member function to test whether a stack is empty. Some stacks may have a limited capacity, and if a program attempts to push an item onto a full stack, the result is an error called **stack overflow**.

Stack Errors

Stack Underflow: The condition resulting from trying to access an item from an empty stack.

Stack Overflow: The condition resulting from trying to push an item onto (add an item to) a full stack.

We could have other operations, but this first version is enough to teach you about stacks.

Stacks are very intuitive—even cute—but are they good for anything besides toy problems? Surprisingly, they have many applications. Most compilers use stacks to analyze the syntax of a program. Stacks are used to keep track of local variables when a program is run. Stacks can be used to search a maze or a family tree or other types of branching structures. In this book, we will discuss examples related to each of these applications. But before we present any complicated applications of the stack class, let us first practice with a simple "toy" problem, so that we can see how a stack is used.

uses for stacks

PROGRAMMING EXAMPLE: **Reversing a Word**

Suppose you want a program to read in a word and then write it out backward. If the program reads in NAT, then it will output TAN. If it reads in TAPS it will output SPAT. The author Roald Dahl wrote a book called ESIOTROT, which our program converts to TORTOISE. One way to accomplish this task is to read the input one letter at a time and place each letter in a stack. After the word is read, the letters in the stack are written out, but because of the way a stack works, they are written out in reverse order. The pseudocode is shown on the next page.

// Reversing the spelling of a word
Declare a stack of characters;

while (there are more characters of the word to read)
    Read a character, and push the character onto the stack.

while (the stack is not empty)
    Write the top character to the screen, and pop it off the stack.

This computation is illustrated in Figure 7.2. At all times in the computation, the only available entry is the entry on "top." Figure 7.2 suggests another intuition for thinking about a stack. You can view a stack as a hole in the ground and view the data entries as being placed in the hole one on top of the other. To retrieve a data entry, you must first remove the entries on top of it.

Self-Test Exercises for Section 7.1

1. What is the meaning of the acronym, LIFO?

2. Give an example of a real-world application in which a stack is used.

3. What is the difference between the top and pop operations of a stack?

4. Suppose a program uses a stack of characters to read in a word and then write the word out backward, as described in this section. Now suppose the input word is DAHL. List all the activations of the push, top, and pop functions. List them in the order in which they will be executed and indicate the character that is pushed or popped. What is the output?

5. Consider the stack class given in Figure 7.1 on page 350. Describe how you can define a new member function that returns the second entry from the top of the stack without changing the stack. Your description will be in terms of top, pop, and push. Give your solution in pseudocode, not in C++.

FIGURE 7.2   Using a Stack to Reverse Spelling

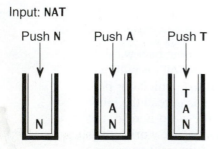

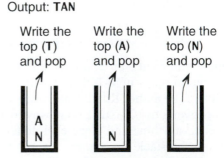

7.2 STACK APPLICATIONS

The STL stack class can be used by any program by including the `<stack>` header file. The example stack applications in this section use only the stack features shown in Figure 7.1 on page 350.

PROGRAMMING EXAMPLE: **Balanced Parentheses**

Later in this chapter we will describe how stacks can be used to evaluate arithmetic expressions. At the moment, we will describe a short function that does a much simpler but closely related task. The function, called `is_balanced`, appears in Figure 7.3, and checks expressions to see if the parentheses match correctly. It checks nothing else. Any symbol other than a right or left parenthesis is simply ignored.

FIGURE 7.3   A Function to Check for Balanced Parentheses

A Function Implementation

```
bool is_balanced(const string& expression)
// Postcondition: A true return value indicates that the parentheses in the given expression
// are balanced. Otherwise the return value is false.
// Library facilities used: stack, string (and using namespace std)
{
    // Meaningful names for constants
    const char LEFT_PARENTHESIS = '(';
    const char RIGHT_PARENTHESIS = ')';

    stack<char> store;        // Stack to store the left parentheses as they occur
    string::size_type i;      // An index into the string
    char next;                // The next character from the string
    bool failed = false;      // Becomes true if a needed parenthesis is not found

    for (i = 0; !failed  &&  (i < expression.length( )); ++i)
    {
        next = expression[i];
        if (next == LEFT_PARENTHESIS)
            store.push(next);
        else if ((next == RIGHT_PARENTHESIS) && (!store.empty( )))
            store.pop( ); // Pops the corresponding left parenthesis
        else if ((next == RIGHT_PARENTHESIS) && (store.empty( )))
            failed = true;
    }

    return (store.empty( ) && !failed);
}
```

For example, consider the string `"((X + Y*(Z + 7))*(A + B))"`. Each of the left parentheses has a corresponding right parenthesis. Also, as the string is read from left to right, there is never an occurrence of a right parenthesis that cannot be matched with a corresponding left parenthesis. Therefore the function call `is_balanced("((X + Y*(Z + 7))*(A + B))")` returns true.

On the other hand, consider the string `"((X + Y*(Z + 7)*(A + B))"`. The parentheses around the subexpression Z + 7 match each other, as do the parentheses around A + B. The second left parenthesis in the expression matches the final right parenthesis, but the first left parenthesis has no matching right parenthesis. Hence, `is_balanced("((X + Y*(Z + 7)*(A + B))")` returns false.

The algorithm used by `is_balanced` is simple: The function scans the characters of the string from left to right. Every time the function sees a left parenthesis, it is pushed onto the stack. Every time the program reads a right parenthesis, the program pops a matching left parenthesis off the stack. All symbols other than parentheses are ignored. If all goes smoothly and the stack is empty at the end of the expression, then the parentheses match. If the stack is empty when the algorithm needs to pop a symbol, or if symbols are still in the stack after all the input has been read, then the parentheses do not match. Now let us see why the algorithm works.

Let us start with some examples. Since no symbols other than parentheses can affect the results, we will use expressions of just parentheses symbols. All of the following are balanced (shading and arrows help find matching parentheses):

If you think about these examples, you can begin to understand the algorithm. In the first example, the parentheses match because they have the same number of left and right parentheses, but the algorithm does more than just count parentheses. The algorithm actually matches parentheses. Every time it encounters a `')'`, the symbol it pops off the stack is the matching `'('`. The parenthesis popped is not just any `'('`, but the one that matches.

The middle example is the same as the first example followed by another pair of matching parentheses. Since the two subexpressions match by themselves, the combination still matches.

The third example is even more revealing. The complete sequence of stack configurations from an execution of the function, using the input `"(()())"`, is shown in Figure 7.4. The stacks shown in the figure show the configuration after processing each character of the expression.

In general the stack works by keeping a stack of the unmatched left parentheses. Every time the program encounters a right parenthesis, the corresponding left parenthesis is deleted (popped) from the stack. If the parentheses in the input match correctly, things work out perfectly, and the stack is empty at the end of the input line.

Our function assumes the input has only one kind of parentheses, but the same technique can be used to check expressions with different kinds of parentheses, such as ( ), [ ], and { }. With different kinds of parentheses, the symbol on top of the stack must match the symbol in the input. For example, when the program encounters a ']' as the next symbol, there must be a '[' on top of the stack. We leave this more general problem as an exercise.

different kinds of parentheses

PROGRAMMING EXAMPLE: Evaluating Arithmetic Expressions

In this programming example we will design and write a calculator program. This will be an example of a program that uses two stacks—one is a stack of characters, and the other is a stack of double numbers.

Evaluating Arithmetic Expressions—Specification

The program takes as input a fully parenthesized numeric expression such as the following:

input to the calculator program

```
((((12 + 9)/3) + 7.2)*((6 - 4)/8))
```

The expression consists of integers or double numbers, together with the operators +, -, *, and /. To focus on the use of the stack (rather than on input details), we require that each input number is non-negative (otherwise it is hard to distinguish the subtraction operator from a minus sign that is part of a negative number). We will assume that the expression is formed correctly so that each operation has two arguments. Finally, we will also assume that the expression is fully parenthesized, meaning that each operation has a pair of matched parentheses surrounding its arguments. We can later enhance our program so that these assumptions are no longer needed.

The output will simply be the value of the arithmetic expression.

output of the calculator program

FIGURE 7.4 Stack Configurations for a Call to is_balanced

Input: (( ) ( ))

| Initial empty stack | Read and push first (| Read and push second (| Read first) and pop matching (| Read and push third (| Read second) and pop matching (| Read third) and pop the last (|

Evaluating Arithmetic Expressions—Design

Most of the program's work will be carried out by a function that reads one line of input and evaluates that line as an arithmetic expression. To get a feel for the problem, let's start by doing a simple example by hand.

do an example by hand

Consider the following expression:

```
(((6 + 9)/3)*(6 - 4))
```

If we evaluate this expression by hand, we might first evaluate the innermost expressions, (6 + 9) and (6 - 4), to produce the smaller expression:

```
((15/3)*2)
```

Next we would evaluate the expression (15/3) and replace this expression with its value of 5. That would leave us with the expression (5*2). Finally, we would evaluate this last operation to get the final answer of 10.

To convert this intuitive approach into a fully specified algorithm that can be implemented, we need to do things in a more systematic way: We need a specific way to find the expression to be evaluated next and a way to remember the results of our intermediate calculations.

First let us find a systematic way of choosing the next expression to be evaluated. (After that, we can worry about how we will keep track of the intermediate results.) We know that the expression to be evaluated first must be one of the innermost expressions—which is a subexpression that has just one operation. Let's decide to evaluate the leftmost of these innermost expressions. For instance, in our example of

```
(((6 + 9)/3)*(6 - 4))
```

the innermost expressions are (6 + 9) and (6 - 4), and the leftmost one of these is (6 + 9). If we evaluate this *leftmost of the innermost expressions*, we obtain

```
((15/3)*(6 - 4))
```

We could now go back and evaluate the other innermost expression (6 - 4), but why bother? There is a simpler approach that spares us the trouble of remembering any other expressions. After we evaluate the leftmost of the innermost expressions, we are left with another simpler arithmetic expression, namely ((15/3)*(6 - 4)), so we can simply repeat the process with this simpler expression: We again evaluate the leftmost of the innermost expressions of our new simpler expression. The entire process will look like the following:

1. Evaluate the leftmost of the innermost expressions in

```
(((6 + 9)/3)*(6 - 4))
```

to produce the simpler expression ((15/3)*(6 - 4)).

2. Evaluate the leftmost of the innermost expressions in

   `((15/3)*(6 - 4))`

   to produce the simpler expression `(5 *(6 - 4))`.

3. Evaluate the leftmost of the innermost expressions in

   `(5*(6 - 4))`

   to produce the simpler expression `(5*2 )`.

4. Evaluate the leftmost of the innermost expressions in

   `(5*2)`

   to obtain the final answer of 10.

translating the hand method to an algorithm

This method works fine with pencil and paper, but the function must read the input one character at a time from left to right. How does the function find *the leftmost of the innermost expressions*? Look at the example on page 356. The end of the expression to be evaluated is always a right parenthesis, ')', and moreover, it is always the *first* right parenthesis. After evaluating one of these innermost expressions, there is no need to back up; to find the next right parenthesis we can just keep reading left to right from where we left off. The next right parenthesis will indicate the end of the next expression to be evaluated.

Now we know how to find the expression to be evaluated next, but how do we keep track of our intermediate values? For this we use two stacks. One stack will contain numbers; there will be numbers from the input as well as numbers that were computed when subexpressions were evaluated. The other stack will hold symbols for the operations that still need to be evaluated. Because a stack processes data in a Last-In/First-Out manner, it will turn out that the correct two numbers are on the top of the numbers stack at the same time that the appropriate operation is at the top of the stack of operations. To better understand how the process works, let's evaluate our sample expression one more time, this time using the two stacks.

We begin by reading up to the first right parenthesis; the numbers we encounter along the way are pushed onto the numbers stack, and the operations we encounter along the way are pushed onto the operations stack. When we reach the first right parenthesis, our two stacks look like this:

Characters read so far (shaded):
`(((6 + 9) / 3) * (6 - 4))`

Numbers   Operations

Whenever we reach a right parenthesis, we combine the top two numbers (on the numbers stack) using the topmost operation (on the characters stack). In our example, we compute 6 + 9, yielding 15, and this number 15 is pushed back onto the numbers stack:

Characters read so far (shaded):
(((6 + 9) / 3) * (6 - 4))

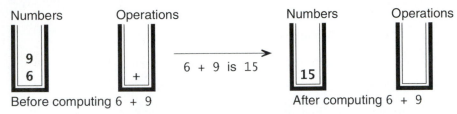

Notice that the leftmost operand (6 in this example) is the *second* number popped off the stack. For addition, this does not matter—who cares whether we have added 6 + 9 or 9 + 6? But the order of the operands does matter for subtraction and division.

Next we simply continue the process: reading up to the next right parenthesis, pushing the numbers we encounter onto the numbers stack and pushing the operations we encounter onto the operations stack. When we reach the next right parenthesis, we combine the top two numbers using the topmost operation. Here's what happens in our example when we reach the second right parenthesis:

Characters read so far (shaded):
(((6 + 9) / 3) * (6 - 4))

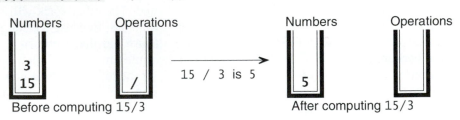

Again, the leftmost operand (15) is the second number popped off the stack, so the correct evaluation is 15/3, not 3/15. Continuing the process, we obtain:

Characters read so far (shaded):
(((6 + 9) / 3) * (6 - 4))

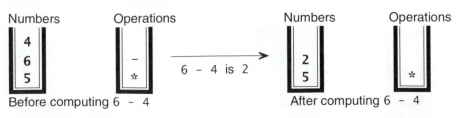

Finally, continuing the process one more time does not add anything to the stacks, but it does read the last right parenthesis and does combine two numbers from the numbers stack with an operation from the operations stack:

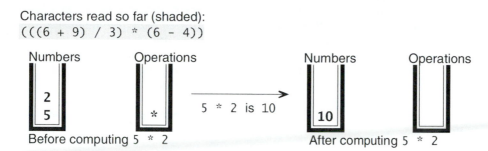

Characters read so far (shaded):
(((6 + 9) / 3) * (6 - 4))

Numbers   Operations

2
5   *

5 * 2 is 10

Numbers   Operations

10

Before computing 5 * 2   After computing 5 * 2

At this point there is no more input, and there is exactly one number in the numbers stack, namely 10. That number is the answer. Notice that when we used the two stacks we performed the exact same evaluations as we did when we first evaluated this expression in a simple pencil-and-paper fashion.

To evaluate our expression we only need to repeatedly handle each input item according to the following cases:

cases for evaluating an arithmetic expression

Numbers.   When a number is encountered in the input, the number is read and pushed onto the numbers stack.

Operation characters.   When one of the four operation characters is encountered in the input, the character is read and pushed onto the operations stack.

Right parenthesis.   When a right parenthesis is read from the input, an "evaluation step" takes place. The step takes the top two numbers from the numbers stack and the top operation from the operations stack. These items are removed from their stacks and the two numbers are combined using the operation (with the second number popped as the left operand). The result of the operation is pushed back onto the numbers stack.

Left parenthesis or blank.   The only other characters that appear in the input are left parentheses and blanks. These are read and thrown away, not affecting the computation. A more complete algorithm would need to process the left parentheses in some way to ensure that each left parenthesis is balanced by a right parenthesis, but for now we are assuming that the input is completely parenthesized in a proper manner.

The processing of input items halts when the end of the input line occurs, indicated by '\n' in the input. At this point, the answer is the single number that remains in the numbers stack.

We now have our algorithm, which we plan to implement as a function meeting this specification:

```
double read_and_evaluate(istream& ins);
// Precondition: The next line of characters in the istream ins is a fully
// parenthesized arithmetic expression formed from non-negative
// numbers and the four operations +, -, *, and /.
// Postcondition: A line has been read from the istream ins, and this line
// has been evaluated as an arithmetic expression. The value of the
// expression has been returned by the function.
```

The implementation of this function appears as part of a complete program in Figure 7.5.

FIGURE 7.5   Basic Calculator Program

A Program

```
// FILE: calc.cxx
// Basic calculator program to evaluate a fully parenthesized arithmetic expression.
// The purpose is to illustrate a fundamental use of stacks.

#include <cctype>      // Provides isdigit
#include <cstdlib>     // Provides EXIT_SUCCESS
#include <cstring>     // Provides strchr
#include <iostream>    // Provides cout, cin, peek, ignore
#include <stack>       // Provides the stack template class
using namespace std;

// PROTOTYPES for functions used by this demonstration program:
double read_and_evaluate(istream& ins);
// Precondition: The next line of characters in the istream ins is a fully parenthesized
// expression formed from non-negative numbers and the four operations +, -, *, and /.
// Postcondition: A line has been read from the istream ins, and this line has been evaluated
// as an arithmetic expression. The value of the expression has been returned by the function.

void evaluate_stack_tops(stack<double>& numbers, stack<char>& operations);
// Precondition: The top of the operations stack contains +, -, *, or /, and the numbers stack
// contains at least two numbers.
// Postcondition: The top two numbers have been popped from the numbers stack, and the top
// operation has been popped from the operations stack. The two numbers have been
// combined using the operation (with the second number popped as the left operand). The
// result of the operation has then been pushed back onto the numbers stack.
```

                                                                (continued)

(FIGURE 7.5 continued)

```
int main( )
{
    double answer;

    cout << "Type a fully parenthesized arithmetic expression:" << endl;
    answer = read_and_evaluate(cin);
    cout << "That evaluates to " << answer << endl;

    return EXIT_SUCCESS;
}


double read_and_evaluate(istream& ins)
// Library facilities used: cstring, iostream, stack
{
    const char DECIMAL = '.';
    const char RIGHT_PARENTHESIS = ')';

    stack<double> numbers;
    stack<char> operations;
    double number;
    char symbol;

    // Loop continues while istream is not "bad" (tested by ins) and next character isn't newline.
    while (ins && ins.peek( ) != '\n')
    {
        if (isdigit(ins.peek( )) || (ins.peek( ) == DECIMAL))
        {
            ins >> number;
            numbers.push(number);
        }
        else if (strchr("+-*/", ins.peek( )) != NULL)
        {
            ins >> symbol;
            operations.push(symbol);
        }
        else if (ins.peek( ) == RIGHT_PARENTHESIS)
        {
            ins.ignore( );
            evaluate_stack_tops(numbers, operations);
        }
        else
            ins.ignore( );
    }

    return numbers.top( );
}
```

(continued)

(FIGURE 7.5 continued)

```
void evaluate_stack_tops(stack<double>& numbers, stack<char>& operations)
// Library facilities used: stack
{
    double operand1, operand2;

    operand2 = numbers.top( );
    numbers.pop( );
    operand1 = numbers.top( );
    numbers.pop( );
    switch (operations.top( ))
    {
        case '+': numbers.push(operand1 + operand2);
                  break;
        case '-': numbers.push(operand1 - operand2);
                  break;
        case '*': numbers.push(operand1 * operand2);
                  break;
        case '/': numbers.push(operand1 / operand2);
                  break;
    }
    operations.pop( );
}
```

A Sample Dialogue

```
Type a fully parenthesized arithmetic expression:
( ( (60 + 40)/50) * (16 - 4) )
That evaluates to 24
```

www.cs.colorado.edu/~main/chapter07/calc.cxx   **WWW**

Evaluating Arithmetic Expressions—Implementation

The implementation of `read_and_evaluate` in Figure 7.5 benefits from three of the `istream` functions:

- The name of the `istream`, `ins`, is used as part of the boolean expression that controls the loop. As we have seen before, the expression `ins` remains true so long as `ins` has not encountered bad input (such as the end of the file).
- The function call `ins.peek( )` returns the next character of the `ins` input stream (without actually reading it).
- The function call `ins.ignore( )` reads and discards the next character from the `ins` input stream.

Our implementation also uses three other functions, which we discuss next.

Functions Used in the Calculator Program

The other three functions used in our implementation are listed here:

- The `isdigit` function (from the facility `<cctype>`) with the prototype:

    bool `isdigit(char c);`

    The function returns true if its argument is one of the digits `'0'` through `'9'`. Otherwise it returns false.

- The `strchr` function (from `<cstring>`) with the prototype:

    char* `strchr(const char s[ ], char c);`

    The function scans the string `s` for an occurrence of the character `c`. If the character `c` is found, then the function returns a pointer to the first occurrence of the character in `s`. Otherwise, the null pointer is returned.

- A function called `evaluate_stack_tops` appears as part of Figure 7.5 on page 362. The function pops two numbers off the numbers stack, combines them with an operation from the operations stack, and pushes the result back on the numbers stack.

Evaluating Arithmetic Expressions—Testing and Analysis

As usual, you should test your program on boundary values that are most likely to cause problems. For this program, one kind of boundary value consists of a single number with no operations. The next simplest kind of expressions are those that combine only two numbers. To test that operations are performed correctly, you should test simple expressions for each of the operations +, –, *, and /. These simple expressions should have only one operation. Be sure to test the division and subtraction operations carefully to ensure that the operations are performed in the correct order. After all, 3/15 is not the same as 15/3, and 3 – 15 is not the same as 15 – 3. These are perhaps the only boundary values. But it is important to also test some cases with nested parentheses. And you can test an illegal division such as 15/0. What does the program do? It probably crashes with a division by zero error. Can you place an assertion in the program that will catch this error, rather than allowing the division by zero to take place? *testing*

Let's estimate the number of operations that our program will use on an input of length n. We will count each of the following as one program operation: reading or peeking at a symbol, performing one of the arithmetic operations (+, –, *, or /), pushing an entry onto one of the stacks, and examining or popping an entry off of one of the stacks. We consider each kind of operation separately. *time analysis*

Time spent reading characters. There are only n symbols in the input, so the program can read at most n symbols. No character is "peeked" at more than once, either, so this part of the program has no more than $2n$ operations.

Time spent evaluating arithmetic operations. Each arithmetic operation performed by the program is the evaluation of an operation symbol in the input. Because there are no more than n arithmetic operations in the input, there are at most n arithmetic operations performed. In actual fact, there are far fewer than n

operations, since many of the input symbols are digits or parentheses. But there are certainly no more than *n* arithmetic operation symbols, so it is safe to say that there are no more than *n* arithmetic operations performed.

Number of push operations. Since there are at most *n* arithmetic operation symbols, we know that there are at most *n* operation symbols pushed onto the operations stack. The numbers stack may contain input numbers and numbers obtained from evaluating arithmetic expressions. Again, an upper bound will suffice: There are at most *n* input numbers and at most *n* arithmetic operations evaluated. Thus, at most, 2*n* numbers are pushed onto the numbers stack. This gives an upper bound of 3*n* total push operations onto the stacks.

Number of top and pop operations. Once we know the total number of entries that are pushed onto the two stacks, we have a bound on how many things can be popped off of the two stacks. After all, you cannot pop off an entry unless it was first pushed onto the stack. Also, our algorithm uses top for each item no more than once. Thus, there is an upper bound of 6*n* total top and pop operations from the stacks.

Total number of operations. Now, let's total things up. The total number of operations is no more than 2*n* reads/peeks, plus *n* arithmetic operations performed, plus 9*n* calls to push, top, and pop—for a grand total of 12*n*. The actual number of operations will be less than this because we have used generous upper bounds in several estimates, but 12*n* is enough to let us conclude that the algorithm for this program is $O(n)$; this is a linear algorithm.

Evaluating Arithmetic Expressions—Enhancements

The program in Figure 7.5 on page 360 is a fine example of how to use stacks. As a computer scientist, you will find yourself using stacks in this manner in many different situations. However, the program is not a fine example of a finished program. Before we can consider it to be a finished product, we need to add a number of enhancements to make the program more robust and friendly.

Some enhancements are easy. It is useful (and easy) to add a loop to the main program that will let the user evaluate more expressions until there is an indication that the user is finished with the calculator. Other enhancements are a bit harder. One nice enhancement would be to permit expressions that are not fully parenthesized, and to use the C++ precedence rules to decide the order of operations when parentheses are missing. We will discuss topics related to this enhancement in Section 7.4, where (surprise!) we'll see that a stack is useful for this purpose, too.

Self-Test Exercises for Section 7.2

6. In the calculator program, what items do the two stacks hold?

7. How would you modify the calculator program in Figure 7.5 on page 360 to allow the symbol ∧ to be used for exponentiation? Describe the changes; do not write out the code.

8. Describe how to modify the calculator program in Figure 7.5 on page 360 to allow for comments in the calculator input. Comments appear at the end of the expression, starting with a double slash // and continuing to the end of the line.

9. What possible errors could cause a stack underflow in the calculator program in Figure 7.5 on page 360?

10. Do an analysis to determine what kind of expressions cause the stack to grow large in the calculator program in Figure 7.5 on page 360.

11. How are the `istream` functions `peek` and `ignore` similar to the `top` and `pop` operations of a stack? How are they different?

12. What is the time analysis, in big-*O* notation, of the arithmetic expressions evaluation algorithm? Explain your reasoning.

7.3 IMPLEMENTATIONS OF THE STACK CLASS

As a programmer, you can use the STL stack without knowing how it works. As a student of computer science, studying the implementations of a stack is good experience for your other programming. We will give two implementations of our stack class: a static implementation using a fixed-sized array, and a dynamic implementation using a linked list. Typical stack implementations in the Standard Library use a third approach (dynamic arrays).

Array Implementation of a Stack

Figure 7.6 gives the header file for a `stack` template class that is similar to the STL stack. The class definition uses two private member variables for the stack:

1. An array, called `data`, that can hold up to `CAPACITY` items (where `CAPACITY` is a static constant of the `stack` class). This is a partially filled array, holding the stack's items in locations `data[0]`, `data[1]`, and so on.

2. A single member variable, `used`, that indicates how much of the partially filled array is currently being used. The entry at `data[0]` is at "the bottom" of the stack. The entry at `data[used-1]` is at "the top" of the stack. If the value of `used` is zero, this will indicate an empty stack.

In other words, our stack implementation is simply a partially filled array implemented in the usual way: an array and a variable to indicate the index of the last array position used. This description is the invariant of our class, so that each member function (except the constructor) may assume that the stack is represented in this way when the operation is activated. Each operation has the responsibility of ensuring that the stack is still represented in this manner when the operation finishes.

the stack entries are stored in a partially filled array

FIGURE 7.6   Header File for the Array Version of the Stack Template Class

A Header File

```
// FILE: stack1.h (part of the namespace main_savitch_7A)
// TEMPLATE CLASS PROVIDED: stack<Item>
//
// TEMPLATE PARAMETER, TYPEDEFS, and MEMBER CONSTANTS for the stack<Item> class:
//     The template parameter, Item, is the data type of the items in the stack, also defined
//     as stack<Item>::value_type. It may be any of the C++ built-in types (int, char, etc.), or a
//     class with a default constructor, a copy constructor, and an assignment operator.
//     The definition stack<Item>::size_type is the data type of any variable that keeps track of
//     how many items are in a stack. For this implementation, stack<Item>::CAPACITY
//     is the maximum capacity of any stack (once CAPACITY is reached, further pushes
//     are forbidden).
//
// CONSTRUCTOR for the stack<Item> template class:
//     stack( )
//         Postcondition: The stack has been initialized as an empty stack.
//
// MODIFICATION MEMBER FUNCTIONS for the stack<Item> template class:
//     void push(const Item& entry)
//         Precondition: size( ) < CAPACITY.
//         Postcondition: A new copy of entry has been pushed onto the stack.
//
//     void pop( )
//         Precondition: size( ) > 0.
//         Postcondition: The top item of the stack has been removed.
//
// CONSTANT MEMBER FUNCTIONS for the stack<Item> template class:
//     Item top( ) const
//         Precondition: size( ) > 0.
//         Postcondition: The return value is the top item of the stack, but the stack is
//         unchanged. This differs slightly from the STL stack (where the top function returns a
//         reference to the item on top of the stack).
//
//     size_type size( ) const
//         Postcondition: The return value is the total number of items in the stack.
//
//     bool empty( ) const
//         Postcondition: The return value is true if the stack is empty, and false otherwise.
//
// VALUE SEMANTICS for the stack<Item> template class:
//     Assignments and the copy constructor may be used with stack<Item> objects.
```

(continued)

(FIGURE 7.6 continued)

```cpp
#ifndef MAIN_SAVITCH_STACK1_H
#define MAIN_SAVITCH_STACK1_H
#include <cstdlib> // Provides size_t

namespace main_savitch_7A
{
    template <class Item>
    class stack
    {
    public:
        // TYPEDEFS AND MEMBER CONSTANT -- See Appendix E if this fails to compile.
        typedef std::size_t size_type;
        typedef Item value_type;
        static const size_type CAPACITY = 30;
        // CONSTRUCTOR
        stack( ) { used = 0; }
        // MODIFICATION MEMBER FUNCTIONS
        void push(const Item& entry);
        void pop( );
        // CONSTANT MEMBER FUNCTIONS
        bool empty( ) const { return (used == 0); }
        size_type size( ) const { return used; }
        Item top( ) const;
    private:
        Item data[CAPACITY];        // Partially filled array
        size_type used;             // How much of array is being used
    };
}

#include "stack1.template" // Include the implementation.
#endif
```

Invariant of the Stack Class (Array Version)

1. The number of items in the stack is stored in the member variable used.

2. The items in the stack are stored in a partially filled array called data, with the bottom of the stack at data[0], the next entry at data[1], and so on to the top of the stack at data[used-1].

FIGURE 7.7   Implementation File for the Array Version of the Stack Template Class

An Implementation File

```
// FILE: stack1.template
// TEMPLATE CLASS IMPLEMENTED: stack<Item> (see stack1.h for documentation)
// This file is included in the header file and not compiled separately.
// INVARIANT for the stack Class:
//     1. The number of items in the stack is in the member variable used.
//     2. The items in the stack are stored in a partially filled array called
//        data, with the bottom of the stack at data[0], the next entry at
//        data[1], and so on to the top of the stack at data[used - 1].

#include <cassert>   // Provides assert

namespace main_savitch_7A
{
    template <class Item>
    const typename stack<Item>::size_type stack<Item>::CAPACITY;


    template <class Item>
    void stack<Item>::push(const Item& entry)
    // Library facilities used: cassert
    {
        assert(size( ) < CAPACITY);
        data[used] = entry;
        ++used;
    }

    template <class Item>
    void stack<Item>::pop( )
    // Library facilities used: cassert
    {
        assert(!empty( ));
        --used;
    }


    template <class Item>
    Item stack<Item>::top( ) const
    // Library facilities used: cassert
    {
        assert(!empty( ));
        return data[used-1];
    }
}
```

www.cs.colorado.edu/~main/chapter7/stack1.template   **WWW**

The member functions that operate on our stack are now straightforward. To initialize the stack, set the private member variable used to zero, indicating an empty array and hence an empty stack. To add an entry to the stack (in the push function), we store the new entry in data[used], and then we increment used by one. To look at the top entry in the stack (function top), we simply look at the entry in array position data[used-1]. To remove an entry from the stack (in the pop function), we decrement used. The member functions to test for emptiness and to return the size are simple inline implementations that examine the value of used.

implementing the stack operations

The implementation file for our stack is given in Figure 7.7 on page 368.

Linked-List Implementation of a Stack

A linked list is a natural way to implement a stack as a dynamic structure whose size can grow and shrink during execution, without a predefined limit that is determined at compilation. The head of the linked list serves as the top of the stack. Figure 7.8 on page 371 contains the header file for a stack template class that is implemented with a linked list. Here is a precise statement of the invariant of this version of the new stack class:

Invariant of the Stack Class (Linked-List Version)

1. The items in the stack are stored in a linked list, with the top of the stack stored at the head node, down to the bottom of the stack at the tail node.

2. The member variable top_ptr is the head pointer of the linked list of items.

As usual, all member functions (except the constructors) assume that the stack is represented in this way when the function is activated, and all functions ensure that the stack continues to be represented in this way when the function finishes.

Because we are using a linked list, there is no predetermined limit to the number of items we can place in our stack. Thus, in the header file we have omitted the constant CAPACITY, but we have added documentation indicating that some of the functions allocate dynamic memory and will throw bad_alloc when dynamic memory is exhausted.

As a further consequence of using a linked list, it makes sense to utilize the node template class from Section 6.4. Thus, in Figure 7.8 you will find this include directive:

```
#include "node2.h"   // Node template class
```

By using the toolkit, many of the stack member functions can be implemented with just a line or two of code, as shown in Figure 7.9 on page 372.

The default constructor, the destructor, `size`, and `empty` are all simple enough to implement as inline member functions in Figure 7.8 on page 371. Since the first node of the list is the top of the stack, the implementation of `top` is easy: `top` just returns the data from the first node. The operations `push` and `pop` work by inserting and deleting nodes, always working at the head of the linked list. Inserting and deleting nodes at the head of the linked list is a straightforward use of `list_head_insert` and `list_head_remove` from the linked-list toolkit. Both the copy constructor and the assignment operator make use of `list_copy` to copy the source stack to the stack that activates the member function. The assignment operator must check for the potential of a self-assignment (such as `s = s`), and the assignment operator is also responsible for calling `list_clear` to release the memory that is currently used by the stack.

The Koenig Lookup

Some functions in the linked-list implementation require a local node variable, such as this:

```
main_savitch_6B::node<Item> *tail_ptr;
```

Since we are inside a template class, we must not have any using directives, and therefore we have the full name `main_savitch_6B::node<Item>` rather than just `node<Item>` (see page 292). However, when we use a node function such as `list_copy`, we do not always need to write the full name `main_savitch_6B:: list_copy`. The reason for this is that compilers can sometimes tell which `list_copy` function is intended since some of its arguments' types are defined in the same `main_savitch_6B` namespace. This use of arguments to determine which function to use is called the **Koenig lookup**.

However, some compilers do not allow the Koenig lookup within template functions, so we have written full names for each of the list functions.

Self-Test Exercises for Section 7.3

13. What is the typical implementation of an STL stack?
14. For the array version of the stack, write a new member function that returns the maximum number of items that can be added to the stack without stack overflow.
15. Describe a simple way to reimplement the array version of the stack without the need for a `CAPACITY` constant.
16. Give the full implementation of a constant member function that returns the second element from the top of the stack without actually changing the stack. Write separate solutions for the two different stack versions.
17. Which functions from the node template class should not be used in the linked-list implementation of a stack? Why?
18. Do a time analysis of the `size` function for the linked-list version of the stack. If the function is not constant time, then can you think of a different approach that is constant time?
19. In the linked-list implementation of the stack, why do some compilers allow `list_copy` without specifying `main_savitch_6B::list_copy`?

FIGURE 7.8   Header File for the Linked-List Version of the Stack Template Class

A Header File

```
// FILE: stack2.h (part of the namespace main_savitch_7B)
```
See Figure 7.6 on page 366 for the other documentation that goes here.
The only difference is that there is no CAPACITY constant.
```
// DYNAMIC MEMORY USAGE by the stack<Item> template class:
//     If there is insufficient dynamic memory, then the following functions throw bad_alloc:
//     the copy constructor, push, and the assignment operator.

#ifndef MAIN_SAVITCH_STACK2_H
#define MAIN_SAVITCH_STACK2_H
#include <cstdlib>    // Provides NULL and size_t
#include "node2.h"    // Node template class from Figure 6.5 on page 317

namespace main_savitch_7B
{
    template <class Item>
    class stack
    {
    public:
        // TYPEDEFS
        typedef std::size_t size_type;
        typedef Item value_type;
        // CONSTRUCTORS and DESTRUCTOR
        stack( ) { top_ptr = NULL; }
        stack(const stack& source);
        ~stack( ) { main_savitch_6B::list_clear(top_ptr); }
        // MODIFICATION MEMBER FUNCTIONS
        void push(const Item& entry);
        void pop( );
        void operator =(const stack& source);
        // CONSTANT MEMBER FUNCTIONS
        size_type size( ) const
            { return main_savitch_6B::list_length(top_ptr); }
        bool empty( ) const { return (top_ptr == NULL); }
        Item top( ) const;
    private:
        main_savitch_6B::node<Item> *top_ptr;   // Points to top of stack
    };
}

#include "stack2.template" // Include the implementation
#endif
```

FIGURE 7.9   Implementation File for the Linked-List Version of the Stack Template Class

An Implementation File

```
// FILE: stack2.template
// TEMPLATE CLASS IMPLEMENTED: stack<Item> (see stack2.h for documentation)
// This file is included in the header file and not compiled separately.
// INVARIANT for the stack class:
//     1. The items in the stack are stored in a linked list, with the top of the stack stored at the
//        head node, down to the bottom of the stack at the final node.
//     2. The member variable top_ptr is the head pointer of the linked list.

#include <cassert>        // Provides assert
#include "node2.h"        // Node template class from Figure 6.5 on page 317

namespace main_savitch_7B
{

    template <class Item>
    stack<Item>::stack(const stack<Item>& source)
    // Library facilities used: node2.h
    {
        main_savitch_6B::node<Item> *tail_ptr; // Needed for argument of list_copy

        main_savitch_6B::list_copy(source.top_ptr, top_ptr, tail_ptr);
    }

    template <class Item>
    void stack<Item>::push(const Item& entry)
    // Library facilities used: node2.h
    {
        main_savitch_6B::list_head_insert(top_ptr, entry);
    }

    template <class Item>
    void stack<Item>::pop( )
    // Library facilities used: cassert, node2.h
    {
        assert(!empty( ));
        main_savitch_6B::list_head_remove(top_ptr);
    }
```

(continued)

(FIGURE 7.9 continued)

```
template <class Item>
void stack<Item>::operator =(const stack<Item>& source)
// Library facilities used: node2.h
{
    main_savitch_6B::node<Item> *tail_ptr; // Needed for argument of list_copy

    if (this == &source) // Handle self-assignment
        return;

    main_savitch_6B::list_clear(top_ptr);
    main_savitch_6B::list_copy(source.top_ptr, top_ptr, tail_ptr);
}


template <class Item>
Item stack<Item>::top( ) const
// Library facilities used: cassert
{
    assert(!empty( ));
    return top_ptr->data( );
}

}
```

www.cs.colorado.edu/~main/chapter7/stack2.template   **W W W**

7.4   MORE COMPLEX STACK APPLICATIONS

Evaluating Postfix Expressions

We normally write an arithmetic operation between its two arguments, for example, the + operation occurs between the 2 and the 3 in the arithmetic expression 2 + 3. This is called *infix notation*. There is another way of writing arithmetic operations that places the operation in front of the two arguments, for example + 2 3 evaluates to 5. This is called **Polish prefix notation** or simply **prefix notation**.

infix versus prefix notation

A **prefix** is something attached to the front of an expression. You may have heard about similar prefixes for words, such as the prefix *un* in *unbelievable*. Thus, it makes sense to call this notation *prefix notation*. But why *Polish*? It is called Polish because it was devised by the Polish mathematician Jan Łukasiewicz. It would be more proper to call it *Łukasiewicz notation*, but apparently non–Polish-speaking people have trouble pronouncing *Łukasiewicz* (lü-kä-**sha**-vēch).

the origin of the notation

Using prefix notation, parentheses are completely avoided. For example, the expression (2 + 3) * 7, when written in this Polish prefix notation, is:

$$* + 2\ 3\ 7$$

The curved lines under the expression indicate groupings of subexpressions (but the lines are not actually part of the prefix notation).

postfix notation

If we prefer, we can write the operations after the two numbers being combined. This is called **Polish postfix notation**, or more simply **postfix notation** (or sometimes **reverse Polish notation**). For example, the expression (2 + 3) * 7 when written in Polish postfix notation is:

$$2\ 3 + 7\ *$$

Once again, the curves merely clarify the groupings of subexpressions, and these curves are not actually part of the postfix notation.

Here's a longer example. The postfix expression 7 3 5 * + 4 - is equivalent to the infix expression (7 + (3*5)) - 4.

Do not intermix prefix and postfix notation. You should consistently use one or the other and not mix them together in a single expression.

our goal: evaluation of postfix expressions

Postfix notation is handy because it does not require parentheses and because it is particularly easy to evaluate (once you learn to use the notation). In fact, postfix notation often is used internally for computers because of the ease of expression evaluation. We will describe an algorithm to evaluate a postfix expression. When converted to a C++ program, the postfix evaluation is similar to the calculator program (Figure 7.5 on page 360)—although, from our comments you might guess that the postfix evaluation is actually simpler than the infix evaluation required in the calculator program.

There are two input format issues that we must handle. When entering postfix notation we will require a space between two consecutive numbers so that you can tell where one number ends and another begins. For example, the input

35 6

consists of two numbers, 35 and 6, with a space in between. This is different from the input

356

which is just a single number, 356. A second input issue: You probably want to restrict the input to non-negative numbers in order to avoid the complication of distinguishing the negative sign of a number from a binary subtraction operation.

postfix evaluation algorithm

Our algorithm for evaluating a postfix expression uses only one stack, which is a stack of numbers. There is no need for a second stack of operation symbols, because *each operation is used as soon as it is read*. In fact, the reason why postfix evaluation is easy is precisely because each operation symbol is immediately used as soon as it is read. In the algorithm we assume that each input entry is either a number or an operation. For simplicity, we will assume that all the operations take two arguments. The complete evaluation algorithm is given in Figure 7.10, along with an example computation.

Let's study the example to see how the algorithm works. Each time an operation appears in the input, the operands for the operation are the two most recently seen numbers. For example, in Figure 7.10(c), we are about to read the * symbol. Since we have just pushed 3 and 2 onto the stack, the * causes a multiplication of 3*2, resulting in 6. The result of 6 is then pushed onto the stack, as shown in Figure 7.10(d).

Sometimes the "most recently seen number" is not actually an input number, but instead it is a number that we computed and pushed back onto the stack. For example, in Figure 7.10(d), we are about to read the first +. At this point, 6 is on top of the stack (as a result of multiplying 3*2). Below the 6 is the number 5. So, the "two most recently seen numbers" are the 6 (that we computed) and the 5 (underneath the 6). We add these two numbers, resulting in 11 (which we push onto the stack, as shown in 7.10(e)).

And so the process continues: Each time we encounter an operation, the operation is immediately applied to the two most recently seen numbers, which always reside in the top two positions of the stack. When the input is exhausted, the number remaining in the stack is the value of the entire expression.

Translating Infix to Postfix Notation

Because it is so easy to evaluate a postfix expression, one strategy for evaluating an ordinary infix expression is to first convert it to postfix notation and then evaluate the postfix expression. This is what compilers often do. In this section, we will present an algorithm to translate an infix expression to a postfix expression. The algorithm's input is an expression in infix notation, and the output is an equivalent expression in postfix notation. We will develop the algorithm as pseudocode and will not specify any precise form of input or output.

infix expression

↓

postfix expression

Until now we have assumed that the operands in our arithmetic expressions were all numbers. That need not be true. For example, an arithmetic expression may also contain variables. In this example, we will assume that the arithmetic expression can also contain variables. In fact, the operands may be anything at all, so long as we have a way of recognizing an operand when our algorithm encounters one. However, in our examples we will assume that the operands are either numbers or variables. We will also assume that all the operations are **binary operations** (which have two operands), such as addition and subtraction. There will be no **unary operations** (which have only one operand), such as sqrt for the square root function. We will present two algorithms, one for fully parenthesized expressions and one for more realistic expressions that omit some parentheses. Our algorithms apply to any sort of operations working on any sort of operands; so, in particular, our algorithms work on boolean expressions as well

FIGURE 7.10   Evaluating a Postfix Expression

Pseudocode

1. Initialize a stack of double numbers.

2. *do*

  if (the next input is a number)
    Read the next input and push it onto the stack.
  else
  {
    Read the next character, which is an operation symbol.
    Use top and pop to get the two numbers off the stack.
    Combine these two numbers with the operation (using the *second* number
    popped as the *left* operand), and push the result onto the stack.
  }
  while (there is more of the expression to read) ;

3. At this point, the stack contains one number, which is the value of the expression.

Example

> Evaluate the postfix expression
> 5 3 2 * + 4 – 5 +

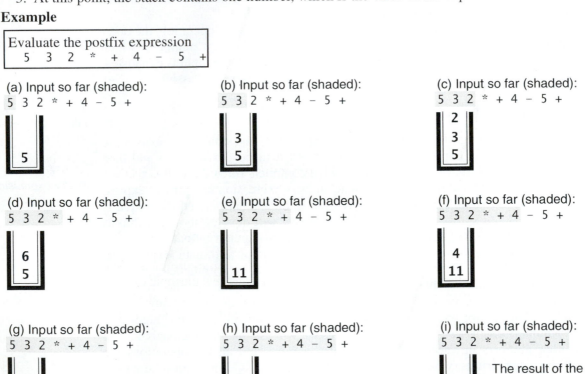

(a) Input so far (shaded):
5 3 2 * + 4 – 5 +

(b) Input so far (shaded):
5 3 2 * + 4 – 5 +

(c) Input so far (shaded):
5 3 2 * + 4 – 5 +

(d) Input so far (shaded):
5 3 2 * + 4 – 5 +

(e) Input so far (shaded):
5 3 2 * + 4 – 5 +

(f) Input so far (shaded):
5 3 2 * + 4 – 5 +

(g) Input so far (shaded):
5 3 2 * + 4 – 5 +

(h) Input so far (shaded):
5 3 2 * + 4 – 5 +

(i) Input so far (shaded):
5 3 2 * + 4 – 5 +

The result of the computation is 12.

as arithmetic expressions. However, in order to keep matters uncluttered, we will consider only arithmetic expressions in our examples.

algorithm for fully parenthesized expressions

If the infix expression is fully parenthesized, the algorithm is simple. All that's needed to convert from infix to postfix notation is to move each operation symbol to the location of the right parenthesis corresponding to that operation and then remove all parentheses. For example, the following infix expression will have its operation symbols moved to the location indicated by the arrows:

The result is the postfix expression:

A 7 + B C / * 2 D * –

This process of moving each operation to the location of its corresponding right parenthesis is more of an idea than a complete algorithm. A complete algorithm should read the expression from left to right and must somehow remember the operations and then determine when the corresponding right parenthesis has been found. We have some work to do before this idea becomes an algorithm.

First, observe that the operands (that is, the numbers and variables) in the equivalent postfix expression are in the same order as the operands in the corresponding infix expression that we start out with. So our algorithm can simply copy the infix expression operands, omitting parentheses and inserting the operations, such as +, *, and so forth, at the correct locations. The problem is finding the location for inserting the operations in the postfix expression. How do we save the operations, and how do we know when to insert them? Look back at our example. If we push the operations onto a stack, then the operations we need will always be on top of the stack. When do we insert an operation? We insert an operation into the output whenever we encounter a right parenthesis in the input. Hence, the heart of the algorithm is to push the operations onto a stack and to pop an operation every time we encounter a right parenthesis. The algorithm is given in Figure 7.11. The algorithm does some checking to ensure that the input expression is fully parenthesized with balanced parentheses, although there is no checking to ensure that each operation appears between its operands (rather than before or after its operands).

Using Precedence Rules in the Infix Expression

So far we have been assuming that our infix expression is fully parenthesized. However, in practice, infix expressions are usually not fully parenthesized, and the computer must rely on precedence rules to determine the order of operations for the missing parentheses. This adds a significant complication.

FIGURE 7.11   Converting a Fully Parenthesized Infix Expression to a Postfix Expression

Pseudocode

1. Initialize a stack of characters to hold the operation symbols and parentheses.

2. *do*

    if (the next input is a left parenthesis)
        Read the left parenthesis and push it onto the stack.
    else if (the next input is a number or other operand)
        Read the operand and write it to the output.
    else if (the next input is one of the operation symbols)
        Read the operation symbol and push it onto the stack.
    else
    {

        Read and discard the next input symbol (which should be a right parenthesis).
        There should be an operation symbol on top of the stack, so write this symbol
        to the output and pop it from the stack. (If there is no such symbol, then print an
        error message indicating that there were too few operations in the infix expression,
        and halt.) After popping the operation symbol, there should be a left parenthesis on
        the top of the stack, so pop and discard this left parenthesis.
        (If there was no left parenthesis, then the input did not have balanced
        parentheses, so print an error message and halt.)

    }
    while (there is more of the expression to read) ;

3. At this point, the stack should be empty. Otherwise print an error message indicating that the expression was not fully parenthesized.

Let's start with an example. We will use the usual C++ precedence rules in our example. Consider the following expression:

```
2 * (A - B) + 3 + C
```

In this case the subtraction is performed first, then the multiplication, and finally the two additions are performed from left to right. The subtraction is first because the parentheses indicate that (A - B) must be evaluated before combining the result with any other operands. The multiplication is performed next—before the additions—because multiplication has *higher precedence* than addition. The two additions are of equal precedence and there are no parentheses to tell us which addition to perform first. The operations (+, -, *, and /) of equal precedence are performed left to right (when parentheses do not indicate otherwise). Thus, the left-hand addition occurs before the right-hand addition. This order of evaluation means the expression is the same as this fully parenthesized expression:

```
(((2 * (A - B)) + 3) + C)
```

To help determine the order of evaluation for arithmetic expressions, we have been referring to the *precedence* of operations, such as +, -, and *. A **precedence** is just an ordering from high to low for the operations. Operations with a higher precedence are evaluated before operations with a lower precedence. Sometimes, two different operations, such as + and -, have equal precedence, in which case we must specify whether the operations are to be evaluated left-to-right or right-to-left. For example, in C++, * and / have equal precedence (with left-to-right evaluation); + and - also have equal precedence (with left-to-right evaluation), but * and / have higher precedence than + and -. That is why we perform multiplication before addition (when there are no parentheses indicating otherwise).

Just to make sure they are fresh in our minds, let us review the C++ rules for evaluating arithmetic expressions that are not fully parenthesized:

rules for using precedence

1. Parentheses, when they are present, determine the order of operations. Everything inside a pair of matching parentheses is evaluated, and that value is then combined with things outside the parentheses.

2. If the order is not indicated by parentheses, operations of higher precedence are performed before operations of lower precedence.

3. Arithmetic operations of equal precedence are performed in left-to-right order, unless parentheses indicate otherwise.

In Figure 7.11 we gave an algorithm to convert a fully parenthesized infix expression to an equivalent postfix expression. Now we can make our algorithm more general. The new version (Figure 7.12 on page 381) does not require full parentheses for the input; the algorithm uses precedence to decide which operation to perform first. In other words, the expressions can be written as we normally write them with parentheses omitted in some cases. Figure 7.13 on page 382 contains an example computation of our algorithm as it translates an infix expression into the corresponding postfix expression. Study the example now, then return here to read the details of the algorithm.

Correctness of the Conversion from Infix to Postfix

For the conversion algorithm to be correct, we must check these items:

1. The postfix expression contains the correct operands in the correct order.
2. The postfix expression evaluates subexpressions in the way indicated by the parentheses in the infix expression.
3. The postfix expression handles operations of differing precedence according to the precedence rules.
4. A string of operations of equal precedence in the infix expression is handled correctly when translated into the postfix expression.

1. The operands are in the right order

2. The parentheses are done correctly

Let's consider each of these four issues. First we need to know that the operands (the numbers and variables) in the postfix expression are in the same order as they were in the input infix expression, but this is easy to see. Because operands are written out as soon as they are read in, they are clearly in the same order as in the input infix expression.

Parentheses are a way of grouping subexpressions. Everything inside a pair of matching parentheses is treated as a single unit by anything outside the parentheses. The parentheses give the following message to the operations outside of the parentheses: *Don't look inside these parentheses. We will work things out among ourselves and deliver a single value for you to combine with other operands.* This means that all operations between a set of matching parentheses in the infix expression should form a subexpression of the postfix expression, and with this algorithm they do just that. To see that they do form a subexpression, we will show the following:

How the Infix-to-Postfix Algorithm Translates Subexpressions

Claim: All of the operations between a pair of matching parentheses (and no other operations) are output between the time the algorithm reads the opening parenthesis and the time that it reads the closing parenthesis.

Once we show that this claim is true, we will know that all the operations between a pair of matching parentheses in the infix expression will be together in a group within the output postfix notation, and so they will form a subexpression of the postfix expression. So, let's see exactly why the claim is valid.

The algorithm keeps track of expressions within matching parentheses by using the stack. When the algorithm encounters an opening parenthesis, that is, a '(', it pushes this parenthesis onto the stack. Now consider what happens between pushing the opening parenthesis and encountering the matching closing parenthesis, that is, the matching ')'. The algorithm will never output an operation from the stack that is below the opening parenthesis, '('. Thus, it only outputs operations that are within the pair of matching parentheses in the input (infix) expression. Moreover, it outputs all of these operations. When it encounters the matching closing parenthesis, it outputs all the remaining operations on the stack all the way down to that matching opening parenthesis.

3. The precedence is handled correctly

When the infix expression contains an operation with low precedence followed by an operation with a higher precedence, then the algorithm should output these operations in reverse order. In other words, the higher precedence operation must be written first. A check of the algorithm will show that the operations are indeed output in reverse order.

When the infix expression contains a sequence of operations of equal precedence, they represent an evaluation that goes from left to right. That means the operations should be output from left to right. If you check the algorithm, you will see that this is true. Operations are pushed onto the stack, but when the next operation of equal precedence is encountered, the operation in the stack is output and the new operation is pushed onto the stack. To confirm this, first check the algorithm in the case where the stack is empty at the time that the operations are encountered. That is the easiest case to see. After that, the other cases will be clearer, because they are similar.

4. Operations of equal precedence are handled correctly

FIGURE 7.12 Converting an Infix Expression to a Postfix Expression (General Case)

Pseudocode

1. Initialize a stack of characters to hold the operation symbols and parentheses.

2. *do*

     if (the next input is a left parenthesis)
           Read the left parenthesis and push it onto the stack.
     else if (the next input is a number or other operand)
           Read the operand and write it to the output.
     else if (the next input is one of the operation symbols)
     {
           do
                 Print the top operation and pop it.
           while none of these three conditions are true:
                 (1) The stack becomes empty, or
                 (2) The next symbol on the stack is a left parenthesis, or
                 (3) The next symbol on the stack is an operation with lower
                       precedence that the next input symbol.

           Read the next input symbol, and push this symbol onto the stack.
     }
     else
     {
           Read and discard the next input symbol (which should be a right parenthesis).
           Print the top operation and pop it; keep printing and popping until the next
           symbol on the stack is a left parenthesis. (If no left parenthesis is encountered, then
           print an error message indicating unbalanced parentheses, and halt.) Finally, pop
           the left parenthesis.
     }
     while (there is more of the expression to read) ;

3. Print and pop any remaining operations on the stack. (There should be no remaining left parentheses; if there are, the input expression did not have balanced parentheses.)

FIGURE 7.13   Example Computation for the Algorithm of Figure 7.12

Example

Convert the infix expression:
3 * X + (Y - 12) - Z

(a) Input so far (shaded):
3 * X + (Y - 12) - Z
The operand 3 is printed.

Output so far:
3

(b) Input so far (shaded):
3 * X + (Y - 12) - Z
The * is pushed.

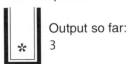

Output so far:
3

(c) Input so far (shaded):
3 * X + (Y - 12) - Z
The operand X is printed.

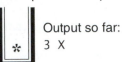

Output so far:
3 X

(d) Input so far (shaded):
3 * X + (Y - 12) - Z
Pop and print the * since it has higher precedence than the +; then push the +.

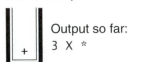

Output so far:
3 X *

(e) Input so far (shaded):
3 * X + (Y - 12) - Z
Push the parenthesis.

Output so far:
3 X *

(f) Input so far (shaded):
3 * X + (Y - 12) - Z
The operand Y is printed.

Output so far:
3 X * Y

(g) Input so far (shaded):
3 * X + (Y - 12) - Z
The - is pushed.

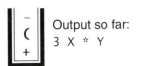

Output so far:
3 X * Y

(h) Input so far (shaded):
3 * X + (Y - 12) - Z
The operand 12 is printed.

Output so far:
3 X * Y 12

(i) Input so far (shaded):
3 * X + (Y - 12) - Z
Pop until left parenthesis.

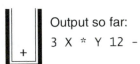

Output so far:
3 X * Y 12 -

(j) Input so far (shaded):
3 * X + (Y - 12) - Z
Pop and print the + since it has precedence equal to the -; then push the -.

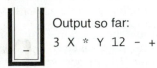

Output so far:
3 X * Y 12 - +

(k) Input so far (shaded):
3 * X + (Y - 12) - Z
The operand Z is printed.

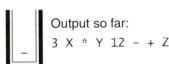

Output so far:
3 X * Y 12 - + Z

(l) Input so far (shaded):
3 * X + (Y - 12) - Z
Pop any remaining operations.

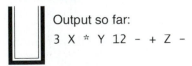

Output so far:
3 X * Y 12 - + Z -

Self-Test Exercises for Section 7.4

20. Evaluate the postfix expression 2 3 - 43 +.
21. Why does a postfix evaluation algorithm only need one stack?
22. Write the following expression in both prefix and postfix notation: ((7+3) * 2)
23. Trace the algorithm from Figure 7.10 on page 376 to evaluate the postfix expression 15 9 6 * + 12 - 15 +. Draw the stack after each push or pop.
24. Trace the algorithm from Figure 7.12 on page 381 to create a postfix expression from 3 / A + (B + 12) - C.

CHAPTER SUMMARY

- A stack is a Last-In/First-Out data structure.
- The accessible end of the stack is called the *top*. Adding an entry to a stack is called a *push* operation. Removing an entry from a stack is called a *pop* operation.
- Attempting to push an entry onto a full stack is an error known as a *stack overflow*. Attempting to pop an entry off an empty stack is an error known as a *stack underflow*.
- A stack can be implemented as a partially filled array.
- A stack can be implemented as a linked list.
- An advantage of a linked-list implementation of a stack over an array implementation is that with the linked list there is no preset limit on the number of entries you can add to the stack. A similar advantage can be obtained by using a dynamic array.
- Stacks have many uses in computer science. The evaluation and translation of arithmetic expressions are two common uses.

Solutions to Self-Test Exercises

1. LIFO refers to a Last-In/First-Out data structure, in which items are taken out in the reverse order of their insertion.

2. Most compilers use stacks to analyze the syntax of a program. Stacks are also used to keep track of local variables when a program is run.

3. The pop operation removes the top item of the stack. The top operation returns a reference to the top item on the stack without removing it.

4. Push a 'D'; push an 'A'; push an 'H'; push an 'L'; top and pop for 'L'; top and pop for 'H'; top and pop for 'A'; top and pop for 'D'. The output is LHAD.

5. Store the top item in a local variable called `t`, then pop it. Look at the next item, storing it in another local variable called `result`. Push the `t` back on the stack, and return the `result`.

6. One stack holds the numbers, and the other stack holds the operations.

7. Within `read_and_evaluate`, there is a call to `strchr` to determine whether the next character is one of the operators. This call should add the symbol `'^'` to its list of operators. Also, add a new case to the switch statement within the function `evaluate_stack_tops`. The new case is for the exponentiation operator. This calculates `operand1` raised to the power of `operand2` and pushes the result back onto the numbers stack. (Use the `pow` function from `<cmath>` to compute the value of a number raised to a power).

8. The modification is most easily accomplished in the function `read_and_evaluate`. Within this function, you can add a bit of code after the line `ins >> symbol;`. This is the line that reads an operator symbol. After reading such a symbol, check whether the symbol is a slash (`'/'`), and peek ahead to see whether the next symbol is also a slash. If so, then read and discard the rest of the line (instead of pushing the operator onto the stack).

9. Any top or pop operation has the potential for a stack underflow. In the evaluation algorithm, these occur in `evaluate_stack_tops`, which is called whenever a right parenthesis is encountered. If the input expression is correctly formed, then at the point of the right parenthesis there will always be at least one operation on the characters stack and at least two operands on the numbers stack—and therefore there can be no stack underflow. But if one of the operations is omitted from the input expression, then when the right parenthesis occurs, there can be a stack underflow on the characters stack. And if one of the operands is omitted from the input expression, then when the right parenthesis occurs, there can be a stack underflow on the numbers stack.

10. The numbers stack grows large if the input expression has parentheses that are nested deeply. For example, consider the input expression (1 + (2 + (3 + (4 + 5)))). By the time the 5 is read and pushed on the stack, the 1, 2, 3, and 4 are already on the numbers stack. In this example, there are four nested subexpressions, and we need to push five numbers onto the numbers stack. So, the general stack size will be one more than the depth of the nesting.

11. The `istream` peek operation is similar to the top operation, in that it returns the next character of the input stream without actually reading it. The `ignore` operation is similar to the pop operation, in that it reads and discards the next character from the input stream. However, an `istream` processes characters in the order they are received, rather than in the LIFO fashion of a stack.

12. The arithmetic expressions evaluation algorithm is a linear algorithm. If n is the length of the input expression, then there are at most n symbols read, n symbols to peek, n arithmetic operations, n pushes onto the numbers stack (once for each input number and once for each evaluation of an operation), n pushes onto the operations stack, and $4n$ top and pop operations (twice the number of pushes). The upper bound is $9n$; ignoring the constant gives $O(n)$.

13. The STL stack is typically implemented using a dynamic array.

14. The function should return `CAPACITY` minus `used`.

15. Use a dynamic array.

16. Here is the solution for the linked-list version. You can write the array version yourself.

```
template <class Item>
Item stack<Item>::second( ) const
// Libraries used: cassert
{
    assert(size( ) >= 2);
    return top_ptr->link( )->data( );
}
```

17. `set_data`, `set_link`, `list_insert`, `list_locate`, `list_remove`, and `list_search` functions should not be used in the stack class, because only the top item of the stack can be accessed.

18. Our `size` implementation calls `list_size`, which is linear time. For a constant time implementation, you could maintain another private member variable to continually keep track of the list length. This variable would be updated each time an item is pushed or popped, and the `size` function can simply return the current value of this variable.

19. See the discussion of the Koenig lookup on page 370.

20. 42

21. There is no need for a second stack of operation symbols, because each operation is used as soon as it is read.

22. Prefix: `* + 7 3 2`   Postfix: `7 3 + 2 *`

23. The trace is the same as the computation at the bottom of Figure 7.10 on page 376, except that the numbers are three times as large.

24. The trace is much the same as the computation in Figure 7.13 on page 382, except that the operations are different.

PROGRAMMING PROJECTS

For more in-depth projects, please see www.cs.colorado.edu/~main/projects/

1 In our first case study on evaluating arithmetic expressions we used two stacks that held different types of data. In some other applications, we might need two stacks with the same type of data. If we implement the stacks as arrays, there is a chance that one array (and hence one stack) becomes filled, causing our computation to end prematurely. This might be a shame, since the other array (stack) might have plenty of room. One way around this problem is to implement two stacks as one large array rather than two smaller arrays. Write a class for a pair of stacks. A pair of stacks is simply an object with two stacks. Call these stacks *StackA* and *StackB*. There should be separate operations for each stack, for example, pop_a and pop_b. Implement the stack pair as a single array. The two stacks grow from the two ends of the array, so for example, one stack could fill up one quarter of the array while the other fills up three quarters.

2 The `top` member function of the STL stack returns a reference to the top item. This is similar to the way that our node class from Chapter 6 has a `data` function that returns a reference to the item in the node (see page 314). For this project, modify both of the stack implementations from Section 7.3 so that the `top` function returns a reference to the top item. With this modification, the prototype of the `top` function changes:

```
Item& top( );
```

Note that `top` is no longer a const function because its return value can now be used to change the top item on a stack. For example, if `s` is a non-empty stack of integers, we can change the top item to 42 by the assignment:

```
s.top( ) = 42;
```

In the case of the Chapter 6 node class, we fixed this problem by adding a second version of the `data` function, and this second version is a const member function (see page 316). Your solutions for this project should do a similar thing for the stack implementations, also providing a const version of the `top` function with this prototype:

```
const Item& top( ) const;
```

This prototype indicates that the return value is a reference to a constant item (and therefore it cannot be used to change the stack). Since the stack cannot be changed, this version of the `top` function is now a const member function.

3 Choose one of the stack implementations from the previous project and implement an iterator that is similar to our bag iterator in Section 6.6.

4 Choose one of the stack implementations and implement a `seek` member function with this specification:

```
Item seek(size_type n = 1);
// Precondition: n < size( ).
// Postcondition: The return value is the
// item that is n from the top (with the top at
// n = 0, the next at n = 1, and so on). The
// stack is not changed.
```

5 In this exercise you will need the `seek` member function from Project 4 or the iterator from Project 3. You could also use the Standard Library stack class (which has an iterator). Write a program that prints all strings with at most *n* letters, where the letters are chosen from a range `first...last`, which is a subrange of the type *char*. Here is an outline for an algorithm to do this using a stack:

```
// Writing all strings of 1 to n letters:
Push first onto the stack.
while (the stack is not empty)
{
    Print the contents of the stack.
    if (the stack contains fewer than n letters)
        Push first onto the stack.
    else
    {
        Pop characters off the stack, until the
        stack is empty, or there is a character
        other than last on the top. (Note: If the
        top character is not last, then nothing is
        popped off the stack.)
        if (the stack is not empty)
            Pop a character c off the stack, and
            push c+1 (i.e., the next letter) onto
            the stack.
    }
}
```

6 Enhance the calculator program given in Figure 7.5 on page 360 so that it has all of the following features: After one expression is evaluated, the user is asked if he or she wants to evaluate another expression and is allowed to choose between evaluating another expression and quitting the program. Expressions need not be fully parenthesized, and when parentheses are missing, the usual C++ precedence rules are followed. If the arithmetic expression entered is not well formed, then the user is told it is not well formed and asked to reenter the expression.

7 In Figure 7.5 on page 360 we presented a program to evaluate arithmetic expressions. In this exercise you will write a similar program to evaluate boolean expressions. Rather than arithmetic operations, the input expressions for this program will use the operations && (the "and" operation), ||(the "or" operation), and !(the "not" operation). Rather than combining numbers, the input expression will combine simple boolean comparisons of numbers such as (1 < 2) and (6 < 3). Assume all the numbers in these simple comparisons are integers. Allow the following comparison operations: <, >, <=, >=, ==, and !=. At first assume that all boolean expressions are fully parenthesized and well formed. Be sure to note that "not" is a unary operation. You can assume that the argument to "not" (which follows the !) is enclosed in parentheses. Your program should allow the user to evaluate additional expressions until the user says he/she wishes to end the program.

For a more difficult assignment, enhance your program by adding any or all of the following features: (a) The numbers need not be integers; (b) the expression need not be fully parenthesized—if parentheses are missing, then the C++ precedence rules apply (note that innermost expressions such as (1 < 2) are still assumed to be in parentheses); (c) the expression need not be well formed—if it is not, then the user is asked to reenter the expression.

8 Write a program that evaluates an arithmetic expression in postfix notation. The basic algorithm is contained in "Evaluating Postfix Expressions" on page 373. Assume the input contains numbers (but no variables) as well as the arithmetic operations +, -, *, and /. Your program should allow the user to evaluate additional expressions until the user wants to end the program. You might also enhance your program so that the expression need not be well formed; if it is not well formed, then the user must reenter the expression.

9 Write a program that takes as input an infix expression and outputs the equivalent postfix expression. The basic algorithm is contained in "Translating Infix to Postfix Notation" on page 375. Assume that the input may contain numbers, variables, arithmetic operations +, -, *, and /, as well as parentheses. However, the expression need not be fully parenthesized, and when parentheses are missing, the usual C++ precedence rules are used to determine the order of evaluation. Your program should allow the user to enter additional expressions until the user says he or she wishes to end the program. For a more difficult assignment, enhance your program so that the expression need not be well formed; if it is not well formed, then the user is asked to reenter the expression.

10 Redo the calculator program given in Figure 7.5 on page 360, but this time implement it in a different way. To evaluate the arithmetic expression, your program will first convert the expression to postfix notation. After that, it will evaluate the postfix expression. Pseudocode for both of these subtasks is given in this chapter. For this exercise, you should not assume that expressions are fully parenthesized. When parentheses are missing, the usual C++ precedence rules are used to determine the order of evaluation. Your program should allow the user to evaluate additional expressions until the user wants to end the program.

11 Suppose that you have n queens from a chessboard. Is it possible to place all n queens on the board so that no two queens are in the same row, no two queens are in the same column, and no two queens are on the same diagonal? For example, a solution with $n = 5$ is shown here:

This problem is called the n-queens problem. For

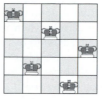

Solution to the
5-queens problem

this project, you are to write a function that has one integer parameter, n, and determines whether there is a solution to the n-queens problem. If a solution is found, then the procedure prints the row and column of each queen. Your program should solve the problem by making a sequence of choices, such as "Try placing the row 1 queen in column 1," or "Try placing the row 7 queen in column 3." Each time a choice is made, the choice is pushed onto a stack that already contains all the previously made choices. The purpose of the stack is to make it easy to fix incorrect choices, using the following pseudocode, with a stack, s, and a boolean variable, success:

Push information onto the stack indicating the first choice is a queen in row 1, column 1.

success = false;

while (!success && !s.empty( ))
{

Check whether the most recent choice (on top of the stack) is in the same row, same column, or same diagonal as any other choices (below the top). If so, then we say there is a conflict; otherwise there is no conflict.

if (there is a conflict)
Pop elements off the stack until the stack becomes empty, or the top of the stack is a choice that is not in column n. If the stack is now not empty, then increase the column number of the top choice by 1.
else if (no conflict, and the stack size is n)
Set success to *true* because we have found a solution to the n-queens problem.
else
Push information onto the stack, indicating that the next choice is to place a queen at row number s.size( )+1, and column number 1.
}

This technique is called **backtracking** since we keep our choices on a stack and *back up* to correct any mistakes that are made. Notice that when you check for a conflict, you will need access to the entire stack (not just the top), so that you should use the seek function from Programming Project 4 or an iterator from Programming Project 3. You could also use the Standard Library stack class (which has an iterator).

12 Choose one of your stack implementations and write a friend function to display the contents of a stack from top to bottom. Then, implement a friend function to display the stack bottom to top.

13 Write a function that compares two stacks for equality. The function takes two stacks as parameters and returns true if they are identical. The stacks should remain unchanged after the function returns to the calling program. Hint: Either write a friend function that can examine the elements directly, or pop the stacks and save the popped elements so that the stacks can be restored. In this second case, the stack parameters will not be const parameters because they are temporarily changed before being restored.

14 In this project, you will use stacks to recognize palindromes. Palindromes are strings that read the same backward as forward (for example, "madam"). Write a program to read a line and print whether or not it is a palindrome. Hint: You will need three stacks to implement the program. (In Chapter 8, you will utilize a stack and a queue to implement the palindrome program more efficiently.)

8

Queues

He who comes first, eats first.

EIKE VON REPKOW
Sachsenspiegel

LEARNING OBJECTIVES

When you complete Chapter 8, you will be able to...

- follow and explain queue-based algorithms using the usual computer science terminology of *enqueue* and *de-queue* (or the unusual C++ queue terms of push and pop).
- use the STL queue class to implement queue-based algorithms such as scheduling first-come, first-serve tasks.
- implement queue and priority queue classes of your own using either an array or a linked-list data structure.

CHAPTER CONTENTS

Queues

A *queue* is a First-In/First-Out data structure similar to a line of people at a ticket window. It can be used whenever you need a data structure that allows entries to "wait their turn." In this chapter we discuss applications of the queue data structure, give two implementations of a queue class, and discuss the differences between queues and stacks. We also discuss a more flexible kind of queue called a *priority queue.*

8.1 INTRODUCTION TO QUEUES AND THE STL QUEUE

The word *queue* is pronounced as if you were saying the letter Q; the word *queue* means the same thing as the word *line* when used in phrases like "waiting in a line." Every time you get in line at a supermarket or in a bank or at a ticket window, you are adding yourself to a queue. If everybody is polite, then people add themselves to the rear of the queue (the rear of the line), and the person at the front of the queue is always the person who is served first. The queue data structure works in exactly the same way, and the abstract definition of a queue reflects this intuition.

Queue Definition

A **queue** is a data structure of ordered entries such that entries can only be inserted at one end (called the **rear**) and removed at the other end (called the **front**). The entry at the front end of the queue is called the **first entry**.

When we say that the entries in a queue are *ordered*, all we mean is that there is a first one (the front one), a second one, a third one, and so forth. We do not require that the entries can be compared using the < operator. The entries may be of any type. In this regard, the situation is the same as it was for a stack.

stacks versus queues

Because entries must be removed in exactly the same order that they were added to the queue, a queue is called a *First-In/First-Out* data structure (abbreviated **FIFO**). This differs from a stack, which is a Last-In/First-Out data structure, but apart from this difference, a stack and a queue are very similar data structures. They differ only in the rule that determines which entry is removed from the list first. The contrast between stacks and queues is illustrated in Figure 8.1. In either structure the entries depicted are entered in the order A, B, C, and D. With a queue, they are removed in the same order: A, B, C, D. With a stack, they are removed in the reverse order: D, C, B, A.

FIGURE 8.1   Contrasting a Stack and a Queue

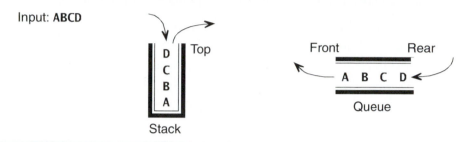

> ## FIFO
>
> A queue is a First-In/First-Out data structure. Items are taken out of the queue in the same order that they were put into the queue.

The Standard Library Queue Class

The C++ Standard Library has a queue template class, part of which is specified in Figure 8.2. The queue's member functions include operations to remove the entry from the front of the queue, to add an entry to the rear of the queue, and so on. The standard queue class has additional operations (not shown in the figure) such as getting a copy of the rear element, but the more traditional operations will satisfy our needs. Later we will discuss the queue implementation.

If a program attempts to add an entry to a queue that is already at its capacity, this is, of course, an error. This error is called **queue overflow**. If a program attempts to remove an entry from an empty queue, that is another kind of error, called **queue underflow**. To help you avoid these errors, the abstract data type provides a boolean function to test for an empty queue and a second function to return the current number of items in the queue. (The function empty is redundant, since the function size can be used to test for an empty queue. However, using the function empty can make the meaning of your code clearer.)

queue overflow and queue underflow

Uses for Queues

Uses for queues are easy to find—we often use queues in our everyday affairs, such as when we wait in line at a bank. To get a feel for using a queue in an algorithm we will first consider a simple example.

Suppose you want a program to read a word and then write the word. This is so simple that you may wonder why we bother to consider this task, but it is best to start with a simple example. One way to accomplish this task is to read the input one letter at a time and place each letter in a queue. After the word is read,

copying a word

the letters in the queue are written out. Because a queue is a First-In/First-Out data structure, the letters are written in the same order in which they were read.

The pseudocode for this approach to copying a word is as follows:

// *Echoing a word*
1. Declare a queue of characters.
2. *while* (there are more characters of the word to read)
   {
       Read a character.
       Push the character into the queue.
   }
3. *while* (the queue is not empty)
   {
       Write the front character to the screen.
       Remove the front character from the queue.
   }

FIGURE 8.2   The Standard Library Queue Class

Partial List of Members for the queue<Item> Class from <queue>

```
// TYPEDEFS
//    value_type:  The data type of the items in the queue from the Item parameter
//    size_type:   The data type for a variable that keeps track of how many items
//                 are in a queue
//
// CONSTRUCTOR
//    Default constructor: Creates an empty queue
//
// VOID FUNCTIONS TO INSERT AND REMOVE ITEMS:
//    pop( ): Removes the front item of the queue (see note*)
//    push(const Item& entry): Adds an item to the rear of the queue (see note*)
//
// FUNCTIONS TO EXAMINE THE QUEUE AND ITS ITEMS:
//    empty( ) const: Returns true if the queue is empty (otherwise returns false)
//    size( ) const:   Returns the number of items in the queue
//    front( ): Returns the front item of the queue (without removing it)
//
// VALUE SEMANTICS:
//    Assignments and the copy constructor may be used with queue<Item> objects.
```

---

* Traditionally, the names *pop* and *push* have been used only with stacks. Other names, such as **enqueue** ("enter queue") and **de-queue** ("delete from queue") were used for queues. However, the new C++ Standard Library uses the names *pop* and *push* for both stacks and queues.

Because queues occur so frequently in real-life situations, they are frequently used in simulation programs. For example, a program to simulate the traffic at an intersection might use a software queue to simulate the real-life situation of a growing line of automobiles waiting for a traffic light to change from red to green.

simulation programs

Queues also appear in computer system software, such as the operating system that runs on your PC. For example, consider a program that reads input from the keyboard. We think of a program as directly reading its input from the keyboard. However, if you think of what actually happens when you give a line of input to a program, you will realize that the program does not necessarily read a character when the corresponding keyboard key is pressed. This allows you to type input to the program, and that input is saved in a queue by software that is part of the operating system. When the program asks for input, the operating system provides characters from the front of its queue. This is called **buffering** the input, and is controlled by the PC's operating system software. In reality, a more sophisticated data structure is used rather than a queue, allowing you to back up and retype part of the line. Also, this form of buffering data in a queue is often used when one computer component is receiving data from another faster computer component. For example, if your fast CPU (central processing unit) is sending data to your printer, which is slow by comparison, then the data is buffered in a queue. By using the queue in this way, the CPU need not wait for the printer to finish printing the first character before the CPU sends the next character.

input/output buffering

In a computer system in which more than one process or component uses a single resource, a queue is often used so that the processes or components wait in line and are served on a "first-come, first-served" basis, just like customers in a bank line. For example, if several computers are networked so that they all use the same printer, then a queue would be used to let them "wait in line" whenever more than one computer wants to use the printer at the same time.

Self-Test Exercises for Section 8.1

1. What is the meaning of FIFO?

2. What are the traditional names for the queue operations that add an item and remove an item from a queue?

3. What queue functions are used to avoid queue overflow and queue underflow?

4. Suppose a program uses a queue of characters to read in a word and then echo it to the screen, as described in the pseudocode on page 392. Now suppose the input word is LINE. Trace the algorithm, giving all the calls to the operations push, front, and pop.

5. Name some common situations where a PC's operating system uses some kind of a queue.

6. Write pseudocode for an algorithm that reads an even number of characters. The algorithm then prints the first character, third character, fifth character, and so on. On a second output line, the algorithm prints the second character, fourth character, sixth character, and so on. Use two queues to store the characters.

8.2   QUEUE APPLICATIONS

Before we actually implement the queue class, we'll show two applications that use the Standard Library queue specified in Figure 8.2 on page 392. Since the queue is a template class, our two applications can use different kinds of queues. The first application uses a queue of characters, and the second uses a queue of integers.

PROGRAMMING EXAMPLE: **Recognizing Palindromes**

A **palindrome** is a string that reads the same forward and backward; that is, the letters are the same whether you read them from right to left or from left to right. For example, the one-word string "radar" is a palindrome. A more complicated example of a palindrome is the following sentence:

```
Able was I ere I saw Elba
```

Palindromes are fun to make up, and they even have applications in at least one area—the analysis of genetic material.

Suppose we want a program to read a line of text and tell us if the line is a palindrome. We can do this by using both a stack and a queue. We will read the line of text into both a stack and a queue, and then write out the contents of the stack and the contents of the queue. The line that is written using the queue is written forward, and the line that is written using the stack is written backward. Now, if those two output lines are the same, then the input string must be a palindrome. Of course, the program need not actually write out the contents of the stack and the queue. The program can simply compare the contents of the stack and the queue character-by-character to see if they would produce the same string of characters.

A program that checks for palindromes in the way we just outlined is given in Figure 8.3. This program uses the Standard Library queue class as well as the stack class. In this program we treat both the upper- and lowercase versions of a letter as being the same character. This is because we want to consider a sentence as reading the same forward and backward even though it might start with an uppercase letter and end with a lowercase letter. For example, the string "Able was I ere I saw Elba" when written backwards reads "ablE was I ere I saw elbA". The two strings match, provided we agree to consider upper- and lowercase versions of a letter as being equal. The treatment of the letters' cases is accomplished with a useful function called `toupper`, from the `<cctype>` library facility. This function has one character as an argument. If this character is a lowercase letter, then the function converts it to the corresponding uppercase letter and returns this value. Otherwise, the function returns the character unchanged.

the toupper function converts lowercase letters to uppercase letters

FIGURE 8.3   A Program to Recognize Palindromes

A Program

```
// FILE: pal.cxx
// A program to test whether an input line is a palindrome. The program ignores spaces,
// punctuation, and the difference between upper- and lowercase letters.

#include <cassert>      // Provides assert
#include <cctype>       // Provides isalpha, toupper
#include <cstdlib>      // Provides EXIT_SUCCESS
#include <iostream>     // Provides cout, cin, peek
#include <queue>        // Provides the queue template class
#include <stack>        // Provides the stack template class
using namespace std;

int main( )
{
    queue<char> q;
    stack<char> s;
    char letter;
    queue<char>::size_type mismatches = 0;   // Mismatches between queue and stack
    cout << "Enter a line and I will see if it's a palindrome:" << endl;

    while (cin.peek( ) != '\n')
    {
        cin >> letter;
        if (isalpha(letter))
        {
            q.push(toupper(letter));
            s.push(toupper(letter));
        }
    }

    while ((!q.empty( )) && (!s.empty( )))
    {
        if (q.front( ) != s.top( ))
            ++mismatches;
        q.pop( );
        s.pop( );
    }

    if (mismatches == 0)
        cout << "That is a palindrome." << endl;
    else
        cout << "That is not a palindrome." << endl;
    return EXIT_SUCCESS;
}
```

www.cs.colorado.edu/~main/chapter8/pal.cxx   **W W W**

FIGURE 8.4   Sample Dialogues from the Palindrome Program

First Sample Dialogue

```
Enter a line and I will see if it's a palindrome:
Straw? No, too stupid a fad. I put soot on warts.
That is a palindrome.
```

Second Sample Dialogue

```
Enter a line and I will see if it's a palindrome:
Able were you ere you saw Elba.
That is not a palindrome.
```

Our program also ignores spaces and punctuation, requiring only that the *letters* on the line read the same forward and backward. This way we can find more palindromes. If we look only at letters, discarding both spaces and punctuation, then there are many more palindromes. However, they are not always easy to spot. For example, you might not immediately recognize the following as a palindrome:

```
Straw? No, too stupid a fad. I put soot on warts.
```

the isalpha function determines which characters are letters

Depending on your current frame of mind, you may think that discovering such sentences is also a stupid fad. Nevertheless, our program ignores blanks and punctuation, so, according to our program, the above is a palindrome. The determination of whether a character is a letter is accomplished with another function from <cctype>. The function, called isalpha, returns true if its single argument is one of the alphabetic characters.

Two sample dialogues from the palindrome program are shown in Figure 8.4. As we often do, we have presented a minimal program to concentrate on the new material being presented. Before the program is released to users, it should be enhanced in a number of ways to make it more friendly (such as allowing more than one sentence to be entered).

Self-Test Exercises for Middle of Section 8.2

7. What C++ function determines if a character is alphabetic? What header provides this function?

8. How would you modify the palindromes program so that it indicates the first position in the input string that violates the palindrome property?

For example, consider the input "Able were you ere you saw Elba." This looks like a palindrome until you see the first "e" in "were," so a suitable output would be

```
That is not a palindrome.
Mismatch discovered at: Able we
```

9. How would you modify the palindromes program so that upper- and lowercase versions of letters are considered different? In the modified program the string "able was I ere I saw elba" would still be considered a palindrome, but the string "Able was I ere I saw Elba" would no longer be considered a palindrome, since, among other things, the first and last letters, "A" and "a," are not the same under these changed rules.

PROGRAMMING EXAMPLE: **Car Wash Simulation**

The *Handy-Dandy Hand Car Wash Company* has decided to modernize and change its image. It has installed a fast, fully automated car-washing mechanism that can wash a car in one to ten minutes. It will soon reopen under its new name *The Automatic Autowash Emporium*. The company wants to know the most efficient way to use its new car-washing mechanism. If the mechanism is used on the fast setting, it can wash a car in one minute, but because of the high pressure required to operate at such speed, the mechanism uses a great deal of water and soap at this setting. At slower settings, it takes longer to wash a car but uses less soap and water. The company wants to know how many customers will be served and how long customers will have to wait in line when the washing mechanism is used at one of the slower speeds. The company also wants to know whether its new motto, "You Ought to Autowash your Auto," will be effective. We respectfully refuse comment on the motto, but we agree to write a program that will simulate automobiles waiting in line for a car wash. This way the manager of the car wash can see how the speed of the car wash, the length of the line, and various other factors interact.

Car Wash Simulation—Specification

The precise program specifications are given by the following input/output descriptions:

Input. The program has three input items: (1) the amount of time needed to wash one car (in total seconds); (2) the probability that a new customer arrives during any given second (we assume that, at most, one customer arrives in a second); and (3) the total length of time to be simulated (in seconds).

Output. The program produces two pieces of output information: (1) the number of customers serviced in the simulated time; and (2) the average time that a customer spent in line during the simulation (in seconds).

Car Wash Simulation—Design

We will carry out a design of the program in a way that is common for many simulation tasks. The approach is to propose a collection of related object types that correspond to real-world objects in the situation that we are simulating. There are many possibilities—our particular approach focuses on the use of our queue class, which will be used to simulate a line of customers waiting to have their cars washed. We first discuss the queue and then propose the other objects needed for the simulation.

the queue

We need to simulate a queue of customers, but we do not have real live customers, so we must decide how we will represent them. There are many ways to represent customers: We could use their names and place them in a queue of names; we could assign an arbitrary number to each customer and store that number in a queue of numbers; we could represent each customer by the make and year of the customer's automobile, or even by how dirty the automobile is. However, none of those representations has any relevance to the specified simulation. For this simulation, all we need to know about a customer is how long the customer waits in the queue. Hence, a good way to represent a customer is to use a number that represents the time that the customer entered the queue. Thus, our queue will be a queue of numbers. In a more complex simulation, it would be appropriate to implement the customers as objects, and one of the customer's member functions would be a function that returns the customer's arrival time.

> **Key Design Concept**
>
> *Determine which properties of a real-world object are relevant to the problem at hand.*

The numbers that record the arrival times are called **time stamps**. Our simulation works in seconds, so a time stamp is just the number of simulated seconds that have passed since the start of the simulation. When the customer (represented by the time stamp) is removed from the queue, we can easily calculate the time the customer spent waiting: The time spent waiting is the total number of seconds simulated so far minus the time stamp.

propose a list of related object types

Figure 8.5 proposes pseudocode for the complete simulation algorithm. In addition to the queue, the pseudocode proposes three other object types: `washer`, `bool_source`, and `averager`. We'll discuss these types one at a time.

Washer. A `washer` is an object that simulates the automatic car-washing mechanism. The simulation program requires one washer object. This washer is initialized with its constructor, and each time another second passes, the simulation program indicates the passage of one second for the washer. This suggests the following constructor and member function:

```
washer::washer(unsigned int s);
// Precondition: The value of s is the number of seconds needed to
//   complete one wash cycle.
// Postcondition: The washer has been initialized so that all other member
//   functions may be used.

void washer::one_second( );
// Postcondition: The washer has recorded (and simulated) the passage of
//   one more second of time.
```

FIGURE 8.5   The Car Wash Simulation

Pseudocode

1. Declare a queue of unsigned integers, which will be used to keep track of arrival times of customers who are waiting to wash their cars. Unsigned integers are the data type used in C++ for numbers that can never be negative. We also declare the following objects:

   (a) A `washer`: The washer's constructor has an argument indicating the amount of time (in seconds) needed by the washer to wash one car.

   (b) A `bool_source`: The constructor has an argument that specifies how frequently the `bool_source` returns true (indicating how often customers arrive).

   (c) An `averager`.

2. `for (current_second = 1; current_second <=` the simulation length`; ++current_second)`
   `{`

   > Each iteration of this loop simulates the passage of one second of time, as follows:
   > Ask the `bool_source` whether a new customer arrives during this second, and
   > if so, enter the `current_second` into the queue.
   > `if` (the `washer` is not busy and the queue is not empty)
   > `{`
   >
   > > Remove the next integer from the queue, and call this integer `next`.
   > > This integer is the arrival time of the customer whose car we will now wash.
   > > So, compute how long the customer had to wait (`current_second - next`),
   > > and send this value to the `averager`. Also, tell the `washer` that it should
   > > start washing another car.
   >
   > `}`
   > Indicate to the `washer` that another simulated second has passed. This allows the
   > `washer` to correctly determine whether it is still busy.

   `}`

3. At this point, the simulation is completed. So we can get and print two items of information from the `averager`: (1) how many numbers the `averager` was given (i.e., the number of customers whose cars were washed); and (2) the average of all the numbers that it was given (i.e., the average waiting time for the customers, expressed in seconds).

Notice that the constructor argument is an *unsigned integer*, which is a data type that forbids negative values. Throughout our simulation, we will use unsigned integers for time values that cannot be negative. As usual, we should provide a default value for this argument (perhaps 60 seconds), so that the constructor can be used as a default constructor.

The other two responsibilities of a washer are to tell the simulation program whether the washing mechanism is currently available and to begin the washing of a new car. These responsibilities are accomplished with two additional member functions:

```
bool washer::is_busy( ) const;
// Postcondition: The return value is true if the washer is busy (in a wash
// cycle); otherwise the return value is false.

void washer::start_washing( );
// Precondition: The washer is not busy.
// Postcondition: The washer has started simulating one wash cycle.
// Therefore, is_busy( ) will return true until the required number of
// simulated seconds has passed.
```

Bool_source. An object of the `bool_source` class provides a sequence of boolean values. Some of the elements in the sequence are true, and some are false. During the simulation, we will have one `bool_source` object that we query once per simulated second. If the query returns true as its response, this indicates that a new customer has arrived during the simulated second; a false return value indicates that no customer has arrived during the simulated second. With this in mind, we propose two functions, described next.

The first function is a constructor for the `bool_source`. This constructor has one argument, which is the probability that the `bool_source` returns true to a query. The probability is expressed as a decimal value between 0 and 1. For example, suppose that our program uses the name `arrival` for its `bool_source`, and we want to simulate the situation where a new customer arrives during 1% of the simulated seconds. Then our program would have the declaration:

```
bool_source arrival(0.01);
```

The argument to this constructor should have a default argument, perhaps 0.5, so that the constructor can also be used as a default constructor.

There is another member function that can be called to obtain the next value in the `bool_source`'s sequence of values. Here is the prototype:

```
bool bool_source::query( ) const;
// Postcondition: The return value is either true or false, with the probability
// of a true value being determined by the argument to the constructor.
```

There are several ways of generating random boolean values, but at this stage we don't need to worry about such implementation details.

Averager. An `averager` computes the average of a sequence of numbers. For example, we might send the following four numbers into an averager: 10, 20, 2, and 12. The averager could then tell us that the average of these numbers is 11.0. The averager can also tell us how many numbers it has processed—in our example the averager processed four numbers. We'll use an averager to keep track of the average waiting time and the total number of cars washed.

The averager has a default constructor that resets the averager so that it is ready to accept a sequence of numbers. The sequence will be given to the averager one number at a time through a member function called `next_number`. For example, suppose that our averager is named `wait_times`, and the next number in the sequence is 10. Then we will activate `wait_times.next_number(10);`. The averager also has two member functions to retrieve its results: One function returns the average of all the numbers that have been given to the averager, and the other function returns the count of how many numbers the averager has been given. Here are the four prototypes:

```
averager::averager( );
// Postcondition: The averager has been initialized so that it is ready to
// accept a sequence of numbers to average.

void averager::next_number(double value);
// Postcondition: The averager has accepted the value as the next number
// in the sequence of numbers that it is averaging.

size_t averager::how_many_numbers( ) const;
// Postcondition: The return value is a count of how many times
// next_number has been activated.

double averager::average( ) const;
// Precondition: how_many_numbers( ) > 0.
// Postcondition: The return value is the average of all the numbers that
// have been given to the averager.
```

Notice that the argument to `next_number` is actually a double number rather than an integer. This will allow us to use the averager in situations where the sequence is more than just whole numbers.

Car Wash Simulation—Implementing the Car Wash Classes

We have completed a specification for the three new classes that will be used in the car wash simulation. We'll define these three types with a header file called `washing.h` (Figure 8.6) and an implementation file called `washing.cxx` (Figure 8.7, starting on page 404). The implementations are straightforward, but we'll provide a little discussion on page 405.

FIGURE 8.6   Header File for the Car Wash Classes

A Header File

```
// FILE: washing.h (part of the namespace main_savitch_8A)
// CLASSES PROVIDED: bool_source, averager, washer
//
// CONSTRUCTOR for the bool_source class:
//    bool_source(double p = 0.5)
//       Precondition: 0 <= p <= 1.
//       Postcondition: The bool_source has been initialized so that p is the approximate
//       probability of returning true in any subsequent activation of the query member function.
//
// CONSTANT MEMBER FUNCTION for the bool_source class:
//    bool query( ) const
//       Postcondition: The return value is either true or false, with the probability of a true
//       value being approximately p (from the constructor).                    (continued)
```

(FIGURE 8.6 continued)

```
//  CONSTRUCTOR for the averager class:
//     averager( )
//        Postcondition: The averager has been initialized so that it is ready to accept a
//        sequence of numbers to average.
//  MODIFICATION MEMBER FUNCTION for the averager class:
//     void next_number(double value)
//        Postcondition: The averager has accepted the value as the next number in the
//        sequence of numbers that it is averaging.
//
//  CONSTANT MEMBER FUNCTIONS for the averager class:
//     size_t how_many_numbers( ) const
//        Postcondition: The return value is a count of how many times next_number has been
//        activated.
//
//     double average( ) const
//        Precondition: how_many_numbers > 0.
//        Postcondition: The return value is the average of all the numbers that have been
//        given to the averager.
//
//  CONSTRUCTOR for the washer class:
//     washer(unsigned int s = 60)
//        Precondition: The value of s is the number of seconds needed for the completion of one
//        wash cycle.
//        Postcondition: The washer has been initialized so that all other member functions may
//        be used.
//
//  MODIFICATION MEMBER FUNCTIONS for the washer class:
//     void one_second( )
//        Postcondition: The washer has recorded (and simulated) the passage of one more
//        second of time.
//
//     void start_washing( )
//        Precondition: The washer is not busy.
//        Postcondition: The washer has started simulating one wash cycle. Therefore, is_busy( )
//        will return true until the required number of simulated seconds has passed.
//
//  CONSTANT MEMBER FUNCTIONS for the washer class:
//     bool is_busy( ) const
//        Postcondition: The return value is true if the washer is busy (in a wash cycle);
//        otherwise the return value is false.
//
//  VALUE SEMANTICS for the bool_source, averager, and washer classes:
//     Assignments and the copy constructor may be used with objects of the three classes.
```

(continued)

(FIGURE 8.6 continued)

```
#ifndef MAIN_SAVITCH_WASHING_H
#define MAIN_SAVITCH_WASHING_H
#include <cstdlib> // Provides std::size_t
namespace main_savitch_8A
{
    class bool_source
    {
    public:
        // CONSTRUCTOR
        bool_source(double p = 0.5);
        // CONSTANT MEMBER FUNCTION
        bool query( ) const;
    private:
        double probability; // Probability of query( ) returning true
    };

    class averager
    {
    public:
        // CONSTRUCTOR
        averager( );
        // MODIFICATION MEMBER FUNCTION
        void next_number(double value);
        // CONSTANT MEMBER FUNCTIONS
        std::size_t how_many_numbers( ) const { return count; }
        double average( ) const;
    private:
        std::size_t count; // How many numbers have been given to the averager
        double sum;        // Sum of all the numbers given to the averager
    };

    class washer
    {
    public:
        // CONSTRUCTOR
        washer(unsigned int s = 60);
        // MODIFICATION MEMBER FUNCTIONS
        void one_second( );
        void start_washing( );
        // CONSTANT MEMBER FUNCTION
        bool is_busy( ) const { return (wash_time_left > 0); }
    private:
        unsigned int seconds_for_wash; // Seconds for a single wash
        unsigned int wash_time_left;   // Seconds until the washer is no longer busy
    };
}

#endif
```

FIGURE 8.7   Implementation File for the Car Wash Classes

An Implementation File

```
// FILE: washing.cxx
// CLASSES implemented: bool_source, averager, washer
//
// INVARIANT for the bool_source class:
//     1. The member variable probability is the approximate probability that query( ) returns
//        true.
//
// INVARIANT for the averager class:
//     1. The member variable count indicates how many numbers the averager has been given.
//     2. The member variable sum is the sum of all the numbers that the averager has been
//        given.
//
// INVARIANT for the washer class:
//     1. The member variable seconds_for_wash is the number of seconds required for one wash.
//     2. The member variable wash_time_left is 0 if the washer is not busy;
//        otherwise it is the number of seconds until the washer is free.

#include <cassert>      // Provides assert
#include <cstdlib>      // Provides rand, RAND_MAX, size_t
#include "washing.h"    // Provides bool_source, averager, washer definitions
using namespace std;

namespace main_savitch_8A
{
    bool_source::bool_source(double p).
    // Library facilities used: cassert
    {
        assert(p >= 0);
        assert(p <= 1);
        probability = p;
    }

    bool bool_source::query( ) const
    // Library facilities used: cstdlib
    {
        return (rand( ) < probability * RAND_MAX);
    }

    averager::averager( )
    {
        count = 0;
        sum = 0;
    }
```

(continued)

(FIGURE 8.7 continued)

```
void averager::next_number(double value)
{
    ++count;
    sum += value;
}

double averager::average( ) const
// Library facilities used: cassert
{
    assert(how_many_numbers( ) > 0);
    return sum/count;
}

washer::washer(unsigned int s)
{
    seconds_for_wash = s;
    wash_time_left = 0;
}

void washer::one_second( )
{
    if (is_busy( ))
        --wash_time_left;
}

void washer::start_washing( )
// Library facilities used: cassert
{
    assert(!is_busy( ));
    wash_time_left = seconds_for_wash;
}
}
```

www.cs.colorado.edu/~main/chapter8/washing.cxx **WWW**

Implementation of the bool_source. The bool_source class has one member variable, probability, which stores the probability that an activation of query will return true. The implementation of the query member function first uses the rand function to generate a random number between 0 and RAND_MAX (including the end points), where RAND_MAX is a constant defined in <cstdlib>. (See the discussion of rand on page 262.) Hence, if the member variable probability is the desired probability of returning true, then query should return true provided the following relationship holds:

```
rand( ) < probability * RAND_MAX
```

For example, suppose we want a 10% chance that `query` returns true, so that `probability` is 0.1. If `rand` returns a value less than `0.1*RAND_MAX`, then `query` will return true. The chance that `rand` returns a value less than `0.1*RAND_MAX` is approximately 10%, since `0.1*RAND_MAX` marks a point that is approximately 10% of the way through `rand`'s output range. Therefore, there is about a 10% chance that the expression `rand( ) < 0.1 * RAND_MAX` will be true. It is this boolean expression that is used in the return statement of `query`.

Implementation of the averager. The implementation of the averager is a direct implementation of the definition of "average" and some straightforward details. The class has two member variables: one to keep track of how many numbers the averager has been given, and another to keep track of the sum of all those numbers. When the `average` member function is activated, the function returns the average calculated as the sum of all the numbers divided by the count of how many numbers the averager was given.

Notice that the averager does not need to keep track of all the numbers individually. It is sufficient to keep track of the sum of the numbers and the count of how many numbers there were.

Implementation of the washer. The `washer` class has two member variables. The first member variable, `seconds_for_wash`, is the number of seconds needed for one complete wash cycle. This variable is set by the constructor and remains constant thereafter. The second member variable, `wash_time_left`, keeps track of how many seconds until the current wash is completed. This value can be zero if the washer is not currently busy.

The washer's `one_second` member function simulates one second of washing time. In our simulation, the only piece of information that might be altered by the `one_second` function is the number of seconds until the washer is no longer busy. So, the `one_second` function checks whether a car is currently being washed. And if there is a car being washed, then the function subtracts one from `wash_time_left`.

The washer's `is_busy` function simply checks whether `wash_time_left` is greater than zero. If so, then there is a car in the washing mechanism. Otherwise, the washing mechanism is ready for another car.

When the car-washing mechanism is not busy, the `start_washing` member function may be activated to start another car through the washer. The function starts the wash by setting `wash_time_left` equal to `seconds_for_wash`.

Car Wash Simulation—Implementing the Simulation Function

We can now implement the simulation pseudocode from Figure 8.5 on page 399. The implementation is shown as a function in Figure 8.8. The function has three parameters, taken from our original specification: (1) an unsigned integer, `wash_time`, which is the amount of time needed to wash one car; (2) a double number, `arrival_prob`, which is the probability that a customer arrives during any particular second; and (3) another unsigned integer, `total_time`, which is the total number of seconds to be simulated. The function writes a copy of its parameters to the screen and then runs the simulation.

Most of the simulation work is carried out in the large for-loop, where the local variable `current_second` runs from 1 to `total_time`. This loop parallels the large loop from the original pseudocode (Step 2 in Figure 8.5 on page 399).

After the loop finishes, the simulation function obtains two pieces of information from the averager and writes these items to `cout`.

Self-Test Exercises for Section 8.2

10. Can a single program use both a stack and a queue?

11. How are time stamps used in simulations?

12. What C++ data type should be used for numbers that can never be negative?

13. Describe at least one assumption we made about the real-world car wash in order to make the simulation more manageable.

14. Use short sentences to describe the three main actions that occur during each second of simulated time in the car wash simulation.

15. What is RAND_MAX? Where is it defined?

16. When the car wash simulation finishes, there could still be some numbers in the queue. What do these numbers represent from the real world? (For a method of handling these leftover numbers, see Programming Project 8 on page 429.)

FIGURE 8.8   Implementation of the Car Wash Function

A Function Implementation

```
void car_wash_simulate
(unsigned int wash_time, double arrival_prob, unsigned int total_time)
// Precondition: 0 <= arrival_prob <= 1.
// Postcondition: The function has simulated a car wash where wash_time is the number of
// seconds needed to wash one car, arrival_prob is the probability of a customer arriving in
// any second, and total_time is the total number of seconds for the simulation. Before the
// simulation, the function has written its three parameters to cout. After the simulation, the
// function has written two pieces of information to cout: (1) the number of cars washed and
// (2) the average waiting time of a customer.
// Library facilities: iostream, queue, washing.h (using namespace std and main_savitch_8A)
{
    queue<unsigned int> arrival_times;    // Time stamps of the waiting customers
    unsigned int next;                    // A value taken from the queue
    bool_source arrival(arrival_prob);
    washer machine(wash_time);
    averager wait_times;
    unsigned int current_second;
```

(continued)

(FIGURE 8.8 continued)

```
// Write the parameters to cout.
cout << "Seconds to wash one car: " << wash_time << endl;
cout << "Probability of customer arrival during a second: ";
cout << arrival_prob << endl;
cout << "Total simulation seconds: " << total_time << endl;

for (current_second = 1; current_second <= total_time; ++current_second)
{   // Simulate the passage of one second of time.

    // Check whether a new customer has arrived.
    if (arrival.query( ))
        arrival_times.push(current_second);

    // Check whether we can start washing another car.
    if ((!machine.is_busy( ))  &&  (!arrival_times.empty( )))
    {
        next = arrival_times.front( );
        arrival_times.pop( );
        wait_times.next_number(current_second - next);
        machine.start_washing( );
    }

    // Tell the washer to simulate the passage of one second.
    machine.one_second( );
}

// Write the summary information about the simulation.
cout << "Customers served: " << wait_times.how_many_numbers( ) << endl;
if (wait_times.how_many_numbers( ) > 0)
    cout << "Average wait: " << wait_times.average( ) << " sec" << endl;
}
```

Sample Output from the Car Wash Simulation Function

```
Seconds to wash one car: 240
Probability of customer arrival during a second: 0.0025
Total simulation seconds: 6000
Customers served: 19
Average wait: 110.211 sec
```

www.cs.colorado.edu/~main/chapter8/carwash.cxx   **WWW**

8.3   IMPLEMENTATIONS OF THE QUEUE CLASS

A queue seems conceptually simpler than a stack because we notice queues in everyday life. However, the implementation of a queue, though similar to that of a stack, is more complicated. As was the case with the stack class, we will give two implementations of our queue class: a static implementation using a fixed-sized array, and a dynamic implementation using a linked list. As usual, our application programs will run with either implementation (although the static version imposes a predetermined capacity on the size of the queue).

Array Implementation of a Queue

As we did with the stack class, we will implement the queue class as a partially filled array. With a queue, we add entries at one end of the array and remove them from the other end. Hence, we will be accessing the used portion of the array at both ends, increasing the size of the used portion at one end and decreasing the size of the used portion at the other end. This differs from our use of a partially filled array for a stack, in that the stack accessed just one end of the partially filled array.

Because we now need to keep track of both ends of the used portion of the array, we will have *two* variables to keep track of how much of the array is used: One variable, called `first`, indicates the first index currently in use, and one variable, called `last`, indicates the last index currently in use. If `data` is the array name, then the queue entries will be in the array components:

keeping track of both ends of the partially filled array

```
data[first], data[first + 1], ... data[last].
```

To add an entry we increment `last` by one, and then store the new entry in the component `data[last]`, where `last` is now one larger than it was before. To get the next entry from the queue, we retrieve `data[first]` and then increment `first` by one, so that `data[first]` is then the entry that used to be second.

There is one problem with this plan. The variable `last` is incremented but never decremented. Hence, it will quickly reach the end of the array. At that point, we will not be able to add any more entries to the queue. Yet, there is likely to be room in the array. In a normal application, the variable `front` would also be incremented from time to time (when entries are removed from the queue). This will free up the array locations with index values less than `first`. There are several ways to reuse these freed locations.

One straightforward approach for using the freed array locations is to maintain all the queue entries so that `first` is always equal to 0 (the first index of the array). When `data[0]` is removed, we move all the entries in the array down one location so the value of `data[1]` is moved to `data[0]`, and then all other entries are also moved down one. This approach will work, but it is inefficient. Every time we remove an entry from the queue, we must move every entry in the queue. Fortunately, there is a better approach.

circular array

We do not need to move all the array elements. When the `rear` index reaches the end of the array, we can simply start reusing the available locations at the front of the array. Think of this arrangement as if the array were bent into a circle with the first component of the array immediately after the last component. In this way, the successor of the final array index is array index [0]. In this circular arrangement, the free index positions are always "right after" `data[last]`.

For example, suppose that we have a queue of characters with a capacity of five, and the queue currently contains three entries 'A', 'B', and 'C'. Perhaps these values are stored with `first` equal to 0 and `last` equal to 2, as shown here:

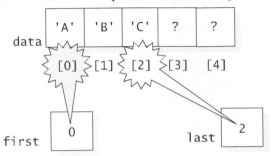

The question marks indicate unused spots in the array.

Let's remove two entries (the 'A' and 'B'), and add two more entries to the rear of this queue, perhaps the characters 'D' and 'E'. The result is shown here:

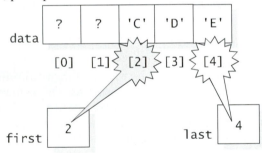

At this point, `first` is 2, `last` is 4, and the queue elements range from `data[2]` to `data[4]`. Suppose that now we add another character, 'F', to the queue. The new entry cannot go after `last`, since we have hit the end of the array. Instead, we go to the front of the array, adding the new 'F' at location `data[0]`, as shown here:

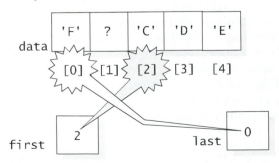

This may look peculiar, with the last index of 0 being before the first index of 2. But keep in mind the circular view of the array. With this view, the queue's entries start at data[first] and continue forward. If you reach the end of the array, then come back to data[0], and keep going until you find the rear. It may help to actually view the array as bent into a circle, with the final array element attached back to the beginning, as shown here:

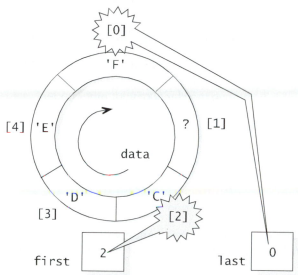

An array used in this way is called a **circular array**.

We now turn to a detailed implementation of our queue using the idea of a circular array. The header file for our queue is given in Figure 8.9. The queue's entries are held in the array, data, which is a private member variable. The private member variables first and last hold the indexes for the front and the rear of the queue, as we have discussed. Whenever the queue is non-empty, the entries begin at the location data[first], continuing forward in the array. If the entries reach the end of the array, then they continue at the first location, data[0]. In any case, data[last] is the last entry in the queue. One other private member variable, count, records the number of items that are in the queue. We will use count to check whether the queue is empty or full, and also to produce the value returned by the size member function.

The queue class definition also has a new feature: a *private* member function called next_index. This is a function that we think will be useful for the implementation, but it is not part of the public interface. We don't want other programmers to use this function; it is just for our own use in implementing a specific kind of queue. A private function such as this is called a **helper function**.

The next_index helper function allows us to step easily through the array, one index after another, with wraparound at the end. The function call next_index(i) usually returns i+1, with one exception. When i is equal to the last index of the array, next_index(i) returns the first index of the array (zero). By the way, you may be wondering, why bother defining next_index at all?

After all, we could simply use the formula "(i+1) % CAPACITY" directly instead of calling `next_index`. The reason for declaring `next_index` is to make the other implementations easier to read. The name `next_index` suggests the purpose it serves, which is to "move to the next index." On the other hand, the formula on its own requires some thought as to its purpose.

ⓘ PROGRAMMING TIP
USE SMALL HELPER FUNCTIONS TO IMPROVE CLARITY

When a class requires some small operation that is implemented as a formula, consider implementing the formula with a helper function (that is, a private member function). This will improve the clarity of your other code.

FIGURE 8.9   Header File for the Array Version of the Queue Template Class

A Header File

```
// FILE: queue1.h (part of the namespace main_savitch_8B)
// TEMPLATE CLASS PROVIDED: queue<Item> (a queue of items)
//
// TEMPLATE PARAMETER, TYPEDEFS, and MEMBER CONSTANTS for the queue<Item> class:
//     The template parameter, Item, is the data type of the items in the queue, also defined
//     as queue<Item>::value_type. It may be any of the C++ built-in types (int, char, etc.), or a
//     class with a default constructor, a copy constructor, and an assignment operator. The
//     definition queue<Item>::size_type is the data type of any variable that keeps track of how
//     many items are in a queue. The static const CAPACITY is the maximum capacity of a
//     queue for this first queue implementation.
//
// CONSTRUCTOR for the queue<Item> template class:
//     queue( )
//         Postcondition: The queue has been initialized as an empty queue.
//
// MODIFICATION MEMBER FUNCTIONS for the queue<Item> template class:
//     void pop( )
//         Precondition: size( ) > 0.
//         Postcondition: The top item of the queue has been removed.
//
//     void push(const Item& entry)
//         Postcondition: A new copy of entry has been inserted at the rear of the queue.
//
// CONSTANT MEMBER FUNCTIONS for the queue<Item> template class:
//     bool empty( ) const
//         Postcondition: The return value is true if the queue is empty.
```

(continued)

(FIGURE 8.9 continued)

```
//    Item front( ) const
//       Precondition: size( ) > 0.
//       Postcondition: The return value is the front item of the queue (but this item is not
//       removed from the queue).
//
//    size_type size( ) const
//       Postcondition: The return value is the total number of items in the queue.

#ifndef MAIN_SAVITCH_QUEUE1_H
#define MAIN_SAVITCH_QUEUE1_H
#include <cstdlib> // Provides size_t

namespace main_savitch_8B
{
    template <class Item>
    class queue
    {
    public:
        // TYPEDEFS and MEMBER CONSTANTS -- See Appendix E if this fails to compile.
        typedef std::size_t size_type;
        typedef Item value_type;
        static const size_type CAPACITY = 30;
        // CONSTRUCTOR
        queue( );
        // MODIFICATION MEMBER FUNCTIONS
        void pop( );
        void push(const Item& entry);
        // CONSTANT MEMBER FUNCTIONS
        bool empty( ) const { return (count == 0); }
        Item front( ) const;
        size_type size( ) const { return count; }
    private:
        Item data[CAPACITY];       // Circular array
        size_type first;           // Index of item at the front of the queue
        size_type last;            // Index of item at the rear of the queue
        size_type count;           // Total number of items in the queue
        // HELPER MEMBER FUNCTION
        size_type next_index(size_type i) const { return (i+1) % CAPACITY; }
    };
}

#include "queue1.template" // Include the implementation.
#endif
```

Discussion of the Circular Array Implementation of a Queue

Figure 8.10 shows the implementation file for the queue class. Once you understand the `next_index` function, it is easy to see that the push and pop implementations add and remove items in the usual way for a circular array.

One point that may seem counterintuitive is the implementation of the queue's constructor. It initializes `last` to the final index of the array (that is, `CAPACITY - 1`). This may seem peculiar, but the reason relates to a requirement in the invariant:

Invariant of the Queue Class (Array Version)

1. The number of items in the queue is in `count`.

2. For a non-empty queue, the items are stored in a circular array beginning at `data[first]` and continuing through `data[last]`. The total capacity of the array is CAPACITY.

3. For an empty queue, `last` is some valid index, and `first` is always equal to `next_index(last)`.

Part of the invariant states: *For an empty queue,* `last` *is some valid index, and* `first` *is always equal to* `next_index(last)`. The queue constructor ensures that this requirement is met by setting `last` to the final index of the array and setting `front` to the first index of the array.

Of course, you may also wonder *why* we imposed this requirement on an empty queue. The answer involves how the insert function works on an empty array. When the first item is inserted into the queue for an empty array, the insert function moves the `last` value to the next available index with the assignment statement `last = next_index(last)`. After this assignment, the new item is placed at `data[last]`. Therefore, by requiring an empty queue to have `first` equal to `next_index(last)`, we have ensured that the first item placed in the queue will reside at `data[first]`.

FIGURE 8.10   Implementation File for the Array Version of the Queue Template Class

An Implementation File

```
// FILE: queue1.template
// TEMPLATE CLASS IMPLEMENTED: queue<Item> (see queue1.h for documentation)
// This file is included in the header file and not compiled separately.
// INVARIANT for the queue class:
//    1. The number of items in the queue is in the member variable count.
//    2. For a non-empty queue, the items are stored in a circular array beginning at data[front]
//       and continuing through data[last]. The total capacity of the array is CAPACITY.
//    3. For an empty array, last is some valid index, and first is always equal to
//       to next_index(last).
```

(continued)

(FIGURE 8.10 continued)

```
#include <cassert> // Provides assert

namespace main_savitch_8B
{
    template <class Item>
    const typename queue<Item>::size_type queue<Item>::CAPACITY;

    template <class Item>
    queue<Item>::queue( )
    {
        count = 0;
        first = 0;
        last = CAPACITY - 1;
    }

    template <class Item>
    Item queue<Item>::front( ) const
    // Library facilities used: cassert
    {
        assert(!empty( ));
        return data[first];
    }

    template <class Item>
    void queue<Item>::pop( )
    // Library facilities used: assert
    {
        assert(!empty( ));
        first = next_index(first);
        --count;
    }

    template <class Item>
    void queue<Item>::push(const Item& entry)
    // Library facilities used: cassert
    {
        assert(size( ) < CAPACITY);
        last = next_index(last);
        data[last] = entry;
        ++count;
    }

}
```

Linked-List Implementation of a Queue

A queue can also be implemented as a linked list. One end of the linked list is the front, and the other end is the rear of the queue. The approach uses two pointers: One points to the first node (front_ptr), and the other points to the last node (rear_ptr), as diagrammed here for a queue with three items:

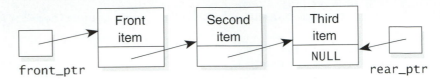

Here is a class definition for a queue template class, which would be part of the queue2.h header file:

```
#include <cstdlib>    // Provides size_t
#include "node2.h"    // Node template class

namespace main_savitch_8C
{
    template <class Item>
    class queue
    {
    public:
        // TYPEDEFS
        typedef std::size_t size_type;
        typedef Item value_type;
        // CONSTRUCTORS and DESTRUCTOR
        queue( );
        queue(const queue<Item>& source);
        ~queue( );
        // MODIFICATION MEMBER FUNCTIONS
        void pop( );
        void push(const Item& entry);
        void operator =(const queue<Item>& source);
        // CONSTANT MEMBER FUNCTIONS
        bool empty( ) const { return (count == 0); }
        Item front( ) const;
        size_type size( ) const { return count; }
    private:
        main_savitch_6B::node<Item> *front_ptr;
        main_savitch_6B::node<Item> *rear_ptr;
        size_type count;        // Total number of items in the queue
    };
}
```

The linked-list version has no CAPACITY constant, but otherwise the specification is the same as the array version. Our proposed invariant for the new queue class is shown here:

Invariant of the Queue Class (Linked-List Version)

1. The number of items in the queue is stored in the member variable count.

2. The items in the queue are stored in a linked list, with the front of the queue stored at the head node, and the rear of the queue stored at the final node.

3. The member variable front_ptr is the head pointer of the linked list of items. For a non-empty queue, the member variable rear_ptr is the tail pointer of the linked list; for an empty list, we don't care what's stored in rear_ptr.

Implementation Details

Each of the queue member functions (except the constructors) may assume that the invariant is valid when the member function is activated, and each member function (except the destructor) must ensure that the invariant is valid when the member function finishes its work. Notice that the invariant includes a member variable called count to keep track of the total number of items in the queue. We could get by without count, but its presence makes the size function quicker.

Most of the member functions' work will be accomplished with the functions of the node template class from Figure 6.5 on page 317. We'll look at the implementations of two functions—push and pop—in some detail.

The queue push member function. The push operation adds a node at the rear of the queue. For example, suppose we start with three items shown here:

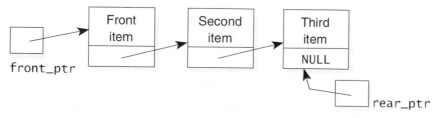

After adding a fourth item, the list would look like this:

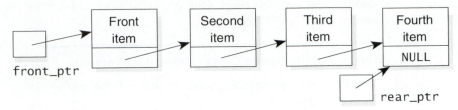

The item for the new fourth entry is placed in a newly created node at the end of the list. Normally, this is accomplished by a function call and an assignment:

```
list_insert(rear_ptr, entry);
rear_ptr = rear_ptr->link( );
```

To add the first item, we need a slightly different approach because the empty list has no rear pointer. In this case we should add the new entry at the head of the list, and then assign `rear_ptr` to also point to the new node, as shown in this segment of code:

```
if (empty( ))
{    // Insert first entry.
    main_savitch_6B::list_head_insert(front_ptr, entry);
    rear_ptr = front_ptr;
}
else
{    // Insert an entry that is not the first.
    main_savitch_6B::list_insert(rear_ptr, entry);
    rear_ptr = rear_ptr->link( );
}
```

In fact, this code is most of the insert function. The only other work is to add one to the `count` member variable.

The queue pop member function. The pop operation removes a node from the front of the queue. For example, suppose we start with this queue:

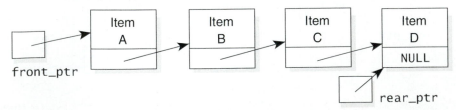

In this example, the pop function will remove the item that is labeled "Item A." When pop returns, the list will have only three items, shown here:

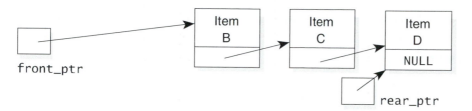

The implementation of pop uses list_head_remove. This implementation is part of the complete queue implementation file in Figure 8.11.

MAKE NOTE OF "DON'T CARE" SITUATIONS

There are often special situations in which we don't care about the value of a member variable. For example, in the special situation of an empty queue, the rear pointer is not used. With some compilers, you may get better error messages if you set such a pointer to NULL. (These compilers provide a message such as "Null pointer access" if you accidentally try to dereference the null pointer.) But in any case—whether you decide to set the rear pointer to NULL or not—you should document the fact that your implementation doesn't care about the value of the rear pointer for an empty queue. In particular, the invariant of the class should include an explicit statement of the "don't care" attitude—otherwise we might inadvertently assume that the rear pointer has some valid value for an empty queue.

WHICH END IS WHICH

We implemented our queue with the front of the queue at the head of the list and the rear of the queue at the tail of the list. As it turns out, this was not an arbitrary choice. Can you see why? What would happen if we had tried to do things the other way around, as shown in this wrong diagram?

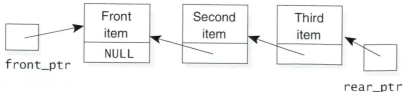

With this wrong arrangement of the queue's front and rear, we can still implement the push operation, adding a new node at the rear of the queue. We also have easy access to the front item. But it will be difficult to actually *remove* the front item. After the removal, the front_ptr must be positioned so that it points to the next node in the queue, and there is no easy way to accomplish that (without starting at the rear and moving through the whole list).

So, keep in mind that it's easy to insert and remove at the head of a linked list, but insertion is the only easy operation at the tail.

FIGURE 8.11   Implementation File for the Linked-List Version of the Queue Template Class

An Implementation File

```
// FILE: queue2.template
// TEMPLATE CLASS IMPLEMENTED: queue<Item> (see queue2.h for documentation)
// This file is included in the header file and not compiled separately.
// INVARIANT for the queue class:
//    1. The number of items in the queue is stored in the member variable count.
//    2. The items in the queue are stored in a linked list, with the front of the queue stored at
//       the head node and the rear of the queue stored at the final node.
//    3. The member variable front_ptr is the head pointer of the linked list of items. For a
//       non-empty queue, the member variable rear_ptr is the tail pointer of the linked list;
//       for an empty list, we don't care what's stored in rear_ptr.

#include <cassert>     // Provides assert
#include "node2.h"     // main_savitch_6B::node from Figure 6.5 on page 317

namespace main_savitch_8C
{
    template <class Item>
    queue<Item>::queue( )
    {
        count = 0;
        front_ptr = NULL;
    }

    template <class Item>
    queue<Item>::queue(const queue<Item>& source)
    // Library facilities used: node2.h
    {
        count = source.count;
        main_savitch_6B::list_copy(source.front_ptr, front_ptr, rear_ptr);
    }

    template <class Item>
    queue<Item>::~queue( )
    // Library facilities used: node2.h
    {
        main_savitch_6B::list_clear(front_ptr);
    }
```

(continued)

(FIGURE 8.11 continued)

```
template <class Item>
void queue<Item>::operator =(const queue<Item>& source)
// Library facilities used: node2.h
{
    if (this == &source) // Handle self-assignment
        return;
    main_savitch_6B::list_clear(front_ptr);
    main_savitch_6B::list_copy(source.front_ptr, front_ptr, rear_ptr);
    count = source.count;
}


template <class Item>
Item queue<Item>::front( ) const
// Library facilities used: cassert
{
    assert(!empty( ));
    return front_ptr->data( );
}


template <class Item>
void queue<Item>::pop( )
// Library facilities used: cassert, node2.h
{
    assert(!empty( ));
    main_savitch_6B::list_head_remove(front_ptr);
    --count;
}


template <class Item>
void queue<Item>::push(const Item& entry)
// Library facilities used: node2.h
{
    if (empty( ))
    {   // Insert the first entry.
        main_savitch_6B::list_head_insert(front_ptr, entry);
        rear_ptr = front_ptr;
    }
    else
    {   // Insert an entry that is not the first.
        main_savitch_6B::list_insert(rear_ptr, entry);
        rear_ptr = rear_ptr->link( );
    }
    ++count;
}
}
```

www.cs.colorado.edu/~main/chapter8/queue2.template   **WWW**

Self-Test Exercises for Section 8.3

17. Under what circumstances is a helper function useful?

18. Write a new constant member function that returns a copy of the item at the rear of the queue. Use the array version of the queue.

19. In a circular array implementation of a queue, why does the constructor set last to the final index of the array?

20. A programmer who sees our array implementation of a queue shown in Figure 8.10 on page 414 gives us the following suggestion: "Why not eliminate the `count` member variable, since the number of elements in the queue can be determined from the values of `front` and `rear`?" Is there a problem with the suggestion?

21. Write a new constant member function that returns a copy of the item at the rear of the queue. Use the linked-list version of the queue.

22. For our implementation, what is the value of the `rear_ptr` in an empty queue?

23. For our implementation, the `front_ptr` must be NULL for an empty queue. Which member functions rely on this requirement?

24. What goes wrong if we try to put the front of the queue at the tail of the linked list?

8.4   PRIORITY QUEUES

Using a queue ensures that customers are served in the exact order in which they arrive. However, we often want to assign priorities to customers and serve the higher priority customers before those of lower priority. For example, a hospital emergency room will handle the most severely injured patients first, even if they are not "first in line." A computer operating system that keeps a queue of programs waiting to use some resource, such as a printer, may give interactive programs a higher priority than batch processing programs that will not be picked up by the user until the next day, or it might give higher priority to short programs and lower priority to longer programs. A **priority queue** is a container class that allows entries to be retrieved according to some specified priority levels. The highest priority entry is removed first. If there are several entries with equally high priorities, then the priority queue's implementation determines which will come out first (sometimes it's the first one that came in; sometimes it's some other criterion).

higher numbers indicate a higher priority

For example, suppose the following customer names and priorities are entered into a priority queue in the order given:

Ginger Snap, priority 0
Natalie Attired, priority 3
Emanual Transmission, priority 2
Gene Pool, priority 3
Kay Sera, priority 2

The higher numbers indicate a higher priority. The names might be removed in the following order: first Natalie Attired (with the highest priority), then Gene Pool, then Emanual Transmission, then Kay Sera, and finally Ginger Snap (with the lowest priority). Note that both Natalie Attired and Gene Pool have priority 3, which is the highest priority, so a different implementation might have Gene Pool removed before Natalie Attired.

How the Priorities Are Specified

The C++ Standard Library has a `priority_queue<Item>` template class that is part of the `<queue>` header file. There are several ways to specify the priority of the elements for a priority queue where the underlying data type is `Item`:

1. If values of the `Item` type can be compared using a built-in "less than" operator, then that operator can be used. For example, a program can create a priority queue of integers (`priority_queue<int>`). As integers are removed from the queue, the implementation will use the "<" operator to determine which is the biggest integer (and the biggest is removed first).

2. If you implement your own class, you can implement the "less than" operator to compare elements. To ensure that the operator is meaningful, the implementation of the "<" operator must meet the rules of a *strict weak ordering* (Figure 6.4 on page 302).

3. A third method for priorities allows the programmer to define a comparison function that is not called "operator <".

The Standard Library Priority Queue Class

Figure 8.12 shows some of the member functions for the Standard Library priority queue class. Notice that the function to get the highest priority element is called `top` (similar to the stack rather than the queue).

Priority Queue Class—Implementation Ideas

A common priority queue implementation uses a tree data structure that achieves high efficiency (logarithmic time for both push and pop). We'll wait until Chapter 11 for that efficient implementation; however, there are several less efficient alternatives. One possibility is to implement the priority queue as an ordinary linked list, where the items are kept in order from highest to lowest priority. We will leave the details of the implementation as another exercise (Programming Project 5 on page 428).

FIGURE 8.12   The Standard Library Priority Queue Class

Partial List of Members for the priority_queue<Item> Class from <queue>

```
// TYPEDEFS
//    value_type: The data type of the items in the priority queue from the Item parameter
//                For this version of the priority queue, the Item must have a "less than"
//                operator < defined, forming a strict weak ordering (see
//                Figure 6.4 on page 302). Appendix H shows other alternatives.
//    size_type:  The data type to keep track of how many items are in a priority queue
//
// CONSTRUCTOR
//    Default constructor: Creates an empty priority queue
//
// VOID FUNCTIONS TO INSERT AND REMOVE ITEMS:
//    pop( ): Removes the highest priority item of the priority queue
//    push(const Item& entry): Adds an item to the priority queue
//
// FUNCTIONS TO EXAMINE THE QUEUE AND ITS ITEMS:
//    empty( ): Returns true if the queue is empty (otherwise returns false)
//    size( ):  Returns the number of items in the queue
//    top( ):   Returns the highest priority item of the queue (without removing it)
//              If there are several equally high priorities, the implementation may
//              decide which one to return.
//
// VALUE SEMANTICS:
//    Assignments and the copy constructor may be used with priority_queue<Item> objects.
```

Self-Test Exercises for Section 8.4

25. Suppose that you create a priority queue of double numbers, inserting the numbers 10, 20, 30. Which number will come out first?

26. Suppose that there are several items with equally high priorities in a priority queue. What does the Standard Library priority queue specify about which item will come out first?

27. What are two ways to compare items in an STL priority queue when using a class for the value_type type?

8.5   REFERENCE RETURN VALUES FOR THE STACK, QUEUE, AND PRIORITY QUEUE CLASSES

Details about the Standard Library stack, queue, and priority queue are listed in Appendix H. We want to point out one difference from our implementations: in the Standard Library, the top and front functions have *reference return values*.

As discussed on page 314 in Chapter 6, this means that the `top` and `front` functions can sometimes be used in a context that allows the actual item in the container to be changed. For example, if `s` is a stack of integers, then this statement changes the top item to 42:

```
s.top( ) = 42;
```

Figure 8.13 shows complete information for the Standard Library `top` and `front` functions. We did not implement return values that are references in our stacks and queues because none of our applications needed it, and some students may read these chapters before Chapter 6. However, it is quick to add the feature yourself (or see `stack3` or `stack4` in `www.cs.colorado.edu/~main/projects/chapter7/`, and `queue3` or `queue4` in the `chapter8` directory).

FIGURE 8.13   Reference Return Values from the Pop and Front Member Functions

For the stack<Item> Template Class

```
stack<Item> b;
const stack<Item> c;
    // For these declarations, the return value of b.top( ) is Item& (a reference to an
    // Item), so that b.top( ) can be used to change the top item (such as the
    // assignment statement: b.top( ) = 42;
    // But the return value of c.top( ) is const Item& (a reference to a constant
    // Item), which cannot be used to change the item in the stack.
```

For the queue<Item> Template Class

```
queue<Item> b;
const queue<Item> c;
    // For these declarations, the return value of b.front( ) is Item& (a reference to an
    // Item), so that b.front( ) can be used to change the front item (such as the
    // assignment statement: b.front( ) = 42;
    // But the return value of c.front( ) is const Item& (a reference to a constant
    // Item), which cannot be used to change the item in the queue.
```

For the priority_queue<Item> Template Class

```
priority_queue<Item> b;
const priority_queue<Item> c;
    // The return values of both b.top( ) and c.top( ) are const Item&
    // (a reference to a constant Item), which cannot be used to change the item in the
    // priority queue.
```

CHAPTER SUMMARY

- A queue is a First-In/First-Out data structure.
- A queue can be used to buffer data that is being sent from a fast computer component to a slower component. Queues also have many other applications: in simulation programs, operating systems, and elsewhere.
- A queue can be implemented as a partially filled circular array.
- A queue can be implemented as a linked list.
- When implementing a stack, you need only keep track of one end of the list of entries, but when implementing a queue, you need to keep track of both ends of the list.
- A priority queue allows items to be removed according to which entry has the highest priority (using a comparison such as the less than operator).

? Solutions to Self-Test Exercises

1. FIFO (First-In/First-Out) refers to a data structure in which entries must be removed in exactly the same order that they were added.

2. enqueue ("enter queue") and de-queue ("delete from queue")

3. The `size` function tests for queue capacity, and the `empty` function tests for an empty queue.

4. The operations are insert 'L', insert 'I', insert 'N', insert 'E', followed by four `front` and `pop` operations for 'L', then 'I', then 'N', then 'E'.

5. Reading input from a keyboard, and sending output to a printer.

6. Read the characters two at a time. Each pair of characters has the first character placed in queue number 1 and the second character placed in queue number 2. After all the reading is done, print all characters from queue number 1 on one line, and print all characters from queue number 2 on a second line.

7. The `cctype` library facility provides the `isalpha` function, which returns true if its single argument is one of the alphabetic characters.

8. A straightforward approach is to use a second queue, called `line`. As the input is being read, each character is placed in the `line` queue (as well as being placed in the original stack and queue). During the comparison phase, we also keep track of how many characters correctly matched. If a mismatch occurs, we can then print an appropriate amount of the `line` queue as part of the error message.

9. Do not apply the `toupper` function.

10. Yes

11. Time stamps are used to record arrival and waiting times for the items in a simulation. The time stamp is the number of simulated seconds that have passed since the start of the simulation. The waiting time of an item is the total number of seconds simulated so far, minus the time stamp.

12. unsigned integer

13. We assumed that no more than one customer arrives during any particular second.

14. (a) Sometimes add a new customer to the arrivals queue. (b) Sometimes start a new car through the washer. (c) Tell the washer that another second has passed.

15. RAND_MAX is a constant defined in cstdlib that specifies the largest return value of rand.

16. These are cars that arrived during the simulation, but they are still waiting in line at the end of the simulation.

17. A helper function is a private member function that is useful when a class requires an operation that should not be part of the public interface.

18. The body of your function should assert that size( ) > 0, and then return data[rear].

19. If last is initialized to the final index of the array, then a new item is inserted correctly into an empty queue. Specifically, the statement last = next_index(last) will place the first item at data[first].

20. The main problem is that you cannot tell the difference between an empty queue (which has front equal to next_index(rear)) and a full queue (which also has front equal to next_index(rear)).

21. The body of your function should assert size( ) > 0, and then return with:
    return rear_ptr->data;

22. It could be any value. Our implementation does not care.

23. The push member function requires that front_ptr is NULL for an empty queue. Otherwise the call to list_head_insert does not work. The destructor also requires a valid NULL pointer for the empty queue (otherwise list_clear does not work).

24. Removals will be hard to implement.

25. 30

26. The class documentation does not say which item will be removed first. The implementation is free to use whatever technique is most convenient.

27. When using your own class for the items in a priority queue, you can implement the operator < to compare elements. Alternatively, you can define a comparison function that is not called operator < .

PROGRAMMING PROJECTS

For more in-depth projects, please see www.cs.colorado.edu/~main/projects/

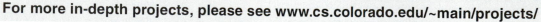

1 In Figure 8.3 on page 395 we presented a program that checks a string to see if the letters in the string read the same forward and backward. These strings are called palindromes. Another kind of palindrome is one in which we look at words, rather than letters. A **word-by-word palindrome** is a string of words such that the words read the same forward and backward. For example, the quote "You can cage a swallow, can't you, but, you can't swallow a cage, can you?" is a word-by-word palindrome. Write a program to test an input string and tell whether or not it is a word-by-word palindrome. Consider upper- and lowercase letters to be the same letter. Define a word as any string consisting of only letters or an apostrophe, and bounded at each end with one of the following: a space, a punctuation mark, the beginning of the line, or the end of the line. Your program should have a friendly interface and allow the user to check more lines until the user says he or she wishes to quit the program.

2 In Figure 8.3 on page 395 we presented a program that checks a string to see if the letters in the string read the same forward and backward. The previous exercise performed a similar check using words in place of letters. In this exercise, you are to write a program that runs a similar check using lines rather than words or letters. Write a program that reads in several lines of text and decides if the passage reads the same whether you read the lines top-to-bottom or bottom-to-top; this is yet another kind of palindrome. For example, the following poem by J. A. Lindon, reads the same whether you read the lines from top to bottom or from bottom to top:

> *As I was passing near the jail*
> *I met a man, but hurried by.*
> *His face was ghastly, grimly pale.*
> *He had a gun. I wondered why.*
> *He had. A gun? I wondered...why,*
> *His face was ghastly! Grimly pale,*
> *I met a man but hurried by,*
> *As I was passing near the jail.*

Consider upper- and lowercase versions of a letter to be the same letter. Consider word boundaries to be significant, so for example, the words in the first line must read the same as the words in the last line in order to pass the test (as opposed to just the letters reading the same); however, consider all word delimiters as being equivalent; that is, a punctuation, any number of spaces, the beginning or end of a line, or any combination of these are all considered to be equivalent. The end of the passage should be marked by a line containing only the word "end," spelled with any combination of upper- and lowercase letters, and possibly with blanks before and/or after it. Your program should have a friendly interface and allow the user to check more passages until the user says he or she wishes to quit the program. Note that to test your program, you don't need to use such well-constructed poems. Your program will check any passage, regardless of its literary merit.

3 Enhance the car-wash simulation procedure in Figure 8.8 on page 407 so that it has the following additional property. There is an additional parameter, which is a maximum length for the queue. When the queue gets as long as this maximum, any customer who arrives will leave without entering the queue (because she or he does not want to wait that long). There should also be one additional simulation result that is printed. In addition to the output shown in Figure 8.8, the function also prints the number of simulated customers who left because the queue was too long. Embed the function in a program that allows the user to repeat simulations with different arguments until the user says she or he wishes to quit the program.

4 Choose one of the queue implementations and implement an iterator that is similar to our bag iterator in Section 6.6.

5 Give a complete implementation of a priority queue, using the idea from page 423.

6 In this chapter we gave a linked-list implementation of a queue. This implementation used two named pointers called `front_ptr` and `rear_ptr` to point to the front and the rear nodes of the queue (linked list). A **circular linked list** is similar to a regular linked list, except that the pointer field in the "last node" points back to the "first node." (Of course, after this change it is no longer clear which node, if any, is intrinsically "first.") If we use a circular linked list, then we need only one pointer to implement a queue, since the front node and the rear node are adjacent nodes, as shown by the following diagram:

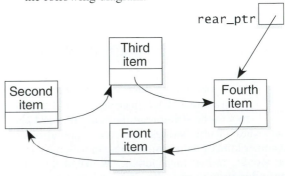

In the diagram we have called the single pointer `rear_ptr`, because it points to the last node in the queue. It turns out that this gives a more efficient implementation than having it point to the first node in the queue. Redo the queue class using a circular linked list.

7 A **double-ended queue** is a list that allows the addition and removal of entries from either end. One end is arbitrarily called the **front** and the other the **rear**, but the two ends behave identically. Specify, design, and implement a template class for a double-ended queue. Include operations to check if it is empty or full. For each end, include operations for adding and deleting entries. Implement the double-ended queue as a doubly linked list. Call your class `deque` (which is pronounced "deck"). By the way, the C++ Standard Library has a deque class.

8 Make improvements to the car-wash simulation program from Section 8.2. One particular improvement that you should make is to handle the customers who are still in the queue at the end of the simulation. These customers should have their cars washed one after another, but no new customers should be allowed to join the queue during this time. The wait times of these leftover customers should be counted along with all the other customers.

9 Write a simulation program for a small airport that has only one runway. There will be a queue of planes waiting to land and a queue of planes waiting to take off. However, only one plane can use the runway at a time. So there can be only one takeoff or one landing in progress at any one time. Assume that all takeoffs take the same amount of time. Assume that all landings take the same amount of time, although this does not need to be the same as the takeoff time. Assume that planes arrive for landing at random times, but with a specified probability of a plane arriving during any given minute. Similarly, assume that planes arrive at the takeoff queue at random times, but with a (possibly different) specified probability of a departure. (Despite the fact that takeoffs and landings are scheduled, delays make this a reasonable assumption.) Since it is more expensive and more dangerous to keep a plane waiting to land than it is to keep a plane waiting to take off, landings will have priority over takeoffs. Thus, as long as some plane is waiting to land, no plane can take off. Use a clock that is an unsigned integer variable that counts the number of minutes simulated. Use the `cstdlib` random number generator to simulate arrival and departure times of airplanes.

This simulation can be used, among other things, for deciding when the air traffic has become so heavy that a second runway must be built. Hence, the simulation will simulate conditions that would be a disaster in which planes crash because they run out of fuel while waiting too long in the landing queue. By examining the simulated situation, the airport authority hopes to avoid the real tragedy. Assume all planes can remain in the queue the same amount of time before they run out of fuel. If a plane runs out of fuel, your simulation will not discover this until the simulated plane is removed from the queue; at that point, the fact that the plane crashed is recorded, that plane is discarded, and the next plane is processed. A crashed plane is not considered in the calculation of waiting time. At the end of the simulated time, the landing queue is examined to see whether any of the planes in the simulated queue have crashed. You can disregard the planes left in the queue at the end of the simulation, other than those that crashed for lack of sufficient fuel. Use the following input and output specification:

Input: (1) The amount of time needed for one plane to land; (2) the amount of time needed for one plane to take off; (3) the average amount of time between arrival of planes to the landing queue; (4) the average amount of time between arrival of planes to the takeoff queue; (5) the maximum amount of time that a plane can stay in the landing queue without running out of fuel and crashing; (6) the total length of time to be simulated.

Output: (1) The number of planes that took off in the simulated time; (2) the number of planes that landed in the simulated time; (3) the number of planes that crashed because they ran out of fuel before they could land; (4) the average time that a plane spent in the takeoff queue; (5) the average time that a plane spent in the landing queue.

10 Do an airport simulation that is more complex than the previous project. In this version, planes arrive for landing with random amounts of fuel, which determines how long they can remain in the air. A plane will crash unless it lands within the time assigned to it. Your simulation will keep planes in a priority queue, where the priority of a plane is equal to the number of minutes before midnight that the plane will crash.

11 Write a simulation program of the lines at a grocery store. The program will be similar to the car wash simulation, except that there are multiple queues instead of one. You might use a vector of queues to simulate the lines. Assume that there are five cashier lines at the grocery store. Customers enter randomly to check out, and then enter the shortest line. If the lines are equal, then the first available line is chosen. Each transaction takes a random amount of time to complete.

For additional work, expand the grocery line program to allow shoppers to
- Avoid a line if all lines are a certain length
- Leave a line if they have waited beyond a certain time
- Check if another line is shorter at specified time intervals
- Switch lines if another line is shorter

12 Redo Programming Project 5 in Chapter 4 using the STL priority queue, so that your list of chores will be prioritized. Create a class chore, which will store the chore as a string, and its priority as an integer. Write a friend function for the chore class that defines the < operator (or define a comparison function). After testing the program, derive a solution to deal with cases in which the priority values of chores are the same. Hint: Use the comparison function to define an additional ordering when two priorities are equal.

CHAPTER **9**

Recursive Thinking

"Well," said Frog. "I don't suppose anyone ever is
completely self-winding. That's what friends are for." He
reached for the father's key to wind him up again.

RUSSELL HOBAN
The Mouse and His Child

LEARNING OBJECTIVES

When you complete Chapter 9, you will be able to...

- recognize situations in which a subtask is nothing more than a simpler version of the larger problem and design recursive solutions for these problems.
- trace recursive calls by drawing pictures of the run-time stack.
- prove that a recursive function has no infinite recursion by finding a valid variant expression and threshold.
- use induction to prove that a recursive function meets its precondition/ postcondition contract.

CHAPTER CONTENTS

Recursive Thinking

*one of the
subtasks is
a simpler version
of the same
problem you are
trying to solve in
the first place*

Often, during top-down design, you'll meet a remarkable situation: One of the subtasks to be solved is nothing more than a simpler version of the same problem you are trying to solve in the first place. In fact, this situation occurs so frequently that experienced programmers start *expecting* to find simpler versions of a large problem during the design process. This expectation is called **recursive thinking**. Programming languages, such as C++, support recursive thinking by permitting a function implementation to contain a call to itself. In such cases, the function is said to use **recursion**.

In this chapter, we start encouraging you to recognize situations where recursive thinking is appropriate. We also discuss recursion in C++, both how it is used to implement recursive designs and the mechanisms that occur during the execution of a recursive function.

9.1   RECURSIVE FUNCTIONS

A First Example of Recursive Thinking

We start with an example. Consider the task of writing a non-negative integer to the screen with its decimal digits stacked vertically. For example, the number 1234 should be written as::

        1
        2
        3
        4

*a case with an
easy
solution . . .
and a case that
needs more
work*

There is one version of this problem that is quite easy: If the integer has only one digit, then we can just print that digit. But if the number has more than one digit, the solution is not immediately obvious, so we might break the problem into two subtasks: (1) First print all digits except the last digit, stacked vertically. (2) Then print the last digit. For example, if the number is 1234, then the first step will write:

        1
        2
        3

and the second step will output the last digit, 4.

Several factors influenced our selection of these two steps. One factor is the ease of providing the necessary data for these two steps. For example, with our input number 1234, the first step needs the digits of 123, which is easily expressed as 1234/10 (since dividing an integer by 10 results in the quotient, with any remainder discarded). In general, if the integer is called number, and number has more than one digit, then the first step prints the digits of number/10, stacked vertically. The second step is equally easy: It requires us to print the last digit of number, which is easily expressed as number % 10 (this is the remainder upon dividing number by 10). Simple expressions, such as number/10 and number % 10, are not so easy to find for other ways of breaking down the problem (such as printing only the first digit in the first step, then printing the rest of the digits in the second step).

The pseudocode for our solution is as follows:

```
// Printing the digits of a non-negative number, stacked vertically
if (the number has only one digit)
    Write that digit.
else
{
    Write the digits of number/10 stacked vertically.
    Write the single digit of number % 10.
}
```

At this point, your recursive thinking cap should be glowing: One of the steps —*write the digits of* number/10 *stacked vertically*—is a simpler instance of the same task of writing a number's digits vertically. It is simpler because number/10 has one fewer digit than number. This step can be implemented by making a recursive call to the function that writes a number vertically. The implementation, with a recursive call, is shown in Figure 9.1. With this function we use the data type *unsigned int* instead of an ordinary *int*. The difference is that an *unsigned int* can never be negative, which is what we want for this function that prints the digits of a *non-negative* integer.

one of the steps is a simpler instance of the same task

In a moment we'll look at the exact mechanism that occurs for a function call such as write_vertical(1234), but first there are two notions to explain:

1. The stopping case. If the problem is simple enough, it is solved without recursive calls. In write_vertical, this occurs when number has only one digit. The case without any recursion is called the **stopping case** or **base case**. In Figure 9.1, the stopping case of write_vertical is implemented with the two lines:

```
if (number < 10)
    cout << number << endl;   // Write the one digit
```

2. The recursive call. In Figure 9.1, the function write_vertical makes a recursive call. The recursive call is the highlighted statement here:

```
else
{
    write_vertical(number/10);    // Write all but the last digit.
    cout << number % 10 << endl; // Write the last digit.
}
```

This is an instance of the write_vertical function calling itself to solve the simpler problem of writing all but the last digit.

| **FIGURE 9.1** | The write_vertical Function |

A Function Implementation

```
void write_vertical(unsigned int number)
// Postcondition: The digits of the number have been written, stacked vertically.
// Library facilities used: iostream (using namespace std)
{
    if (number < 10)
        cout << number << endl; // Write the one digit
    else
    {
        write_vertical(number/10);        // Write all but the last digit
        cout << number % 10 << endl;      // Write the last digit
    }
}
```

Sample Results of `write_vertical(1234)`

```
1
2
3
4
```

www.cs.colorado.edu/~main/chapter09/vertical.cxx   **WWW**

Tracing Recursive Calls

During a function call, such as `write_vertical(3)`, what actually occurs? The first step is that the argument 3 is copied to function's formal parameter, `number`. This is the way that all value parameters are handled in a function call: The argument provides an initial value for the formal parameter.

Once the formal parameter has its initial value, the function's code is executed. Since 3 is less than 10, the boolean expression in the if-statement is true. So in this case, it is easy to see that the function just prints 3 and does no more work.

Next, let's try an argument that causes the function to enter the else-part, such as the function call:

```
write_vertical(37);
```

When the function is called, the value of `number` is set equal to 37, and the code is executed. Since 37 is not less than 10, the two statements of the else-part are executed. Here is the first statement:

```
write_vertical(number/10);   // Write all but the last digit.
```

example of a recursive call

In this statement, (number/10) is (37/10), which is 3. So, this function call is `write_vertical(3)`. We already know the action of `write_vertical(3)`:

Print 3 on a single line of output. After this call to `write_vertical` is completely finished, the second line in the else-part executes:

```
cout << number % 10 << endl;
```

This just writes `number % 10`. In our example, `number` is 37, so the statement prints the digit 7. The total output of the two lines in the else-part is:

```
3
7
```

The function `write_vertical` uses recursion. Yet we did nothing new or different in evaluating the function call `write_vertical(37)`. We treated it just like any other function call. We simply substituted the actual argument for `number` and then executed the code. When we reached the recursive call `write_vertical(3)`, we simply repeated this process one more time.

FIGURE 9.2   The super_write_vertical Function

A Function Implementation

```
void super_write_vertical(int number)
// Postcondition: The digits of the number have been written, stacked vertically.
// If a number is negative, then a negative sign appears on top.
// Library facilities used: iostream (using namespace std)
{
    if (number < 0)
    {
        cout << '-' << endl;                    // Print a negative sign.
        super_write_vertical(abs(number));      // abs computes absolute value.
        ‖ This is Spot #1 referred to in the text.
    }
    else if (number < 10)
        cout << number << endl;                 // Write the one digit.
    else
    {
        super_write_vertical(number/10);        // Write all but the last digit.
        ‖ This is Spot #2 referred to in the text.
        cout << number % 10 << endl;            // Write the last digit.
    }
}
```

Sample Results of `super_write_vertical(-361)`

```
-
3
6
1
```

PROGRAMMING EXAMPLE: **An Extension of write_vertical**

Suppose we want to extend `write_vertical` to a more powerful function, called `super_write_vertical`, which handles all integers including negative integers. With a negative input, the new function prints the negative sign on the first line of output, above any of the digits. For example,

```
super_write_vertical(-361)
```

produces this output with a minus sign on the first line:

```
-
3
6
1
```

How do we handle a negative number? The first step seems clear enough: Print the negative sign. After this, we must print the digits of `number`, which are the same as the digits of abs(`number`). (The abs function is the "absolute value" function from `<cstdlib>`. It leaves positive numbers unchanged and removes the negative sign from negative numbers.) So, the pseudocode for `super_write_vertical` is an extension of our original pseudocode:

> *if* (the number is negative)
> {
>   Write a negative sign.
>   Write the digits of abs(`number`) stacked vertically.
> }
> *else if* (the number has only one digit)
>   Write that digit.
> *else*
> {
>   Write the digits of `number`/10 stacked vertically.
>   Write the single digit of number % 10.
> }

If you think recursively, you will recognize that the step *write the digits of* abs(`number`) *stacked vertically* is a simpler version of our original problem (simpler because the negative sign does not need to be written). This suggests the implementation in Figure 9.2 on page 435, with two recursive calls: one for the new case that writes the digits of abs(`number`) and a second call for the original case that writes the digits of `number`/10. We also have added some highlighted comments, identifying two particular locations, Spot #1 and Spot #2, to aid in taking a closer look at recursion.

A Closer Look at Recursion

The computer keeps track of function calls in the following way: When a function call is encountered, the first step is to save some information that will allow the computation to return to the correct location after the function call is completed. The computer also provides memory for the called function's formal parameters and any local variables that the called function uses. Next, the actual arguments are plugged in for the formal parameters, and the code of the called function begins to execute.

If the execution should encounter *another* function call—recursive or otherwise—then the first function's computation is stopped temporarily. This is because the second function call must be executed before the first function call can continue. Information is saved that indicates precisely where the first function call should resume when the second call is completed. The second function is given memory for its own parameters and local variables. The execution then proceeds to the second function call. When the second function call is completed, the execution returns to the correct location within the first function. And the first function resumes its computation.

how function calls are executed

This mechanism is used for both recursive and nonrecursive function calls. As an example of the function-call mechanism in a recursive function, let's completely trace the function call `super_write_vertical(-36)`. Initially, we call `super_write_vertical` with `number` set to `-36`. The actual argument, `-36`, is copied to the formal parameter, `number`, and we start executing the code with `number` having the value `-36`. At the moment when the function's execution begins, all of the important information that the function needs to work is stored in a special memory block called the function's **activation record**. The activation record contains information as to where the function should return when it is done with its computation, and it also contains the values of the function's local variables and parameters. For example, if our `super_write_vertical` function was called from a main program, then the activation record might contain this information:

> Activation record for first call to
> super_write_vertical
> ────────────────────────────
> Number: −36
>
> When the function returns, the
> computation should continue at
> line 57 of the main function.

The "return location" specified in a real activation record does not actually refer to lines of code in the main function, but when you're imagining an activation record you can think of a return location in this manner.

With the activation record in place, the function starts executing. Because the number is negative, the boolean test of the if-statement is true, and the negative sign is printed. At this point, the computation is about to make a recursive call, indicated here:

```
if (number < 0)
{
    cout << '-' << endl;
    super_write_vertical(abs(number));
    ‖ This is Spot #1 referred to in the text.
}
```

A recursive call is made in the super_write_vertical function.

This function call generates its own activation record with its own value of number (which will be 36) and its own return location. The new activation record is placed on top of the other activation record, like this:

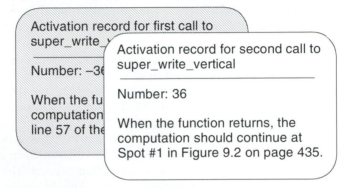

Activation record for first call to
super_write_

Number: –36

When the fu
computation
line 57 of the

Activation record for second call to
super_write_vertical

Number: 36

When the function returns, the computation should continue at Spot #1 in Figure 9.2 on page 435.

In fact, the collection of activation records is stored in a *stack* data structure called the **run-time stack**. Each function call pushes the next activation record on top of the run-time stack.

In our example, the second call of super_write_vertical executes with its own value of number equal to 36. The function's code executes, taking the last branch of the if-else control structure, arriving at another recursive call shown here:

Another recursive call is made in the super_write_vertical function.

```
else
{
    super_write_vertical(number/10);
    ‖ This is Spot #2 referred to in the text.
    cout << number % 10 << endl;
}
```

To execute this recursive call, another activation record is created (with `number` now set to 3), and this activation record is pushed onto the run-time stack:

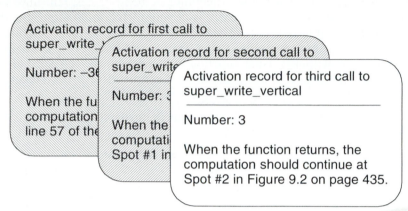

The `super_write_vertical` function begins executing once more. With `number` set to 3, the function enters the section to handle a one-digit number. At this point, the digit 3 is printed, and no other work is done during this function call.

When the third function call ends, its activation record is popped off the stack. But just before it is popped, the activation record provides one last piece of information—telling where the computation should continue. In our example, the third activation record is popped off the stack, and the computation continues at Spot #2 in Figure 9.2 on page 435. At this point we have the two remaining activation records shown here:

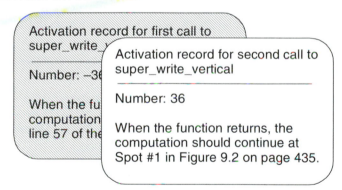

As we said, the computation is now at Spot #2 in Figure 9.2 on page 435. This is the highlighted location shown here:

```
else
{
    super_write_vertical(number/10);
    || This is Spot #2 referred to in the text.
    cout << number % 10 << endl;
}
```

The next statement is an output statement. What does it print? From the activation record on top of the stack, we see that number is 36, so the statement prints 6 (which is 36 % 10). The second function call then finishes, returning to Spot #1 in Figure 9.2 on page 435. But there is no more work to do after Spot #1, so the first function call also returns. The total effect of the original function call was to print three characters: a minus sign, then 3, and finally 6. The tracing was all accomplished with the usual function call mechanism—no special treatment was needed to trace recursive calls. In the example there are two levels of recursive calls:

1. super_write_vertical(-36) made a recursive call to
   super_write_vertical(36);

2. super_write_vertical(36) made a recursive call to
   super_write_vertical(3).

In general, function calls may be much deeper than this, but even at the deepest levels the function call mechanism remains the same as the example that we have traced.

Key Design Concept

Find smaller versions of a problem within the larger problem itself.

General Form of a Successful Recursive Function

C++ places no restrictions on how recursive calls are used in function definitions. However, in order for a recursive function definition to be useful, any call of the function must ultimately terminate with some piece of code that does not depend on recursion—in other words, there must be a *stopping case*. The function may call itself, and that recursive call may call the function again. The process may be repeated any number of times. However, the process will not terminate unless eventually one of the recursive calls does not itself make a recursive call. The general outline of a recursive function definition is as follows:

Recursive Thinking

Suppose that a problem has one or more cases in which some of the subtasks are simpler versions of the same problem you are trying to solve in the first place. These subtasks are solved by recursive calls.

A function that makes recursive calls must also have one or more cases in which the entire computation is accomplished without recursion. These cases without recursion are called **stopping cases** or **base cases**.

Often a series of if-else statements determines which of the cases will be executed. A typical scenario is for the original function call to execute a case that includes a recursive call. That recursive call may in turn execute a case that requires another recursive call. For some number of times each recursive call produces another recursive call, but eventually one of the stopping cases applies.

Every call of the function must eventually lead to a stopping case or else the function call will never end because of an infinite sequence of recursive calls. (In practice, a call that includes infinite recursion will terminate abnormally rather than actually running forever because the computation no longer has enough memory for the run-time stack of activation records.)

Self-Test Exercises for Section 9.1

1. What is the output produced by the function call `exercise(3)`, for each of the following three definitions?

```
void exercise(int n)
{
    cout << n << endl;
    if (n > 1)
        exercise(n-1);
}
```

```
void exercise(int n)
{
    if (n > 1)
        exercise(n-1);
    cout << n << endl;
}
```

```
void exercise(int n)
{
    cout << n << endl;
    if (n > 1)
        exercise(n-1);
    cout << n << endl;
}
```

2. What information does an activation record contain?

3. What type of data structure is used to store activation records? Why?

4. What happens if a recursive function does not have a base case?

5. What is the output of the following function with an argument of 3?

```
void cheers(int n)
{
    if (n <= 1)
        cout << "Hurrah" << endl;
    else
    {
        cout << "Hip" << endl;
        cheers(n-1);
    }
}
```

6. Modify the `cheers` function from the previous exercise so that it first prints "Hurrah" followed by n-1 "Hip"s. Make a further modification so that n-1 "Hip"s occur both before and after the "Hurrah". Make another modification so that approximately half of the "Hip"s occur before the "Hurrah", and half appear after.

7. Write a recursive function that has one parameter that is a non-negative integer. The function writes out that number of asterisks '*' to the screen, followed by that number of exclamation points '!'. Do not use any loops or local variables.

8. Write a recursive function that takes a string as a parameter and prints its reversal. The base case is an empty string.

9.2 STUDIES OF RECURSION: FRACTALS AND MAZES

Recursive thinking makes its biggest impact on problems in which one of the *subtasks* is a simpler version of the *same* problem that you are working on. For example, when we write the digits of a long number, our first step is to write the digits of the smaller number, number/10. This section provides additional examples of recursive thinking and the functions that recursion leads to.

FIGURE 9.3

The First Few Steps in Generating a Random Fractal

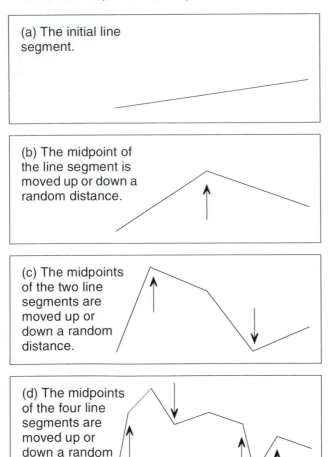

(a) The initial line segment.

(b) The midpoint of the line segment is moved up or down a random distance.

(c) The midpoints of the two line segments are moved up or down a random distance.

(d) The midpoints of the four line segments are moved up or down a random distance.

Programming Example:
Generating Random Fractals

Fractals are one of the tools that graphics programmers use to artificially produce remarkably natural scenes of mountains, clouds, trees, and other objects. We'll explain fractals in a simple setting and develop a recursive function to produce a certain kind of fractal.

To understand fractals, think about a short line segment, as shown in Figure 9.3(a). Imagine grabbing the middle of the line and moving it vertically a random distance. The two endpoints of the line stay fixed, so the result might look like Figure 9.3(b). This movement has created two smaller line segments: the left half of the original segment and the right half. For each of these smaller line segments, we'll grab the midpoint and move it up or down a random distance. Once again, the endpoints of the line segments remain fixed, so the result of this second step might look like Figure 9.3(c). One more step might produce Figure 9.3(d). The process continues as long as you like, with each step creating a slightly more jagged line.

After several more steps, the line could appear as shown here:

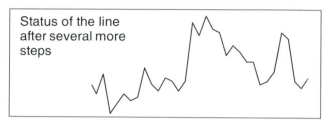

Status of the line
after several more
steps

Perhaps you can imagine that this jagged line is the silhouette of a mountain skyline.

The line that we're generating has an interesting property. Suppose that we carry out thousands of steps to create our line and then magnify a small portion of the result, as shown here:

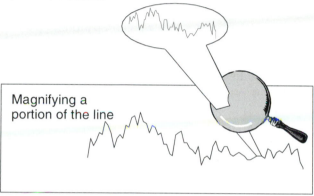

Magnifying a
portion of the line

The magnified portion is not identical to the entire line, but there is a lot of similarity. **Fractal** is the term coined by the mathematician Benoit Mandelbrot to describe objects, such as our line, that exhibit some kind of similarity under magnification. In fact, the first fractals studied were mathematically defined sets that remain *completely unchanged* when magnified to certain powers. In nature, objects don't generally remain completely unchanged under magnification, but magnified views commonly exhibit similarities with the larger object (such as our line, or a cloud, or a fern). Also, in nature (and our line), the powers of magnification where the similarities occur are limited, so nature's fractals are really rough approximations to the more formal mathematical fractals. Even so, the term *fractal* is often applied to any object that exhibits similarities under some magnification. The jagged line that we have described is called a **random fractal** because of the randomness in its generation.

fractals, nature's fractals, and random fractals

A Function for Generating Random Fractals—Specification

We wish to write a function that can draw or otherwise represent the random fractal that we have described. The input to this function includes the height of the two endpoints of the original line, measured from a fixed baseline, and the horizontal width from the left endpoint to the right endpoint. For example, consider the line segment shown here:

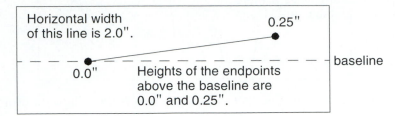

The height of the left endpoint is exactly at the baseline, and the height of the right endpoint is 0.25 inches above the same baseline. The horizontal width of the line is 2.0 inches. The heights of both endpoints and the width of the line segment will be three of the parameters to the fractal-generating function. The function also has a fourth parameter that we call epsilon. Once the width of the line segment becomes less than or equal to epsilon, we will stop the process of grabbing and moving midpoints. (We use the name *epsilon* because that is the Greek letter that mathematicians use for a small positive quantity.)

We can now write the prototype of the fractal generator as shown here:

```
void random_fractal(
    double left_height,
    double right_height,
    double width,
    double epsilon
);
```

Now we must consider the function's behavior. Let's look at an example using the initial line segment drawn earlier and an epsilon of 0.6 inches. Here is one possible result of the process, which divides the total 2.0" line into four pieces, each spanning a width of 0.5":

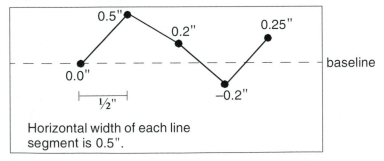

The process stops when the width of a line segment reaches 0.5", since 0.5" is less than our specified epsilon of 0.6". The endpoints of each 0.5" segment have heights above or below the baseline. Our function will be responsible for generating and displaying the height of the right endpoint of each tiny line segment. So, in this example, we expect `random_fractal` to display the four heights 0.5", 0.2", -0.2", and 0.25". For the moment we won't pin down the actual method of displaying these heights—a graphical program might display the heights by actually drawing the random fractal, whereas a simpler program might simply print each height as a double number.

Design and Implementation of the Fractal Function

Sometimes, generating a random fractal is simple. In particular, suppose that we call `random_fractal` with the line segment's width less than or equal to epsilon. For example, we might use a 2.0" initial line segment, with epsilon set to 3.0", as in this function call:

```
random_fractal(0.0, 0.25, 2.0, 3.0);
```

This is simple because when `width <= epsilon`, we don't continue dividing the segment. Instead, we simply "display the heights of the right endpoints of each segment." Moreover, we have only *one* segment (which we won't divide anymore), and the height of the right endpoint of that one segment is just the parameter `right_height`. So, we have the first step of our algorithm:

```
if (width <= epsilon)
    display right_height;
```

As with our previous recursive functions, this first step of the design is vital to recursive thinking. You must be able to identify a *stopping case* of the problem that can be solved with little or no work. In `random_fractal`, the stopping case occurs when `width` is no more than `epsilon`.

stopping case for the random fractal function

Now for the larger problem. We must design an algorithm to handle a `width` that is no larger than `epsilon`. Our first step is to find the current height of the midpoint of the segment and move it up or down a random amount. We'll call the height of the displaced point the `mid_height`, as shown here:

The value of `mid_height` will be computed in two steps:

1. Compute the average of `left_height` and `right_height` with the assignment:
   ```
   mid_height = (left_height + right_height)/2;
   ```

2. Add a random real number to `mid_height`, as shown here:

`mid_height += random_real(-width, width);`

the random_real function

The function `random_real` is one that we have written as part of a small toolkit of useful functions. This toolkit does not have to do with recursion, so we have placed it in an appendix (`useful.h` and `useful.cxx` in Appendix I) rather than giving the details here. At the moment we just need to know the value returned by the function call `random_real(-width, width)`. The function returns a random real number that lies in the range defined by its two arguments. In particular, `random_real(-width, width)` provides a random value from the range `-width` to `width`. We chose this particular range so that the random fractal does not take huge jumps when the width gets smaller.

After computing the height of the displaced midpoint, we have two segments: (a) from the left endpoint of the original segment to the displaced midpoint, and (b) from the displaced midpoint to the right endpoint of the original segment. The horizontal width of each smaller line segment is `width/2`. And what work do we have left to do? *We must generate a random fractal for each of these two smaller line segments.* This work can be accomplished with two recursive calls:

```
random_fractal(left_height, mid_height,  width/2, epsilon);
random_fractal(mid_height,  right_height, width/2, epsilon);
```

two recursive calls solve two smaller versions of the original problem

The first of these recursive calls generates a random fractal for the leftmost smaller line segment. Let's examine the arguments of the first recursive call: The first two arguments are the heights of the endpoints of the leftmost segment (`left_height` and `mid_height`), and the third argument is the horizontal width of the leftmost segment (`width/2`). When we generate the random fractal for this smaller segment, we use the same value of `epsilon` that we were given originally. The second recursive call handles the rightmost line segment in a similar way.

The entire `random_fractal` function is implemented in Figure 9.4. Let's discuss its method of displaying numbers.

How the Random Fractals Are Displayed

In the `random_fractal` function we have called a function named `display` to display the actual numbers. The `display` function (also part of `useful.h` in Appendix I) displays a number with a simple bar drawn out of stars. For example, here are several sample function calls with their output:

```
display(8)   prints:                    |********
display(-4)  prints:                ****|
display(-3)  prints:                 ***|
display(0)   prints:                    |
display(2)   prints:                    |**
```

As a general rule, each call of `display(x)` prints one line of output with a vertical bar in the middle of the line. If x is positive, then approximately x stars are printed to the right of the vertical bar. If x is negative, then approximately x stars are printed to the left of the vertical bar.

Figure 9.5 on page 448 shows a complete sample output from the call:

```
random_fractal(10.0, 10.0, 16.0, 1.0);
```

If you tip your head right 90 degrees, you'll see a nice random fractal landscape.

FIGURE 9.4   A Function to Generate a Random Fractal

A Function Implementation

```
void random_fractal(
    double left_height,
    double right_height,
    double width,
    double epsilon
)
// Precondition: width and epsilon are both positive.
// Postcondition: The function has generated a random fractal from a line segment. The
// parameters left_height and right_height are the heights of the line segment, and the
// parameter width is the segment's width. The generation of the random fractal stops when
// the width of the line segments reaches epsilon or less.
// Method of displaying the output: The height of the right endpoint of each line segment in
// the random fractal is displayed by calling the function display(...).
// Library facilities used: cassert, useful.h (from Appendix I)
{
    double mid_height;    // Height of the midpoint of the line segment

    assert(width > 0);
    assert(epsilon > 0);

    if (width <= epsilon)
        display(right_height);
    else
    {
        mid_height = (left_height + right_height) / 2;
        mid_height += random_real(-width, width);
        random_fractal(left_height, mid_height,  width/2, epsilon);
        random_fractal(mid_height,  right_height, width/2, epsilon);
    }
}
```

| **FIGURE 9.5** | Sample Output of the Random Fractal Function |

A Sample Result of `random_fractal(10.0, 10.0, 16.0, 1.0)`

```
                              |************
                              |*************
                              |***************
                              |**********
                              |*****
                              |***
                              |
                          ***|
                           **|
                        *****|
                         ****|
                            *|
                              |*
                              |***
                              |********
                              |**********
```

PROGRAMMING EXAMPLE: **Traversing a Maze**

Suppose that your friend Jervis has a maze in his backyard. One day, Jervis mentions two facts about the maze:

1. Somewhere in the maze is a magic tapestry that contains the secret of the universe.
2. You may keep this tapestry (and its secret) if you can enter the maze, find the tapestry, and return to the maze's entrance. (So far, many have entered, but none has returned.)

The maze is built on a rectangular grid. At each point of the grid, there are four directions to move: north, east, south, or west. Some directions, however, may be blocked by an impenetrable wall. You decide to accept Jervis's challenge and enter the maze—but only with the help of your portable computer and a function that we'll write to guide you into the maze, *and back out.*

Traversing a Maze—Specification

We plan to write a function, `traverse_maze`, that you can execute on a portable computer that you carry through the maze. The function will give you directions and ask you questions to take you to the magic tapestry and back out. The complete specification appears at the top of the next page.

```
bool traverse_maze( );
// Precondition: The user of the program is facing an unblocked spot in the
// maze, and this spot has not previously been visited by the user.
// Postcondition: The function has asked a series of queries and provided
// various directions to the user. The queries and directions have led the
// user through the maze and back to the exact same position where the
// user started. The return value of the function is a true/false value
// indicating whether the user found a magic tapestry in the maze.
```

This recursive function will return a boolean value (rather than being a void functon). A function that returns a value can be recursive in situations like this where the answer to a smaller problem will help to solve the complete problem. In this particular case, we'll see that searching part of the maze can help us determine whether the tapestry is present in the entire maze.

FIGURE 9.6   Script for the Maze Traversal Function

A Sample Dialogue

```
Step forward & write your name on the ground.
Have you found the tapestry? [Yes or No]
No
Please turn left 90 degrees.
Are you facing a wall? [Yes or No]
No
Is your name written ahead of you? [Yes or No]
No
Step forward & write your name on the ground.
Have you found the tapestry? [Yes or No]
No
Please turn left 90 degrees.
Are you facing a wall? [Yes or No]
Yes
Please turn right 90 degrees.
Are you facing a wall? [Yes or No]
No
Is your name written ahead of you? [Yes or No]
No
Step forward & write your name on the ground.
Have you found the tapestry? [Yes or No]
Yes
Pick up the tapestry, and take a step backward.
Please turn right 90 degrees.
Please turn right 90 degrees.
Please step forward, then turn 180 degrees.
Please turn right 90 degrees.
Please turn right 90 degrees.
Please turn right 90 degrees.
Please step forward, then turn 180 degrees.
```

This dialogue supposes that the user starts at the entrance to the maze drawn below. The starting point of the user is represented by the arrow in a circle, with the arrow pointing in the direction that the user is facing. The large X is the magic tapestry.

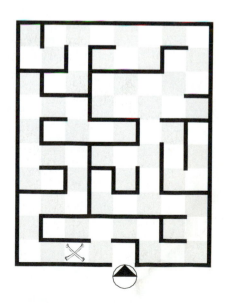

Figure 9.6 shows a drawing of what the maze might look like, along with a sample dialogue. A sample dialog written at this point—before we've written the function—is called a **script**, and it can help clarify a loose specification. As you might suspect, Jervis's actual maze is rather more complex than this script might suggest, but simplicity often results in the best scripts.

Traversing a Maze—Design

The `traverse_maze` function appears to perform a pretty complex task. When the function starts, all that's known is that the user of the program is facing some spot in the maze, and that spot has not been previously visited. The function must take the user into the maze, eventually leading the user back to the exact starting spot. Hopefully, along the way the user will find the magic tapestry. Recursive thinking can make the task easier.

We'll call the program's user Judy. We'll always start by asking Judy to take a step forward onto the spot that she hasn't visited before. We'll also ask her to write her name on the ground so later we can tell whether she's been to this spot before. After these two steps we will ask her whether she has found the tapestry at this new spot and place her true or false answer in a local variable named `found`.

the stopping case

Now there is one easy case: If the tapestry is at this spot, we will have Judy pick up the tapestry and ask her to take a step backward to her starting spot. This is the stopping case. The function returns true to indicate that the tapestry was found.

But what if Judy does not find the tapestry at this spot? In this case, there are three possible directions for Judy to explore: going forward, leftward, or rightward. We won't worry about exploring backward because that is the direction that Judy just came from. Also, sometimes we do not need to explore all three directions (forward, left, and right). A direction is a "dead end" if (a) there is a wall blocking that direction, or (b) Judy's name is written on the ground in that direction (indicating she has already been there)—and there is no need to explore dead ends. We also don't need to explore a direction if Judy already found the tapestry in one of the other directions.

This description suggests the following steps if the user has not found the tapestry at this spot:

1. Have the user face left (the first direction to explore).

2. *for* each of the three directions
   {
         if (!found && the direction that is now being faced isn't a dead end)
         {
             Explore the direction that is now being faced, returning
             to this exact spot after the exploration and setting
             found to true if the tapestry was found.
         }
         Have the user turn 90 degrees to the right (the next direction).
   }

3. The user is now facing the direction she came from, so ask her to step forward and turn around (so that she is facing this spot, as she was before this function was called).

Are you thinking recursively? The highlighted step "Explore the direction that is now being faced. . ." is a simpler instance of the problem that we are trying to solve. The instance is simpler because one spot in the maze has been eliminated from consideration—namely, the spot that the user is at does not contain the tapestry. In our implementation, we'll solve this simpler problem with a recursive call.

Traversing a Maze—Implementation

Our implementation benefits from some functions to carry out various subtasks:

- `dead_end`: This function determines whether the direction in front of the user is a dead end. Remember that dead ends are caused by a wall or by a direction that the user has already explored. The function returns true (for a dead end) or false (for no dead end).

- `eat_line`: This function (from `useful.h` in Appendix I) reads characters from standard input until a newline character is encountered.

- `inquire`: This function (from `useful.h` in Appendix I) asks the user a yes/no question; it returns true if the user answers "yes," and returns false if the user answers "no."

The implementation of `dead_end` (shown in Figure 9.7) makes two calls of the `inquire` function and returns the "or" of the results (using the `||` operation). When the "or" expression is evaluated, the `inquire` function is called to ask the user "Are you facing a wall?" If the user answers "yes," then the `inquire` function returns true and the rest of the "or" expression will not be executed. This follows the general rule of **short-circuit evaluation** that we have seen before—meaning that the evaluation of a logical expression stops when there is enough information to determine whether the expression is true or false. On the other hand, if the user answers "no" to the first query, then the `inquire` function returns false, and the rest of the "or" expression will be executed (asking the second question "Is your name written in front of you?").

In all, the function returns true if the user answers "yes" to the first question, or if the user first answers "no" to the first question (there is no wall) and then answers "yes" to the second question (the user's name is written in front of herself).

FIGURE 9.7 The dead_end Function Used in the Maze Traversal

A Function Implementation

```
bool dead_end( )
// Postcondition: The return value is true if the direction directly in front is a dead end.
// Library facilities used: useful.h (from Appendix I)
{
    return inquire("Are you facing a wall?")
           ||
           inquire("Is your name written in front of you?");
}
```

FIGURE 9.8   A Function to Traverse a Maze

A Function Implementation

```
bool traverse_maze( )
```
// Precondition: The user of the program is facing an unblocked spot in the maze that has not
// previously been visited by the user.
// Postcondition: The function has asked a series of questions and provided various directions
// to the user. The questions and directions have led the user through the maze and back to
// the exact same position where the user started. The return value of the function is a
// true/false value indicating whether the user found a magic tapestry in the maze.
// Library facilities used: iostream (using namespace std), useful.h (from Appendix I)
// Also uses dead_end from Figure 9.7 on page 451.
```
{
    int direction;   // Counts 1, 2, 3 for the three directions to explore
    bool found;      // Will be set to true if we find the tapestry

    cout << "Step forward & write your name on the ground." << endl;
    found = inquire("Have you found the tapestry?");

    if (found)
    {   // Pick up the tapestry and step back from whence you came.
        cout << "Pick up the tapestry and take a step backward." << endl;
    }
    else
    {   // Explore the three directions (not counting the one that you just
        // came from). Start with the direction on your left, and then
        // turn through each of the other possible directions one at a time.

        cout << "Please turn left 90 degrees." << endl;
        for (direction = 1; direction <= 3; ++direction)
        {
            if ( !found && !dead_end( ) )
                found = traverse_maze( );
            cout << "Please turn right 90 degrees." << endl;
        }

        // You're now facing the direction from whence you came, so step
        // forward and turn around. This will put you in the exact
        // spot that you were at when the function call began.
        cout << "Please step forward, then turn 180 degrees." << endl;
    }
    return found;
}
```

The actual `traverse_maze` function is given in Figure 9.8 on page 452. It follows our pseudocode quite closely. You might enjoy knowing that the magic tapestry really does exist in a book called *Castle Roogna* (Ballantine Books) by Piers Anthony. The hero of the book actually becomes part of the tapestry, whereupon his quest leads him to a *smaller* version of the *same* tapestry.

The Recursive Pattern of Exhaustive Search with Backtracking

The `traverse_maze` function of Figure 9.8 follows a recursive pattern that you may find useful elsewhere. The pattern is useful when a program is searching for a goal within a space of individual points that have connections between them. In the maze problem, the "points" are the individual squares of the maze, and the "connections" are the possible steps that the explorer can take in the four compass directions. Later you'll run into many data structures that have the form of "points and connections."

The task of searching such a structure can often follow this pattern:

- Start by *marking* the current point in some way. In the maze, the mark was obtained by asking the explorer to write her name on the ground. The purpose of the mark is to ensure that we don't mistakenly return to this point and end up going around in circles, continually returning to this same spot. This marking step is not always necessary; sometimes there are other mechanisms to prevent unbounded repetitions of searching the same direction.

- Check whether the current point satisfies the goal. If so, return some value that indicates the success of the search.

- On the other hand, if the current point does not satisfy the goal, then one by one examine the other points that are connected to the current point. For each such point, check to see whether the point is marked; if so, we can ignore the point because we have already been there. On the other hand, if a connected point is not marked, then make a recursive call to continue the search from the connected point onward. If the recursive call finds the goal, then we won't bother checking any other points, but if the recursive call fails, then we will check each of the other unmarked connected points by further recursive calls.

This pattern is called **exhaustive search with backtracking**. The term *exhaustive search* means that all possibilities are tried. *Backtracking* is the process of a recursive call returning without finding the goal. When such a recursive call returns, we are back where we started, and we can explore other directions with further recursive calls.

Exhaustive search with backtracking is most useful when the known search space doesn't get too large. But even with huge search spaces, programmers often use variants that try to cut down the search space in an intelligent manner. You'll find successful variants in programs that play games such as chess. As one more recursive example, we'll write a method to play a game with a definite, small search space, so we won't need to cut down this space at all.

PROGRAMMING EXAMPLE: **The Teddy Bear Game**

Here are the rules of the Teddy Bear game: Your friend is going to give you a certain number of bears. The number of bears is called `initial`, and your goal is to end up with a particular number of bears, called the `goal` number.

There are two other integer parameters to the game: `increment` and n. At any point in the game, you have two choices: (a) You can ask for (and receive) `increment` more bears, or (b) if you have an even number of bears, then you can give half of them back to your friend. Each time you do (a) or (b), that is called a *step* in the game, and the goal must be reached in n steps or fewer. For example, if `initial` is 99, `increment` is 53, and n is at least 4, then the following sequence of steps will reach the goal of 91:

$$99 \quad \underset{\text{step a}}{\rightarrow} \quad 152 \quad \underset{\text{step b}}{\rightarrow} \quad 76 \quad \underset{\text{step b}}{\rightarrow} \quad 38 \quad \underset{\text{step a}}{\rightarrow} \quad 91$$

We want to write a recursive function, `bears`, that determines whether it is possible to reach a `goal` starting with some `initial` and `increment` numbers (allowing no more than n steps). The implementation follows the pattern from the previous page, although the "marking" step of the pattern is not needed since we can prevent going around in circles by stopping when the parameter n reaches zero. So the pattern has only these two steps:

- Check whether the `initial` value is equal to the `goal`. If so, return `true` to indicate that the goal can be reached.

- On the other hand, if the `initial` value does not equal the `goal`, then we'll check that n is positive (otherwise we have no more moves to make and must return `false` because the goal cannot be reached). When n is positive, we'll solve the problem by making some recursive calls. One call starts by taking an (a)-step and the other starts by taking a (b)-step— although this second call is made only if `initial` is an even number.

The implementation of the bear function appears in Figure 9.9. Notice the expression (`inital % 2 == 0`) to determine whether the initial number of bears is even. Also note that the bear function returns a bool value. Therefore, each time we make a recursive call, we must use the return value of the recursive call in some way (such as controlling an if-statement).

⊍ PITFALL

FORGETTING TO USE THE RETURN VALUE FROM A RECURSIVE CALL

When a nonvoid function is recursive, the return value of each recursive call should be used in some way. Don't make the recursive call as if it were a void function.

FIGURE 9.9 A Function to Play the Teddy Bear Game

A Function Implementation

```
bool bears(int initial, int goal, int increment, int n)
// Precondition: All parameters are non-negative integers.
// Postcondition: The method has determined whether it is possible to reach the goal in the
// following Teddy Bear game. In the game, your friend gives you a certain number of bears.
// The number of bears is called initial, and your goal is to end up with a particular number of
// bears, called the goal number. At any point in the game, you have two choices: (a) You can
// ask for (and receive) increment more bears, or (b) if you have an even number of bears,
// then you can give half of them back to your friend. Each time you do (a) or (b), that is called
// a step in the game.
// The return value is true if and only if the goal can be reached in n steps or fewer.
{
    if (initial == goal)
        return true;
    else if (n == 0)
        return false;
    else if (bears(initial+increment, goal, increment, n-1))
        return true;
    else if ((initial % 2 == 0) && bears(initial/2, goal, increment, n-1))
        return true;
    else
        return false;
}
```

www.cs.colorado.edu/~main/chapter09/bears.cxx   **W W W**

Self-Test Exercises for Section 9.2

9. Suppose you call `random_fractal` with a width of 8 and an epsilon of 1. Then `random_fractal` will make two recursive calls, and each of those will make two more calls, and so on until `width` is less than or equal to epsilon. How many total calls will be made of `random_fractal`, including the original call?

10. Draw a copy of the maze from Figure 9.6 on page 449, moving the magic tapestry to a more difficult location. Run the `traverse_maze` function, pretending that you are in this maze and following the function's directions. (Do not peek over the walls.)

11. Revise the `random_fractal` function so that the movements of the midpoints are no longer random. Instead, the first midpoint should be moved upward by the amount `width`, the midpoints at the next level of recursion should be moved down by the amount `width`, the next level will move up again, then down, and so on.

12. Suppose that you are exploring a rectangular maze containing 10 rows and 20 columns. What is the maximum number of recursive calls that can be generated if you start at the entrance of the maze and call `traverse_maze`?

9.3   REASONING ABOUT RECURSION

After a lecture on cosmology and the structure of the solar system, William James was accosted by a little old lady.

"Your theory that the sun is the center of the solar system, and the earth is a ball which rotates around it has a very convincing ring to it, Mr. James, but it's wrong. I've got a better theory," said the little old lady.

"And what is that, madam?" inquired James politely.

"That we live on a crust of earth which is on the back of a giant turtle."

Not wishing to demolish this absurd little theory by bringing to bear the masses of scientific evidence he had at his command, James decided to gently dissuade his opponent by making her see some of the inadequacies of her position.

"If your theory is correct, madam," he asked, "what does this turtle stand on?"

"You're a very clever man, Mr. James, and that's a very good question," replied the little old lady, "but I have an answer to it. And it is this: the first turtle stands on the back of a second, far larger, turtle, who stands directly under him."

"But what does this second turtle stand on?" persisted James patiently.

To this the little old lady crowed triumphantly. "It's no use, Mr. James—it's turtles all the way down."

J. R. ROSS
Constraints on Variables in Syntax

In all our examples of recursive thinking, the series of recursive calls eventually reached a call that did not involve further recursion (that is, it reached a *stopping case*). If, on the other hand, every recursive call produces another recursive call, then a recursive call will, in theory, run forever. This is called **infinite recursion**. In practice, such a function will run until the computer runs out of memory for the activation records and terminates the program abnormally. Phrased another way, a recursive declaration should not be "recursive all the way down." Otherwise, like the lady's explanation of the solar system, a recursive call will never end, except perhaps in frustration.

In this section, we will show you how to reason about recursive functions, both to show that there is no infinite recursion and to show that a recursive function's results are correct. As an example, we'll start with a new recursive function called power that computes powers of the form x^n, where x is any double number and n is an integer. So, power(3.0, 2) is 3.0^2 (which is 9.0), and power(4.2, 3) is 4.2^3 (which is 74.088). For any nonzero value of x, the value of x^0 is defined to be 1, so for example power(9.1, 0) is 1. For a negative exponent, $-n$, the value returned is defined by:

$$x^{-n} = 1/x^n \quad \{ \ x \text{ is any real number, and } -n \text{ is a negative integer } \}$$

For example, `power(3.0, -2)` is $1/3.0^2$ (which is 1/9). The only forbidden power is taking 0^n when *n* is not positive. Here is the function's complete specification:

```
double power(double x, int n);
// Precondition: If x is zero, then n must be positive.
// Postcondition: The value returned is x raised to the power n.
```

Our implementation begins by checking the precondition, and then deals with several cases. The first case, when n is non-negative, is easy. This case is computed by setting a local variable, `product`, to 1, and then repeatedly multiplying `product` by x. The repeated multiplication occurs n times, in the for-loop shown here:

```
if (n >= 0)
{
    product = 1;
    for (count = 1, count <= n; ++count)
        product = product * x;
    return product;
}
```

To understand what is needed for a negative exponent, let's consider a concrete case. Suppose that we are computing `power(3.0, -2)`, which must return the value 3.0^{-2}. But this value is equal to $1/3.0^2$. Negative powers are the same as positive powers in the denominator. This means that if we know that the function returns the correct answer when n is positive, then we can calculate the correct value for `power(3.0, -2)` by the expression `1/power(3.0, 2)`. By thinking recursively, whenever n is negative, `power` can compute its answer with a recursive call, like this:

```
return 1/power(x, -n);  // When n is negative (and so -n is positive)
```

Remember, in this statement, n is negative (such as -2), so that -n is positive, and therefore, the recursive function call in the expression `1/power(x, -n)` has a positive second argument. With a positive second argument, our `power` function makes no further recursive calls (i.e., a stopping case), and so the recursion ends.

This brings us to our first general technique for reasoning about recursion, which can be applied to the complete `power` function of Figure 9.10:

One Level Recursion

Suppose that every case is either a stopping case or it makes a recursive call that is a stopping case. Then the deepest recursive call is only one level deep, and therefore no infinite recursion occurs.

FIGURE 9.10   Implementation of the Power Function with Only One Level of Recursion

A Function Implementation

```
double power(double x, int n)
// Precondition: If x is zero, then n must be positive.
// Postcondition: The value returned is x raised to the power n.
// Library facilities used: cassert
{
    double product; // The product of x with itself n times
    int count;

    if (x == 0)
        assert(n > 0);

    if (n >= 0)
    {
        product = 1;
        for (count = 1; count <= n; ++count)
            product = product * x;
        return product;
    }
    else
        return 1/power(x, -n);
}
```

Sample Results of the Function

Call with these arguments		Return value of function call
x	n	
3.0	2	9.0
2.0	-3	0.125
4.1	0	1.0
-2.0	3	-8.0

www.cs.colorado.edu/~main/chapter09/powers.cxx   **WWW**

How to Ensure That There Is No Infinite Recursion

In general, recursive calls don't stop at just one level deep. A recursive call does not need to reach a stopping case immediately. Programmers have developed methods to reason about recursive calls that go beyond one level deep, based on the principles of *mathematical induction*. The reasoning can increase your confidence that a recursive function avoids infinite recursion. As an example to show that there is no infinite recursion, let's rewrite the function power so that it uses more recursion. The revision is based on the observation that for any number x and any positive integer n, the following relation holds:

$$x^n = x(x^{n-1})$$

This formula means that an alternative way to define x^n is as follows:

The Value of x^n

The value is undefined when $n \leq 0$ and $x = 0$;

otherwise the value is 0 when $x = 0$;

otherwise the value is 1 when $n = 0$;

otherwise the value is x times x^{n-1} when $n > 0$;

otherwise the value is $1 / x^{-n}$ when $n < 0$.

The C++ version of a recursive function that computes in this way is given in Figure 9.11. To avoid confusion, we have used a slightly different name, pow, for this version of the function.

an alternative algorithm for computing powers

Tracing a recursive function such as pow can quickly overwhelm you, but there are relatively simple ways of showing that there is no infinite recursion without actually tracing through the execution. The most common way to ensure that a stopping case is *eventually* reached is to define a numeric quantity called the *variant expression*. This quantity must associate each legal recursive call to a single number. In a moment we'll discuss the properties that the variant expression should have; but first let's look at the kind of quantity we have in mind for the variant expression of the pow function. The value of the variant expression for pow is as follows.:

The Variant Expression for pow

The variant expression is abs(n) + 1 (when n is negative), and the variant expression is n (when n is non-negative).

FIGURE 9.11   Alternative Implementation of a Function to Compute Powers

A Function Implementation

```
double pow(double x, int n)
// Precondition: If x is zero, then n must be positive.
// Postcondition: The value returned is x raised to the power n.
// Library facilities used: cassert
{
    if (x == 0)
    {    // x is zero, and n should be positive
        assert(n > 0);
        return 0;
    }
    else if (n == 0)
        return 1;
    else if (n > 0)
        return x * pow(x, n-1);
    else // x is nonzero, and n is negative
        return 1/pow(x, -n);
}
```

www.cs.colorado.edu/~main/chapter09/powers.cxx   **W W W**

With this definition we can examine a sequence of recursive pow calls, beginning with pow(2.0, -3):

A Sequence of Recursive Calls

pow(2.0, -3) has a variant expression abs(n) + 1, which is 4; it makes a recursive call of pow(2.0, 3).

pow(2.0, 3) has a variant expression n, which is 3; it makes a recursive call of pow(2.0, 2).

pow(2.0, 2) has a variant expression n, which is 2; it makes a recursive call of pow(2.0, 1).

pow(2.0, 1) has a variant expression n, which is 1; it makes a recursive call of pow(2.0, 0).

pow(2.0, 0) has a variant expression n, which is 0; this is the stopping case.

There are two important points to this example: (a) Each time a recursive call is made, the variant expression is reduced by at least one; and (b) When the variant expression reaches zero, there is a stopping case that terminates with no further recursive calls.

In general, a **variant expression** is a numeric quantity that is decreased by at least some fixed amount on each recursive call. And, once the variant expression reaches a small enough value, a stopping case occurs. The "small enough value," which guarantees a stopping case, is called the **threshold**. In the pow example, the threshold is zero, and each recursive call reduces the variant expression by one. Here's a summary of the general technique for proving that a recursive call terminates:

variant expression and threshold

Ensuring That There Is No Infinite Recursion

To prove that a recursive call does not lead to infinite recursion, it is enough to find a *variant expression* and a *threshold* with the following properties:

1. Between one call of the function and any succeeding recursive call of that function, the value of the variant expression decreases by at least some fixed amount.

2. If the function is called and the value of the variant expression is less than or equal to the threshold, then the function terminates without making any recursive calls.

It is important that the reduction is at least a fixed amount. Otherwise, the variant expression might start at 1, then decrease to one-half, then to one-quarter, then to one-eighth, and so on, decreasing by ever-smaller amounts and never reaching the threshold. In the most common case, such as pow, the variant expression always decreases by at least one, and the threshold is zero.

To see that these two conditions guarantee no infinite recursion, reason as follows: Suppose the two conditions hold. Since Condition 1 is true, every recursive call will decrease the variant expression. This means that either the function will terminate, which is fine, or else the variant expression will decrease until it reaches the threshold. But if Condition 2 holds, then once the variant expression reaches the threshold, the function will terminate. That covers all the cases.

Inductive Reasoning About the Correctness of a Recursive Function

In addition to checking that a recursive function terminates, you should also check that it always behaves correctly—in other words, that it meets its precondition/postcondition contract. The usual method for showing correctness of a recursive function is called **induction**. (And, in fact, the technique is the same as *mathematical induction*, which you may have used in math classes.) The

induction

induction method requires a programmer to demonstrate the following facts about the function's behavior:

**Induction Method
To Show That a Recursive Function is Correct**

To show that a recursive function meets its precondition/postcondition contract, first show that there is no infinite recursion (by showing the previous Conditions 1 and 2), and then show that the following two conditions are also valid:

3. Whenever the function makes no recursive calls, then it meets its precondition/postcondition contract. (This is called the **base step**.)

4. Whenever the function is called and all the recursive calls it makes meet their precondition/postcondition contracts, then the original call will also meet its precondition/postcondition contract. (This is called the **induction step**.)

The conditions are numbered 3 and 4 to emphasize that they ensure correctness only if you know that there is no infinite recursion. You must also ensure that Conditions 1 and 2 hold for an appropriate variant expression and threshold.

Let's return to the function pow defined in Figure 9.11 on page 460. To complete our demonstration so that it performs as desired, we must show that 3 and 4 hold.

It is easy to see that Condition 3 holds. The only way that the function can terminate without a recursive call is if the value of x is zero or n is zero. If x is zero the function returns 0, which is the correct answer; and if n is zero (and x is not zero) the function returns 1, which is also correct.

To see that Condition 4 holds we need only recall the algebraic identities:

$$x^n = x(x^{n-1}) \quad \text{and} \quad x^n = 1/x^{-n}$$

To summarize how to reason about recursion: First check that the function always terminates (no infinite recursion); next make sure that the stopping cases work correctly; finally, for each recursive case, pretend that you know the recursive calls will work correctly, and use this to show that each recursive case works correctly.

Self-Test Exercises for Section 9.3

13. What is a variant expression?

14. Write a recursive function that finds the sum of the first *n* odd positive integers. Find a variant expression and a threshold for this function.

15. Use inductive reasoning to show that your function from the previous exercise is always correct.

16. Write a recursive function that computes the number of digits in an integer *n*. (You might recall from page 20 that this is $\lfloor \log_{10} n \rfloor + 1$.) Do not use any local variables in your function declaration. Find a variant expression and threshold to show that the function has no infinite recursion.

17. Use inductive reasoning to show that your function from the previous exercise is always correct.

18. Find variant expressions and thresholds to show that the functions `random_fractal` and `traverse_maze` (Section 9.2) never result in infinite recursion.

19. Use induction to show that `random_fractal` meets its precondition/postcondition contract.

CHAPTER SUMMARY

- If a problem can be reduced to smaller instances of the same problem, then a recursive solution is likely to be easy to find and implement.
- A recursive algorithm for a function implementation contains two kinds of cases: one or more cases that include a *recursive call* and one or more *stopping cases* in which the problem is solved without the use of any recursive calls.
- When writing recursive functions, always check to see that the function will not produce infinite recursion. This can be done by finding an appropriate *variant expression* and *threshold*.
- *Inductive reasoning* can be used to show that a recursive function meets its precondition/postcondition contract.

Solutions to Self-Test Exercises ?

1. The top-left function prints 3, then 2, then 1. The top-right function prints 1, then 2, then 3. The bottom function prints 3, then 2, then 1, then 1 again, then 2 again, then 3 again.

2. The activation record contains the return location of the function after it is finished. It also contains the values of the function's local variables and parameters.

3. A stack is used to store activation records, because the last function called is the first one that returns.

4. The function call will never end because of an infinite sequence of recursive calls. In reality, the recursive calls will terminate abnormally when the memory storage for the run-time stack runs out.

5. The output is Hip, then Hip, then Hurrah, on three separate lines.

6. For the first modification, change the two lines in the else-block to
```
cheers(n-1);
cout << "Hip" << endl;
```
For the second modification, change the lines to
```
cout << "Hip" << endl;
cheers(n-1);
cout << "Hip" << endl;
```
For the third modification, change the lines to
```
if (n % 2 == 0)
    cout << "Hip" << endl;
cheers(n-1);
if (n % 2 == 1)
    cout << "Hip << endl";
```

7. The function implementation is
```
void exercise4(unsigned int n)
{
    if (n > 0)
    {
        cout << '*';
        exercise4(n-1);
        cout << '!';
    }
}
```

8. The function implementation is shown below. Note that s.substr(1) gives the substring that begins at location s[1] and continues to the end of the string.
```
void reverse(const string s)
{
    if (s.length( ) > 0 )
    {
        reverse(s.substr(1));
        cout << s[0]);
    }
}
```

9. The original call makes two calls with a width of 4. Each of those calls makes two calls with a width of 2, so there are four calls with a width of 2. Each of those four calls makes two more calls, again cutting the width in half, so there are eight calls with a width of 1. These eight calls do not make further calls since width has reached epsilon. The total number of calls, including the original call, is 1 + 2 + 4 + 8, which is 15 calls.

10. Did you peek?

11. The easiest solution requires an extra parameter, called level, which indicates how deep the recursion has proceeded. When the revised function is called from a program, the value of level should be given as zero. Each recursive call increases the level by one. When the level is an even number, then the midpoint is moved upward; when the level is odd, then the midpoint is moved downward. The code to do the movement is as follows:
```
if (level % 2 == 0)
    mid_height += width;
else
    mid_height -= width;
```

12. Each recursive call steps forward into a location that has not previously been visited. Therefore, the number of calls can be no more than the number of locations in the maze, which is 200.

13. A variant expression is a numeric quantity that is used to ensure that a stopping case is eventually reached.

14. The function implementation is:
```
unsigned int sum_odds(unsigned int n)
{
    if (n == 1)
        return 1;
    else
        return
            sum_odds(n-1)+(2*n - 1);
}
```
One possibe variant expression is n, and the threshold is 1.

15. The stopping case is correct, because the first odd positive integer is 1. For the induction step, assume that the recursive call sum_odds(n-1) returns the correct value of the first n-1 odd integers. The nth odd integer is 2*n-1, so the sum sum_odds(n-1) plus (2*n-1) is the correct sum of the first n odd integers.

16. The function implementation is:
```
int digits(int n)
{
    if (n < 10) && (n > -10))
        return 1;
    else
        return 1 + digits(n/10);
}
```
A good variant expression is "the number of digits in n," with the threshold of 1.

17. The base case includes numbers that are less than 10 and more than −10. All these numbers have one digit, and the function correctly returns the answer 1. For the induction case, we have a number *n* with more than one digit. The number of digits will always be one more than *n*/10 (using integer division), so if we assume that the recursive function call digits(n/10) returns the right answer, then 1 + digits(n/10) is the correct number of digits in *n*.

18. For random_fractal, a good variant expression is the ratio width/epsilon. When this ratio is greater than one, each recursive call cuts width in half, which subtracts at least 0.5 from the ratio. When the ratio reaches 1 (or less), the recursion stops since width is then no more than epsilon. Therefore, 1 is the threshold.

The function traverse_maze has a variant expression that is expressed in English as "the number of locations in the maze that do not yet have your name written on the ground." This value is reduced by at least one during each recursive call, and when this value reaches zero, there can be no further recursive calls. Therefore, 0 is the threshold.

19. We have already found a variant expression and threshold for Conditions 1 and 2, showing that random_fractal does not result in infinite recursion. For Condition 3, we must show that the function has correct behavior for the stopping case. In this case, width is no more than epsilon, and therefore the line segment does not need further dividing. We only need to output the height of the right endpoint of the current line segment, which is what the function does. In Condition 4 of the inductive reasoning, we assume that the two recursive calls correctly generate a random fractal for the two smaller line segments that we have created. Putting these two smaller random fractals together correctly gives us the larger random fractal.

PROGRAMMING PROJECTS

For more in-depth projects, please see www.cs.colorado.edu/~main/projects/

1 Write a function that produces the following output:

```
This was written by call number 1.
 This was written by call number 2.
  This was written by call number 3.
   This was written by call number 4.
   This ALSO written by call number 4.
  This ALSO written by call number 3.
 This ALSO written by call number 2.
This ALSO written by call number 1.
```

In this example, the recursion stopped when it reached four levels deep, but your function should be capable of continuing to any specified level.

2 Write a function with two parameters, prefix (a string, using the string class from <string>) and levels (an unsigned integer). The function prints the string prefix followed by "section numbers" of the form 1.1., 1.2., 1.3., and so on. The levels argument determines how many levels the section numbers have. For example, if levels is 2, then the section numbers have the form x.y. If levels is 3, then the section numbers have the form x.y.z. The digits permitted in each level are always '1' through '9'. As an example, if prefix is the string "BOX:" and levels is 2, then the function would start by printing

```
BOX:1.1.
BOX:1.2.
BOX:1.3.
```

and finish by printing

```
BOX:9.7.
BOX:9.8.
BOX:9.9.
```

The stopping case occurs when `levels` reaches zero. The primary string manipulation technique that you will need is the ability to create a new string that consists of `prefix` followed by a digit and a period. If `s` is the string you want to create and `i` is the digit (an integer in the range 1 to 9), then the following statements will perform this task:

```
s = prefix;
s += '.';
s += char('0' + i);
```

The third statement puts the character ('0' + i) on the end of the string, and this character is the ASCII value for the digit that corresponds to the integer i. This new string, s, can be passed as a parameter to recursive calls of the function.

3 Write a recursive function that has two inputs, `first` and `second`, which are both strings (from `<string>`). The function should print all rearrangements of the letters in `first`, followed by `second`. For example, if `first` is the string "CAT" and `second` is the string "MAN", then the function would print the strings CATMAN, CTAMAN, ACTMAN, ATCMAN, TACMAN, and TCAMAN. The stopping case of the function occurs when the length of `first` has zero characters. We'll leave the recursive thinking up to you, but we should mention that two string member functions will make things go smoother. These member functions are

```
void string::insert(
    size_type position,
    size_type number_of_copies,
    char c
);
// Postcondition: The specified number of
// copies of c have been inserted into the
// string at the indicated position. Chars
// that used to be at or after the given
// position have been shifted right one spot.

void string::erase
(size_type position, size_type n);
// Postcondition: n characters have been
// removed from the string, beginning at the
// specified position.
```

4 Write an interactive program to help you count all of the boxes in a room. The program should begin by asking something like *How many unnumbered boxes can you see?* Then the program will have you number those boxes from 1 to *m*, where *m* is your answer. But, remember that each box might have smaller boxes inside, so once the program knows you can see *m* boxes, it should ask you to open box number 1 and take out any boxes you find, numbering those boxes 1.1, 1.2, and so on. It will also ask you to open box number 2 and take out any boxes you find there, numbering those boxes 2.1, 2.2, and so on. This continues for box 3, 4, up to *m*. And, of course, each time you number a box 1.1 or 3.8 or something similar, *that* box might have more boxes inside. Boxes that reside inside of 3.8 would be numbered 3.8.1, 3.8.2, and so on. At the end, the program should print a single number telling you the total number of boxes in the room.

5 Write a recursive function called `sumover` that has one argument *n*, which is an unsigned integer. The function returns a double value, which is the sum of the reciprocals of the first *n* positive integers. (The reciprocal of *x* is the fraction $1/x$.) For example, `sumover(1)` returns `1.0` (which is $1/1$); `sumover(2)` returns `1.5` (which is $1/1 + 1/2$); `sumover(3)` returns approximately `1.833` (which is $1/1 + 1/2 + 1/3$). Define `sumover(0)` to be zero. Do not use any local variables in your function.

6 The formula for computing the number of ways of choosing *r* different things from a set of *n* things is the following:

$$C(n, r) = \frac{n!}{r!(n-r)!}$$

In this formula, the factorial function is represented by an exclamation point (!), and defined as the product:

$$n! = n \times (n-1) \times (n-2) \times \ldots \times 1$$

Discover a recursive version of the $C(n, r)$ formula and write a recursive C++ function that computes the value of the formula. Embed the function in a program and test it.

7 Write a recursive function that has as arguments an array of characters and two bounds on array indices. The function should reverse the order of those entries in the array whose indices are between the two bounds. For example, suppose that the array is

```
a[0] = 'A'   a[1] = 'B'   a[2] = 'C'
a[3] = 'D'   a[4] = 'E'
```

and the bounds are 1 and 4. Then after the function is run the array elements should be

```
a[0] = 'A'   a[1] = 'D'   a[2] = 'C'
a[3] = 'B'   a[4] = 'e'
```

Embed the function in a program and test it.

8 Write a recursive function to produce a pattern of *n* lines of asterisks. The first line contains one asterisk, the next line contains two, and so on up to the *n*th line, which contains *n* asterisks. Line number *n*+1 again contains *n* asterisks, the next line has *n*−1 asterisks, and so on until line number 2*n*, which has just one asterisk.

9 Examine this pattern of asterisks and blanks, and write a recursive function that can generate exactly this pattern:

```
*
*  *
   *
*  *  *  *
      *
      *  *
         *
*  *  *  *  *  *  *  *
         *
         *  *
            *
         *  *  *  *
            *
            *  *
               *
```

10 This is a number puzzle project. Here are the rules: Your instructor is going to give you a certain number of floppy disks. The number of disks is called `initial`. You then have two choices: (a) you ask for (and receive) 53 more disks, or (b) if you have an even number of disks, then you may give half of them back to your instructor. Each time you do (a) or (b), that is called a *step* in the game. Your goal is to end up with exactly 91 disks in n steps or fewer. For example, if `initial` is 99 and n is 4, then the following sequence of steps will reach the goal of 91:

$$99 \xrightarrow[\text{step a}]{} 152 \xrightarrow[\text{step b}]{} 76 \xrightarrow[\text{step b}]{} 38 \xrightarrow[\text{step a}]{} 91$$

For this project, write a recursive function, `goal`, which determines whether it is possible to reach the goal (91) starting with some `initial` number, and allowing no more than n steps. The base case occurs when `initial` is 91 (since in this case, the answer is yes), or when n is zero and `initial` is not 91 (since in this case, the answer is no). If you do not have a base case, then solve the problem by making one or two recursive calls (one to `goal(initial+53, n-1)` and the other to `goal(initial/2, n-1)`—although this second call is made only if `initial` is an even number).

11 Let's think about your computer science class for a moment. You might know several students, perhaps Judy, Jervis, Walter, and Michael. Each of those students knows several other students, and each of those knows more students and so on. Now, there is one particular student named Dor that you would like to meet. One way to meet Dor would be if you had a mutual acquaintance: For example, you know Judy, and Judy knows Dor, so Judy could introduce you to Dor. Or, there might be a longer path of acquaintances: For example, you know Judy, and Judy knows Harry, and Harry knows Cathy, and Cathy knows Dor. In this case, Judy can introduce you to Harry, Harry can introduce you to Cathy, and Cathy can introduce you to Dor.

Write an interactive program to help you figure out whether there is a path of acquaintances from you to Dor. The program should include a recursive function that has one argument, `person`, which is the name of a person in your class. The function determines whether there is a path of acquaintances from person to Dor. Hint: This problem is similar to the maze problem in Section 9.2. But beware of potential infinite recursion! One way to avoid infinite recursion is to include a bag of student names, which keeps track of the names of the students you have already visited on your search for a path to Dor.

12 A *pretty print* program takes a program, which may not be indented in any particular way, and produces a copy with the same program indented so that bracket pairs ({ and }) line up with inner pairs indented more than outer pairs, so that if-else statements are indented as we have been doing, and so that other indenting is as we have been doing. Write a program that reads a C++ program from one text file and produces a pretty print version of the program in a second text file. To make it easier, simply do this for the body of the program, ignoring the declarations, and assume that all substatements of complex statements (other than compound statements themselves) are compound statements (that is, are enclosed by brackets).

13 Rewrite the recursive pow function from Figure 9.11 on page 460, so that the time to compute pow(x, n) is log(*n*). Hint: Use the formula $x^{2n} = x^n \times x^n$.

14 Write a recursive function to convert a character string of digits to an integer. Example: convert("1234") returns 1234. Hint: To convert a character to a number, subtract the ASCII value '0' from the character. For example, if the string s has but one character, then the function can return the value s[0] - '0'.

15 Ackermann's function, named after the German mathematician Wilhelm Ackermann, is used in the theory of recursive functions. There are several variants of this function. Their common properties are that the function takes two parameters (*x* and *y*) and grows very fast (much faster than polynomials or exponentials). Here is one variant:

1. If $x = 0$ then Ackermann(x, y) = $2y$
2. If $x >= 1$ and $y = 0$ then Ackermann(x, y) = 0
3. If $x >= 1$ and $y = 1$ then Ackermann(x, y) = 2
4. If $x >= 1$ and $y >= 2$ then Ackermann(x, y) = Ackermann(x-1, Ackermann(x, y-1))

Implement this variant of Ackermann's function with a recursive function.

CHAPTER **10**

Trees

Some people call it the Tree of Heaven. No matter where its seed fell, it made a tree which struggles to reach the sky.

BETTY SMITH
A Tree Grows in Brooklyn

LEARNING OBJECTIVES

When you complete Chapter 10, you will be able to...

- follow and explain tree-based algorithms using the usual computer science terminology.
- design and implement classes for binary tree nodes and nodes for general trees.
- list the order in which nodes are visited for the three common binary tree traversals (in-order, pre-order, post-order) and implement these algorithms.
- list the rules for a binary search tree and determine whether a tree satisfies these rules.
- carry out searches, insertions, and removals by hand on a binary search tree and implement these algorithms using your binary tree node class.

CHAPTER CONTENTS

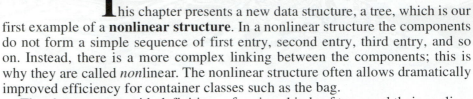

nonlinear
structures

This chapter presents a new data structure, a tree, which is our first example of a **nonlinear structure**. In a nonlinear structure the components do not form a simple sequence of first entry, second entry, third entry, and so on. Instead, there is a more complex linking between the components; this is why they are called *non*linear. The nonlinear structure often allows dramatically improved efficiency for container classes such as the bag.

The chapter starts with definitions of various kinds of trees and their applications. We then show how to represent trees and implement a node class for building and manipulating binary trees. The binary trees are useful for many classes such as the new bag implementation in the final section of this chapter.

10.1 INTRODUCTION TO TREES

a real tree. . .

Binary Trees

The first kind of tree that we'll look at is a *binary tree*, which is the most commonly used tree data structure. A binary tree is not too different from a real tree. The real tree starts at its root, growing upward. At some point, the trunk splits into two smaller branches. Each of the smaller branches continues, perhaps splitting into two still smaller branches, and so forth until each branch ends with some leaves.

. . .and a
computer
scientist's tree

If you take that tree, pull it out of the ground, and stick its root in the air, you will have a computer scientist's tree. You see, a computer scientist draws a tree with the root at the top, branches below that, and leaves at the very bottom. And, of course, a computer scientist's tree contains data of one kind or another. Let's be more specific, with a concrete example of a binary tree of integers, shown in Figure 10.1.

FIGURE 10.1 A Binary Tree of Integers

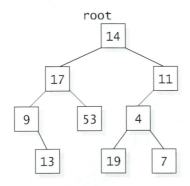

Each of the boxes in the Figure 10.1 is called a **node** of the tree, and each node contains some data—in this case each piece of data is an integer, but we might also have trees of double numbers, trees of strings, even trees where each node's data is a complex type like a stack or a queue. The node at the top of the diagram, which has the number 14, is called the **root**. Each node in a binary tree may have up to two nodes below it, one linked on its left and one linked on its right. These are called the node's **left child** and **right child**. For example, the root's left child is the node containing 17, and its right child contains 11. Some nodes have only a left child, some have only a right child, and some have no children at all. A node with no children is called a **leaf**. In more general kinds of trees, a node may have more than two children, but for the **binary** trees that we're discussing, each node is limited to at most two children. One other point: With the exception of the root, each node is the child of just one node; the root is not the child of any node.

Much of the terminology for trees comes from family relations, such as the word "child." Perhaps you can guess the meaning of some other terms: *parent, sibling, ancestor, descendant*. These definitions are given below, but first we'll provide a complete definition of a binary tree:

Binary Trees

A **binary tree** is a finite set of nodes. The set might be empty (no nodes, which is called the **empty tree**). But if the set is not empty, it follows these rules:

1. There is one special node, called the **root**.

2. Each node may be associated with up to two other different nodes, called its **left child** and its **right child**. If a node *c* is the child of another node *p*, then we say that "*p* is *c*'s **parent**."

3. Each node, except the root, has exactly one parent; the root has no parent.

4. If you start at a node and move to the node's parent (provided there is one), then move again to that node's parent, and keep moving upward to each node's parent, you will eventually reach the root.

Here are some other terms used with trees, with examples selected from Figure 10.1 on page 470 and Figure 10.2 on page 472.

tree terminology

Parent. The **parent** of a node is the node linked above it. More precisely, if a node *c* is the child of another node *p*, then we say that "*p* is *c*'s **parent**." Except for the root, every node has just one parent, and the root has no parent. In Figure 10.1, the node containing 17 is the parent of the nodes containing 9 and 53.

Sibling. Two nodes are **siblings** if they have the same parent. In Figure 10.1, the nodes containing 9 and 53 are siblings.

FIGURE 10.2   More Examples of Binary Trees

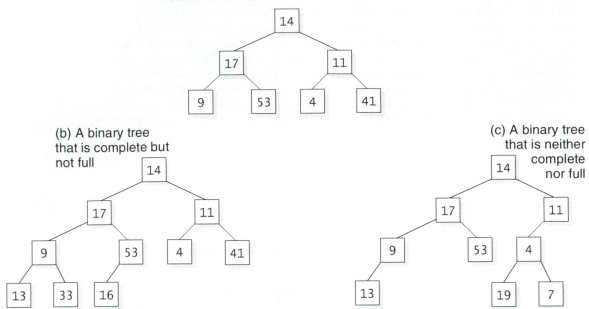

Ancestor.   A node's parent is its first **ancestor**. The parent of the parent is the next ancestor. The parent of the parent of the parent is the next ancestor . . . and so forth, until you reach the root. The root is an ancestor of each other node.

Descendant.   A node's children are its first **descendants**. The children's children are its next descendants. The children of the children of the children are. . . well, you get the idea.

Subtree.   Any node in a tree also can be viewed as the root of a new, smaller tree. This smaller tree contains the node that we've picked as the new root and all of the new root's descendants. This is called a **subtree** of the original tree. In Figure 10.2(a), we may choose 17 as the root of a new subtree, and that subtree has three nodes: the nodes containing 17, 9, and 53.

Left and right subtrees of a node.   For a node in a binary tree, the nodes beginning with its left child and below are its **left subtree**. The nodes beginning with its right child and below are its **right subtree**.

Depth of a node.   Suppose you start at a node *n* and move upward to its parent. We'll call this "one step." Then move up to the parent of the parent—that's a second step. Eventually, you will reach the root, and the number of steps taken is called the **depth of the node** *n*. The depth of the root itself is zero; a child of the root has depth one. In Figure 10.2(b), the node containing 13 has depth three.

Depth of a tree. The **depth of a tree** is the maximum depth of any of its leaves. In Figure 10.2(b), the leaf containing 13 has depth three, and there is no deeper leaf. So the depth of the example tree is three. If a tree has only one node, the root, then its depth is zero (since the depth of the root is zero). The empty tree doesn't have any leaves, so we use –1 for its depth. Just to confuse things, you'll often see the term *height* of a tree used instead of *depth*, but they mean the same thing.

Full binary trees. In a **full binary tree**, every leaf has the same depth, and every nonleaf has two children. Figure 10.1 on page 470 is not a full tree because it has leaves at different depths—some with depth two and some with depth three. Also, some of the nonleaves have only one child. In Figure 10.2, part (a) is full, but parts (b) and (c) are not full.

Complete binary trees. Suppose you take a full binary tree and start adding new leaves at a new depth from left to right. All the new leaves have the same depth—one more than where we started—and we always add leftmost nodes first. For example, if you add three nodes to Figure 10.2(a), then one possible result is Figure 10.2(b). The tree is no longer a full tree because some leaves are a bit deeper than others. Instead, we call this a **complete binary tree**. In order to be a complete tree, every level except the deepest must contain as many nodes as possible; and at the deepest level, all the nodes are as far left as possible.

Binary Taxonomy Trees

Binary trees are useful in many situations. We'll look at one example, **binary taxonomy trees**, which can be used to store certain kinds of knowledge. The particular example we have in mind stores information about a collection of animals. Each leaf in a binary taxonomy tree contains the name of an animal, and each nonleaf node contains a question about animals.

binary taxonomy trees store knowledge about a collection of animals

For example, suppose that we want a taxonomy tree for four animals: a kangaroo, a mouse, a trout, and a robin. The tree might look like Figure 10.3. To use a binary taxonomy tree, you start at the root and ask the question that is written there. If the answer is "yes," you move to the left child, and if the answer is "no,"

FIGURE 10.3 A Small Binary Taxonomy Tree

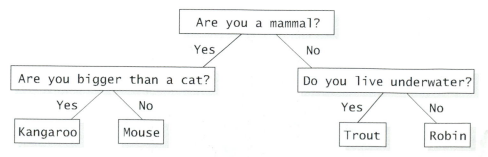

you move to the right child. Eventually, you will reach a leaf, and the name at the leaf tells you which animal you have been examining—or at least it does if the animal is one of the animals that the tree knows about.

General Trees

Each node in a binary tree has at most two children. In fact, that's why the word "binary'" is used. But in general, a node in a tree may have any number of children. Figure 10.4 shows an example where some nodes have one child, some have two, and some have three. A node in a general tree might even have more than three children (although three is the most in Figure 10.4). In Figure 10.4 we have not written any data at the nodes—but we could have written integers or strings or whatever data type we were interested in storing.

Trees

A **tree** is a finite set of nodes. The set might be empty (no nodes, which is called the **empty tree**). But if the set is not empty, then it must follow these rules:

1. There is one special node, called the **root**.

2. Each node may be associated with one or more different nodes, called its **children**. If a node *c* is the child of another node *p*, then we say that "*p* is *c*'s **parent**."

3. Each node except the root has exactly one parent; the root has no parent.

4. If you start at any node and move to the node's parent (provided there is one), then move again to that node's parent (provided there is one), and keep moving upward to each node's parent, you will eventually reach the root.

FIGURE 10.4 A General Tree

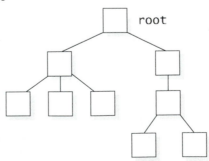

There are other special kinds of trees. For example, Section 11.2 uses B-trees, which are trees where the number of children of each node must lie between a certain minimum and a certain maximum.

Self-Test Exercises for Section 10.1

1. Draw a binary tree with 12 nodes. Circle the root, and put asterisks at each leaf. Find two nodes that are siblings, and connect them with a wiggly line. Choose one of the leaves, and shade all of its ancestors.

2. Consider the tree in the margin. Which nodes are leaves? Which nodes are siblings with each other? What is the depth of the tree?

3. For the tree in the margin, what additions will make the tree full? What additions will make the tree complete?

4. What is the depth of a tree with only a root node? What is the depth of a tree with no nodes?

5. Draw a tree that contains members of your family. The root should contain your mother's mother. Her children nodes contain her actual children, and those nodes contain her children's children, and so on.

6. What is the depth of the tree from Exercise 5? What is the depth of the node that contains *you*? Draw a circle around all nodes that are your ancestor nodes. Do each of these nodes contain one of your real-life ancestors? Draw a big square around all nodes that are descendants of your mother. Does each of these nodes contain one of her real-life descendants?

7. Create a binary taxonomy tree with 16 animals. Is your tree full? Is it complete?

a tree...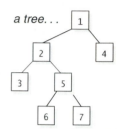

10.2 TREE REPRESENTATIONS

This section discusses two kinds of trees and how they typically are represented in a data structure. For the most part, if you understand these two representations, you can also manage other kinds of trees.

Array Representation of Complete Binary Trees

Complete binary trees have a simple representation using arrays. The representation can use a fixed-sized array (as in the classes of Chapter 3), which means that the size of the data structure is fixed during compilation, and during execution it does not grow larger or smaller. Or the representation can use a dynamic array (as in the classes of Chapter 4), allowing the representation to grow and shrink as needed during the execution of a program.

Remember that in a complete binary tree, all of the depths are full, except perhaps for the deepest. At the deepest depth, the nodes are as far left as possible.

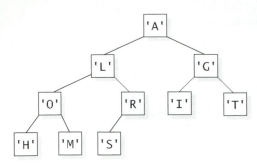

For example, in the margin is a complete binary tree with 10 nodes where the item contained in each node is a character.

In this example, the first seven nodes completely fill the levels at depth zero (the root), depth one (the root's children), and depth two. There are three more nodes at depth three, and these nodes are as far left as possible.

The 10 characters that the tree contains can be stored in an array of characters, starting with the root's character in the [0] location of the array, as shown below:

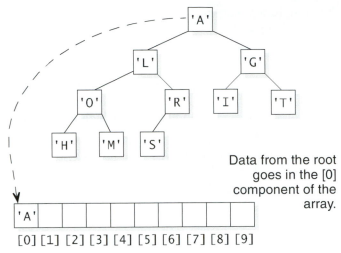

Data from the root goes in the [0] component of the array.

After the root, the two nodes with depth one are placed in the array, as shown here:

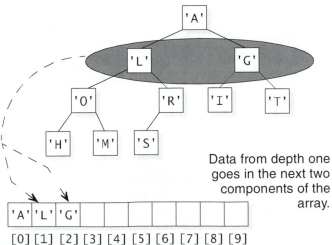

Data from depth one goes in the next two components of the array.

We continue in this way, placing the four nodes of depth two next and finishing off with the nodes of depth three. The entire representation of the tree by an array is shown here:

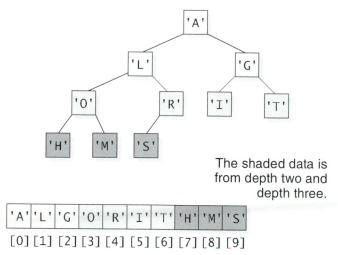

The shaded data is from depth two and depth three.

There are several reasons why the array representation is convenient:

formulas for storing data from a complete binary tree in the components of an array

1. The data from the root always appears in the [0] component of the array.

2. Suppose that the data for a nonroot node appears in component [i] of the array. Then the data for its parent is always at location [(i-1)/2] (using integer division).

3. Suppose that the data for a node appears in component [i] of the array. Then its children (if they exist) always have their data at these locations:

   Left child at component [2i+1];

   Right child at component [2i+2].

These formulas make it easy to implement algorithms that traverse the tree, moving from node to node in various ways, processing data along the way.

Before long you will implement some classes that store data in a tree. If the tree is a complete binary tree, then the class can store the complete binary tree in a fixed-sized array, using the formulas that we have written. Such a class will have at least two private member variables: (1) The array itself is one member variable, and (2) a second member variable keeps track of how much of the array is used. The actual links between the nodes are not stored. Instead, these links exist only via the formulas that determine where an item is stored in the array based on the item's position in the tree.

the tree can use a dynamic array or a static array

As an alternative to a fixed-sized array, the implementation can use a dynamic array. Using a dynamic array entails a third member variable to keep track of the complete size of the dynamic array.

Noncomplete binary trees can also be implemented using an array, although a problem arises in determining which children of a node actually exist. We'll address this problem in the Programming Project 4 on page 530. But for now, let's look at the other alternative: a dynamic implementation of binary trees that allocates and releases nodes as needed.

Representing a Binary Tree with a Class for Nodes

A binary tree can be represented by its individual nodes, where each node is stored in an object of a `binary_tree_node` class, similar to the way that we used a node to build linked lists. Here is the basic idea:

Node Representation of Binary Trees

Each node of a tree is stored in an object of a new `binary_tree_node` class. Each node contains pointers that link it to other nodes in the tree. An entire tree is represented as a pointer to the root node.

For a binary tree, we'll link each node to its left child and right child. The node also has a member variable to hold some data. The type of the data can be declared with a template parameter, as shown here:

```
template <class Item>
class binary_tree_node
{
public:
    || Public member functions will give access to the data and links.
private:
    Item data_field;
    binary_tree_node *left_field;
    binary_tree_node *right_field;
};
```

The `data_field` of a node holds some information that occurs in the node. Each binary tree node also contains two pointers which point to the left and right children of the node. When a child pointer is NULL, it indicates that the particular child does not exist. We could include other links in a binary tree node: perhaps a pointer to the node's parent, or to the root of the entire tree, or even to siblings. But many applications need only the children links.

We can draw a boxes-and-arrows representation of a small tree, as in Figure 10.5. Each node is stored in one object of type `binary_tree_node`, and the entire tree is accessed through a pointer that points to the root node of the tree. Within the diagram, a null pointer is drawn as a slash. The pointer to the root node is similar to the head pointer of a linked list, providing a starting point to access all the nodes in the tree. If the tree was empty (with no nodes), then the root pointer would be null.

FIGURE 10.5 A Binary Tree Represented with binary_tree_node Objects

(a) Example binary tree of characters

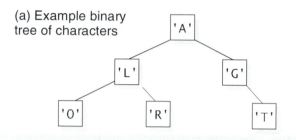

(b) Representation of the binary tree using binary_tree_node objects. Each large box is a binary_tree_node object, and each of the small shaded boxes is a pointer to a binary_tree_node.

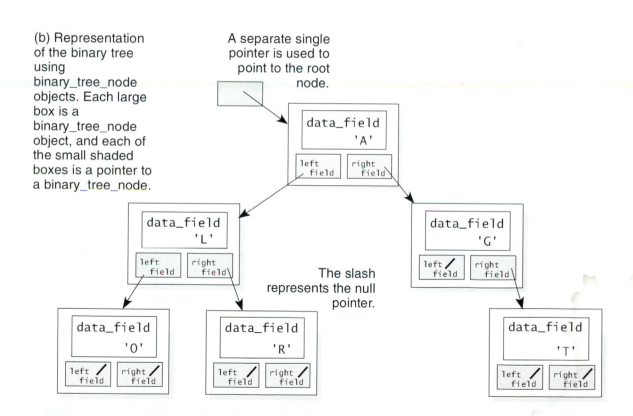

A separate single pointer is used to point to the root node.

The slash represents the null pointer.

Self-Test Exercises for Section 10.2

8. Describe one problem with representing noncomplete binary trees using the array implementation described in this section.

9. Consider a complete binary tree with exactly 10,000 nodes, implemented with an array. Suppose that a node has its value stored in location 4999. Where is the value stored for this node's parent? Where is the value stored for its left child? What can you say about its right child?

10. Draw a representation of a small binary tree with three nodes containing integers. Put 10 in the root, 20 in the left child of the root, and 30 in the right child of the root. Use the binary tree node definition from this section.

11. Write the member variables for a new node definition that could be used for a tree where each node has up to four children, and each node also has a pointer to its parent. Store the children pointers in an array of four pointers.

10.3 BINARY TREE NODES

Figure 10.6 shows the `binary_tree_node` definition that we plan to use. As we did with the linked-list node, the `data` function returns a reference to the actual data. In Chapter 6, we had a short discussion (page 314) of functions that return a reference. We can provide some more details now. For the `data` function's return value of `Item&` (which is a reference to an `Item`), the return statement (`return data_field`) arranges for the function to return a *reference* to the `data_field` member variable of a node. A reference is like a pointer, but it can be used with no need for the dereferencing asterisk (`*`). Therefore, any time we have a `binary_tree_node` n, the expression `n.data( )` will directly access the node's `data_field`. For example, with integer items, the assignment `n.data( ) = 42` puts the value 42 in the node's `data_field`. The non-const versions of these functions return a reference to the left or right pointer in the node, so that, for example, an assignment such as `p->left( ) = q;` is an alternative to `p->set_left(q);`.

As we saw in Chapter 6, since the `data` function returns a reference, we require both a const `data` function (to be used when we are forbidden from changing a node) and a non-const `data` function (to be used when we are allowed to change a node). Therefore, the function may be used with a pointer that was declared with the const keyword (`const binary_tree_node* p`) or with an ordinary pointer. The non-const versions of the functions to obtain the left and right links also return references (to `left_field` or `right_field`). This allows us to use the `left` or `right` function to change a link (for example, `n.left( ) = NULL`).

By the way, in the first printing of this text, the `left` and `right` functions did not return references, but without the references, certain recursive functions are harder to write in Section 10.5.

In addition to the expected functions to access and modify a node, we have one more member function, `is_leaf`, with this implementation:

```
bool is_leaf( ) const
    { return (left_field == NULL) && (right_field == NULL); }
```

This function returns true if the given node has no children (both pointers to left and right are null).

With the binary tree node definition in hand, we can define a small collection of functions for creating and manipulating trees. Primarily, the functions are meant to help a programmer who is writing a class that uses a binary tree to store data. The functions are similar to the linked-list functions that we wrote in Chapter 5 and subsequently used in linked-list versions of the bag class, sequence class, stack class, and queue class.

FIGURE 10.6   The Binary Tree Node Definition

A Class Definition

```
template <class Item>
class binary_tree_node
{
public:
    // TYPEDEF
    typedef Item value_type;
    // CONSTRUCTOR
    binary_tree_node(
        const Item& init_data = Item( ),
        binary_tree_node* init_left = NULL,
        binary_tree_node* init_right = NULL
    )
    {
        data_field = init_data;
        left_field = init_left;
        right_field = init_right;
    }
    // MODIFICATION MEMBER FUNCTIONS
    Item& data( ) { return data_field; }
    binary_tree_node*& left( ) { return left_field; }
    binary_tree_node*& right( ) { return right_field; }
    void set_data(const Item& new_data) { data_field = new_data; }
    void set_left(binary_tree_node* new_left) { left_field = new_left; }
    void set_right(binary_tree_node* new_right) { right_field = new_right; }
    // CONSTANT MEMBER FUNCTIONS
    const Item& data( ) const { return data_field; }
    const binary_tree_node* left( ) const { return left_field; }
    const binary_tree_node* right( ) const { return right_field; }
    bool is_leaf( ) const
        { return (left_field == NULL) && (right_field == NULL); }
private:
    Item data_field;
    binary_tree_node *left_field;
    binary_tree_node *right_field;
};
```

www.cs.colorado.edu/~main/chapter10/bintree.h   **WWW**

We will start with only two functions, but we'll add more later. After we specify and implement the functions, we'll collect them together with a header file and implementation file.

Returning nodes to the heap. Our first function returns the nodes of a tree to the heap. The function has one parameter, which is the root pointer of the tree. Here is the specification:

```
template <class Item>
void tree_clear(binary_tree_node<Item>*& root_ptr);
// Precondition: root_ptr is the root pointer of a binary tree (which may be
// NULL for the empty tree).
// Postcondition: All nodes at the root or below have been returned to the
// heap, and root_ptr has been set to NULL.
```

The implementation is easier than it seems—the ease comes from recursive thinking. First notice that there is one easy case: When `root_ptr` is NULL, the function does no work. On the other hand, if the root pointer is not null, then there are four steps:

1. Clear the left subtree, returning all its nodes to the heap.
2. Clear the right subtree, returning all its nodes to the heap.
3. Return the root node to the heap.
4. Set the root pointer to null.

Steps 1 and 2 are examples of "smaller versions of the problem that we are trying to solve in the first place." Think recursively, and you will write this:

```
template <class Item>
void tree_clear(binary_tree_node<Item>*& root_ptr)
{
    if (root_ptr != NULL)
    {
        tree_clear( root_ptr->left( ) );
        tree_clear( root_ptr->right( ) );
        delete root_ptr;
        root_ptr = NULL;
    }
}
```

The base case (when the root pointer is null) does no work.

Copying a tree. Our second function also has a simple recursive implementation. The function copies a tree, as specified here:

```
template <class Item>
binary_tree_node<Item>* tree_copy
    (const binary_tree_node<Item>* root_ptr);
// Precondition: root_ptr is the root pointer of a binary tree (which may be
// NULL for the empty tree).
// Postcondition: A copy of the binary tree has been made, and the return
// value is a pointer to the root of this copy.
```

Once again, there is a simple base case: When `root_ptr` is null, the function simply returns `NULL`. On the other hand, if the root pointer is not null, then the tree has at least one node. The tree can be copied with these three steps (using local variables `l_ptr` and `r_ptr`, which are both pointers to nodes):

1. Make `l_ptr` point to a copy of the left subtree (which might be empty).
2. Make `r_ptr` point to a copy of the right subtree (which might be empty).
3. *return new* `binary_tree_node(root_ptr->data(), l_ptr, r_ptr);`

Once again, the first two steps of the pseudocode are smaller versions of the problem we are solving in the first place. Therefore these two steps can be solved with recursive calls. Here's the complete implementation of `tree_copy`:

```
template <class Item>
binary_tree_node<Item>* tree_copy
    (const binary_tree_node<Item>* root_ptr)
{
    binary_tree_node<Item> *l_ptr;
    binary_tree_node<Item> *r_ptr;

    if (root_ptr == NULL)
        return NULL;
    else
    {
        l_ptr = tree_copy( root_ptr->left( ) );
        r_ptr = tree_copy( root_ptr->right( ) );
        return new binary_tree_node<Item>
                        (root_ptr->data( ), l_ptr, r_ptr);
    }
}
```

Later we will place the `tree_clear` and `tree_copy` functions in an implementation file (`bintree.template`) along with a header (`bintree.h`).

NOT CONNECTING ALL THE LINKS

Any time you are implementing a dynamic structure with pointers, there is a potential pitfall: forgetting to set all of the pointer fields of a node. With a linear structure, such as a list or a stack, the pitfall is not so common, since each node has only one pointer field. But as the structures become more complex, such as our binary tree node, the potential for forgetting to correctly set a pointer becomes more likely.

For example, the `binary_tree_node` constructor must set both the left and right pointers of a newly created node. When you allocate a node that is part of a dynamic structure, any unused pointers should immediately be set to the null pointer. This will prevent you from mistakenly thinking that unused pointers are pointing to a valid node.

PROGRAMMING EXAMPLE: **Animal Guessing**

Now we'll write a small program that uses the binary tree toolkit. The program is a simple guessing game: You pretend that you are an animal, and the program asks questions to try to guess what animal you are. If the program guesses correctly, another round of the game is started. And if the program can't figure out what you are, you provide some more knowledge to the program so that the next time the game is played, the program is a bit smarter.

an animal guessing program that gets smarter and smarter

As an example, suppose you are pretending to be a raccoon. The program might start by asking *"Are you a mammal?"* and you answer, "Yes." Next, the program wants to know *"Are you bigger than a cat?"* and again you answer, "Yes." Finally, the program guesses: *"Are you a kangaroo?"* and with a smug smile you reply, "No, don't be ridiculous."

At this point, the program says, *"I give up. What are you?"* You explain that you are a raccoon. You then provide the program with a question that the program can use in the future to distinguish a kangaroo from a raccoon—perhaps *"Are you a marsupial?"*—and you tell the program that the answer to this question is "yes" for a kangaroo but "no" for a raccoon. The next time that you are a raccoon, the program will have enough information to guess correctly. A sample dialogue with the program is given in Figure 10.7.

FIGURE 10.7   Part of a Sample Dialogue with the Animal Guessing Program

A Sample Dialogue

```
Are you a mammal? Please answer [Yes or No]
Yes
Are you bigger than a cat? Please answer [Yes or No]
Yes
My guess is Kangaroo. Am I right? [Yes or No]
No
I give up. What are you?
Raccoon
Please type a yes/no question that will distinguish a Raccoon from a Kangaroo.
Your question:
Are you a marsupial?
As a Raccoon, Are you a marsupial? Please answer [Yes or No]
No
Shall we play again? [Yes or No]
No
Thank you for teaching me a thing or two.
```

As you might guess, the data used by the program is stored in a binary taxonomy tree, as described on page 473, with each nonleaf node containing a question. When the program begins, it will only know about four animals, and the taxonomy tree will look like this:

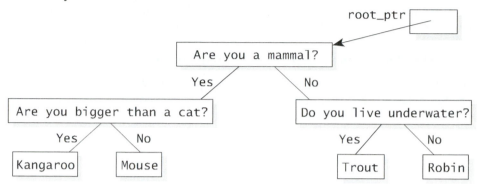

The program maintains a root pointer that always points to the root of the binary taxonomy tree. As the game is being played, the program also maintains a second pointer called `current_ptr`. The current pointer starts at the root and travels down the tree according to the answers that the user provides.

For example, suppose that the user answers yes to the first question "Are you a mammal?" Then the program will move its current pointer to the left subtree, as shown here:

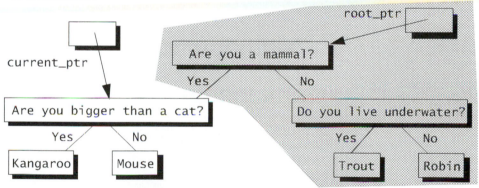

In the drawing we have hidden part of the tree to indicate that only the left subtree is now relevant to the game. The rest of the tree and the root pointer are still present, but they are not needed at this point in the game.

The program continues asking questions. Each time the user answers yes to a question, the current pointer is moved left. Each no answer moves the current pointer right. This continues until the program reaches a leaf. When a leaf is reached, the program guesses that you are the animal whose name is stored at the leaf. If the leaf contains the correct animal, then all is well. But if the guess is wrong, then the program elicits information from the user, and that information is used to update the taxonomy tree.

In the example, where you were a raccoon, the program would use the information to modify the taxonomy tree, resulting in the larger taxonomy tree of Figure 10.8(a). After several rounds of the game, the taxonomy tree might contain quite a few animals. Figure 10.8(b) shows what the tree could look like with seven animals. As an exercise, pretend you are a squid, and follow the route that would be taken from the root to the squid leaf in this tree.

Animal Guessing Program—Design and Implementation

Now that we have a general idea of how the program works, let's carry out a top-down design. The main program has three steps, shown in the pseudocode at the top of the next page.

FIGURE 10.8 Two Possible Taxonomy Trees

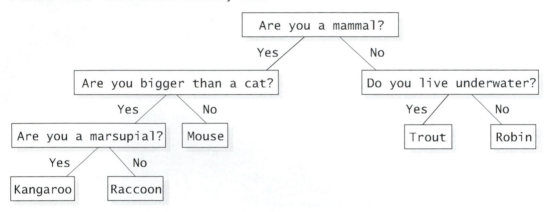

(a) Taxonomy tree after adding a raccoon

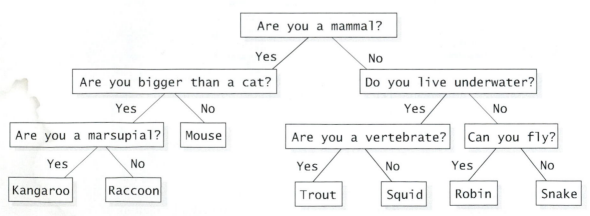

(b) Taxonomy tree with seven animals

1. Print the instructions for the user.

2. Create a small initial taxonomy tree with four animals; the pointer variable `taxonomy_root_ptr` points to the root of this initial tree.

3. Repeat the following steps as often as the user wants:

    a. Play one round of the game, perhaps adding information to the bottom of the tree.

    b. Ask the user, "Shall we play again?" and read the answer.

The first two steps from our outline will be accomplished by functions that we call `instruct` and `beginning_tree`. For Step 3a, we'll design a function called `play`. Step 3b can be accomplished with the `inquire` function, which is part of the toolkit of useful functions that we have used before (`useful.h` from Appendix I). That function asks a yes/no question, returning true if the user replies yes, and returning false if the user replies no.

Putting these steps together, we can write the main function, using a root pointer to the binary taxonomy tree, as shown here:

```
int main( )
{
    binary_tree_node<string> *taxonomy_root_ptr;

    instruct( );
    taxonomy_root_ptr = beginning_tree( );
    do
        play(taxonomy_root_ptr);
    while (inquire("Shall we play again?"));

    cout << "Thanks for teaching me a thing or two." << endl;
    return EXIT_SUCCESS;
}
```

Notice that the type of the data in each node is a `string` object from the Standard Library `<string>` facility.

the data at each node is a string

Next, we discuss the functions `instruct`, `beginning_tree`, and `play`.

The instruct function. This is a function with output to the screen to explain the game. You can write it yourself with the prototype: *void* `instruct( );`

The beginning_tree function. This function creates the initial binary taxonomy tree and returns a pointer to the root of this tree, as shown in this outline:

```
binary_tree_node<string>* beginning_tree( )
// Postcondition: The function has created a small taxonomy tree.
// The return value is the root pointer of the new tree.
{
    binary_tree_node<string> *root_ptr;
    binary_tree_node<string> *child_ptr;
```

1. Make root_ptr point to a new node with the data "Are you a mammal?" Both child pointers are initially null.

2. Make child_ptr point to a new node with the data "Are you bigger than a cat?" Give it two leaves as children with the data "Kangaroo" on the left and "Mouse" on the right. Then activate root_ptr->set_left(child_ptr);

3. Make child_ptr point to a new node with the data "Do you live underwater?" Give it two leaves as children with the data "Trout" on the left and "Robin" on the right. Then activate root_ptr->set_right(child_ptr);

4. *return* root_ptr;
```
}
```

The complete implementation will be shown as part of a program in a moment. For now, you should notice beginning_tree can create its new nodes by using the binary tree node constructor. When beginning_tree finishes, the root pointer in the main program will point to the root node of our initial taxonomy tree.

The play function. The play function has one parameter, which initially is the root pointer of the binary taxonomy tree, as shown in this prototype:

```
void play(binary_tree_node<string>* current_ptr);
```

The function causes the current pointer to move down the tree in response to the user's replies. (The root pointer, back in the main program, will stay pointing at the root since current_ptr is an ordinary value parameter.) When the current pointer reaches a leaf, an animal is guessed.

We'll use two other functions to carry out most of play's work. The first function, named ask_and_move, asks the question that's contained at the current node of the tree and then shifts the current pointer to the left or right child, based on the user's answer. Here is the specification for ask_and_move:

```
void ask_and_move(binary_tree_node<string>*& current_ptr);
// Precondition: current_ptr points to a nonleaf node in a binary taxonomy
// tree.
// Postcondition: The question at the current node has been asked. The
// current pointer has been shifted left (if the user answered yes) or right
// (for a no answer).
```

specification of the ask_and_move function

The second important function used by `play` is called `learn`. The `learn` function is used after the game reaches a leaf and the animal at the leaf is wrong. The function elicits information from the user and thereby improves the tree, as specified here:

```
void learn(binary_tree_node<string>* leaf_ptr);
// Precondition: leaf_ptr is a pointer to a leaf in a taxonomy tree.
// This leaf contains a wrong guess that was just made.
// Postcondition: Information has been elicited from the user,
// and the tree has been improved.
```

specification of the learn function

Using the two functions, the implementation of `play` is relatively short, as shown here:

```
void play(binary_tree_node<string>* current_ptr)
// Precondition: current_ptr points to the root of a binary taxonomy tree
// with at least two leaves.
// Postcondition: One round of the animal game has been played,
// and maybe the tree has been improved.
{
    cout << "Think of an animal, then press the return key.";
    eat_line( );

    while (!current_ptr->is_leaf( ))
        ask_and_move(current_ptr);

    cout << ("My guess is " + current_ptr->data( ) + ". ");
    if (!inquire("Am I right?"))
        learn(current_ptr);
    else
        cout << "I knew it all along!" << endl;
}
```

Within this implementation we used the `inquire` function to ask the question "Am I right?". A function named `eat_line` is also used to read and throw away all characters up to the next newline character. Both of these functions are part of our toolkit of useful functions (see Appendix I).

So what's left to do? Implement the two functions `ask_and_move` and `learn`, which we'll do now.

The ask_and_move function.   This function has one argument, which is the current pointer to a node in the taxonomy tree. The function asks the question at this node and shifts the current pointer down to a subtree based on the user's answer. Using the `inquire` function from `useful.h`, the implementation is short:

```
void ask_and_move(binary_tree_node<string>*& current_ptr)
{
    cout << current_ptr->data( );
    if (inquire(" Please answer:"))
        current_ptr = current_ptr->left( );
    else
        current_ptr = current_ptr->right( );
}
```

The learn function.   This function is called when the game reaches a leaf and makes a wrong guess. The function takes several steps to improve the taxonomy tree. The function's argument is a pointer to the node that contains the incorrect guess, as shown in this prototype:

```
void learn(binary_tree_node<string>* leaf_ptr);
```

For example, suppose we just made an incorrect guess of a kangaroo from this tree:

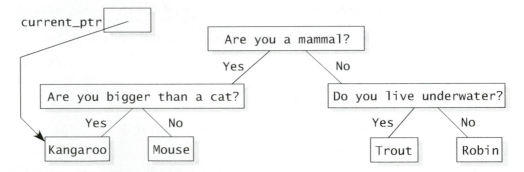

The `learn` function first sets three local `string` variables:

1. What animal was guessed? This comes from `current_ptr->data( )` and is stored in a local variable called `guess_animal`. For this example, the `guess_animal` is "Kangaroo."

2. What is the correct animal? The user's answer to this question is read into a local `string` variable called `correct_animal`. To read the answer, we use the string's `getline` function. This function reads an entire line of input, including blanks, and places this line in a string. For this example, suppose that the user's answer is "Raccoon."

3. What is a yes/no question that can distinguish the right animal from the animal that was guessed? In our example, we need a question that can distinguish a kangaroo from a raccoon. The user might provide the question "Are you a marsupial?" and we'll store this question in another local string variable called `new_question`.

With the three strings set, we need one more piece of information. In particular, we need to know whether the new animal answers yes or no to the question that the user has just provided. In our example, we need to know whether a raccoon answers yes or no to the question "Are you a marsupial?" Of course, a raccoon is not a marsupial, so based on this no answer, we can proceed as follows:

1. Copy the new question into `current_ptr`'s data field.

2. Copy the *guessed* animal into a new leaf, which is created to be the left child of the current node.

3. Copy the *correct* new animal into a new leaf, which is created to be the right child of the current node.

In our example, these steps improve the taxonomy tree as shown here:

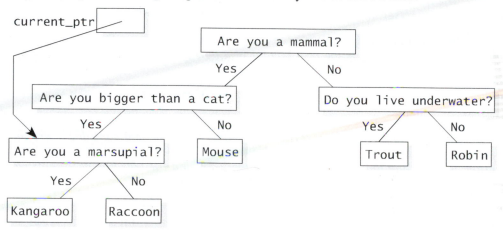

The other possibility is that the new animal has a yes answer to the new question. For example, the question to distinguish a raccoon from a kangaroo could be "Do you have a ringed tail?" In this case, the new animal (raccoon) would be added as the left child of the new question, and the old animal (kangaroo) added on the right.

The implementation of the `learn` function is part of the complete animal-guessing program in Figure 10.9.

Animal Guessing Program—Improvements

Our animal program suffers from one problem: Each time the program is executed, it starts out by knowing only four animals. An improvement will allow it to store the current taxonomy tree in a file and read that file whenever the program starts. This way the program remembers all the animals it was taught.

FIGURE 10.9   The Animal Guessing Program

A Program

```
// FILE: animal.cxx
// This animal guessing program illustrates the use of the binary tree node class.

#include <cstdlib>      // Provides EXIT_SUCCESS
#include <iostream>     // Provides cout
#include <string>       // Provides string class
#include "bintree.h"    // Provides the binary tree node class
#include "useful.h"     // Provides eat_line, inquire (from Appendix I)
using namespace std;
using namespace main_savitch_10;        // binary_tree_node

// PROTOTYPES for functions used by this game program:
void ask_and_move(binary_tree_node<string>*& current_ptr);
// Precondition: current_ptr points to a nonleaf node in a binary taxonomy tree.
// Postcondition: The question at the current node has been asked. The current pointer has
// been shifted left (if the user answered yes) or right (for a no answer).

binary_tree_node<string>* beginning_tree( );
// Postcondition: The return value is the root pointer of a new small taxonomy tree.

void instruct( );
// Postcondition: Instructions for playing the game have been printed to the screen.

void learn(binary_tree_node<string>* leaf_ptr);
// Precondition: leaf_ptr is a pointer to a leaf in a taxonomy tree. The leaf contains a wrong
// guess that was just made.
// Postcondition: Information has been elicited from the user, and the tree has been improved.

void play(binary_tree_node<string>* current_ptr);
// Precondition: current_ptr points to the root of a binary taxonomy tree with at least two leaves.
// Postcondition: One round of the animal game has been played, and maybe the tree has
// been improved.

int main( )
{
    binary_tree_node<string> *taxonomy_root_ptr;

    instruct( );
    taxonomy_root_ptr = beginning_tree( );
    do
        play(taxonomy_root_ptr);
    while (inquire("Shall we play again?"));
    cout << "Thank you for teaching me a thing or two." << endl;
    return EXIT_SUCCESS;
}
```

(continued)

(FIGURE 10.9 continued)

```
void ask_and_move(binary_tree_node<string>*& current_ptr)
// Library facilities used: bintree.h, string, useful.h
{
    cout << current_ptr->data( );
    if (inquire(" Please answer"))
        current_ptr = current_ptr->left( );
    else
        current_ptr = current_ptr->right( );
}

binary_tree_node<string>* beginning_tree( )
// Library facilities used: bintree.h, string
{
    binary_tree_node<string> *root_ptr;
    binary_tree_node<string> *child_ptr;

    const string root_question("Are you a mammal?");
    const string left_question("Are you bigger than a cat?");
    const string right_question("Do you live underwater?");
    const string animal1("Kangaroo");
    const string animal2("Mouse");
    const string animal3("Trout");
    const string animal4("Robin");

    // Create the root node with the question "Are you a mammal?"
    root_ptr = new binary_tree_node<string> (root_question);

    // Create and attach the left subtree.
    child_ptr = new binary_tree_node<string> (left_question);
    child_ptr->set_left( new binary_tree_node<string> (animal1) );
    child_ptr->set_right( new binary_tree_node<string> (animal2) );
    root_ptr->set_left(child_ptr);

    // Create and attach the right subtree.
    child_ptr = new binary_tree_node<string> (right_question);
    child_ptr->set_left( new binary_tree_node<string> (animal3) );
    child_ptr->set_right( new binary_tree_node<string> (animal4) );
    root_ptr->set_right(child_ptr);

    return root_ptr;
}

void instruct( )
   The implementation of this function is omitted—write it yourself!
```

(continued)

(FIGURE 10.9 continued)

```
void learn(binary_tree_node<string>* leaf_ptr)
// Library facilities used: bintree.h, iostream, string, useful.h
{
    string guess_animal;      // The animal that was just guessed
    string correct_animal;    // The animal that the user was thinking of
    string new_question;      // A question to distinguish the two animals

    // Set strings for the guessed animal, correct animal, and a new question.
    guess_animal = leaf_ptr->data( );
    cout << "I give up. What are you? " << endl;
    getline(cin, correct_animal);
    cout << "Please type a yes/no question that will distinguish a" << endl;
    cout << correct_animal << " from a " << guess_animal << "." << endl;
    cout << "Your question: " << endl;
    getline(cin, new_question);

    // Put the new question in the current node, and add two new children.
    leaf_ptr->set_data(new_question);
    cout << "As a " << correct_animal << ", " << new_question << endl;
    if (inquire("Please answer"))
    {
        leaf_ptr->set_left( new binary_tree_node<string> (correct_animal) );
        leaf_ptr->set_right( new binary_tree_node<string> (guess_animal) );
    }
    else
    {
        leaf_ptr->set_left( new binary_tree_node<string> (guess_animal) );
        leaf_ptr->set_right( new binary_tree_node<string> (correct_animal) );
    }
}

void play(binary_tree_node<string>* current_ptr)
// Library facilities used: bintree.h, iostream, string, useful.h
{
    cout << "Think of an animal, then press the return key.";
    eat_line( );

    while (!current_ptr->is_leaf( ))
        ask_and_move(current_ptr);

    cout << ("My guess is " + current_ptr->data);
    if (!inquire(". Am I right?"))
        learn(current_ptr);
    else
        cout << "I knew it all along!" << endl;
}
```

Self-Test Exercises for Section 10.3

12. What is the base case for the recursive functions `tree_clear` and `tree_copy`?

13. Write a new function to compute the number of children that a node has.

14. Write a new function to compute the number of nodes in a binary tree. Write another function to compute the depth of a binary tree. Both functions have one argument, which is the tree's root pointer. Think recursively.

10.4   TREE TRAVERSALS

> *And then he got up, and said: "And the only reason for making honey is so as I can eat it." So he began to climb the tree.*
>
> *He climbed and he climbed and he climbed, and as he climbed he sang a little song to himself.*
>
> A. A. MILNE
> *Winnie-the-Pooh*

Traversals of Binary Trees

Programs that use tree structures often need to process all of the nodes in a tree, applying the same operation to each node. This processing is called a **tree traversal**. For example, suppose we have a tree where each node contains an integer, and we need to print a list of all the integers in the tree. For a binary tree, there are three common ways of doing this kind of processing: **pre-order traversal**, **in-order traversal**, and **post-order traversal**. This section defines and implements the three traversal methods for binary trees. We also implement an unusual fourth traversal method (a **backward in-order traversal**), which is useful for printing a tree. We start with a description of each method.

Pre-order traversal. The word "pre-order" means the root is processed *pre*vious to its two subtrees. So, a pre-order traversal has these three steps for a non-empty tree:

1. Process the root.
2. Process the nodes in the left subtree with a recursive call.
3. Process the nodes in the right subtree with a recursive call.

pre-order: the root is processed prior to its two subtrees

At the end of this section we'll give an extremely general implementation of these three steps, which will allow you to do any kind of processing on each node. For now, let's look at a simpler case, where we just want to print the contents of each node. In this case we would add this template function to the binary tree functions of Section 10.3:

```
template <class Item>
void preorder_print(const binary_tree_node<Item>* node_ptr)
// Precondition: node_ptr is a pointer to a node in a binary tree (or
// node_ptr may be NULL to indicate the empty tree).
// Postcondition: If node_ptr is non-NULL, then the data of *node_ptr and
// all its descendants have been written to cout with the << operator, using
// a pre-order traversal.
// Library facilities used: cstdlib, iostream
{
    if (node_ptr != NULL)
    {
        std::cout << node_ptr->data( ) << std::endl;
        preorder_print( node_ptr->left( ) );
        preorder_print( node_ptr->right( ) );
    }
}
```

Notice how the processing of the two subtrees is accomplished with recursive calls. It's also important to see that pointers to the roots of the left and right subtrees of the original node are passed as arguments to the recursive calls.

Let's look at an execution of the pre-order traversal in more detail. We'll trace `preorder_print`, applied to the binary tree shown here:

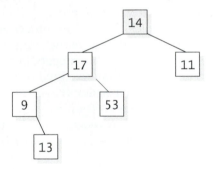

Suppose that our `node_ptr` points to the shaded root in the diagram. The function's first step is to print the number at the root, so after this step, the only number printed is 14 (from the root).

The function's second step makes a recursive call, with a pointer to the root node of the left subtree. In effect, the recursive call says "do a pre-order traversal of the left subtree." To illustrate that we are now doing a traversal of a subtree, we will temporarily hide everything except the left subtree, as shown here:

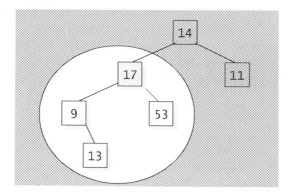

In this recursive call, the node_ptr points to the shaded node containing 17.
The first step of the recursive call is to print the number at the node_ptr, so
after that step the total output contains two numbers:

    14
    17

The second step of the recursive call is to make yet another recursive call,
with the argument being its own node_ptr->left( ). In other words, this second recursive call will begin at the shaded node containing 9 in this drawing:

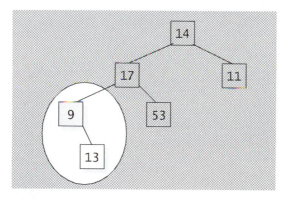

We now have three function calls that are active: The original function call with
the pointer to the root (containing 14), the first recursive call with a pointer to
the left child of the root (containing 17), and the second recursive call with a
pointer to the shaded node as shown (containing 9). This second recursive call
carries out its appointed task by first printing a 9. After this, the total output consists of these three lines:

    14
    17
    9

Once again, the function makes a recursive call. But this time the argument node_ptr->left( ) is NULL, indicating that there is no left subtree of the current node_ptr, so the function call returns. Where does it return to? It returns to the place where it was called, with the node_ptr pointing to the node with 9, and executing the code at the spot marked here with an arrow:

when the
recursive call
returns,
execution
continues at this
spot

```
if (node_ptr != NULL)
{
    std::cout << node_ptr->data( ) << std::endl;
    preorder_print( node_ptr->left( ) );
    preorder_print( node_ptr->right( ) );
}
```

At this point in the recursive call, we have already printed the 9 and processed the empty left subtree. So the next step will make another recursive call to process the right subtree. The node_ptr in this recursive call points to the node with 13, in this drawing:

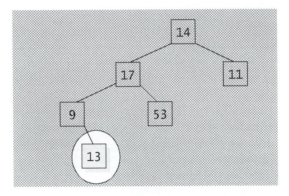

This function call prints the number 13, so that the entire output now has four numbers:

```
14
17
9
13
```

Both the left and right subtrees are empty for the node containing 13. So the recursive calls made at this level (to process those two empty subtrees) will do no work. The recursive call, which printed 13, returns. Where do matters go from there? Can you finish tracing the pre-order traversal? By the time the last recursive call has returned, we've "visited" every node in the tree, and the numbers have been printed out, in this order:

14
17
9
13
53
11

In-order traversal.   The only change for an in-order traversal is that the root is processed *in* between the processing of its two subtrees. Here are the three steps for a non-empty tree:

in-order: the root is processed in between its two subtrees

1. Process the nodes in the left subtree with a recursive call.
2. Process the root.
3. Process the nodes in the right subtree with a recursive call.

The implementation of an in-order print function is a rearrangement of the pre-order print:

```
template <class Item>
void inorder_print(const binary_tree_node<Item>* node_ptr)
// Precondition: node_ptr is a pointer to a node in a binary tree (or
// node_ptr may be NULL to indicate the empty tree).
// Postcondition: If node_ptr is non-NULL, then the data of *node_ptr and
// all its descendants have been written to cout with the << operator, using
// an in-order traversal.
// Library facilities used: cstdlib, iostream
{
    if (node_ptr != NULL)
    {
        inorder_print( node_ptr->left( ) );
        std::cout << node_ptr->data( ) << std::endl;
        inorder_print( node_ptr->right( ) );
    }
}
```

Post-order traversal.   In a post-order traversal, the processing of the root is *post*poned until last in a non-empty tree:

post-order: the root is processed after its two subtrees

1. Process the nodes in the left subtree with a recursive call.
2. Process the nodes in the right subtree with a recursive call.
3. Process the root.

We'll leave the implementation as an exercise in rearrangement.

Can you work out the order of the output numbers for the in-order and post-order traversals on an example such as Figure 10.5 on page 479? You'll be asked to work that out in Self-Test Exercise 15 at the end of this section.

Printing the Data from a Tree's Node

In debugging a program, the nodes of a tree are generally printed using a pre-order traversal, printing each parent prior to its children. For example, consider the small tree shown here, along with the output from the pre-order traversal:

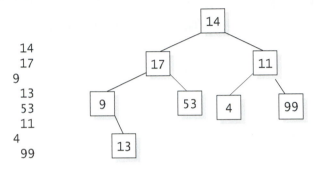

```
14
17
 9
   13
   53
11
 4
   99
```

There are two items that will make the output easier to read. The first trick is to print some indication when a node is a leaf or when a node has only one child. The second trick is to indent each number according to its depth in the tree. Each number will have an indentation of four times the depth of the node, as shown here:

```
14
    17
        9
            [Empty]
            13 [leaf]
        53 [leaf]
    11
        4 [leaf]
        99 [leaf]
```

Each leaf node has the word [leaf] printed after the data. Each nonleaf node has its two children printed below it with an extra four spaces of indentation. For example, the node containing 17 has a left child (containing 9) and a right child (containing 53). Notice that the node containing 9 has only a right child. In the spot where the left child would be printed if it existed is the word [Empty].

The function to carry out this kind of printing is a pre-order traversal with one extra parameter to carry information about the depth of each node. The implementation is shown at the top of the next page.

```
template <class Item, class SizeType>
void print
    (const binary_tree_node<Item>* node_ptr, SizeType depth)
// Precondition: node_ptr is a pointer to a node in a binary tree (or
// node_ptr may be NULL to indicate the empty tree). If the pointer is not
// NULL, then depth is the depth of the node pointed to by node_ptr.
// Postcondition: A representation of *node_ptr and all its descendants have
// been written to cout with the << operator. Each node is indented four
// times its depth.
// Library facilities used: cstdlib, iomanip, iostream
{
    std::cout << std::setw(4*depth) << ""; // Indentation
    if (node_ptr == NULL)
    {   // Fallen off the tree
        std::cout << "[Empty]" << std::endl;
    }
    else if (node_ptr->is_leaf( ))
    {   // A leaf
        std::cout << node_ptr->data( );
        std::cout << " [leaf]" <<std::endl;
    }
    else
    {   // A nonleaf
        std::cout << node_ptr->data( ) << std::endl;
        print(node_ptr->right( ), depth+1);
        print(node_ptr->left( ),  depth+1);
    }
}
```

The statement `std::cout << std::setw(4*depth) << "";` prints the empty string (that is, `""`), with a "field width" of `4*depth`. The result is that `4*depth` spaces are printed before printing the node's data. (The `setw` function from `iomanip` sets the field width of the next item that is printed.).

The Problem with Our Traversals

The different binary tree traversals visit each node in a tree, and processing is done at each node. For the specific traversals that we have seen, the "processing" was simply printing the value of the contents of the node. But in general, we'd like to be able to do *any* kind of processing—not just printing. On the surface, this is not difficult. We can just replace the `cout` statement in the traversal function with some other form of processing (or perhaps we could get our efficient friend Jervis to do this). But there are two problems with the replacement strategy:

1. Suppose that our boss Judy wants to do three different kinds of processing, or worse yet, 3000 kinds of processing. Jervis would need to write 3000 different functions, each of which is nearly the same as all the others.

2. The writer of the binary tree class should not have to anticipate every kind of processing that a user may desire. In fact, the writer of the class often will have no contact with the programmer (Judy) who uses the class. Even if there is contact, Judy might not want to tell the other programmer about this processing. "Mind your own business," Judy would say to the other programmer. "Just give me *one* function that is capable of doing any kind of processing."

a different approach uses function objects

In C++, it is possible to write just one function that is capable of doing a tree traversal and carrying out virtually any kind of processing at the nodes. One approach, using C++ function objects, is described in the online projects at www.cs.colorado.edu/~main/projects/chapter10. Another solution uses a new kind of parameter, which is actually a function itself. A few examples can help explain how a parameter can be a function.

A Parameter Can Be a Function

Here is the interesting idea that will lead us to a solution to the traversal problem:

> *A parameter of a function may be a function itself.*

The idea underlies the fact that some problems cannot be solved by any algorithm. If you want to pursue that startling result you might read Douglas Hofstadter's book *Gödel, Escher, Bach: An Eternal Golden Braid*. But our own use for the idea is more mundane. We merely want to write some simple functions where some of the parameters are other functions.

As a first example, we'll write a function called apply, with three arguments:

- The first argument is actually a *void* function that we'll call f. The function f has one integer reference parameter of its own.
- The second argument is an array of integers called data.
- The third argument is a size_t value called n, indicating the number of components in the array.

You can see these three parameters in the prototype of the apply function. We have highlighted the first parameter:

```
void apply( void f(int&), int data[ ], size_t n);
```

The first parameter of our apply function is no ordinary parameter. We list this first parameter as *void* f(*int*&), which means that the first parameter, f, must be a *void* function with one reference parameter (an integer). The key syntactic feature is that the parameter name, f, is followed by parentheses. Inside these parentheses we give the types of f's own parameters.

When a *parameter is a function*, we list that parameter as shown here:

Parameters That Are Functions

A parameter to a function may be a function itself. Such a parameter is declared by writing the name of the function's return type (or *void*), then the name of the parameter, and finally a pair of parentheses ( ). Inside the parentheses is a list of the parameter types that the function needs.

Example:
```
void apply( void f(int&), ...
```

Within the implementation of the `apply` function, the parameter `f` can be used like any other *void* function with a single integer argument. Our intention is for the `apply` function to take the parameter `f`, and apply it to each of the data elements `data[0]`, `data[1]`, and so on up to `data[n-1]`. Here is the implementation:

```
void apply( void f(int&), int data[ ], size_t n)
// Precondition: data is an array with at least n components.
// Postcondition: The function f has been applied to the first
// n components of the data array.
{
    size_t i;

    for (i = 0; i < n; ++i)          ← f can be used
        f(data[i]);   ←                 just like any
}                                       other function.
```

As an example of how `apply` is used, suppose we have this function:

```
void seven_up(int& i)
// Postcondition: i has had 7 added to its value.
{
    i += 7;
}
```

The `seven_up` function adds 7 to its reference parameter `i`. Now suppose that `numbers` is an array of 10 integers. How can we easily add 7 to each of the 10 integers in the `numbers` array? Here's the solution, using `apply`:

```
apply(seven_up, numbers, 10);
```

This use of the `apply` function executes `seven_up(data[0])`, and then `seven_up(data[1])`, and so on through `seven_up(data[9])`, adding 7 to each of the components of the `numbers` array.

The power of the `apply` function comes from the fact that its first argument can be any *void* function with a single integer reference parameter. For example, suppose we have a function with this prototype:

```
void triple(int& i);
// Postcondition: i has been increased by a factor of 3.
```

Then the call `apply(triple, numbers, 10)` will increase each of the components of `numbers` by a factor of 3.

A Template Version of the Apply Function

At the moment, the `apply` function applies a function to every component in an array of integers. The function becomes more useful if we write it as a template function, where the component type of the array is specified by the template parameter. Here is one way to write the new version of `apply`:

```
template <class Item, class SizeType>
void apply(void f(Item&), Item data[ ], SizeType n)
// Precondition: data is an array with at least n components.
// Postcondition: The function f has been applied to the first
// n components of the data array.
// Note: Item may be any type. SizeType may be any of the
// integer or const integer types.
{
    size_t i;

    for (i = 0; i < n; ++i)
        f(data[i]);
}
```

In this template function, the template parameter `Item` is the component type of the array, and a second template parameter `SizeType` is the data type of the argument that specifies the array size. (See the Pitfall on page 287 for the reason to use a template parameter instead of simply using `size_t`.)

The new `apply` function works fine. For example, suppose we have a function with this prototype:

```
void convert_to_upper(char& c);
// Postcondition: If c was a lowercase letter, then it has been converted to
// the corresponding uppercase letter; otherwise c is unchanged.
```

Now suppose that `name` is an array of 10 characters. We can convert all these characters to uppercase with a single call to the `apply` template function:

```
apply(convert_to_upper, name, 10);
```

This statement instantiates the `apply` function with the `Item` type as a character and the `SizeType` as an integer. The function call then applies `convert_to_upper` to each of the 10 characters of `name`.

More Generality for the Apply Template Function

There's another improvement we can make to the `apply` function. At the moment, the first argument to the `apply` function must have the form:

```
void f(Item&);
```

This strict form precludes many functions that we might want to use. For example, `f` cannot have a value parameter (it must have a *reference* parameter). To obtain more generality with the function `f`, we can add a third template parameter, as shown in the highlights here:

```
template <class Process, class Item, class SizeType>
void apply(Process f, Item data[ ], SizeType n)
// Precondition: data is an array with at least n components.
// Postcondition: The function f has been applied to the first
// n components of the data array.
// Note: Process is the type of a function f that may be called with a
// single Item argument. Item may be any type. SizeType may be any of
// the integer or const integer types.
{
    size_t i;

    for (i = 0; i < n; ++i)
        f(data[i]);
}
```

> **Compatibility with Different C++ Compilers**
>
> *Some C++ compilers don't support the use of a template function with a parameter that is a function itself. Templates still seem to be a sticky point in compatibility between different compilers.*

We now have an extra template parameter, `Process`, which is used as the type of the first argument `f`. Using a template parameter in this way allows the type of the actual first argument to vary. In particular, the first argument to `apply` can be any function that "may be called with a single `Item` argument." Here are some common examples using the `numbers` array of 10 integers:

```
void triple(int& i); // Postcondition: i has been multiplied by three.

// Multiply each number in the array by three:
apply(triple, numbers, 10);
```

As a second example, the function may have a value parameter (instead of a reference parameter):

```
void print(int i); // Postcondition: i has been printed to cout.

// Print all the numbers to cout:
apply(print, numbers, 10);
```

As one last example, consider an array called words containing 10 strings:

```
void print(const string& s); // Postcondition: s has printed to cout.

// Print all the words to cout:
apply(print, words, 10);
```

Template Functions for Tree Traversals

Our apply function applies a specified function to each of the components of an array. We can use the same technique to apply a specified function to every item in a binary tree. For example, this template function will apply a function f to all the items in a binary tree, using a pre-order traversal:

```
template <class Process, class BTNode>
void preorder(Process f, BTNode* node_ptr)
// Precondition: node_ptr is a pointer to a node in a binary tree (or
// node_ptr may be NULL to indicate the empty tree).
// Postcondition: If node_ptr is non-NULL, then the function f has been
// applied to the contents of *node_ptr and all of its descendants, using a
// pre-order traversal.
// Note: BTNode may be a binary_tree_node or a const binary tree node.
// Process is the type of a function f that may be called with a single
// Item argument (using the Item type from the node).
// Library facilities used: cstdlib
{
    if (node_ptr != NULL)
    {
        f( node_ptr->data( ) );
        preorder(f, node_ptr->left( ) );
        preorder(f, node_ptr->right( ) );
    }
}
```

Within the implementation of preorder, we can use f just like any other function that needs a single Item argument. In particular, look at the statement:

```
f( node_ptr->data( ) );
```

This statement passes the data from one node to the function f. We don't even need to know exactly what f does. Perhaps it is simply a function to print the data, or maybe it does a more complicated computation. As the writer of the preorder function, we don't need to worry about those details. We have truly managed to provide just *one* function that is capable of doing *any* kind of processing.

We can add our new `preorder` function to the binary tree toolkit from Section 10.3. We can also add similar `inorder` and `postorder` functions, plus the nice print function that we developed with a backward in-order traversal. All these items are collected together in the header file (Figure 10.10, `bintree.h`) and implementation file (Figure 10.11, `bintree.template`). We also added a function called `tree_size` to compute the number of nodes in a binary tree.

Self-Test Exercises for Section 10.4

15. Look at the tree in Figure 10.5 on page 479. In what order are the letters printed for an in-order traversal? What about a post-order traversal? What about a backward in-order traversal?

16. Suppose we do a traversal of the tree in Figure 10.1 on page 470, printing out the numbers in the order 13, 9, 53, 17, 19, 7, 4, 11, 14. What kind of traversal did we do? In what order are the numbers printed for the other kinds of traversals?

17. Suppose that you have a tree where the left subtree contains 3000 nodes and the right subtree contains 100 nodes. For each kind of traversal, how many nodes are processed before the root node?

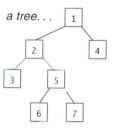

a tree...

18. Consider the tree in the margin. Write the order of the nodes processed in a pre-order, in-order, and post-order traversal. Draw the output that would result from this tree with the tree-printing function from this section.

19. Write a function with the prototype *void* `stars(int i);` . The function prints a line of i stars. How can you easily apply the `stars` function to every node in a binary tree using an in-order traversal?

20. Here is an output from the tree-printing function for a tree of integers:

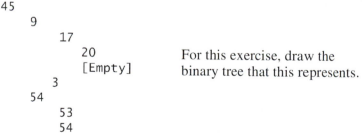

For this exercise, draw the binary tree that this represents.

21. Which of the traversal methods make sense for general trees where there is no limit to the number of children that a node may have?

FIGURE 10.10 Header and Implementation Files for the Binary Tree Node

A Header File

```
// FILE: bintree.h (part of the namespace main_savitch_10)
// PROVIDES: A template class for a node in a binary tree and functions for
// manipulating binary trees. The template parameter is the type of data in each node.
//
// TYPEDEF for the binary_tree_node<Item> template class:
//     Each node of the tree contains a piece of data and pointers to its children. The
//     type of the data (binary_tree_node<Item>::value_type) is the Item type from the template
//     parameter. The type may be any of the C++ built-in types (int, char, etc.), or a class with
//     a default constructor, and an assignment operator.
//
// CONSTRUCTOR for the binary_tree_node<Item> class:
//     binary_tree_node(
//         const Item& init_data = Item( ),
//         binary_tree_node<Item>* init_left = NULL,
//         binary_tree_node<Item>* init_right = NULL
//     )
//         Postcondition: The new node has its data equal to init_data,
//         and its child pointers equal to init_left and init_right.
//
// MEMBER FUNCTIONS for the binary_tree_node<Item> class:
//     const Item& data( ) const          <----- const version
//     and
//     Item& data( )                      <----- non-const version
//         Postcondition: The return value is a reference to the data from this binary_tree_node.
//
//     const binary_tree_node* left( ) const  <----- const version
//     and
//     binary_tree_node* left( )               <----- non-const version
//     and
//     const binary_tree_node* right( ) const <----- const version
//     and
//     binary_tree_node* right( )              <----- non-const version
//         Postcondition: The return value is a pointer to the left or right child (which will be
//         NULL if there is no child).
//
//     void set_data(const Item& new_data)
//         Postcondition: The binary_tree_node now contains the specified new data.
//
//     void set_left(binary_tree_node* new_link)
//     and
//     void set_right(binary-tree_node* new_link)
//         Postcondition: The binary_tree_node now contains the specified new link to a child.
```
(continued)

(FIGURE 10.10 continued)

```
//      bool is_leaf( )
//         Postcondition: The return value is true if the node is a leaf; otherwise the return value
//         is false.
//
//   NONMEMBER FUNCTIONS to maniplulate binary tree nodes:
//      template <class Process, class BTNode>
//      void inorder(Process f, BTNode* node_ptr)
//         Precondition: node_ptr is a pointer to a node in a binary tree (or node_ptr may be NULL
//         to indicate the empty tree).
//         Postcondition: If node_ptr is non-NULL, then the function f has been applied to the
//         contents of *node_ptr and all of its descendants, using an in-order traversal.
//         Note: BTNode may be a binary_tree_node or a const binary tree node.
//         Process is the type of a function f that may be called with a single
//         Item argument (using the Item type from the node).
//
//      template <class Process, class BTNode>
//      void postorder(Process f, BTNode* node_ptr)
//         Same as the in-order function, except with a post-order traversal.
//
//      template <class Process, class BTNode>
//      void preorder(Process f, BTNode* node_ptr)
//         Same as the in-order function, except with a pre-order traversal.
//
//      template <class Item, class SizeType>
//      void print(const binary_tree_node<Item>* node_ptr, SizeType depth)
//         Precondition: node_ptr is a pointer to a node in a binary tree (or node_ptr may be
//         NULL to indicate the empty tree). If the pointer is not NULL, depth is the depth of the
//         node pointed to by node_ptr.
//         Postcondition: A representation of *node_ptr and all its descendants have been written
//         to cout with the << operator. Each node is indented four times its depth.
//
//      template <class Item>
//      void tree_clear(binary_tree_node<Item>*& root_ptr)
//         Precondition: root_ptr is the root pointer of a binary tree (which may be NULL for the
//         empty tree).
//         Postcondition: All nodes at the root or below have been returned to the heap, and
//         root_ptr has been set to NULL.
//
//      template <class Item>
//      binary_tree_node<Item>* tree_copy(const binary_tree_node<Item>* root_ptr)
//         Precondition: root_ptr is the root pointer of a binary tree (which may be NULL for the
//         empty tree).
//         Postcondition: A copy of the binary tree has been made, and the return value is a
//         pointer to the root of this copy.                              (continued)
```

(FIGURE 10.10 continued)

```
//    template <class Item>
//    size_t tree_size(const binary_tree_node<Item>* node_ptr)
//      Precondition: node_ptr is a pointer to a node in a binary tree (or node_ptr may be
//      NULL to indicate the empty tree).
//      Postcondition: The return value is the number of nodes in the tree.

#ifndef BINTREE_H
#define BINTREE_H
#include <cstdlib> // Provides NULL and size_t

namespace main_savitch_10
{
    template <class Item>
    class binary_tree_node
    {
        || See Figure 10.6 on page 481 for the class definition that goes here.
    };

    // NONMEMBER FUNCTIONS for the binary_tree_node<Item>:
    template <class Process, class BTNode>
    void inorder(Process f, BTNode* node_ptr);

    template <class Process, class BTNode>
    void preorder(Process f, BTNode* node_ptr);

    template <class Process, class BTNode>
    void postorder(Process f, BTNode* node_ptr);

    template <class Item, class SizeType>
    void print(const binary_tree_node<Item>* node_ptr, SizeType depth);

    template <class Item>
    void tree_clear(binary_tree_node<Item>*& root_ptr);

    template <class Item>
    binary_tree_node<Item>* tree_copy(const binary_tree_node<Item>* root_ptr);

    template <class Item>
    std::size_t tree_size(const binary_tree_node<Item>* node_ptr);
}

#include "bintree.template"   // Include the implementation.
#endif
```

FIGURE 10.11   Second Version of the Implementation File for the Binary Tree Toolkit

An Implementation File

```
// FILE: bintree.template
// IMPLEMENTS: The binary_tree node class (see bintree.h for documentation).
#include <cassert>      // Provides assert
#include <cstdlib>      // Provides NULL, std::size_t
#include <iomanip>      // Provides std::setw
#include <iostream>     // Provides std::cout

namespace main_savitch_10
{
    template <class Process, class BTNode>
    void inorder(Process f, BTNode* node_ptr)
    // Library facilities used: cstdlib
    {
        if (node_ptr != NULL)
        {
            inorder(f, node_ptr->left( ));
            f( node_ptr->data( ) );
            inorder(f, node_ptr->right( ));
        }
    }

    template <class Process, class BTNode>
    void postorder(Process f, BTNode* node_ptr)
    // Library facilities used: cstdlib
    {
        if (node_ptr != NULL)
        {
            postorder(f, node_ptr->left( ));
            postorder(f, node_ptr->right( ));
            f( node_ptr->data( ) );
        }
    }

    template <class Process, class BTNode>
    void preorder(Process f, BTNode* node_ptr)
    // Library facilities used: cstdlib
    {
        if (node_ptr != NULL)
        {
            f( node_ptr->data( ) );
            preorder(f, node_ptr->left( ));
            preorder(f, node_ptr->right( ));
        }
    }
```

(continued)

(FIGURE 10.11 continued)

```cpp
template <class Item, class SizeType>
void print(const binary_tree_node<Item>* node_ptr, SizeType depth)
// Library facilities used: iomanip, iostream, stdlib
{
    std::cout << std::setw(4*depth) << ""; // Indentation
    if (node_ptr == NULL)
    {   // Fallen off the tree
        std::cout << "[Empty]" << std::endl;
    }
    else if (node_ptr->is_leaf( ))
    {   // A leaf
        std::cout << node_ptr->data( );
        std::cout << " [leaf]" <<std::endl;
    }
    else
    {   // A nonleaf
        std::cout << node_ptr->data( ) << std::endl;
        print(node_ptr->right( ), depth+1);
        print(node_ptr->left( ),  depth+1);
    }
}
```

```cpp
template <class Item>
void tree_clear(binary_tree_node<Item>*& root_ptr)
```
See the implementation on page 482.

```cpp
template <class Item>
binary_tree_node<Item>* tree_copy(const binary_tree_node<Item>* root_ptr)
```
See the implementation on page 483.

```cpp
template <class Item>
std::size_t tree_size(const binary_tree_node<Item>* node_ptr)
// Library facilities used: cstdlib
{
    if (node_ptr == NULL)
        return 0;
    else
        return
        1 + tree_size(node_ptr->left( )) + tree_size(node_ptr->right( ));
}
```

10.5 BINARY SEARCH TREES

Lucy looked very hard between the trees and could just see
in the distance a patch of light that looked like daylight.
"Yes," she said, "I can see the wardrobe door."

C.S. LEWIS
The Lion, the Witch and the Wardrobe

Perhaps you thought that you would never see another bag after Chapter 3 (the bounded bag), Chapter 4 (the bag with a dynamic array), Chapter 5 (the linked-list bag), and Chapter 6 (the bag as a template class). But binary trees offer yet another way to improve our bag class, so we will have one last look at bags (the *last* look, we promise).

The Binary Search Tree Storage Rules

Binary trees offer an improved way of implementing the bag class. The improvement generally performs faster than our previous bags. Or at least *sometimes* the improved approach may be taken. The improved implementation requires that the bag's entries can be compared with the usual comparison operators <, >, ==, and so on. These operators must form a *strict weak ordering,* as described in Figure 6.4 on page 302. Apart from requiring a strict weak ordering, the new bag class has a specification that is identical to our earlier bags. Therefore, a programmer who is using the bag class may switch to the new, improved bag without difficulty.

So, what good do we obtain from the ordering of the elements? We'll take advantage of the order to store the items in the nodes of a binary tree, using a strategy that will make it easy to find items. The strategy is to follow a collection of rules called the **binary search tree storage rules**, defined here:

Binary Search Tree Storage Rules

In a **binary search tree**, the entries of the nodes can be compared with a strict weak ordering. These two rules are followed for every node *n*:

1. The entry in node *n* is never less than an entry in its left subtree (though it may be equal to one of these entries).

2. The entry in node *n* is less than every entry in its right subtree.

For example, suppose we want to store the numbers {3, 9, 17, 20, 45, 53, 53, 54} in a binary search tree. Figure 10.12(a) shows a binary search tree with these numbers. You can check that each node follows the binary search tree storage rules. Binary search trees also can store a collection of strings, or real numbers, or *anything* that can be compared using some sort of less-than comparison.

Can you see an advantage to storing a bag in a binary search tree rather than in an array or a linked list? The previous implementations of the bag class, using

FIGURE 10.12 Using a Binary Search Tree

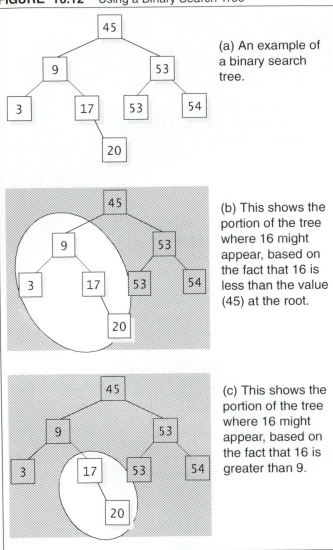

(a) An example of a binary search tree.

(b) This shows the portion of the tree where 16 might appear, based on the fact that 16 is less than the value (45) at the root.

(c) This shows the portion of the tree where 16 might appear, based on the fact that 16 is greater than 9.

an array or a linked list, have a striking inefficiency: When we count the number of occurrences of an entry in the bag, it is necessary to examine *every* entry of the bag. Even if we are interested only in whether or not an entry appears in the bag, we will often look at many entries before we stumble across the one we seek.

With a binary search tree, searching for an entry is often much quicker. For example, suppose we're looking for the number 16 in the tree of Figure 10.12(a). We'll start at the root and compare 16 to the root's number. Since 16 is less than the root's number (45), we immediately know that 16 can appear only in the left subtree—if it appears at all. In Figure 10.12(b), we show the area where 16 might appear, based on knowing that 16 is less than the value at the root. Next we'll compare 16 with the root of the left subtree. Since 16 is greater than 9, this eliminates another portion of the tree, as shown in 10.12(c).

The number 16 is smaller than the next point on the tree (17), so we should continue to the left . . . but we've run out of tree. At this point, we can stop and conclude that 16 is nowhere in the binary search tree even though we only looked at the three numbers 45, 9, and 17. In fact, the most we'll ever have to look at is the depth of the tree plus one—four entries in this case.

This efficiency is the motivation for representing bags with a binary search tree. In the remainder of this section, we'll use binary search trees to implement the bag class, as specified in the header file of Figure 10.13. This is the same specification we have used before, but we have added a restriction on the item type, requiring the correct kind of less-than operator.

FIGURE 10.13   Header File for Our Sixth Bag Class

A Header File

```
// FILE: bag6.h (part of the namespace main_savitch_10)
// TEMPLATE CLASS PROVIDED: bag<Item> (a container template class for a collection of items)
//
// TYPEDEFS for the bag<Item> class:
//   bag<Item>::value_type
//     bag<Item>::value_type is the data type of the items in the bag. It may be any of the
//     C++ built-in types (int, char, etc.), or a class with a default constructor, a copy
//     constructor, an assignment operator, and a less-than operator forming a strict
//     weak ordering.
//
//   bag<Item>::size_type
//     bag<Item>::size_type is the data type of any variable that keeps track of how many
//     items are in a bag.
//
// CONSTRUCTOR for the bag<Item> class:
//   bag( )
//     Postcondition: The bag is empty.
//
// MODIFICATION MEMBER FUNCTIONS for the bag<Item> class:
//   size_type erase(const Item& target)
//     Postcondition: All copies of target have been removed from the bag. The return value
//     is the number of copies removed (which could be zero).
//
//   bool erase_one(const Item& target)
//     Postcondition: If target was in the bag, then one copy of target has been removed from
//     the bag; otherwise the bag is unchanged. A true return value indicates that one copy
//     was removed; false indicates that nothing was removed.
//
//   void insert(const Item& entry)
//     Postcondition: A new copy of entry has been inserted into the bag.
//
//   void operator +=(const bag& addend)
//     Postcondition: Each item in addend has been added to this bag.
//
// CONSTANT MEMBER FUNCTIONS for the bag<Item> class:
//   size_type size( ) const
//     Postcondition: Return value is the total number of items in the bag.
//
//   size_type count(const Item& target) const
//     Postcondition: Return value is number of times target is in the bag.
//
// NONMEMBER FUNCTIONS for the bag class:
//   bag operator +(const bag& b1, const bag& b2)
//     Postcondition: The bag returned is the union of b1 and b2.
```

(continued)

(FIGURE 10.13 continued)

```
// VALUE SEMANTICS for the bag class:
//     Assignments and the copy constructor may be used with bag objects.
// DYNAMIC MEMORY USAGE by the bag:
//     If there is insufficient dynamic memory, then the following functions throw bad_alloc:
//     The constructors, insert, operator +=, operator +, and the assignment operator.

#ifndef BAG6_H
#define BAG6_H
#include <cstdlib>      // Provides NULL and size_t
#include "bintree.h"    // Provides binary_tree_node and related functions

namespace main_savitch_10
{
    template <class Item>
    class bag
    {
    public:
        // TYPEDEFS
        typedef std::size_t size_type;
        typedef Item value_type;
        // CONSTRUCTORS and DESTRUCTOR
        bag( );
        bag(const bag& source);
        ~bag( );
        // MODIFICATION functions
        size_type erase(const Item& target);
        bool erase_one(const Item& target);
        void insert(const Item& entry);
        void operator +=(const bag& addend);
        void operator =(const bag& source);
        // CONSTANT functions
        size_type size( ) const;
        size_type count(const Item& target) const;
    private:
        binary_tree_node<Item> *root_ptr;  // Root pointer of binary search tree
        | Other private members may be added if you need them.
    };

    // NONMEMBER functions for the bag<Item> template class
    template <class Item>
    bag<Item> operator +(const bag<Item>& b1, const bag<Item>& b2);
}

#include "bag6.template" // Include the implementation.
#endif
```

Our Sixth Bag—Class Definition

The second part of Figure 10.13 on page 516 shows the class definition for our sixth and final bag. In our definition, the bag's only member variable is a root pointer for the binary search tree. This tree's nodes contain the entries of the bag. If the bag is empty, then the root pointer will be NULL. We could add other member variables—for example, a count of the number of nodes would be convenient. But limiting ourselves to only the root pointer will allow us to clearly focus on the necessary tree algorithms. So, the bag definition in Figure 10.13 looks like this:

```
template <class Item>
class bag
{
public:
    || Prototypes of public member functions go here.
private:
    binary_tree_node<Item> *root_ptr; // Root pointer
};
```

Here's a formal statement of the invariant of our new bag:

Invariant for the Sixth Bag ADT

1. The items in the bag are stored in a binary search tree.
2. The root pointer of the binary search tree is stored in the member variable `root_ptr` (which may be NULL for an empty tree).

Our Sixth Bag—Implementation of Some Simple Functions

Now we're ready to dive into the implementations of the bag functions. For the most part, we will provide only pseudocode that you can implement yourself.

Constructors. The default constructor sets the root pointer to NULL. The copy constructor needs to make a new copy of the source's tree, and point `root_ptr` to the root of this copy. Use the `tree_copy` function to do the copying.

The destructor. The destructor needs to return all nodes to the heap. Again, you should make use of an appropriate function from `bintree.h`.

Overloading the assignment operator. Since our bag uses dynamic memory, we must overload the assignment operator. The assignment operator works like the copy constructor with two preliminary steps: (1) First check for the possibility of a self-assignment by comparing (`this == &source`). If these two pointers are equal, then we have a self-assignment such as b = b. In this case, the function returns with no further work. (2) If there is no self-assignment, then before we copy the source tree we must release all memory used by the nodes of the current tree. Use tree_clear to release memory.

The size member function. The size member function simply returns the answer from tree_size(root_ptr) using the tree_size function from bintree.h.

Counting the Occurrences of an Item in a Binary Search Tree

The count member function counts the number of occurrences of an item called target. We'll keep track of these occurrences in a local variable called many (which is initialized to zero). The important point to keep in mind is that we will not look at every entry in the binary search tree. Instead, we'll have a local pointer called cursor, which is initialized to the root pointer. We'll use a loop to move the cursor down through the tree, always moving along the path where the target might occur. At each point in the tree we have four possibilities:

1. The cursor can become NULL, indicating that we've moved off the bottom of the tree. In this case, we have counted all the occurrences of the target. So the loop can end, and we should return the current value of many.

2. The target might be smaller than the data at the cursor node. In this case, the target can appear only in the left subtree. For example, suppose we are counting occurrences of the string Denver in a binary search tree of strings (using the lexicographic order on our string class). The cursor's data might be Pittsburgh, and the situation looks like this:

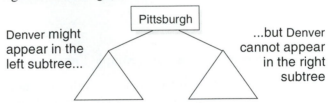

In this situation, we'll continue our search by assigning:

```
cursor = cursor->left( );
```

3. The data at the cursor node might be smaller than the target. This is similar to the previous case, except that we must continue our search to the right instead of the left, using the assignment:

```
cursor = cursor->right( );
```

4. The target might equal the data at the cursor node. In this case we add one to many and continue the search to the left (since items to the left are less than *or equal to* the item at the cursor node).

The implementation of these steps is straightforward using a while-loop.

Inserting a New Item into a Binary Search Tree

The `insert` member function adds a new item to a binary search tree, using this prototype:

```
void insert(const Item& entry);
```

We suggest that you handle one special case first: When the first entry is inserted, simply call `root_ptr = new binary_tree_node<Item>(entry)`.

The other case is when there are already some other entries in the tree. In this case, we'll set a `cursor` equal to the current root pointer, then we pretend to search for the exact entry that we are trying to insert. But the search runs a bit differently than a real search. The main difference is that we stop the search just before the cursor falls off the bottom of the tree, and we insert the new entry at the spot where the cursor was about to fall off. For example, consider the task of inserting 16 into this binary search tree:

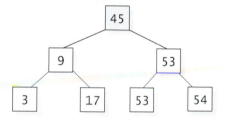

The cursor starts at the shaded node (with 45). If we were searching for the 16, we would continue the search to the left. So, we move our cursor to the left, resulting in the cursor pointing to the node that contains 9:

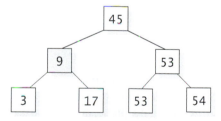

Again pretend that you are searching for the 16 instead of inserting it, so that now the cursor moves right to the node containing 17:

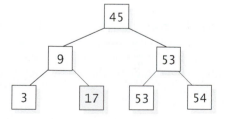

At this point, an ordinary search would continue to the left, stepping off the bottom of the tree. But instead, we insert the new entry at this position, resulting in this tree:

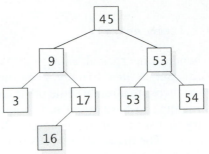

To implement the scheme, we suggest a boolean variable called done, which is initialized to false. We then have a loop that continues until done becomes true. Each iteration of the loop handles these two cases:

1. Suppose the new entry is less than or equal to the data at the cursor node. In this case, check the left pointer. If the pointer to the left child is NULL, then create a new node containing the entry, make this node the left child, and set done to true. On the other hand, if the left pointer is not NULL, then move the cursor to the left and continue the search with the single assignment statement:

    ```
    cursor = cursor->left( );
    ```

2. Suppose the new entry is greater than the data at the cursor node. In this case, follow the same procedure as Case 1, but use the right pointer instead of the left pointer.

After the loop ends, the function returns.

Removing an Item from a Binary Search Tree

The erase member function removes all copies of a specified item from the tree, and the erase_one member function allows us to remove a specified item from a binary search tree. Their implementations are similar, so we will focus on just erase_one, with this prototype:

```
bool erase_one(const Item& target);
```

It is possible to implement the erase_one function on its own, but the direct solution deals with many special cases and must also maintain a precursor similar to the precursor for removing a node from a linked list. Because of these complications, we prefer an indirect method that uses two auxiliary functions with the following specifications.

```
template <class Item>
bool bst_remove(
    binary_tree_node<Item>*& root_ptr,
    const Item& target
);
// Precondition: root_ptr is a root pointer of a binary search tree (or may
// be NULL for the empty tree).
// Postcondition: If target was in the tree, then one copy of target has been
// removed, root_ptr now points to the root of the new (smaller) binary
// search tree, and the function returns true. Otherwise, if target was not
// in the tree, then the tree is unchanged, and the function returns false.

template <class Item>
void bst_remove_max(
    binary_tree_node<Item>*& root_ptr,
    Item& removed
);
// Precondition: root_ptr is a root pointer of a non-empty binary search
// tree.
// Postcondition: The largest item in the binary search tree has been
// removed, and root_ptr now points to the root of the new (smaller) binary
// search tree. The reference parameter, removed, has been set to a copy
// of the removed item.
```

You will need to implement these two functions at the top of your implementation file, `bag6.template`. The only purpose of these functions is for *your* use, making the bag's removal function easier. Since you don't intend for other programmers to use these functions, there is no need to mention them in your header file. Instead, you should list their precondition/postcondition contracts with their implementations.

With these two functions in place, the bag's `erase_one` function is simply implemented with a function call `bst_remove(root_ptr, target)`. Now we can turn to our two auxiliary functions.

The bst_remove function. The `bst_remove` function has a recursive implementation to remove the `target`. Here are the cases:

1. The binary search tree could be empty, indicated by a root pointer that is NULL. If there's nothing in the tree, then there's nothing to remove, and the function returns with no work.

2. The tree could be non-empty, with the target *less than* the root entry. In this case, make a recursive call to delete the target from the left subtree, like this:

   ```
   bst_remove(root_ptr->left( ), target);
   ```

   This recursive call works correctly because `root_ptr->left( )` is the root pointer for a smaller binary search tree (that is, the left subtree).

3. The tree could be non-empty, with the root entry *less than* the target. Again, make a recursive call, using the pointer to the right subtree.

4. The tree could be non-empty, with the target *equal to* the root entry. We have found a copy of the target and must somehow remove it from the tree. But be careful! We can't simply delete this node because it may have children, and we don't want those children to be disconnected from the rest of the tree. To avoid orphaning those children, we'll deal with Case 4 in two separate cases:

Case 4a: The root node has no left child.

Case 4b: The root node does have a left child.

The pseudocode for these two cases is described below.

Case 4a. In this case of the `bst_remove` function, the root data is equal to the target, and the root node has no left child. For example, we might be deleting Pittsburgh from this subtree:

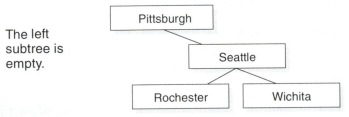

The left
subtree is
empty.

In this case, we can delete the root entry and make the right child (Seattle) the new root node. To actually implement this root shift requires three steps:

```
oldroot_ptr = root_ptr;
root_ptr = root_ptr->right( );
delete oldroot_ptr;
```

The variable `oldroot_ptr` is a local variable that we make point to the old root (the root that we are about to get rid of). We then move the actual root pointer down to its right child. And finally we execute *delete* `old_root_ptr`, which returns the old root node to the heap.

Does this scheme work correctly even if there is no right child? Yes, it does. With no right child, the statement `root_ptr = root_ptr->right( )` will set the root pointer to NULL, indicating that there are no nodes left in this particular tree.

Case 4b. In this case, the root node does have a left child, so we can't simply move the root pointer to the right (as we did in case 4a). We could check whether there is a right child, and if not, we could certainly move the root pointer left—but we have a more general plan in mind. The plan is to find some entry in the non-empty left subtree, and move this entry up to the root. But which entry? Here's an example to help you figure out which entry should be taken from the left subtree to replace the root entry. In this example, we are deleting Pittsburgh from this subtree:

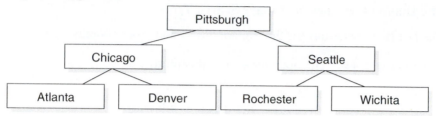

The plan is to replace the root with one of the three entries from the left subtree. Which of these entries can safely be moved to the root? Not Atlanta, because the remaining entries in the left subtree (Chicago and Denver) would be larger than the new root (Atlanta). Not Chicago, because that would leave the larger string Denver in the left subtree. What about Denver? Yes, that will do, since none of the entries that remain in the left subtree are larger than Denver. Here is the resulting subtree after removing Denver from the left subtree and placing it at the root:

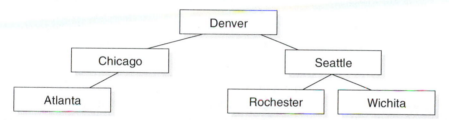

The string Denver is the correct choice because it is the *largest entry in the left subtree.* Any other choice from the left subtree will violate the binary search tree storage rules. So, how do we delete the largest item from the left subtree, and place this same item at the root? We can use our own `bst_remove_max` function with the call:

```
bst_remove_max(root_ptr->left( ), root_ptr->data( ));
```

Now you know why we proposed the `bst_remove_max` function. Used in this way, it removes the largest item from the tree with `root_ptr->left( )` as its root pointer, and it places this largest item in the root's data field.

The bst_remove_max function. The `bst_remove_max` function remains to be implemented. We'll leave that as an exercise in recursive thinking, with just two cases: (1) The base case occurs if there is no right child. In this case, the largest item is at the root, so you can set `removed` equal to the data from the root, move the root pointer down to the left, and delete the root node. (2) On the other hand, if there is a right child, then there are larger items in the right subtree. In this case, make a recursive call to delete the largest item from the right subtree.

The Union Operators for Binary Search Trees

The last two operations for the bag are the += and + operators.

The operator +=. The operator += has this prototype:

```
template <class Item>
void operator +=(const bag<Item>& addend);
```

This is another example of a function that will benefit from an auxiliary function. The auxiliary function that we propose is actually another bag member function, with this specification:

```
template <class Item>
void bag::insert_all
(const binary_tree_node<Item>* addroot_ptr);
// Precondition: addroot_ptr is the root pointer of a binary search tree that
// is separate from the binary search tree of the bag that activated this
// method.
// Postcondition: All the items from the addroot_ptr's binary search tree
// have been added to the binary search tree of the bag that activated this
// method.
```

Our intention is that this method is a new *private* member function of the bag. Since the function is private, the specification can use private information, such as the fact that the bag is implemented with a binary search tree. As a private method, the prototype for `insert_all` must be placed with other private members in the bag's definition, as shown here:

```
template <class Item>
class bag
{
public:
    ...
private:
    binary_tree_node<Item>* root_ptr; // Root pointer
    void insert_all
        (const binary_tree_node<Item>* addroot_ptr);
};
```

A private member function is sometimes called a **helper function** because it will help the other member functions do their work. In the case of the bag, the operator += can be implemented by using `insert_all`, as shown next:

```
template <class Item>
void bag<Item>::operator +=(const bag& addend)
{
    binary_tree_node<Item> *addroot_ptr;

    if (this == &addend)
    {
        addroot_ptr = tree_copy(addend.root_ptr);
        insert_all(addroot_ptr);
        tree_clear(addroot_ptr);
    }
    else
        insert_all(addend.root_ptr);
}
```

Notice that we do have a bit of complication when the addend is the same bag as the bag that activated the operator += (as in the statement b += b). In this case we must make a second copy of the addend's tree and call insert_all, using the second copy rather than using the addend's tree directly. The reason for this complication is the restriction of insert_all's precondition, which requires that the tree that's being added "is separate from the binary search tree of the bag that activated this method."

Now we can look at the implementation of the private member function insert_all. The approach is to traverse the tree that we are adding, inserting a copy of each traversed item into the bag that activated the operator. For example, if we use a pre-order traversal, then the pseudocode for insert_all is:

```
if (addroot_ptr != NULL)
{
    insert(addroot_ptr->data( ));
    Make a recursive call to insert all of addroot_ptr's left subtree.
    Make a recursive call to insert all of addroot_ptr's right subtree.
}
```

Our pseudocode explicitly uses a pre-order traversal of the nodes. If you wish, you may use a post-order traversal instead. But avoid an in-order traversal. The problem with an in-order traversal is that the nodes of the addend tree will be processed in order from smallest to largest. Therefore, these nodes will be inserted into the other bag from smallest to largest. This is a bad way to build a binary search tree. The resulting tree ends up with a single long narrow path, with only right children. Sometimes such long narrow trees are hard to avoid. But do avoid such trees when you can, because searching and other algorithms are inefficient when the trees lose their branching structure. In the next chapter we will examine some specific ways to ensure that long narrow trees are not created.

The operator +. This is an ordinary function (not a member function) with the prototype:

```
bag<Item> operator +(const bag& b1, const bag& b2);
```

The function is easy to implement by using the operator +=. Look back at the operator + from a previous bag implementation if you are uncertain.

Time Analysis and an Iterator

With the descriptions that we've given, you can put together the implementation file for the new bag. We'll carry out a time analysis of the operations after we've seen a few more trees (see Section 11.3).

   You might also want to add an iterator to the new bag, to allow a programmer to step through the items of the bag one at a time. One method for implementing an iterator is described in Programming Project 7 on page 530.

Self-Test Exercises for Section 10.5

22. Why is it bad to insert nodes from smallest to largest in a binary search tree?

23. Build a binary search tree with the following words (inserted in this order): *blueberry, peach, apricot, pear, cherry, mango,* and *papaya.*

24. How many comparisons are needed to search for these words in the search tree you created in the previous exercise: *pear, orange, blueberry.*

25. Add a new member function to the bag. The function should print all items in the bag from smallest to largest. (Hint: Use a traversal.)

26. Write a bag friend function called `join` with this prototype:
    ```
    template <class Item>
    void join(
        bag<Item>& top,
        bag<Item>& left,
        bag<Item>& right
    );
    ```
    The precondition of the function requires that `top` has just one item, that everything in `left` is less than or equal to the item in `top`, and that everything in `right` is greater than the item in `top`. The postcondition requires that `top` now contains everything from `left` and `right`, and that `left` and `right` are now both empty. Your function should take constant time.

CHAPTER SUMMARY

- *Trees* are a nonlinear structure, with many applications, including organizing information (such as taxonomy trees) and implementing an efficient version of the bag class (using binary search trees).

- Trees may be implemented with either fixed-sized arrays or dynamic data structures. An array is particularly appropriate for *complete binary trees* because of the conditions that require the nodes of a complete tree to occur in specific locations.

- A *tree traversal* consists of processing a tree by applying some action to each node. Three common traversal methods—pre-order traversal, in-order traversal, and post-order traversal—differ only in the order in which the nodes are processed. A backward in-order traversal is a quick and convenient way to print the data from a tree in a readable format.

- A parameter of a function may be a function itself.

- Using parameters that are functions, we can write extremely flexible tree traversals, where the action applied to each node is determined by a parameter to the traversal function.

- Binary search trees are one common application of trees, which permit us to store a bag of ordered items in a manner where adding, deleting, and searching for entries is potentially much faster than with a linear structure.

- Operations on trees are good candidates for recursive thinking. This is because many tree operations include a step to process one or more subtrees, and this step is "a smaller version of the same problem."

Solutions to Self-Test Exercises

1. Here is one possible solution:

2. Leaves: 3, 4, 6, and 7. Siblings: 2 and 4; 3 and 5; 6 and 7. Depth: 3.

3. To make a full tree, add a left child and right child to node 3, and a left and right child to the node 4 (call them 10 and 11); add a left and right child to each of the new nodes 10 and 11. To make a complete tree, add a left and right child to node 3.

4. The depth of a tree with only a root is zero. The depth of an empty tree is often called −1.

5 and 6. Here is a solution. The depth of this tree is 3. The node containing me has a depth of 2. My ancestors are circled, and my mother's descendants have a big square around them.

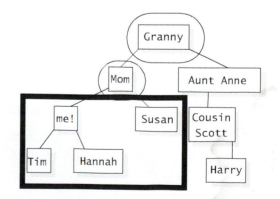

7. This solution is both full and complete. "Yes" answers move left, and "no" answers move right.

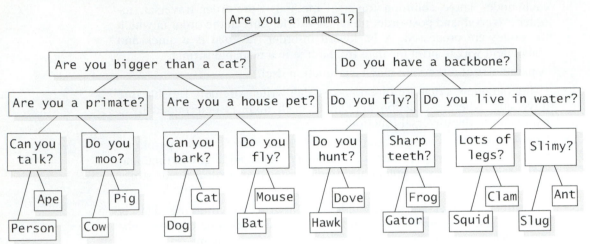

8. One problem is determining which children of a node actually exist.

9. We use the formulas from page 477. The parent is stored at index 2499, which is (4999–1)/2. The left child is stored at index 9999, which is (2*4999)+1. If there were a right child, it would be stored at index 10,000 (which is (2*4999)+2). But since the last index is 9999, there is no right child.

10. A separate single pointer is used to point to the root node.

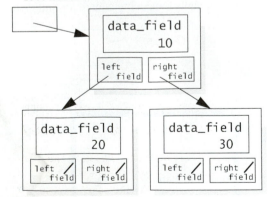

11. ...
```
private:
    Item data_field;
    tree_node *parent_ptr;
    tree_node *links[4];
    ...
```

12. The base case is when the tree is empty (the root pointer is NULL).

13. Here is one solution:
```
template <class Item>
int kids(binary_tree_node<Item> node)
// Postcondition: The return value is
//   the number of children of the node.
// Libraries used: cstdlib
{
    int answer = 0;
    if (node->left( )!= NULL) ++answer;
    if (node->right( )!= NULL) ++answer;
    return answer;
}
```

14. The node counting function is `tree_size` from the bottom of Figure 10.11 on page 512. The depth function has a similar recursive implementation.

15. The in-order traversal prints O, L, R, A, G, T. The post-order traversal prints O, R, L, T, G, A. The backward in-order traversal prints T, G, A, R, L, O.

16. This would be a post-order traversal. For in-order: 9, 13, 17, 53, 14, 19, 4, 7, 11. For pre-order: 14, 17, 9, 13, 53, 11, 4, 19, 7.

17. Pre-order: 1, 2, 3, 5, 6, 7, 4. In-order: 3, 2, 6, 5, 7, 1, 4. Post-order: 3, 6, 7, 5, 2, 4, 1. The output from the print function is

```
1
    2
        3 [leaf]
        5
            6 [leaf]
            7 [leaf]
    4
```

18. Pre-order: zero. Post-order: 3100. In-order: 3000.

19.
```
void stars (int i)
{
    int j;
    for (j = 0; j < i; ++j);
        cout << '*';
    cout << endl;
}
```
To apply the function to every node in a tree: `in_order(stars, r)`, where `r` is the root pointer.

20.

```
        54
    54
        53
  45
        3
    9
        17
            20
```

21. Pre-order would process a node before any of its children are processed. Post-order would process a node after all of its children are pro-

cessed. In-order doesn't really make sense for a general tree.

22. The nodes will be inserted into the bag from smallest to largest, resulting in a tree with a single path with only right children.

23.

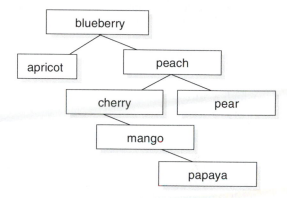

24. pear: 3. orange: 5. blueberry: 1.

25. The body of your function should call
```
inorder(print_item, root_ptr);
```
where `print_item` is a function that you write to print one item.

26. The function needs four statements, as shown here:
```
top.root_ptr->set_left
        (left.root_ptr);
left.root_ptr = NULL;
top.root_ptr->set_right
        (right.root_ptr);
right.root_ptr = NULL;
```

PROGRAMMING PROJECTS

For more in-depth projects, please see www.cs.colorado.edu/~main/projects/

1 This project deals with a simple kind of *expression tree*, where there are two kinds of nodes:

(a) Leaf nodes, which contain a real number as their entry;

(b) Nonleaf nodes, which contain either the character '+' or the character '*' as their entry, and have exactly two children.

For this project, implement a class for expression trees, including operations for building expression trees. Also include a recursive function to "evaluate" a non-empty expression tree using these rules:

(a) If the tree has only one node (which must be a leaf), then the evaluation of the tree returns the real number that is the node's entry;

(b) If the tree has more than one node, and the root contains '+', then first evaluate the left subtree, then evaluate the right subtree, and add the results. If the root contains '*', then evaluate the two subtrees and multiply the results.

For example, consider the small expression tree shown to the right. The left subtree evaluates to 3+7, which is 10. The right subtree evaluates to 14. So the entire tree evaluates to 10*14, which is 140.

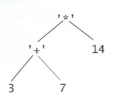

2 Design and implement a class for binary trees, following the specification of Figure 10.14 on page 531. Your design should use the binary tree node class from this chapter. If you wish, you may also add other member functions, such as a function to remove a node. However, the collection of functions in Figure 10.14 is sufficient for many applications, such as writing a version of the animal guessing program from Section 10.3.

3 Specify, design, and implement a class for *complete* binary trees using the array representation from Section 10.2. You should have only one member function that adds a new node (since there is only one place where a node may be added), and one member function that removes the last node of the tree.

4 Design and implement a class for binary trees, following the specification of Figure 10.14 on page 531. Your design should use a dynamic array to hold the data from the nodes in the same way that a complete binary tree is usually represented. However, these binary trees do *not* need to be complete. Instead, you should have a second private member variable that is a dynamic array of boolean values called is_present. The is_present array indicates which nodes actually exist in the tree. For example, if the tree has a root node, then location is_present[0] is true. If the root has a left child, then is_present[1] is true. If the root has a right child, then is_present[2] is true.

5 Revise the animal guessing program from Figure 10.9 on page 492 so that the initial knowledge tree is obtained by reading information from a file. Also, when the program ends, the knowledge tree at that point is written to the same file. You must carefully specify the format of the data in this file. The format should make it easy to do two things: (a) read the file and set the initial tree, and (b) write the knowledge tree to the file, using some kind of traversal.

6 This project requires that you know how to determine the actual time taken for a function to execute. Write a test program for the bag class from Section 10.5. The program should allow the user to specify an integer, n. The program then adds n randomly selected integers to a bag and then counts the number of occurrences of each integer between 1 and n, keeping track of the amount of time needed for the entirety of these operations. Also use the test program to test one of the earlier bag implementations. Graph the results of your tests on a plot that has elapsed time on the y-axis and n on the x-axis. (In the next chapter, we will do an analysis to explain these times.)

7 One of our previous bags had an *iterator* that allows a programmer to step through the items of a bag one at a time (see bag5.h from Figure 6.8 on page 336). For this project, add an iterator to the bag from Section 10.5. The implementation of the iterator uses two private member variables called s and i. The member variable s is a dynamic array of pointers to binary tree nodes. Each of the array elements points to one of the nodes in the bag's binary tree. The current item of the iterator is always in the node that s[i] points to.

The bag's start function creates the initial array, which will be given to the iterator. For an empty tree, this is just an empty array. For a non-empty tree, do an in-order traversal of the tree's nodes, putting pointers to each node into the array.

Adding or removing elements from the bag should invalidate all of its iterators.

FIGURE 10.14 Specification of a Binary Tree Class for Programming Project 2 on page 530

Documentation for a Header File

```
// FILE: bt_class.h
// TEMPLATE CLASS PROVIDED: binary_tree<Item> (a binary tree where each node has an item)
//     The template parameter, Item, is the data type of the items in the tree's nodes.
//     It may be any of the C++ built-in types (int, char, etc.), or a class with a default
//     constructor, a copy constructor, and an assignment operator.
//
// NOTE: Each non-empty tree always has a current node.  The location of the current node is
// controlled by three member functions: shift_up, shift_to_root, shift_left, and shift_right.
//
// CONSTRUCTOR for the binary_tree<Item> template class:
//     binary_tree( )
//         Postcondition: The binary tree has been initialized as an empty tree (with no nodes).
//
// MODIFICATION MEMBER FUNCTIONS for the binary_tree<Item> template class:
//     void create_first_node(const Item& entry)
//         Precondition: size( ) is zero.
//         Postcondition: The tree now has one node (a root node), containing the specified entry.
//         This new root node is the current node.
//
//     void shift_to_root( )
//         Precondition: size( ) > 0.
//         Postcondition: The current node is now the root of the tree.
//
//     void shift_up( )
//         Precondition: has_parent( ) returns true.
//         Postcondition: The current node has been shifted up to the parent of the old current
//         node.
//
//     void shift_left( )
//         Precondition: has_left_child( ) returns true.
//         Postcondition: The current node has been shifted down to the left child of the
//         original current node.
//
//     void shift_right( )
//         Precondition: has_right_child( ) returns true.
//         Postcondition: The current node has been shifted down to the right child of the
//         original current node.
//
```

(continued)

(FIGURE 10.14 continued)

```
//      void change(const Item& new_entry)
//        Precondition: size( ) > 0.
//        Postcondition: The data at the current node has been changed to the new entry.
//
//      void add_left(const Item& entry)
//        Precondition: size( ) > 0, and has_left_child( ) returns false.
//        Postcondition: A left child has been added to the current node, with the given entry.
//
//      void add_right(const Item& entry)
//        Precondition: size( ) > 0, and has_right_child( ) returns false.
//        Postcondition: A right child has been added to the current node, with the given entry.
//
// CONSTANT MEMBER FUNCTIONS for the binary_tree<Item> template class:
//      size_t size( ) const
//        Postcondition: The return value is the number of nodes in the tree.
//
//      Item retrieve( ) const
//        Precondition: size( ) > 0.
//        Postcondition: The return value is the data from the current node.
//
//      bool has_parent( ) const
//        Postcondition: Returns true if size( ) > 0, and the current node has a parent.
//
//      bool has_left_child( ) const
//        Postcondition: Returns true if size( ) > 0, and the current node has a left child.
//
//      bool has_right_child( ) const
//        Postcondition: Returns true if size( ) > 0, and the current node has a right child.
//
// VALUE SEMANTICS for the binary_tree<Item> template class:
//      Assignments and the copy constructor may be used with binary_tree objects.
//
// DYNAMIC MEMORY USAGE by the binary_tree<Item> template class:
//      If there is insufficient dynamic memory, then the following functions throw bad_alloc:
//      create_first_node, add_left, add_right, the copy constructor, and the
//      assignment operator.
```

www.cs.colorado.edu/~main/chapter10/bt_class.h   **WWW**

8 Write a function that takes a binary search tree as input and produces a linked list of the entries, with the entries sorted (smallest entries at the front of the list and largest entries at the back). Hint: use in-order traversal.

9 Binary search trees have their best performance when they are *balanced*, which means that at each node, *n*, the size of the left subtree of *n* is within one of the size of the right subtree of *n*. Write a function that takes a sorted linked list of entries and produces a balanced binary search tree. If useful, you may add extra parameters to the procedure, such as the total number of entries in the list. Hint: First build the left subtree of the root, then the right subtree of the root, then put the pieces together with the `join` function from Self-Test Exercise 26 on page 526. Think recursively!

11 Redo Programming Project 17 in Chapter 3 using a binary search tree. Use the employee's ID number as the search key. A template function should print out various statistics on the tree by taking an appropriate function as a parameter.

12 Create a class to store the contact phone numbers/email of your friends and relatives. Use the new class in a program that maintains a list of contacts.

13 Design and implement a concordance program, which stores a library of book records. Create a book class with name, ISBN, author, and publication date. Use a binary search tree to store the records, where the author name is the search key. Revise the binary search tree to be able to store and retrieve duplicate search keys.

11

Tree Projects

*The great, dark trees of the Big Woods stood all around
the house, and beyond them were other trees and beyond
them were more trees.*

LAURA INGALLS WILDER
The Little House in the Big Woods

LEARNING OBJECTIVES

When you complete Chapter 11, you will be able to...

- list the rules for a heap or B-tree and determine whether a tree satisfies these rules.
- insert a new element into a heap or remove the largest element by following the insertion algorithm (with reheapification upward) and the removal algorithm (with reheapification downward).
- do a simulation by hand of the algorithms for searching, inserting, and removing an element from a B-tree.
- use the heap data structure to implement a priority queue.
- use the B-tree data structure to implement a set class.
- recognize which operations have logarithmic worst-case performance on balanced trees.

CHAPTER CONTENTS

Tree Projects

$\mathbf{T}$his chapter describes two programming projects involving trees. The projects are improvements of classes that we've seen before: the priority queue class (Section 8.4) and the set class (which is like a bag, but does not allow more than one copy of an item). Both projects take advantage of *balanced* trees, in which the different subtrees below a node are guaranteed to have nearly the same height. We also analyze the time performance of tree algorithms, concentrating on a connection between trees and logarithms, and explaining the advantages obtained from balanced trees.

11.1 HEAPS

The Heap Storage Rules

In some ways, a **heap** is like a binary search tree: It is a binary tree where a less-than operator forms a *strict weak ordering* that can be used to compare the nodes' entries. (For a reminder of the rules of a strict weak ordering, see Figure 6.4 on page 302.) But the arrangement of the elements in a heap follows some new rules that are different from a binary search tree:

Heap Storage Rules

A **heap** is a binary tree where the entries of the nodes can be compared with the less-than operator of a strict weak ordering. In addition, these two rules are followed:

1. The entry contained by a node is never less than the entries of the node's children.

2. The tree is a complete binary tree, so that every level except the deepest must contain as many nodes as possible; and at the deepest level, all the nodes are as far left as possible (see "Complete Binary Trees" on page 473).

As an example, suppose that entries are integers. The top of the next page shows three trees with six entries. Only one is a heap—which one?

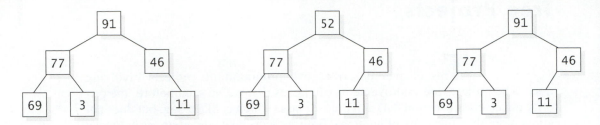

The tree on the left is not a heap because it is not complete—a complete tree must have the nodes on the bottom level as far left as possible. The middle tree is not a heap because one of the nodes (containing 52) has a value that is smaller than its child (which contains 77). The tree on the right *is* a heap.

A heap could be implemented with the binary tree nodes from Chapter 10. But wait! A heap is a *complete* binary tree, and a complete binary tree is implemented more easily with an array than with the node toolkit (see "Array Representation of Complete Binary Trees" on page 475). If we know the maximum size of a heap in advance, then the array implementation can use a fixed-sized array. If we are uncertain about the heap's maximum size, then the array implementation can use a dynamic array that grows and shrinks as needed.

implement heaps with a fixed array or with a dynamic array

In Self-Test Exercise 2, you'll be asked to write definitions that would support each of these implementations. The rest of this section will show how heaps can be used to implement an efficient priority queue—and we won't worry much about which heap implementation we are using.

The Priority Queue ADT with Heaps

Priority queues were introduced in Section 8.4. A priority queue behaves much like an ordinary queue: Entries are placed in the queue and later taken out. But unlike an ordinary queue, each entry in a priority queue can be compared with the other entries using a less-than operator. When entries leave a priority queue, the highest priority entries always leave first. We have seen one suggested implementation of a priority queue in Section 8.4. Now we'll give an alternative implementation that uses a heap.

an alternative way to implement priority queues

In the heap implementation of a priority queue, each node of the heap contains one entry, which can be compared to each of the other entries by the less-than operator. The tree is maintained so that it follows the heap storage rules using the entries' priorities to compare nodes. Therefore:

1. The entry contained by a node is never less than the entries of the node's children.

2. The tree is a complete binary tree.

We'll focus on two priority queue operations: adding a new entry, and removing the entry with the highest priority. In both operations, we must ensure that the structure remains a heap when the operation concludes. Also, both operations can be described without worrying about precisely how we've implemented the underlying heap.

Adding an Entry to a Heap

Let's start with the operation that adds a new entry. For our examples, we will use heaps where the entries are integers, with the usual less-than operation. Suppose that we already have nine entries that are arranged in a heap as follows:

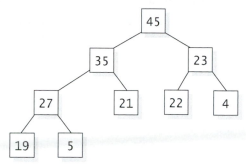

In an actual priority queue, each entry might be more complex, but they would still be comparable by some less-than operator.

Suppose that we are adding a new entry of 42. The first step is to add this entry in a way that keeps the binary tree complete. In this case the new entry will be the left child of the entry with priority 21:

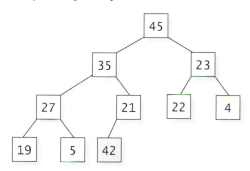

add the new entry in a way that keeps the binary tree complete

But now the structure is no longer a heap, since the node with 21 is less than its child with 42. The algorithm for the insertion operation fixes this by causing the new entry (42) to rise upward until it reaches an acceptable location. This is accomplished by swapping the new entry with its parent:

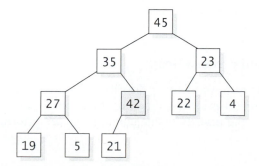

FIGURE 11.1   Adding an Entry to a Priority Queue

Pseudocode for Adding an Entry

The priority queue has been implemented as a heap.

1. Place the new entry in the heap in the first available location. This keeps the structure as a complete binary tree, but it might no longer be a heap since the new entry's parent might be less than the new entry.

2. `while` (the new entry's parent is less than the new entry)
   Swap the new entry with its parent.

Notice that the process in Step 2 will stop when the new entry reaches the root, or when the new entry's parent is no longer less than the new entry.

The new entry's parent is *still* less than 42, so a second swap is done:

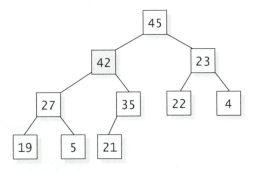

reheapification upward

Now the new entry stops rising, because its parent (45) is no longer less than the new entry. In general, the "new entry rising" stops when the new entry has a parent with a higher or equal priority, or when the new entry reaches the root. The rising process is called **reheapification upward**.

The steps for adding an entry are outlined in Figure 11.1. Some of the details depend on how the underlying heap is implemented. For example, if the heap is implemented with a fixed-sized array, then the first step must check that there is room for a new entry. With a dynamic array, the first step might need to increase the size of the array.

Removing an Entry from a Heap

When an entry is removed from a priority queue, we must always remove the entry with the highest priority—the entry that stands "on top of the heap." For example, suppose the priority queue contains the ten priorities drawn at the top of the next page.

The entry at the root, with priority 45, will be removed, and this is the entry that is returned by the operation:

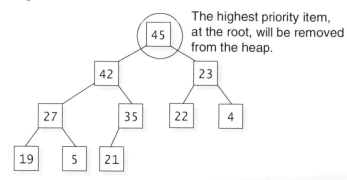

But here we are ignoring a potential problem: There might be several entries with the highest priority. One possibility is to have the equal entries leave the priority queue in First-In/First-Out (FIFO) order. But our adding and deleting mechanisms do not provide a way to determine which of several entries arrived first. So, we will not specify any particular requirement about how equal entries leave the priority queue.

The problem of removing the root from a heap remains. During the removal, we must ensure that the resulting structure remains a heap. If the root entry is the only entry in the heap, then there is really no more work to do except to decrement the member variable that is keeping track of the size of the heap. But if there are other entries in the tree, then the tree must be rearranged because a heap is not allowed to run around without a root. The rearrangement begins by moving the last entry in the last level up to the root, like this:

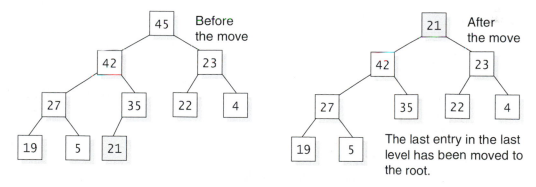

The structure is now a complete tree, but it is not a heap because the root is less than its children. To fix this, we can swap the root with its larger child, as shown here:

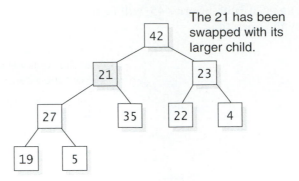

The structure is not yet a heap, so again we swap the out-of-place node with its larger child, giving this tree:

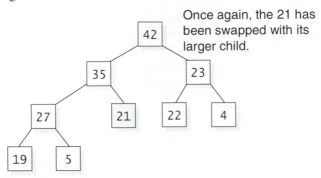

reheapification downward

At this point, the node that has been sinking has reached a leaf so we can stop, and the structure is a heap. The process would also stop when the sinking node is no longer less than one of its children. This process, called **reheapification downward**, is summarized in Figure 11.2.

Heaps have several other applications, including a sorting algorithm that is discussed in Chapter 13.

FIGURE 11.2   Removing an Entry from a Priority Queue

Pseudocode for Removing an Entry

The priority queue has been implemented as a heap.

1. Copy the entry at the root of the heap to the variable that is used to return a value.
2. Copy the last entry in the deepest level to the root, and then take this last node out of the tree. This entry is called the "out-of-place" entry.
3. `while` (the out-of-place entry is less than one of its children)
        Swap the out-of-place entry with its highest child.
4. Return the answer that was saved in Step 1.

Notice that the process in Step 3 will stop when the out-of-place entry reaches a leaf or when the out-of-place entry is no longer less than one of its children.

Self-Test Exercises for Section 11.1

1. How does a heap differ from a binary search tree?

2. Write a C++ class definition that would be appropriate for a priority queue of values that is implemented as a heap with up to 50 entries. Write a second definition that does not have any predefined limit to the number of entries in the heap. Use a dynamic array for the second class.

3. Where is a new entry to a heap initially placed? Why?

4. After an item is removed from a heap, which item is placed in the root?

5. Start with an empty heap of integers, and enter the ten numbers 1 through 10. Draw the resulting heap.

6. Remove three entries from the heap that you created in the previous exercise. Draw the resulting heap.

7. In the description of reheapification downward, we specified that the out-of-place entry must be swapped with the larger of its two children. What goes wrong if we swap with the smaller child instead?

11.2 B-TREES

Binary search trees were used in Section 10.5 to implement a bag class. But the efficiency of binary search trees can go awry. This section explains the potential problem and shows one way to fix it. Most of the presentation is not tied to any particular programming language.

FIGURE 11.3 Two Troublesome Search Trees

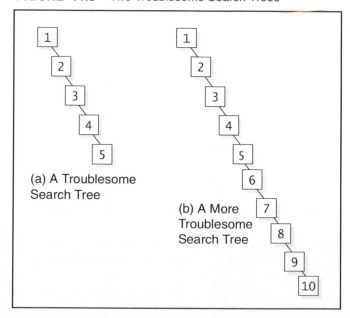

(a) A Troublesome Search Tree

(b) A More Troublesome Search Tree

The Problem of Unbalanced Trees

Let's create a troublesome binary search tree of integers. The first number is 1, then we add 2, then 3, 4, and 5, in that order. The result appears in Figure 11.3(a). Perhaps you've spotted the problem. Suppose next we add 6, 7, 8, 9, and 10, in that order, ending up with Figure 11.3(b). The problem is that the levels of the tree are only sparsely filled, resulting in long, deep paths and defeating the purpose of binary trees in the first place. For example, if we are searching Figure 11.3(b) for the number 12, then we'll end up looking at every node in the tree. In effect, we are no better off than the linked-list implementation. Similar problems arise for adding and deleting entries.

The problem has several possible solutions, all of which involve trees where the depth of the leaves remains small. For example, one solution is to periodically balance the search trees, as described in Programming Project 9 in Chapter 10 (page 533). Another solution uses a particular kind of tree called a B-tree, where leaves cannot become too deep (relative to the number of nodes). These trees were proposed by R. Bayer and E.M. McCreight in 1972 (see "Organization and Maintenance of Large Ordered Indexes" in *Acta Informatica,* Volume 1, Number 3 [1972], pages 173–189). The rest of this section provides a B-tree implementation.

The B-Tree Rules

B-trees are <u>not</u> binary trees

A B-tree is a special kind of tree, similar to a binary search tree, where each node holds entries of some type. As with binary search trees, the implementation requires the ability to compare two entries via a less-than operator. But a B-tree is not a binary search tree—in fact, a B-tree is not even a *binary* tree because *B-tree nodes have many more than two children.* Another important property of B-trees is that *each node contains more than just a single entry.* The rules for a B-tree make it easy to search for a specified entry, and the rules also ensure that leaves do not become too deep.

B-tree rules may be formulated for either a bag or a set

The precise B-tree rules may be formulated so that the B-tree stores a bag of entries similar to the bag implementations that we have seen before. Alternatively, a B-tree may be formulated to store a *set* of entries. The difference between a set and a bag is that two or more equal entries can occur many times in a bag but not in a set. For example, the C++ Standard Library has a set template class where equal entries are forbidden (see Appendix H for details). We'll look at a "set formulation" of the B-tree rules, but keep in mind that a "bag formulation" is also possible.

The entries in a B-tree node. Every B-tree depends on a positive constant integer called MINIMUM. The purpose of the constant is to determine how many entries are held in a single node, as shown in the first two B-tree rules:

> **B-tree Rule 1:** The root may have as few as one entry (or even no entries if it also has no children); every other node has at least MINIMUM entries.

> **B-tree Rule 2:** The maximum number of entries in a node is twice the value of MINIMUM.

Although MINIMUM may be as small as 1, in practice much larger values are used—perhaps several hundred, or even a couple thousand.

The many entries of a B-tree node are stored in an array, so that we can talk about "the entry at index 0," or "the entry at index 1," and so on. Within the array, the entries must be sorted from smallest to largest. This provides our third B-tree rule:

> **B-tree Rule 3:** The entries of each B-tree node are stored in a partially filled array, sorted from the smallest entry (at index 0) to the largest entry (at the final used position of the array).

The subtrees below a B-tree node. The number of subtrees below a node depends on how many entries are in the node. Here is the rule:

> **B-tree Rule 4:** The number of subtrees below a nonleaf node is always one more than the number of entries in the node.

For example, suppose a node has 42 entries. Then this node will have 43 children. We will refer to the many subtrees of a node from left to right as "subtree number 0, subtree number 1, . . ." and so on up to the last subtree.

The entries in each subtree are organized in a way that makes it easy to search the B-tree for any given entry. Here is the rule for that organization:

> **B-tree Rule 5:** For any nonleaf node: (a) An entry at index i is greater than all the entries in subtree number i of the node, and (b) an entry at index i is less than all the entries in subtree number $i+1$ of the node.

Let's look at an example to illustrate Rules 4 and 5. Suppose that a nonleaf node contains two integer entries, the numbers 93 and 107. This node must have three subtrees, organized as follows:

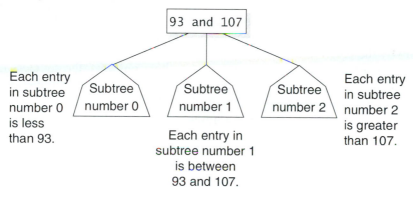

A B-tree is balanced. The final B-tree rule ensures that a B-tree avoids the problem of an unbalanced tree:

> **B-tree Rule 6:** Every leaf in a B-tree has the same depth.

An Example B-Tree

As another example, here is a B-tree of ten integers (with `MINIMUM` set to 1). Can you verify that all six B-tree rules are satisfied?

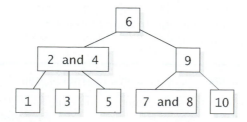

The Set ADT with B-Trees

The rest of this section discusses the algorithms for implementing a set class using B-trees. The class is a template class that depends on the underlying type of the items in the set. There are public member functions for adding and removing items, and also for checking whether a given item is in the set. As you can see in our complete header file (Figure 11.4), there are also several private member functions that will simplify the implementations of the other member functions. We'll discuss these "helper" functions at the point where they are used, but first let's examine the private member variables and member constants that we have in mind.

The set class has two private member constants, shown here with a selection of 200 for MINIMUM:

two private member constants of the set

```
static const size_t MINIMUM = 200;
static const size_t MAXIMUM = 2 * MINIMUM;
```

These constants are *private* because a programmer who *uses* the set class does not need to know about their existence. Access to these private values is needed only by the programmer who *implements* the set class.

After the declaration of the private member constants, the set class has four private member variables. The purpose of these four member variables is to store all the information about the root node of the B-tree that contains the set's entries. Here are the first three member variables from the set class in Figure 11.4 on page 546:

member variables store information about the root of the B-tree

```
size_t data_count;
Item data[MAXIMUM+1];
size_t child_count;
```

Keep in mind that the member variables store information about the *root* node. For example, data_count stores the number of entries in the B-tree's root (not in the entire B-tree). The root's entries are stored in the partially filled array called data, ranging from data[0] through data[data_count-1]. The complete size of the data array is MAXIMUM + 1, which allows space for one extra entry beyond the usual maximum number. You'll see the benefit of this extra space when we discuss the implementations of the member functions.

The number of children of the root node is stored in the member variable child_count. The children of the root have an important property that will allow us to use *recursive thinking* in our implementations. Here is the property that you should burn into your memory:

> Every child of the root node is also the root of a smaller B-tree.

(text continues on page 547)

FIGURE 11.4   Header File for the Set Template Class

A Header File

```
// FILE: set.h (part of the namespace main_savitch_11)
// TEMPLATE CLASS PROVIDED: set<Item> (a container template class for a set of items)
//
// TYPEDEFS for the set<Item> class:
//    set<Item>::value_type
//       set<Item>::value_type is the data type of the items in the set. It may be any of the
//       C++ built-in types (int, char, etc.), or a class with a default constructor, a copy
//       constructor, an assignment operator, and a less-than operator forming a strict
//       weak ordering.
//
// CONSTRUCTOR for the set<Item> class:
//    set( )
//       Postcondition: The set is empty.
//
// MODIFICATION MEMBER FUNCTIONS for the set<Item> class:
//    void clear( )
//       Postcondition: The set is empty.
//
//    bool insert(const Item& entry)
//       Postcondition: If an equal entry was already in the set, the set is unchanged and the
//       return value is false. Otherwise, entry was added to the set and the return value is true.
//       This is slightly different than the C++ Standard Library set (see Appendix H).
//
//    size_t erase(const Item& target)
//       Postcondition: If target was in the set, then it has been removed from the set and the
//       return value is 1. Otherwise the set is unchanged and the return value is zero.
//
// CONSTANT MEMBER FUNCTIONS for the Set<Item> class:
//    size_t count(const Item& target) const
//       Postcondition: Returns the number of items equal to the target (either 0 or 1 for a set).
//
//    bool empty( ) const
//       Postcondition: Returns true if the set is empty; otherwise returns false.
//
// VALUE SEMANTICS for the set<Item> class:
//    Assignments and the copy constructor may be used with set<Item> objects.
//
// DYNAMIC MEMORY USAGE by the set<Item> class:
//    If there is insufficient dynamic memory, then the following functions throw bad_alloc:
//    The constructors, insert, and the assignment operator.
```

(continued)

(FIGURE 11.4 continued)

```cpp
#ifndef MAIN_SAVITCH_SET_H
#define MAIN_SAVITCH_SET_H
#include <cstdlib>    // Provides size_t

namespace main_savitch_11
{
    template <class Item>
    class set
    {
    public:
        // TYPEDEFS
        typedef Item value_type;
        // CONSTRUCTORS and DESTRUCTOR
        set( );
        set(const set& source);
        ~set( ) { clear( ); }
        // MODIFICATION MEMBER FUNCTIONS
        void operator =(const set& source);
        void clear( );
        bool insert(const Item& entry);
        std::size_t erase(const Item& target);
        // CONSTANT MEMBER FUNCTIONS
        std::size_t count(const Item& target) const;
        bool empty( ) const { return (data_count == 0); }
    private:
        // MEMBER CONSTANTS
        static const std::size_t MINIMUM = 200;
        static const std::size_t MAXIMUM = 2 * MINIMUM;
        // MEMBER VARIABLES
        std::size_t data_count;
        Item data[MAXIMUM+1];
        std::size_t child_count;
        set *subset[MAXIMUM+2];
        // HELPER MEMBER FUNCTIONS
        bool is_leaf( ) const { return (child_count == 0); }
        bool loose_insert(const Item& entry);
        bool loose_erase(const Item& target);
        void remove_biggest(Item& removed_entry);
        void fix_excess(std::size_t i);
        void fix_shortage(std::size_t i);
```

As an alternative to fixed arrays, you might consider using a vector as described in Appendix H. The advantage of the vector is that it has useful member functions such

The private member functions are discussed in the text.

‖ The programmer who implements the class may add other private members.

```cpp
    };
}
#include "set.template" // Include the implementation.

#endif
```

Let's look at an example to illustrate the rule "Every child of the root node is also the root of a smaller B-tree." For the example, consider the following B-tree (with MINIMUM equal to 1):

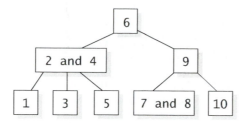

The root of this B-tree has two children, and each of these children is also the root of a smaller B-tree. These two smaller B-trees are clearly shown here:

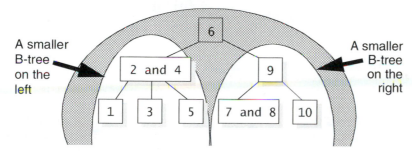

Each of the smaller B-trees also contains a set of entries. We will call these two smaller sets "subset number 0" and "subset number 1." If there were more children, we would continue with "subset number 2," and so on. The last subset is "subset number child_count-1."

Now consider how to store the subsets. The best solution is to store each subset as *an actual set object.* In the root node itself, we will store *pointers* to these smaller set objects. These pointers are stored in the fourth member variable of the set class, declared here:

```
set *subset[MAXIMUM+2];
```

The member variable subset is a partially filled array of pointers to smaller subsets. It is able to hold up to MAXIMUM + 2 such pointers—which is one more than the maximum number of children that a B-tree node may have. As with the entries, the benefit of this "space for one extra" will become evident shortly.

As an example, suppose a B-tree root has two children. Then subset[0] is a pointer to "subset number 0," and subset[1] is a pointer to "subset number 1." With this in mind, let's again consider the following B-tree:

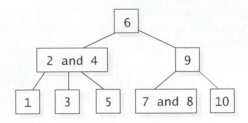

The root contains one entry and two children, so the member variables of the set object for this B-tree will look like this:

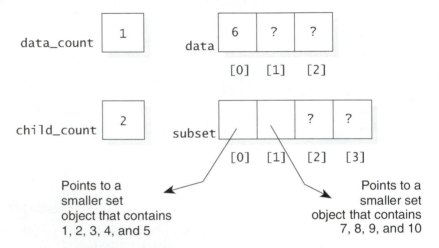

The important idea is that each subset[i] is a pointer to another set object. We will be able to use all of the set member functions with these objects in various recursive calls. Here is the complete invariant for our set class:

Invariant for the Set Class Implemented with a B-Tree

1. The items of the set are stored in a B-tree, satisfying the six B-tree rules.

2. The number of entries in the tree's root is stored in the member variable data_count, and the number of sub-trees of the root is stored in the member variable child_count.

3. The root's entries are stored in data[0] through data[data_count-1].

4. If the root has subtrees, then these subtrees are stored in sets pointed to by the pointers subset[0] through subset[child_count-1].

Searching for an Item in a B-Tree

The set class has a member function, `count`, that determines whether an item called `target` appears in the set. We use the name `count` to be consistent with the multiset class, but keep in mind that the set's `count` function always returns zero (if the target is not found) or one (if the target is found).

Searching for an item in a B-tree follows the same idea as searching a binary search tree, although there's more work needed to handle nodes that contain many entries instead of just one. The basic idea: Start with the entire B-tree, checking to see whether the target is in the root. If the target does appear in the root, then the search is done—the function can return one to indicate that it found the target. A second possibility is that the target is not in the root, and the root has no children. In this case, the search is also done—the function can return zero to indicate that the target is not in the set. The final possibility is that the target is not in the root, but there are subtrees below. In this case, there is only one possible subtree where the target can appear, so the function makes a recursive call to search that one subtree for the target.

The entire function can benefit from one preliminary step, shown as the first step of this pseudocode:

// Searching for a target in a set

1. Make a local variable, `i`, equal to the first index such that `data[i]` is not less than the `target`. If there is no such index, then set `i` equal to `data_count`, indicating that all of the entries are less than the target.

2. *if* (we found the target at `data[i]`)
      return 1;
   else if (the root has no children)
      return 0;
   else
      return `subset[i]->count(target);`

Be careful how you test the condition at the start of Step 2. In order to "find the target at `data[i]`," you must ensure that `i < data_count` and also that the target is actually equal to `data[i]`. But the `Item` data type is not required to have an `==` operator. Instead, you already know that `data[i]` is not less than the target, so if the target is also not less than `data[i]`, then we have found the target. One implementation is: *if* (`(i < data_count) && !(target < data[i])`).

The recursive call in the pseudocode above is highlighted. Notice the form that the activation requires, using the member selection operator (`->`) rather than a simple dot. The reason is that `subset[i]` is a *pointer* to a set (rather than an actual set). The recursive call works well in this situation because the subset is *smaller* than the entire set. Thus, the recursive call is solving a *smaller* version of the original problem.

As an example of executing the pseudocode, suppose we are searching for 10 in this B-tree:

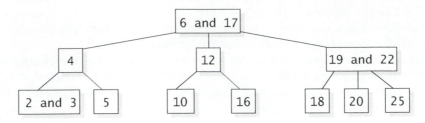

The search begins by finding the first item in the root that is not less than the target 10. This is the item 17, which occurs at data[1] in the root, so Step 1 sets i to the index 1. In Step 2 we notice that we have not found the target at data[1], but the root does have children. So, we make a recursive call, searching subtree number 1 for the target 10. You can visualize the recursive call subtree[1]->count(10) as searching for a 10 in this part of the tree:

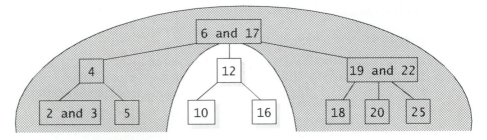

The recursive call of the count member function has its own copy of the local variable i. This variable i is set to 0 in Step 1 of the recursive call (since data[0] of the subtree is greater than or equal to the target 10). Again, we have not found the target, so the recursion continues, activating the count member function for the still smaller subtree shown here:

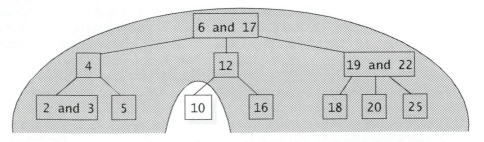

The recursive call finds the target, returning one to the previous recursive call. That previous recursive call then returns one to the original call, and the original call can also return one, indicating that the target was found somewhere in the set.

There are several parts for you to clarify in your implementation. How do you find the correct value of i in the first step of the pseudocode? (Make sure that your approach uses only the less-than operator to compare items since the `Item` data type is not required to have other comparison operations.) How do you determine whether the root has children? (Use the private `is_leaf` member function.)

Inserting an Item into a B-Tree

The `insert` member function of the set class adds a new item to the B-tree. It is easier to add a new entry to a B-tree if we relax one of the B-tree rules. In particular, we will allow a somewhat "loose insertion" function to complete its work with the possibility that there is one entry too many in the root node of the B-tree. In other words, a loose insertion might result in `MAXIMUM + 1` entries in the root. For example, consider this B-tree where `MAXIMUM` is 2:

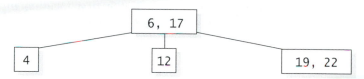

Suppose that we want to add 18 to the tree. The end result of a loose insertion could be the following illegal B-tree:

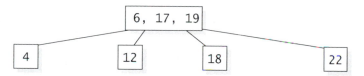

The B-tree is illegal because the root node has three entries, which is one more than the definition of `MAXIMUM`. Notice that *only the root* may have an extra entry after the "loose insertion." Our plan is for the insert member function to begin by calling another member function that carries out a loose insertion. After the loose insertion, the usual insert member function will examine the root node. If the root node has too many entries, then the insert member function will fix that problem in a way that we'll describe later. For now, though, we'll turn our attention to the design of the loose insertion function.

The Loose Insertion into a B-Tree

From our previous discussion, you can design a specification for a loose insertion. The function will be a private member function called `loose_insert`. The specification is given here:

```
template <class Item>
bool set<Item>::loose_insert(const Item& entry);
// Precondition: The entire B-tree is valid.
// Postcondition: If entry was already in the set, then the set is unchanged
//   and the return value is false. Otherwise, the entry has been added to the
//   set, the return value is true, and the entire B-tree is still
//   valid EXCEPT that the number of entries in the root of this set might be
//   one more than the allowed maximum.
```

Since this is a *private* member function, it may violate the usual invariant for the set class. As you can see, the precondition does satisfy the usual invariant, but the postcondition allows for a violation of the invariant. This precondition/postcondition contract will not appear in the set's header file. It is present only in the implementation file, as an aid to the programmer who implements the class.

The first step of our approach for the loose insertion is identical to the first step of the searching function. This step finds the first location in the root's entries that is not less than the new entry. Once we have this location, there are three possibilities listed in Step 2 of the pseudocode:

pseudocode for the loose insert

// *Inserting a new entry in a Set*

1. Make a local variable, `i`, equal to the first index such that `data[i]` is not less than `entry`. If there is no such index, then set `i` equal to `data_count`, indicating that all of the entries are less than the target.

2. `if` (we found the new entry at `data[i]`)
      2a. Return false with no further work (since the new entry is already in the set).
   `else if` (the root has no children)
      2b. Add the new entry to the root at `data[i]`. (The original entries at `data[i]` and afterwards must be shifted right to make room for the new entry.) Return true to indicate that we added the entry.
   `else`
   {   2c. Save the value from this recursive call:
      `subset[i]->loose_insert(entry);`
      Then check whether the root of `subset[i]` now has an excess entry; if so, then fix that problem.
      Return the saved value from the recursive call.
   }

Looking through the pseudocode, Steps 2a and 2b are fairly easy.

The more interesting work occurs in Step 2c, where we have not found the new entry, nor are we ready to insert the new entry. In this case, we make a recursive call to do a loose insertion of the new entry in the appropriate subset. Since the recursive call is a *loose* insertion, we may end up with one excess entry in the root of our subset. This excess entry must be dealt with before returning because the postcondition does not allow *subsets* to have nodes with extra entries.

As an example of executing the pseudocode, suppose we are making a loose insertion of 18 into this B-tree (with MAXIMUM set to 2):

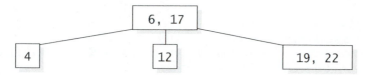

Step 1 of the pseudocode finds the first item in the root that is not less than the new entry 18. As you see, all of the root entries are less than 18, so what does Step 1 do instead? From the pseudocode, you see that the index i will be set to 2 (the number of entries in the root node).

In Step 2 we notice that we have not found the new entry in the root, nor are we at a leaf. So we proceed to Step 2c, making a recursive call to insert 18 into subtree number 2, as shown here:

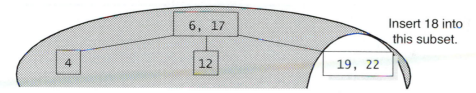

Insert 18 into this subset.

The recursive call finds a small subtree with just a root. Following Step 2b, the recursive call inserts the number 18 into the root of the subtree and then returns true. After the recursive call returns, the entire tree looks like this:

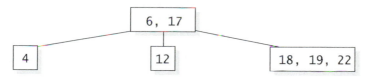

When the recursive call returns, we carry out the rest of Step 2c, checking whether the root of the subtree now has too many entries. Indeed, the root of subset[2] now has three entries, which is one more than the allowed maximum. We must fix this problem child, but how? It seems that fixing the child may take quite a bit of work, so we will propose another private member function to carry out this work.

A Private Member Function to Fix an Excess in a Child

Here's the specification for the private member function that we have in mind:

```
template <class Item>
void set<Item>::fix_excess(std::size_t i);
// Precondition: (i < child_count) and the entire B-tree is valid EXCEPT that
// subset[i] has MAXIMUM + 1 entries.
// Postcondition: The tree has been rearranged so that the entire B-tree is
// valid EXCEPT that the number of entries in the root of this set might be
// one more than the allowed maximum.
```

Looking at the specification, you can see that the function starts with a problem child. When the function finishes, the child no longer has a problem, although the *root* may now have a problem. The approach of the fix_excess function can be simply stated:

Fixing a Child with an Excess Entry

To fix a child with MAXIMUM + 1 entries, the child node is split into two nodes that each contain MINIMUM entries. This leaves one extra entry, which is passed upward to the parent.

Let's examine an example of this approach. In the example, suppose that MINIMUM is 2, so that the maximum number of entries in a node is 4 (which is 2*MINIMUM). We want to fix subtree number 1 (the shaded subtree) in this example tree:

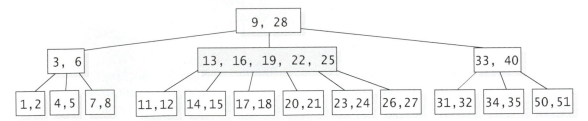

The approach taken by fix_excess is to split the problem node (with 2*MINIMUM + 1 entries) into two smaller nodes (with MINIMUM entries each). This leaves one entry unaccounted for, and that one extra entry will be passed upward to the parent of the split node. Therefore, the parent of the split node gains one additional child (from splitting the full node) and also gains one additional entry (the extra entry that is passed upward). In the example shown above, the result of the splitting is shown here:

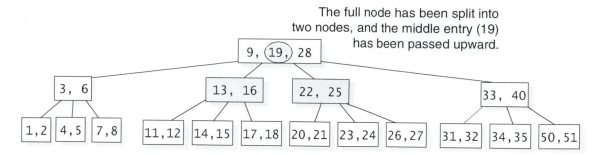

The full node has been split into two nodes, and the middle entry (19) has been passed upward.

It is always the *middle* entry of the split node that moves upward. Also, notice that the children of the split node have been equally distributed between the two smaller nodes.

As another example of fix_excess in action, suppose that MAXIMUM is 2, and we have the problem child shown here:

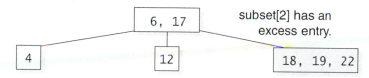

subset[2] has an excess entry.

After calling fix_excess(2), the problem child will be split into two nodes, with the middle entry passed upward, as shown here:

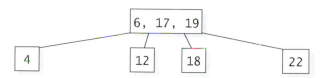

As you can see in this example, fixing the problem child can create a root with an excess entry—but that is all right because the postcondition of fix_excess permits the root to have an extra entry.

Back to the Insert Member Function

We need to finish the discussion of the original insert function. By using the loose_insert function, the public insert function has just two steps:

```
// Pseudocode for the public insert member function
if (!loose_insert(entry))
    Return false since loose_insert did not add a new entry to the set.
if (data_count > MAXIMUM)
    Fix the root of the entire tree so that it no longer has too many entries.
Return true.
```

pseudocode for insert

In this pseudocode, how do we "fix the root of the entire tree so that it no longer has too many entries"? The step can be accomplished in two parts. The first part copies all entries and child pointers from the root to a newly allocated node and clears out the root, leaving it with one child (which is the newly allocated node) and no entries. For example, suppose that we do a loose insertion, and then the B-tree looks like this (with MAXIMUM set to 2):

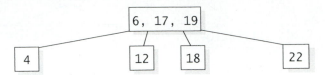

We will copy everything from the root to a new node and clear out the root. In the resulting tree, the root will have no entries, and everything else has moved down one level, as shown here:

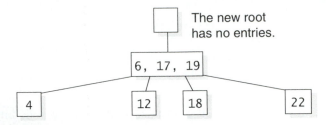

Once we have shifted things in this way, the problem is now with the child of the root. We can fix this problem by splitting the subset[0] of the root into two nodes and passing the middle entry upward. In fact, if you are careful in writing fix_excess, this splitting can be carried out by calling fix_excess(0). Care must be taken because this root has no entries, so fix_excess must be prepared to deal with such a situation. (If you take this approach, you should document the extended ability of fix_excess in its precondition.)

In this example, after splitting subset[0] we have the completely valid B-tree shown here:

B-trees gain height only at the root

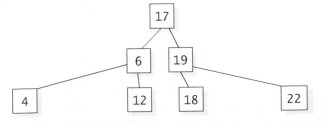

By the way, this growth at the root (within the insert member function) is the only point where a B-tree gains height.

Employing Top-Down Design

As you work on the project, keep in mind the top-down design that we have employed. As shown in Figure 11.5, the original insert member function calls the private member function `loose_insert`. Both the ordinary insert and the loose insert functions call `fix_excess`. At several points in the design of `fix_excess`, you should propose and implement smaller functions to carry out the basic work of copying and shifting elements in an array. You might be able to use some functions from the `<algorithm>` facility to do this array work (see Appendix I).

> **FIGURE 11.5** Top-Down Design for the `insert` Member Function
>
> The `insert` function calls:
> - `loose_insert`
> - `fix_excess`
>
> The `loose_insert` function is recursive and also calls:
> - `fix_excess`
> - various array functions
>
> The `fix_excess` function calls:
> - various array functions

Removing an Item from a B-Tree

The `erase` member function of the set removes an entry from the B-tree. Most of the work will be accomplished with a private member function, `loose_erase`, which performs a "loose removal" that is analogous to the loose insertion. The looseness in `loose_erase` occurs because it is allowed to leave a root that has one entry too few. In other words, it might leave the root of the whole tree with zero entries (which is not permitted unless there are also no children), or it might leave the root of an internal subtree with fewer than MINIMUM entries. The specification of `loose_erase` is given here:

```
template <class Item>
bool set<Item>::loose_erase(const Item& target);
// Precondition: The entire B-tree is valid.
// Postcondition: If target was not in the set, then the set is unchanged and
// the return value is false. Otherwise, the target has been removed, the
// return value is true, and the entire B-tree is still valid
// EXCEPT that the number of entries in the root of this set might be one
// less than the allowed minimum.
```

Our complete erase function will first call `loose_erase`. Afterwards, if necessary, we can fix a root that may have been left with zero entries and one child. Thus, the erase pseudocode has these steps:

```
// Pseudocode for the public erase member function
if (loose_erase(target))
        Return zero since loose_erase did not remove an entry from the set.
if ((data_count == 0) && (child_count == 1))
        Fix the root of the entire tree so that it no longer has zero entries.
Return one since one entry was removed from the set.
```

pseudocode for remove

In this pseudocode, how do we "fix the root of the entire tree so that it no longer has zero entries"? For example, we might have a tree that looks like this:

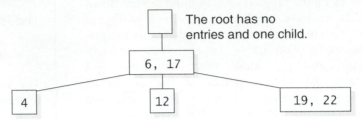

Our solution for this problem is to first set a temporary pointer that points to the only child. Next, copy everything from the only child up to the root node. Finally, delete the original child. After this rearrangement, our tree will be one level shorter, as shown here:

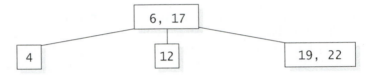

B-trees lose height only at the root

This shrinking at the root (within the remove member function) is the only point where a B-tree loses height.

Now we are left with the task of designing the loose erase function.

The Loose Erase from a B-Tree

The private `loose_erase` function starts in the same way as the search and insert functions, by finding the first index i such that `data[i]` is not less than the target. Once we have found this index, there are four possibilities, shown here:

pseudocode for loose erase

// *Removing a target entry from a set (loose erase)*

1. Make a local variable, i, equal to the first index such that `data[i]` is not less than `target`. If there is no such index, then set i equal to `data_count`, indicating that all of the entries are less than the target.

2. Deal with one of these four possibilities:

   2a. The root has no children, and we did not find the target: In this case, there is no work to do, since the target is not in the set (return false).

   2b. The root has no children, and we found the target: In this case, remove the target from the data array, and return true.

   2c. The root has children, and we did not find the target (see below).

   2d. The root has children, and we found the target (see below).

Cases 2c and 2d require further development.

Case 2c. In this case, we did not find the target in the root, but the target still might appear in `subset[i]`. We will make a recursive call (and save its answer for us to return ourselves):

    subset[i]->loose_erase(target)

This call will remove the target from `subset[i]`, but we are then left with the problem that the root of `subset[i]` might have only MINIMUM − 1 entries. If so, then we'll fix the problem by calling another private member function with the specification shown here:

```
template <class Item>
void set<Item>::fix_shortage(std::size_t i);
// Precondition: (i < child_count) and the entire B-tree is valid EXCEPT that
// subset[i] has MINIMUM − 1 entries.
// Postcondition: The tree has been rearranged so that the entire B-tree is
// valid EXCEPT that the number of entries in the root of this set might be
// one less than the allowed minimum.
```

We'll look at the design of `fix_shortage` later.

Case 2d. In this case, we have found the target in the root, but we cannot simply remove it from the data array because there are children below (and removing an entry would thereby violate B-tree Rule 4 on page 543). Instead, we will go into `subset[i]` and remove the *largest* item in this subset. We will take a copy of this largest item and place it into `data[i]` (which contains the target). The total effect is the same as removing the target.

For example, suppose we have found the target 28 at `data[1]` in the root of this B-tree:

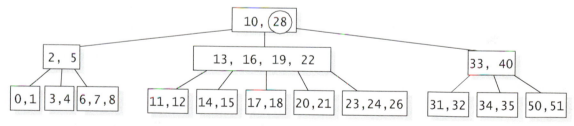

Our plan is to go into `subset[1]`, remove the largest item (the 26), and place a copy of this 26 on top of the target. After these steps, the B-tree no longer has the 28:

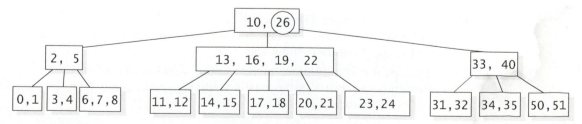

The combination of removing the largest item from subset[i] and placing a copy of the largest item into data[i] can be accomplished by calling another new private member function, remove_biggest, with this specification:

```
template <class Item>
void set<Item>::remove_biggest(Item& removed_entry);
// Precondition: (data_count > 0) and the entire B-tree is valid.
// Postcondition: The largest item in the set has been removed, and a copy
// of this removed entry has been placed in removed_entry. The entire
// B-tree is still valid, EXCEPT that the number of entries in the root of this
// set might be one less than the allowed minimum.
```

By using remove_biggest, most of Step 2d is accomplished with one function call:

```
subset[i]->remove_biggest(data[i]);
```

After this function call returns, we have deleted the largest entry from subset[i] and placed a copy of this item into data[i] (replacing the target). The work that remains is to fix the possible shortage that may occur in the root of subset[i] (since the postcondition of subset[i]->remove_biggest allows for the possibility that the root of subset[i] ends up with MINIMUM - 1 entries). How do we fix such a shortage? We can use the same fix_shortage member function that we used at the end of Step 2c. Thus, the entire code for Step 2d is the following:

```
subset[i]->remove_biggest(data[i]);
if (subset[i]->data_count < MINIMUM)
    fix_shortage(i);
return true; // Indicate that we removed the target.
```

We have two more issues to deal with: the designs of fix_shortage and remove_biggest.

A Private Member Function to Fix a Shortage in a Child

four situations for the fix_shortage pseudocode

When fix_shortage(i) is called, we know that subset[i] has only MINIMUM - 1 entries. How can we correct this problem? There are four situations that you can consider:

Case 1 of fix_shortage: Transfer an extra entry from subset[i-1].
Suppose that subset[i-1] has more than the minimum number of entries. Then we can carry out these transfers:

    a. Transfer data[i-1] down to the front of subset[i]->data. Remember to shift over the existing entries to make room, and add one to subset[i]->data_count.

b. Transfer the final item of `subset[i-1]->data` up to replace `data[i-1]`, and subtract one from `subset[i-1]->data_count`.

c. If `subset[i-1]` has children, transfer the final child of `subset[i-1]` over to the front of `subset[i]`. This involves shifting over the existing array `subset[i]->subset` to make room for the new child pointer at `subset[i]->subset[0]`. Also add one to `subset[i]->child_count`, and subtract one from `subset[i-1]->child_count`.

For example, let's call `fix_shortage(2)` for this tree (with `MINIMUM` set to 2):

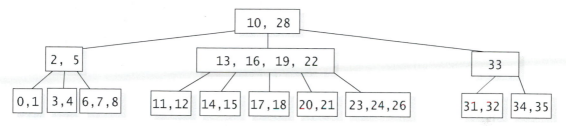

In this example, we need to fix `subset[2]`, which has only one entry. Following the steps outlined above, we can transfer an entry from `subset[1]`. This transferred entry is the 22, which gets passed up to `data[1]`, and the 28 (from `data[1]`) comes down to be the new first entry of the problem node. One child is also transferred from the end of `subset[1]` to the front of `subset[2]`, as shown here:

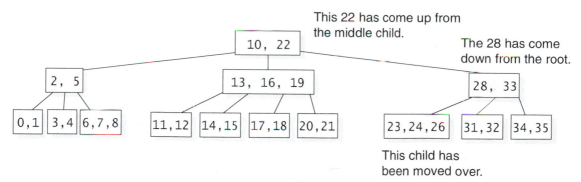

This 22 has come up from the middle child.

The 28 has come down from the root.

This child has been moved over.

Case 2 for fix_shortage: Transfer an extra entry from subset[i+1].
Another possibility is to transfer an extra entry from `subset[i+1]`. The work is similar to what you have just seen for transferring an entry from `subset[i-1]`.

Case 3 for fix_shortage: Combine subset[i] with subset[i-1].
Suppose that `subset[i-1]` is present (in other words, `i > 0`), but it has only `MINIMUM` entries. In this case, we cannot transfer an entry from `subset[i-1]`, but we can combine `subset[i]` with `subset[i-1]`. The combining occurs in three steps:

a. Transfer data[i-1] down to the end of subset[i-1]->data. This actually removes the item from the root, so shift data[i], data[i+1], and so on, leftward to fill in the gap. Also remember to subtract one from data_count, and add one to subset[i-1]->data_count.

b. Transfer all the items and children from subset[i] to the end of subset[i-1]. Remember to update the values of subset[i-1]->data_count and subset[i-1]->child_count. Also set subset[i]->data_count and subset[i]->child_count to zero.

c. Delete the node subset[i], and shift subset[i+1], subset[i+2], and so on leftward to fill in the gap. Also reduce child_count by one.

For example, let's call fix_shortage(2) for this tree (with MINIMUM set to 2):

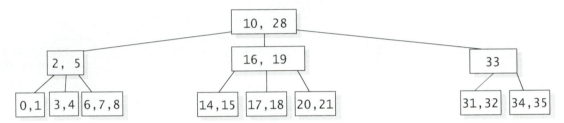

In this example, subset[2] is merged with its sibling to the left. During the merge, the 28 also is passed down from the root to become a new entry of the merged nodes. The result is the following tree:

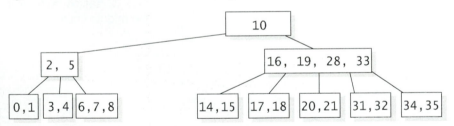

As you can see, this tree has too few entries in its own root, but that is okay because the postcondition of fix_shortage allows the root of the resulting tree to have one less than the required number of entries.

Case 4 for fix_shortage: Combine subset[i] with subset[i+1].
Our fourth case is to combine the problem subset with subset[i+1]. The work is similar to what you have just seen for combining with subset[i-1].

You now have enough information to write the fix_shortage member function. You should emphasize a clear logical structure to determine which of the four cases is appropriate. Your implementation will be cleaner if you provide four new private member functions to do the actual work in each of the four cases.

Removing the Biggest Item from a B-Tree

Our final member function has this specification:

```
template <class Item>
void set<Item>::remove_biggest(Item& removed_entry);
// Precondition: (data_count > 0) and the entire B-tree is valid.
// Postcondition: The largest item in the set has been removed, and a copy
// of this removed entry has been placed in removed_entry. The entire
// B-tree is still valid, EXCEPT that the number of entries in the root of this
// set might be one less than the allowed minimum.
```

The work of `remove_biggest` is easy if the root has no children. In this case, we copy the last item of `data` into the reference parameter, `removed_entry`. Then we subtract one from `data_count`. That's all! We might be left with a node that has one less than the allowed minimum number of entries, but according to the postcondition, that is okay.

What if the root has children? In this case, we make a recursive call to remove the largest entry from the rightmost child. The recursive call is:

```
subset[child_count-1]->remove_biggest(removed_entry);
```

Notice the argument, `removed_entry`, that we use in the recursive call. This argument will be set equal to the item that is removed from the subtree. This is exactly what we need, and there is only one remaining problem. The recursive call might leave the root of `subset[child_count-1]` with one entry too few. How can we fix a child that has a shortage of entries? The `fix_shortage` function can fix such a node. So, after the recursive call, you should check the number of entries in the root of `subset[child_count-1]`. If the number of entries is less than `MINIMUM`, then call `fix_shortage(child_count-1)`.

🕐 PROGRAMMING TIP

WRITE AND TEST SMALL PIECES

If you are implementing the entire set class, don't try to do the whole thing at once. Instead, you should write and test functions one at a time. In this project, you should also carry out a major testing after you have completed the `insert` and `count` functions, and before you have started on any of the erasing machinery.

When you start on the erasing functions, draw a diagram of the top-down design that you are implementing.

Test pieces as soon as you can. This early testing can be aided by initially implementing all of your planned functions with a single line that simply prints the name of the function, indicating that the function has been activated. A single line such as this is called a **stub**. With stubs in place, you can test any function as soon as you have written the complete version. For example, as soon as you implement the erase function, you can test it. You know that it should call the `loose_erase` function, so you expect the `loose_erase` stub to print a message indicating that `loose_erase` has been called.

Throughout your implementation work, it will be useful if you can print some representation of a B-tree. We suggest that you temporarily add a public print function, similar to the function shown in Figure 11.6.

In order for the output of the print function to be understandable, keep the value of MINIMUM small during testing—perhaps 1 or 2.

PROGRAMMING TIP

CONSIDER USING THE STL VECTOR

As an alternative to fixed arrays in your B-tree implementation, you might consider using a vector as described in Appendix H. The advantage of the vector is that it has useful member functions such as insert. Use the vector's reserve member function to allocate the maximum number of items that the vector will ever need.

External B-Trees

Programmers may use B-trees to ensure quick behavior from the fact that the trees are always balanced (all the leaves are at the same depth). If a balanced tree is your only objective, then the choice of the MINIMUM constant is

---

FIGURE 11.6 Implementing a Temporary Member Function That Prints a Set's B-Tree

A Function Implementation

```
template <class Item>
void set<Item>::print(int indent) const
// This is a temporary public function for use by the programmer who implements the set
// class. The function prints a representation of the set's B-tree. The entries of the root node
// are printed with an indentation given by the parameter, and each subtree has an extra
// four spaces of indentation.
// Library facilities used: iostream (provides cout), and iomanip (provides setw)
{
    const int EXTRA_INDENTATION = 4;
    size_t i;

    std::cout << std::setw(indent) << ""; // Print the indentation.

    // Print the data from the root.
    for (i = 0; i < data_count; ++i)
        std::cout << data[i] << " ";
    std::cout << std::endl;

    // Print the subtrees.
    for (i = 0; i < child_count; ++i)
        subset[i]->print(indent+EXTRA_INDENTATION);
}
```

not critical. Sometimes `MINIMUM` is simply 1, meaning that each node has one or two entries, and nonleaf nodes have *two or three* children. This situation is called a **2-3 tree**, which was proposed by John E. Hopcroft several years before B-trees were devised.

most of the nodes reside in slower secondary memory

Sometimes B-trees become large—so large that the entire tree cannot reside in the computer's main memory at one time. For example, a residential phone book of the United States contains over 100 million entries. The set of entries can still be organized as a B-tree, but most of the nodes must be stored in slower secondary memory such as a hard drive or a CD-ROM. Typically, the root node is loaded into main memory, where it stays for the life of the program. But nonroot nodes must be loaded from the secondary memory whenever they are needed. This situation is called an **external B-tree**.

A primary consideration with external B-trees is to reduce the total number of accesses to the secondary memory device. Therefore, the `MINIMUM` constant will be set quite large. With `MINIMUM` set to 1000, we can store more than one billion (10^9) entries with just the root and two levels below it. Because the root is always kept in memory, no search will ever require more than two nodes from the secondary memory device.

Another factor concerns the retrieval mechanism used by the secondary storage device. When a request is made to read from a hard disk or CD-ROM, there is a relatively long initial *access time* to position the disk's read head over the requested section of the disk. Once the head has been positioned, contiguous data can be read fairly quickly. This data is transferred in fixed-sized blocks, using a relatively high *sustained transfer rate*. For example, a 40x CD-ROM has an access time of about $\frac{1}{10}$ of a second. Once the head is positioned, the drive transfers about 6 million bytes per second. With this in mind, you need to ensure that each node is stored in a contiguous area of the disk—for if the node is spread out in several different areas, each area will require $\frac{1}{10}$ of a second access time to reposition the head.

Self-Test Exercises for Section 11.2

8. What are two major differences between a B-tree and a binary search tree? How do these differences affect searching for an item?

9. Suppose `MINIMUM` is 200 for a B-tree. What is the maximum number of entries that a node may contain? What is the minimum number of entries that a nonroot node may have? What is the maximum number of children that a node may have? What is the minimum number of children that a nonleaf, nonroot node may have?

10. Suppose `MINIMUM` is 1000 for a B-tree. The tree has a root and one level of 1000 nodes below that. What is the minimum number of entries that this tree might have? What is the maximum?

11. Suppose a nonleaf node in a B-tree contains the integers 17, 39, and 76 as entries. `MINIMUM` is set to 2. Give one possible set of values for the entries in the children of the node.

12. Start with an empty B-tree, with `MINIMUM` set to 1. Enter the integers 1 through 10. Draw the resulting tree.

13. Remove the numbers 8, 3, and 6 from the tree that you created in the previous exercise. Draw the resulting tree after each removal.

14. How are subtrees stored in the B-tree set implementation in this chapter?

15. What is meant by loose insertion? How is a loose insertion eventually fixed?

16. What is a stub? Why is it useful?

17. What are two factors to consider when using external B-trees?

11.3   TREES, LOGS, AND TIME ANALYSIS

The implementations in this chapter—heaps and B-trees—are efficient for a simple reason: The depth of the trees is kept small so that following a path from the root to a leaf does not examine too many nodes. In fact, we can make a strong statement relating the depth of a tree to the worst-case time required for the operations we have implemented:

Worst-Case Times for Tree Operations

The worst-case time performance for the following operations are all $O(d)$, where d is the depth of the tree:

1. Adding an entry in a binary search tree, a heap, or a B-tree.

2. Deleting an entry from a binary search tree, a heap, or a B-tree.

3. Searching for a specified entry in a binary search tree or a B-tree.

For example, consider adding an entry to a heap. The new entry is placed at the next available location of the heap at the deepest level, d. The priority of the new entry is then compared with its parent's priority, and the new entry might be swapped with its parent. In the worst case, this process continues, comparing the new entry with its parent and swapping, until the new entry reaches the root. In this worst case, the new entry had to be compared with its parent and swapped d times, where d is the depth at which the new entry began its life. Since one comparison and swap requires a fixed number of operations, the total number of operations in the algorithm is a fixed number times d, which is $O(d)$. You can carry out a similar analysis for each of the other tree operations.

Time analyses for these operations are more useful if they are given in terms of the number of entries in the tree, rather than in terms of the tree's depth. To express the time analyses in these terms, we must first answer a secondary question: *What is the maximum depth for a tree with n entries?* We'll answer this question for binary search trees and heaps, leaving the case of B-trees for your exercises. Once this question is answered, we can provide worst-case time analyses in terms of the number of entries in a tree.

Time Analysis for Binary Search Trees

Suppose a binary search tree has n entries. What is the maximum depth the tree could have? A binary tree must have at least one node at each level. For example, a binary tree with depth 2 must have a root (at level 0), at least one child of the root (at level 1), and at least one child of the child (at level 2). If a tree has n nodes, then the first node may appear at the root level, the second node at level 1, the third node at level 2, and so on until the nth node, which appears at depth $n-1$. So, a binary tree with n entries could have a depth as big as $n-1$.

What does this say about the worst-case time analysis of the binary search tree operations in terms of the number of entries in a tree? Here's the analysis:

Worst-Case Times for Binary Search Trees

Adding an entry, deleting an entry, or searching for an entry in a binary search tree with n entries is $O(d)$, where d is the depth of the tree. Since d is no more than $n-1$, the operations are $O(n-1)$, which is $O(n)$ (since we can ignore constants in big-O notation).

Time Analysis for Heaps

In a heap, we can examine the relationship between depth and number of entries by first computing the smallest number of entries required for a heap to reach a given depth d. Remember that a heap is a complete binary tree so that each level must be full before proceeding to the next level. The first entry goes at level 0 (the root level). The next two entries must go at level 1, the next four entries at level 2, the next 8 entries at level 3, and so on. Let's present this information in a table.

Level	Number of nodes to fill the level
0	1 node
1	2 nodes
2	4 nodes
3	8 nodes
4	16 nodes
...	
d	2^d nodes

The values in the table are the maximum number of nodes that may occur at each level. Using the table, we can obtain the total number of nodes needed to reach level d:

Number of nodes needed for a heap to reach depth d is

$$(1 + 2 + 4 + \ldots + 2^{d-1}) + 1$$

The first part of the formula, up to 2^{d-1}, is the number of entries required to completely fill the first d–1 levels, and the extra "+ 1" at the end is required because there must be at least one entry in level d.

This formula can be simplified by shifting the +1 to the front:

Number of nodes needed for a heap to reach depth d is

$$1 + 1 + 2 + 4 + \ldots + 2^{d-1}$$

Why is this a simplification? Look at the start of the formula, which begins $1 + 1\ldots$ Then combine the two 1's, like this:

$$1 + 1 + 2 + 4 + \ldots + 2^{d-1} \quad = \quad 2 + 2 + 4 + \ldots + 2^{d-1}$$

Now we have a formula that begins with two 2's, which can also be combined:

$$2 + 2 + 4 + \ldots + 2^{d-1} \quad = \quad 4 + 4 + \ldots + 2^{d-1}$$

Now we have a formula that begins with two 4's, and if we combine the 4's we get two 8's, and so on until we eventually end up with just $2^{d-1} + 2^{d-1}$. So:

Number of nodes needed for a heap to reach depth d is

$$= (1 + 2 + 4 + \ldots + 2^{d-1}) + 1$$
$$= 2^{d-1} + 2^{d-1}$$

This last formula, $2^{d-1} + 2^{d-1}$, is the same as 2^d, so we have the following result:

The number of nodes needed for a heap to
reach depth d is 2^d.

Expressed another way: The number of nodes in a heap is at least 2^d, where d is the depth of the heap.

This is certainly a simple formula, but in order to use it, we need to explain a bit about **base 2 logarithms**. For any positive number, x, the base 2 logarithm of x is an exponent r such that:

$$2^r = x$$

The number r in this equation is usually written $\log_2 x$. For example:

$$2^0 = 1, \text{ so that } \quad \log_2 1 = 0$$
$$2^1 = 2, \text{ so that } \quad \log_2 2 = 1$$
$$2^2 = 4, \text{ so that } \quad \log_2 4 = 2$$
$$2^3 = 8, \text{ so that } \quad \log_2 8 = 3$$
$$2^4 = 16, \text{ so that } \quad \log_2 16 = 4$$
$$2^d = 2^d, \text{ so that } \quad \log_2 2^d = d$$

The last line of this table is the key to our heap analysis. We know that in a heap, the number of entries, n, is at least 2^d, where d is the depth of the heap. Therefore:

$$\log_2 n \;\geq\; \log_2 2^d \;(\text{since } n \geq 2^d)$$

Since $\log_2 2^d = d$, this implies that:

$$\log_2 n \;\geq\; d.$$

This is the relationship that we need between the number of entries, n, and the depth of a heap. Here's the analysis:

Worst-Case Times for Heap Operations

Adding or deleting an entry in a heap with n entries is $O(d)$, where d is the depth of the tree. Because d is no more than $\log_2 n$, the operations are $O(\log_2 n)$, which is $O(\log n)$ (since we can ignore log bases in big-O notation).

The time analysis for B-trees will also result in $O(\log n)$ time, as you'll be asked to show in Self-Test Exercise 19.

Omitting the subscript, 2, from $O(\log_2 n)$ may be a bit confusing, but to explain why the omission is valid, we need to look at logarithms in more depth. This look at logarithms will also give us a good understanding of the behavior that is expected from logarithmic algorithms, such as adding and deleting from a heap.

Logarithms

The definition of $\log_2 x$ is a number r such that $2^r = x$. The number 2 is called the **base of the logarithm**, and the definition extends to other bases. For example, $\log_{10} x$ is the number r such that $10^r = x$. Or consider base 16, where $\log_{16} x$ is the number r such that $16^r = x$.

Here are some specific examples for base 10:

$$10^0 = 1, \qquad \text{so that } \log_{10} 1 = 0$$
$$10^1 = 10, \qquad \text{so that } \log_{10} 10 = 1$$
$$10^{1.5} = \text{about } 32, \quad \text{so that } \log_{10} 32 = \text{about } 1.5$$
$$10^3 = 1000, \qquad \text{so that } \log_{10} 1000 = 3$$

From these examples, you can see why we said in Chapter 1 that the number of digits in a positive integer n is approximately $\log_{10} n$. You can work out a little table:

For n in the range 1 to 9,	$0 \le \log_{10} n < 1$
For n in the range 10 to 99,	$1 \le \log_{10} n < 2$
For n in the range 100 to 999,	$2 \le \log_{10} n < 3$
For n in the range 1000 to 9999,	$3 \le \log_{10} n < 4$

Extrapolating from this table, you can find a precise relationship between the number of digits in a positive integer and base 10 logarithms (using $\lfloor \log_{10} n \rfloor$ to indicate rounding down the logarithm to an integer):

> The number of digits in a positive integer n is $\lfloor \log_{10} n \rfloor + 1$.

There is also a relationship between logarithms in one base and logarithms in another base:

> For any two bases, a and b, and a positive number x:
> $$(\log_b a) \times (\log_a x) = \log_b x$$

This equation is the reason why bases generally are omitted from big-O notation. For example, if an algorithm requires $\log_2 n$ operations, then that is the same as $4 \times \log_{16} n$ operations, since $\log_2 16$ is 4. In big-O notation, the multiplication by a constant (such as 4) is ignored, and this is why we write simply $O(\log n)$ rather than $O(\log_2 n)$.

Logarithmic Algorithms

Logarithmic algorithms are algorithms with worst-case time $O(\log n)$, such as adding and deleting from a heap. These algorithms have a characteristic time behavior:

> **Time Behavior of Logarithmic Algorithms**
>
> For a logarithmic algorithm, doubling the input size will make the time increase by a fixed number of new operations.

For example, consider adding a new entry to a heap with n entries. The algorithm may look at as many as $\log_2 n$ nodes. If we double the number of nodes to $2n$, then the algorithm may look at as many as $\log_2 2n$ nodes—but $\log_2 2n$ is just one more than $\log_2 n$. (For example, $\log_2 1024 = 10$, and $\log_2 2048 = 11$). So we can double the number of entries in a heap, and the process of adding a new entry requires us to examine only one extra node.

Self-Test Exercises for Section 11.3

18. Evaluate the following logarithms:

$$\log_2 32 \qquad \log_5 125 \qquad \log_{16} 256$$
$$\log_{10} 100 \qquad \log_{37} 1 \qquad \log_9 81$$

19. Show that adding, deleting, and searching in a B-tree have worst-case time $O(\log n)$.

20. Why are logarithmic bases generally omitted from big-O notation?

21. Use the definition of logarithms to show that $\log_2 2n$ is always just one more than $\log_2 n$.

CHAPTER SUMMARY

- A *heap* is a complete binary tree that follows the rule that the entry at any node is never less than any of its children's entries. Heaps provide an efficient implementation of priority queues.

- A *B-tree* is a tree for storing entries in a manner that follows six rules. The first two rules specify the minimum and maximum number of entries for each node. The third rule requires each node's entries to be sorted from smallest to largest. Rules 4 and 5 indicate how many subtrees a nonleaf node must have and provides an order on the elements of the subtrees. The last rule requires each leaf to be at the same depth.

- The tree algorithms that we have seen for binary search trees, heaps, and B-trees all have worst-case time performance of $O(d)$, where d is the depth of the tree.

- The depth of a heap or B-tree is never more than $O(\log n)$, where n is the number of nodes. Hence, the operations on these structures are also $O(\log n)$.

? Solutions to Self-Test Exercises

1. Heaps are always complete binary trees. In addition, the ordering rule is different, requiring that an entry contained by a node is never less than the entries of the node's children.

2. The priority queue class needs a private member variable that is an array of objects that can be compared with a less-than operator. Our solution is based on the interface from Figure 8.12 on page 424. Here is the solution with a fixed-sized array:

```
template <class Item>
class simple_priority_queue
{
public:
    // TYPEDEFS and MEMBER CONSTANT
    typedef Item value_type;
    typedef std::size_t size_type;
    static const size_type CAPACITY=50;
    // CONSTRUCTOR
    priority_queue( );
    // MODIFICATION MEMBER FUNCTIONS
    void pop( );
    void push(const Item& entry);
    // CONSTANT MEMBER FUNCTIONS
    bool empty( ) const;
    size_type size( ) const;
    Item top( ) const;
private:
    Item data[CAPACITY];
    size_type used;
};
```

For the version with no fixed capacity, you can change the data array to a dynamic array. You'll also need to add a copy constructor, an assignment operator, and a destructor.

3. A new entry to a heap is initially placed in the leftmost available location in the deepest level, in order to maintain a complete binary tree. (Later, the new entry is pushed upward to ensure that the heap rules are still valid.)

4. When an item is removed from a heap, the last entry of the deepest level is placed in the root. This item is then pushed downward to ensure

that the heap rules are still valid. After the reheapification downward, the largest remaining item is at the root.

5. With our insertion algorithm, you end up with this heap:

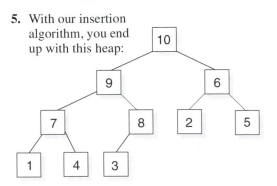

6. With our removal algorithm, you end up with this heap:

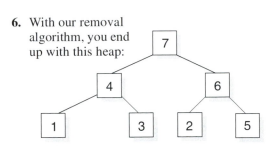

7. If we swap with the smaller child, then the larger child will still have a priority that exceeds its parent's priority.

8. There are many differences that you might choose for this answer, but two fundamental differences are that each node in a B-tree may contain more than one entry (whereas a binary search tree has one entry per node), and the number of children for a non-leaf node in a B-tree is exactly one more than the number of entries (whereas in a binary search tree, each node has at most two children).

   When searching for an item in a binary search tree, the searcher must always choose between going left or right at each node. In a B-tree, the searcher must choose among more than just two possible children.

9. The maximum number of entries that a node may contain is 400, although during an insertion we may temporarily have a node with 401 entries. The minimum number of entries that a nonroot node may have is 200, although during a removal we may temporarily have a node with 199 entries. The maximum number of children that a node may have is 401, although during an insertion, we may temporarily have a node with 402 children. The minimum number of children that a nonleaf, nonroot node may have is 201, although during a removal we may temporarily have a node with 200 children.

10. The root has 999 entries, and each of the 1000 nodes at the next level has between 1000 and 2000 entries. Therefore, the total number of entries in the tree is between 1,000,999 and 2,000,999 entries.

11. Child 0: 15, 16; Child 1: 25, 26; Child 3: 50, 51; Child 4: 80, 81.

12. With our insertion algorithm, you end up with this B-tree:

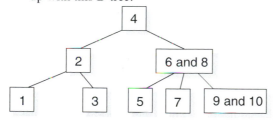

13. After removing the 8:

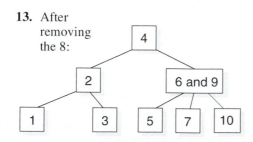

13. (continued)

After removing the 3:

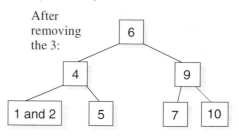

After removing the 6:

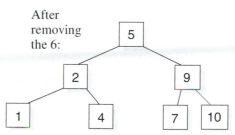

14. Each subtree is stored as an set object. The parent of each subset stores pointers to the smaller set objects.

15. A loose insertion allows the top node of a subtree to temporarily hold one too many entries. The problem is fixed by splitting the node with two many entries. After the split, one new node contains the entries before the middle, another new node contains the entries after the middle, and the middle entry itself has been passed upward to a higher level.

16. A stub is a function with a single line that simply prints the name of the function, indicating that it has been activated. It is useful for writing and testing functions one at a time.

17. The total number of accesses to the secondary memory devices should be minimized. Also, ensure that each node is stored in a contiguous area of the disk.

18. The logarithms are:

$$\log_2 32 = 5 \quad \log_5 125 = 3 \quad \log_{16} 256 = 2$$
$$\log_{10} 100 = 2 \quad \log_{37} 1 = 0 \quad \log_9 81 = 2$$

19. In all three functions, the number of total steps is a constant times the depth of the B-tree. For non-empty trees, this depth is no more than $\log_M n$, where M is the MINIMUM constant and n is the number of entries in the tree. Thus, the functions all require no more than $O(\log n)$ operations.

20. Bases are not generally used in big-O notation because a relationship exists between logarithms of different bases, such that they can be equated using a constant. In other words, for any two bases b and d, a logarithm in base b is always equal to a constant times the same logarithm in base d. (This constant is $\log_b d$.) Big-O notation ignores multiplicative constants.

21. All logarithms in this solution are base 2:
$$2^{1+\log n} = 2 \times 2^{\log n} = 2n = 2^{\log 2n}$$
Therefore, $1 + \log n = \log 2n$.

PROGRAMMING PROJECTS
For more in-depth projects, please see www.cs.colorado.edu/~main/projects/

---

1 Using a heap, implement the priority queue class from Section 8.4. The class should have a static constant member variable, CAPACITY, which is the maximum size of the heap (as in the solution to Self-Test Exercise 1) and an array, data, that contains the heap with the entries. We also want to have FIFO behavior for entries with equal priority. To obtain this behavior, the class should have an extra private member variable which is an array, order, where order[i] contains the order in which data[i] was added to the queue. For example, if entry[7] was the 33rd item added to the priority queue, then order[7] would be 33. When you are comparing two entries with equal priority, use the order number to "break the tie," (so that if two entries have the same priority number, then the one with the earlier order number will come out of the priority queue first).

2 Repeat Project 1, with no predefined limit on the size of the heap. Use a dynamic array.

3 Use a B-tree to implement the set class from Figure 11.4 on page 545. Follow the programming tips from page 563.

4 The <math> facility provides a standard function log(x), which returns the natural logarithm of x (with a base that is approximately 2.71828). This base is written e, and the logarithms with this base are called **natural logarithms**. The number e may seem like a strange choice for the base of a logarithm, but the choice is motivated by the fact that natural logarithms are easy to approximate as the sum of a series, and they also occur as the limits of series such as the computation of compound interest. In your math class, you probably used the notation *ln x* for the natural logarithm of x.

Anyway, in this project, you are to write a function:

```
double logb(double base, double x);
```

The function returns the logarithm of x to the given base. Make use of the log function and the formulas in Section 11.3.

5 The heap in this chapter is referred to as a maxheap, because the highest priority value is also the maximum value. Implement the heap as a minheap, in which the entry of the node with the highest priority has the minimum value in the heap, and an entry of a node is never more than the entries of the node's children.

6 Redo Programming Problem 12 in Chapter 8, using the heap implementation of the priority queue. Break the tie of equal elements using the method in Programming Problem 1.

CHAPTER **12**

Searching

His reasons are as two grains of wheat hid in two bushels
of chaff: you shall seek all day ere you find them, and,
when you have them, they are not worth the search.

WILLIAM SHAKESPEARE
The Merchant of Venice

LEARNING OBJECTIVES

When you complete Chapter 12, you will be able to...

- do a simulation by hand of a serial search (to find an element in an array) or a binary search (to find an element in a sorted array) and be able to implement these algorithms.
- demonstrate why binary search has a logarithmic worst-case performance.
- do a simulation by hand of an insertion or removal of an element from an open-address or chained hash table and be able to implement these algorithms.
- implement a hash table class using open-address hashing or chained hashing with an underlying data structure that is either an array or a vector.
- use template parameters that are classes, constant values, or functions.
- calculate the expected number of elements that will be examined to find an element in an open-address or chained hash table with a specified load factor.
- use the STL map and multimap classes as an alternative to hash tables in situations where the keys are from a data type that can be sorted.

CHAPTER CONTENTS

Searching a list of values is a common computational task. An application program might retrieve a student record, bank account record, credit record, or any other type of record using a search algorithm. In this chapter, we present and analyze some of the most common (and some of the most efficient) methods of searching for a particular item. The algorithms include serial search, binary search, and search by hashing.

We also use the search algorithms to develop additional techniques for analyzing the running times of algorithms, particularly average-time analyses and the analysis of recursive algorithms.

12.1 SERIAL SEARCH AND BINARY SEARCH

Serial Search

Our starting point is the searching algorithm, shown in Figure 12.1. This algorithm, called a **serial search**, steps through part of an array one item at a time looking for a desired item. The search stops when the item is found or when the search has examined each item without success. The technique is often used because it is easy to write and is applicable to many situations.

Serial Search—Analysis

The running time of the serial search is easy to analyze, but some care is needed to specify the precise kind of analysis. As always, we will count the number of operations required by the algorithm rather than measuring actual elapsed time. For searching an array, a common approach is to count one operation each time that the algorithm accesses an element of the array. With the serial search, the size of the array is one important factor in determining the number of array accesses, but even if we use a particular fixed array, the number of array accesses will still vary depending on precisely which target we are looking for. If the target is the first element in the array, then there will be only one array access. If the target is near the middle of the array, then the serial search accesses about half of the array elements.

worst case

Usually when we discuss running times, we consider the "hardest" inputs, for example, a target that requires the algorithm to access the largest number of array elements. This is called the **worst-case** running time. For the serial search, the worst-case running time occurs when the target is not in the array. In this case, the algorithm accesses every element, and we have the following formula:

Worst-Case Time for Serial Search

For an array of *n* elements, the worst-case time for serial search requires *n* array accesses.

---

average case

With serial search, searches of an *n*-element array usually require fewer than *n* array accesses. Thus, the worst-case expression "*n* array accesses" makes serial search sound worse than it often is. An alternative is the **average-case** running time, which is obtained by averaging the running times for all different inputs of a particular kind. For example, we can develop an expression for the average-case running time of serial search based on all the targets that are actually in the array. To be concrete in this first example, suppose that the array has 10 elements, so that there are 10 possible targets. If we are searching for the target that occurs at the first location, then there is just one array access. If we are searching for the target that occurs at the second location, then there are two array accesses. And so on, through the final target, which requires 10 array accesses. In all, there are 10 possible targets, which require 1, 2, 3, 4, 5, 6, 7, 8, 9, or 10 array accesses. The average of all these searches is

$$\frac{1 + 2 + 3 + 4 + 5 + 6 + 7 + 8 + 9 + 10}{10} = 5.5$$

FIGURE 12.1   Serial Search Algorithm

Pseudocode for Serial Search

// *Searches for a desired item in the n array elements starting at a[first]*

Set a `size_t` variable i to 0, and set a boolean variable found to false.

```
while ((i < n) && !found)
{
     if (a[first+i] is the desired item)
          found = true;
     else
          ++i;
}

if (found)
     The desired item is in a[first+i].
else
     The desired item does not appear in the n items starting at a[first].
```

We can generalize this example so that the average-case running time of the serial search is written as an expression with part of the expression being the size of the array. Using n as the size of the array, this expression for the average-case running time is

$$\frac{1 + 2 + \ldots + n}{n} = \frac{n(n + 1)/2}{n} = (n + 1)/2$$

The first equality in this formula is obtained from the formula that we developed on page 19. We can summarize the average-case running time for serial search:

Average-Case Time for Serial Search

For an array of n elements, the average-case time for serial search to find an element that is in the array requires $(n + 1)/2$ array accesses.

You may have noticed that both the worst-case time and the average-case time are $O(n)$ expressions; nevertheless, the average case is about half the time of the worst case.

best case   A third way to measure running times is called **best-case** running time, and as the name suggests, it takes the most optimistic view possible. The best-case running time is defined as the smallest of all the running times on inputs of a particular size. For serial search, the best case occurs when the target is found at the front of the array, requiring only one array access:

Best-Case Time for Serial Search

For an array of n elements, the best-case time for serial search is just one array access.

Unless the best-case behavior occurs with high probability, the best-case running time generally is not used during an analysis.

Binary Search

Serial search is easy to implement, easy to analyze, and fine to use if you are only searching a small array a few times. However, if a search algorithm will be used over and over, it is worthwhile to find a faster algorithm. A dramatically faster search algorithm is sometimes available. The algorithm, called *binary search,* may be used only if the array is sorted. Here are three examples for which binary search is applicable:

- Searching an array of integers, where the array is sorted from the smallest integer (at the front) to the largest integer (at the end of the array).

- Searching an array of strings, where the strings are sorted alphabetically.

- Searching an array where each component is an object containing information about an auto part, and the array is sorted by "part numbers" from the smallest to the largest.

For concreteness, we'll develop the algorithm for the first of these three cases (searching a sorted array of integers), but keep in mind that the same algorithm applies to any other kind of sorted array.

Our integer version of the binary search will be implemented with a function called `search`. The prototype for `search` requires six parameters. The first three parameters provide the array itself, the starting index of the portion of the array that we are searching, and the number of elements to search. The fourth parameter is the target that we are searching for. For example, consider:

```
search(b, 17, 10, 42, ...
```

This example shows the first four arguments needed to search for the number 42 occurring somewhere in the 10 elements from `b[17]` through `b[26]`.

The fifth and sixth parameters are reference parameters, used to return the result of the search. The fifth parameter is a boolean value, indicating whether the target was found. If the target was found, then the sixth parameter indicates the index where the target occurs in the array. Here is the prototype:

```
void search(
    const int a[ ],
    size_t first,
    size_t size,
    int target,
    bool& found,
    size_t& location
);
// Precondition: The array segment starting at a[first] and containing size
// elements is sorted from smallest to largest.
// Postcondition: The array segment starting at a[first] and containing size
// elements has been searched for the target. If the target was present,
// then found is true, and location is set so that target == a[location].
// Otherwise found is set to false.
```

Binary Search—Design

Let us produce an algorithm to perform this search task. It will help to visualize the problem in concrete terms. Suppose that the list of numbers is a list of invalid credit card numbers, and it is so long that it takes a book to list them all. This is in fact how invalid credit card numbers are distributed to stores that do

FIGURE 12.2 The Binary Search Function

A Function Implementation

```
void search(
    const int a[ ],
    size_t first,
    size_t size,
    int target,
    bool& found,
    size_t& location
)
// Precondition: The array segment starting at a[first] and containing size elements is sorted
// from smallest to largest.
// Postcondition: The array segment starting at a[first] and containing size elements has been
// searched for the target. If the target was present, then found is true, and location is set so
// that target == a[location]. Otherwise, found is set to false.
// Library facilities used: cstdlib (provides size_t from namespace std)
{
    size_t middle;

    if (size == 0)
        found = false;
    else
    {
        middle = first + size/2;
        if (target == a[middle])
        {
            location = middle;
            found = true;
        }
        else if (target < a[middle])
            // The target is less than a[middle], so search before the middle.
            search(a, first, size/2, target, found, location);
        else
            // The target must be greater than a[middle], so search after the middle.
            search(a, middle+1, (size-1)/2, target, found, location);
    }
}
```

Sample Results of search(b, 2, 5, 42, ...) **when b contains**

-7	3	8	39	42	63	70
[0]	[1]	[2]	[3]	[4]	[5]	[6]

found will be set to true;
location will be set to 4.

www.cs.colorado.edu/~main/chapter12/search.cxx   **WWW**

not have access to a computer. If you are a clerk and are handed a credit card, you must check to see if it is on the list and hence invalid. How would you proceed? Open the book to the middle and see if it is there. If not and it is smaller than the middle number, then work toward the beginning of the book. If it is larger than the middle number, work your way toward the back of the book. This idea produces our first draft of an algorithm:

```
if (size == 0)
    found = false;
else
{
    middle = index of the approximate midpoint of the array segment;
    if (target == a[middle])
        the target has been found at a[middle];
    else if (target < a[middle])
        search for the target in the area before the midpoint;
    else if (target > a[middle])
        search for the target in the area after the midpoint;
}
```

It is natural to use recursive calls for the two substeps that "search smaller lists," and that is what our implementation will do. As with any recursive function, we must ensure that the function terminates rather than producing infinite recursion. This insurance is provided by noting that each recursive call searches a shorter list, and when the list length reaches zero there can be no further recursive calls. This reasoning can be formalized as in Chapter 9 (see "Ensuring That There Is No Infinite Recursion" on page 461). Using the Chapter 9 technique, we see that the parameter `size` is a valid *variant expression*, with a *threshold* of zero. In other words, the `size` parameter is always reduced by at least one on each recursive call, and when `size` reaches zero, there is no further recursion.

Our complete implementation of the pseudocode is shown in Figure 12.2.

PITFALL

COMMON INDEXING ERRORS IN BINARY SEARCH IMPLEMENTATIONS

Binary search and similar array-based algorithms are notorious for having errors involving the array indices. Two of the most common problems are listed here:

Calculating the size of the array for the recursive call. The implementation in Figure 12.2 has two recursive calls. It's important to double-check your expression for the size of the array segment that is being searched in the recursive call. For example, one of our recursive calls searches the segment that occurs before a[middle]. This segment begins at a[first] going up to (but not including) a[middle]. How many entries are there in this segment? The answer is middle-first, which is the same as size/2, according to this calculation:

```
middle - first = (first + size/2) - first = size/2
```

In our recursive call, we use the expression `size/2` for the argument that expresses the size of the array, since this expression conveys the idea that the recursive call searches about half of the original array.

You should carry out a similar calculation to verify that the number of elements after a`[middle]` is `(size-1)/2`. Hence, the size argument in our second recursive call is the expression `(size-1)/2`.

Ensuring that size_t values do not become negative. A second common error is writing a size_t expression that could end up with a negative value. For example, `first`, `size`, and `middle` might all be as small as zero, so it would be a mistake to write any of these expressions: `first - 1`, `size - 1`, `middle - 1`. We did not need any of these expressions, but it may be tempting to use these expressions in other implementations of binary search (particularly if you change the prototype so that the first and last indices are both parameters).

Avoid these possibly negative `size_t` values, as the run-time results are unpredictable.

Binary Search—Analysis

We want to estimate the running time for the binary search algorithm given in Figure 12.2. The algorithm tests to see if the middle entry of the array has the target that we are looking for. If it does, the algorithm stops, returning the index of this middle entry. If our sought-after target is not in the middle of the array, the algorithm searches either the "half" above or the "half" below this midpoint. This narrows the search to about half of the array elements, then another recursive call can take it to half of that, then half of that, and so forth. The algorithm runs longest if the target is not in the array. If the target is not in the array, then eventually the algorithm will make a recursive call to search an array with zero elements. Of course, the target cannot occur in an empty array, so at that point the algorithm returns and tells us that the target could not be found. We want to analyze this algorithm for worst-case running time.

The binary search algorithm is a recursive algorithm so we need to compute the amount of time taken by all recursive calls, and recursive calls of recursive calls, etc. As in other cases, we will simply count the number of operations performed. The only operations mentioned in the algorithm are addition, subtraction, division, assignment, tests for equality or "less than," and the array access operation.

Let n be the number of elements in the array segment being searched (i.e., the value of `size`). We want to know how many operations the algorithm will perform in the worst case. As it turns out, the worst case is when the target is not in the array so we will assume that `target` is not in the array.

When the algorithm starts out, it tests to see if the array segment is empty *one operation* (`size == 0`). This is a stopping case for the recursion. We'll charge one operation for this test for emptiness.

After that, the algorithm computes the midpoint index as follows: *three more operations*

```
middle = first + size/2;
```

This adds an additional three operations, one each of division, addition, and assignment.

Next the algorithm tests to see whether the target equals `a[middle]`. This *two more* requires one array access, and one application of `==`, and so counts as two more *operations* operations.

We are assuming that the target is not in the array. So the algorithm then goes on to do the comparison:

another two operations

```
(target < a[middle])
```

This also requires two operations—one for the array access and one for the comparison.

The algorithm then makes a recursive call, which requires a few operations to *10 more* provide the arguments. The exact number of operations depends on the way *operations* function calls are implemented, but 10 operations should handle all the arithmetic and passing of arguments. And, of course, there will be the operations carried out by the recursive call, but we have not begun to worry about that yet.

If we total up all the operations used, we've estimated that the algorithm performs no more than 18 operations before each recursive call. The recursive call can produce another recursive call, which in turn produces another recursive call, which in turn produces another recursive call, until the procedure gets to a stopping case. Each of these recursive calls is preceded by 18 (or fewer) operations. The total number of operations is thus no more than 18 times the length of this chain of recursive calls plus the number of operations performed in the stopping case. Using the symbol $T(n)$ for the worst-case running time to search an array of n elements, we therefore have:

$T(n) = 18 \times$ (the length of the longest chain of recursive calls)
$+$
the number of operations performed in the stopping case

There are two possible stopping cases—when the size becomes zero, or when the target is found. Since the worst case is when the key is not in the array, we assume that the key is not found. The stopping case when the key is not found requires two operations (an equality test and an assignment to `found`).

Thus, the running time function can be expressed by

$T(n) = 18 \times$ (the length of the longest chain of recursive calls) $+ 2$

There is a standard term for the long phrase in parentheses, namely the **depth of recursive calls**:

Depth of Recursive Calls

The length of the longest chain of recursive calls in the execution of an algorithm is called the **depth of recursive calls** for that algorithm.

This definition allows us to replace the long phrase in our formula with this standard term and so obtain the slightly more compact formula:

$$T(n) = 18 \times \text{(the depth of recursive calls)} + 2$$

Rather than compute the exact value for the depth of recursive calls, we will determine an upper bound approximation to the number of recursive calls. The figure we obtain may be slightly larger than the actual number of calls but will be a close approximation. This is common practice when analyzing running times. It is often easier to calculate an upper bound than it is to calculate the exact running time. As long as we use an upper bound so that we are estimating higher than the true value, then we will always be safe. This way our algorithm might turn out to be a bit faster than we thought, but never slower. Now let us calculate this upper bound on the length of the longest string of recursive calls.

The array contains n elements to be searched. Each recursive call is made on an array segment that contains, at most, half of the elements. Hence, to approximate the depth of recursive calls, all we need to do is determine how many times we can divide n in half, and then divide that half in half again, then divide that result in half yet again, and so on until the array is "all gone." The array is "all gone" when there are no entries to divide in half (that is, when size is zero). Thus:

**Depth of Recursive Calls for Binary Search
of an *n*-Element Array**

The depth of recursive calls is, at most, the number of times that n can be divided by 2, stopping when the result is less than 1.

We can now estimate the number of operations performed by the binary search algorithm on an array with n elements. We know that the number of operations performed is at most

$$T(n) = 18 \times \text{(the depth of recursive calls)} + 2$$

$$= 18 \times \text{(the number of times that } n \text{ can be divided by}$$
$$2, \text{ stopping when the result is less than 1)} + 2$$

Let us denote the second expression in parentheses by $H(n)$ and call it the **halving function**. In other words:

The Halving Function

The **halving function** $H(n)$ is defined by $H(n)$ = (the number of times that n can be divided by 2, stopping when the result is less than 1).

With this new definition, we can express our estimate of the running time for the binary search algorithm compactly. The worst-case running time is closely approximated by:

$$T(n) = 18\,H(n) + 2$$

To get a feel for how fast or slow this running time is, we must know a little about this function $H(n)$. As it turns out, $H(n)$ is almost exactly equal to the base 2 logarithm of n, which is written $\log_2 n$. To be even more precise, for any positive integer n:

Value of the Halving Function

$H(n)$ = (the number of times that n can be divided by 2, stopping when the result is less than 1) has the value:
$$H(n) = \lfloor \log_2 n \rfloor + 1$$

The symbols $\lfloor\ \rfloor$ mean that we round fractional numbers down to the next lowest whole number. For example, $\lfloor 3.7 \rfloor$ is 3. The notation $\lfloor\ \rfloor$ is called the **floor function**, and we have used it before, in Chapter 1 when we noted that the number of digits in a positive integer n is $\lfloor \log_{10} n \rfloor + 1$. Since $H(n)$ is a whole number and $\log_2 n$ might include a fractional part, they cannot always be exactly equal, but the above equality means that $H(n)$ and $\log_2 n$ will never differ by more than one. Let's explore what this equality tells us about the running time of binary search.

For an array with n elements ($n > 0$), we have seen that the worst-case running time of the binary search algorithm is

$$T(n) = 18\,H(n) + 3 = 18(\lfloor \log_2 n \rfloor + 1) + 2$$

If we throw out the constants, the result says that the worst-case running time is *logarithmic* (that is, $O(\log n)$).

Worst-Case Time for Binary Search

For an array of n elements, the worst-case time for binary search is logarithmic.

An algorithm with logarithmic running time is fast because the logarithm of *n* is much smaller than *n*. Moreover, the larger *n* is, the more dramatic this difference becomes. For example, the base 2 logarithm of 2 is 1, the base 2 logarithm of 8 is 3, the base 2 logarithm of 64 is 6, the base 2 logarithm of a thousand is less than 10, and the base 2 logarithm of a million is less than 20.

binary search is an O(log n) algorithm

This means that the binary search algorithm is very efficient. On an array with a thousand elements, our binary search algorithm with a running time of $18(\lfloor \log_2 n \rfloor + 1) + 2$ will perform no more than 182 operations. Even with a million entries, the worst-case time is fewer than 400 operations.

average time is also O(log n)

We won't give a rigorous analysis of the average running time for binary search, but we can tell you that the average running time for actually finding a number is $O(\log n)$. It is not hard to see why this is true. We have already seen that, when a target is not found, the depth of recursion is $\lfloor \log_2 n \rfloor + 1$. In the worst case, even a found target requires a recursion depth of $\lfloor \log_2 n \rfloor$ (just one less than not finding a target). In some cases, the algorithm will not need that many recursive calls. If the sought-after target is found, the algorithm can terminate without additional recursive calls. Thus, on some inputs the depth of recursive calls will be 0, on others it will be 1, on others 2, and so forth up to $\lfloor \log_2 n \rfloor$. However, a more complete analysis would show that nearly half the keys in the array end up taking a recursion depth of $\lfloor \log_2 n \rfloor$. Even if the other half of the keys had no recursion at all, this would still result in an *average* recursion depth of one half of $\lfloor \log_2 n \rfloor$. Thus, the average number of recursive calls for finding a key is at least one half of $\lfloor \log_2 n \rfloor$. So, the average case can only save us a factor of ½ or less over the worst case. But constants like ½ do not matter in big-*O* expressions; therefore the average-case running time is $O(\log n)$, the same as the worst-case running time.

Standard Library Search Functions

The Standard Template Library provides operations in `<algorithm>` to find elements within both sorted and unsorted ranges. These functions work with forward iterators, bidirectional iterators, and random-access iterators (see Section 6.3).

Functions for Sorted Ranges

The following functions each have two versions. One version uses the operator < to compare items. A second version, which we won't discuss, uses an extra parameter at the end to provide a comparison function. In each case, two iterators, `first` and `last`, provide a range of elements [`first..last`), which includes all the elements from `*first` up to but not including `*last`, and these elements must be sorted from smallest to largest.

```
bool binary_search
     (Iterator first, Iterator last, const Item& target);
```

```
Iterator lower_bound
        (Iterator first, Iterator last, const Item& target);

Iterator upper_bound
        (Iterator first, Iterator last, const Item& target);
```

The `binary_search` function returns true if a specified value appears in the sorted range, and false otherwise.

binary search

The `lower_bound` and `upper_bound` functions both return an iterator in the range [`first..last`).

Normally, the iterator returned by `lower_bound` is an iterator that refers to the first occurrence of the target in the range [`first..last`). For example, suppose the elements in our sequence are the integers 2, 4, 6, 6, 7, 9, and 11; if our target is the number 6, then `lower_bound` will return an iterator that refers to the first occurrence of the number 6. If the target does not appear in the range, then the iterator returned by `lower_bound` will refer to the first item that is bigger than the target. With the same sequence (2, 4, 6, 6, 7, 9, 11) and a target of 8, the `lower_bound` function will return an iterator that refers to the number 9. If all of the sequence items are less than the target, then the return value will be equal to the `last` iterator. Another way to view the lower bound iterator is that it is the leftmost spot in the sequence before which the target can be inserted with the numbers still staying in order.

lower bound

The iterator returned by `upper_bound` is an iterator that refers to the first item that is bigger than the target. In our example sequence (2, 4, 6, 6, 7, 9, 11) and the target of 6, the `upper_bound` function will return an iterator that refers to the number 7. Once again, if no such element can be found, then the return value is the `last` iterator. Another way to view the upper bound iterator is that it is the rightmost spot in the sequence before which the target can be inserted with the numbers staying in order.

upper bound

Here's another example that uses a vector of strings:

```
vector<string> pets;

// Put some strings into alphabetical order:
pets.push_back("cat");
pets.push_back("dog");
pets.push_back("dog");
pets.push_back("fish");
pets.push_back("snake");
pets.push_back("turtle");
```

The vector now contains six strings, sorted alphabetically:

"cat"	"dog"	"dog"	"fish"	"snake"	"turtle"

At this point, we can find the first occurrence of "dog" and the first item after all the dogs, like this:

```
vector<string>::iterator first_dog =
    = lower_bound(pets.begin( ), pets.end( ), "dog");

vector<string>::iterator after_dog =
    = upper_bound(pets.begin( ), pets.end( ), "dog");
```

At this point in the code, *first_dog will be the first occurrence of "dog" and *after_dog will be "fish".

By the way, the only time that lower_bound and upper_bound return the same iterator is when the target does not appear in the sorted range. The technique used by both of these functions is a binary search, so their behavior is guaranteed to be logarithmic in the size of the range.

Functions for Unsorted Ranges

The STL find and count functions work with any STL sequence class that has an iterator, regardless of whether the sequence is sorted. Note that some containers, such as set and map, implement their own versions of the find and count functions. The prototypes for these functions are

```
difference_type count
    (Iterator first, Iterator last, const Item& target);
iterator find
    (Iterator first, Iterator last, const Item& target);
```

count

The count function's return type is a special integer type that allows the computer to store integers that might be too large for an int. The return value of the count function is the number of times that the target value appears in the range [first..last). It uses the == operator of the Item type to determine whether an item is equal to the target.

find

The find function returns an iterator that refers to the first occurrence of the target. If the target is not found, the last iterator is returned. The find and count functions may be used with any of the STL container classes or with arrays. Even the STL string class can be searched with these functions, as shown in Figure 12.3.

The STL search Function

An STL function called search can be used to determine whether a copy of one sequence (determined by two iterators [target_first..target_last)) occurs as a contiguous piece somewhere within a second sequence (determined by two other iterators [first..last)). The prototype is shown here:

```
iterator1 search(
    iterator1 first, iterator1 last,
    iterator2 target_first, iterator2 target_last
);
```

The return value is an iterator in [first..last) which is the start of an occurrence of a copy of [target_first..target_last). If there is no such occurrence, the the return value is the last iterator.

FIGURE 12.3   Using the find Function with a String

A Program

```cpp
#include <algorithm>    // Provides the find function
#include <iostream>     // Provides getline and cout
#include <string>       // Provides the string class
using namespace std;

int main( )
{
    string line;
    string:: iterator i, where_is_e;

    cout << "Please enter a line of text: ";
    getline(cin, line);
    where_is_e = find(line.begin(), line.end(), 'e');

    cout << "You entered the following before entering an e: ";
    for (i = line.begin(); i != where_is_e; ++i)
        cout << *i;
    cout << endl;

    cout << "The rest of your input was: ";
    for (i = where_is_e; i != line.end(); ++i)
        cout << *i;
    cout << endl;

    return 0;
}
```

A Sample Dialogue

Please enter a line of text: **Cyclops has just one eye.**
You entered the following before entering an e: Cyclops has just on
The rest of your input was: e eye.

www.cs.colorado.edu/~main/chapter12/testfind.cxx   **W W W**

Self-Test Exercises for Section 12.1

1. When is a serial search an acceptable choice?

2. What is the worst-case, average-case, and best-case running time for a successful serial search?

3. Reimplement the search function from Figure 12.2 on page 580 as a serial search. Use the pseudocode from Figure 12.1 on page 577, and make appropriate adjustments to the precondition/postcondition contract.

4. Why does a binary search function require parameters of the first array index and the size of the array?

5. What are the stopping cases in the recursive binary search function?

6. This exercise requires familiarity with template functions (Section 6.1). Rewrite the search function from Figure 12.2 on page 580 so that it is a template function. There is a template parameter for the type of the array's component.

7. Consider the search function from Figure 12.2 on page 580. Rewrite the function so that there is no `size` parameter. Instead, there is a parameter called `last`, which is the last index of the array segment that is being searched. Your precondition may require `first <= last`.

8. Compute the following values (H is the halving function): $H(1)$, $H(2)$, $H(4)$, $H(7)$, $H(8)$, $H(9)$.

12.2 OPEN-ADDRESS HASHING

In this section we will present another approach to storing and searching for values. The technique, called *hashing*, has a worst-case behavior that is linear for finding a target, but with some care, hashing can be dramatically fast in the average case. Hashing also makes it easy to add and delete elements from the collection that is being searched, providing an advantage over binary search (since binary search must ensure that the entire list stays sorted when elements are added or deleted).

Introduction to Hashing

The Sixth Column Tractor Company sells all kinds of tractors with various stock numbers, prices, and other details. They want us to store information about each tractor in an inventory so that they can later retrieve information about any particular tractor simply by entering its stock number. To be specific, suppose the information about each tractor is an object of the following form, with the stock number stored in the key field:

```
struct tractor
{
    int key;              // The stock number
    double cost;          // The price, in dollars
    int horsepower;       // Size of the engine
};
```

In this example, we have used the keyword *struct* rather than *class*. A struct is the same as a class, with one difference: Unless you state otherwise, *struct members are public*. Therefore, even without the keyword *public*, our tractor definition has three public member variables.

unless you state otherwise, struct members are public

As a kind of programming pact, C++ programmers tend to use a struct only when all the members are public. For example, you will see this use of structs by the Hewlett-Packard programmers who provided the first implementation of the C++ Standard Library.

Struct

A **struct** is a special kind of class. The special feature is that struct members are all public (unless you state otherwise).

C++ programmers tend to use a struct only when *all* the members are public.

Of course there might be other information in each tractor object, but this will do for our example. If the stock numbers have values ranging from 0 to 49, we could store the tractor objects in an array of the following type, placing stock number i in location data[i]:

```
tractor data[50]; // Array of 50 tractor records
```

The individual elements of our array are called the **records** of our data collection. The record for stock number i can be retrieved immediately since we know it is in data[i].

But what if the stock numbers do not form a neat range like 0...49. Suppose that we know there will be 50 or fewer different stock numbers, but that they will be distributed in the range 0 through 4999. We could use an array with 5000 components, but that seems wasteful since only a small fraction of the array would be used. It appears that we have no alternative but to store the records in an array with 50 elements and to use a serial search through the array whenever we wish to find a particular stock number. Things are not that bad. If we are clever, we can store the records in a relatively small array and yet retrieve particular stock numbers much faster than we would by serial search.

To illustrate the trick involved, suppose that an inside informer at the Sixth Column Tractor Company tells us that the stock numbers will be these:

```
0, 100, 200, 300, ... 4800, 4900
```

In this case, we can store the records in an array called `data` with only 50 components. The record with stock number `i` can be stored at this location:

```
data[i / 100]
```

With the aid of integer division, we can make do with the indexes 0 through 49, even though the numbers become as large as 4900. If we want stock number 700, we compute 700/100 and obtain the index 7. The record for stock number 700 is stored in array component `data[7]`.

hash function

This general technique is called **hashing**. Each record requires a unique identifying value called its **key**. In our example, the key was the stock number stored in a member variable called `key`, but other, more complex keys are sometimes used. A function, called the **hash function**, maps key values to array indexes. Suppose we name our hash function `hash`. If a record has a key value of `i`, then we will try to store that record at location `data[hash(i)]`. Using the hash function to compute the correct array index is called **hashing the key to an array index**. The hash function must be chosen so that its return value is always a valid index for the array. The hash function may be either a declared C++ function or a simple arithmetic expression. In our example, `hash(i)` was this expression:

```
i / 100
```

collisions

In our example, every key produced a different index value when it was hashed. That is a perfect hash function, but unfortunately a perfect hash function cannot always be found. Suppose we change the example so that we no longer have stock number 400, but we have 399 instead. Then the record with stock number 300 will be placed in `data[3]` as before, but where will stock number 399 be placed? Stock number 399 is supposed to be placed in `data[399/100]`. In other words, the record for stock number 399 is supposed to be placed in `data[3]`. There are now two different records that belong in `data[3]`. This situation is known as a **collision**. In this case we could redefine the hash function to avoid the collision. But in practice, you do not know the exact numbers that will occur as keys, and therefore you cannot design a hash function that is guaranteed to be free of collisions (unless, perhaps, your insider at the tractor company has a lot of pull). Something must be done to cope with the tractor collisions.

Typically you do not know what numbers will be used as the key values, but you do know an upper bound on how many there will be. The usual approach is to use an array size that is larger than needed—later we will see formulas that indicate how many extra positions are needed. The extra array positions make collisions less likely. A good hash function will distribute the key values uniformly through the index range of the array. If the array indexes range from 0 to 99, then you might use the following hash function to produce an array index for a record with a given `key`:

```
key % 100
```

This hash function always produces a value in the range 0 to 99 (that is, the remainder when `key` is divided by 100).

One way of dealing with collisions is the algorithm given here:

dealing with collisions

// *Basic storage by hashing algorithm*

1. For a record with key value given by `key`, compute the index `hash(key)`.
2. If `data[hash(key)]` does not already contain a record, then store the record in `data[hash(key)]` and end the storage algorithm.
3. If the location `data[hash(key)]` already contains a record, then try `data[hash(key)+1]`. If that location already contains a record, try `data[hash(key)+2]`, and so forth until a vacant position is found. When the highest numbered array position is reached, simply go to the start of the array. For example, if the array indexes are 0...99, and 98 is the key, then try 98, 99, 0, 1, and so on, in that order.

This storage algorithm is called **open-address hashing**, or more simply **open addressing**. In open addressing, collisions are resolved by placing the item in the next *open* spot of the array. Open addressing requires that the array be initialized so that the program can test to see if an array position already contains a record. For example, if the key will always be a non-negative integer, the key field of each array element can be initialized to a negative number, perhaps −1. As long as the key field contains a negative number, the program knows that the array location does not contain a record.

The Table Class—Specification

Storage by hashing forms the basis to implement a new container class called a table. A **table** is a container of records with operations for inserting, deleting, and locating records. This sounds a lot like a bag, but the difference is that each table operation is controlled by a single key field of the record rather than being controlled by the entire item value.

The `table` class will actually be a template class that depends on the data type of the records that are being stored. We use the name `RecordType` for the name of these records, so the actual `table` class definition will begin like this:

```
template <class RecordType>
class table
{    ...
```

The `RecordType` has some requirements: It must have a public integer member called `key`, and this member holds the key of each record. Each key must be a non-negative integer, and two different records cannot have the same key.

We will implement the table using a hash function as we outlined. When a table is implemented in this way, it is called a **hash table**. The next few paragraphs specify the operations for our `table` class.

The constructor. The `table` class has a default constructor that creates a table with a capacity of 811 records. The number 811 will be defined as a static constant named `CAPACITY` in the `table` class. There are several ways that we could allow for larger tables, but we will postpone that in order to focus on the table mechanism itself. So, a typical `table` declaration using the `tractor` data type would be as follows:

```
table<tractor> deere; // Can hold up to 811 tractors
```

The insert function. The `table` class has an insert function to place a new record into the table. There are two possible outcomes from an insertion:

- There might already be a record with the same key as the new record. In this case, the old record is replaced by the new record with the same key.
- If the new record has a key that is not already in the table, then the new record is added to the table.

The specification of the insert member function is shown here:

```
void insert(const RecordType& entry);
// Precondition: entry.key >= 0. Also if entry.key is not already a
//   key in the table, then the table has space for another record
//   (that is, size( ) < CAPACITY).
// Postcondition: If the table already had a record with a key
//   equal to entry.key, then that record is replaced by entry.
//   Otherwise entry has been added as a new record of the table.
```

The precondition requires that `entry.key` is a valid key (not negative), and if the key is a new key, then the table must not be already full (otherwise there won't be room for the new record).

The is_present and find functions. There are two constant functions called `is_present` and `find`. These functions search the table for a record with a particular key. Here are the specifications of the member functions:

```
bool is_present(int key) const;
// Postcondition: The return value is true if the table contains a record with
//   the specified key. Otherwise the return value is false.
```

```
void find(int key, bool& found, RecordType& result) const;
// Postcondition: If the table contains a record with the specified key, then
//   result is a copy of the record with that key, and found is true.
//   Otherwise found is false, and the result contains garbage.
```

The remove function. This function removes a particular record from the table. Here is the specification of the member function:

```
void remove(int key);
// Postcondition: If a record was in the table with the specified key, then
// that record has been removed. Otherwise the table is unchanged.
```

The Table Class—Design

Now we'll move on to the design and implementation of our `table` class. The complete header file for this first version of our table is shown in Figure 12.4.

Invariant for the Table Class. The records of the table are stored in an array called `data`, which is a private member variable. The number of array locations actually being used is stored in the private member variable `used`. Here is our complete invariant:

Invariant for the Table Class

1. The number of records in the table is in the member variable `used`.

2. The actual records of the table are stored in the array data, with a maximum of CAPACITY entries. Each used spot in the array has a non-negative key. An unused record in the array has its key field set to the constant NEVER_USED (if it has never been used) or the constant PREVIOUSLY_USED (if it once was used but is now vacant).

The second rule of the invariant needs some discussion. We have restricted valid keys to be non-negative integers. So, any unused spot in the array can be indicated by using a negative key. It turns out that we'll gain some efficiency if we distinguish between two different kinds of negative keys. We will use the constant `NEVER_USED` (defined as −1) in the key field to indicate a location that has *never* held a record. On the other hand, the constant `PREVIOUSLY_USED` (defined as −2) in the key field indicates a location that once held a record that has since been removed. You'll see the purpose of `NEVER_USED` versus `PREVIOUSLY_USED` when we implement the `find` function.

Five private member functions. The table definition also has five private member functions. We think these five functions will be useful for the implementation, but they are not part of the public interface. We don't want other programmers to use these functions; they are just for our own use in implementing a specific kind of table—a hash table. We have used similar "helper" functions in the past (such as `next_index` for one of the queue classes in Chapter 8).

The first helper function is the hash function, called `hash`. The function takes a key (which is an *int*) and hashes the key to an array index.

FIGURE 12.4   Header File for the Table Template Class

A Header File

```
// FILE: table1.h (part of the namespace main_savitch_12A)
// TEMPLATE CLASS PROVIDED: table<RecordType> (a table of records with keys)
//      This class is a container template class for a table of records.
//      The template parameter, RecordType, is the data type of the records in the table.
//      It may be any of the bulit-in C++ types (int, char, etc.), or a class with a default
//      constructor, an assignment operator, and an integer member variable called key.
//
// TYPEDEFS and MEMBER CONSTANT for the table<RecordType> class:
//    static const size_t CAPACITY = _____
//      table<RecordType>::CAPACITY is the maximum number of records held by a table.
//
// CONSTRUCTOR for the table<RecordType> template class:
//    table( )
//      Postcondition: The table has been initialized as an empty table.
//
// MODIFICATION MEMBER FUNCTIONS for the table<RecordType> class:
//    void insert(const RecordType& entry)
//      Precondition: entry.key >= 0. Also if entry.key is not already a key in the table, then
//      the table has space for another record (that is, size( ) < CAPACITY).
//      Postcondition: If the table already had a record with a key equal to entry.key, then that
//      record is replaced by entry. Otherwise, entry has been added as a new record of the
//      table.
//
//    void remove(int key)
//      Postcondition: If a record was in the table with the specified key, then that record has
//      been removed. Otherwise the table is unchanged.
//
// CONSTANT MEMBER FUNCTIONS for the table<RecordType> class:
//    bool is_present(int key) const
//      Postcondition: The return value is true if there is a record in the table with the
//      specified key. Otherwise, the return value is false.
//
//    void find(int key, bool& found, RecordType& result) const
//      Postcondition: If a record is in the table with the specified key, then found is true, and
//      result is set to a copy of the record with that key. Otherwise found is false,
//      and the result contains garbage.
//
//    size_t size( ) const
//      Postcondition: Return value is the total number of records in the table.
```

(continued)

(FIGURE 12.4 continued)

```
//  VALUE SEMANTICS for the table<RecordType> template class:
//     Assignments and the copy constructor may be used with table<RecordType> objects.

#ifndef TABLE1_H
#define TABLE1_H
#include <cstdlib>        // Provides size_t

namespace main_savitch_12A
{
    template <class RecordType>
    class table
    {
    public:
        // MEMBER CONSTANT -- See Appendix E if this fails to compile.
        static const std::size_t CAPACITY = 811;
        // CONSTRUCTOR
        table( );
        // MODIFICATION MEMBER FUNCTIONS
        void insert(const RecordType& entry);
        void remove(int key);
        // CONSTANT MEMBER FUNCTIONS
        bool is_present(int key) const;
        void find(int key, bool& found, RecordType& result) const;
        std::size_t size( ) const { return used; }
    private:
        // MEMBER CONSTANTS -- These are used in the key field of special records.
        static const int NEVER_USED = -1;
        static const int PREVIOUSLY_USED = -2;
        // MEMBER VARIABLES
        RecordType data[CAPACITY];
        std::size_t used;
        // HELPER FUNCTIONS
        std::size_t hash(int key) const;
        std::size_t next_index(std::size_t index) const;
        void find_index(int key, bool& found, std::size_t& index) const;
        bool never_used(std::size_t index) const;
        bool is_vacant(std::size_t index) const;
    };
}

#include "table1.template" // Include the implementation.
#endif
```

The second helper function, called `next_index`, is used to step through the array one index after the other with wraparound at the end. The function call `next_index(i)` usually returns i + 1, with one exception. When i is equal to the last index of the array, `next_index(i)` returns the first index of the array (zero).

The third helper function, `find_index`, is intended to find the array index of a record with a particular key. The function call `find_index(key, found, i)` searches for a record with the specified key. If such a record is found, the function sets the reference parameter `found` to true and sets i to the index of the record. Otherwise the function sets `found` to false and leaves i as garbage. This helper function is similar to the public `find` member function. The difference is that `find` returns a copy of the record with the specified key, whereas `find_index` returns the array index of the record that contains the specified key. The `find_index` function is useful for the implementor of the class because the implementor often needs to know where a particular record is located in the array. On the other hand, the programmer who uses the class doesn't need to know where a record is stored—in fact, that programmer doesn't even know that the records happen to be stored in an array.

The last two helper functions are boolean functions. The value of `never_used(i)` is true if `data[i]` has never been used (indicated by the NEVER_USED value in its key field). The value of `is_vacant(i)` is true if `data[i]` is not currently being used (indicated by any negative value in the key field).

🛈 Programming Tip

Using size_t Can Indicate a Value's Purpose

Can you tell that the return value of the hash function is intended to be used as an array index? Yes, you can—because the return value is a `size_t` value (rather than a mere *int*). In a similar manner, both the parameter and the return value of `next_index` are `size_t` values, because both of these items are array indexes. The parameters of `find_index`, `never_used`, and `is_vacant` follow the same practice.

We use `size_t` values for array indexes because doing so helps us easily identify the purpose of various values. Later, we could change the type of the keys to something other than an *int*, but each of the `size_t` values (used for array indexes and sizes) would remain `size_t`.

The Table ADT—Implementation

The constructor. Most of the table constructor's work involves filling the key fields of each array component with NEVER_USED, to indicate that the locations are not now used and have never been used previously. The constructor will also set used to zero.

The insert member function. The insert member function uses two local variables: (1) A boolean variable, called already_present, is set to true or false to indicate whether there is already an entry with the same key as the new entry. (2) A size_t variable, called index, is set so that data[index] is the right location for the new entry. The complete pseudocode has three steps:

1. find_index(entry.key, already_present, index);

2. *if* (!already_present)
    a. Check that the size of the array is less than its capacity.
    b. Use a loop to set index so that data[index] is the first vacant location at or after data[hash(entry.key)]. If the loop reaches the end of the array, then it should continue searching at data[0].
    c. ++used;

3. data[index] = entry;

This pseudocode is implemented in the top of Figure 12.5. Notice that the loop in Step 2b uses this assignment statement:

index = next_index(index);

This assignment moves index to the next available array index, wrapping back to the start of the array when index reaches the last valid array index. Also notice how the insert works if there is already a record with the same key as the new entry. In this case, the new entry replaces the old record (and the private member variable used remains unchanged).

The remove member function. In our insert function, we made use of the helper function, find_index. This function also simplifies the remove function, which has only two steps in its pseudocode (using local variables found and index):

1. find_index(key, found, index);

2. *if* (found)
    Remove the entry by setting data[index].key to PREVIOUSLY_USED (indicating a spot that's no longer used), and subtract 1 from used.

The remove implementation appears in the bottom of Figure 12.5.

The find_index function. We have pushed substantial work into the find_index function, which we will now implement. The function is

FIGURE 12.5   Implementation of insert and remove Functions for the Open-Address Hash Table

Two Function Implementations

```
template <class RecordType>
void table<RecordType>::insert(const RecordType& entry)
// Library facilities used: cassert, cstdlib
{
    bool already_present;     // True if entry.key is already in the table
    std::size_t index;           // data[index] is location for the new entry

    assert(entry.key >= 0);

    // Set index so that data[index] is the spot to place the new entry.
    find_index(entry.key, already_present, index);

    // If the key wasn't already there, then find the location for the new entry.
    if (!already_present)
    {
        assert(size( ) < CAPACITY);
        index = hash(entry.key);
        while (!is_vacant(index))
            index = next_index(index);
        ++used;
    }

    data[index] = entry;
}

template <class RecordType>
void table<RecordType>::remove(int key)
// Library facilities used: cassert, cstdlib
{
    bool found;            // True if key occurs somewhere in the table
    std::size_t index;    // Spot where data[index].key == key

    assert(key >= 0);

    find_index(key, found, index);
    if (found)
    {   // The key was found, so remove this record and reduce used by 1.
        data[index].key = PREVIOUSLY_USED; // Indicates a spot that's no longer in use.
        --used;
    }
}
```

www.cs.colorado.edu/~main/chapter12/table1.template   **WWW**

responsible for finding the location in the array that contains a particular key value. Here is the full specification of the private member function:

```
void find_index(int key, bool& found, std::size_t& index) const;
// Precondition: key >= 0.
// Postcondition: If a record is in the table with the specified key, then
// found is true, and index is set so that data[index].key is the specified
// key. Otherwise found is false, and i is garbage.
```

The function begins by hashing the key value to an array index and assigning this index to its reference parameter, i. The function then uses a loop to advance i through the array until we find the key or determine that the key is not in the array. If the loop finds the key, then the index i will be exactly at the spot where data[i].key == key, so the function can set found to true and return. On the other hand, if data[i] is not equal to key, then the function should set found to false before returning.

In our description of this work, just what does it mean to "determine that the key is not in the array"? One possibility is that we have examined every record in the array without finding the key. But sometimes it is possible to determine that the key is not in the array even though some records have not been examined. Recall that if there is a record with its key equal to the parameter key, then this record should be in position hash(key) or in the first available position after that. Our function starts searching at array index hash(key). Should it ever encounter a position that has *never* held a record, then we have an interesting fact: If the key were ever inserted in the array, then it would have been inserted at or before this vacant spot. Hence, the function knows that it has looked at every place that the key could possibly occur. Therefore, in the find_index implementation, the loop terminates if it reaches a position that has never been used, as shown in this implementation of the loop (count is a local variable that keeps track of how many records we have examined):

```
count = 0;
i = hash(key);
while((count < CAPACITY) && (!never_used(i)) && (data[i].key != key))
{
    ++count;
    i = next_index(i);
}
```

Notice that this technique for terminating the search cannot simply stop when it encounters a position that is *currently* vacant, but the loop must continue until it encounters a position that has *never* held a record.

The find_index implementation is shown as part of the complete implementation file in Figure 12.6. The figure also implements the other member functions that we have not yet discussed.

FIGURE 12.6   Implementation File for the Table Template Class

An Implementation File

```
// FILE: table1.template
// TEMPLATE CLASS IMPLEMENTED: table (see table1.h for documentation)
// INVARIANT for the table class:
//     1. The number of records in the table is in the member variable used.
//     2. The actual records of the table are stored in the array data, with a maximum of
//        CAPACITY entries. Each used spot in the array has a non-negative key. Any unused
//        record in the array has a key field of NEVER_USED (if it has never been used) or
//        PREVIOUSLY_USED (if it once was used, but is now vacant).
#include <cassert>    // Provides assert
#include <cstdlib>    // Provides size_t

namespace main_savitch_12A
{
    template <class RecordType>
    const std::size_t table<RecordType>::CAPACITY;
    template <class RecordType>
    const int table<RecordType>::NEVER_USED;
    template <class RecordType>
    const int table<RecordType>::PREVIOUSLY_USED;

    template <class RecordType>
    table<RecordType>::table( )
    // Library facilities used: cstdlib
    {
        std::size_t i;

        used = 0;
        for (i = 0; i < CAPACITY; ++i)
            data[i].key = NEVER_USED;   // Indicates a spot that's never been used.
    }

    template <class RecordType>
    void table<RecordType>::insert(const RecordType& entry)
```
‖ See the implementation in Figure 12.5 on page 600.

```
    template <class RecordType>
    void table<RecordType>::remove(int key)
```
‖ See the implementation in Figure 12.5 on page 600.

```
    template <class RecordType>
    bool table<RecordType>::is_present(int key) const
```
‖ See the solution to Self-Test Exercise 9 on page 618.

```
    template <class RecordType>
    void table<RecordType>::find(int key, bool& found, RecordType& result) const
```
‖ See the solution to Self-Test Exercise 13 on page 618.   *(continued)*

(FIGURE 12.6 continued)

```
template <class RecordType>
inline std::size_t table<RecordType>::hash(int key) const
// Postcondition: The return value is the hash value for the given key.
{
    return (key % CAPACITY);
}


template <class RecordType>
inline std::size_t table<RecordType>::next_index(std::size_t index) const
// Precondition: index < CAPACITY.
// Postcondition: The return value is either index+1 (if this is less than CAPACITY) or zero
// (if index+1 equals CAPACITY).
{
    return ((index+1) % CAPACITY);
}


template <class RecordType>
void table<RecordType>::find_index
    (int key, bool& found, std::size_t& i) const
// Precondition: key >= 0.
// Postcondition: If a record is in the table with the specified key, then found is true and index
// is set so that data[index].key is the specified key. Otherwise found is false, and i is garbage.
{
    std::size_t count; // Number of entries that have been examined

    count = 0;
    i = hash(key);
    while((count < CAPACITY) && (!never_used(i)) && (data[i].key != key))
    {
        ++count;
        i = next_index(i);
    }
    found = (data[i].key == key);
}


template <class RecordType>
inline bool table<RecordType>::never_used(std::size_t index) const
|| See the solution to Self-Test Exercise 14 on page 618.

template <class RecordType>
inline bool table<RecordType>::is_vacant(std::size_t index) const
|| See the solution to Self-Test Exercise 14 on page 618.
}
```

★✦ C++ Feature

Inline Functions in the Implementation File

Four of the five `table` helper functions are short—just one line of code each. Because of their shortness, you might want to provide quicker execution by declaring the helper functions to be inline member functions. On the other hand, you could be unwilling to put the implementations of the functions in the header file (where we have previously put inline member functions). After all, a programmer who uses the `table` class doesn't need to know about the helper functions and certainly doesn't need to see their implementations.

In such a case, you can get the best of both worlds by putting the implementations in the usual implementation file and including the keyword *inline* just before the function definition. For example, here is the start of one of the helper functions from the implementation file of Figure 12.6:

```
template <class RecordType>
inline std::size_t table<RecordType>::hash(int key) const
```

The keyword *inline* causes most compilers to provide a faster implementation of the short function (by avoiding the actual function call and putting the code for the function body at each location where the function is called).

Remember, you normally do not provide documentation for a helper function in the header file. Instead, the documentation goes with the implementation in the implementation file, where it can help the programmer who is implementing the class.

Choosing a Hash Function to Reduce Collisions

We have used a simple hash function that hashes a given key to the array index:

```
key % CAPACITY
```

This kind of hash function depends on the remainder upon division, and is therefore called a **division hash function**.

With a division hash function, certain table sizes are better than others at avoiding collisions that arise in data taken from real examples. C.E. Radke's 1970 study suggests that a good choice is a table size that is a prime number of the form $4k+3$. For example, 811 is a prime number equal to $(4 \times 202) + 3$.

Although division hash functions are the most common, you may sometimes encounter data that produces many collisions regardless of the table size. In this case, you can try two other common kinds of hash functions:

- **Mid-square hash function.** The key is multiplied by itself. The hash function returns some middle digits of the result.

- **Multiplicative hash function.** The key is multiplied by a constant less than one. The hash function returns the first few digits of the fractional part of the result.

Double Hashing to Reduce Clustering

Consider what happens during an insertion with a collision. The insertion function moves forward from the original index until a vacant spot is found in the array. For example, suppose that a new key hashes to location 330, but this location is full. Then the insertion tries 331, then 332, then 333, and so on. Searching for a vacant spot in this manner is called **linear probing**.

There is a problem with linear probing. When several different keys are hashed to the same array location, the result is a small cluster of elements, one after another. As the table approaches its capacity, these clusters tend to merge into larger and larger clusters. This is the problem of **clustering**. If the key values happen to be consecutive numbers (such as a run of consecutive stock numbers in an inventory), then a "division hash function" makes clustering even worse. As clustering gets worse, insertions take longer because the insert function must step all the way through a cluster to find a vacant location. Elements are inserted farther and farther from their correct hashed index, and searches require more time.

The most common technique to avoid clustering is called **double hashing**. The technique uses a second hash function to determine how we move through an array to resolve a collision. To see how this works, let's call the original hash function `hash1,` and call the second hash function `hash2`. When an item is inserted, double hashing begins by hashing the key to an array index using `hash1`. If there is a collision, then we calculate `hash2(key)` using the result to tell us how far forward to move through the array in looking for a vacant spot. For example, suppose that a new key hashes to location 330, and that `hash2(key)` is 7. If location 330 is occupied, then we move forward 7 spots and try location 337. If 337 is also occupied, then we move forward another 7 spots to location 344, and so on.

As we are stepping through the array, adding `hash2(key)` to the index at each step, there are two considerations:

- The array index must not leave the valid range of 0 to `CAPACITY - 1`. We can keep the index in this range with the "%" operation. In particular, suppose that `i` is the index that we have just examined (with a collision). Then the next index to examine is

  `(i + hash2(key)) % CAPACITY`

  For example, suppose that `CAPACITY` is 811, and `hash2(key)` is 14. If a new key hashes to spot 787, and there is a collision, then the next few spots that we will try are 801, then 4, then 18, then 32. Notice that the 4 is calculated as (801 + 14) % `CAPACITY`.

- As we step through the array, we must ensure that every array position is examined. With double hashing, this is a potential problem. We could come back to our starting position before we have examined every available location. There is an easy way to avoid this problem: Make sure that the array's capacity is *relatively prime* with respect to the value returned by hash2 (in other words, these two numbers must not have any common factors, apart from 1). One way to accomplish this is to choose CAPACITY as a prime number, and have hash2 return values in the range 1 through CAPACITY - 1. With this in mind, the preeminent computer scientist Donald Knuth suggests the following possibility:

1. Both CAPACITY and CAPACITY - 2 should be prime numbers. For example, 811 is prime and so is 809. (Two such primes, separated by 2, are called **twin primes**.)

2. hash1(key) = key % CAPACITY.

3. hash2(key) = 1 + (key % (CAPACITY-2)). This particular hash2 function will never return a value above CAPACITY-2, although in general, the hash2 values could be as large as CAPACITY-1.

With our table class from Figure 12.4 on page 596, double hashing can be incorporated in several ways. The easiest approach is to add another private member function to compute hash2, and change next_index to return:

```
(i + hash2(key)) % CAPACITY
```

This next_index function needs key as another parameter.

At this point, you know enough to implement open-address hashing with linear probing or with double hashing. We'll delay the analysis of hashing until after the presentation of *chaining*, which is another way to resolve collisions.

Self-Test Exercises for Section 12.2

9. What are the advantages of hashing over performing a binary search?

10. When should a programmer use a struct rather than a class?

11. How are collisions resolved in open-address hashing?

12. Write the table's is_present member function.

13. Write the table's find member function.

14. Write the two table helper functions: never_used and is_vacant. These functions appear in the implementation file of Figure 12.6 on page 602, but they are also inline functions (as described in the C++ Feature on page 604). The never_used function returns true if data[index] has never been used. The is_vacant function returns true if data[index] is not currently being used.

15. Suppose that a hash table is full and you try to insert a new entry. What happens if the new entry's key is already in the table? What happens if the new entry's key is not already in the table?

16. In the implementation of the table's find_index function, the function may sometimes find a key field that has been used previously (but not currently). Why does the function need to continue to search?

17. Describe one problem with linear probing. How can this be solved?

18. An empty hash table has a capacity of 103, and you insert six entries with keys 103, 0, 205, 308, 411, and 2. Using linear probing and a division hash function, where will these entries be placed in the table? Where will they be placed with double hashing (with `hash2(key)` returning the value `1 + (key % 101)`).

19. Write a quick program to determine whether there is a pair of twin primes between 1200 and 1250, with the upper prime having the form $4k+3$ for some k. With this information, can you suggest a good size for a hash table that uses double hashing and has a capacity around 1225?

12.3 CHAINED HASHING

In open-address hashing, a collision is handled by probing the array for an unused position. Each array component can hold just one entry. When the array is full, no more items can be added to the table. We could handle this problem by resizing the array and rehashing all the entries, placing each entry in a new, larger array. But this would require a careful choice of the new size and probably would require each entry to have a new hash value computed. Another approach is to use a different collision resolution method called chained hashing.

In **chained hashing**, also called **chaining**, each component of the hash table's array can hold more than one entry. As with all hashing, we still hash the key of each entry to obtain an array index. But if there is a collision, we don't worry too much. We simply place the new entry in its proper array component along with other entries that happened to hash to the same array index.

How does chaining place more than one entry in each component of the array? The answer is that each array component must have some underlying structure. The most common structure that you will see for the array's components is to have each `data[i]` be a head pointer for a linked list. The nodes of the linked list each have an item that is the `RecordType` of the table, as diagrammed here:

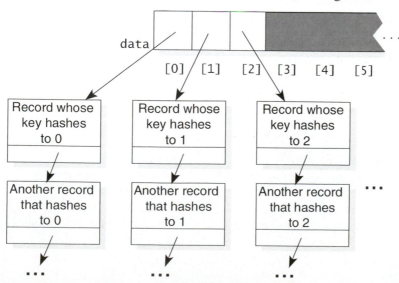

In this scheme, all the records that hash to location i are placed on the linked list, which has its head pointer stored in data[i]. To maintain the linked lists, we can use the template version of our node class (from Section 6.4). With this approach, the table class definition is shown in Figure 12.7.

In the figure we have included the file node2.h from Figure 6.5 on page 317 to provide the node class. We also have defined a static member constant called TABLE_SIZE, which determines the size of the table's array. We used the name TABLE_SIZE rather than CAPACITY since "CAPACITY" suggests a limit to the number of entries—but in fact, the chaining hash table can hold more than TABLE_SIZE entries.

FIGURE 12.7   Definition of the Table Template Class Using Chaining and the Linked-List Toolkit

A Template Class Definition

```
#include <cstdlib>      // Provides size_t
#include "node2.h"      // Provides the node type, from Figure 6.5 on page 317

namespace main_savitch_12B
{
    template <class RecordType>
    class table
    {
    public:
        // MEMBER CONSTANT -- See Appendix E if this fails to compile.
        static const std::size_t TABLE_SIZE = 811;
        // CONSTRUCTORS AND DESTRUCTOR
        table( );
        table(const table& source);
        ~table( );
        // MODIFICATION MEMBER FUNCTIONS
        void insert(const RecordType& entry);
        void remove(int key);
        void operator =(const table& source);
        // CONSTANT MEMBER FUNCTIONS
        void find(int key, bool& found, RecordType& result) const;
        bool is_present(int key) const;
        std::size_t size( ) const { return total_records; }
    private:
        main_savitch_6B::node<RecordType> *data[TABLE_SIZE];
        std::size_t total_records;
        // HELPER MEMBER FUNCTION
        std::size_t hash(int key) const;
    };
}
```

↖ *Each component of the array is a head pointer for a linked list.*

In our example, the table size is 811, so that the `data` array consists of 811 head pointers for 811 linked lists. Each list is a linked list where the nodes contain `RecordType` values.

Our class definition has one other private member variable, `total_records`, which keeps track of the total number of records in all 811 linked lists. You can complete this implementation yourself.

Self-Test Exercises for Section 12.3

20. Consider the chaining version of the table that we have described. What value will the constructor place in each component of `data`?

21. Write the insert member function for the chaining version of the table.

22. Use your insert function to place six items in a hash table with a table size of 811. Use the keys 811, 0, 1623, 2435, 3247, and 2.

23. In our new `table` class, the array is still a fixed size. So why do we need the copy constructor, destructor, and overloaded assignment operator?

24. Suppose that the keys can be compared with the usual "less than" operator. Can you think of some advantage to keeping each linked list of the table sorted from smallest key to largest key?

12.4 TIME ANALYSIS OF HASHING

The worst-case for hashing occurs when every key gets hashed to the same array index. In this unfortunate case, we may end up searching through all the items to find the one we are after—a linear operation, just like serial search. However, with some reasonable assumptions, the average time for a search of a hash table is dramatically fast, requiring us to examine just a handful of elements. This section provides the information needed for an average-time analysis of our three hashing methods.

The Load Factor of a Hash Table

The average-time performance of hashing is complex, particularly if deletions are allowed. However, Knuth's *The Art of Programming*, Volume 3, provides formulas that can guide our choice of hash-table algorithms. Knuth's most useful formulas provide the average number of table elements that must be examined during a successful search for a key. There are three different formulas for the three versions of hashing: open addressing with linear probing, open addressing with double hashing, and chained hashing.

These three formulas depend on how many items are in the table. When the table has many items, there are many collisions, and the average time for a search is longer. With this in mind, we first define a fraction called the **load factor**, which is written α and defined by the formula at the top of the next page.

definition of the load factor, α

$$\alpha = \frac{\text{Number of occupied table locations}}{\text{The size of the table's array}}$$

For open-address hashing, each array element holds at most one item, so the load factor can never exceed 1. But with chaining, each array position can hold many items, and the load factor might be higher than 1.

Average search time for open addressing (linear probing). Open-address hash tables with linear probing have just one hash function. Collisions are resolved by stepping forward, probing consecutive array elements. With linear probing, and no deletions, Knuth's formula for the average time of a successful search is as follows:

Searching with Linear Probing

In open-address hashing with linear probing, a nonfull hash table, and no deletions, the average number of table elements examined in a successful search is approximately

$$\frac{1}{2}\left(1 + \frac{1}{1-\alpha}\right)$$

This formula is not exact, but it is a good approximation when the load factor (α) is below 1. You might notice that the formula completely fails when α is 1, since there is then a division by zero. But that situation would indicate a full hash table, and you should avoid getting close to full anyway. If you insist on a full hash table of n elements, Knuth shows that the average time for a successful search is approximately $\sqrt{n(\pi/8)}$ —but better yet, steer clear of full tables, and you can use the preceding formula. In addition to a nonfull table, the formula's derivation also assumes that we have not deleted any items, and that the hash function does a good job of uniformly distributing all possible keys throughout the array (which is called **uniform hashing**).

As an example of how to use the formula, suppose that we plan to put 649 entries in a table with a capacity of 811. This provides a load average of 649/811, or about 80%. On average, we expect successful searches to examine three table elements, as shown here:

$$\frac{1}{2}\left(1 + \frac{1}{1-\alpha}\right) = \frac{1}{2}\left(1 + \frac{1}{1-0.8}\right) = 3.0$$

Average search time for open addressing (double hashing). You have seen that open-address hash tables with double hashing provide some relief from clustering. The result is a smaller average time, given by the following formula (which uses "ln" to denote the natural logarithm of a number):

Searching with Double Hashing

In open-address hashing with double hashing, a nonfull hash table, and no deletions, the average number of table elements examined in a successful search is approximately:

$$\frac{-\ln(1 - \alpha)}{\alpha}$$

As with the previous formula, this estimate is approximate. It depends on a nonfull hash table, no deletions, and using a hash function with uniform hashing.

You don't need to memorize the formula, but you should know how to use it along with the ln key on your calculator. For example, $\ln(0.2)$ is about -1.6, so with a load factor of 0.8 we expect to examine an average of two elements in a successful search, as shown here:

$$\frac{-\ln(1 - \alpha)}{\alpha} = \frac{-\ln(0.2)}{0.8} = \frac{1.6}{0.8} = 2$$

This is an improvement over the linear probing with the same load factor.

Average search time for chained hashing. With chaining, each element of the table's array is a head pointer for a linked list, and each of these linked lists may have several items. Therefore, the load factor may be higher than one in this formula:

Searching with Chained Hashing

In open-address hashing with chained hashing, the average number of table elements examined in a successful search is approximately

$$1 + \frac{\alpha}{2}$$

Once again, this estimate is approximate, and it depends on using uniform hashing. Unlike the other two formulas, the chaining formula remains valid even with deletions.

With a load factor of 0.8, chained hashing expects to examine only 1.4 items during a successful search. Some other possible load factors are shown in Figure 12.8, where you can compare the average numbers for the three different hashing methods.

FIGURE 12.8 Average Number of Table Elements Examined During a Successful Search

Load factor (α)	Open addressing with linear probing $\frac{1}{2}\left(1 + \frac{1}{1-\alpha}\right)$	Open addressing with double hashing $\frac{-\ln(1-\alpha)}{\alpha}$	Chained hashing $1 + \frac{\alpha}{2}$
0.5	1.50	1.39	1.25
0.6	1.75	1.53	1.30
0.7	2.17	1.72	1.35
0.8	3.00	2.01	1.40
0.9	5.50	2.56	1.45
1.0			1.50
2.0	Not applicable		2.00
4.0			3.00

Self-Test Exercises for Section 12.4

25. Suppose that you place 180 items in a hash table with an array size of 200. What is the load factor? For each of the three hash methods, what is the average number of table elements that you expect to have examined during a successful search?

26. You want to place 1000 elements in a hash table, and you'd like an average search to examine just two table elements. How big does the table's array need to be? Give separate answers for the three hash methods.

12.5 PROGRAMMING PROJECT: A TABLE CLASS WITH STL VECTORS

A New Table Class

We have discussed table classes implemented with an array of records (for open-address hashing) and an array of linked lists (for chained hashing). A table class can be also implemented with existing STL containers. This is advantageous in that the table can easily access and modify data items using the member functions of the containers. We suggest the STL vector class to implement a new version of the table class. The STL vector class is analogous to a dynamic array for which certain member functions automatically increase the size of the array. It uses subscripting to access elements (such as `v[2] = 10` for a vector v of integer values). Appendix H provides details for using the vector template class. Like the table in Figure 12.7 on page 608, this table will use chained hashing, but there are a few changes in the design.

Using Vectors in the New Table

In the original version, the table was an array called `data`. Each location, `data[i]`, was the head pointer for a linked list of all the records with a hash value of `i`. The new version will use vectors instead of linked lists:

The New Table Is an Array of Vectors

Each `data[i]` will be a *vector* that contains all the records with a hash value of `i`.

Template Parameters That Are Constants

Until now, all our template parameters have been data types, such as the `RecordType` for our table. However, a template parameter can also be a constant value that is used throughout the class definition. This will change our template prefix as shown here:

```
template <class RecordType, size_t TABLE_SIZE>
class table
{ // In this definition, we'll use RecordType and the constant TABLE_SIZE .
. .
```

The syntax consists of the data type of the constant (such as `size_t`) followed by the name that you want to use for the constant (such as `TABLE_SIZE`).

Template Parameters Can Be Constant Values

A template parameter can be a constant value, and that constant can then be used throughout the template's definition. Our new table will have a template parameter for the `TABLE_SIZE` constant.

Template Parameters That Are Functions

We no longer require `RecordType` to have an explicit key member variable. This gives us more flexibility in the kinds of records that can be stored. However, we will need a new mechanism to compute the key of a record. This will be done by a function with the following prototype:

```
int hashkey(const RecordType& r);
```

When we need to compute a key for a record `r` it will use `hashkey(r)`.

But how does the new table class obtain the `hashkey` function? The programmer who writes the table class can't write `hashkey` because the `RecordType` is unknown. The answer is that the hashkey function can be provided as a third template parameter for the table class, like this:

```
template <
    class RecordType,
    size_t TABLE_SIZE,
    int hashkey(const RecordType&)
>
class table
{ // In this definition, we'll use RecordType, the constant TABLE_SIZE,
  // and the function: int hashkey(const RecordType&).
```

The syntax for that third template parameter is the prototype for the function that you want another programmer to provide to the template class.

Template Parameters Can Be Functions

A template parameter can be a function, and that function can then be used throughout the template's definition. Our new table will have a template parameter for the `hashkey` function.

Implementing the New Table Class

Within the new definition of the class, the programmer who implements the new table may use `RecordType`, `TABLE_SIZE` and the function `hashkey` whenever they are needed without worrying about where they came from. It is the responsibility of the programmer who uses our table class to provide those three items.

A suggested class definition for the new table is shown in Figure 12.9. A programmer who wants to create a hash table of tractors using the tractor struct from page 590 must first write the `hashkey` function for tractors and then declare whatever tables are needed:

```
int hashkey(const tractor& t)
{
    return t.key;
}

// Declare a hash table of size 811 for tractors:
main_savitch_12C::table<tractor, 811, hashkey> my_table;

//...now my_table can be used.
```

Hash tables of other kinds of records can also be created, so long as the programmer provides the record type, the table size, and the `hashkey` function.

FIGURE 12.9 The Table Template Class Using a Vector and Additional Template Parameters

A Template Class Definition

```
#include <cstdlib>     // Provides size_t
#include <vector>      // Provides the STL vector class

namespace main_savitch_12C
{
    template <class RecordType, size_t TABLE_SIZE, int hashkey(const RecordType&>
    class table
    {
    public:
        // CONSTRUCTORS (no destructor needed, uses automatic copy constructor)
        table( );
        // MODIFICATION MEMBER FUNCTIONS
        void insert(const RecordType& entry);
        void remove(int key);
        // CONSTANT MEMBER FUNCTIONS
        void find(int key, bool& found, RecordType& result) const;
        bool is_present(int key) const;
        std::size_t size( ) const { return total_records; }
    private:
        vector<RecordType> data[TABLE_SIZE];
        std::size_t total_records;
        // HELPER MEMBER FUNCTION
        std::size_t hash(int key) const;
    };
}
```

Each component of the array is a vector.

Self-Test Exercises for Section 12.5

27. Name three different kinds of template parameters.

28. Write a simple hash function for strings to use as a template parameter for the table class in Figure 12.8. One option is to add the ASCII integer values of all the characters in the string. Use the expression static_cast<int>(s[i]) to obtain the ASCII integer value of character i in a string s.

29. Implement the is_present function for the new table.

30. Why doesn't the new table need a copy constructor, destructor, or assignment operator?

12.6 MAPS AND MULTIMAPS FROM THE STL

The first version of the STL does not have a hash table class, although there are proposals to add one. There are, however, two other classes—map and multip-map from <map>—which can be used to store key/value pairs provided that the keys have a less-than operator forming a strict weak ordering (see Figure 6.4 on page 302). This allows keys that are numbers or strings or many other types. For example, if you want to store the months of the year as keys, with their number of days as values, you could declare a map object as follows:

```
map<string, int> months;
```

The first template parameter is the type of the key, and the second is the type of the data that is stored with each key.

The map class provides subscripting through its keys. Because of the subscripting functionality provided in map, values can be entered into a map either through the insert function or through array-type assignment, such as here:

```
months["July"] = 31;
```

The multimap is like a map, except that it allows multiple values to be associated with a single key (and therefore, you can't use the cool subscripting notation that comes with a map). Multiple data with one key is useful in cases where a key might need to have more than one value associated with it. For example, a multimap for cities and their area codes might be declared, assigned, and printed with the following code:

```
multimap<string, int> cities;
multimap<string, int>::const_iterator i;

cities.insert(make_pair("Denver", 303));
cities.insert(make_pair("Denver", 720));

for (i = cities.begin(); i != cities.end(); ++i)
{
    cout << i->first << '\t' << i->second << endl;
}
```

Multiple area codes for Denver will be assigned to the multimap, whereas a map would overwrite the first entry with a duplicate key. Note that the items in the map are structs with two parts, the key (called first) and the value (called second), so these parts can be obtained through an iterator with the notation i->first and i->second.

A partial list of map and multimap functions can be found in Appendix I.

CHAPTER SUMMARY

- Serial search is quick to program but requires linear time to find an item in both the worst case and the average case.

- Binary search works well on a sorted array of items, requiring $O(\log n)$ time in both the worst case and the average case. But as items are added or deleted, keeping the array in order may take considerable time (linear time for each insertion or deletion in the worst case).

- Hash tables are a good strategy for storing and retrieving records. In fact, it would be perfect if there were no collisions.

- One way to deal with collisions is *open addressing*. This scheme handles collisions by placing the new entry in the first open location that is at or after the spot where the key hashes to. Two methods of searching for an open location are *linear probing* (which examines the array locations in consecutive order) and *double hashing* (which uses a second hash function to determine the size of the steps that are taken through the array). Double hashing is the better method, because it avoids clustering.

- Another way to deal with collisions is *chaining*. In the chaining approach, each location of the hash table's array is able to hold multiple entries. A common way to implement chaining is for each array location to be a head pointer for a linked list of entries.

- The worst-case search time for a hash table is linear. But the average-case time is quite fast. Depending on the load factor and the precise method of hashing, the average case requires about two to five table elements to be examined during a successful search (see Figure 12.8 on page 612).

- A new class, such as a table, can sometimes be effectively implemented using existing classes from the STL.

- Template parameters can be classes, constant values, or functions.

- The STL includes two classes, map and multimap, which allow a programmer to store key/value pairs.

Solutions to Self-Test Exercises

?

1. A serial search is acceptable when you are searching a small array only a few times.

2. Worst-case: $O(n)$. Average case looks at half the items, which is still $O(n)$. Best case is constant time (looks at but one item).

3. The precondition is modified so that the array no longer needs to be sorted. Here's the code:
```
void search(
    const int a[ ],
    size_t first, size_t size,
    int target, bool& found,
    size_t& location
)
```

```
{
    size_t i;
    bool found;
    i = 0;
    found = false;
    while ((i < size) && !found)
    {
        if (a[first+i] == target)
        {
            found = true;
            location = first+i;
        }
        else
            ++i;
    }
}
```

4. Because of the recursive calls in a binary search, the array is repeatedly split in half. The `first` and `size` parameters keep track of the portion of the array that is currently being searched.

5. When size becomes zero, or when the target is found

6. The following template prefix is placed before the function:
   `template <class Item, class SizeType>`
   In the implementation, change every occurrence of *int* to `Item`, and change the `size_t` parameters to `SizeType`. (See "Parameter Matching for Template Functions" on page 284 for an explanation of the need for the `SizeType`.)

7. The function is not difficult to write, but pay attention to the potential pitfalls from page 581.

8. $H(1)=1$, $H(2)=2$, $H(4)=3$, $H(7)=3$, $H(8)=4$, $H(9)=4$.

9. Hashing can be fast in the average case. Adding and deleting elements is easier in a container that provides hashing, because a binary search requires that the items remain sorted. Use a struct only when all the members are public.

10. Programmers tend to use a struct only when all the members are public.

11. Here's the body of the implementation:
    ```
    {
        bool found;
        std::size_t index;
        assert(key >= 0);
        find_index(key, found, index);
        return found;
    }
    ```

12. Collisions are resolved by placing the item in the next open spot of the array.

13. Here's the body of the implementation:
    ```
    {
        std::size_t index;
        assert(key >= 0);
        find_index(key, found, index);
        if (found)
            result = data[index];
    }
    ```

14. Here is the `never_used` member function:
    ```
    template <class RecordType>
    inline bool Table<RecordType>::
    never_used(size_t index) const
    // Library facilities used: stdlib.h
    // Precondition: index < CAPACITY.
    // Postcondition: If data[index] has never
    // been used, then the return value is true.
    // Otherwise the return value is false.
    {
        return
            (data[index].key == NEVER_USED);
    }
    ```

Here is the `is_vacant` member function:
```
template <class RecordType>
inline bool Table<RecordType>::
is_vacant(size_t index) const
// Library facilities used: stdlib.h
// Precondition: index < CAPACITY.
// Postcondition: If data[index] is not now
// being used, then the return value is true.
// Otherwise the return value is false.
{
    return
        (data[index].key < 0);
}
```

15. If the key was already present, then the record with that key is overwritten. If the key was not already present, then the assertion tests whether `size( )` < CAPACITY is true, and this assertion fails, halting the program.

16. Suppose we start looking in the data array at some index, say 34, and we move forward until we find an unoccupied location. Perhaps this first unoccupied location is at index 36. If position 36 has a key of NEVER_USED, then that indicates that the position has never been used, and therefore no record with the given key appears in the array (since it would have been placed in this unused position, or perhaps in position 34 or 35 which we already examined).

On the other hand, if position 36 has a key of PREVIOUSLY_USED, then this position has previously been used and since removed. In this case, it is possible that there is a record with the given key in the array at a position after `data[36]`. It might be after this position, because at the time it was inserted, `data[36]` might have been in use.

17. Linear probing can result in clustering of elements when several different keys are hashed to the same location. Insertions and searching take longer as clustering gets worse. Double hashing can solve this problem by using a second hash function to resolve a collision.

18. For linear probing, the key/index pairs are 103 at [0], 0 at [1], 205 at [102], 308 at [2], 411 at [3], and 2 at [4]. For double hashing the key/index pairs are 103 at [0], 0 at [1], 205 at [102], 308 at [5], 411 at [7], and 2 at [2].

19. There is a twin prime pair at 1229 and 1231, which suggests that 1231 is a good table capacity.

20. NULL

21. We suggest that you first write a helper function with one parameter that is a key. The function returns a pointer to a node with the specified key (or returns NULL if there is no such node). Using this function (which we call `find_ptr`):

```
template <class RecordType>
void Table<RecordType>::
insert(const RecordType& entry)
{
    main_savitch_6B::node<RecordType>
    *cursor;

    cursor = find_ptr(entry.key);
    if (cursor == NULL)
    {
        list_head_insert
          (data[hash(entry.key)], entry);
        ++used;
    }
    else
        cursor->setdata(entry);
}
```

22. The `data[0]` list will have the keys 0 and 811. The `data[1]` list will have the key 1623. The `data[2]` list will have the keys 2 and 2435. The `data[3]` list will have the key 3247. All other lists are empty.

23. The ADT does use dynamic memory (the linked lists).

24. If the lists are kept in order, then a search can stop as soon as it reaches a key that is greater than the target.

25. The load factor is 0.9 (i.e., 180/200). With linear probing, the expected average is 5.50; with double hashing, the expected average is 2.56; with chained hashing, the expected average is 1.45.

26. For linear probing, we need a load factor of 2/3, which requires a table capacity of 1500. For double hashing, we need a load factor of just less than 0.8, requiring a table capacity of about 1250. For chaining, we need a load factor of 2, requiring an array size of 500.

27. A template parameter can be a data type, a constant data value, or a function.

28. Here is one implementation:

```
int hashkey(const string& s)
{
    int result = 0;

    for (int i = 0; i < s.length(); ++i)
        result = result + static_cast<int>(s[i]);
    return (result % table_size);
}
```

29. Here is one implementation:

```
bool table::is_present(int key) const;
{
    size_t i = hash(key); // If key exists, it will be in data[i].
    vector<RecordType>::const_iterator it;

    for (it = data[i].begin( ); it != data[i].end( ); ++it)
    {
        if (hashkey(*it) == key)
            return true;
    }
    return false;
}
```

30. A copy constructor, destructor, and assignment operator are needed only when a class makes direct use of dynamic memory. The new table class uses dynamic memory, but only through the vector class, which is another great reason to use the STL classes.

PROGRAMMING PROJECTS
For more in-depth projects, please see www.cs.colorado.edu/~main/projects/

1 Reimplement the binary search using a loop and no recursion. If you are familiar with template functions, then your implementation should be a template function that can search any array that is sorted from smallest to largest (using the < operator).

2 Use a binary search technique to rewrite the guess_game function from Figure 1.4 on page 24. The function may ask questions such as "Is your number bigger than 42?" Your result should have worst-case time of $O(\log n)$.

3 Use **double hashing** to reimplement the hash table from Figure 12.4 on page 596.

4 In our open-address hash tables, we have used linear probing or double hashing. Another probing method, which avoids some clustering, is called **quadratic probing**. The simplest version of quadratic probing works like this: Start by hashing the key to an array index. If there is a collision, then move to the next array index. If there is a *second* collision, then move forward *two* more spots through the array. After a *third* collision, we move forward *three* more spots, and so on. For example, suppose that a new key hashes to location 327, and this location is full. The next location that we try is 328. If 328 is a second collision, then we move two spots forward to location 330. If 330 is a third collision, then we move three spots forward to location 333. If our calculation of the next spot takes us beyond the end of the array, then we "wrap around" to the front of the array (similar to double hashing). In general, if `data[i]` is the location that has just caused a collision, and we have already examined `count` elements, then we increase `i` according to the assignment:

```
i = (i + count) % CAPACITY;
```

In this formula, the "% `CAPACITY`" causes the "wrap around" to the front of the array. In order for this approach to work correctly, the capacity must be a power of 2, such as $2^{10} = 1024$. Otherwise, the sequence of probes does not correctly examine all array items.

For this project, use quadratic hashing to reimplement the hash table from Figure 12.4 on page 596.

5 Implement a dictionary program using a table. The user inputs a word, and the word's definition is displayed. You will need to revise one of the table implementations to use a string as the search key. Use a hash function similar to the one you implemented for Self-Test Exercise 28.

6 Redo Programming Problem 13 of Chapter 10 to allow the user to search for books using the ISBN, book title, or author search key. One way to accomplish this would be to create a separate hash table of book objects for each search key; however, this would result in duplicated data and wasted memory. A better implementation would be to store the actual data in a list, and use separate hash tables for each search key. The value associated with each key is not the book itself, but just the position of the book in the long list of books. Assume that there are no duplicates in the search keys.

7 Design a scheme that allows for duplicate keys in the previous project.

13

Sorting

A place for everything and everything in its place.

ISABELLA MARY BEETON
The Book of Household Management

LEARNING OBJECTIVES

When you complete Chapter 13, you will be able to...

- do a simulation by hand of selectionsort, insertionsort, mergesort, quicksort, and heapsort.
- implment each of these sorting algorithms to sort an array of numbers or to sort any collection of objects that provides a random access iterator.
- explain the run-time advantage of insertionsort for the situation in which an array is nearly sorted to begin with.
- explain the advantage of mergesort for sorting a collection of data that is too large to fit in memory all at once.
- demonstrate situations where the poor choice of a pivot element can cause quadratic behavior for quicksort.

CHAPTER CONTENTS

Sorting

$\mathbf{O}$ne, commonly encountered programming task is sorting a list of values. By way of examples, the list might consist of exam scores, and we may want to see them sorted from lowest to highest, or from highest to lowest; the list might be a list of words that we have misspelled, and we may want to see them in alphabetical order; the list might be a list of student records, and we may want them sorted by student number or alphabetically by student name. In this chapter we present and analyze a number of different sorting algorithms.

To maintain a sharp focus on the sorting algorithms, we will consider only arrays of integers and design algorithms to sort the integers into order from smallest to largest. However, if you are familiar with templates (Chapter 6), then you may easily adapt the algorithms to sort arrays of values of other types, or to sort values according to other ordering relations. Other adaptations are also possible. For example, one common way of ordering records is to choose one special field, which is then called the **key field**, and to sort the records according to that key field. Using a key field, we could sort a list of student records by student number (with the student number serving as the key field). We could sort the same records alphabetically by name (with the student name serving as the key field).

sorting by key value

We'll finish the chapter with a discussion of the sorting utilities in the C and C++ Standard Libraries.

13.1 QUADRATIC SORTING ALGORITHMS

In this section we develop and implement two algorithms to sort a list of numbers into increasing order.

Selectionsort—Specification

We have an array of integers to sort into order from smallest to largest. To be concrete, we'll use this prototype and precondition/postcondition contract:

```
void selectionsort(int data[ ], size_t n);
// Precondition: data is an array with at least n components.
// Postcondition: The elements of data have been rearranged so
//   that data[0] <= data[1] <= ... <= data[n-1].
```

Selectionsort—Design

The problem is to sort an array, such as data, from smallest to largest. That means rearranging the values so that data[0] is the smallest, data[1] the next smallest, and so forth up to data[n-1], which is the largest. That definition yields an outline for a straightforward algorithm (i is a local variable):

```
for (i = 0; i < n; ++i)
    Put the next smallest element in location data[i].
```

This approach finds the smallest element, then the next smallest, and so on, placing the items in data[0], data[1],... as they are found. We can also work the approach the other way, finding the largest item, then the next largest, and so on:

```
for (i = n-1; i >= 0; --i)
    Put the next largest element in location data[i].
```

There are many ways to realize this general approach. We could use two arrays, copying the elements from one array to the other in sorted order. However, one array is both adequate and economical. To help in exploring this approach, we will use the concrete example shown here:

data

10	8	6	2	16	4	18	11	14	12
[0]	[1]	[2]	[3]	[4]	[5]	[6]	[7]	[8]	[9]

Consider sorting this array with a pencil and eraser according to the second version of the pseudocode that we have outlined (finding and placing the largest element, then the next largest, and so on).

We begin by searching the array for the largest element, and we find this largest element at data[6], which is the 18. We next want to set the last element of the array equal to this value of 18. In doing so, we must be careful to not lose the original value of 12 that was stored in array location data[9]. A simple assignment statement like the following would destroy the 12:

```
data[9] = data[6]; // No good: destroys the original data[9].
```

The algorithm must not simply destroy the original value 12 that was in the final spot of the array. Fortunately we have an array location in which to store it. We can place it in the location that used to have the largest element. In other words, we actually want to "swap" the largest element with the final element of the array. After the swap, the array looks like this:

The largest value has been
swapped with the final value
in the array.

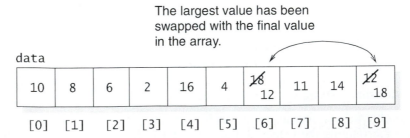

data

10	8	6	2	16	4	18̸ 12	11	14	1̸2̸ 18
[0]	[1]	[2]	[3]	[4]	[5]	[6]	[7]	[8]	[9]

The values of data[6] and data[9] have simply been swapped. A similar thing is done with the second-largest value of the array. We find this second-largest value (the 16 at data[4]) and swap it with the next-to-last element of the array (data[8]), resulting in this array:

The second-largest value has been
swapped with the next-to-last value
in the array.

data

10	8	6	2	16 14	4	12	11	14 16	18
[0]	[1]	[2]	[3]	[4]	[5]	[6]	[7]	[8]	[9]

The entire array can be sorted by a series of swaps such as these. Any sorting algorithm that is based on swapping is referred to as an **interchange sort**.

The simplest interchange sorting algorithm, which we have been describing, is called **selectionsort**. The algorithm's basic pseudocode is shown here:

```
for (i = n-1; i > 0; --i)
    swap(data[i], data[suitable index]);
```

These two lines of pseudocode have two refinements from our original pseudo-code. First, we are using the swap function from the <algorithm> facility. The function interchanges the values of its two arguments. The second refinement is that the loop executes only n-1 times, stopping when i drops to zero. There is no need to execute the loop with i equal to zero because when i reaches zero, all the larger elements are already in their correct spots. Therefore, data[0] must already have the smallest value.

the swap function

All that remains is to calculate the expression for the "suitable index." When the loop considers data[i] and looks for a suitable value to interchange, the locations with indexes above i already contain the correct values for a sorted array. So the sought-after index is the index of the largest of the remaining elements data[0], data[1], . . . , data[i]. There are i+1 of these elements to examine, searching for the index of the largest one. This search is carried out by a loop, keeping track of the largest item that has been found, and also keeping track of the index of that item. Here is the refinement of our pseudocode:

```
for (i = n-1; i > 0; --i)
{
    index_of_largest = 0;
    largest = data[0];
    for (j = 1; j <= i; ++j)
    {
        if (data[j] > largest)
            Change largest to data[j] and index_of_largest to j
    }
    swap(data[i], data[index_of_largest]);
}
```

Selectionsort—Implementation

The complete sorting algorithm is implemented by the function selectionsort, which is shown in Figure 13.1, along with a small demonstration program.

FIGURE 13.1 Selectionsort

A Program

```
// FILE: select.cxx
// An interactive test program for the selectionsort function

#include <algorithm>   // Provides swap
#include <cstdlib>     // Provides EXIT_SUCCESS, size_t
#include <iostream>    // Provides cout and cin
using namespace std;

// PROTOTYPE of the function used in this test program:
void selectionsort(int data[ ], size_t n);
// Precondition: data is an array with at least n components.
// Postcondition: The elements are rearranged so that data[0] <= data[1] <= ... <= data[n-1].

int main( )
{
    const char BLANK = ' ';
    const size_t ARRAY_SIZE = 10;   // Number of elements in the array to be sorted
    int data[ARRAY_SIZE];           // Array of integers to be sorted
    int user_input;                 // Number typed by the user
    size_t number_of_elements;      // How much of the array is used
    size_t i;                       // Array index

    // Provide some instructions.
    cout << "Please type up to " << ARRAY_SIZE << " positive integers. ";
    cout << "Indicate the list's end with a zero." << endl;

    // Read the input numbers.
    number_of_elements = 0;
    cin >> user_input;
    while ((user_input != 0) && (number_of_elements < ARRAY_SIZE))
    {
        data[number_of_elements] = user_input;
        ++number_of_elements;
        cin >> user_input;
    }

    // Sort the numbers, and print the result with two blanks after each number.
    selectionsort(data, number_of_elements);
    cout << "In sorted order, your numbers are: "<< endl;
    for (i = 0; i < number_of_elements; ++i)
        cout << data[i] << BLANK << BLANK;
    cout << endl;

    return EXIT_SUCCESS;
}
```

(continued)

(FIGURE 13.1 continued)

```
void selectionsort(int data[ ], size_t n)
// Library facilities used: algorithm, cstdlib
{
    size_t i, j, index_of_largest;
    int largest;

    if (n == 0)
        return; // No work for an empty array

    for (i = n-1; i > 0; --i)
    {
        largest = data[0];
        index_of_largest = 0;
        for (j = 1; j <= i; ++j)
        {
            if (data[j] > largest)
            {
                largest = data[j];
                index_of_largest = j;
            }
        }
        swap(data[i], data[index_of_largest]);
    }
}
```

Sample Dialogue

```
Please type up to 10 positive integers. Indicate the list's end with a zero.
80  10  50  70  60  90  20  30  40 0
In sorted order, your numbers are:
10  20  30  40  50  60  70  80  90
```

www.cs.colorado.edu/~main/chapter13/select.cxx   **WWW**

In the selectionsort implementation, you will notice that i and n are both size_t, so we have added an extra if-statement to handle the case of "sorting an empty array" (the case where n is zero). In this case, the function has no work to do (there are no elements to sort), but since size_t values may not be negative, we must avoid the assignment i = n-1.

Selectionsort—Analysis

We want to analyze the worst-case running time for the selectionsort algorithm that we implemented as the function selectionsort shown in Figure 13.1. Let us use n for the number of items to be sorted. In the function selectionsort, n is the value of the size_t parameter n.

In outline form, the main work of the selectionsort algorithm is given here:

```
for (i = n-1; i > 0; --i)
    swap(data[i], data[suitable index]);
```

When i is equal to n-1, then data[suitable index] is the largest element in the array; when i is equal to n-2, then data[suitable index] is the second-largest element in the array, and so forth.

How many operations are performed by this for-loop? The answer is not easy. Many of the operations are hidden. The loop control variable, i, is compared to zero at the start of each loop iteration. The swap function uses some number of assignment operations, and the calculation of the "suitable index" requires some work. The value of i is decremented at the end of each loop iteration. We could determine the precise number of operations for each of these subtasks in the loop. However, that is more detail than we need. We are only looking for a big-O approximation, which means that we do not need the exact values for constants. This will simplify our analysis significantly.

During each iteration of the loop, there is some constant number of operations in managing the loop control variable, and there is some constant number of operations involved in the call to the swap function. So *the number of operations in each loop iteration is the sum:*

some constant + the cost of finding the suitable index

Since there are $n-1$ loop iterations, the total count of the number of operations performed is given by the product:

$(n - 1) \times$ (some constant + the cost of finding the suitable index)

To change this into a nice formula expressed in terms of n, we need to determine the cost of finding the "suitable index."

As it turns out, when the algorithm is looking for the value to place in location data[i], the "suitable index" is the index of the largest of the values

data[0], data[1], ..., data[i]

The selectionsort algorithm uses a for-loop to determine the location of this largest element and thereby the value of the "suitable index." This loop looks at each of these array elements and performs some constant number of operations with each of them. Since i can be as large as $n-1$, in the worst case, the loop will look at all n array elements from data[0] to data[n-1] and perform a constant number of operations on each one. Hence, our estimate of the number of operations to find this "suitable index" is *at most a constant times n.*

Putting this information together, we see that the total count of the number of operations performed in the selectionsort is this:

Total = $(n - 1) \times$ (some constant + the cost of finding the suitable index)

$\leq (n - 1) \times$ [some constant + (some other constant) $\times n$]

Now we need to estimate the quantity:

$(n - 1) \times$ [some constant + (some other constant) $\times n$]

If you multiply this out, you will get an n^2 term, an n term, and a constant term without any n. Thus, the number of operations performed is:

$n^2 \times$ (some new constant)

$+$

$n \times$ (some other new constant)

$+$

(yet another new constant)

This is our estimate of the worst-case running time for selectionsort. Because we are doing a big-O analysis, we can ignore the constants and only consider the highest exponent of n. Hence, we see that the worst-case running time for selectionsort is $O(n^2)$.

This analysis of the running time for selectionsort did not depend on the initial values in the array. The selectionsort algorithm performs the same number of operations no matter what values are in the array that it sorts. Thus, the average-case running time (and even the best-case running time) is the same as the worst-case running time.

Selectionsort Running Time

The worst-case running time, the average-case running time, and the best-case running time for selectionsort are all quadratic.

PROGRAMMING TIP

ROUGH ESTIMATES SUFFICE FOR BIG-*O*

We have just computed big-*O* expressions for the worst-case running time of the selectionsort algorithm. Notice that when we performed the big-*O* analyses, we did not compute exact formulas for the running times. For example, when we estimated the number of operations in one iteration of the primary loop used in the algorithm, we decided that the algorithm performed the following number of operations in each loop iteration:

some constant + the cost of finding the suitable index

Notice that we never computed the exact value of "some constant." Because big-*O* expressions are accurate only to "within a constant multiple," the exact value of the constant does not matter. If we want only a big-*O* expression, there is no reason to spend time computing an exact value for this constant.

Insertionsort

Another simple and natural sorting algorithm is based on the following illustration of sorting an array that contains this list of 10 integers:

(8,   2,   5,   3, 10,   7,   1,   4,   6,   9)

One way to proceed is to take the numbers one at a time and build up another sorted list of values. The first number is 8, so make a list that contains only the one number 8. That is certainly a sorted list. Next take the 2 and combine it with the 8 to obtain a longer sorted list, namely (2, 8). Next, add the 5 to obtain the list: (2, 5, 8).

If you keep adding numbers to the list, you will eventually obtain a sorted list containing all the numbers. The original list decreases by one on each iteration, and the list we are building increases by one on each iteration. The progress of this process is shown here for the example list:

( )   (8,   2,   5,   3, 10,   7,   1,   4,   6,   9)

(8)   (2,   5,   3, 10,   7,   1,   4,   6,   9)

(2,   8)   (5,   3, 10,   7,   1,   4,   6,   9)

(2,   5,   8)   (3, 10,   7,   1,   4,   6,   9)

(2,   3,   5,   8)   (10,   7,   1,   4,   6,   9)

(2,   3,   5,   8, 10)   (7,   1,   4,   6,   9)

(2,   3,   5,   7,   8, 10)   (1,   4,   6,   9)

(1,   2,   3,   5,   7,   8, 10)   (4,   6,   9)

(1,   2,   3,   4,   5,   7,   8, 10)   (6,   9)

(1,   2,   3,   4,   5,   6,   7,   8, 10)   (9)

(1,   2,   3,   4,   5,   6,   7,   8,   9, 10)   ( )

With the insertionsort, your first thought might be to use an additional array and copy values from one array to the other. The numbers in the left-hand lists in our drawings would be in one array, and the numbers in the right-hand lists would be in the other array. But if you look carefully at the drawings, you will see that one list grows at exactly the same rate that the other list shrinks. So we need only one array. If we have 10 numbers, we need only 10 positions. One list can be kept at the front of the array and the other at the back of the array.

We can redraw the progress of the insertionsort in a way that makes it evident that one array is sufficient. At the start of the insertionsort, we have the same 10-element array that we have been working with:

data

8	2	5	3	10	7	1	4	6	9
[0]	[1]	[2]	[3]	[4]	[5]	[6]	[7]	[8]	[9]

We have called the array data. The first component, data[0], is shaded to indicate that even at the start, the front part of the array—with only the one shaded item—can be viewed as a tiny sorted array on its own. The first actual work will be to insert the second element (data[1], which is a 2) into the tiny sorted array, increasing the "sorted part" of the array to encompass two elements, as shown here:

data

2	8	5	3	10	7	1	4	6	9
[0]	[1]	[2]	[3]	[4]	[5]	[6]	[7]	[8]	[9]

So, at this point, the first two elements (2, 8) form a small sorted list, and we still need to insert the remaining elements (5, 3, 10, 7, 1, 4, 6, 9). After the insertion of the 5, we have the situation shown here:

data

2	5	8	3	10	7	1	4	6	9
[0]	[1]	[2]	[3]	[4]	[5]	[6]	[7]	[8]	[9]

The insertion process continues, taking the next element from the unsorted side of the array and inserting it into the sorted side of the array. Each insertion increases the size of the sorted side and decreases the unsorted side until the entire array is sorted. The following pseudocode describes the whole process:

```
for (i = 1; i < n; ++i)
    Insert data[i] into the elements before data[i] (which are already sorted)
```

The insertion of data[i] can be done in three steps, which we'll illustrate when i is 3 for the sample array:

2	5	8	3	10	7	1	4	6	9
[0]	[1]	[2]	[3]	[4]	[5]	[6]	[7]	[8]	[9]

1. Save a copy of the number to be inserted. For our example, this step copies data[3] into a temporary local variable, as shown here:

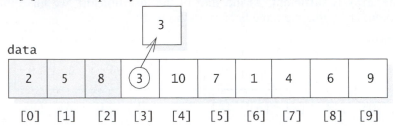

2. Move up the elements before data[i] until you reach the spot to insert the new number. In our example, we move the 8 and then the 5, as shown here:

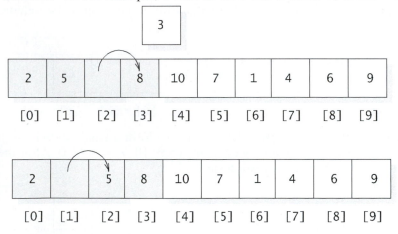

3. Insert the new number into the open spot. For our example, the 3 is inserted:

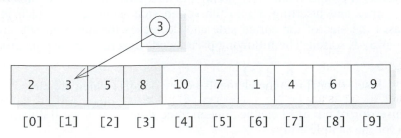

Insertionsort—Analysis

You can convert these ideas into the actual insertionsort function yourself (see Self-Test Exercise 4 on page 635). We'll finish this section by analyzing the insertionsort in a slightly different manner, determining how many times the algorithm must access an element of the array—either for a comparison, or for a swap of some sort. For many sorting algorithms, such as insertionsort, the count of array accesses is proportional to the total number of operations. Therefore, the final big-O analysis comes out the same.

We start by asking how many array accesses are required to insert just one new element. If you analyze the insertion process, you will see that the function starts by comparing the new element to the final element from the sorted portion of the array. After this comparison, the algorithm works backward through the array until it finds the correct spot to insert a new element. In the worst case, the algorithm could compare and shift each element of the array once, and therefore the total number of array accesses is limited to a constant times n. In fact, an insertion may need significantly fewer than $O(n)$ accesses as an insertion examines only the elements in the sorted portion rather than all n. But $O(n)$ operations is a good overestimate because it is easy to express and easy to work with.

So, the insertion of one new element takes $O(n)$ time, and there are n elements to insert. Thus the total time for n separate insertions is no more than this:

$$\text{Total} = n \times (\text{the number of operations in an } O(n) \text{ algorithm})$$
$$= n \times (\text{some constant times } n)$$
$$= \text{some constant times } n^2$$
$$= O(n^2)$$

This analysis shows one important trick to remember:

Analysis for Quadratic Time

An $O(n)$ process that is performed n times results in a quadratic number of operations ($O(n^2)$).

In the case of insertionsort, we actually perform $n-1$ insertions rather than n, but the time for $n-1$ insertions is also quadratic.

Our analysis has used one major overestimation. We assumed that each insertion was required to examine the full n elements of the array, but some insertions require the examination of far fewer elements. Will a more accurate estimate reduce the time analysis? The answer is no. A precise analysis of the worst-case running time still results in a quadratic formula. To see this, suppose that all the original elements are far from their correct places. In fact, these elements might be completely backward, as shown here:

10	9	8	7	6	5	4	3	2	1
[0]	[1]	[2]	[3]	[4]	[5]	[6]	[7]	[8]	[9]

The first insertion must insert the 9 before the 10, resulting in this array:

9	10	8	7	6	5	4	3	2	1
[0]	[1]	[2]	[3]	[4]	[5]	[6]	[7]	[8]	[9]

The next insertion must insert the 8 in front of everything else. And then the 7 is inserted, again at the front. With the elements starting out backward, each insertion must compare and shift all the elements in the currently sorted part of the array, placing the new element at the front. So, for an insertionsort to work on a completely backward array requires these comparisons and shifts:

1 compare and shift to insert the 1st element
+
2 compares and shifts to insert the 2nd element
+
. . .
+
n–1 compares and shifts to insert the (n–1) element

The total number of compares and shifts is thus $1 + 2 + 3 + \ldots + (n{-}1)$. You can use a technique similar to Figure 1.2 on page 19 to evaluate this sum. The result is $n(n{-}1)/2$, which is $O(n^2)$. So the worst case for insertionsort is indeed quadratic time, the same as selectionsort.

The analysis of the average-case running time for insertionsort is essentially the same as that for the worst case. The only difference is that a single insertion will, on the average, stop after accessing half of the elements from the sorted side, rather than accessing them all. This means that the average-case running time is half that of the worst-case running time, but we know that a constant multiple, such as ½, does not affect a big-O expression. Thus, the average-case running time for insertionsort is quadratic, the same as the worst-case running time.

On the other hand, the best-case running time for insertionsort is much better than quadratic. In particular, suppose that the array is *already sorted* before we begin our work. This is certainly an advantage, though the advantage does not help all sorting algorithms. For example, starting with a sorted array does not help selectionsort, which still requires quadratic time. But starting with a sorted array does help insertionsort. In this case, each insertion of a new element will examine only a single element from the array. This single-element examination is carried out once to insert each new element, and the result is an $O(n)$ time.

You probably think that starting with an already sorted array does not happen too often. But frequently an array is *nearly* sorted—perhaps a few new elements are out of place. Insertionsort is also quite quick for nearly sorted arrays.

Insertionsort Running Time

Both the worst-case running time and the average-case running times are quadratic. But the best-case (when the starting array is already sorted) is linear, and the algorithm is also quick when the starting array is nearly sorted.

Self-Test Exercises for Section 13.1

1. Compare the worst-case, average-case, and best-case running time for selectionsort and insertionsort.

2. Show the following array after each iteration of selectionsort, using the largest element version of swapping: 5 19 13 36 23 2

3. Show the following array after each iteration of insertionsort: 5 19 13 36 23 2

4. Give a complete function implementation for insertionsort.

5. The `selectionsort` function in Figure 13.1 on page 626 sorts integers into increasing order. How would you change the function so that it sorts integers into decreasing order?

6. The `selectionsort` function in Figure 13.1 on page 626 sorts integers into increasing order. How would you change the function so that it sorts an array of lowercase strings into alphabetical order?

13.2 RECURSIVE SORTING ALGORITHMS

Divide-and-Conquer Using Recursion

Let's start with an explicit statement of a recursive design technique called **divide-and-conquer**. Here's the idea: When a problem is small, simply solve it. When the problem is large, divide the problem into two smaller subproblems, each of which is about half of the original problem. Solve each subproblem with a recursive call. After the recursive calls, extra work is often needed to combine the solutions of the smaller problems, resulting in a solution to the larger problem.

Divide-and-conquer can work in slightly different ways, perhaps having more than two subproblems or having subproblems with unequal size, but the basic approach—two subproblems with roughly equal size—works best.

Applied to sorting, divide-and-conquer results in the following pattern:

> **Key Design Concept**
>
> *Divide-and-conquer works best with two equally sized subproblems, each of which is solved with a recursive call.*

The Divide-and-Conquer Sorting Paradigm

1. Divide the elements to be sorted into two groups of equal (or almost equal) size.

2. Sort each of these smaller groups of elements (by recursive calls).

3. Combine the two sorted groups into one large sorted list.

As an illustration, we can see how these three steps will sort a small array. The first step divides the array into two equally sized groups, as shown in this cut:

| 9 | 12 | 31 | 25 | 5 | 8 | 20 | 2 | 3 | 6 |

After the cut, we have two smaller arrays, with five elements each. These smaller arrays can separately be sorted with recursive calls, providing this result:

| 5 | 9 | 12 | 25 | 31 |

| 2 | 3 | 6 | 8 | 20 |

When the recursive calls return, the two half-arrays somehow need to be put together into one sorted array, as shown here:

| 2 | 3 | 5 | 6 | 8 | 9 | 12 | 20 | 25 | 31 |

We will present two recursive sorting functions based on this divide-and-conquer paradigm. But first there is a C++ feature that we will discuss to make the recursive calls easier.

C++ FEATURE

SPECIFYING A SUBARRAY WITH POINTER ARITHMETIC

Our sorting functions will require recursive calls to sort various portions of the array. This raises an interesting problem regarding the arguments of a sorting function. As an example of the problem, look at the specification of one of our sorts:

```
void selectionsort(int data[ ], size_t n);
// Precondition: data is an array with at least n components.
// Postcondition: The elements of data have been rearranged so
//   that data[0] <= data[1] <= ... <= data[n-1].
```

Is it possible to use this function to sort only *part* of an array? Certainly we can sort the *first part* of an array. For example, suppose that data is an array of 10 integers. This function call will sort the first five elements of data:

```
selectionsort(data, 5);
```

This function call will rearrange the elements data[0] through data[4] so that the values are smallest to largest. But can we use the function to sort the second part of the array (from data[5] through data[9]) or a middle piece (such as data[2] through data[6])? The answer is yes, but we'll need a C++ feature called *pointer arithmetic*.

To illustrate pointer arithmetic, we'll continue with our array, data, of 10 integers. Suppose that data has these values:

data

9	12	31	25	5	8	20	11	3	6
[0]	[1]	[2]	[3]	[4]	[5]	[6]	[7]	[8]	[9]

For any value i from 0 to 9, the expression data[i] refers to *one* of the 10 components. For example, data[5] refers to the value 8 in the array. This is not new. But another use of the index i is new: For any value i from 0 to 9, the expression (data + i) refers to the small array that starts at data[i] and continues to the end of the array. For example, (data + 5) refers to that part of data that begins at data[5] and includes 8, 20, 11, 3, 6. A small array, which is actually part of a larger array, is called a **subarray**. The expression (data + 5) is an example of **pointer arithmetic**, which allows a programmer to combine a pointer or an array with integer values. Pointer arithmetic has many interesting uses, but we'll only use it for this one purpose of *specifying a subarray*.

Consider the subarray (data + 5). This is part of the complete data array, containing the last five elements of data. Moreover, (data + 5) can be used just like any other five-element array. Here are some examples:

```
cout << (data + 5)[0]; // Prints the 8
cout << (data + 5)[2]; // Prints the 11
++((data + 5)[1]);     // Adds one to the array element
```

The third statement, ++((data + 5)[1]), adds one to the [1] element of the subarray, increasing it from 20 to 21. After this statement, the data array has these values:

data

9	12	31	25	5	8	21	11	3	6
[0]	[1]	[2]	[3]	[4]	[5]	[6]	[7]	[8]	[9]

Notice that (data + 5)[1] is the [1] element of the subarray, but it is also the [6] element of the whole array. So changing (data + 5)[1] will actually change data[6]. In other words: *A subarray is always part of a complete array. Changing the subarray will change the complete array.*

Why did we want to use subarrays in the first place? Using a subarray, we can make a function call that sorts *part* of an array. Here are two examples:

```
selectionsort((data + 5), 4); // Sorts data[5] through data[8]
selectionsort((data + 2), 5); // Sorts data[2] through data[6]
```

For example, the second function call sorts five elements starting at data[2].

With subarrays in hand, we can develop our two recursive sorting algorithms.

Specifying Subarrays with Pointer Arithmetic

Suppose that data is an array with at least n elements. For any integer i from 0 to n, the expression (data + i) refers to the subarray that begins at data[i] and continues to the end of the array.

In the subarray, (data + i)[0] is the same as data[i]; (data + i)[1] is the same as data[i+1]; and so on.

A subarray is always part of a complete array. Changing the subarray will change the complete array.

Mergesort

The most straightforward implementation of the divide-and-conquer approach to sorting is the **mergesort** algorithm. The mergesort algorithm divides the array near its midpoint, sorts the two half-arrays by recursive calls to the algorithm, and then merges the two halves to get a new sorted array of elements. The final "merging" step of the process will require some thought, so we'll postpone that part of the implementation by assuming that we have a separate function to carry out the merging. The prototype for the merging function is shown here:

```
void merge(int data[ ], size_t n1, size_t n2);
// Precondition: data is an array (or subarray) with at least n1 + n2
//   elements. The first n1 elements (from data[0] to data[n1-1]) are sorted
//   from smallest to largest, and the last n2 (from data[n1] to
//   data[n1 + n2 - 1]) are also sorted from smallest to largest.
// Postcondition: The first n1 + n2 elements of data have been rearranged
//   to be sorted from smallest to largest.
// NOTE: If there is insufficient dynamic memory, then bad_alloc is
//   thrown.
```

This merge function will be used as the last step of our mergesort. Notice that the merge function will use some dynamic memory, so there is a possibility of failure that we have indicated in the specification. Can you predict where the dynamic memory will come into play? You'll see the answer shortly, but for now, examine the mergesort function in Figure 13.2.

The stopping case for mergesort's recursion is when the array to be sorted consists of only one element. In this stopping case, there is no work to do because a single element does not need to be "rearranged." On the other hand, if there is more than one element, then the mergesort function carries out these steps:

1. Calculate the sizes of the two subarrays. The first size, n1, is approximately half of the entire size (calculated by n/2, using integer division). The second size, n2, is whatever is left over (calculated by n - n1).

2. Use recursive calls to sort the two subarrays. Notice that the second recursive call, `mergesort((data + n1), n2)`, uses pointer arithmetic to specify the subarray that begins at `data[n1]`.

3. Finally, a call to the `merge` function combines the two sorted halves.

The operation of the `merge` function has some issues that we discuss next.

The Merge Function

The algorithm for the merge function uses a second temporary array that we will call `temp`. Elements will be copied from the array `data` to the array `temp` in such a way that the array `temp` is correctly sorted. (After that, the values are simply copied back to the array `data`.) The merging algorithm uses the precondition that the two halves of the array (`data[0]` through `data[n1 - 1]`, and `data[n1]` through `data[n1 + n2 -1]`) are each sorted. Since they are both sorted, we know that `data[0]` contains the smallest element in the first half, and `data[n1]` contains the smallest element in the second half. Therefore, we know that the

---

FIGURE 13.2   Mergesort

A Function Implementation

```
void mergesort(int data[ ], size_t n)
// Precondition: data is an array with at least n components.
// Postcondition: The elements of data have been rearranged so
// that data[0] <= data[1] <= ... <= data[n-1].
// NOTE: If there is insufficient dynamic memory, then bad_alloc is thrown.
// Library facilities used: cstdlib
{
    size_t n1;  // Size of the first subarray
    size_t n2;  // Size of the second subarray

    if (n > 1)
    {
        // Compute sizes of the subarrays.
        n1 = n / 2;
        n2 = n - n1;

        mergesort(data, n1);           // Sort from data[0] through data[n1-1]
        mergesort((data + n1), n2);    // Sort from data[n1] to the end

        // Merge the two sorted halves.
        merge(data, n1, n2);
    }
}
```

This function calls merge, which uses dynamic memory, so we must indicate the possibility of failure.

The two subarrays are sorted with recursive calls.

www.cs.colorado.edu/~main/chapter13/merge.cxx   **WWW**

smallest element in the *entire* array is either data[0] or data[n1]. The algorithm compares these two elements and copies the smallest one to position temp[0]. The algorithm then somehow marks the copied element as being "already copied." For example, suppose that data contains ten integers. After the first one is copied to temp, we might have this situation:

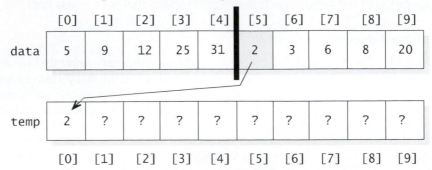

The drawing has a thick black line to separate the two halves of the data array. The 2 (at the front of the second half) is smaller than the 5 (at the front of the first half), so this 2 is copied to the front of the temporary array. We marked the 2 as "already copied" by shading it in the diagram. In the actual algorithm, we'll keep track of which items have been copied by maintaining three variables: copied (total number of elements copied from data to temp), copied1 (the number of elements copied from the first half of data), and copied2 (the number of elements copied from the second half of data). All three local variables are initialized to zero in the merge function. Each time we copy an element from the first half of data to the temporary array, we add one to both copied and copied1. Each time we copy an element from the second half of data to the temporary array, we add one to both copied and copied2. So, after copying the 2 in our example, copied and copied2 are both 1, but copied1 remains zero.

The merge algorithm proceeds by looking at the next uncopied elements from each half of the data array. The smaller of these two elements is copied to the next spot in the temporary array. In our example, we would next compare the 5 (from the first half) to the 3 (the next uncopied element from the second half). Since the 3 is smaller, we copy the 3 to the next spot in temp, as shown here:

At this point we have copied a total of two elements (since `copied` is 2). Both of the copied elements came from the second half (since `copied1` is 0 and `copied2` is 2).

The next step of the algorithm will compare the 5 (from the first half) to the 6 (from the second half). The 5 is lower, so it gets copied to the temporary array, as shown here:

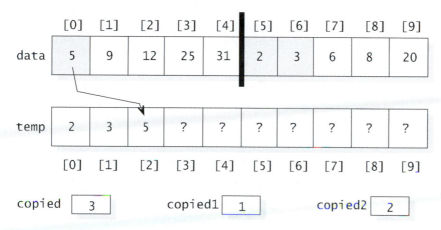

The loop proceeds in this way, moving through the two array halves. With this idea, we can write our first version of the pseudocode, as shown here:

1. Initialize `copied`, `copied1`, and `copied2` to zero.

2. *while* (both halves of the array have more elements to copy)
   if ((next element of the first half) <= (next element of the second half))
   {
       Copy the next element of the first half to the next spot in `temp`.
       Add 1 to both `copied` and `copied1`.
   }
   else
   {
       Copy the next element of the second half to the next spot in `temp`.
       Add 1 to both `copied` and `copied2`.
   }

Using the local variables `copied`, `copied1`, and `copied2`, we can refine the pseudocode a bit. The "next spot in temp" is `temp[copied]`; the "next element in the first half" is `data[copied1]`. And the "next element in the second half" is part of the subarray (`data + n1`)—that is, the subarray that begins at `data[n1]`. In fact, the element that we want to examine from the second half is the element (`data + n1`) `[copied2]`, as shown in this refinement:

1. Initialize `copied`, `copied1`, and `copied2` to zero.

```
2. while (both halves of the array have more elements to copy)
     if (data[copied1] <= (data + n1)[copied2])
     {
         temp[copied] = data[copied1];
         Add 1 to both copied and copied1.
     }
     else
     {
         temp[copied] = (data + n1)[copied2];
         Add 1 to both copied and copied2.
     }
```

In our actual implementation, the two assignment statements can be modified to also add 1 to `copied` and to the appropriate one of the other two local variables (`copied1` or `copied2`). The modified assignment statements make use of the `++` operator, as shown here:

1. Initialize `copied`, `copied1`, and `copied2` to zero.

2. *while* (both halves of the array have more elements to copy)

```
     if (data[copied1] <= (data + n1)[copied2])
         temp[copied++] = data[copied1++];
     else
         temp[copied++] = (data + n1)[copied2++];
```

Using an index such as `copied++` has the effect of using the *current* value of the variable `copied` as the index and *afterward* adding 1 to the variable. (If we wanted to add 1 before using the index, we would write `++copied` instead of `copied++`).

This part of our algorithm works fine as long as neither half of the array runs out of elements. However, eventually one of the two halves will run out of elements. For our example, this will occur after we copy the last element (20) from the second half of the `data` array to the temporary array, as shown here:

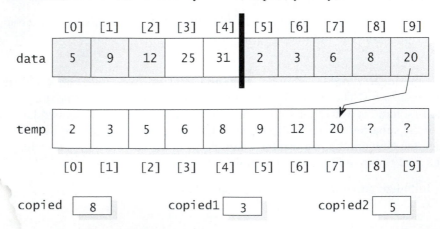

FIGURE 13.3   A Function to Merge Two Sorted Arrays

A Function Implementation

```
void merge(int data[ ], size_t n1, size_t n2)
// Precondition: data is an array (or subarray) with at least n1 + n2 elements. The first n1
// elements (from data[0] to data[n1 - 1]) are sorted from smallest to largest, and the last n2
// (from data[n1] to data[n1 + n2 - 1]) also are sorted from smallest to largest.
// Postcondition: The first n1 + n2 elements of data have been rearranged to be sorted from
// smallest to largest.
// NOTE: If there is insufficient dynamic memory, then bad_alloc is thrown.
// Library facilities used: cstdlib
{
    int *temp;              // Points to dynamic array to hold the sorted elements
    size_t copied  = 0;     // Number of elements copied from data to temp
    size_t copied1 = 0;     // Number copied from the first half of data
    size_t copied2 = 0;     // Number copied from the second half of data
    size_t i;               // Array index to copy from temp back into data

    // Allocate memory for the temporary dynamic array.
    temp = new int[n1+n2];

    // Merge elements, copying from two halves of data to the temporary array.
    while ((copied1 < n1) && (copied2 < n2))
    {
        if (data[copied1] < (data + n1)[copied2])
            temp[copied++] = data[copied1++];              // Copy from first half
        else
            temp[copied++] = (data + n1)[copied2++];  // Copy from second half
    }

    // Copy any remaining entries in the left and right subarrays.
    while (copied1 < n1)
        temp[copied++] = data[copied1++];
    while (copied2 < n2)
        temp[copied++] = (data+n1)[copied2++];

    // Copy from temp back to the data array, and release temp's memory.
    for (i = 0; i < n1+n2; ++i)
        data[i] = temp[i];
    delete [ ] temp;
}
```

www.cs.colorado.edu/~main/chapter13/merge.cxx   **WWW**

At a point like this, we want to copy the elements remaining in the nonempty half into the temporary array. This yields the following final version of our pseudocode for the `merge` function:

1. Initialize `copied`, `copied1`, and `copied2` to zero.

2. *while* (both halves of the array have more elements to copy)
   if (data[copied1] <= (data + n1)[copied2])
       temp[copied++] = data[copied1++];
   else
       temp[copied++] = (data + n1)[copied2++];

3. Copy any remaining entries from the left or right subarray.

4. Copy the elements from `temp` back to `data`.

This pseudocode translates to the C++ function shown in Figure 13.3. The only additional items deal with allocating the memory for the temporary array. This temporary array is a dynamic array containing `n1` + `n2` elements. At the end of the function, the dynamic array is released via the *delete* operator.

Dynamic Memory Usage in Mergesort

During a mergesort, our merge function will be called many times. A complete analysis would show that a mergesort of an *n*-element array makes $O(n)$ calls to the merge function. Each call to merge allocates a temporary dynamic array, uses the array, and then releases the array. With some computers, this repeated allocation and release of dynamic memory takes a significant amount of execution time. A solution is given in Programming Project 6 on page 672.

Mergesort—Analysis

A complete analysis of mergesort's running time is beyond the scope of this book, but we can give the final result and hint at its derivation. First the result:

Mergesort Running Time

The worst-case running time, the average-case running time, and the best-case running time for mergesort are all $O(n \log n)$.

As usual, *n* is the number of items to be sorted. Let us try to motivate this formula. In the case of the mergesort, the algorithm performs similarly on all inputs; so our motivation will apply to both the worst-case, average-case, and best-case running times. Let's diagram the first few levels of recursive calls made by a typical mergesort:

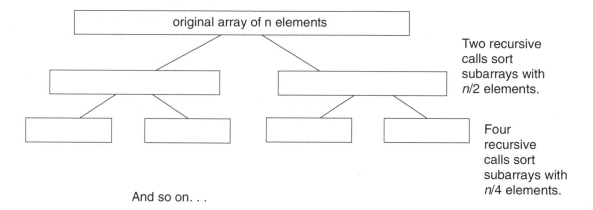

original array of n elements

Two recursive calls sort subarrays with *n*/2 elements.

Four recursive calls sort subarrays with *n*/4 elements.

And so on. . .

At the top level, we make two recursive calls to sort subarrays with *n*/2 elements each. At this level, we call merge once to merge those two *n*/2 arrays into a single *n* element array. At the second level, each *n*/2 array is broken into two *n*/4 arrays. At this level there will be two merge calls, each of which merges a pair of *n*/4 arrays to create the two *n*/2 arrays. Continuing this pattern, you will see a total of these calls to merge:

At the top level, 1 call to merge creates an array with *n* elements
+
At the next level, 2 calls to merge to create two $^n/_2$ arrays
+
At the next level, 4 calls to merge to create four $^n/_4$ arrays
+
At the next level, 8 calls to merge to create eight $^n/_8$ arrays
+
. . .

The pattern continues until we cannot further subdivide the arrays (because we have only a single element).

At each level of the pattern, the *total* work done by merging is $O(n)$. For example, at the top level we have one merge call to create an array with *n* elements, and the number of operations in this one call is proportional to *n*. At the next level, there are two merge calls, but each of the calls does work that is proportional to *n*/2, so again the *total* work done at that level is $O(n)$. At the next level we have four merge calls that each do work that is proportional to *n*/4. And so on.

Each level does *total* work proportional to *n*. So the total cost of the mergesort is given by this formula:

(some constant) $\times n \times$ (the number of levels in the pattern)

The size of the array pieces is halved on each step down the pattern. So the number of levels in the pattern is approximately equal to the number of times that n can be halved, stopping when the result is less than or equal to one. That number of "halvings" is approximated by $\log_2 n$ (the base 2 logarithm of n). Therefore, mergesort appears to perform the following number of operations:

(some constant) $\times n \times \log_2 n$

As a big-O formula, we can throw out the multiplicative constant and also the constant 2 in the base of the logarithm. So the time is $O(n \times \log n)$. This time of n multiplied by a logarithm of n is usually written more simply as $O(n \log n)$, pronounced "big-O of $n \log n$."

Our analysis has not been formal, but it is the correct answer, and a rigorous demonstration would follow the same outline as our intuitive explanation.

Mergesort has a worst-case running time of $O(n \log n)$ operations, which is faster than the $O(n^2)$ running times for the selectionsort and insertionsort algorithms. But, how much faster is it? We can get a feel for the difference by comparing the function $n \log_2 n$ with n^2. The table in Figure 13.4 gives some representative values for comparison. As you can see by studying the table, an $n \log_2 n$ running time is substantially faster than an n^2 running time, particularly if the array to be sorted is large.

FIGURE 13.4

Value of $n \log_2 n$ versus n^2

n	$n \log_2 n$	n^2
2	2	4
8	24	64
32	160	1024
128	896	16,384
512	4608	262,144
2048	22,528	4,194,304

Mergesort for Files

The mergesort algorithm is not actually a good choice for sorting arrays. The quicksort and heapsort, which we will describe in a moment, are better because they don't require a temporary array for the merge step. However, mergesort can be modified to sort a file, even if the file is too large to fit in the largest possible array. In the mergesort of a file, the file is divided into several pieces, and each piece is sorted (perhaps with a recursive call of the mergesort function). The sorted pieces are then merged into a single sorted file, and the separate pieces can be removed.

With this use of mergesort, the separate file pieces get smaller and smaller with each recursive call. Eventually, a piece gets small enough to fit into an array. At this point, the piece should be read into an array and sorted using quicksort.

Quicksort

We developed the mergesort algorithm as a special case of a general sorting technique that is called divide-and-conquer sorting. In this section we will develop another sorting algorithm based on this same basic divide-and-conquer approach. This sorting algorithm is called **quicksort**, first devised by the computer scientist C. A. R. Hoare. It is similar to mergesort in many ways. It divides the elements to be sorted into two groups, sorts the two groups by two recursive calls, and combines the two sorted groups into a single array of sorted values. However, the method for dividing the array in half is much more sophisticated than the simple method we used for mergesort. On the other hand, the method for combining these two groups of sorted elements is trivial compared to the method used in mergesort. In mergesort the division is trivial and the combining complicated. With quicksort the division is complicated and the combining is trivial.

The basic idea of quicksort is simple: Suppose you know some particular value that belongs in the middle of the array, or at least the approximate middle of the array. We will call this value the **pivot element**, or simply, the **pivot**. Suppose we somehow put this pivot element into its correct location in the array, somehow put all the values less than or equal to the pivot in array positions before the pivot, and somehow put all the values greater than the pivot in array positions after the pivot element. At this point we have not sorted the values less than the pivot element, we simply placed them, in any order, in array positions before the pivot element. Similarly, we have not yet sorted the values greater than the pivot, but we simply placed them, in any order, in array positions after the pivot element.

pivot element

After this initial moving of array elements, we have moved the array closer to being sorted. We know that the pivot element of the array is in the correct position. We also know that all other values are in the correct segment of the array, either the segment before the pivot element or the segment after the pivot element. However, although we know they are in the correct segment, those segments are still not sorted. One way to proceed is to sort the two segments separately. This works because we know that all values in the first segment are less than all values in the second segment, so no value ever needs to move from one segment to the other. How do we sort the two segments? These are smaller versions of the original sorting task, and so we can sort the two smaller array segments by recursive calls. If we continue to divide the array into smaller portions in the way we outlined, we will eventually get down to array segments of size one and we can use that as a stopping case (requiring no work).

This idea is sound except for one problem. How do we find a pivot element and its correct final position in the sorted array? There is no obvious way to quickly find the midpoint value until after the array is sorted. Our solution will be to take an arbitrary array value and use it as the pivot element. As a result, we may not be dividing the array exactly in half, but as long as we do divide it into smaller pieces, our algorithm will eventually sort the array. We perform the subtask of dividing the array elements with a function called `partition`. The `partition` function chooses some arbitrary pivot element, places it at the correct index position, and divides the remaining array elements as we have described. The function will not necessarily do those three things in that order, but it will do them all. The function prototype and specification is as follows:

```
void partition(int data[ ], size_t n, size_t& pivot_index);
// Precondition: n > 1, and data is an array (or subarray) with at least n
// elements.
// Postcondition: The function has selected some "pivot value" that occurs
// in data[0]. . .data[n-1]. The elements of data have then been
// rearranged and the pivot index set so that
//      -- data[pivot_index] is equal to the pivot;
//      -- each item before data[pivot_index] is <= the pivot;
//      -- each item after data[pivot_index] is > the pivot.
```

We will formulate our sorting algorithm as a recursive function called quicksort, which makes a call to the partition function. After the partitioning, the array and the pivot index look like this:

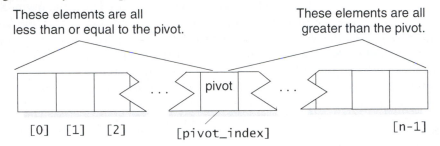

After the partition, our quicksort function makes two recursive calls. The first recursive call sorts the elements before the pivot element, from data[0] to data[pivot_index - 1]. The second recursive call sorts the elements after the pivot element, from data[pivot_index + 1] to data[n - 1]. The recursive calls are part of the quicksort implementation in Figure 13.5. We still need to derive the code for the partition function.

The Partition Function

Since we have no information about the values in the array, all values have an equal probability of being the value that belongs in the middle of the array. Moreover, we know that the algorithm will work no matter what value we use for the pivot element. So, we arbitrarily choose the first array element to use as the pivot element. (On page 654 we discuss why this is not always the best choice and propose a method to fix the problem.)

The partition function will move all the values that are less than or equal to this pivot element toward the beginning of the array, that is, toward positions with lower numbered indexes. All values that are greater than this pivot element are moved the other way, toward the tail end of the array, with higher numbered indexes. Because the pivot element is not necessarily the value that belongs at the exact midpoint position of the array, we do not know where the dividing line between the two array portions belongs. Hence, we do not know how far forward we need to move elements less than or equal to the pivot element, nor do we know how far toward the end of the array we must move elements that are greater than the pivot element. We solve this dilemma by working inward from the two ends of the array. We move smaller elements to the beginning of the array, and we move larger elements to the tail end of the array. In this way we obtain two segments—one segment of smaller elements growing to the right from the beginning of the array, and one segment of larger elements growing to the left from the tail end of the array. When these two segments meet, we have correctly partitioned the array. The correct location for the pivot element is at the boundary of these two segments.

Starting at the beginning of the array, the algorithm passes over smaller elements at the beginning of the array until it encounters an element that is larger than the pivot element. This larger element is not in the correct segment and must somehow move to the tail end segment. Starting at the tail end of the array, the algorithm passes over larger elements at that end of the array until it encounters an element that is smaller than (or equal to) the pivot element. This smaller element is not in the correct segment and must somehow move to the beginning segment. At that point we know that the elements in the two segments up to, but not including, these out-of-place elements are in the correct segment of the array. If we switch these two out-of-place elements, we will know that they also are in the correct portion of the array. Using this technique of locating and switching

FIGURE 13.5   Quicksort

A Function Implementation

```
void quicksort(int data[ ], size_t n)
// Precondition: data is an array with at least n components.
// Postcondition: The elements of data have been rearranged so that
// data[0] <= data[1] <= data[2] <= ... <= data[n-1].
// Library facilities used: cstdlib
{
    size_t pivot_index;  // Array index for the pivot element
    size_t n1;           // Number of elements before the pivot element
    size_t n2;           // Number of elements after the pivot element

    if (n > 1)
    {
        // Partition the array, and set the pivot index.
        partition(data, n, pivot_index);

        // Compute the sizes of the subarrays.
        n1 = pivot_index;
        n2 = n - n1 - 1;

        // Recursive calls will now sort the subarrays.
        quicksort(data, n1);
        quicksort((data + pivot_index + 1), n2);
    }
}
```

www.cs.colorado.edu/~main/chapter13/quick.cxx   **W W W**

incorrectly placed elements at the ends of the array, our algorithm proceeds to continually expand the segment at the beginning of the array and the segment at the tail end of the array, until these two segments meet.

For example, suppose the following represents our array:

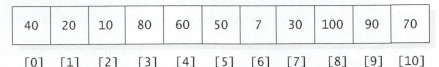

We choose the first value, 40, as our pivot element. Starting at the beginning of the array, we look for the first element that is greater than the pivot. That is the 80. Starting from the other end we look for the first value that is less than or equal to the pivot. That is the 30. We use two variables called too_big_index and too_small_index to hold the indexes of these two array elements. After finding the two out-of-place elements, the array can be represented as follows:

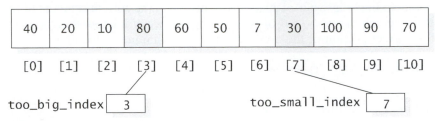

The two shaded elements are in incorrect segments of the array. If we interchange them, the array will be closer to being divided correctly. After the exchange the array will contain these elements:

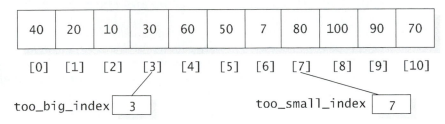

We now repeat the process. Continuing from the places we left off, we increment too_big_index until we find another element larger than the pivot; we decrement too_small_index until we find another element less than or equal to the pivot element. This changes the values of the two index variables as shown here:

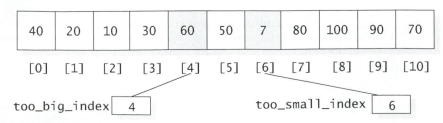

Exchanging these two elements places them in the correct array portions and yields the following array value:

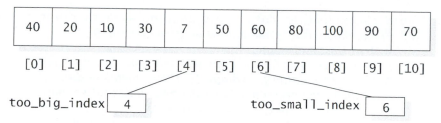

If we continue to look for elements to exchange, we will increment the `too_big_index` until it reaches the element that contains 50, and we will decrement the `too_small_index` past the element 50 to the index of the element 7. At this point the two indexes have crossed each other, as shown here:

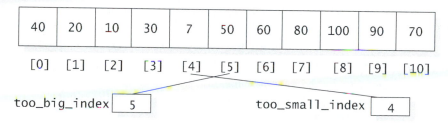

Once the indexes cross each other, we have partitioned the array. All elements less than or equal to the pivot element of 40 are in the first five positions. All elements greater than the pivot element of 40 are in the last six positions. However, the pivot is not yet at the dividing point between the two parts of the array. At this point, the correct spot for the pivot will always be at the location given by the variable `too_small_index`. The reason is because the `too_small_index` has just hit the tail end of the first of the two array segments.

So, we exchange the values of `data[0]` and `data[too_small_index]`. After moving the pivot element, the array configuration is as follows:

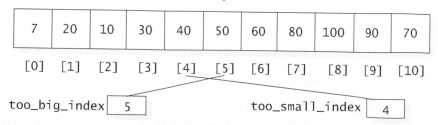

In addition to the local variables `too_small_index` and `too_big_index`, our pseudocode for the complete partition function will also have a local variable called `pivot` to hold a copy of the pivot element. The array itself is called `data`, and the total number of elements is n. The precondition guarantees that n is at least 2. Here is the pseudocode:

```
void partition(int data[ ], size_t n, size_t& pivot_index)
// Precondition: n > 1, and data is an array (or subarray)
//  with at least n elements.
//  Postcondition: The function has selected some "pivot value"
//  that occurs in data[0]...data[n-1]. The elements of data
//  have then been rearranged and the pivot index set so that
//     -- data[pivot_index] is equal to the pivot;
//     -- each item before data[pivot_index] is <= the pivot;
//     -- each item after data[pivot_index] is > the pivot.
```

1. Initialize values:
   ```
   pivot = data[0];
   too_big_index = 1;      // Index of first item after pivot
   too_small_index = n-1;  // Index of last item
   ```

2. Repeat the following until the two indexes cross each other (in other words, keep going while `too_big_index <= too_small_index`):

   2a. *while* `too_big_index` has not yet reached n, and `data[too_big_index]` is less than or equal to the pivot, move `too_big_index` up to the next index.

   2b. *while* `data[too_small_index]` is greater than the pivot, move `too_small_index` down to the previous index.

   2c. *if* (`too_big_index < too_small_index`), then there is still room for both end portions to grow toward each other, so swap the values of `data[too_big_index]` and `data[too_small_index]`.

3. Move the pivot element to its correct position:

   3a. `pivot_index = too_small_index;`

   3b. Move `data[pivot_index]` (which still contains a value that is less than or equal to the pivot) to `data[0]` (which still contains the pivot).

   3c. `data[pivot_index] = pivot;`

Quicksort—Analysis

We want to estimate the running time of quicksort from Figure 13.5 on page 649. As always, *n* will be the number of items to be sorted, and we will express our running times in terms of *n*. In the best situation, the analysis of quicksort is much like our mergesort analysis from page 645. In this situation, each partition places the pivot element in the precise middle of the current subarray so that each recursive call sorts about half of the current subarray, as shown here:

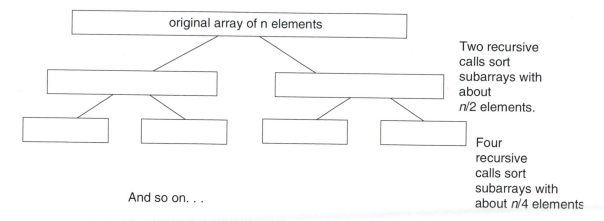

original array of n elements

Two recursive
calls sort
subarrays with
about
n/2 elements.

Four
recursive
calls sort
subarrays with
about *n*/4 elements

And so on. . .

The total work carried out by the partitions on each level is $O(n)$, so that the total time for quicksort is

(some constant) $\times n \times$ (the number of levels in the pattern)

In the ideal case, with the pivot element near the middle of each subarray, the number of levels is about $\log_2 n$ (just like the mergesort analysis). This results in a running time of $O(n \log n)$, which is the *best* that quicksort can manage.

But sometimes quicksort is significantly worse than $O(n \log n)$. In fact, the worst time behavior occurs when the array is already sorted before calling `quicksort`. In this case, the first element is smaller than everything else. Because we have been using the first element for the pivot, the pivot element is smaller than everything else. This causes a miserable partition, with everything to the right of the pivot, as shown here:

No elements
are less than
or equal to the pivot.

n-1 elements
are greater than
the pivot.

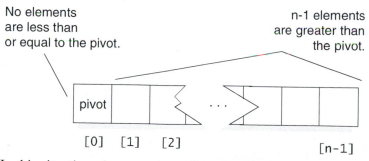

pivot

[0] [1] [2]   [n-1]

In this situation, the recursive call to sort the right-hand subarray has a lot of work to do. It must sort $n-1$ elements. Even worse, when the recursive call does its own partitioning, its pivot element will be the smallest of its $n-1$ elements, and again a bad partitioning occurs. The recursive call at the next level will have to sort $n-2$ elements. This pattern of bad partitions continues with recursive calls to sort $n-3$, $n-4$, and so on right down to 1. The total work done by all these recursive calls is proportional to the familiar sum: $n + (n-1) + (n-2) + (n-3) + \ldots + 1$.

What's the big-O analysis for this sum? It is $O(n^2)$ (see Figure 1.2 on page 19). So the *worst*-case running time for quicksort is quadratic.

Despite a poor worst-case time, quicksort generally is quite good. In fact, the average time (which we won't develop) turns out to be $O(n \log n)$. This is the same as mergesort, and we have the bonus of not needing to allocate an extra array for the merging process.

Quicksort Running Time

The worst-case running time of quicksort is $O(n^2)$. But the average-case running time and the best-case running time for quicksort are both $O(n \log n)$. Obtaining a good running time requires the choice of a good pivot element.

Quicksort—Choosing a Good Pivot Element

Our analysis of running times points out that the choice of a good pivot element is critical to the efficiency of the quicksort algorithm. If we can ensure that the pivot element is near the median of the array values, then quicksort is very efficient. One technique that is often used to increase the likelihood of choosing a good pivot element is to choose three values from the array and then use the middle of these three values as the pivot element. For example, if the three values chosen from the array are 10, 107, and 53—then 53 would be used as the pivot element. One possibility for the three values is to use the first array value, the last array value, and the value in the array position nearest to the midpoint of the array. However, with our particular partitioning pseudocode, using these three values actually has poor performance when the array starts in reverse order. A better choice is to use three randomly selected values from the array.

Several other common techniques to speed up quicksort are discussed in the Self-Test Exercises and Programming Projects.

Self-Test Exercises for Section 13.2

7. Use pointer arithmetic to print the ninth element of an array data. Give two ways to write this.

8. Suppose that `data` is an array of 1000 integers. Write a single function call that will sort the 100 elements `data[222]` through `data[321]`.

9. Which recursive sorting technique always makes recursive calls to sort subarrays that are about half the size of the original array?

10. Why is mergesort not a good choice for sorting arrays? Why is it a good choice for sorting files?

11. Compare the running times of mergesort and quicksort.

12. In quicksort, what kind of time performance is obtained when the good "splitting" of arrays continues for all recursive calls? What time performance occurs if there is bad splitting, so that many recursive calls reduce the array size by only one?

13. The `quicksort` function in Figure 13.5 on page 649 produces its worst-case running time when the array is already sorted. Suppose you know that the array might already be sorted or almost sorted. How should you modify the algorithm for quicksort?

14. One problem with both of our recursive sorting algorithms is that the recursion continues all the way down until we have a subarray with only one entry. The one-entry subarray is our stopping case. This works fine, but once the size of the subarrays becomes fairly small, a lot of time is wasted making more and more recursive calls. To fix this problem, actual implementations usually stop making recursive calls when the size of the array becomes small. The definition of "small" can vary, but experiments have shown that somewhere around 15 entries is a good choice for small arrays. For this exercise, modify the recursive quicksort algorithm so that any small array is sorted using insertion sort, and the process of partitioning and making recursive calls is done only for arrays that are not small.

stopping recursion before the subarrays get too small

13.3   AN *O(N LOG N)* ALGORITHM USING A HEAP

Heapsort

Both mergesort and quicksort have an average-case running time that is $O(n \log n)$. Mergesort also has a worst-case running time that is $O(n \log n)$, whereas the worst-case running time for quicksort is $O(n^2)$. That makes mergesort sound preferable to quicksort. However, mergesort requires more storage since it requires an extra array. In this section we present a sorting algorithm, called *heapsort*, that combines the time efficiency of mergesort and the storage efficiency of quicksort. Like mergesort, heapsort has a worst-case running time that is $O(n \log n)$, and like quicksort it does not require an additional array.

Like selectionsort, heapsort is an interchange sorting algorithm that works by repeatedly interchanging pairs of array elements. Thus, heapsort needs only some small constant amount of storage in addition to the array that holds the items to be sorted. Heapsort is similar to selectionsort in another way as well. Selectionsort locates the largest value and places it in the final array position. Then it locates the next largest value and places it in the next-to-last array position, and so forth. Heapsort uses a similar strategy, locating the largest value, then the next largest, and so on. However, heapsort uses a much more efficient algorithm to locate the array values to be moved.

heapsort is an interchange sorting algorithm

Heapsort works by first transforming the array to be sorted into a *heap*. This notion of a heap is the same data structure that was used in Section 11.1 to implement a priority queue. As a quick review, here is the definition of a heap:

the array is made into a heap

Heap Review (from Section 11.1)

A **heap** is a binary tree where the entries of the nodes can be compared with the less-than operator of a strict weak ordering. In addition, these two rules are followed:

1. The entry contained by a node is never less than the entries of the node's children.

2. The tree is a complete binary tree, so that every level except the deepest must contain as many nodes as possible; and at the deepest level, all the nodes are as far left as possible (see "Complete Binary Trees" page 473).

A heap is a *complete* binary tree, and we have an efficient method for representing a complete binary tree in an array. This representation was first shown in Section 10.2, following these rules:

- Data from the root of the complete binary tree goes in the [0] component of the array.

- Data from the root's children is put in the next two components of the array.

- We continue in this way, placing the four nodes of depth two in the next four components of the array, and so forth. For example, a heap with 10 nodes can be stored in a 10-element array, as shown here:

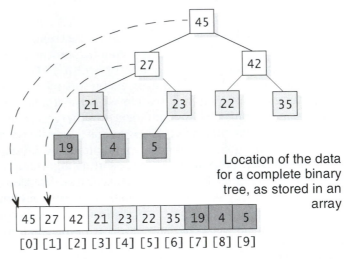

Location of the data for a complete binary tree, as stored in an array

45	27	42	21	23	22	35	19	4	5
[0]	[1]	[2]	[3]	[4]	[5]	[6]	[7]	[8]	[9]

To be more precise about the location of data in the array, we have these rules:

1. The data from the root always appears in the [0] component of the array.

2. Suppose that the data for a nonroot node appears in component [i] of the array. Then the data for its parent is always at location [(i-1)/2] (using integer division).

3. Suppose that the data for a node appears in component [i] of the array. Then its children (if they exist) always have their data at these locations:
Left child at component [2i+1]; Right child at component [2i+2].

With these facts in mind, we can easily state the general idea that underlies the heapsort algorithm. We start with an array of values to be sorted. The heapsort algorithm treats the array values as if they were values in a complete binary tree using the three rules listed above. That much is easy since any array of *n* values represents some complete binary tree with *n* nodes.

The first step of the heapsort algorithm is to rearrange the values in the array so that the corresponding complete binary tree is a heap. In other words, we rearrange the array so that the corresponding complete binary tree follows the heap storage rule: *The value contained in a node is never less than an entry from one of the node's children.* For example, suppose the array begins with these values:

first, the array is made into a heap

21	35	22	27	23	45	42	19	4	5
[0]	[1]	[2]	[3]	[4]	[5]	[6]	[7]	[8]	[9]

This array can be interpreted as representing this complete binary tree:

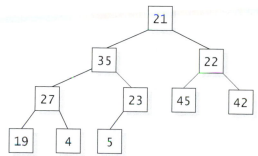

Of course, this complete binary tree is *not* a heap—for example, the data in the root's left child (35) is larger than the data in the root (21). So, the first step of the heapsort is to rearrange the array elements so that the corresponding complete binary tree is a heap.

For the 10-element example that we have just seen, the first step of the heapsort might rearrange the array so that the elements are in the following order:

45	27	42	21	23	22	35	19	4	5
[0]	[1]	[2]	[3]	[4]	[5]	[6]	[7]	[8]	[9]

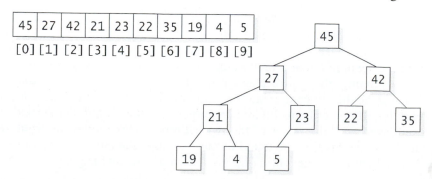

After the rearrangement of the array elements, the corresponding complete binary tree is a heap, and to aid your visualization, we have drawn the corresponding tree beside the array. But keep in mind that the only place that the numbers are stored is in the array. The tree is just our visualization of how those elements are structured. In a moment, we'll provide the details of how the rearrangement into a heap occurs, but first let's look at the rest of the heapsort algorithm.

find the largest element, and move it to the end of the array

Recall that the largest value in a heap is stored in the root, and that in our array representation of a complete binary tree, the root node is stored in the first array position. Thus, since the array represents a heap, we know that the largest array element is in the first array position. To get the largest value into the correct array position, we simply interchange the first and the final array elements. After interchanging these two array elements, we know that the largest array element is in the final array position, as shown here:

5	27	42	21	23	22	35	19	4	45
[0]	[1]	[2]	[3]	[4]	[5]	[6]	[7]	[8]	[9]

The dark vertical line in the array separates the "unsorted side" of the array (on the left) from the "sorted side." Moreover, the unsorted side (on the left) still represents a complete binary tree, which is *almost* a heap, as shown at the top of the next page.

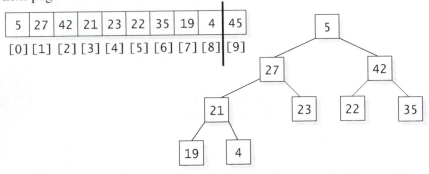

fix the heap

When we consider the *unsorted* side as a complete binary tree, it is only the root that violates the heap storage rule. This root is smaller than its children. So, the next step of the heapsort is to reposition this one out-of-place value in order to restore the heap. In Section 11.1 we discussed this process of restoring the heap by repositioning the out-of-place root. The process, called *reheapification downward*, begins by comparing the value in the root with the value of each of its children. If one or both children are larger than the root, then the root's value is exchanged with the larger of the two children. This moves the troublesome value down one level in the tree. For our example, the out-of-place value (5) is exchanged with its larger child (42), as shown on the next page.

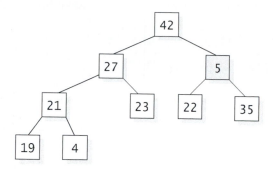

Of course, this "exchange" of values actually occurs within the array that represents the heap, so that the array now looks like this:

42	27	5	21	23	22	35	19	4	45
[0]	[1]	[2]	[3]	[4]	[5]	[6]	[7]	[8]	[9]

In this example, the 5 is still out of place, so we will once again exchange it with its largest child, resulting in the array (and heap) shown here:

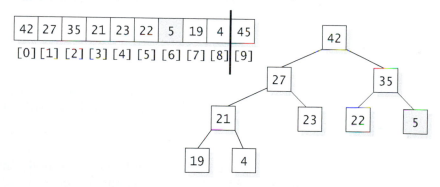

42	27	35	21	23	22	5	19	4	45
[0]	[1]	[2]	[3]	[4]	[5]	[6]	[7]	[8]	[9]

Keep in mind that only the unsorted side of the array must be maintained as a heap. In general, the reheapification continues until the troublesome value reaches a leaf or it reaches a spot where it is no larger than its children.

When the unsorted side of the array is once again a heap, the heapsort continues by exchanging the largest element in the unsorted side with the rightmost element of the unsorted side. For our example, the 42 is exchanged with the 4, as shown here:

4	27	35	21	23	22	5	19	42	45
[0]	[1]	[2]	[3]	[4]	[5]	[6]	[7]	[8]	[9]

As you can see, the "sorted side" now has the two largest elements, and the unsorted side is once again *almost* a heap, as shown here:

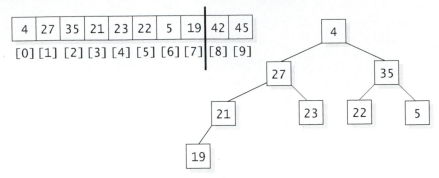

4	27	35	21	23	22	5	19	42	45
[0]	[1]	[2]	[3]	[4]	[5]	[6]	[7]	[8]	[9]

Only the root (4) is out of place, and that may be fixed by another reheapification downward. After the reheapification downward, the largest value of the unsorted side will once again reside at location [0], and we can continue to pull out the *next* largest value.

Here is the pseudocode for the heapsort algorithm we have been describing:

// Heapsort for the array called data with n elements
1. Convert the array of *n* elements into a heap.

2. `unsorted = n;` *// The number of elements in the unsorted side*

3. `while (unsorted > 1)`
   `{`
       // Reduce the unsorted side by one.
       `--unsorted;`
       Swap `data[0]` with `data[unsorted]`.
       The unsorted side of the array is now a heap with the root out of place.
       Do a reheapification downward to turn the unsorted side back into
       a heap.
   `}`

The implementation of this pseudocode is shown in Figure 13.6. In the implementation, we use two functions, `make_heap` and `reheapify_down`, which we will discuss next.

Making the Heap

At the start of the heapsort algorithm, we must rearrange the array elements so that they form a heap. This rearrangement is accomplished by calling a function with the following specification:

`void make_heap(int data[ ], size_t n);`
// Precondition: data is an array with at least n elements.
// Postcondition: The elements of data have been rearranged so that the
// complete binary tree represented by this array is a heap.

There are two common ways to build an initial heap from the array. One method is relatively easy to program, and we will show that method here. A second, more efficient method requires more difficult programming that we will outline in Programming Project 5 on page 671.

The simple approach to make_heap builds the heap one element at a time, starting at the front of the array. Initially we start with just one element, and this one element forms a small heap of one node. For example, we might start with the array shown here:

21	35	22	27	23	45	42	19	4	5
[0]	[1]	[2]	[3]	[4]	[5]	[6]	[7]	[8]	[9]

In this array, the area to the left of the vertical bar can be viewed as a heap with just one node, and the area to the right is still a jumble of random values.

The make_heap algorithm adds the array nodes to the heap one at a time. In our example, we will next add the 35 to the heap, resulting in the following

the first array element forms a heap with one node

FIGURE 13.6   Heapsort

A Function Implementation

```
void heapsort(int data[ ], size_t n)
// Precondition: data is an array with at least n components.
// Postcondition: The elements of data have been rearranged so
// that data[0] <= data[1] <= ... <= data[n-1].
// Library facilities used: algorithm, cstdlib (using the namespace std)
// NOTE: The implementation also uses the two functions, make_heap and reheapify_down,
// which are discussed in the text.
{
    size_t unsorted;

    make_heap(data, n);

    unsorted = n;

    while (unsorted > 1)
    {
        --unsorted;
        swap(data[0], data[unsorted]);
        reheapify_down(data, unsorted);
    }
}
```

www.cs.colorado.edu/~main/chapter13/heapsort.cxx   **WWW**

configuration. In this illustration, we have drawn both the array and the state of the heap that is formed from the elements to the left of the vertical bar.

21	35	22	27	23	45	42	19	4	5

[0] [1] [2] [3] [4] [5] [6] [7] [8] [9]

```
        21
       /
     35
```

As you can see, just adding the node in this way does not actually create a heap because the newly added node (35) has a value that is larger than its parent. However, we can fix this problem by pushing the out-of-place node upward until it reaches the root or it reaches a place with a larger parent. This process of pushing a new node upward is called *reheapification upward*. We have seen reheapification upward before, in Section 11.1. In that section, reheapification upward was used whenever a new item was added to the priority queue (which was represented as a heap).

The pseudocode for make_heap uses reheapification upward, as shown here (with two local size_t variables called i and k):

```
// Making a heap from an array called data with n elements
for (i = 1; i < n; ++i)
{
    k = i; // The index of the new entry
    while (data[k] is not yet the root, and data[k] is bigger than its parent)
        Swap data[k] with its parent, and reset k to be the index of its parent.
}
```

The complete implementation of this pseudocode as the function make_heap is left up to you. The readability of your implementation can be improved if you also implement another function called parent, as shown here:

```
inline size_t parent(size_t k)
// Precondition: k > 0.
// Postcondition: The function assumes that k is the index of an array
// element, where the array represents a complete binary tree. The return
// value is the index of the parent of node k, using the formula from
// Rule 3 on page 657.
// Library facilities used: cstdlib
{
    return (k-1)/2;
}
```

Whenever k is an index of an element in the array and k is not zero, the value of parent(k) is the array index of the parent of data[k]. You can use this function whenever you need to calculate the index of the parent of a node.

By the way, you may have noticed the keyword *inline* at the front of the *inline function* parent function. This keyword has the same effect that we have seen before for inline member functions, causing the compiler to make the function calls a bit faster by putting the actual code for the function body at each location where the function is called. We suggest that you use inline functions for any one-line function that returns the value of a simple formula.

Reheapification Downward

We have one more function to implement, the reheapification downward, with this specification:

```
void reheapify_down(int data[ ], size_t n);
// Precondition: n > 0, and data is an array with at least n elements. These
// elements form a heap, except that data[0] may be in an incorrect location.
// Postcondition: The data values have been rearranged so that the first
// n elements of data now form a heap.
```

The function works by continually swapping the out-of-place element with its largest child, as shown in this pseudocode:

```
// Reheapification downward (for a heap where the root is out of place)
size_t current;            // Index of the node that's moving down
size_t big_child_index;    // Index of current's larger child
bool heap_ok;              // Will become true when heap is correct

current = 0;
heap_ok = false;

while ((!heap_ok) && (the current node is not a leaf))
{
    Set big_child_index to be the index of the larger child of the current
    node. (If there is only one child, then big_child_index will be set to
    the index of this one child.)

    if (data[current] < data[big_child_index])
    {
        Swap data[current] with data[big_child_index].
        current = big_child_index;
    }
    else
        heap_ok = true;
}
```

The swapping stops when the out-of-place element reaches a leaf, or when the out-of-place element is larger than both of its children. If you implement this function, use two auxiliary functions (left_child and right_child) to compute the indexes of the left and right child of a node.

Heapsort—Analysis

Let us count operations for the worst-case running time for the heapsort algorithm. As usual, we take the problem size n to be the number of items to be sorted. If you look back at the implementation from Figure 13.6 on page 661, you will see that the total number of operations can be given as this sum:

(The operations to build the initial heap)

+

(The operations to pull the items out of the heap one at a time)

+

(Some fixed number of operations for a few other assignments)

To refine this formula, we must calculate the number of operations to build the initial heap and the number of operations required when an element is pulled out of the heap.

Building the initial heap.   To build the heap we add the items one at a time, using reheapification upward to push the new item upward until it reaches the root or it reaches an acceptable spot (where the parent has a larger value). Since we actually add n–1 elements (rather than n), the total time is this:

$(n - 1) \times$ (number of operations for one reheapification upward)

The maximum number of operations for one reheapification upward is a constant times the depth of the heap. In Section 11.3, we showed that the depth of a heap is no more than $\log_2 n$. Therefore, the worst-case time for building the heap is the following:

$(n - 1) \times$ a constant $\times (\log_2 n)$

Removing the constants from this formula results in an $O(n \log n)$ running time to build the initial heap.

Pulling the items out of the heap.   Once the initial heap is built, we pull items out of the heap one at a time. After each item is removed, we perform a reheapification downward. We pull out a total of n–1 items, and the number of operations in each reheapification downward is never more than a constant times the depth of the tree. Therefore, pulling all the items out of the tree also requires $(n - 1) \times$ a constant $\times (\log_2 n)$ operations, which is an $O(n \log n)$ running time.

worst case for heapsort

Total time for heapsort.   We can now give a final estimate for the worst-case running time for the entire heapsort algorithm. Building the initial heap requires $O(n \log n)$ operations, and then pulling the items out of the heap requires another $O(n \log n)$ operations. You might be tempted to write that the sum of all this work is $O(2n \log n)$, and you would be right. But remember that multiplication by a constant (such as 2) can be ignored in big-O notation, so in fact the entire algorithm from start to finish requires $O(n \log n)$ operations.

We won't give a derivation, but it turns out that the average-case running time for heapsort is also $O(n \log n)$, the same as the worst-case running time.

average case for heapsort

Heapsort Running Time

The worst-case running time and the average-case running time for heapsort are both $O(n \log n)$.

Self-Test Exercises for Section 13.3

15. How is the heapsort algorithm similar to the selectionsort algorithm? How is it different?

16. How would you modify the heapsort algorithm so that it sorts integers into decreasing order rather than increasing order?

17. What features of the mergesort and quicksort algorithms does the heapsort algorithm have?

13.4 SORTING WITH LIBRARY FUNCTIONS AND RANDOM ACESSS ITERATORS

The Original C qsort Function

The original C Standard Library has a quicksort function that is still widely used. The prototype is part of `<cstdlib>`, along these lines:

```
void qsort(
    void* base,
    size_t number_of_elements,
    size_t element_size,
    int compare(const void*, const void*)
);
```

The first parameter is a pointer to an element of an array. The data type *void** indicates that the type of elements in the array remains unspecified. It could be an array of integers, or an array of doubles, or some more complex type.

The second parameter is the number of elements in the array to be sorted (starting with the element that `base` points to).

The third parameter tells how many bytes of memory are required for each element of the array. In C++, this number can be obtained by applying the *sizeof* operator to the data type. For example, *sizeof(int)* is the number of bytes for one integer.

The final parameter, `compare`, is a parameter that is a function itself, as described on page 502. As the name suggests, the `compare` function is used to compare two elements of the array. In particular, the two parameters to the compare function are pointers to elements in the array. The return value must be an integer such that:

- A negative integer indicates that the first element is the smaller of the two.

- A zero return value indicates that the two elements are equal to each other.

- A positive integer indicates that the first element is the larger of the two.

Typically, the programmer who uses the `qsort` function will write the comparison function. For example, a programmer who is sorting an array of integers can write and use this comparison function:

```
int compare_integers(const void* p1, const void* p2)
{
    return *( (int *)p1 )  -  *( (int *)p2) );
}
```

The first part of the return statement, `*( (int *)p1 )`, obtains a copy of the integer that `p1` points to. The `(int *)` phrase is needed to convert the pointer from a void pointer to a pointer to an integer. The overall return value is created by a subtraction (subracting the second integer from the first). This is just what we need because the result will be negative (if the first number is smaller), or zero (if the two numbers are equal), or positive (if the first number is larger).

Once we've written the `compare` function, we can use the `qsort` function to sort an array of integers, for example:

```
int numbers[7] = { 0, 10, 2, 0, 4, 15, 6 };
// This will sort all of the numbers array. Note that numbers is considered
// to be a pointer to the first element of the array. We convert it to a
// void pointer by the phrase (void *)numbers:
qsort( (void *)numbers, 7, sizeof(int), compare_integers);
```

The STL Sort Function

There are several sort functions in the STL. The simplest is from `<algorithm>`:

```
void sort(Iterator begin, Iterator end);
```

The function has two iterators as parameters, which must be random access iterators from some container, as described on page 310. The elements of the container are sorted, starting at the `begin` element and going up to but not including the end iterator.

Every pointer to an array element is considered to be a random access iterator, so we can use the sort function to sort some or all of an array. For example:

```
int numbers[7] = { 0, 10, 2, 0, 4, 15, 6 };
// This will sort all of the numbers array. Note that numbers is considered
// to be a pointer to the first element of the array, and numbers + 7 is a
// pointer to the element that is one spot past the end of the array.
sort(numbers, numbers+7);
```

Within <algorithm> there are also several functions for performing various parts of the sorting algorithms that we've seen in this chapter. There are functions for partitioning a sequence (as in quicksort), creating or maintaining a heap, and merging two sorted sequences.

Writing a Sort Function That Uses Iterators

We wrote all of our sort algorithms to sort an array of integers, but each of these algorithms can be generalized to sort any type of data. Sometimes, the general algorithm requires a random access iterator that can traverse the sequence to be sorted. Other algorithms can manage with a less powerful iterator such as the implementation of a selectionsort in Figure 13.7. Here are a few notes on that implementation:

- The algorithm differs from the selectionsort in Figure 13.1 on page 626. The new algorithm works by repeatedly selecting the smallest item from part of the array and swapping this item with the item at the front of the array segment.

- The function is a template function with a template parameter called ForwardIterator. This name informs a programmer that the function is compatible only with iterators that have all the properties of a forward iterator as described on page 309. You should always use the complete name of the iterator type (such as ForwardIterator), or always use the abbreviations suggest by Bjarne Stroustrup: Out, In, For, Bi, and Rand.

- Notice that the algorithm uses only the operations that are guaranteed for a forward iterator.

- Normally, we declare variables at the top of a function. In this case, however, we declared i, j, and location_of_smallest at a lower point when we knew what value to assign to these items initially. The reason for delaying the declarations is so that the ForwardIterator does not require a default constructor.

- The function uses std::iter_swap from <algorithm> to swap the current items of two iterators.

FIGURE 13.7   Selectionsort Implemented with a ForwardIterator

A Function Implementation

```
template <class ForwardIterator>
void selectionsort(ForwardIterator first, ForwardIterator last)
// Precondition: first and last are ForwardIterators that define a sequence
// of items that can be compared with the < operator.
// Postcondition: The elements of [first..last) have been sorted from smallest to largest.
// Library facilities used: algorithm
{
    for (ForwardIterator i = first; i != last; ++i)
    {   // Find smallest from [i..last) and swap it with *i.
        ForwardIterator location_of_smallest = i;
        for (ForwardIterator j = i+1; j != last; ++j)
        {
            if (*j < *location_of_smallest)
                location_of_smallest = j;
        }
        // location_of_smallest is now at the smallest item in [i..last).
        std::iter_swap(i, location_of_smallest);
    }
}
```

www.cs.colorado.edu/~main/chapter13/selectit.cxx   **WWW**

CHAPTER SUMMARY

- All the sorting algorithms presented in this chapter apply to any type of values sorted according to any reasonable ordering relation. The array values do not need to be integers.

- In divide-and-conquer sorting methods, the values to be sorted are split into two approximately equal groups, the groups are sorted by a recursive call, and then the two sorted groups are combined into the final sorted list. Mergesort and quicksort are examples of divide-and-conquer sorting algorithms.

- Selectionsort and insertionsort have quadratic running times in both the worst case and the average case. This is comparatively slow. However, if the arrays to be sorted are short, or if the sorting program will only be used a few times, then they are reasonable algorithms to use. Insertionsort is particularly good if the array is nearly sorted beforehand.

- Mergesort and quicksort are much more efficient than selectionsort and insertionsort. They have an average-case running time that is $O(n \log n)$. If you need to sort a large number of long lists, it would be worth the extra effort of coding and debugging one of these more complicated algorithms.

- Mergesort has the advantage that its worst-case running time is $O(n \log n)$, but it has the disadvantage of needing to allocate a second array to use in the merging process.

- Quicksort has the disadvantage of a quadratic worst-case time. However, with some care in the pivot selection process, we usually can avoid this bad time. Quicksort can be further improved by stopping the recursive calls when the subarrays become small (around 15 elements). These small subarrays can be sorted with an insertionsort.
- Heapsort works by creating a heap from all the array elements and then pulling the largest element out of the heap, then the next largest, and so on. The worst-case and average-case times for heapsort are $O(n \log n)$.

Solutions to Self-Test Exercises ?

1. The worst-case, average-case, and best-case running times for selectionsort are all quadratic. The worst-case and average-case running times for insertionsort are also quadratic, but the best case is linear. The insertionsort algorithm is quicker for arrays that are partially sorted, whereas the selectionsort algorithm performs the same number of operations no matter what values are in the array.

2.
```
5   19   13   36   23    2  (at start)
5   19   13    2   23   36
5   19   13    2   23   36
5    2   13   19   23   36
5    2   13   19   23   36
2    5   13   19   23   36
```

3.
```
5   19   13   36   23    2  (at start)
5   19   13   36   23    2
5   13   19   36   23    2
5   13   19   36   23    2
5   13   19   23   36    2
2    5   13   19   23   36
```

4. Here is one solution:
```
void insertionsort
(int data[ ], size_t n)
{
    size_t i, j;
    int next;

    for (i = 1; i < n; ++i)
    {
        next = data[i];
        j = i;
        while(j>0 && next<data[j-1])
        {
            data[j] = data[j-1];
            --j;
        }
        data[j] = next;
    }
}
```

5. In Figure 13.1 on page 626, we should find the index of the smallest element rather than the index of the largest.

6. To sort strings, change each declaration of the array to an array of strings rather than an array of integers. Alternatively, if you are familiar with template functions (Chapter 6), you could implement the selectionsort as a template function that depends on the underlying type of items in the array. This underlying type could be any type with a copy constructor, an assignment operator, and with a less-than operator that is a strict weak ordering.

7. `cout << (data + 9)[0];`
   `cout << (data + 6)[3];`

8. `quicksort((data + 222), 100);`

9. Mergesort always makes recursive calls to sort subarrays that are about half the size of the original array, resulting in $O(n \log n)$ time.

10. Mergesort is not a good choice for sorting arrays because of the additional memory required for the temporary array in the merge step. However, a large file may be sorted effectively by mergesort by dividing the file into several pieces, and merging the sorted pieces into a single file. The individual pieces can be removed after the file is sorted.

11. The worst-case, average-case, and best-case running times for mergesort are all $O(n \log n)$. The average-case and best-case running times for quicksort are both $O(n \log n)$, but the worst-case running time of quicksort is $O(n^2)$. The running time of the quicksort depends on the pivot element. The running time of mergesort does not depend on the array elements, but on the array length.

12. When there is good splitting in quicksort, the resulting time is $O(n \log n)$. When there is bad splitting in quicksort, the result can be quadratic time.

13. See "Quicksort—Choosing a Good Pivot Element" on page 654.

14. Your new quicksort function should have an if-statement that tests whether (n <= 15). If so, then call insertionsort; otherwise, proceed as in the original quicksort.

15. Heapsort is also an interchange algorithm that repeatedly swaps pairs of array elements. Heapsort locates the largest value, then the next largest, and so on, as the selection sort. However, heapsort uses a heap to store, locate, and swap values, which results in a much more efficient implementation.

16. Change the heap rule so that the value in every node is less than or equal to its children. Modify make_heap to build this new kind of heap by changing the test in the while-loop to this:

    (k>0 && data[k] < data[parent(k)])

    In reheapify_down, change the series of if-statements so that they find the index of the smaller child. If this smaller child is less than the current node, then swap the current node with the smaller child and continue. Otherwise, the heap is okay.

17. Like mergesort, heapsort has a worst-case running time that is $O(n \log n)$ and like quicksort, it does not require an additional array.

PROGRAMMING PROJECTS

For more in-depth projects, please see www.cs.colorado.edu/~main/projects/

 If you are familiar with template functions (Chapter 6), then rewrite one of the sorting functions as a template function. You may choose selectionsort, insertionsort, mergesort, quicksort, or heapsort. For example, with selectionsort you would have the specification shown here:

```
template <class Item, class SizeType>
void selectionsort
(Item data[ ], SizeType n);
// Precondition: data is an array with at
// least n components.
// Postcondition: The elements of data
// have been rearranged so that
// data[0] <= data[1] <= ... <= data[n-1].
// NOTE: Item may be any of the C++ built-in
// types (int, char, etc.), or any class with a
// copy constructor, an assignment operator,
// and the six comparison operators forming a
// total order semantics.
```

2 Redo the insertionsort algorithm so that the values are inserted into a linked list rather than an array. This eliminates the need to move other values when a new value is inserted, since your algorithm can simply insert a new node where the new value should go. Analyze your algorithm to obtain a big-O expression of the worst-case running time. Code your algorithm to produce a complete C++ program that reads in a list of 10 integers, sorts the integers, and then writes out the sorted list. Your program should allow the user to repeat the process and sort another list until the user says he or she wants to exit the program.

3 One of the advantages of mergesort is that it can easily be adapted to sort a linked list of values. This is because the algorithm retrieves the values from the two lists being merged in the order that they occur in the lists. If the lists are linked lists, then that algorithm can simply move down the list node after node. With heapsort or quicksort the algorithm needs to move values from random locations in the array so they do not adapt as well to sorting a linked list. Write a program that sorts a linked list of integers using mergesort. The program will read the integers into a linked list and then sort the linked list using mergesort. This will require additional linked lists, but you should use linked lists, not arrays, for all your list storage.

 Rewrite quicksort so that there are no recursive calls. The technique is to use a stack to keep track of which portions of the array still need to be sorted. Whenever we identify a portion of the array that still needs to be sorted, we will push two items onto the stack: (1) the starting index of the array segment and (2) the length of the array segment. The entire quicksort can now work as follows (with no recursion):

1. Push 0 and n onto the stack (indicating that we must sort the n-element array segment starting at data[0]).

2. *while* (the stack is not empty)

   a. Pop a size n and a starting index i off the stack. We must now sort the n-element array segment starting at data[i]. To do this sort, first call partition(data+i,n,pivot_index)

   b. If the area before the pivot index has more than one element, then we must sort this area. This area begins at data[i] and has pivot_index elements, so push i and pivot_index onto the stack.

   c. If the area after the pivot index has more than one element, then we must sort this area. This area begins at data[i + pivot_index + 1] and has (n - pivot_index - 1) elements, so push (i + pivot_index + 1) and (n - pivot_index - 1) onto the stack.

With this approach, in the worst case, the stack must be as big as the array that's being sorted. This worst case occurs when we keep pushing two-element array segments onto the stack. However, there is a modification that reduces the maximum stack size. When you do steps 2b and 2c, make sure that the *larger* array segment gets pushed onto the stack first. With this modification, the maximum necessary stack size is just $2 \log_2 n$. With this in mind, you can use a stack with a fixed size—for example, a 100-element stack is enough to sort an array with 2^{50} elements.

5 The discussion on page 660 shows our algorithm for building the initial heap in the heapsort algorithm. The algorithm is reasonably efficient, but we can be even more efficient. The more efficient algorithm uses a function that creates a heap from a subtree of the complete binary tree. This function has the following specification:

```
void heapify_subtree(
    int data[ ],
    size_t root_of_subtree,
    size_t n
);
// Precondition: data is an array with at least
// n elements, and root_of_subtree < n. We will
// consider data to represent a complete
// binary tree, and in this representation the
// node at data[root_of_subtree] is the root of
// a subtree called s. This subtree s is already
// a heap, except that its root might be out of
// place.
// Postcondition: The subtree s has been
// rearranged so that it is now a valid heap.
```

You can write the heapify_subtree function yourself. Using this function, you can make an entire *n*-element array into a heap with the algorithm:

```
for (i = (n/2); i > 0; --i)
    heapify_subtree(data, i-1, n);
```

For example, with *n*=10, we will end up making the following sequence of calls:

```
heapify_subtree(data, 4, 10);
heapify_subtree(data, 3, 10);
heapify_subtree(data, 2, 10);
heapify_subtree(data, 1, 10);
heapify_subtree(data, 0, 10);
```

It turns out that this method is actually $O(n)$ rather than $O(n \log n)$.

For this project, reimplement make_heap, as outlined above.

6 On page 644, we discussed problems with the dynamic memory usage of mergesort. One solution to the problem is to rewrite the mergesort according to the following specification:

```
void mergesort(
    int data[ ],
    size_t first_index,
    size_t last_index,
    int temp[ ]
);
// Precondition: data[first_index] through
// data[last_index] are array elements in no
// particular order. The temp array has
// locations temp[first_index] through
// temp[last_index].
// Postcondition: The elements
// data[first_index] through data[last_index]
// have been rearranged so that they are
// ordered from smallest to largest. The array
// elements temp[first_index] through
// temp[last_index] have been used as
// temporary storage and now contain a
// copy of data[first_index] through
// data[last_index].
```

7 Rewrite the quicksort partition function so that the pivot is chosen by selecting the median of three random values from the array (see page 654). Next, write a version using five random values. This may reduce the running time. Test both of these versions with sorted arrays, random arrays, and reverse order arrays and display your results.

8 Write a program to compare the running time of the heapsort and quicksort algorithms in this chapter with each other and with the library sorting algorithms. Test each algorithm with n random integers (using the rand( ) function) and n sorted numbers. You can use the clock_t variable and clock function from the <ctime> library facility to time each sort in terms of CPU ticks. Display your results in a table.

CHAPTER 14

Derived Classes and Inheritance

*It is indeed a desirable thing to be well descended, but the
glory belongs to our ancestors.*

PLUTARCH
Morals

LEARNING OBJECTIVES

When you complete Chapter 14, you will be able to...

- recognize situations in which inheritance can simplify the implementation of a group of related classes.
- implement derived classes.
- recognize situations in which creating an abstract base class will allow the later implementation of many derived classes that share underlying functions.
- use our abstract game class to implement many derived classes for playing two-player strategy games such as chess, checkers, Othello, and Connect Four.

CHAPTER CONTENTS

14

Derived Classes and Inheritance

Object-oriented languages provide support that allows programmers to easily create new classes that acquire some or many of their properties from an existing class. The original class is called the **base class** (or
parent class, or *ancestor class*, or *superclass*) and the new, slightly different
class is the **derived class** (or *child class*, or *descendant class*, or *subclass*).

The first section of this chapter provides an introduction to derived classes.
The next two sections show two detailed programming examples: an ecosystem
simulation using a variety of animal classes, and a powerful game class that
forms the base class for many different two-player strategy games.

14.1 DERIVED CLASSES

One of the exercises in Chapter 2 was a clock class to keep track of a time
value such as 9:48 P.M. (see Self-Test Exercise 19 on page 62). One possible definition for this class is shown in Figure 14.1 on page 675. Now suppose you're
writing a program with various kinds of clocks: 12-hour clocks, 24-hour clocks,
alarm clocks, cuckoo clocks, and so on. Each of these things is a clock, but
each also has additional properties that don't apply to clocks in general. For
example, a cuckoo_clock might have an extra function, is_cuckooing, that
returns true if its cuckoo bird is currently making noise. How would you implement a cuckoo_clock, which is a clock with one extra member function?

One possible solution uses no new ideas: Modify the original clock definition
by adding an extra member function. With this solution, the cuckoo_clock definition looks a lot like the ordinary clock.

```
class cuckoo_clock
{
public:
    // CONSTRUCTOR
    cuckoo_clock ( );
    // MODIFICATION MEMBER FUNCTIONS
    void set_time(int hour, int minute, bool morning);
    void advance(int minutes);
    // CONSTANT MEMBER FUNCTIONS
    int get_hour( ) const;
    int get_minute( ) const;
    bool is_morning( ) const;
    bool is_cuckooing( ) const;
    ...
```

Can you think of some potential problems with this solution? Problems occur
when a program has a cuckoo_clock but also has an ordinary clock and

FIGURE 14.1 The Clock Class

Documentation for the Clock Class

```
// CONSTRUCTOR for the clock class (part of namespace main_savitch_14):
//    clock( )
//       Postcondition: The clock is set to 12:00 (midnight).
//
// MODIFICATION MEMBER FUNCTIONS for the clock class:
//    void set_time(int hour, int minute, bool morning)
//       Precondition: 1 <= hour <= 12, and 0 <= minute <= 59.
//       Postcondition: The clock's time has been set to the given hour and minute (using usual
//       12-hour time notation). If the third parameter, morning, is true, then this time is from
//       12:00 midnight to 11:59 A.M. Otherwise this time is from 12:00 noon to 11:59 P.M.
//
//    void advance(int minutes)
//       Postcondition: The clock has been moved forward by the indicated number of minutes.
//       Note: A negative argument moves the clock backward.
//
// CONSTANT MEMBER FUNCTIONS for the clock class:
//    int get_hour( ) const
//       Postcondition: The value returned is the current hour using a 12-hour clock.
//
//    int get_minute( ) const
//       Postcondition: The value returned is the current minute on the clock.
//
//    bool is_morning( ) const
//       Postcondition: If the clock's time lies from 12:00 midnight to 11:59 A.M. (inclusive),
//       the function returns true; otherwise it returns false.
//
// VALUE SEMANTICS for the clock class:
//       Assignments and the copy constructor may be used with clock objects.
```

Class Definition

```
class clock
{
public:
    // CONSTRUCTOR
    clock( );
    // MODIFICATION MEMBER FUNCTIONS
    void set_time(int hour, int minute, bool morning);
    void advance(int minutes);
    // CONSTANT MEMBER FUNCTIONS
    int get_hour( ) const;
    int get_minute( ) const;
    bool is_morning( ) const;
private:
    | For this example, we don't care what private implementation is used.
};
```

www.cs.colorado.edu/~main/chapter14/clocks.h **WWW**

perhaps other kinds of clocks as well. We'll end up writing a separate class definition for each different type of clock. Even though all of these have similar or identical constructors and member functions, we'll still end up repeating the member function implementations for each different kind of clock.

The solution to the clock problem is a new concept, called derived classes, described here:

Derived Classes

Derived classes use a concept called inheritance. In particular, once we have a class, we can then declare new classes that contain all of the members of the original class—plus any extras that you want to throw in. This new class is called a **derived class** of the original class. The original class is called the **base class**. And the members that the derived class receives from its base class are called **inherited members**.

How to Declare a Derived Class

In the definition of the derived class, the name of the derived class is followed by a single colon, the keyword *public*, and then the name of the base class. For example, suppose that we want to declare a derived class cuckoo_clock using the existing clock class as the base class. The beginning of the cuckoo_clock class definition would then look like this:

```
class cuckoo_clock : public clock
{
    ...
```

This definition indicates that every cuckoo_clock is also an ordinary clock. The primary consequence is that all of the public members of an ordinary clock are *immediately available as public members* of a cuckoo_clock. These members are said to be **inherited** from the clock.

public base class versus private base class

In the clock example, we used the keyword *public*, which creates a **public base class**. An alternative is to use the keyword *private* instead of *public*, resulting in a **private base class**. With a private base class, all of the public members of an ordinary clock are immediately available as *private* members of a cuckoo_clock. In both cases—public base class or private base class—it is the public members of the clock that are accessible to the cuckoo_clock. In some sense, the private members of the clock are also present in a cuckoo_clock—they must be present because some of the public members make use of the private members. But, these private members cannot be accessed directly in a cuckoo_clock, not even by the programmer who implements a cuckoo_clock. This is why we did not even list the clock's private members in Figure 14.1.

protected members

For future reference, you should know that there is a third kind of member called a **protected member**. In most respects, a protected member is just like a private member, but the programmer of a derived class has direct access to protected members. We'll use protected members in Section 14.3.

FIGURE 14.2   The CuckooClock Is Derived from the Ordinary Clock

A Derived Class Definition

```
class cuckoo_clock : public clock
{
public:
    bool is_cuckooing( ) const;
};
```

The definition could be added to the same header file that contains the clock class, or be placed anywhere else that has access to the clock class.

A Member Function Implementation

```
bool cuckoo_clock::is_cuckooing( ) const
{
    return (get_minute( ) == 0);
}
```

The new member function is in an implementation file.

Part of www.cs.colorado.edu/~main/chapter14/clocks.h and clocks.cxx   **W W W**

Now, let's finish our cuckoo_clock definition and see how it can be used in a program. Our complete cuckoo_clock is shown in Figure 14.2. As you can see, a cuckoo_clock has one extra public member function: a boolean function called is_cuckooing, which returns true when the clock's cuckoo is making noise. In the implementation of is_cuckooing, you can see that our cuckoos make noise whenever the current minute of the time is zero. In this implementation, we use the ordinary clock function, get_minute, to determine whether the current minute is zero.

Once the cuckoo_clock definition is available, a program may declare cuckoo_clock objects using all the public clock member functions and also using the new is_cuckooing function. In this usage, there are some special considerations for the constructors, the destructor, and the assignment operator. We'll discuss these considerations over the next few pages.

The Automatic Constructors of a Derived Class

A derived class may declare its own constructors, or it may use the automatic default constructor and the automatic copy constructor that are provided for every C++ class. Later we will examine the case of derived classes with their own declared constructors, but for the cuckoo clock, the automatic constructors are sufficient. We get the following automatic constructors.

The automatic default constructor.   If we don't declare *any* constructors for a derived class, then C++ will automatically provide a default constructor. This default constructor will carry out two steps: (1) activate the default constructor for the base class (to initialize any member variables that the base class uses), then (2) activate default constructors for any new member variables that the derived class has, but the base class does not have.

For example, our cuckoo clock has an automatic default constructor that is activated in an object declaration such as this:

```
cuckoo_clock noisy;
```

The `cuckoo_clock`'s automatic default constructor will activate the ordinary `clock` default constructor for `noisy`, initializing any private member variables of the ordinary clock. Remember, these private member variables are present in any cuckoo clock, and therefore they must be initialized even though there is no way to directly access these member variables.

The automatic copy constructor. If a derived class does not define a copy constructor of its own, then C++ will automatically provide a copy constructor. This copy constructor is similar to the automatic default constructor in that it carries out two steps: (1) activate the copy constructor for the base class (to copy any member variables that the base class uses), then (2) activate copy constructors for any new member variables that the derived class has but the base class does not have. The copy constructors that are activated in Steps 1 and 2 may themselves be automatic copy constructors, or they may be specially written to accomplish correct copying of dynamic data structures.

Using a Derived Class

We now know enough to write a bit of sample code that uses a derived class:

```
cuckoo_clock noisy;
int minutes;

cout << "How many minutes should I advance the clock? ";
cin >> minutes;
noisy.advance(minutes);

if (noisy.is_cuckooing( ))
    cout << "Cuckoo cuckoo cuckoo." << endl;
else
    cout << "All's quiet on the cuckoo front." << endl;
```

The key feature is that a cuckoo clock may use ordinary clock member functions (such as `advance`), and it may also use the new `is_cuckooing` function. The inheritance is accomplished with little work on our part. We need to write only the body of `is_cuckooing`; none of the ordinary clock functions need to be rewritten for the cuckoo clock.

There's another advantage to derived classes: An object of the derived class may be used at any location where the base class is expected. For example, suppose we overload the "less than" operator to compare the times on two clocks, as shown in Figure 14.3 on page 679. We can use this relational operator to compare two ordinary clocks, but we can also compare any of the clock's derived classes. Here is some sample code:

```
cuckoo_clock sunrise, your_time;
int minutes;

sunrise.advance(60 * 6); // Set the sunrise for 6 A.M.
cout << "How many minutes do I advance your clock?" << endl;
cin >> minutes;
your_time.advance(minutes);

if (sunrise < your_time)
    cout << "That's before sunrise!" << endl;
else
    cout << "That's not before sunrise." << endl;
```

FIGURE 14.3   Implementation of the Less-Than Operator for Clocks

A Function Implementation

```
bool operator < (const clock& c1, const clock& c2)
// Postcondition: Returns true if the time on c1 is earlier than the time on c2
// over a usual day (starting at midnight); otherwise returns false.
{
    // Check whether one is morning and the other is not.
    if (c1.is_morning( ) && !c2.is_morning( ))
        return true;
    else if (c2.is_morning( ) && !c1.is_morning( ))
        return false;

    // Check whether one is 12 o'clock and the other is not.
    else if ((c1.get_hour( ) == 12) && (c2.get_hour( ) != 12))
        return true;
    else if ((c2.get_hour( ) == 12) && (c1.get_hour( ) != 12))
        return false;

    // Check whether the hours are different from each other.
    else if (c1.get_hour( ) < c2.get_hour( ))
        return true;
    else if (c2.get_hour( ) < c1.get_hour( ))
        return false;

    // The hours are the same, so check the minutes.
    else if (c1.get_minute( ) < c2.get_minute( ))
        return true;
    else
        return false;
}
```

www.cs.colorado.edu/~main/chapter14/clocks.cxx   **WWW**

In fact, we can even use the "less than" operator to compare an ordinary clock with a cuckoo_clock, or to compare two objects from different derived classes.

Any functions that you write to manipulate a clock will also be able to manipulate all of the clock's derived classes. Without derived classes, we would need to write a separate function for each kind of clock that we want to manipulate.

The Automatic Assignment Operator for a Derived Class

If a derived class does not define its own assignment operator, then C++ will automatically provide an assignment operator. This automatic assignment operator is similar to the automatic constructors, carrying out two steps: (1) activate the assignment operator for the base class (to copy any member variables that the base class uses), then (2) activate the assignment operator for any new member variables that the derived class has but the base class does not have. The assignment operators that are activated in Steps 1 and 2 may themselves be automatic assignment operators, or they may be specially written to accomplish correct copying of dynamic data structures.

Assignments are also allowed from a derived class to the base class, for example:

```
clock ordinary;
cuckoo_clock fancy;

fancy.advance(60);
ordinary = fancy;
```

Advance the fancy clock to 1 A.M. and assign the ordinary clock to equal the fancy clock.

The assignment ordinary = fancy is permitted because a cuckoo clock (such as fancy) can be used at any point where an ordinary clock is expected. Therefore, the assignment will activate the assignment operator for an ordinary clock (using fancy as if it were just an ordinary clock).

On the other hand, an assignment in the other direction, fancy = ordinary, is *forbidden* because an object of the base class (the ordinary clock) cannot be used as if it were an object of the derived class (the cuckoo clock).

Allowed:	Forbidden:
When a base class is public, an object of a derived class may be used as if it were an object of the base class.	But an object of the base class cannot usually be used as if it were an object of the derived class.

The Automatic Destructor of a Derived Class

Derived classes have one last automatic feature. If a class does not have a declared destructor, then C++ provides an automatic destructor that carries out two steps: (1) the destructors are called for any member variables that the derived class has, but the base class does not have, then (2) the destructor is called for the base class. Notice that an automatic destructor works differently than an automatic constructor: An automatic destructor first activates the destructors for member variables and then activates the destructor for the base class. But an automatic constructor first activates the constructor for base class, and then activates the constructors for member variables.

Overriding Inherited Member Functions

A derived class must sometimes perform some actions differently from the way the base class does. For example, the original clock provides the current hour via `get_hour`, using a 12-hour clock. Suppose we want to implement a derived class that provides its hour on a 24-hour basis, ranging from 0 to 23. The new clock can be defined as a derived class called `clock24`. The `clock24` class inherits everything from the ordinary clock, but it provides a new `get_hour` member function. This is called **overriding** an inherited member function.

To override an inherited member function, the derived class uses a new prototype for the overridden function, as shown here:

```
class clock24 : public clock
{
public:
    int get_hour( ) const;  // Overridden from the clock class
};
```

Now we are free to define a new implementation of `clock24::get_hour`. Within this implementation, we can use any of the ordinary clock functions, and we can even use the `get_hour` member function from the ordinary clock. The notation for using the ordinary clock's `get_hour` function is to place the scope resolution operator, `clock::`, in front of the function call. So, when we write `clock::get_hour( )`, we are activating the original clock's `get_hour` function. Here's the complete implementation of `clock24::get_hour`:

use the scope resolution operator to call the original version of the function

```
int clock24::get_hour( ) const
{
    int ordinary_hour;

    ordinary_hour = clock::get_hour( );
    if (is_morning( ))
    {
        if (ordinary_hour == 12)
            return 0;
        else
            return ordinary_hour;
    }
    else
    {
        if (ordinary_hour == 12)
            return 12;
        else
            return ordinary_hour + 12;
    }
}
```

🕐 **PROGRAMMING TIP**

MAKE THE OVERRIDING FUNCTION CALL THE ORIGINAL

In the example of the `clock24::get_hour` function, the first action of the overriding function is to call the original function. Often, the overriding function will call the original function to do some of its work. Frequently the call to the original function will be the *first* action of an overriding member function.

Several features of derived classes remain to be seen, such as derived classes that require new private member variables. These considerations will arise in the examples from the next sections of this chapter.

Self-Test Exercises for Section 14.1

1. What are the similarities and difference between a public base class and a private base class?

2. Design and implement a derived class called `daylight_clock`. A daylight clock is like a clock except that it has one extra boolean member function to determine whether it is currently daylight. Assume that daylight stretches from 7 A.M. through 6:59 P.M.

3. Suppose a derived class does not declare any constructors of its own. What constructors is it given automatically?

4. If `jacket` is a derived class of `clothes`, are the following statements legal? Why or why not?

   ```
   clothes coat;
   jacket blazer;
   blazer = coat;
   ```

5. Describe the actions of the automatic assignment operator and the automatic destructor for a derived class.

6. Design and implement a derived class called `noon_alarm`. A noon alarm object is just like a clock, except that whenever the `advance` function is called to advance the clock forward through 12 o'clock noon, an alarm message is printed (by the advance member function).

14.2 SIMULATION OF AN ECOSYSTEM

A is-a B means that A is a particular kind of B

There are many potential uses for derived classes, but one of the most frequent uses comes from the is-a relationship. "A is-a B" means that each A object is a particular kind of B object. For example, a cuckoo clock is a particular kind of clock. Some other examples of is-a relationships for living organisms are shown in Figure 14.4. The relationships are drawn in a tree called an **object hierarchy** tree. In this tree, each base class is placed as the parent of its derived classes.

Implementing Part of the Organism Object Hierarchy

We will implement four classes from the object hierarchy tree of living organisms and use these four classes in a program that simulates a small ecosystem. The four classes that we will implement are

- A general class, called organism, that can be used by a program to simulate the simplest properties of organisms, such as being born, growing, and eventually dying.

- Two classes that are derived from an organism. The classes, called animal and plant, can do everything that an ordinary organism can do—but they also have extra abilities associated with animals and plants.

- The final class, called herbivore, is derived from the animal class. It is a special kind of animal that eats plants.

FIGURE 14.4 An Object Hierarchy

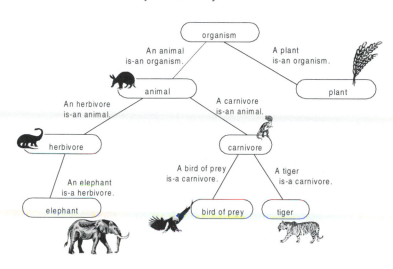

These four classes might fit into a larger hierarchy as shown in Figure 14.4. Keep in mind that each of the derived classes might have new member variables as well as new member functions.

The Organism Class

At the top of our object hierarchy tree is a class called organism. Within a program, every organism is given an initial size, measured in ounces. Each organism is also given a growth rate, measured in ounces per week. A program that wants to simulate the growth of an organism will start by specifying an initial size and growth rate as arguments to the organism's constructor. Throughout a computation, a program may call a member function named simulate_week, which causes the organism to simulate the passage of one week in its life—in other words, activating simulate_week makes the organism grow by its current growth rate. The organism class has a few other member functions specified in Figure 14.5, and a usage of the organism class is shown in Figure 14.6.

The organism class has functions to assign a new growth rate, to alter the organism's current size by a specified amount, and to return information about the organism's current size and growth rate. Also notice that the constructor has default arguments (one ounce for the initial size and zero ounces per week for the initial growth rate); therefore the constructor may be used with no arguments (that is, a default constructor).

FIGURE 14.5   Documentation for the Organism Class

Documentation for the Organism Class

```
//  CLASS PROVIDED: organism (part of the namespace main_savitch_14)
//     An organism object can simulate a growing organism such as a plant or an animal.
//
//  CONSTRUCTOR for the organism class:
//     organism(double init_size = 1, double init_rate = 0)
//        Precondition: init_size >= 0. Also, if init_size is 0, then init_rate is also zero.
//        Postcondition: The organism being simulated has been initialized. The value returned
//        from get_size( ) is now init_size (measured in ounces), and the value returned from
//        get_rate( ) is now init_rate (measured in ounces per week).
//
//  MODIFICATION MEMBER FUNCTIONS for the organism class:
//     void simulate_week( )
//        Postcondition: The size of the organism has been changed by its current growth rate.
//        If the new size is less than zero, then the actual size is set to zero rather than to a
//        negative value, and the growth rate is also set to zero.
//
//     void assign_rate(double new_rate)
//        Postcondition: The organism's growth rate has been changed to new_rate
//        (measured in ounces per week).
//
//     void alter_size(double amount)
//        Postcondition: The given amount (in ounces) has been added to the organism's current
//        size. If this results in a new size less than zero, then the actual size is set to zero
//        rather than to a negative value, and the growth rate is also set to zero.
//
//     void death( )
//         Postcondition: The organism's current size and growth rate have been set to zero.
//
//  CONSTANT MEMBER FUNCTIONS for the organism class:
//     double get_size( ) const
//        Postcondition: The value returned is the organism's current size (in ounces).
//
//     double get_rate( ) const
//        Postcondition: The value returned is the organism's current growth rate (in oz/week).
//
//     bool is_alive( ) const
//        Postcondition: If the current size is greater than zero, then the return value is true.
//        Otherwise the return value is false.
//
//  VALUE SEMANTICS for the organism class:
//     Assignments and the copy constructor may be used with organism objects.
```

www.cs.colorado.edu/~main/chapter14/organism.h   **WWW**

FIGURE 14.6   Sample Program from the Movie, *The Blob*

A Program

```
// FILE: blob.cxx
// This small demonstration shows how the organism class is used.
#include <cstdlib>          // Provides EXIT_SUCCESS
#include <iostream>         // Provides cout and cin
#include "organism.h"       // Provides the organism class
using namespace std;

int main( )
{
    main_savitch_14::organism blob(20.0, 100000.0);
    int week;

    // Untroubled by conscience or intellect, the Blob grows for three weeks.
    for (week = 1; week <= 3; ++week)
    {
        blob.simulate_week( );
        cout << "Week " << week << ":" << " the Blob is ";
        cout << blob.get_size( ) << " ounces." << endl;
    }

    // Steve McQueen reverses the growth rate to -80000 ounces per week.
    blob.assign_rate(-80000.0);
    while (blob.is_alive( ))
    {
        blob.simulate_week( );
        cout << "Week " << week << ":" << " the Blob is ";
        cout << blob.get_size( ) << " ounces." << endl;
        ++week;
    }

    cout << "The Blob (or its son) shall return." << endl;
    return EXIT_SUCCESS;
}
```

Can anyone stop the Blob?!

Sample Dialogue

```
Week 1: The Blob is 100020 ounces.
Week 2: The Blob is 200020 ounces.
Week 3: The Blob is 300020 ounces.
Week 4: The Blob is 220020 ounces.
Week 5: The Blob is 140020 ounces.
Week 6: The Blob is 60020 ounces.
Week 7: The Blob is 0 ounces.
The Blob (or its son) shall return.
```

Steve McQueen comes to the rescue at the end of week 3!

The organism class is not hard to implement, and we'll leave its implementation up to you. But we will give one example of using the class. Movie buffs may recall the 1958 film, *The Blob*. The Blob came to Earth from outer space at a mere 20 ounces, but "untroubled by conscience or intellect," it absorbs anything and anyone in its path. Without giving away the whole plot, let's suppose that the Blob grows at the astonishing rate of 100,000 ounces per week for three weeks. Then our hero (Steve McQueen) manages to reverse its growth to a rate of negative 80,000 ounces per week. A program to simulate the movie plot is shown in Figure 14.6. The program assumes that the organism class is implemented with a header file called organism.h.

The Animal Class: A Derived Class with New Private Member Variables

Now we will implement a class that can be used to simulate an animal. Since an animal *is-an* organism, we will declare the animal class as a derived class of the organism. In our design, an animal is an organism that must consume a given amount of food each week to survive. If a week has passed and the animal has consumed less than its required amount of food, then death occurs. With this in mind, the animal class will have two new private member variables, which are not part of the organism class, as shown in this partial definition:

the derived class has two new private member variables

```
class animal : public organism
{
public:
    ‖ We discuss the animal's public members in a moment.
private:
    double need_each_week;
    double eaten_this_week;
};
```

The first new member variable, need_each_week, keeps track of how many ounces of food the animal must eat each week in order to survive. The second new member variable, eaten_this_week, keeps track of how many ounces of food the animal has eaten so far this week.

When a derived class has some new member variables, it will usually need a new constructor to initialize those member variables. This is the first example that we have seen where a derived class has a new constructor rather than using the automatic constructors that were described on page 677.

How to Provide a New Constructor for a Derived Class

When a derived class has a new constructor, the prototype for the new constructor appears in the public portion of the class definition, just like any other constructor. In the case of the animal, the new constructor will have three arguments. The first two arguments are the same as the arguments for any organism, providing the initial size and the initial growth rate. The third argument will indicate how much food the animal needs, in ounces per week. Thus, the start of the animal's public section is given next.

```
class animal : public organism
{
public:
    animal(double init_size = 1, double init_rate = 0, double init_need = 0);
```

Each parameter has a default argument, so that this constructor can also be used as a default constructor. The constructor has no argument for `eaten_this_week`, since we plan to have that member variable initialized to zero (indicating that a newly constructed animal has not eaten).

The work of the animal's constructor is easy enough to describe: The first two arguments must somehow initialize the size and growth rate of the animal; the last argument initializes `need_each_week`; the value of `eaten_this_week` is initialized to zero. But how do we manage to use `init_size` and `init_rate` to initialize the size and growth rate of the animal? Most likely the size and growth rate are stored as private member variables of the `organism` class, but the animal has no direct access to the `organism`'s private member variables.

There is a solution to this problem, called the **member initialization list**. This list is an extra line in the constructor of a derived class. The purpose is to *provide initialization, including a call to the constructor of the base class.* The details of the member initialization list are given in Figure 14.7.

FIGURE 14.7   How to Write a Member Initialization List

The Member Initialization List

A member initialization list is used by a constructor to call the constructor of the base class and initialize other member variables. The rules are as follows:

1. The member initialization list appears in the implementation of a constructor, after the closing parenthesis of the parameter list and before the opening bracket of the constructor's body.
2. The list begins with a colon, followed by a list of items separated by commas.
3. For a derived class, the list can contain the name of the base class, followed by an argument list (in parentheses) for the base class constructor.
4. The list can also contain any member variable followed by its initial value in parentheses.
5. When the derived class constructor is called, the member variables are initialized with the specified values and the constructor for the base class will be activated before anything else is done.
6. If a base class constructor is not activated in the member initialization list, then the default constructor for the base class will automatically be activated before any of the rest of the derived class constructor is executed.

Example:
```
animal::animal(double init_size, double init_rate, double init_need)
: organism(init_size, init_rate), // Activate base class constructor
  need_each_week(init_need),       // Initial value for need_each_week
  eaten_this_week(0)               // Initial value for eaten_this_week is 0
{ // Because of the initialization list, the body of this constructor has no work to do. }
```

Here is the implementation of our animal constructor, with the member initialization list highlighted:

```
animal::animal
(double init_size, double init_rate, double init_need)
: organism(init_size, init_rate), // Activate base class constructor
  need_each_week(init_need), // Initial value for need_each_week
  eaten_this_week(0)          // Initial value for eaten_this_week is 0
{
    // Because of the initialization list, this constructor has no work.
}
```

By the way, in the `animal` class definition, we will provide each of the parameters with a default argument, so that this constructor can be used as a default constructor for the animal.

The Other Animal Member Functions

The animal has four new member functions that deal with eating, and the `simulate_week` member function must also be overridden. The four new functions are called `assign_need`, `eat`, `still_need`, and `total_need`. We'll discuss each of these member functions now.

The assign_need function. This member function has this prototype:

```
void assign_need(double new_need);
```

The member function is activated when a simulation needs to specify how much food an animal must eat to survive a week. For example, if `spot` is an animal that needs 30 ounces of food to survive a week, then `spot.assign_need(30)` is activated. During a simulation, the food requirements may change, so that `assign_need` can be activated several times with different arguments.

The eat function. Whenever the animal, `spot`, eats `m` ounces of food, the member function `spot.eat(m)` records this event. Here's the prototype of the member function:

```
void eat(double amount);
```

The amount of food that has been eaten during the current week is stored in a private member variable, `eaten_this_week`. So, activating `eat(m)` will simply add `m` to `eaten_this_week`.

Overriding the simulate_week function. The animal must do some extra work in its `simulate_week` member function. Therefore, it will override the organism's `simulate_week` function. The animal's `simulate_week` will first activate `organism::simulate_week` to carry out whatever work an ordinary organism does to simulate one week. Next, the animal's `simulate_week` determines whether the animal has had enough food to eat this week. If `eaten_this_week` is less than `need_each_week`, then `death` is activated. Also, `eaten_this_week` is reset to zero to restart the recording of food eaten for the animal's next week.

Here's some example code to show the coordination of the new member functions. It begins by declaring a 160-ounce animal `spot` (perhaps a cat). Spot is not currently growing (since `init_rate` is zero in the constructor), but she does require 30 ounces of food per week:

```
animal spot(160, 0, 30);

spot.eat(10);
spot.eat(25);
spot.simulate_week( );
if (spot.is_alive( ))
    cout << "Spot lives!\n";
else
    cout << "Spot has died.\n";
```

Spot catches a 10-ounce fish and steals 25 ounces of chicken from the kitchen.

Spot still lives at the end of her first week.

```
spot.eat(10);
spot.eat(15);
spot.simulate_week( );
if (spot.is_alive( ))
    cout << "Spot lives!\n";
else
    cout << "Spot has died.\n";
```

Spot catches another 10-ounce fish, but gets only 15 ounces of chicken this week.

Sadly, Spot dies at the end of her second week.

Two constant functions. The last two animal member functions are constant functions called `total_need` and `still_need`. The `total_need` function returns the total amount of food that the animal needs in a week, and the `still_need` function returns the amount of food that the animal still needs in the current week (which is the total need minus the amount already eaten).

The complete documentation and definition for the animal appears in Figure 14.8. The documentation and class definition could be placed in the same header file as the `organism` class (`organism.h`), and the member function implementations would then appear along with the organism member functions in `organism.cxx`. Alternatively, the animal class could have a separate header file and a separate implementation file. If the animal files are separate, then `organism.h` must be given in an include directive in the animal files.

The next derived class that we'll build is a class to simulate a plant. The plant class is derived from an organism, and it has one extra member function—but the work is left up to you in the Self-Test Exercises on page 692.

FIGURE 14.8   The Animal Class

Documentation for the Animal Class

```
//  CLASS PROVIDED: animal (part of the namespace main_savitch_14)
//     animal is a derived class of the organism class. All the organism public member functions
//     are inherited by an animal. In addition, an animal has these extra member functions:
//
//  CONSTRUCTOR for the animal class:
//     organism(double init_size = 1, double init_rate = 0, double init_need = 0)
//        Precondition: init_size >= 0, and init_need >= 0. If init_size is 0, then init_rate is zero
//        too.
//        Postcondition: The organism being simulated has been initialized. The value returned
//        from get_size( ) is now init_size (measured in ounces), the value returned from
//        get_rate( ) is now init_rate (measured in ounces per week), and the animal must eat
//        at least init_need ounces of food each week to survive.
//
//  MODIFICATION MEMBER FUNCTIONS for the animal class:
//     void assign_need(double new_need)
//        Precondition: new_need >= 0.
//        Postcondition: The animal's weekly food requirement has been changed to new_need
//        (measured in ounces per week).
//
//     void eat(double amount)
//        Precondition: amount >= 0.
//        Postcondition: The given amount (in ounces) has been added to the amount of food
//        that the animal has eaten this week.
//
//     void simulate_week( )  -- overridden from the organism class
//        Postcondition: The size of the organism has been changed by its current growth rate.
//        If the new size is less than zero, then the actual size is set to zero rather than to a
//        negative value, and the growth rate is also set to zero. Also, if the animal has eaten
//        less than its required need over the past week, then death has been activated.
//
//  CONSTANT MEMBER FUNCTIONS for the animal class:
//     double still_need( ) const
//        Postcondition: The return value is the ounces of food that the animal still needs to
//        survive the current week (which is the total need minus the amount eaten so far).
//
//     double total_need( ) const
//        Postcondition: The return value is the total amount of food that the animal needs to
//        survive one week (measured in ounces).
//
//  VALUE SEMANTICS for the animal class:
//     Assignments and the copy constructor may be used with animal objects.
```

(continued)

(FIGURE 14.8 continued)

Class Definition

```
class animal : public organism
{
public:
    // CONSTRUCTOR
    animal(double init_size = 1, double init_rate = 0, double init_need = 0);
    // MODIFICATION MEMBER FUNCTIONS
    void assign_need(double new_need);
    void eat(double amount);
    void simulate_week( ); // Overridden from the Organism class
    // CONSTANT MEMBER FUNCTIONS
    double still_need( ) const;
    double total_need( ) const { return need_each_week; }
private:
    double need_each_week;
    double eaten_this_week;
};
```

Implementation of the Member Functions

```
animal::animal(double init_size, double init_rate, double init_need)
: organism(init_size, init_rate),
  need_each_week(init_need),
  eaten_this_week(0)
{
    // Because of the initialization list, the body of this constructor has no work.
}


void animal::assign_need(double new_need)
// Library facilities used: cassert
{
    assert(new_need >= 0);
    need_each_week = new_need;
}


void animal::eat(double amount)
// Library facilities used: cassert
{
    assert(amount >= 0);
    eaten_this_week += amount;
}
```

(continued)

(FIGURE 14.8 continued)

```
void animal::simulate_week( )
{
    organism::simulate_week( );
    if (eaten_this_week < need_each_week)
        death( );
    eaten_this_week = 0;
}

double animal::still_need( ) const
{
    if (eaten_this_week >= need_each_week)
        return 0;
    else
        return need_each_week - eaten_this_week;
}
```

www.cs.colorado.edu/~main./chpater14/organism.h and organism.cxx   **WWW**

Self-Test Exercises for Middle of Section 14.2

7. Draw an object hierarchy diagram for various kinds of people.

8. The object hierarchy in the previous exercise might be used to track people in a health club facility. Provide a class definition of the base class. Private data members should include name, birthdate, weight, and gender. Include public function prototypes to calculate the age of a person from the birthdate, and to set and retrieve the weight and gender.

9. Write the constructor for one of the derived classes from Exercises 7 and 8. Use a member initialization list.

10. Declare a new class called `plant`, which is derived from an organism and has one extra member function:

    > `void nibbled_on(double amount);`
    > `// Precondition: 0 <= amount <= get_size( ).`
    > `// The plant's size has been decreased by amount. If this reduces`
    > `// the size to zero, then death is activated.`

    Suppose `fern` is a plant. Activating `fern.nibbled_on(m)` corresponds to some beast eating m ounces of `fern`. Notice that `nibbled_on` differs from the existing `alter_size` member function, since in the `nibbled_on` function, the amount is removed from the size (rather than added), and there is also a strict precondition on the amount eaten.

    Your `plant` class should have one constructor with the same parameters as the `organism` constructor. The plant's constructor merely calls the organism constructor (in the member initialization list). The actual body of the plant constructor has no lines (though you may want to put a comment). Provide default arguments of zero for both parameters.

11. Write a function with one argument, which is a list of plants, as shown in this prototype:

    `double total_mass(const vector<plant>& collection);`

    This uses the vector template class from the C++ Standard Library, which is a container class that is similar to a dynamic array (see Appendix H). The function should calculate and return the mass of all the plants on the list. Your function may use `collection.size( )` to determine the number of plants in the vector and then use the notation `collection[i]` to access plant number i (starting at `collection[0]`). Or you can use a vector iterator to step through the plants. (The use of iterators is described in Section 6.3).

The Herbivore Class

We're almost ready to start designing a simulation program for a small ecosystem. The ecosystem will be a small pond containing weeds and weed-eating fish. The weeds will be modeled by the `plant` class from Self-Test Exercise 10 on page 692, and the fish will be a new class that is derived from the animal class that we have just completed.

The new class for the fish, called `herbivore`, is an animal that eats plants. This suggests that an herbivore should have one new member function, which we call `nibble`. The member function will interact with a plant object that the herbivore is nibbling, and this plant object is a parameter to the new member function. Here is the specification we have in mind:

```
void herbivore::nibble(plant& meal);
// Postcondition: eat(amount) and meal.nibbled_on(amount) have both
// been activated. The amount is usually half of the plant, but it will not be
// more than 10% of the herbivore's weekly need nor more than the
// amount that the herbivore still needs to eat to survive this week.
```

For example, suppose that `carp` is an herbivore, and `bushroot` is a plant. If we activate `carp.nibble(bushroot)`, then `carp` will eat some of `bushroot`, by activating two other functions: (1) its own `eat` member function and (2) the `bushroot.nibbled_on( )` function.

The `nibble` function follows a few rules about how much of the plant is eaten. The rules state that `carp.nibble(bushroot)` will usually cause `carp` to eat half of `bushroot`, but a single nibble will not eat more than 10% of the animal's weekly need nor more than the amount that the animal still needs to eat in order to survive the rest of the week. In an actual model, these rules would be derived from behavior studies of real herbivores.

The complete herbivore documentation is shown in Figure 14.9, along with the class definition and the implementation of the herbivore's member functions.

FIGURE 14.9   The Herbivore Class

Documentation for the Herbivore Class

```
//  CLASS PROVIDED: herbivore (part of the namespace main_savitch_14)
//     herbivore is a derived class of the animal class. All the animal public member functions
//     are inherited by an herbivore. In addition, an herbivore has these extra member
//     functions:
//
//  CONSTRUCTOR for the herbivore class:
//     herbivore(double init_size = 1, double init_rate = 0, double init_need = 0)
//        Same as the animal constructor.
//
//  MODIFICATION MEMBER FUNCTIONS for the herbivore class:
//     void nibble(plant& meal)
//        Postcondition: eat(amount) and meal.nibbled_on(amount) have been activated. The
//        amount is usually half of the plant, but it will not be more than 10% of the
//        herbivore's weekly need nor more than the amount that the animal still needs to eat to
//        survive this week.
//
//  VALUE SEMANTICS for the herbivore class:
//     Assignments and the copy constructor may be used with herbivore objects.
```

Class Definition

```
class herbivore : public animal
{
public:
    // CONSTRUCTOR
    herbivore(double init_size = 1, double init_rate = 0, double init_need = 0);
    // MODIFICATION MEMBER FUNCTIONS
    void nibble(plant& meal);
};
```

Implementation of the Member Functions

```
herbivore::herbivore(double init_size, double init_rate, double init_need)
: animal(init_size, init_rate, init_need)
{
    // No work is done here, except calling the animal constructor.
}
```

(continued)

(FIGURE 14.9 continued)

```
void herbivore::nibble(plant& meal)
{
    const double PORTION = 0.5;       // Eat no more than this fraction of plant
    const double MAX_FRACTION = 0.1;  // Eat no more than this fraction of weekly need
    double amount;                    // How many ounces of the plant will be eaten

    // Set amount to some portion of the plant but no more than a given maximum fraction
    // of the total weekly need and no more than what the herbivore still needs to eat this
    // week.
    amount = PORTION * meal.get_size( );
    if (amount > MAX_FRACTION * total_need( ))
        amount = MAX_FRACTION * total_need( );
    if (amount > still_need( ))
        amount = still_need( );

    // Eat the plant.
    eat(amount);
    meal.nibbled_on(amount);
}
```

www.cs.colorado.edu/~main/chapter14/organism.h and organism.cxx   **WWW**

The Pond Life Simulation Program

A simulation program can use objects such as our herbivores to predict the effects of changes to an ecosystem. We'll write a program along these lines to model the weeds and fish in a small pond. The program stores the pond weeds in a container of plants, using the vector container class that is part of the C++ Standard Library (see Appendix H). For example, suppose the pond has 2000 weeds with an initial size of 15 ounces each and a growth rate of 2.5 ounces per week. Then we will create a list of 2000 plants, as shown here:

```
const size_t MANY_WEEDS = 2000;  // Number of weeds in the pond
const double WEED_SIZE   =   15; // Initial size of each weed (ounces)
const double WEED_RATE   =  2.5; // Weed growth rate (ounces/week)

// Create a sample plant and initialize the vector to contain MANY_WEEDS
// copies of this sample plant:
const plant SAMPLE(WEED_SIZE, WEED_RATE);
vector<plant> weeds(MANY_WEEDS, SAMPLE);
```

Our vector of plants is initialized by the vector constructor with two arguments: `vector<plant> weeds(MANY_WEEDS, SAMPLE)`. This version of the constructor creates an initial vector that contains MANY_WEEDS copies of the SAMPLE plant.

Our simulation has a second vector, called `fish`, which is a vector of herbivores. Initially, we'll stock the fish vector with 300 full-grown fish.

With the vectors initialized, our simulation may proceed. Throughout the simulation, various fish nibble on various plants. Each week, every weed increases by its growth rate (stated as 2.5 ounces/week in the code). Some weeds will also be nibbled by fish, but during our simulation no weed will ever be completely eaten, so the weeds never die, nor do we ever create new weeds beyond the initial 2000. On the other hand, the number of fish in the pond may vary throughout the simulation. When a fish dies (because of insufficient nibbling), that fish is removed from the fish vector. New fish are also born each week at a rate that we'll explain in a moment. For now, though, you should be getting a good idea of the overall simulation. Let's lay out these ideas precisely with some pseudocode:

// Pseudocode for the pond life simulation

1. Create a vector, called `weeds`, containing a bunch of plants. The exact number of weeds, their initial size, and their growth rate are determined by constants called `MANY_WEEDS`, `WEED_SIZE`, and `WEED_RATE`.

2. Create a vector, called `fish`, containing a bunch of herbivores. The number of fish and their initial size are determined by constants `INIT_FISH` and `FISH_SIZE`. In this simple simulation, the fish will not grow (their growth rate is zero), and their weekly need will be their initial size times a constant called `FRACTION`.

3. For each week of the simulation, we will first cause some randomly selected fish to nibble on randomly selected weeds. On average, each fish will nibble on `AVERAGE_NIBBLES` weeds (where `AVERAGE_NIBBLES` is yet another constant in our program). After all these nibbles, we will activate `simulate_week` for each fish and each weed. Dead fish will be removed from the fish vector. At the end of the week, we will give birth to some new fish. The total number of new fish is the current number of fish times a constant called `BIRTH_RATE`. To simplify the simulation, we will have the new fish born fully grown with a growth rate of zero.

At the end of each week (simulated in Step 3), our program prints a few statistics. These statistics show the number of fish that are currently alive and the total mass of the weeds.

Our program implementing the pseudocode is given in Figure 14.10. The top of the program lists the various constants that we have mentioned, from `MANY_WEEDS` to `BIRTH_RATE`. After the constants, we list prototypes for two functions that we found useful in the implementation. One of the functions, called `pond_week`, carries out the simulation of one week in the pond, as described in Step 3 of the pseudocode. The other function, `total_mass`, computes the total mass of all the plants in the bag of weeds.

We discuss a few of the implementation details starting on page 700.

FIGURE 14.10 The Pondlife Simulation

A Program

```
// FILE: pondlife.cxx
// A simple simulation program to model the fish and weeds in a pond

#include <iostream>      // Provides cin, cout
#include <iomanip>       // Provides setw
#include <cstdlib>       // Provides EXIT_SUCCESS, rand, size_t
#include <vector>        // Provides the vector template class
#include "organism.h"    // Provides Herbivore, Plant classes
using namespace std;
using namespace main_savitch_14;

// PROGRAM CONSTANTS
const size_t MANY_WEEDS     = 2000;  // Number of weeds in the pond
const double WEED_SIZE      =   15;  // Initial size of each weed, in ounces
const double WEED_RATE      =  2.5;  // Growth rate of weeds, in ounces/week
const size_t INIT_FISH      =  300;  // Initial number of fish in the pond
const double FISH_SIZE      =   50;  // Fish size, in ounces
const double FRACTION       =  0.5;  // A fish must eat FRACTION times its size
                                     // during one week or it will die.
const int    AVERAGE_NIBBLES =  30;  // Average number of plants nibbled by
                                     // a fish over one week
const double BIRTH_RATE     = 0.05;  // At the end of each week, some fish have
                                     // babies. The total number of new fish born is
                                     // the current number of fish times the
                                     // BIRTH_RATE (rounded down to an integer).

// Samples weed and fish objects to copy into the vectors of the main program:
const plant SAMPLE_WEED(WEED_SIZE, WEED_RATE);
const herbivore SAMPLE_FISH(FISH_SIZE, 0, FISH_SIZE * FRACTION);

// PROTOTYPES for the functions used in the program:
void pond_week(vector<herbivore>& fish, vector<plant>& weeds);
// Precondition: weeds.size( ) > 0.
// Postcondition: On average, each fish has nibbled on AVERAGE_NIBBLES plants, and then
// simulate_week has been activated for each fish and each weed. Any fish that died are
// removed from the fish bag, and then BIRTH_RATE * fish.size( ) new fish have been added to
// the fish bag.


double total_mass(const vector<plant>& collection);
// Postcondition: The return value is the total mass of all the plants in the collection.
```

(continued)

(FIGURE 14.10 continued)

```cpp
int main( )
{
    vector<plant> weeds(MANY_WEEDS, SAMPLE_WEED);        // A vector of weeds
    vector<herbivore> fish(INIT_FISH, SAMPLE_FISH);      // A vector of weeds
    int many_weeks;     // Number of weeks to simulate
    int i;              // Loop control variable

    // Get number of weeks, and format the output.
    cout << "How many weeks shall I simulate? ";
    cin >> many_weeks;
    cout.setf(ios::fixed, ios::floatfield);
    cout << "Week     Number     Plant Mass" << endl;
    cout << "         of Fish    (in ounces)" << endl;

    // Simulate the weeks.
    for (i = 1; i <= many_weeks; ++i)
    {
        pond_week(fish, weeds);
        cout << setw(4) << i;
        cout << setw(10) << fish.size( );
        cout << setw(14) << setprecision(0) << total_mass(weeds);
        cout << endl;
    }

    return EXIT_SUCCESS;
}


double total_mass(const vector<plant>& collection)
{
    double answer;
    vector<plant>::const_iterator p;

    answer = 0;
    for (p = collection.begin( ); p != collection.end( ); ++p)
        answer += p->get_size( );

    return answer;
}
```

(continued)

(FIGURE 14.10 continued)

```
void pond_week(vector<herbivore>& fish, vector<plant>& weeds)
{
    // Variables for an index and an iterator for the weeds:
    vector<plant>::iterator        wi;
    vector<plant>::size_type       weed_index;

    // Variables for an index, an iterator, and counters for the fish:
    vector<herbivore>::iterator   fi;
    vector<herbivore>::size_type  fish_index;
    vector<herbivore>::size_type  new_fish_population;

    size_t many_iterations;    // How many random nibbles to simulate
    size_t i;                  // Loop counter

    // Have randomly selected fish nibble on randomly selected plants.
    many_iterations = AVERAGE_NIBBLES * fish.size( );
    for (i = 0; i < many_iterations; ++i)
    {
        fish_index = rand( ) % fish.size( );    // Index of a random fish
        weed_index = rand( ) % weeds.size( );   // Index of a random weed
        fish[fish_index].nibble(weeds[weed_index]);
    }

    // Simulate the weeks for the weeds.
    for (wi = weeds.begin( ); wi != weeds.end( ); ++wi)
        wi->simulate_week( );

    // Simulate the weeks for the fish, and count how many died.
    fi = fish.begin( );
    while (fi != fish.end( ))
    {
        fi->simulate_week( );
        if (!fi->is_alive( ))
            fish.erase(fi);
        else
            ++fi;
    }

    // Calculate the new number of fish, and reset the fish vector to this size.
    // If this adds new fish to the vector, then those new fish will be equal to the
    // SAMPLE_FISH that is used for all our fish:
    new_fish_population = (1 + BIRTH_RATE) * fish.size( );
    fish.resize(new_fish_population, SAMPLE_FISH);
}
```

Pondlife—Implementation Details

we use the vector's ability to access an element with array notation, and we use a vector iterator

The implementations of pond_week and total_mass are at the end of Figure 14.10. These implementations show a few features of the Standard Library vector class from Appendix H. In particular, we need the ability to access a random item from a vector and the ability to step through the items of a vector one at a time.

The vector permits quick access of an arbitrary element using array notation. For example fish[i] is a reference to the item at position i in the fish vector (where i can range from 0 to fish.size( ) - 1). Note that this is a reference to the item, as discussed on page 314. This means that when we use the array notation to access an item, any changes made to the item will change the actual item in the vector. For example, consider the statement:

```
fish[fish_index].nibble(weeds[weed_index]);
```

This statement activates the nibble member function of a fish (which will change the fish) and the argument to the function is a weed (so this weed is also changed by being nibbled on).

The use of the iterator is also important. For example, within the pond_week function, we activate simulate_week for each plant by using the iterator to step through the weeds one at a time, as shown here:

```
// Simulate the weeks for the weeds.
for (wi = weeds.begin( ); wi != weeds.end( ); ++wi)
    wi->simulate_week( );
```

the member selection operator can be used with an iterator to activate a member function of the iterator's current object

For the iterator wi, we can use the notation *wi to access its element, or we can use notation such as wi->simulate_week( ). This is the same member selection operator that is avialable to use with pointers. It is equivalent to writing the longer expression (*wi).simulate_week( ). In either case, we activate the simulate_week method of the weed that wi refers to.

Using the Pond Model

No doubt you have noticed that our pond model is not entirely rooted in reality. For example, each fish is born full grown and does not continue to grow. This simplification makes it easier to handle the fish vector when we need to add or remove fish at the end of the pond_week function. Some extensions to make the model more realistic are given in the Programming Projects of this chapter. Nevertheless, even our simple program illustrates the principles of simulation programs. Let's look at one way that a simulation program such as ours could be used.

Suppose that your friend Judy owns a pond with 2000 weeds, about 15 ounces each. And perhaps the pond is too choked with weeds for Judy's taste. One way to control the weeds is to introduce a weed-eating species of fish—the pond life program can help us predict what will happen when a certain number of fish are put in the pond. For example, suppose we have a species of fish where the program's constants (Figure 14.10 on page 697) are accurate. When we run the program with these constants, the output in Figure 14.11 occurs.

Actually, if you run the program, you may get slightly different output because of the use of the random factor in the bag's grab function. What does the program predict will happen in the pond if we introduce 300 of this kind of fish? Each output line gives the fish population and the plant mass at the end of one more week. The model predicts that the mass of the weeds will decrease fairly rapidly. This is followed by a period of some oscillation in both the fish and plant populations, including a rather catastrophic week for the fish when their population drops from 359 to 144. Sudden declines such as this are observed in real ecosystems when a species is allowed to expand, limited only by its food supply.

This kind of model can provide predictions as well as testing theories of interactions in an ecosystem. It's also important to remember that any predictions are only as accurate as the underlying model.

Dynamic Memory Usage

The pondlife program requires a lot of dynamic memory—enough room for about 6000 double numbers, plus room for the bags of pointers. For example, an older version of our program required the "huge memory model" for Borland's 4.5 compiler (-mh option on the compile line). If you receive abnormal program termination with your pondlife program, it is probably due to an insufficient dynamic memory.

FIGURE 14.11 Pond Program Dialogue

Sample Dialogue

How many weeks shall I simulate? **38**

Week	Number of Fish	Plant Mass (in ounces)
1	315	27500
2	330	24625
3	346	21375
4	363	17725
5	379	13654
6	359	9286
7	144	6462
8	109	7960
9	112	10245
10	117	12445
11	122	14520
12	128	16470
13	134	18270
14	140	19920
15	147	21420
16	154	22745
17	161	23895
18	169	24870
19	177	25645
20	185	26220
21	194	26595
22	203	26745
23	213	26670
24	223	26345
25	234	25770
26	245	24920
27	257	23795
28	268	22374
29	281	20674
30	292	18656
31	306	16356
32	313	13720
33	301	10984
34	244	8689
35	189	7812
36	163	8225
37	161	9176
38	164	10159

Self-Test Exercises for Section 14.2

12. Write code to declare a vector of organisms. Put 10 new organisms in the vector, with an initial size of 16 ounces and a growth rate of 1 ounce per week. Grab five random organisms, and alter their growth rates to 2 ounces per week. Finally, calculate the total of all the organisms' growth rates, and print the result.

13. In the previous exercise, you started with 10 organisms growing at 1 ounce per week. Five random organisms had their growth rates changed to 2 ounces per week, so you might think that the total of all the organisms' rates would be 5*1 + 5*2, which is 15. But when we ran the program, the total was only 14. Why?

14. Design and implement a new class derived from the animal class. The new class, called `carnivore`, has one new member function with the prototype shown here:

```
void carnivore::chase(animal& prey, double chance);
```

When `chase(prey, chance)` is activated for some carnivore, the carnivore chases the prey. The probability of actually catching the prey is given by the parameter `chance` (which should lie between 0 and 1—for example 0.75 for a 75% chance). If the prey actually is caught, then this will also activate the carnivore's `eat` member function and (sadly) activate the prey's `death` member function.

Note: You can use the `rand` function (from `<cstdlib>`) to determine whether the animal is caught, as shown here:

```
if (rand( )/double(RAND_MAX) < chance)
{
    || Code for catching and eating the prey
}
```

14.3 VIRTUAL MEMBER FUNCTIONS AND A GAME CLASS

This section demonstrates *virtual member functions*, which are a new kind of member function that allows certain aspects of activating a function to be delayed until a program is actually running.

Introduction to the Game Class

To make the explanation of virtual functions concrete, we'll present an example of a class called `game`, which will make it easier for us to write programs that play various two-player games such as chess, checkers, or Othello. The games we have in mind will pit a human player against the computer, with the computer making moves that are, hopefully, intelligent.

The key to the game class is the realization that many aspects of these different games can be handled in a uniform way. For example, each game needs a general procedure for going back and forth between the human player and the computer, and each game needs a sensible procedure for selecting the computer's move from among the alternatives. So our proposal is to have a game class that provides all these common operations and will serve as a base class for many derived classes that play various two-player games.

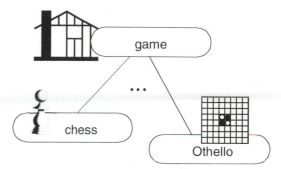

The game class provides a framework for other games to be implemented. For example, a programmer who is writing a chess-playing program can implement a derived chess class that uses the game as the base. Another programmer, writing a program to play Othello, can implement a derived othello class that also uses the game as its base.

The definition of our proposed game class is given in Figure 14.12.

There's a lot of information in the game class definition and it uses several new techniques. We'll briefly explain each part of the definition, and then we'll come back to concentrate on the parts of the defintion that must be understood in order to write a derived class such as chess, or Othello, or—as we'll actually do in an example—a derived class to play a game called Connect Four.

FIGURE 14.12   Definition for the Game Class

Class Definition

```
class game
{
public:
    // ENUM TYPE
    enum who { HUMAN, NEUTRAL, COMPUTER }; // Possible game outcomes

    // CONSTRUCTOR and DESTRUCTOR
    game( ) { move_number = 0; }
    virtual ~game( ) { }

    // PUBLIC MEMBER FUNCTIONS
    // The play function should not be overridden. It plays one game, with the human player
    // moving first and the computer second. The computer uses an alpha-beta look ahead
    // algorithm to select its moves. The return value is the winner of the game (or
    // NEUTRAL for a tie).
    who play( );
```

(continued)

(FIGURE 14.12 continued)

```
protected:
        // OPTIONAL VIRTUAL FUNCTIONS (overriding these is optional)
        virtual void display_message(const std::string& message) const;
        virtual std::string get_user_move( ) const;
        virtual who last_mover( ) const;
        virtual int moves_completed( ) const;
        virtual who next_mover( ) const;
        virtual who opposite(who player) const;
        virtual who winning( ) const;

        // VIRTUAL FUNCTIONS THAT MUST BE OVERRIDDEN:
        // The overriding function should call the original when it finishes.

        // Have the next player make a specified move:
        virtual void make_move(const std::string& move) { ++move_number; }

        // Restart the game from the beginning:
        virtual void restart( ) { move_number = 0; }

        // PURE VIRTUAL FUNCTIONS (these must be provided for each derived class)

        // Return a pointer to a copy of myself:
        virtual game* clone( ) const = 0;

        // Compute all the moves that the next player can make:
        virtual void compute_moves(std::queue<std::string>& moves) const = 0;

        // Display the status of the current game:
        virtual void display_status( ) const = 0;

        // Evaluate a board position (positive values are good for the player who just moved):
        virtual int evaluate( ) const = 0;

        // Return true if the current game is finished:
        virtual bool is_game_over( ) const = 0;

        // Return true if the given move is legal for the next player:
        virtual bool is_legal(const std::string& move) const = 0;

private:
        int move_number; // Number of moves made so far
        || Other private items could go here, too.
};
```

www.cs.colorado.edu/~main/chapter14/game.h   **W W W**

The who type.   The class starts with this definition:

```
enum who { HUMAN, NEUTRAL, COMPUTER }; // Possible game outcomes
```

This definition defines an **enum type**, which you might not have used before. An enum type defines a simple new data type along with values that variables of that type can be assigned. In our example, the new enum type is called who, and a variable of type who can be assigned one of the three constants called HUMAN, NEUTRAL, and COMPUTER. We'll use variables of this type to keep track of who won a game (using NEUTRAL for a tie), or whose turn it is to move.

enum type

The constructor.   The game class has a simple constructor that assigns the value zero to its one private member variable (move_number). This variable keeps track of how many moves have been made while a game is being played.

The public play function.   The game class has one public member function:

```
who play( );
```

This function is activated to cause one game to be played. For example, later we will write a class called connect4, which is derived from the game class and plays a game called Connect Four. A simple main function that plays a Connect Four game looks like this:

```
int main( )
{
    connect4 instance;
    connect4::who winner;

    winner = instance.play( );
    switch (winner)
    {
    case connect4::HUMAN:    cout << "You win" << endl; break;
    case connect4::COMPUTER: cout << "I win"   << endl; break;
    case connect4::NEUTRAL:  cout << "A draw"  << endl; break;
    }

    return EXIT_SUCCESS;
}
```

This plays one game of Connect Four.

The game is interactive, letting the user type game moves at the keyboard (or, as we will see, the input can come in other ways). A member function of the game class directs the computer's moves, searching through all possible moves, looking at responses that the human might make to those moves, and looking at possible responses to the human's responses, and so on.

You are probably wondering about the details of directing the computer's moves. We will discuss that at the end of this section, but for now, let's assume that some wise and generous programmer has given us the complete game class, which we are going to use to implement games such as Connect Four. The wonderful feature of the game class is that we don't need to know the details of how `play` works in order to write our derived class. We can just trust that our wise and generous programmer wrote the `play` function correctly. This is one of the big benefits of a well-written base class:

The Benefit of a Well-Written Base Class

With a well-written base class in hand, a programmer can write derived classes without worrying about how the base class accomplishes its work.

So, we're planning to write a class that is derived from the game class. Among other things, our derived class will inherit the powerful `play` function. We have no immediate need to understand the details of the `play` function, but we do need to know more about the next part of the game class definition, which provides a series of protected, virtual functions.

Protected Members

The next part of the game class definition begins like this:

```
protected:
    // OPTIONAL VIRTUAL FUNCTIONS (overriding these is optional)
    virtual void display_message
        (const std::string& message) const;
```

The keyword *protected* indicates that the items that follow will be a new kind of member, somewhat between *public* and *private*. In particular, a **protected member** can be used (and overridden) by a derived class; but apart from within a derived class, any protected member is private. It cannot be used elsewhere.

Virtual Member Functions

The first protected member function in the game class is `display_message`. The game class implements this function is a simple way by printing the message (which is an argument) to the standard output (`cout`). This works fine, and whenever the `play` function needs to print a message, it does so by activating `display_message`. In fact, the beginning of our play function looks like this:

```
game::who game::play( )
{
    display_message("Welcome!");
    ...
```

This works fine. When we play the game, the welcome message is printed at the start. But, suppose that we write a game that needs to display messages by some other method. Perhaps the messages go to a graphical window, or the messages are embellished in some other manner before being printed. This sounds as if it won't be a problem. Our derived class will inherit all the game class members, but it can override any method that it doesn't like. As an example, perhaps we want our Connect Four game to print "***" before each displayed message (just to make the messages more exciting). We could override the `display_method` function so that `connect4::display_method` first prints "***" and then prints the message.

With this approach, when the `play` method begins, it will activate `display_message("Welcome!")`, but what will this print? If it uses `game::display_message`, then the word "Welcome!" appears by itself. If it uses `connect4::display_message`, then "***Welcome!" is printed. So which version is used? Here is the usual rule:

When One Member Function Activates Another

Normally, when a member function f activates another member function g, the version of g that is actually activated comes from the same class as the function f. This behavior occurs even if the activated function g is later overridden, and f is activated by an object of the derived class.

In this example, this means that `game::play` normally would use `game::display_message`, even if a derived object activates the `play` method. This is where virtual member functions come to the rescue. When a member function is declared with the *virtual* keyword, you are anticipating that the method will be overridden in some derived class. And you are also demanding a bit more:

Activating a Virtual Member Function

Whenever a *virtual* member function is activated, the data type of the activating object is examined when the program is running, and the correct version of the function is used.

In other words: For a **virtual member function**, the choice of which version of the function to use is never made until the program is running. At run time, the program examines the data type of the object that activated the method, and thereby uses the correct version of the function.

There are several situations that require virtual member functions. The most common situation is the case we have described, where one member function activates another member function, and the programmer anticipates that this other member function will be overridden in the future.

Virtual Destructors

Whenever a class has virtual methods, it's a good idea to also provide a virtual destructor, even if the base class has no need for a destructor. With a virtual destructor, the compiler arranges for the right destructor to be called at run time, even when the compiler is uncertain about the exact data type of the object. This is why our game includes a destructor: `virtual ~game( ) { } .`

The Protected Virtual Member Functions of the Game Class

All of the protected functions of the game class are virtual member functions, because we anticipate that the programmer who implements a derived game will override some or all of these protected functions. In fact, we're almost ready to implement our derived Connect Four game, which will override eight virtual functions. But first, let's examine the three broad groups of virtual functions that the game class provides:

Optional virtual functions. The `display_message` function is one of seven optional virtual functions. The programmer of a derived class may override these to obtain different behavior (such as a different method of displaying messages). But for our Connect Four game, we'll accept the game class's implementations, not overriding any of the seven methods.

Virtual functions that must be overridden. The game class requires that two other virtual functions must be overridden by any derived class. In each case, the game class has done a little bit of the work needed for these functions, but most of the work must be done by the derived class.

When these two methods are overridden, the new method in the derived class must activate the original version of the method (otherwise the little bit of work that the game class does will be omitted). For these two functions, there is no way that the game class can actually require the derived class to provide the overriding versions, except by making this request in the game class documentation.

Pure virtual functions. The final six virtual functions are examples where the game class cannot do any of the work. Such a function is called a **pure virtual function**, and it is indicated by the notation "= 0" before the semicolon of the prototype. For example:

```
// Return true if the given move is legal for the next player:
virtual bool is_legal(const string& move) const = 0;
```

Pure Virtual Functions and Abstract Classes

A **pure virtual function** is indicated by = 0 before the end of the semicolon in the prototype. The class does not provide any implementation of a pure virtual function. Because there is no implementation, any class with a pure virtual function is called an **abstract class** and no instances of an abstract class may appear in a program.

Abstract classes are used as base classes, and it is up to the derived class to provide an implementation for each pure virtual function.

A Derived Class to Play Connect Four

We're ready to implement a connect4 class that is derived from the game class. The derived class will have member variables to keep track of the status of a Connect Four game as it is being played. The derived class will also override eight virtual member functions to provide the tasks that the game class needs for examining and manipulating the status of the game.

the rules of Connect Four

The rules of Connect Four are easy to describe. The game board consists of a transparent vertical tray with seven slots at the top. The players alternate dropping checkers into the slots: white (for player one), then black (player two), then white (player one), black (player two) and so on. The game ends when someone gets four of their checkers in a row (horizontally, vertically, or diagonally). For example, after the first player's third move, the board might look like this:

In this situation, the black player needs to make the next move in the rightmost column, otherwise the white player can win by getting four-in-a-row horizontally on the next move. Each slot can hold up to six checkers, so it is possible that the game ends with no player having four-in-a-row (that would be a tie).

The Private Member Variables of the Connect Four Class

what the game class requires from its derived classes

Our connect4 class definition will be derived from game. To write this class, we need to know what the game class requires from each of its derived classes. The requirements are easy to describe: The derived class must have member variables to keep track of the status of a single game. In the case of Connect Four, the connect4 class must have member variables to keep track of the status of a single game of Connect Four as the game is played.

In addition, the derived class must implement at least the eight virtual functions that allow the game class to access the game status. Our overall plan for the connect4 class is shown in Figure 14.13, including three private member variables. Our intention with these variables is to refer each location on the board by a column number (from 0 to 6) and a row number (from 0 to 5). It may seem

---

FIGURE 14.13   Class Definition for the Connect Four Game

Class Definition

```
class connect4 : public game
{
public:
    // STATIC CONSTANTS
    static const int ROWS = 6;
    static const int COLUMNS = 7;

    // CONSTRUCTOR
    connect4( );

protected:
    // Return a pointer to a copy of myself:
    virtual game* clone( ) const;

    // Compute all the moves that the next player can make:
    virtual void compute_moves(std::queue<std::string>& moves) const;

    // Display the status of the current game:
    virtual void display_status( ) const;

    // Evaluate a board position (positive values are good for the player who just moved)
    virtual int evaluate( ) const;

    // Return true if the current game is finished:
    virtual bool is_game_over( ) const;

    // Return true if the given move is legal for the next player:
    virtual bool is_legal(const std::string& move) const;

    // Have the next player make a specified move:
    virtual void make_move(const std::string& move);

    // Restart the game from the beginning:
    virtual void restart( );

private:
    // MEMBER VARIABLES TO TRACK THE STATE OF THE GAME
    who data[ROWS][COLUMNS];
    int many_used[COLUMNS];
    int most_recent_column;

    ‖ Other private items could go here, too.
};
```

www.cs.colorado.edu/~main/chapter14/connect4.h   **WWW**

strange to start our numbers at zero instead of one, but doing so will make our programming easier because we store information about the board in this two-dimensional array (which is a private member variable):

```
who data[ROWS][COLUMNS];
```

Remember that the who data type came from the game class. It is an enum type that has three possible values (HUMAN, NEUTRAL, COMPUTER). The ROWS and COL-UMNS constants are defined as static member constants of the connect4 class (ROWS is 6 and COLUMNS is 7), so that each spot in the data array corresponds to one spot on the game board. For example, if the game board has a black checker at row 1 and column 6, then data[1][6] will be set to COMPUTER (since the computer is the second player, using black checkers). Any location without a checker will be recorded as NEUTRAL in the data array.

the purpose of the three member variables

In addition to the data array, we have two other private member variables:

```
int many_used[COLUMNS];
int most_recent_column;
```

The value of many_used[i] is the number of checkers in column number i (which is useful when you're calculating where the next checker in that column should go). After the game is started, the value of most_recent_column will be the column where the last checker was placed. This is useful for reducing the calculations about whether the game has ended.

The only remaining work is to understand and implement the eight virtual functions and the constructor. We'll do this over the next few pages, sometimes providing an implementation and other times providing only a discussion.

The Connect Four Constructor and Restart Function

The connect4 default constructor activates the game constructor (using the member initialization list described in Figure 14.7 on page 687) and then activates the restart member function. The restart function initializes the connect4 member variables; for example, the data array is set to all NEUTRAL values. As indicated in the documentation for the game class (Figure 14.12 on page 703), the restart function of any derived class must also activate game::restart( ), which will re-initialize the game's member variables.

Three Connect Four Functions That Deal with the Game's Status

Each class that is derived from the game must implement three virtual member functions that allow the game class to access the current state of the game:

The display_status function.   This *void* function has no parameters. It merely displays the current status of the game. Our implementation of display_status prints a grid representing the game, like this:

```
Current game status
(HUMAN = #  and  COMPUTER = @):
Most recent move in column 5
    .   .   .   .   .   .   .
    .   .   .   .   .   .   .
    .   .   .   .   .   .   .
    .   .   .   .   .   .   .
    .   .   .   @   .   .   .
    .   .   @   #   #   #   .
    0   1   2   3   4   5   6
Computer's turn to move...
```

In this grid, we used the character '@' to represent a computer checker and the character '#' to represent the human's checker.

The is_game_over function. This *bool* function also has no parameters. Its return value is true if the current game is over. The game is over if the most recently placed checker is part of a four-in-a-row, or if all the columns are full.

The evaluate function. This function is the heart of the game. It examines the current status and provides a numerical estimate of how favorable the current status seems, providing a positive answer if the status is good for the computer and a negative answer if the status is good for the human. Larger magnitudes indicate a more certain answer, and an evaluation of zero indicates that the game is more-or-less even for both players.

The evaluation should be done in fixed way that doesn't try to look ahead at possible future moves (because looking ahead is already built into the game class's *play* function). There's no one right way to evaluate the game status, but we can tell you the idea we used, which was suggested by our colleague John Gillett: We examine each possible sequence of four consecutive locations, giving each such sequence a value as follows:

If the four locations have...	then the value is...
...four computer checkers	+500
...1 to 3 computer checkers and none of the human's	+1 to +3
...no checkers or a mixture of both players	zero
...1 to 3 human checkers and none of the computer's	-1 to -3
...four of the human's checkers	-500

The result of our evaluation function is the sum of all these values from examining each of the possible sequences of four locations in the current game. The large numbers (+500 and –500) were selected so that the total evaluation would always favor the player who obtained four-in-a-row, even if the other locations completely favor the other player.

Three Connect Four Functions That Deal with Moves

Our game class needs some way to represent a move in the game. Since the programmer of the game class doesn't know much about the exact game being played, we decided to use strings to represent moves. The exact format of these "move strings" can be decided by the programmer who implements a derived class. In the case of Connect Four, our move strings will just be simple strings that contain one digit specifying the slot in which the player wants to place the next checker. For example, the string "3" represents the move of putting a checker into slot number 3.

Each derived class must provide three virtual member functions that deal with its move strings:

The is_legal_move function. This *bool* function has a string as its parameter. It returns true if the string is currently a legal move for the next player. Among other things, the game class uses this function to determine whether a move typed by the user is currently legal. For Connect Four, a move is legal provided that it is a number from 0 to COLUMNS-1, and that that column is not already full.

The make_move function. This *void* function has a string move as its parameter. The string has already been checked to ensure that it is a legal move. The function is responsible for making this move (by updating the member variables that represent the status of the game). The function must also activate game::make_move, so that that base class can update any of its member variables that deal with the status of the game.

The compute_moves function. The prototype for this function is

```
void compute_moves(std::queue<std::string>& moves) const;
```

The function examines the current status of the game and determines what moves are currently legal. All these legal moves are then placed into the queue. The function does not actually make any of these moves (it just puts these moves into the queue), so compute_moves can be a const member function.

If the game is not yet over, there should always be at least one legal move put into the queue (although in some games, such as Othello, this one legal move could be a "pass" move).

The Clone Function

Each class derived from our game class must provide one more function:

```
virtual game* clone( ) const;
```

The purpose of this function is to make a complete copy of the current game, and return a pointer to this copy. Such copies are needed by the game class when it is exploring possible future moves. (These potential moves are made to copies of the game, so that the actual game is not altered during the mere exploration of future possibilities).

The implementation of the connect4 clone function can use the automatic copy constructor, so there is not much work to making a copy:

```
game*  connect4::clone( )  const
{
    return new connect4(*this);
}
```

This call of the *new* operator uses the `connect4` automatic copy constructor to create a copy of *`this`. The notation *`this` is always the object that activated the current method; in other words, the object that activated the `clone` method. So, the overall effect is to create a copy of the `connect4` object that activated the `clone` method, and return a pointer to this new object.

another reason why we used virtual member functions

Notice that the actual return type of the `clone` function is a pointer to a `game` object. This is fine because a pointer to a `game` object (the base class) can be used to point to a `connect4` object (the derived type). Moreover, if we activate member functions of this object, we will always use the correct `connect4` member functions (because we used virtual member functions).

virtual constructors are forbidden

Finally, notice that the `clone` method is simple, but it cannot be implemented by the `game` itself because the game base class cannot use the copy constructor of the derived class. We might get around this problem if constructors could be virtual, but C++ does not allow virtual constructors.

Writing Your Own Derived Games from the Game Class

You can now write the `connect4` class yourself (for comparison to ours), or you could write other games that are derived from the game class. Some useful resources are online:

http://www.cs.colorado.edu/~main

/chapter14/game.h	our game class header file
/chapter14/game.cxx	our game class implementation file
/chapter14/connect4.h	our connect4 header file
/chapter14/connect4.cxx	our connect4 implementation file
/projects/chapter14/	ideas for other games to implement

It's interesting that you can write such clever games without knowing the details of the game class's `play` function. In fact, we encourage you to write your derived classes without much concern for the workings of the base. On the other hand, it might be interesting to know a bit more about the game class's algorithm. You can download and read the entire game class, or read our short discussion, next.

The Game Class's Play Algorithm with Minimax

The play algorithm alternates between getting a human move and a computer move. The interesting part is the computer move, which starts by using `compute_moves` to calculate all the possible moves. For example, if the computer has three possible moves, then we can draw the situation as shown in the margin. Our first version of the game class had a private member function, `eval_with_look_ahead`, which was used to evaluate each of the possible new positions, with this specification:

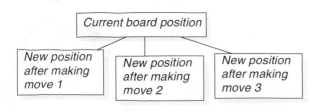

```
int eval_with_look_ahead(int look_ahead);
// The return value of the current board position is evaluated from the
// viewpoint of the player who just moved. Positive values are good for this
// player, and negative values are bad. The look_ahead parameter
// determines how far we should examine possible future moves.
```

For each possible move, the game class creates a copy of the current game, makes the move in the copy, and calls `eval_with_look_ahead` to evaluate how good the game seems to be after the possible move. In our implementation, the game class uses a value of 4 for the `look_ahead` parameter, meaning that the evaluation will look at the possible responses to the move, and the responses to the responses, and so on (ending with four levels of responses).

Base cases. The `eval_with_look_ahead` function has two easy cases: when `look_ahead` is zero or when the game is over. In these cases, we don't need to look at any future moves. Instead, we simply call `evaluate`, which is the virtual member function that evaluates the game status without looking ahead. (If we are using `eval_with_look_ahead` to evaluate for the computer, then we just return the `evaluate` value directly. If we're evaluating from the human's viewpoint, then we multiply `evaluate`'s answer times -1 since the documentation specifies that `evaluate` always does its work from the computer's viewpoint).

Recursive cases. When the game is not over and `look_ahead` is more than zero, we use recursion to evaluate all the responses that the other player might make in the current board position. For example, suppose that `eval_with_look_ahead` was asked to evaluate the current board position from the viewpoint of the computer, with a `look_ahead` value of 4. Here are the steps of the algorithm, carried out for our example:

1. Generate a queue of all moves that the human opponent could now make:
   ```
   queue<string> moves;
   compute_moves(moves);
   ```

2. For each move in the queue, create a copy of the current game, and apply the move to this copy. Then evaluate how this altered game looks to the opponent, keeping track of the biggest value that the opponent finds. We use a recusive call of `eval_with_look_ahead` to evaluate the altered state, reducing the `look_ahead` by one:
   ```
   game* future;
   int value, best_value;
   best_value = INT_MIN; // INT_MIN is smallest int from <climits>
   while (!moves.empty( ))
   {
       future = clone( );
       future->make_move(moves.front( ));
       value = future->eval_with_look_ahead(look_ahead-1);
       delete future;
       if (value > best_value)
           best_value = value;
       moves.pop( );
   }
   ```

3. In our example, suppose that Step 1 found three possible moves, and that the values of these moves were −7, +10, and +42 (from the opponent's viewpoint). Which of these three moves do you think that the opponent will choose? The opponent's best move is the +42, so let's assume that the +42 is selected. From our viewpoint, that move would result in a value of −42, so that's what we'll return as our value. In general, our return value will be −1 times the best value that the opponent found:

```
return -1*best_value;
```

As we said, these three steps are the pseudocode for our first implementation of `eval_with_look_ahead`. The steps are a variation of a common game playing algorithm called **minimax search** (which means that we assume that the opponent will move to try to minimize our value, and then we move to try to maximize our value).

If you get the game class from `www.cs.colorado.edu/~main/chapter14/`, you'll find that the actual `eval_with_look_ahead` has one other improvement by using a second parameter:

```
int eval_with_look_ahead(int look_ahead, int beat_this);
```

The extra parameter, `beat_this`, is the value of another move that we have been considering. If we discover that we can't beat the value of that other move, then we'll stop the evaluation process—there's no point in continuing if we know that we can't do better than some other move that we've already examined. This process of cutting short a minimax search is called **alpha-beta pruning**. You might analyze alpha-beta pruning in detail in an artificial intelligence class. For now, you can just study our complete function in Figure 14.14.

Self-Test Exercises for Section 14.3

15. Where can a protected member of a class be used?
16. What was one situation where a virtual member function is required?
17. When a virtual member function is activated, how is the correct version of the function chosen?
18. What is a pure virtual function and when is it used?
19. For the base class definition in Exercise 8, write a pure virtual function prototype that calculates the BMR (basal metabolic rate). The function has no parameters and returns a float. You will implement this function as part of Programming Project 5.
20. Implement the `make_move` function for the `connect4` game.
21. What is alpha-beta pruning?

FIGURE 14.14   Evaluate with Look Ahead Using Alpha-Beta Pruning

Member Function Implementation

```
int game::eval_with_look_ahead(int look_ahead, int beat_this)
// Evaluate a board position with look ahead.
// --int look_ahead: How deep the look ahead should go to evaluate the move.
// --int beat_this: Value of another move that we're considering. If the current board position
//    can't beat this, then cut it short.
// The return value is large if the position is good for the player who just moved.
{
    queue<string> moves;     // All possible opponent moves
    int value;               // Value of a board position after opponent moves
    int best_value;          // Evaluation of best opponent move
    game* future;     // Pointer to a future version of this game

    // Base case:
    if (look_ahead == 0 || is_game_over( ))
        if (last_mover( ) == COMPUTER)
            return evaluate( );
        else
            return -evaluate( );

    // Recursive case:
    compute_moves(moves);
    best_value = INT_MIN;
    while (!moves.empty( ))
    {
        future = clone( );
        future->make_move(moves.front( ));
        value = future->eval_with_look_ahead(look_ahead-1, best_value);
        delete future;
        if (value > best_value)
        {
            if (-value <= beat_this)
                return INT_MIN + 1; // Alpha-beta pruning
            best_value = value;
        }
        moves.pop( );
    }

    // The value was calculated from the opponent's perspective.
    // The answer we return should be from the player's perspective, so multiply times -1:
    return -best_value;
}
```

www.cs.colorado.edu/~main/chapter14/game.cxx   **WWW**

CHAPTER SUMMARY

- Object-oriented programming supports the use of *reusable components* by permitting new *derived classes* to be declared, which automatically *inherit* all members of an existing base class.
- All members of a base class are inherited by the derived class, but only the nonprivate members of the base class can be accessed by the programmer who implements the derived class. This is why most of our examples of base classes do not specify the precise form of the private members of the base class.
- The connection between a derived class and its base class can often be characterized by the *is-a* relationship. For example, an herbivore *is-a* particular kind of animal, so it makes sense to implement `herbivore` as a derived class of the `animal` base class.
- An abstract base class (such as the game class) can provide a common framework that is needed by many derived classes. An abstract base class has one or more pure virtual functions, which are functions that must be overridden before the class can be used.

FURTHER READING

This chapter has introduced the concept of derived classes and inheritance, which is a central concept for OOP programming. In your future programming, further extensions of inheritance are likely to be important. For example, C++ permits **multiple inheritance**, where a single derived class inherits members from several base classes. To learn more about inheritance, multiple inheritance, and virtual member functions, you can consult a comprehensive C++ language guide such as *C++ Primer* by Stanley B. Lippman and Josée Lajoie.

Further analysis of minimax and alpha-beta pruning is covered in textbooks such as *Artificial Intelligence* by Patrick Henry Winston.

? Solutions to Self-Test Exercises

1. In both cases, the public members of the base class are available to the derived class. In a public base class, the public members are available as public members of the derived class. In a private base class, the public members of the base class are only available as private members of the derived class.

2. The definition for the derived class is shown here, along with the implementation of the new member function:

```cpp
class daylight_clock : public clock
{
public:
    bool is_day( ) const;
};

bool daylight_clock::is_day( ) const
{
    if (is_morning( ))
        return (get_hour( ) >= 7);
    else
        return (get_hour( ) < 7);
}
```

3. The derived class receives an automatic default constructor (which calls the default constructor for the base class and then calls the default constructor for any member variables of the derived class). The derived class also receives an automatic copy constructor (which calls the copy constructor for the base class and then calls the copy constructor for any member variables of the derived class).

4. The assignment is not legal, because an object of the base class (coat) cannot be used as if it were an object of the derived class.

5. The automatic assignment operator calls the assignment operator for the base class and then calls the assignment operator for any member variables of the derived class. The automatic destructor first calls the destructor for any member variables of the derived class, and then calls the destructor for the base class.

6. The NoonAlarm overrides the advance member function of the ordinary clock:

```cpp
class noon_alarm : public clock
{
public:
    void advance(int minutes);
};

void noon_alarm::advance(int minutes)
// Library facilities used: iostream
{
    int until_noon;

    // Calculate number of minutes until
    // noon.
    if (is_morning( ))
        until_noon =
            60 * (12-get_hour( ))
            - get_minute( );
    else if (get_hour( ) != 12)
        until_noon =
            60 * (24 - get_hour( ))
            - get_minute( );
    else
        until_noon =
            60 * 24
            - get_minute( );

    // Maybe print an alarm message.
    if (minutes > 0)
        if (minutes >= until_noon)
            cout << "Alarm!";
    // Call the base member function.
    clock::advance(minutes);
}
```

7.

8. A class definition of person:

```cpp
class person
{
public:
    person();
    person(string name, double weight,
           date birthdate, char gender);
    double set_weight(double weight);
    double get_weight() const;
    int get_age() const;
private:
    string name;
    date birthdate;
    double weight;
    char gender;
};
```

9. A constructor for the derived class adult:

```cpp
adult::adult(
        string name,
        double weight,
        date birthdate,
        char gender)
        :person
          (name, weight, birthdate, gender)
{}
```

10. The plant definition is

```cpp
class plant : public organism
{
public:
    // CONSTRUCTOR
    plant(double init_size = 0,
          double init_rate = 0);
    // MODIFICATION FUNCTIONS
    void nibbled_on(double amount);
};
```

The member functions are implemented here:

```cpp
plant::plant(double init_size,
             double init_rate)
: organism(init_size, init_rate)
{
    // All work is done by the organism
    // constructor.
}
```

```
void plant::
nibbled_on(double amount)
// Library functions used: cassert
{
    assert(amount >= 0);
    assert(amount <= get_size( ));
    alter_size(-amount);
}
```

11. See the solution in Figure 14.10 on page 699.

12. Here is one solution:
```
const int N = 10;
const int SELECT = 5;
const organism SAMPLE(16, 1);
vector<organism> blobs(N, SAMPLE);
int i, index;
double answer;
vector<organism>::iterator it;

for (i = 1; i <= SELECT; ++i)
{
    index = rand( ) % N;
    blobs[index].assign_rate(2);
}

answer = 0;
for (it = blobs.begin( );
     it != blobs.end( );
     ++it)
        answer +=
        it->get_rate();

cout << answer << "total of rates\n";
```

13. rand selected one organism twice (and three other organisms were selected once each).

14. We'll leave some of this to you, but here is the new member function:
```
void carnivore::chase
(animal& prey, double chance)
// Library facilities used: cassert, cstdlib
{
    assert(chance >= 0);
    assert(chance <= 1);
    if (chance > 0)
        if (rand()/double(RAND_MAX)
                        < chance)
        {
            eat(prey.get_size( ));
            prey.death( );
        }
}
```

15. A protected member can be used (and overridden by a derived class) but cannot be used outside of a derived class.

16. The base class has a member function f, which activates another member function g. This g member function will be overridden in a derived class. When an object of the derived class activates f, it will use the base class version of f. But within f, we want it to use the overridden g from the derived class.

17. The correct version of a virtual member function is only determined during run time. During execution, the program selects a member function based on the data type of the object that activated the method.

18. The class does not provide any implementation of a pure virtual function. Because there is no implementation, any class with a pure virtual function is called an abstract class and no instances of an abstract class may appear in a program. The pure virtual fuctions are expected to be overriden in the derived classes.

19. `virtual double calculate_bmr() = 0;`

20. Here is one solution using the Standard Library function atoi to convert a string to an integer (see Appendix G):
```
void connect4::make_move
(const string& move)
// Library facilities used: cassert, cstdlib
{
    int row, column;

    assert(is_legal(move));
    column = atoi(move.c_str( ));
    row = many_used[column]++;
    data[row][column] = next_mover( );
    most_recent_column = column;
    game::make_move(move);
}
```

21. Alpha-beta pruning is the process of stopping an evaluation, such as a minimax search, if it cannot produce a better solution than one that has already been determined.

1 A *set* is like a *bag*, except that a set does not allow multiple copies of any element. If you try to insert a new copy of an item that is already present in a set, then the set simply remains unchanged. For this project, implement a set as a new class that is derived from one of your bags. Your implementation should override only the `insert` member function.

2 Rewrite the pond life program from Figure 14.10 on page 697 so that the values declared at the start of the program are no longer constant. The program's user should be able to enter values for all of these constants. Also, extend the program so that the fish are more realistic. In particular, the fish should be born at a small size and grow to some maximum size. Each fish should also have a weekly food requirement that is proportional to its current size.

3 Extend the `organism` object hierarchy from Section 14.2 so that there is a new class `carnivore` as described in Self-Test Exercise 14 on page 702. Use the hierarchy in a model of life on a small island that contains shrubs, geese that eat the shrubs, and foxes that eat the geese. The program should allow the user to vary the initial conditions on the island (such as number of foxes, the amount of food needed to sustain a fox, and so on).

4 Implement a bag template class as a derived class of a list. Use the list from Figure 14.12 on page 703. The bag should have all of the operations from Figure 6.8 on page 336.

5 Implement the people base class of Self-Test Exercise 8 on page 692. Also, implement male and female derived classes and calculate BMR based on the following formulas:
Male: $66 + (30.14 \times$ weight in pounds$) + (1.97 \times$ height in inches$) - (6.8 \times$ age$)$; Female: $655 + (21.12 \times$ weight in kilos$) + (.71 \times$ height in inches$) - (4.7 \times$ age$)$.

Expand the class hierarchy to include a function to calculate recommended daily calorie intake. The calorie intake equals the BMR multiplied by a constant that indicates physical activity levels. The multiplicative constants are sedentary (1.2), moderately active (1.55), lightly active (1.35), and highly active (1.725).

6 Write a program that maintains a vector of people (from the previous project) to represent health club members. The program should give the user menu choices to modify and view a person's health information. Also include functions to compute the average age, weight, and activity level of all club members by gender.

7 Redo Programming Project 13 of Chapter 10 to store other forms of media (such as CD, DVD, VHS, and cassette tape). Create a base class item, and derive the other forms, including books, as you see fit. The base class should contain the ISBN, but derived classes may contain different members depending on their media type. Users should be able to view and modify items as before, but also provide functionality to view items of a particular media.

15

Graphs

So many gods, so many creeds,
So many paths that wind and wind,
When just the art of being kind
Is all this sad world needs.

ELLA WHEELER WILCOX
The World's Need

LEARNING OBJECTIVES

When you complete Chapter 15, you will be able to...

- follow and explain graph-based algorithms using the usual computer science terminology.
- design and implement classes for labeled or unlabeled graphs.
- list the order in which nodes are visited for the two common graph traversals (breadth-first and depth-first) and implement these algorithms.
- simulate the steps of simple path algorithms (such as determining whether a path exists) and be able to design and implement such algorithms.
- simulate the steps of Dijkstra's shortest-path algorithm and be able to implement it.

CHAPTER CONTENTS

Graphs

Graphs are the most general data structure in this text. In fact, it's fair to say that graphs are the ultimate commonly used data structure. Many of the data structures that you will study in the future can be expressed in terms of graphs. This chapter provides an introduction to graphs and their algorithms, including the implementation of a graph class in C++.

15.1   GRAPH DEFINITIONS

A graph, like a tree, is a nonlinear data structure consisting of nodes and links between the nodes. In the trees that we have already seen, the nodes are somewhat orderly: The root is linked to its children, which are linked to their children, and so on to the leaves. But in a graph, even this modicum of order is gone. Graph nodes may be linked in any pattern—or lack of pattern—dependent only upon the needs of an application.

Graphs occur in several varieties. We'll start with the simplest form: *undirected graphs.*

graphs occur in several varieties, the simplest of which is an undirected graph

Undirected Graphs

An undirected graph is a set of nodes and a set of links between the nodes. Each node is called a **vertex**, each link is called an **edge**, and each edge connects two vertices. Undirected graphs are drawn by putting a circle for each vertex and a line for each edge. For example, here is a drawing of an undirected graph with five vertices and six edges:

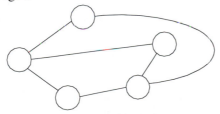

Often we'll need to refer to the vertices and edges of a graph, and we can do this by writing names next to each vertex and edge. For example, the following graph has vertices named v_0, v_1, v_2, v_3, and v_4, whereas its edges are named e_0, e_1, e_2, e_3, e_4, and e_5:

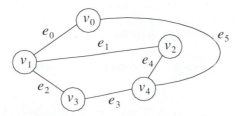

in a drawing, the placement of the vertices and edges is unimportant

In a drawing such as this, the actual placement of the vertices and edges is unimportant. The only important points are which vertices are connected and which edges are used to connect them. So, when you are feeling like a contortionist, you might draw the graph differently:

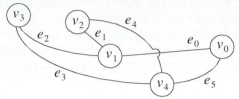

This is the same as the previous graph—we have just drawn it differently.

Here's a formal definition of these graphs:

Undirected Graphs

An **undirected graph** is a finite set of vertices together with a finite set of edges. Both sets might be empty (no vertices and no edges), which is called the **empty graph**.

Each edge is associated with two vertices. We sometimes say that the edge **connects** its two vertices. The order of the two connected vertices is unimportant, so it does not matter whether we say "This edge connects vertices *u* and *v*," or "This edge connects vertices *v* and *u*."

An edge is even allowed to connect a single vertex to itself—we'll see examples of this later, and we'll also see several different variants of graphs. Many applications will require additional data to be attached to each vertex or to each edge, but even without these extras, we can give the flavor of a graph application with an example.

PROGRAMMING EXAMPLE: **Undirected State Graphs**

As an example of a problem where graphs are useful, we'll look at a little game. To start the game, you place three coins on the table in a line, as shown here:

     The start of the game

At the start of the game, the middle coin is "tails" and the other two are "heads." The goal is to change the configuration of the coins so that the middle coin is heads and the other two are tails, like this:

     The goal of the game

Now, this wouldn't be much of a game without a few rules. Here are the rules:

1. You may flip the middle coin (from heads to tails or vice versa) whenever you want to.

2. You may flip one of the end coins (from heads to tails or vice versa) only if the other two coins are the same as each other (both heads or both tails).

You are not allowed to change the coins in any other way, such as shuffling them around. But within these rules you may flip coins. For example, if you start with the position *head-tail-head*, then the first rule allows you to flip the middle coin resulting in three heads:

       From the start position, flip the middle coin.

If you play the game for a while, you'll soon figure out how to get from the starting position (*head-tail-head*) to the goal position (*tail-head-tail*) within the limits of the rules. But our *real* goal is to figure out how a graph can aid in solving this kind of problem—even if the rules were beyond human manageability. The graph we'll use is called an undirected state graph, which is a graph where each of the vertices represents one of the possible configurations of the game. These configurations are called "states," and the coin game has eight states ranging from *head-head-head* to *tail-tail-tail*. Therefore, these eight states are the vertices of the state graph for the coin game. Figure 15.1 shows each vertex as a large oval so that we have room inside the oval to draw the state of the coins. Two vertices of the undirected state graph are connected by an edge whenever it is possible to move back and forth between the two states using one of the rules. For example, Rule 1 allows us to move between *head-head-head* and *head-tail-head*, so one of the edges in the graph goes from the topmost state

a graph may represent the legal moves in a game

FIGURE 15.1   Undirected State Graph for the Coin Game

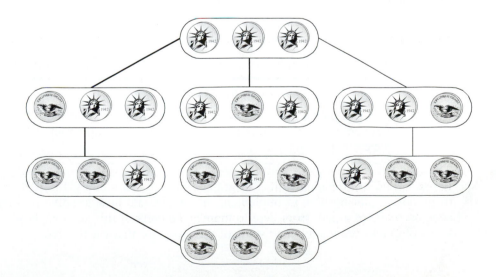

in Figure 15.1 (*head-head-head*) to the state directly below it (*head-tail-head*). Figure 15.1 shows a total of eight edges: The four vertical edges come from Rule 1, and the four diagonal edges come from Rule 2. You may have noticed a curious fact about our rules: Whenever it is possible to move from one state to another (such as moving *head-head-head* to *head-tail-head*), it is also possible to move in the other direction (such as *head-tail-head* to *head-head-head*). If you study the rules, you will see that this is true. The way we have drawn the edges reflects this symmetry. The edges are drawn as line segments connecting two vertices, with no indication as to which direction a movement must proceed. In this game, if an edge connects two vertices v_0 and v_1, then a movement is permitted in both directions, from v_0 to v_1, or from v_1 to v_0. This property of the coin game is the reason why we may use an undirected state graph. Later, we will see more complex games where movements might be permitted in only one direction, and hence we will need more complex graphs.

Once we know the undirected state graph, the game becomes a problem of finding a path from one vertex to another, where the path is only allowed to follow edges. According to our rules, we need to find a path from the vertex *head-tail-head* to the vertex *tail-head-tail*, and one such path consists of edges 1 through 5, highlighted here:

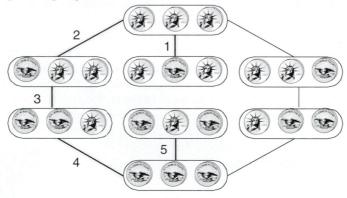

The coin game is a small problem, and the state graph isn't vital to the solution. But the important idea of the example goes beyond this small game:

Graphs in Problem Solving

Often, a problem can be represented as a graph, and the solution to the problem is obtained by solving a problem on the corresponding graph.

Because of this wide applicability of graphs, we will study many different kinds of graphs, exploring how to implement the graphs and how to solve problems such as "Is there a path from here to there?" The rest of this section shows the kinds of graphs we'll study and some of the problems that we'll solve.

Directed Graphs

The graphs we have seen so far are all **undirected**, which means that each edge connects two vertices with no particular orientation or direction. An edge just connects two vertices—there is no "first vertex" or "second vertex." But there is another kind of graph called a **directed graph**, where each edge has an orientation connecting its first vertex (called the edge's **source**) to its second vertex (the edge's **target**). Here is the formal definition of a directed graph:

Directed Graphs

A **directed graph** is a finite set of "vertices" together with a finite set of "edges." Both sets might be empty (no vertices and no edges), which is called the **empty graph**.

Each edge is associated with two vertices, called its **source** and **target** vertices. We sometimes say that the edge **connects** its source to its target. The order of the two connected vertices *is* important, so it *does* matter whether we say "This edge connects vertex *u* to vertex *v*," or "This edge connects vertex *v* to vertex *u*."

Directed graphs are drawn as diagrams with circles representing the vertices and *arrows* representing the edges. Each arrow starts at an edge's source and has the arrowhead at the edge's target, for example:

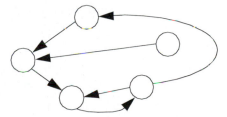

One application of directed graphs is a state graph for a game where reversing a move is sometimes forbidden. For such a game, the state graph might have an edge from a source v_1 to a target v_2 but *not* include the reverse edge from v_2 to v_1. This would indicate that the game's rules permit a move from state v_1 to state v_2, but not the other way around. For example, we could use a large state graph to represent the different states in a game of tic-tac-toe. Two of the many possible states are shown next, with a directed edge between them.

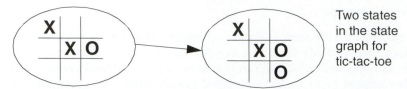

Two states in the state graph for tic-tac-toe

There is a directed arrow between these two states, since it is possible to move from the first state to the second state (by placing an O), but it is not possible to move in the other direction (since once an O is placed, it may not be removed).

More Graph Terminology

Loops. A **loop** is an edge that connects a vertex to itself. In the diagrams that we've been using, this is drawn as a line (or arrow) with both ends at the same location. The highlighted edges at the left of these two graphs are both loops:

Path. A **path** in a graph is a sequence of vertices, $p_0, p_1, \ldots p_m$, such that each adjacent pair of vertices p_i and p_{i+1} are connected by an edge. In a directed graph, the connection must go from the source p_i to the target p_{i+1}.

Multiple edges. In principle, a graph may have two or more edges connecting the same two vertices in the same direction. These are called **multiple edges**. In a diagram, each edge is drawn separately, for example:

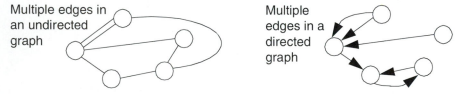

Multiple edges in an undirected graph

Multiple edges in a directed graph

Note that the two edges at the bottom of the directed graph are not multiple edges because they connect the two vertices in different directions. Many applications do not require multiple edges. In fact, many implementations of graphs do not permit multiple edges. Throughout the graph implementations of this chapter, we will specify which implementations permit multiple edges and which implementations forbid them.

Simple graphs. The simplest of graphs have no loops and no multiple edges. Appropriately enough, these graphs are called **simple graphs**. Many applications require only simple directed graphs, or even simple undirected graphs.

Airline Routes Example

Let's examine a directed graph that represents the flights of a small airline called Crocodile Airlines. Each vertex in the graph is a city, and each edge represents a regularly scheduled flight from one city to another. Crocodile's complete collection of flights is shown below. Notice that the graph is directed; for example, it's possible to fly from Darwin to Canberra on a nonstop flight, but not the other way around.

airline routes form a directed graph

The point of expressing the flights as a graph is that questions about the airline can be answered by carrying out common algorithms on the graph. For example, a sheep farmer might wonder what is the fewest number of flights required to fly from Black Stump to Melbourne. This is an example of a *shortest path* problem that we will solve in Section 15.4. With a small graph such as this one you can probably see that the shortest path from Black Stump to Melbourne consists of four edges, but a manual examination might not suffice for a larger graph.

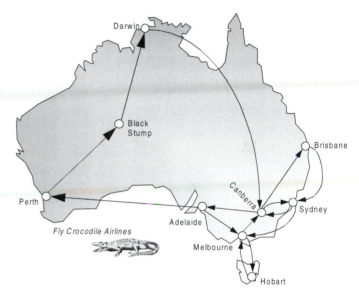

Self-Test Exercises for Section 15.1

1. How many vertices and edges does the airline graph have? How many loops? How would you interpret a loop in this graph?

2. Is the airline graph a directed graph? Why or why not?

3. Is the airline graph a simple graph? Why or why not?

4. The degree of a vertex *v* in an undirected graph is the number of times *v* is an endpoint of an edge. A loop at the vertex contributes twice to the degree. What is the degree of each vertex in the graph in the margin?

5. A vertex in a directed graph has an in-degree, which is the number of edges with *v* as the target vertex, and an out-degree, which is the number of edges with *v* as their source vertex. What are the in-degree and out-degree of the following vertices in the airline graph: Canberra, Sydney, and Melbourne?

6. A *cycle* in a directed graph is a path that begins and ends at the same vertex. The *length* of the cycle is the number of edges. Give example cycles of length 3 and 5 in the airline graph by naming the vertices in the cycle.

7. Suppose we have four coins in the coin game instead of just three. At the start of the game, the coins are in a line, with the two end coins heads

and the other two coins tails. The goal is to change the configuration so that the two end coins are tails, and the other two coins are heads. There are three rules for this game: (1) Either of the end coins may be flipped whenever you want to. (2) A middle coin may be flipped from heads to tails only if the coin to its immediate right is already heads. (3) A middle coin may be flipped from tails to heads only if the coin to its immediate left is already tails. Your mission: Draw the directed state graph for this game, and determine whether it is possible to go from the start configuration to the goal. Why does the graph need to be directed?

15.2 GRAPH IMPLEMENTATIONS

"I could spin a web if I tried," said Wilbur, boasting. "I've just never tried."

E. B. WHITE
Charlotte's Web

Different kinds of graphs require different kinds of implementations, but the fundamental concepts of all graph implementations are similar. We'll look at several representations for one particular kind of graph: directed graphs in which loops are allowed. Some of the representations allow multiple edges, and some do not. In each of the representations, the vertices of the graph are named with numbers 0, 1, 2, ..., so that we may refer to each vertex individually by saying "vertex 0," "vertex 1," and so on.

Representing Graphs with an Adjacency Matrix

Let's start with a directed graph with no multiple edges. The graph's edges may be represented in a square grid of boolean (true/false) values, called the graph's **adjacency matrix**. Here is an example of a graph with four vertices and its adjacency matrix:

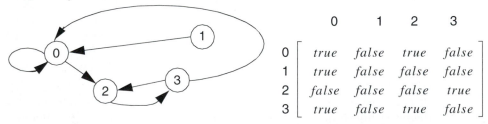

	0	1	2	3
0	*true*	*false*	*true*	*false*
1	*true*	*false*	*false*	*false*
2	*false*	*false*	*false*	*true*
3	*true*	*false*	*true*	*false*

a true component at row i and column j indicates an edge from vertex i to vertex j

Each component of the adjacency matrix indicates whether a certain edge is present. For example, is there an edge from vertex 0 to vertex 2? Yes, because true appears at row 0 of column 2. But is there also an edge from vertex 2 to vertex 0? No, because false appears at row 2 of column 0. The general rule for using an adjacency matrix is given here:

> ### Adjacency Matrix
>
> An **adjacency matrix** is a square grid of true/false values that represent the edges of a graph. If the graph contains *n* vertices, then the grid contains *n* rows and *n* columns. For two vertex numbers *i* and *j*, the component at row *i* and column *j* is true if there is an edge from vertex *i* to vertex *j*; otherwise the component is false.

Using a Two-Dimensional Array to Store an Adjacency Matrix

In C++, an adjacency matrix can be stored in a **two-dimensional array** in which every component has two indexes rather than the usual one index. Programmers usually view a two-dimensional array as a grid of elements, where the first index provides the row number of a component, and the second index provides the column number of a component. In a declaration of a two-dimensional array, the number of rows is given in square brackets, followed by the number of columns (also in square brackets). For example, a program might require a two-dimensional array of double numbers with 12 rows and 8 columns, as declared here:

in a two-dimensional array, every component has two indexes

```
double budget[12][8];
```
Declaring a two-dimensional array with 12 rows and 8 columns

Within the program, the individual components of the two-dimensional array can be accessed by specifying both indexes. For example, we can assign 3.14 to row number 2 and column number 6 with this assignment statement:

```
budget[2][6] = 3.14;
```

As with an ordinary array, the index numbers begin with zero, so our budget has rows numbered from 0 to 11, and columns numbered from 0 to 7.

For an adjacency matrix, we use a two-dimensional array with one row and one column for each vertex of the graph. The components of the array are boolean true/false values. For example, the adjacency matrix for a graph with four vertices can be stored using this declaration of a two-dimensional array:

```
bool adjacency_matrix[4][4];
```

The component `adjacency_matrix[i][j]` contains true if there is an edge from vertex *i* to vertex *j*. A false value indicates no edge. Edges of a graph can be added (by placing true in a location of the matrix) or removed (by placing false). Once the adjacency matrix has been set, an application can examine locations of the matrix to determine which edges are present and which are missing.

Representing Graphs with Edge Lists

Again, suppose we have a directed graph with no multiple edges. Such a graph can be represented by creating a linked list for each vertex. An example appears at the top of the next page.

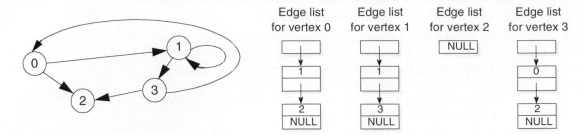

To understand the example, look at the linked list for vertex number 0. This list contains 1 and 2, which means that there is an edge from vertex 0 to vertex 1, and a second edge from vertex 0 to vertex 2. In general, the linked list for vertex number *i* is a list of vertex numbers following this rule:

Linked List Representation of Graphs

A directed graph with *n* vertices can be represented by *n* different linked lists. List number *i* provides the connections for vertex *i*. To be specific: For each entry *j* in list number *i*, there is an edge from *i* to *j*.

Loops are allowed in this representation; for example, look at the list for vertex 1 in the edge lists just given. Number 1 appears on this list itself, so there is an edge from vertex 1 to vertex 1 in the graph. We may also have vertices that are not the source of any edge—for example, vertex 2 in the graph above. Since vertex 2 is not the source of any edge, the edge list for vertex 2 is empty. If we allow the same element to appear more than once on the list, then multiple edges could also be allowed. But often, multiple edges are not allowed.

In a graph with *n* vertices, there are *n* edge lists. The head pointers for the *n* edge lists can be stored in an array of *n* head pointers. When we need to determine whether an edge exists from vertex *i* to vertex *j*, we check to see whether *j* appears on list number *i*.

Representing Graphs with Edge Sets

Another implementation of graphs uses the set class from the C++ Standard Library. To represent a graph with 10 vertices, we can declare an array of 10 sets of integers, as shown here:

```
set<int> connections[10];
```

Using this representation, a set such as `connections[i]` contains the vertex numbers of all of the vertices that vertex *i* is connected to. For example, suppose that `connections[3]` contains the numbers 1 and 2. In this case, there is an edge from vertex 3 to vertex 1, and another edge from vertex 3 to vertex 2.

Which Representation Is Best?

If the space is available, then an adjacency matrix is easier to implement and generally easier to use than edge lists or edge sets. But sometimes there are other considerations. For example, how often will you be doing each of these operations:

1. Adding or removing edges
2. Checking whether a particular edge is present
3. Iterating a loop that executes one time for each edge with a particular source vertex i

The first two operations require only a small constant amount of time with the adjacency matrices. But in the worst case, both (1) and (2) require $O(n)$ operations with the edge list representation (where n is the number of vertices). This worst case occurs when the operation must traverse an entire edge list, and that edge list might contain as many as n edges. With edge sets, both (1) and (2) are somewhat fast ($O(\log n)$) because the Standard Library set implementations generally store items in a balanced tree as discussed in Chapter 11).

On the other hand, the edge lists are efficient for the third operation. With an edge list, the third operation can be carried out by simply stepping through the list one element at a time. The time required is $O(e)$, where e is the number of edges that have vertex i as their source. The set class also provides operations to step through the elements of the set one at a time (using an iterator). In this way, both edge lists and edge sets are likely to require just $O(e)$ operations to step through the edges with a particular source vertex. But with an adjacency matrix, the act of stepping through the edges with source vertex i requires each entry in row i to be examined. This traversal of the entire row is necessary just to see whether each entry is true or false. This always requires $O(n)$ time, where n is the number of vertices.

In general, your choice of representations should be based on your expectations as to which operations are most frequent. One last consideration is the average number of edges originating at a vertex. If each vertex has only a few edges (a so-called **sparse graph**), then an adjacency matrix is mostly wasted space filled with the value false.

PROGRAMMING EXAMPLE: Labeled Graph Class

Now we'll implement a class for directed graphs with no multiple edges. This class has only a few member functions; for example, there is no way to remove vertices. The simple form of the first `graph` class provides a sharp focus on graphs and their algorithms.

With our `graph` class, each graph is initially created with no vertices and no edges. There is a member function to add new vertices. For an n-vertex graph, these vertices are always numbered from zero to $n-1$. Once a graph has some vertices, other functions add or remove edges. Each graph has a maximum number of vertices specified by the constant `graph::MAXIMUM`. We could avoid a maximum number of vertices by using dynamic memory, but doing so will detract from our primary focus, so we leave it for the Programming Projects in this chapter.

When we implement the graph, the number of vertices will be stored in the member variable named `many_vertices`, which may be anywhere from zero to `MAXIMUM` minus one. A graph's edges are stored in an adjacency matrix, which is implemented as the two-dimensional boolean array called `edges`. The `edges` array has `MAXIMUM` rows and `MAXIMUM` columns, but keep in mind that we might not be using all of this array. For example, if `many_vertices` is 3, then we will use only the nine components ranging from `edges[0][0]` to `edges[2][2]`.

Our `graph` class will have one extra feature: The vertices will have information attached to them in the same way that we attached information to tree nodes. For example, in the airline route graph on page 729, each vertex is associated with a city name. The placement of information at each vertex makes the graph a **labeled graph**, and the information itself is called a vertex's **label**. Of course, the information might be any data type—integers, doubles, strings, you name it—which suggests that a class for labeled graphs should be implemented as a template class, with the type of the labels determined by a template parameter.

The labels of the vertices will be stored in a private member variable named `labels`, which is an ordinary one-dimensional array. The label for vertex number `i` will be stored in `labels[i]`. Thus, our graph definition has a total of three member variables, listed in the private section shown here:

```
template <class Item>          If your compiler does not permit
class graph                    initialization of static constants,
{                              see Appendix E.
public:
    // MEMBER CONSTANTS
    static const std::size_t MAXIMUM = 20;
    ‖ We'll discuss the member functions in a moment.
private:
    bool edges[MAXIMUM][MAXIMUM];
    Item labels[MAXIMUM];
    std::size_t many_vertices;
};
```

Member Functions to Add Vertices and Edges

When a graph is initialized with the constructor, it has no vertices and no edges. At any time, the current number of vertices can be obtained from a constant member function named `size`. Thus, a newly constructed graph g has `g.size( )` equal to zero.

Two member functions, `add_vertex` and `add_edge`, allow us to add new vertices and edges, with these specifications:

```
void add_vertex(const Item& label);
// Precondition: size( ) < MAXIMUM.
// Postcondition: The size of the graph has been increased by adding
// one new vertex. This new vertex has the specified label and no edges.

void add_edge(size_t source, size_t target);
// Precondition: (source < size( )) and (target < size( )).
// Postcondition: The graph has all the edges that it originally had, and
// also has another edge from the specified source to the specified target.
// (If this edge was already present, then the graph is unchanged.)
```

For example, the following four statements create the two-vertex graph shown in the picture. In this graph, vertex number zero (v_0) contains the *double* number 3.14, and vertex number one (v_1) contains the double number 2.17:

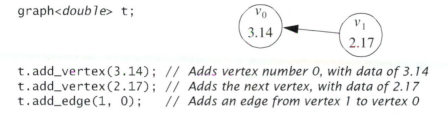

```
graph<double> t;
```

```
t.add_vertex(3.14);  // Adds vertex number 0, with data of 3.14
t.add_vertex(2.17);  // Adds the next vertex, with data of 2.17
t.add_edge(1, 0);    // Adds an edge from vertex 1 to vertex 0
```

As you can see from the example, the add_vertex member function of the graph class requires an argument, which is the label of the newly added vertex.

Labeled Graph Class—Overloading the Subscript Operator

Once a graph is created, we want to access its vertex labels by using the usual "square bracket" notation from C++. For example, suppose that g is a 10-vertex labeled graph. To print the label of vertex 3, we would like to write this:

```
cout << g[3];
```

When used this way, the square brackets are called the **subscript operator**.

We also want the subscript operator to allow assignments and other changes to the labels. For example, suppose that g's labels are integers. We want to be able to change the label of a vertex with a simple assignment statement such as this:

```
g[3] = 42;◄———Change the label of vertex 3 to 42.
```

In C++, we can overload the subscript operator to behave in exactly this way. The overloading of the subscript operator is accomplished with the highlighted prototype in the following class definition:

```
template <class Item>
class graph
{
public:
    ...
    Item& operator [ ] (std::size_t vertex);
    ...
```

In this definition, you can see the prototype for the overloaded subscript operator. Note that the return value is a reference. As discussed on page 314, this
allows us to use the operator to actually change a label (such as the assignment
statement g[3] = 42). An ordinary return value of Item would permit us to get
a current value, but it would not provide any way to change a label.

The full implementation of the overloaded subscript operator is shown here:

```
template <class Item>
Item& graph<Item>::operator [ ] (std::size_t vertex)
{
    assert(vertex < size( ));
    return labels[vertex];
}
```

The return statement, return labels[vertex], indicates that any changes
that the calling program makes directly on the return result will actually change
the component labels[vertex] in the private member variable labels.

A Const Version of the Subscript Operator

The subscript operator described above returns a reference to the label of the
vertex, allowing the label to be changed. Therefore the operator is not a constant
member function, and it cannot be used with a graph that is declared with the
const keyword (such as const graph<int> g). This is similar to the data
member function from our node class for linked lists (see page 316). The solution is to provide a second version of the subscript operator, which returns only
a copy of the vertex's label, as shown here:

```
template <class Item>
Item  graph<Item>::operator [ ] (std::size_t vertex) const
{
    assert(vertex < size( ));
    return labels[vertex];
}
```

The only difference between this and the earlier version is that the return type of
the new version is Item (rather than a reference Item&). Therefore, it is not possible to use the new version to change a vertex, and the new version can be
declared as a constant member function.

Labeled Graph Class—Neighbors Function

Even though we're implementing our graph using an adjacency matrix, the class will also have a member function, called `neighbors`, that computes an edge list for a specified vertex. This edge list will be provided as a set of integers, using the Standard Library set class. The vector will contain all of the vertex numbers for the targets of edges that start at a specified source. Here's an example to show the integer array that's computed and returned by `g.neighbors(3)` for a particular graph:

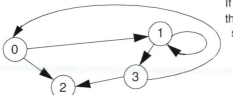

If g is the graph shown here, then `g.neighbors(3)` returns the set containing 0 and 2.

This means that vertex 3 is the source of two edges, going to vertices 0 and 2.

The `neighbors` method may take $O(n)$ time to compute one of its sets, but once an array is available, it can be used to quickly traverse all the neighbors of a vertex. Notice that the size of the set computed by `g.neighbors(i)` is equal to the number of edges that have vertex `i` as the source, and this could even be zero (resulting in a set with zero elements).

As an example, suppose that `flight` is a graph with `string` labels and at least four vertices. The following code will print the vertex numbers of all of the neighbors of vertex 3:

```
set<size_t> connections;
set<size_t>::iterator it;
connections = flight.neighbors(3);

for (it = connections.begin( ); it != connections.end( ); ++it)
    cout << *it << endl;
```

A slightly different loop will print the *labels* of the neighbors of vertex 3:

```
for (it = connections.begin( ); it != connections.end( ); ++it)
    cout << flight[*it] << endl;
```

Labeled Graph Class—Implementation

The header file and implementation file for the graph class are given in Figure 15.2. In addition to the member functions that we have already mentioned, there is also a function to remove an edge from a graph, and a function to determine whether a particular edge exists.

Note that throughout the class definition and implementation we have used the notation `std::size_t` and `std::set` since `size_t` and `set` are part of the `std` namespace and we must not place a using directive in a template class (see page 292).

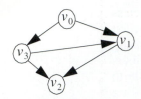

Self-Test Exercises for Section 15.2

8. Write an adjacency matrix for the graph drawn in the margin.

9. Consider this adjacency matrix. Are there any loops in the graph?

	[0]	[1]	[2]	[3]
[0]	false	true	false	true
[1]	false	true	true	false
[2]	false	false	false	false
[3]	false	true	true	true

Which node has the highest in-degree? Which node has the highest out-degree?

10. Write a new `graph` member function to remove the highest-numbered vertex from a graph.

11. We have assumed that there are no multiple edges in a graph, and therefore we could store simple true/false in the adjacency matrix. Describe how adjacency matrixes might be used if the graphs have multiple edges.

12. Compare and contrast the adjacency lists and edge lists.

13. Write a function with one parameter that is a graph. The return value of the function is the total number of edges in the graph.

14. Suppose that g is a graph with integer labels. What is the label of vertex 3 at the three points marked here? Assume that the statements are executed one after another, and i is an integer variable.

```
g[3] = 42;  // Point 1
i = g[3];   // Point 2
i = 43;     // Point 3
```

FIGURE 15.2   Header File for the Graph Class

A Header File

```
// FILE: graph.h (part of the namespace main_savitch_15)
// TEMPLATE CLASS PROVIDED: graph<Item> (a class for labeled graphs)
//     The vertices of an n-vertex graph are numbered from zero to n-1. Each vertex has a
//     label of type Item. It may be any of the C++ built-in types (int, char, etc.), or any
//     class with a default constructor and an assignment operator. The graph may not have
//     multiple edges.
//
// MEMBER CONSTANTS for the graph<Item> template class:
//     static const size_t MAXIMUM = _____
//        graph::MAXIMUM is the maximum number of vertices that a graph can have.
//
// CONSTRUCTOR for the graph<Item> template class:
//     graph( )
//        Postcondition: The graph has been initialized with no vertices and no edges.
```

(continued)

(FIGURE 15.2 continued)

```
//   MODIFICATION MEMBER FUNCTIONS for the graph<Item> template class:
//     void add_vertex(const Item& label)
//        Precondition: size( ) < MAXIMUM.
//        Postcondition: The size of the graph has been increased by adding one new vertex.
//        This new vertex has the specified label and no edges.
//
//     void add_edge(size_t source, size_t target)
//        Precondition: (source < size( )) and (target < size( )).
//        Postcondition: The graph has all the edges that it originally had, and it also has
//        another edge from the specified source to the specified target. (If this edge was
//        already present, then the graph is unchanged.)
//
//     void remove_edge(size_t source, size_t target)
//        Precondition: (source < size( )) and (target < size( )).
//        Postcondition: The graph has all the edges that it originally had except for the edge
//        from the specified source to the specified target. (If this edge was not originally
//        present, then the graph is unchanged.)
//
//     Item& operator [ ] (size_t vertex)
//        Precondition: vertex < size( ).
//        Postcondition: The return value is a reference to the label of the specified vertex.
//
// CONSTANT MEMBER FUNCTIONS for the graph<Item> template class:
//     size_t size( ) const
//        Postcondition: The return value is the number of vertices in the graph.
//
//     bool is_edge(size_t source, size_t target) const
//        Precondition: (source < size( )) and (target < size( )).
//        Postcondition: The return value is true if the graph has an edge from source to target.
//        Otherwise the return value is false.
//
//     set<size_t> neighbors(size_t vertex) const
//        Precondition: (vertex < size( )).
//        Postcondition: The return value is a set that contains all the vertex numbers of
//        vertices that are the target of an edge whose source is at the specified vertex.
//
//     Item operator [ ] (size_t vertex) const
//        Precondition: vertex < size( ).
//        Postcondition: The return value is a reference to the label of the specified vertex.
//        NOTE: This function differs from the other operator [ ] because its return value is
//        simply a copy of the Item (rather than a reference of type Item&). Since this function
//        returns only a copy of the Item, it is a const member function.
//
// VALUE SEMANTICS for the graph<Item> template class:
//     Assignments and the copy constructor may be used with graph<Item> objects.
```

(continued)

(FIGURE 15.2 continued)

```
#ifndef MAIN_SAVITCH_GRAPH_H
#define MAIN_SAVITCH_GRAPH_H
#include <cstdlib>   // Provides size_t
#include <set>       // Provides set

namespace main_savitch_15
{
    template <class Item>
    class graph
    {
    public:
        // MEMBER CONSTANTS
        static const std::size_t MAXIMUM = 20;
        // CONSTRUCTOR
        graph( ) { many_vertices = 0; }
        // MODIFICATION MEMBER FUNCTIONS
        void add_vertex(const Item& label);
        void add_edge(std::size_t source, std::size_t target);
        void remove_edge(std::size_t source, std::size_t target);
        Item& operator [ ] (std::size_t vertex);
        // CONSTANT MEMBER FUNCTIONS
        std::size_t size( ) const { return many_vertices; }
        bool is_edge(std::size_t source, std::size_t target) const;
        std::set<std::size_t> neighbors(std::size_t vertex) const;
        Item operator[ ] (std::size_t vertex) const;
    private:
        bool edges[MAXIMUM][MAXIMUM];
        Item labels[MAXIMUM];
        std::size_t many_vertices;
    };
}

#include "graph.template" // Include the implementation.
#endif
```

If your compiler does not permit initialization of static constants, see Appendix E.

An Implementation File

```
// FILE: graph.template (part of the namespace main_savitch_15)
// TEMPLATE CLASS IMPLEMENTED: graph<Item> (See graph.h for documentation.)
// This file is included in the header file and not compiled separately.
// INVARIANT for the graph class:
//     1. The number of vertices in the graph is stored in the member variable many_vertices.
//        These vertices are numbered from 0 to many_vertices-1.
//     2. edges is the adjacency matrix for the graph (with true in edges[i][j] to indicate an
//        edge from vertex i to vertex j).
//     3. For each i < many_vertices, labels[i] is the label of vertex i.       (continued)
```

(FIGURE 15.2 continued)

```cpp
#include <cassert>       // Provides assert
#include <cstdlib>       // Provides size_t
#include <set>           // Provides set

namespace main_savitch_15
{
    template <class Item>
    const std::size_t graph<Item>::MAXIMUM;

    template <class Item>
    void graph<Item>::add_edge(std::size_t source, std::size_t target)
    // Library facilities used: cassert, cstdlib
    {
        assert(source < size( ));
        assert(target < size( ));
        edges[source][target] = true;
    }

    template <class Item>
    void graph<Item>::add_vertex(const Item& label)
    // Library facilities used: cassert, cstdlib
    {
        std::size_t new_vertex_number;
        std::size_t other_number;

        assert(size( ) < MAXIMUM);
        new_vertex_number = many_vertices;
        ++many_vertices;
        for (other_number = 0; other_number < many_vertices; ++other_number)
        {
            edges[other_number][new_vertex_number] = false;
            edges[new_vertex_number][other_number] = false;
        }
        labels[new_vertex_number] = label;
    }

    template <class Item>
    bool graph<Item>::is_edge(std::size_t source, std::size_t target) const
    // Library facilities used: cassert, cstdlib
    {
        assert(source < size( ));
        assert(target < size( ));
        return edges[source][target];
    }
```

(continued)

(FIGURE 15.2 continued)

```
template <class Item>
Item& graph<Item>::operator [ ] (std::size_t vertex)
// Library facilities used: cassert, cstdlib
{
    assert(vertex < size( ));
    return labels[vertex];       // Returns a reference to the label
}


template <class Item>
Item graph<Item>::operator [ ] (std::size_t vertex) const
// Library facilities used: cassert, cstdlib
{
    assert(vertex < size( ));
    return labels[vertex];       // Returns only a copy of the label
}


template <class Item>
std::set<std::size_t> graph<Item>::neighbors(std::size_t vertex) const
// Library facilities used: cassert, cstdlib, set
{
    std::set<std::size_t> answer;
    std::size_t i;

    assert(vertex < size( ));

    for (i = 0; i < size( ); ++i)
    {
        if (edges[vertex][i])
            answer.insert(i);
    }
    return answer;
}


template <class Item>
void graph<Item>::remove_edge(std::size_t source, std::size_t target)
// Library facilities used: cassert, cstdlib
{
    assert(source < size( ));
    assert(target < size( ));
    edges[source][target] = false;
}
}
```

www.cs.colorado.edu/~main/chapter15/graph.template   **WWW**

15.3 GRAPH TRAVERSALS

In the chapter on trees, we saw three different binary tree traversals. Each traversal visits all of a binary tree's nodes and does some processing at each node. The three traversals had similar recursive implementations, with the distinguishing factor being whether a node was visited before, after, or in between its two children. A graph vertex doesn't have children like a tree node, so the tree traversal algorithms are not immediately applicable to graphs. But there are two common ways of traversing a graph. One of the methods (breadth-first search) uses a queue to keep track of vertices that still need to be visited, and the other method (depth-first search) uses a stack. The depth-first search can also be implemented recursively in a way that does not explicitly use a stack of vertices.

This section discusses the two traversal algorithms and provides implementations of the algorithms (using the `graph` class—Figure 15.2 on page 738). Both of the traversal algorithms have the same underlying purpose: to start at one vertex of a graph (the "start" vertex), process the information contained at that vertex, and then move along an edge to process a neighbor. When the traversal finishes, all of the vertices that can be reached from the start vertex have been processed.

A traversal algorithm must be careful that it doesn't enter a repetitive cycle—for example, moving from the start vertex to a neighbor, from there to the neighbor's neighbor, and possibly from there back to the starting point and back to the same neighbor, and back to the same neighbor's neighbor, and so on. To prevent this potential "spinning your wheels," we will include an ability to *mark* each vertex as it is processed. If a traversal ever returns to a vertex that is already marked, then reprocessing is not done. In drawings, we will indicate a marked vertex by shading it. For example, consider this graph:

when the traversal finishes, all of the vertices that can be reached from the start vertex have been processed

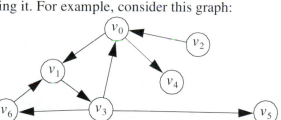

A traversal might begin by processing vertex number 0. We don't really care what kind of processing occurs—maybe the labels are printed out, or perhaps there is more complicated processing. In any case, there will be some processing of vertex number 0, and then we will mark it as processed, looking like this:

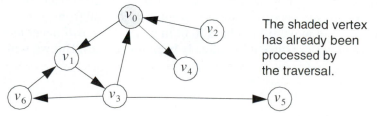

The shaded vertex has already been processed by the traversal.

The progress of a traversal after the start vertex depends on the traversal method being used. We'll start by looking at how a depth-first search proceeds.

Depth-First Search

After processing vertex 0, a depth-first search moves along a directed edge to one of vertex 0's neighbors. In our example, there are two possibilities: moving to vertex 1 (along the edge from 0 to 1) or moving to vertex 4 (along the edge from 0 to 4). In our example, it is not possible to move from vertex 0 to 3, or from vertex 0 to 2, because the edges go in the wrong direction. So the traversal has a choice: Move to vertex 1 or move to vertex 4. Right now we won't worry about exactly how the choice is made—let's just assume that the next vertex processed is vertex 1. After processing vertex 1, the picture looks like this:

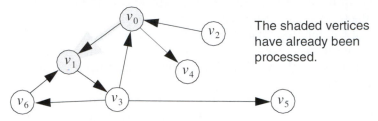

The shaded vertices have already been processed.

In the drawing we have highlighted the edge from vertex 0 to vertex 1 to indicate the intuitive notion of "moving from one vertex to another."

From here, the traversal moves to one of vertex 1's neighbors. You may think of vertex 1 as being at the "leading edge" of the depth-first traversal. It is the vertex that has most recently been processed, and so we will continue pushing forward from vertex 1, moving to one of vertex 1's unprocessed neighbors. In this example, there is only one unprocessed neighbor to consider, vertex 3. So we will move to vertex 3 and process it. At this point, we have processed three of the vertices, as shown here:

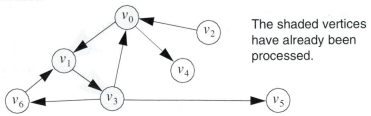

The shaded vertices have already been processed.

to prevent going around in circles, never move forward to a marked vertex

One of vertex 3's neighbors is vertex 0—but vertex 0 has already been marked as previously processed. So, to prevent the traversal from going around in circles, we will not move from 3 back to 0. In general, *we will never move forward to a marked vertex* (since it has already been processed). But we will move to vertex

3's other neighbors (vertices 5 and 6). Suppose we move to vertex 5 first. After processing vertex 5, the picture looks like this:

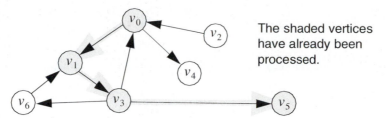

The shaded vertices have already been processed.

Since vertex 5 has no neighbors, the depth-first traversal cannot proceed forward any farther. Instead, the traversal comes back to see if the previous vertex— vertex 3—has any more unmarked neighbors:

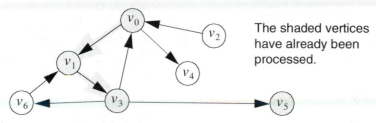

The shaded vertices have already been processed.

Does v_3 have any more
unmarked neighbors?

In this drawing, you can see that four vertices have been processed. And the "leading edge" of the search has pulled back to vertex v_3. Does v_3 have any more unmarked neighbors where the search can proceed? Yes—v_6 is an unmarked neighbor of v_3, so again the search plunges forward, along the edge from v_3 to v_6. Vertex 6 is processed, giving this picture:

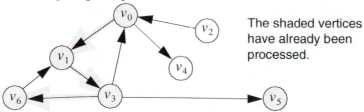

The shaded vertices have already been processed.

What now? Vertex 6 does have a neighbor—vertex 1—but v_1 has already been marked. So, since vertex 6 has no *unmarked* neighbors, the traversal again backs up to see if v_3 has any more unmarked neighbors. After the backup, we have the situation shown next.

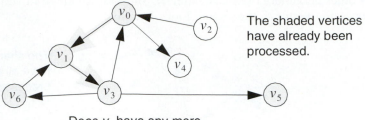

The shaded vertices have already been processed.

Does v_3 have any more unmarked neighbors?

Vertex 3 has no more unmarked neighbors (thank goodness!). So back we go to the previous vertex—vertex 1—to check whether it has any unmarked neighbors:

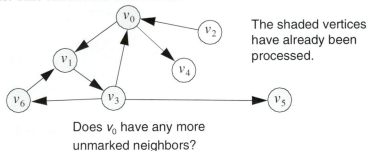

The shaded vertices have already been processed.

Does v_1 have any more unmarked neighbors?

You can see that the leading edge of the search is now at v_1, and that v_1 has no more unmarked neighbors, so back we go to vertex 0, to see if it has any unfinished business. This situation is drawn here:

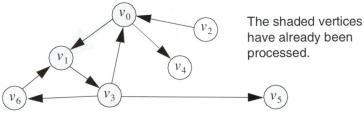

The shaded vertices have already been processed.

Does v_0 have any more unmarked neighbors?

From vertex 0 we can still travel to the unmarked vertex 4 and process it, as shown here:

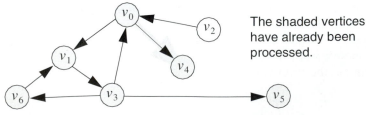

The shaded vertices have already been processed.

Vertex 4 has no neighbors, so we back up once more to vertex 0:

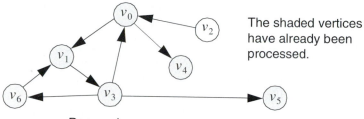

The shaded vertices
have already been
processed.

Does v_0 have any more
unmarked neighbors?

Vertex 0 has no more unmarked neighbors—and since this was the starting point there is no place left to back up to. That's the end of the traversal.

In this example, vertex 2 was never processed because there was no path from the start vertex (vertex 0) to vertex 2. A traversal only processes those vertices that can be reached from the start vertex.

There's one other important point about a depth-first search: From the starting vertex, the traversal proceeds to a neighbor and from there to another neighbor and so on, always going as far as possible before it ever backs up. In describing this behavior, it seems as if there's a lot to keep track of: where we start, where we go from there, and where we go from there. But the actual implementation can use recursion to keep track of most of these details in a simple way. We'll tackle that recursive implementation after looking at an alternative method: breadth-first search.

some vertices are not processed because they can't be reached from the start vertex

Breadth-First Search

A breadth-first search uses a queue to keep track of which vertices might still have unprocessed neighbors. The search begins with a starting vertex, which is processed, marked, and placed in the queue. For example, suppose we are processing this graph with vertex 0 as our starting point, so that vertex 0 is the first vertex to be processed, marked, and placed into the queue:

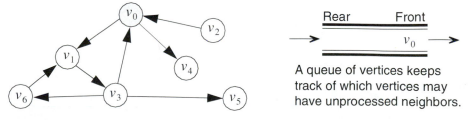

A queue of vertices keeps
track of which vertices may
have unprocessed neighbors.

Once the starting vertex has been processed, marked, and placed in the queue, the main part of the breadth-first search begins. This consists of repeatedly carrying out the following steps:

1. Remove a vertex, v, from the front of the queue.

2. For each unmarked neighbor, u of v: Process u, mark u, and then place u in the queue (since u may have further unprocessed neighbors)

These two steps are repeated until the queue becomes empty. Let's look at our example to see how these two steps are carried out when vertex 0 is at the head of the queue. The vertex 0 is removed from the queue, and we note that it has two unprocessed neighbors: vertices 1 and 4. Vertices 1 and 4 will each be processed, marked, and placed in the queue. Let's assume that vertex 1 is placed in the queue first, and then vertex 4. (The queuing could also occur the other way, with vertex 4 placed first; the algorithm is correct either way.) After 1 and 4 are in the queue, the situation looks like this:

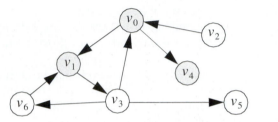

Since the queue still has entries, we repeat the two steps again: Remove the front entry (vertex 1), process and mark any unmarked neighbors of vertex 1, and enter these neighbors into the queue. The only unmarked neighbor of vertex 1 is vertex 3, so after processing, marking, and entering vertex 3, the situation looks like this:

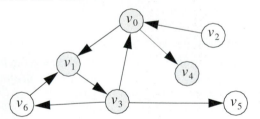

Next we remove vertex 4 from the front of the queue. Since vertex 4 has no neighbors, no new entries are processed or placed in the queue. The situation is now:

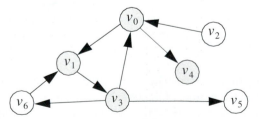

Vertex 3 comes out of the queue next. It has two unmarked neighbors (vertices 5 and 6) which are processed, marked, and placed in the queue, like this:

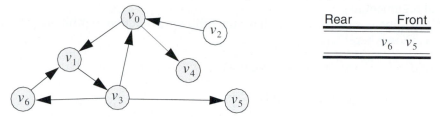

Rear	Front
v_6	v_5

Notice that vertex 0 (which is also a neighbor of vertex 3) does not get reprocessed because it is already marked.

At this point, we remove vertex 5 from the front of the queue, but it has no unmarked neighbors to worry about. We then remove vertex 6 from the queue. It also has no unmarked neighbors. The queue is finally empty, which ends the breadth-first search.

The effect of the breadth-first search is similar to the depth-first search: Vertices 0, 1, 3, 4, 5, and 6 have all been processed since they could all be reached from the starting point (vertex 0). Vertex 2 was not processed since there is no directed path from vertex 0 to vertex 2. However, the breadth-first search processes the vertices in a different order than the depth-first search. The breadth-first search first processed vertex 0, then processed the neighbors of the start point (1 and 4), then processed *their* neighbors (vertex 3), and so on. This contrasts with a depth-first search that processed the vertices 0, 1, 3, and 5 to start with (in that order).

You should now be able to carry out depth-first and breadth-first searches by hand on a directed graph. Next we will specify and implement the two searches as template functions that can be applied to any labeled graph.

the effects of breadth-first and depth-first search are similar—only the order of processing vertices differs

Depth-First Search—Implementation

One way to implement a depth-first search is with the following template function:

```
template <class Process, class Item, class SizeType>
void depth_first(Process f, graph<Item>& g, SizeType start);
// Precondition: start is a vertex number of the labeled graph g.
// Postcondition: A depth-first search of g has been executed, starting at
// the start vertex. The function f has been applied to the label of each
// vertex visited by the search.
```

In this prototype, the parameter g may be any graph. For example, g could be a graph with integer labels, so that the actual type of g is graph<int>. The parameter f is a function with one argument. This function, which is a parameter to the traversal function, is similar to the functions for tree traversals in Figure 10.10 on page 508. The function has an argument itself, which must be the same data type as the labels of the graphs. During a search, each time a vertex v is reached, that vertex is "processed" by calling f with the label of v as the actual argument to f.

For example, suppose that we have the following function to print integer values, as shown here:

```
void print_int_line(int value)
{
    cout << value << endl;
}
```

With this function in hand, we can carry out a depth-first search of a graph g, starting at vertex 0, and print all the values that we encounter. The function call for the search is as follows:

```
depth_first(print_int_line, g, 0);
```

The implementation of `depth_first` uses an array of boolean values declared as a local variable of the function, shown here:

```
bool marked[g.MAXIMUM];
```

This array has one component for each possible vertex of the graph g, and its purpose is to keep track of which vertices have been marked as visited by the search. In general, for a vertex number v, the component `marked[v]` is true if v has already been visited by the search, and false otherwise. The complete pseudocode for `depth_first` is short:

pseudocode for depth-first search

1. Check that the start vertex is a valid vertex number of the graph.

2. Set all the components of `marked` to false.

3. Call a separate function to actually carry out the search.

You may be wondering, "Why call a separate function in Step 3? Why can't we just carry out the search in the body of the `depth_first` function itself?" Good question. The answer is that we plan to use recursion: The start vertex is processed and then recursive calls are made to process each of the start vertex's neighbors. Further recursive calls are made to process the neighbors' neighbors, and so on. So, if the work were carried out in the body of the `depth_first` function, each time a recursive call is made, we would do Step 2—clearing the marked array—and . . . oops! Clearing the marked array at every recursive call will definitely lead to trouble.

The new function, executed in Step 3, will be called `rec_dfs` with this prototype:

```
template <class Process, class Item, class SizeType>
void rec_dfs(
    Process f, graph<Item>& g, SizeType v, bool marked[ ]
);
// Precondition: g is a labeled graph that is being traversed by a depth-
// first search. For each vertex x, marked[x] is true if x has already been
// visited by this search; otherwise marked[x] is false. The vertex v is an
// unmarked vertex that the search has just arrived at.
// Postcondition: The depth-first search of g has been continued through
// vertex v and beyond to all the vertices that can be reached from v via a
// path of unmarked vertices. The function f has been applied to the label
// of each vertex visited by the search, and each such vertex x has also
// been marked by setting marked[x] to true.
```

Now let's examine the body of the rec_dfs function. The first task is to mark and process the vertex v. After this we will examine each of vertex v's neighbors. Each time we find an unmarked neighbor we will make a recursive call to continue the search through that neighbor and beyond. The phrase "and beyond" is important because if a neighbor has another unmarked neighbor, then there will be another recursive call at that level, and so on until we reach a vertex with no unmarked neighbors. This description of rec_dfs is implemented in the top of Figure 15.3, and the actual depth_first function is implemented afterward.

Breadth-First Search—Implementation

The breadth-first search is implemented with a queue of vertex numbers. The start vertex is processed, marked, and placed in the queue. Then the following steps are repeated until the queue is empty: (1) remove a vertex, v, from the front of the queue, and (2) for each unmarked neighbor u of v: process u, mark u, and then place u in the queue (since u may have further unprocessed neighbors).

These steps are implemented in the end of Figure 15.3.

Self-Test Exercises for Section 15.3

15. What would happen if the visited vertices were not marked in the breadth and depth-first search? What type of path produces this effect?

16. Does a depth-first or breath-first search process all vertices in a graph? Why or why not?

17. Do a depth-first search of the Australia graph (page 729), starting at Sydney. List the order in which the cities are processed. Do the same for a breadth-first search.

18. Suppose you are doing a breadth-first search of a graph with n vertices. How large can the queue get?

19. What kind of search occurs if you replace breadth-first search's queue with a stack?

FIGURE 15.3   Depth-First Search and Breadth-First Search

Function Implementations

```
template <class Process, class Item, class SizeType>
void rec_dfs(Process f, graph<Item>& g, SizeType v, bool marked[ ])
// Precondition: g is a labeled graph that is being traversed by a depth-first search. For each
// vertex x, marked[x] is true if x has already been visited by this search, otherwise marked[x]
// is false. The vertex v is an unmarked vertex that the search has just arrived at.
// Postcondition: The depth-first search of g has been continued through vertex v and beyond
// to all the vertices that can be reached from v via a path of unmarked vertices. The function
// f has been applied to the label of each vertex visited by the search, and each such vertex x
// has also been marked by setting marked[x] to true.
// Library facilities used: cstdlib, graph.h, set
{
    std::set<std::size_t> connections = g.neighbors(v);
    std::set<std::size_t>::iterator it;

    marked[v] = true;    // Mark vertex v.
    f(g[v]);             // Process the label of vertex v with the function f.

    // Traverse all the neighbors, looking for unmarked vertices:
    for (it = connections.begin( ); it != connections.end( ); ++it)
    {
        if (!marked[*it])
            rec_dfs(f, g, *it, marked);
    }
}


template <class Process, class Item, class SizeType>
void depth_first(Process f, graph<Item>& g, SizeType start)
// Precondition: start is a vertex number of the labeled graph g.
// Postcondition: A depth-first search of g has been executed, starting at the start vertex.
// The function f has been applied to the label of each vertex visited by the search.
// Library facilities used: algorithm, cassert, graph.h
{
    bool marked[g.MAXIMUM];

    assert(start < g.size( ));
    std::fill_n(marked, g.size( ), false);
    rec_dfs(f, g, start, marked);
}
```

(continued)

(FIGURE 15.3 continued)

```
template <class Process, class Item, class SizeType>
void breadth_first(Process f, graph<Item>& g, SizeType start)
// Same as the depth_first function, but using a breadth-first search instead
// Library facilities used: algorithm, cassert, cstdlib, graph.h, queue
{
    bool marked[g.MAXIMUM];
    std::set<std::size_t> connections;
    std::set<std::size_t>::iterator it;
    std::queue<std::size_t> vertex_queue;

    assert(start < g.size( ));

    std::fill_n(marked, g.size( ), false);

    marked[start] = true;
    f(g[start]);
    vertex_queue.push(start);
    do
    {
        connections = g.neighbors(vertex_queue.front( ));
        vertex_queue.pop( );
        // Mark and process the unmarked neighbors, and place them in the queue.
        for (it = connections.begin( ); it != connections.end( ); ++it)
        {
            if (!marked[*it])
            {
                marked[*it] = true;
                f(g[*it]);
                vertex_queue.push(*it);
            }
        }
    }
    while (!vertex_queue.empty( ));
}
```

www.cs.colorado.edu/~main/chapter15/searches.template   **WWW**

15.4   PATH ALGORITHMS

Determining Whether a Path Exists

Frequently, a problem is represented by a graph, and the answer to the problem can be found by answering some question about paths in the graph. For example, a network of computers can be represented by a graph, with each vertex representing one of the machines in the network, and each edge representing a communication wire between two machines. The question of whether one machine can send a message to another machine boils down to whether the corresponding vertices are connected by a path.

Either breadth-first search or depth-first search may be used to determine whether a path exists between two vertices u and v. The idea is to use u as the start vertex of the search and proceed with a breadth-first or depth-first search. If the vertex v is ever visited, then the search may stop and announce that there is a path from u to v. On the other hand, if v is never visited, then there is no path from u to v.

Graphs with Weighted Edges

Often we need to know more than just "Does a path exist?" In the network example described above, each edge represents a communication wire between machines. Such a wire might have a "cost" associated with using the wire. The cost could be the amount of energy required to use the path, or perhaps the amount of time required for the wire to transmit a message, or even a dollars-and-cents cost required to use the wire to send one message. In any case, there could be many paths from one vertex to another, and we might want to find the path with the lowest total cost (that is, the path with the lowest possible sum of its edge costs).

This kind of question can be solved by using a graph where each edge has a non-negative integer value attached to it, called the **weight** or **cost** of the edge. Here's an example of a graph with edge weights:

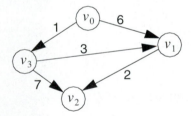

the shortest path between two vertices is the path with lowest total cost

In this example, there are several paths from vertex v_0 to vertex v_2. The path with the lowest total cost traverses the edge from v_0 to v_3 (with a cost of 1), then from v_3 to v_1 (with a cost of 3), and finally from v_1 to v_2 (with a cost of 2). The total cost of this path is $1 + 3 + 2$, which is 6. There is a path with fewer edges (such as the path from v_0 to v_1 to v_2), but no other path has a lower total cost. The path with the lowest total cost is called the **shortest path**. (If you think of the weights as distances, then the term *shortest path* will sound sensible.) The problem of finding the shortest path between two vertices of a graph occurs often in computer science (such as the network example) and in applications (such as finding the shortest driving distance between two points on a road map).

Here is a summary of the concepts we have introduced:

Weighted Edges and Shortest Paths

A **weighted edge** is an edge together with a non-negative integer called the edge's **weight**.

The **weight of a path** is the total sum of the weights of all edges in the path. (Note: The weight of the empty path, with no edges, is always zero.)

If two vertices are connected by at least one path, then we can define the **shortest path** between two vertices. This is the path that has the smallest weight. (There may be several paths with equally small weights, in which case each of the paths is called "smallest.")

Shortest-Distance Algorithm

In this section we will present an efficient algorithm called *Dijkstra's algorithm* (named for computer scientist Edsgar Dijkstra, who proposed the algorithm) for finding the shortest path between two vertices. Throughout the section we will use graphs with weighted edges where each weight is a non-negative integer. We will use pseudocode rather than a particular language such as C++.

We start with a problem that's simpler than actually finding the shortest path from one vertex to another. We'll concentrate on simply finding the *weight* of the shortest path—in other words the smallest possible sum of edge weights along a path from one vertex to another. This weight is called the **shortest distance**.

Dijkstra's algorithm actually provides more information than just the shortest distance from one vertex to another. In fact, the algorithm provides the shortest distance from a starting vertex (which we call `start`) to *every* vertex in the graph. The algorithm uses an integer array called `distance`, with one component for each vertex in the graph. Here is the algorithm's goal:

we'll actually find shortest distances rather than shortest paths

---

Goal of the Shortest-Distance Algorithm

The goal is to completely fill the distance array so that for each vertex v, the value of `distance[v]` is the weight of the shortest path from `start` to v.

We'll illustrate how the algorithm works with this small graph:

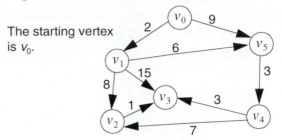

The starting vertex is v_0.

The algorithm begins by filling in one value in the distance array. We fill in zero for the component that is indexed by the `start` vertex itself, indicating that the weight of the shortest path from the `start` vertex to the `start` vertex itself is zero. This is correct since the empty path exists from the `start` vertex to itself. At this point, the distance array has one known value:

0	?	?	?	?	?

distance

[0]　[1]　[2]　[3]　[4]　[5]

At this point we have one correct value, `distance[0]`. In the other locations we will write a value based on what we know so far. Because we don't know too much, our initial values won't be too accurate, but that's okay. In fact, the values that we fill in will all be *infinity*, represented by the symbol ∞. The distance array, with mostly ∞, is shown here:

0	∞	∞	∞	∞	∞

distance

[0]　[1]　[2]　[3]　[4]　[5]

In an actual implementation, we would use some special integer value for ∞. For example, we could use -1 and make sure that all the rest of our programming always treats an occurrence of -1 as if it were infinity.

Now we are ready to do some processing that will steadily improve the values in the distance array. We begin with an observation about the initial values that we've placed in the distance array: These initial values are actually correct, *if we are permitting only the empty path and ignoring all other paths.* In other words, if the empty path is the only path that we are permitting, then there is a path from the start vertex to itself (namely the empty path with weight zero). But there is no way to get from the start vertex to any other vertex, and the fact that there is no path is represented by ∞ in the distance array.

Of course, permitting *only* the empty path is an overwhelming restriction. The key to the algorithm is in gradually relaxing this restriction, allowing more vertices to appear in permitted paths. As more and more vertices are allowed, we will continually revise the distance array so that its values are correct, *for paths that pass through only allowed vertices*. By the end of the algorithm, all vertices are allowed, and the distance array has values that are entirely correct.

the algorithm gradually improves the values in the distance array

The idea we have described needs some refinement. How are newly allowed vertices selected? How do we keep track of which vertices are currently allowed? How is the distance array revised at each step? These questions are addressed in the following list of three steps for the complete algorithm:

Step 1. Fill in the distance array with ∞ at every location with the exception of distance[Start], which is assigned the value zero.

Step 2. Initialize a *set* of vertices, called allowed_vertices, to be the empty set. Throughout the algorithm a **permitted path** is a path that starts at the start vertex, and where each vertex on the path (except perhaps the final vertex) is in the set of allowed vertices. The final vertex on a permitted path does not need to be in the allowed_vertices set. At this point, allowed_vertices is the empty set, so the only permitted path is the empty path without any edges. (This empty path does contain one vertex, the start vertex. But since this vertex is the *final* vertex on the path, the vertex is not required to be in the allowed vertices set.)

Step 3. The third step is a loop. Each time through the loop we will add one more vertex to allowed_vertices and then update the distance array so that all the allowed vertices may appear on paths. Here's a brief summary of the loop:

```
// Loop in Step 3 of the shortest-distance algorithm:
// n is the number of vertices in the graph

for (allowed_size = 1; allowed_size <= n; ++allowed_size)
{
    // At this point, allowed_vertices contains allowed_size - 1 vertices,
    // which are the allowed_size  - 1 closest vertices to the start vertex.
    // Also, for each vertex v, distance[v] is the shortest distance from the
    // start vertex to vertex v, provided that we are considering only
    // permitted paths (i.e., paths where each vertex except the final
    // vertex must be in allowed_vertices).
```

Step 3a. Let next be the closest vertex to the start vertex that is not yet in the set of allowed vertices (if several vertices are equally close, then you may choose next to be any of them).

Step 3b. Add the vertex next to the set allowed_vertices.

Step 3c. Revise the distance array so that the new vertex (next) may appear on permitted paths.

```
}
```

The loop's computation hinges on the condition written just before Step 3a. The condition indicates that the `allowed_vertices` set actually contains the `allowed_size-1` vertices that are *closest* to the start vertex. The condition also indicates that `distance[v]` is always the shortest distance from the start vertex to vertex v, provided that we are considering only permitted paths (that is, paths where all vertices except the final vertex must be in the set of allowed vertices). This condition is true the first time the loop is entered, and it is also true at the start of each subsequent iteration. The responsibility of the three steps—3a, 3b, and 3c—is to ensure that the condition remains valid at the start of each iteration. Let's examine the three steps in some detail.

Step 3a. This step must determine which of the *unallowed* vertices is closest to the start vertex. There is a simple rule for choosing this vertex:

How to Choose the Next Vertex in Step 3a

In Step 3a, we will always choose the unallowed vertex that has the *smallest* current value in the distance array. (If several vertices have equally small distances, then we may choose any of them.)

For example, suppose we reach Step 3a, and we have this situation:

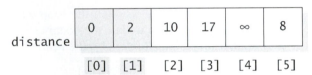

In this example, the two shaded vertices, 0 and 1,
are already in the set of allowed vertices.

Since vertices 0 and 1 are already in the allowed set, we may not choose them as the next vertex. Among the other vertices, vertex 5 has the smallest current value in the distance array (the value is 8). So, we would choose vertex 5 as the next vertex. In the answer to Self-Test Exercise 21, we will explain precisely *why* this rule works, but for now it is sufficient to know that this is the correct way to select the next vertex.

Step 3b. In this step we "add the vertex `next` to the set `allowed_vertices`." The implementation of this step depends on how the set of allowed vertices is represented. One possibility is to implement `allowed_vertices` as a set of vertex numbers, using `set<int>` from the Standard Template Library. In this case, Step 3b merely inserts `next` into the set.

Step 3c. Finally, we must revise the distance array so that the newly allowed vertex, `next`, is permitted on a path from the start vertex to another vertex. An example will explain the necessary revisions. Suppose that vertices 0, 1, and 5 are already in the `allowed_vertices` set, and that we have just added vertex 2 as our next vertex, as shown here:

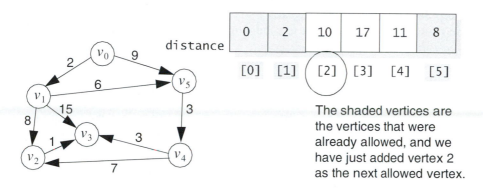

0	2	10	17	11	8
[0]	[1]	[2]	[3]	[4]	[5]

distance

The shaded vertices are the vertices that were already allowed, and we have just added vertex 2 as the next allowed vertex.

Since we have just added vertex 2 as a newly allowed vertex, we must now update the distance array to reflect the fact that vertex 2 may now appear on paths.

For example, `distance[3]` is currently 17. This means that there is a path from the start vertex to vertex 3 that uses only vertices 0, 1, and 5, and that has a length of 17. Here's the key question: *If we also allow vertex 2 to appear on a path from the start vertex to vertex 3, can we obtain a distance that is smaller than 17?* A smaller distance might be possible by taking a two-part path, shown here:

The first part of the path goes from the start vertex v_0 to the newly allowed vertex v_2 . . .

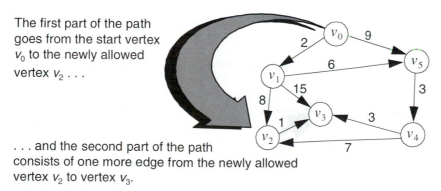

. . . and the second part of the path consists of one more edge from the newly allowed vertex v_2 to vertex v_3.

This path has two parts: the part from the start vertex to vertex 2, followed by the part that has the single edge from vertex 2 to vertex 3. The total weight of this path is:

`distance[2]` + (weight of the edge from vertex 2 to vertex 3)

In our example, this sum is 11, which is smaller than the current "best distance to vertex 3." Therefore we should replace distance[3] with this smaller sum. We must also create similar two-part paths for each of the other unallowed vertices, and if the two-part path is smaller than the current distance, then we modify the distance array. This provides the following refined pseudocode for Step 3c:

Step 3c. Revise the distance array so that the new vertex (next) may appear on permitted paths. The integer n is the number of vertices; v and sum are local integer variables, as shown in this code:

```
for (v = 0; v < n; ++v)
    if ((v is not an allowed vertex) and (there is an edge from next to v))
    {
        sum = distance[next] + (weight of the edge from next to v);
        if (sum < distance[v])
            distance[v] = sum;
    }
```

Notice that we do not consider a possible new smaller distance to vertices that are already allowed vertices. That is because these vertices are all closer to the start vertex than next is, so that distance[next] is going to be larger than the shortest distance to any of these vertices.

Also, when we are creating the new two-part paths, we consider only the case where the second part of the path is a *single edge* from next to the end vertex. The reason for this is that a longer path from next to the end vertex would have to pass through other allowed vertices, meaning that we have a path that goes from the start vertex, through next, through *another* allowed vertex, and finally to the end vertex. But such a path will always be shorter by avoiding the next vertex altogether—just go from the start vertex to that other allowed vertex (using the shortest path) and then to the end vertex. Such a path, which does not go through the next vertex, is already permitted. We don't need to consider such a path again—we need to consider only new paths that pass through the next newly allowed vertex.

The complete pseudocode for the algorithm is shown in Figure 15.4. The main loop actually stops at the number of vertices minus 1 because at that point there is only one unallowed vertex, and this must be the farthest vertex from the start vertex so that no shortest paths can go through this farthest vertex.

We'll execute the algorithm on our example graph. Here's the situation after initializing the distance array:

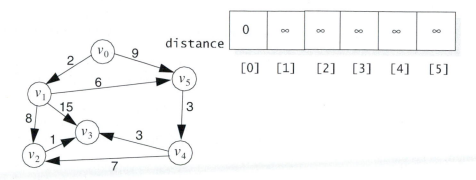

At this point, the set of allowed vertices is empty, and we will enter the main loop for the first time. In Step 3a, the value of `next` is set to vertex 0 (since `distance[0]` is the smallest value in the distance array). We then look at each unallowed vertex v with an edge from vertex 0 to vertex v. These are vertices 1 and 5, so we check to see whether we need to revise `distance[1]` and `distance[5]`:

- `distance[0]` + (the weight of the edge from 0 to 1) is 2. Since this is smaller than the current value of `distance[1]`, we replace `distance[1]` with 2.

- `distance[0]` + (the weight of the edge from 0 to 5) is 9. Since this is smaller than the current value of `distance[5]`, we replace `distance[5]` with 9.

At this point, the distance array is as shown here (with the allowed vertices shaded):

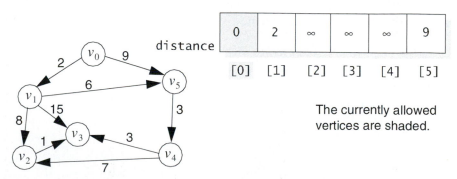

The currently allowed vertices are shaded.

FIGURE 15.4   Dijkstra's Shortest-Distance Algorithm

Pseudocode

Input. A directed graph with positive, integer edge weights and n vertices. One of the vertices, called start, is specified as the start vertex.

Output. A list of the shortest distances from the start vertex to every other vertex in the graph.

The algorithm uses an array of n integers (called distance) and a set of vertices (called allowed_vertices). The variables v, allowed_size, and sum are local integer variables. There is some special value (∞) that we can place in the distance array to indicate an infinite distance (which means there is no path).

Step 1. Initialize the distance array to contain all ∞, except distance[start], which is set to zero.

Step 2. Initialize the set of allowed vertices to be the empty set.

Step 3. Compute the complete distance array:

```
for (allowed_size = 1; allowed_size < n; ++allowed_size)
{
    // At this point, allowed_vertices contains allowed_size - 1 vertices, which are the
    // allowed_size - 1 closest vertices to the start vertex. Also, for each vertex v, distance[v]
    // is the shortest distance from the start vertex to vertex v, provided that we are
    // considering only permitted paths (i.e., paths where each vertex except the final vertex
    // must be in allowed_vertices).
```

Step 3a. Let next be the closest vertex to the start vertex, which is not yet in the set of allowed vertices (if several vertices are equally close, then you may choose next to be any of them).

Step 3b. Add the vertex next to the set allowed_vertices.

Step 3c. Revise the distance array so that the new vertex (next) may appear on permitted paths:

```
    for (v = 0; v < n; ++v)
        if ((v is not an allowed vertex) and (there is an edge from next to v))
        {
            sum = distance[next] + (weight of the edge from next to v);
            if (sum < distance[v])
                distance[v] = sum;
        }
}
```

Step 4. Output the values in the distance array. (Each distance[v] is the shortest distance from the start vertex to vertex v.)

The second time we enter the main loop, the value of next is set to vertex 1 (since distance[1] is the smallest value of the unallowed vertices). We then look at each unallowed vertex v with an edge from vertex 1 to vertex v. These are vertices 2, 3, and 5, so we check to see whether we need to revise distance[2], distance[3], and distance[5]:

- distance[1] + (the weight of the edge from 1 to 2) is 10. Since this is smaller than the current value of distance[2], we replace distance[2] with 10.

- distance[1] + (the weight of the edge from 1 to 3) is 17. Since this is smaller than the current value of distance[3], we replace distance[3] with 17.

- distance[1] + (the weight of the edge from 0 to 5) is 8. Since this is smaller than the current value of distance[5], we replace distance[5] with 8.

At this point, the distance array is:

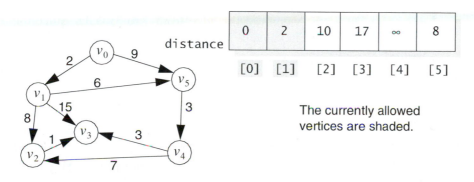

	0	2	10	17	∞	8
	[0]	[1]	[2]	[3]	[4]	[5]

distance

The currently allowed vertices are shaded.

The third time we enter the main loop, the value of next will be set to vertex 5 (since distance[5] is the smallest value of the unallowed vertices). We then look at each unallowed vertex v with an edge from vertex 5 to vertex v. Vertex 4 is the only vertex that is the target of an edge from vertex 5, so we check to see whether we need to revise distance[4]:

- distance[5] + (the weight of the edge from 5 to 4) is 11. Since this is smaller than the current value of distance[4], we replace distance[4] with 11.

At this point, we have this situation:

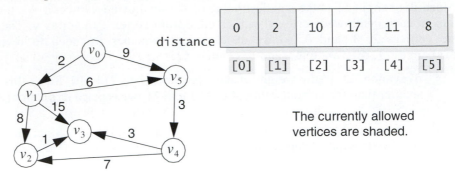

0	2	10	17	11	8
[0]	[1]	[2]	[3]	[4]	[5]

distance

The currently allowed
vertices are shaded.

The fourth time we enter the main loop, the value of `next` will be set to vertex 2 (since `distance[2]` is the smallest value of the unallowed vertices). We then look at each unallowed vertex v with an edge from vertex 2 to vertex v. Vertex 3 is the only such vertex, so we check to see whether we need to revise `distance[3]`:

- `distance[2]` + (the weight of the edge from 2 to 3) is 11. Since this is smaller than the current value of `distance[3]`, we replace `distance[3]` with 11.

At this point, the situation is:

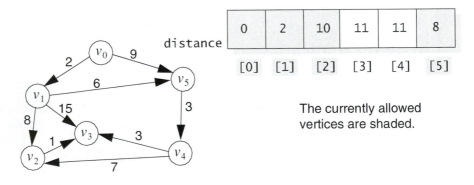

0	2	10	11	11	8
[0]	[1]	[2]	[3]	[4]	[5]

distance

The currently allowed
vertices are shaded.

The fifth time we enter the main loop, the value of `next` will be set to either vertex 3 or vertex 4 (since both `distance[3]` and `distance[4]` are 11). It doesn't matter which one we choose, so let's choose vertex 4. We then look at each unallowed vertex v with an edge from vertex 4 to vertex v. This is only vertex 3, so we check to see whether we need to revise `distance[4]`:

- `distance[4]` + (the weight of the edge from 4 to 3) is 14. Since this is *larger* than the current value of `distance[3]`, we do not replace `distance[3]`.

At this point, we are nearly done:

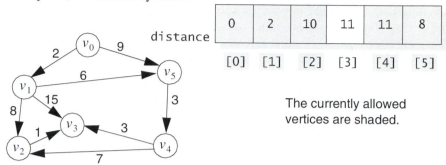

0	2	10	11	11	8
[0]	[1]	[2]	[3]	[4]	[5]

distance

The currently allowed vertices are shaded.

The main loop of the algorithm now stops. We don't need to process that last unallowed vertex (3), since it is the farthest vertex from the start vertex. For each vertex v, the value of distance[v] is the shortest distance from the start vertex (vertex 0) to v.

Shortest-Path Algorithm

We have shown how to compute the *weight* of the shortest path from a start vertex to each other vertex in a graph. But how can we compute the actual sequence of vertices that occurs along the shortest path? It turns out that Dijkstra's shortest-distance algorithm contains enough information to actually print the shortest path from the start vertex to any other vertex, provided that we keep track of one extra piece of information:

Predecessor Information for Shortest Paths

For each vertex v, we will keep track of which vertex was the next vertex when distance[v] was given a new smaller value. We will keep track of these values in an array called predecessor, so that for each vertex v, predecessor[v] is the value of next at the time when distance[v] was given a new smaller value. (Note: predecessor[start] does not need to have a value, since distance[start] is never updated.)

The predecessor information is easy to keep track of. Each time that we update distance[v] with the assignment distance[v] = sum , we must also update predecessor[v] with this assignment:

```
predecessor[v] = next;
```

When the algorithm finishes, the value of distance[v] is the weight of the shortest path from the start vertex to vertex v. Or distance[v] might be ∞, indicating that there is no path from the start vertex to vertex v. But when distance[v] is not ∞, we can actually print out the vertices on the shortest path from the start vertex to vertex v, using the following method:

```
// Printing the vertices on the shortest path from the start vertex to v:
// Vertices are printed in reverse order, starting at v, and going to start.

vertex_on_path = v; // The last vertex on the path
cout << vertex_on_path << endl; // Print the final vertex.
while (vertex_on_path != start)
{
    vertex_on_path = predecessor[vertex_on_path];
    cout << vertex_on_path << endl;
}
```

In other words, the last vertex on the path to v is vertex v itself. The next-to-last vertex is predecessor[v]. And the vertex before that is obtained by applying predecessor to the next-to-last vertex—and so on, right back to the start vertex. As indicated, this algorithm, manages to print the vertices in reverse order, from vertex v back to the start vertex.

Self-Test Exercises for Section 15.4

20. What value indicates that there is no path between vertices in Dijkstra's algorithm? Why is this value used?

21. When we select the next vertex in the shortest-distance algorithm, we need to select the unallowed vertex that is closest to the start vertex. How is this selection done?

22. Consider the graph that we have been using throughout this section, except change the weight of the edge that goes from 0 to 5. Its new weight is 4. Go through the entire algorithm to compute the new distance array.

23. Compute the complete predecessor array for the previous exercise, and use it to find the actual shortest path from vertex 0 to vertex 3.

CHAPTER SUMMARY

- Graphs are a flexible data structure with many occurrences in computer science and in applications. Many problems can be solved by asking an appropriate question about paths in a graph.

- There are several different kinds of graphs: undirected graphs (where edges have no particular orientation), directed graphs (where each edge goes from a source vertex to a target vertex), graphs with loops (i.e., an edge connecting a vertex to itself), graphs with multiple edges (i.e., more than one edge may connect the same pair of vertices), labeled graphs (where each vertex has an associated label), and graphs with weighted edges (where each edge has an associated number called its weight).

- There are two common ways to implement a graph: an adjacency matrix or edge lists. The different implementations have different time performance for common operations such as determining whether two vertices are connected.

- There are two common ways to traverse a graph: depth-first search and breadth-first search.

- Dijkstra's algorithm provides an efficient way to determine the shortest path from a given start vertex to every other vertex in a graph with weighted edges.

Solutions to Self-Test Exercises

1. The airline route graph has nine vertices, 14 edges, and no loops. A loop would be an excursion flight that takes off and lands at the same city.

2. It is directed because each edge (drawn as an arrow) has an orientation, going from its source to its target.

3. It is simple (no loops, no multiple edges).

4. The degree of (a) is 5; (b), (c), and (d) have degree of 2; the degree of (e) is 3.

5. Canberra's degrees are both 3; Sydney's degrees are both 2; Melbourne's degrees are 3 (in) and 2 (out).

6. Length 3: Sydney, Canberra, Brisbane, Sydney. Length 5: Canberra, Adelaide, Perth, Black Stump, Darwin, Canberra.

7. Your state graph should have 16 vertices and 48 directed edges. (There are 32 edges from Rule 1, and eight edges each from Rules 2 and 3.) It is possible to go from the start state to the goal state in four moves.

8.

	[0]	[1]	[2]	[3]
[0]	false	true	false	true
[1]	false	false	true	false
[2]	false	false	false	false
[3]	false	true	true	false

9. Yes, there is a loop on vertex 3. Vertex 1 has the highest in-degree (3). Vertex 3 has the highest out-degree (also 3).

10. The function need only subtract 1 from the member variable `many_vertices`.

11. The adjacency matrix, a, could be a two-dimensional array of unsigned integers with a[i][j] storing the number of edges from vertex i to vertex j.

12. This is an open-ended question, but your answer should consider space requirements for each representation, and time requirements for common operations.

13. One solution would call neighbors for each node. Each call to neighbors returns a set, and your function can return the sum of the sizes of all these sets. Another solution could call is_edge for each possible source and target node. The return value from this function would be the number of times that is_edge returns true.

14. At point 1, the label is 42. At point 2, the label is still 42, and the integer variable i is also 42. At point 3, the i has changed to 43, but the label is still 42. (To change the label, the change must be made to g[3] itself.)

15. A traversal will loop indefinitely on a graph with a cycle if visited vertices are not marked.

16. Not always. A vertex *v* in a graph will not be processed by a DFS or BFS if there is no path from the start vertex to *v*.

17. Traversals sometimes make choices about which vertex to visit next. When we have such a choice, we will visit the vertex that is alphabetically first, giving these two orders: *Depth-first:* Sydney, Canberra, Adelaide, Melbourne, Hobart, Perth, Black Stump, Darwin, Brisbane. *Breadth-first:* Sydney, Canberra, Melbourne, Adelaide, Brisbane, Hobart, Perth, Black Stump, Darwin.

18. If *n* is 1, then the queue needs room for only one vertex. If *n* is more than 1, then the queue will never have more than *n*–1 entries. Here is why: The start vertex is only in the queue once (by itself), and then we remove the start vertex from the queue. Each other vertex is placed in the queue at most once, so the largest queue needed would occur if all *n*–1 vertices are neighbors of the start vertex.

19. A depth-first search

20. The infinity symbol indicates that there is no path between two vertices. An actual algorithm would use some unused number, such as –1, for this infinity. The shortest distances algorithm gradually reduces the values in the distance array, so the largest possible value should be the initial value.

21. From among the unallowed vertices, we select the vertex with the smallest current value in the distance array. This works because the current distance array contains the correct distance values if we are permitting only allowed vertices, and the currently allowed vertices are the *n*–1 closest vertices. Therefore, the shortest path to the nth closest vertex must pass through only currently allowed vertices, and therefore the distance array contains the correct value for that nth closest vertex.

22. The new final distance array: (0, 2, 10, 10, 7, 4).

23. The new shortest path to vertex 3: vertex 0 to vertex 5, vertex 5 to vertex 4, vertex 4 to vertex 3.

PROGRAMMING PROJECTS
For more in-depth projects, please see www.cs.colorado.edu/~main/projects/

1 Consider our graph objects from Figure 15.2 on page 738. These graphs have a maximum number of vertices, determined by the static constant graph::MAXIMUM. This constant determines the number of rows and columns of the adjacency matrix, and the size of the array for the labels. These two arrays are declared in the highlighted lines of the graph definition:

```
template <class Item>
class graph
{
public:
    // MEMBER CONSTANTS
    static const std::size_t MAXIMUM=20;
    ...
```

```
private:
    bool edges[MAXIMUM][MAXIMUM];
    Item labels[MAXIMUM];
    std::size_t many_vertices;
};
```

There are several ways to change `edges` to a dynamic array, which can grow and shrink as vertices are added and removed. This project describes one approach for you to carry out. The approach is to eliminate the static constant, and change the private member variables as shown here:

```
template <class Item>
class graph
{
public:
    ...
private:
    bool **edges;
    Item *labels;
    std::size_t allocated;
    std::size_t many_vertices;
};
```

The array of labels has been changed to an ordinary dynamic array. But what is the meaning of the declaration *bool **edges*? This declaration says that `edges` is more than a pointer to a boolean value; in fact, it is a *pointer to a pointer* to a boolean. A "pointer to a pointer" can be made to act like a two-dimensional array. For example, suppose that we want `edges` to act like an array with *n* rows and *n* columns. Using a `size_t` variable i, we could write this code to allocate the needed memory:

```
edges = new (bool*)[n];
for (i = 0; i < n; ++i)
    edges[i] = new bool[n];
```

In this code, the first statement has an interesting effect. The statement `edges = new (bool*)[n]` makes `edges` point to an array of *n* pointers. The for-loop then makes each of these pointers point to a dynamic array of *n* boolean values. After the for-loop, we can use `edges` just as if it was an *n* by *n* two-dimensional array of boolean values. For example, we could fill the entire "array" with *false* using the loop shown here (i and j are both `size_t` variables):

```
for (i = 0; i < n; ++i)
    for (j = 0; j < n; ++j)
        edges[i][j] = false;
```

For example, with *n* equal to 3, then the above code constructs the dynamic arrays shown below. The key point is that with this structure, we can use `edges` as if it were a two-dimensional array.

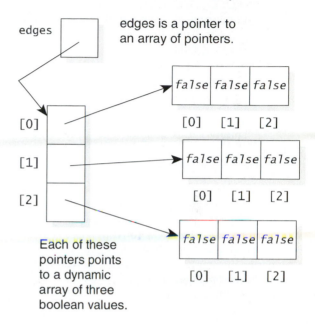

edges is a pointer to an array of pointers.

Each of these pointers points to a dynamic array of three boolean values.

For this project, rewrite the `graph` class so that `edges` is implemented as we have described. You should also add another private member variable called `allocated`. The value of `allocated` is the number of rows and columns in `edges`. This number must be no less than the actual number of vertices (which is still stored in the private member variable `many_vertices`).

Your implementation should include a constructor with one argument. This argument is a `size_t` value that specifies the initial allocation for the number of rows and columns in the adjacency matrix. There should also be a `resize` function to allow a programmer to explicitly change the allocation. If `add_vertex` is called and the matrix is already full, then `add_vertex` should call `resize` to allocate a larger adjacency matrix.

2 Use edge lists to reimplement the `graph` class from Figure 15.2 on page 738. There should be no limit to the number of vertices.

Alternatively, you could reimplement the graph class so that each vertex has a set of edges (using the set class from the Standard Library).

3 Implement a new template class that is derived from the graph. The new class should permit both edges and vertices to have labels.

4 Implement a function with three arguments: a graph, a starting vertex number, and an ending vertex number. The function determines whether there is a directed path from the starting vertex to the ending vertex.

5 Implement a new class for graphs with weighted edges. Use the ordinary graph class as a base type for your implementation. After implementing the new class, provide two extra functions to implement Dijkstra's shortest-distance and shortest-path algorithms.

6 Write a program to help a traveler plan the shortest traveling path from one city to another. The program should read a file of data containing a list of cities and a list of roads connecting the cities. Each road has a distance attached to it. Allow the user to enter queries of the form "City1, City2" and have the program print the shortest sequence of roads to travel from City1 to City2.

7 Write a program to help you make better social connections. The program should read a file of data containing a list of people in your community and a list of who-knows-who. Allow the user to enter various queries about which people know each other, such as "How many people does Harry know?" or "Is there anyone that both Harry and Cathy know?"

8 Choose some graph implementation and implement a graph member function to delete a vertex from the graph. The function should not only remove the vertex, but all edges that have the vertex as the source or target.

9 Implement an undirected graph class by modifying any of the graph implementations discussed in this chapter.

10 Rewrite the maze program in Chapter 9 (page 448) using a graph class to represent the maze. A path should be generated with the entrance and exit as endpoints. Use a depth-first search to travel through the maze.

Appendix A
ASCII Character Set

Most implementations of C++ provide the standard ASCII (American Standard Code for Information Interchange) character set as the first 128 characters. Characters 0 through 31 and 127 are standard signals to control devices such as a printer.

Your programming should not depend on the ASCII characters being present. However, the language does guarantee that the integer codes for the digits '0' through '9' will be numerically ordered and consecutive. So, for example, '0'+3 must be the character '3'.

0	null '\0'	22	syn	44	comma	66	B	88	X	110	n
1	soh	23	etb	45	minus	67	C	89	Y	111	o
2	stx	24	can	46	period	68	D	90	Z	112	p
3	etx	25	em	47	/	69	E	91	[	113	q
4	end transmission	26	sub	48	0	70	F	92	\	114	r
5	enquire	27	escape	49	1	71	G	93	]	115	s
6	acknowledge	28	fs	50	2	72	H	94	^	116	t
7	ring a bell '\a'	29	gs	51	3	73	I	95	underscore	117	u
8	backspace '\b'	30	rs	52	4	74	J	96	back quote	118	v
9	tab '\t'	31	us	53	5	75	K	97	a	119	w
10	new line '\n'	32	blank	54	6	76	L	98	b	120	x
11	vertical tab '\v'	33	!	55	7	77	M	99	c	121	y
12	form feed '\f'	34	"	56	8	78	N	100	d	122	z
13	carriage return '\r'	35	#	57	9	79	O	101	e	123	{
14	so	36	$	58	:	80	P	102	f	124	|
15	si	37	%	59	;	81	Q	103	g	125	}
16	dle	38	&	60	<	82	R	104	h	126	~
17	dc1	39	single quote	61	=	83	S	105	i	127	delete
18	dc2	40	(	62	>	84	T	106	j		
19	dc3	41	)	63	?	85	U	107	k		
20	dc4	42	*	64	@	86	V	108	l		
21	nak	43	+	65	A	87	W	109	m		

Appendix B
Further Big-*O* Notation

Formal Definition of Big-*O*

Throughout the text, we analyze the running times of algorithms in terms of the size of an algorithm's input. For example, in Section 11.1 we developed a binary search algorithm to search an array of *n* elements, looking for a specified target. On page 585, we saw that the maximum number of operations for the binary search is given by the formula:

$T(n)$ = the maximum number of operations to search an *n*-element array
  $= 18(\lfloor \log_2 n \rfloor + 1) + 2$

Big-*O* notation is a way of analyzing a function such as $T(n)$. The analysis throws away some information about the function, but keeps other information that is most relevant to determining algorithm performance. In an informal way, you know enough to examine the function $T(n)$ for the binary search; you can "throw out the constants" and conclude that $T(n)$ is an $O(\log n)$ function.

In general, when we examine a function, such as $T(n)$, the big-*O* analysis results in some simpler expression, such as log *n*. The simpler expression is also a function of *n*. If we call this $F(n)$, then a typical big-*O* analysis provides a result of the form "$T(n)$ is an $O(F(n))$ function." In mathematical terms, this kind of result has a precise definition, as follows:

Formal Definition of Big-*O*

When we say that "$T(n)$ is an $O(F(n))$ function," we mean that there is some fixed number that we call the *threshold*, and some constant multiplier that we call *c*, such that

$$\text{Whenever } n \geq threshold, \text{ then } T(n) \leq cF(n).$$

For example, consider the function $T(n) = 3n^2 + 9n$. Some arithmetic shows that whenever $n \geq 5$, then $3n^2 + 9n \leq 4n^2$. Therefore, using a threshold of 5, and a constant multiplier of 4, we can see that

$$3n^2 + 9n \text{ is an } O(n^2) \text{ function.}$$

The graph at the top of the next page illustrates the meaning of a big-*O* expression. Notice that before the threshold, either of the two functions may be larger; anything can happen before this threshold value. But once *n* exceeds the threshold, the function $cF(n)$ is always greater than $T(n)$. Also notice that it is *c* multiplied by $F(n)$, and not simply $F(n)$, that we are comparing to $T(n)$. So, the graph illustrates the fact that "$T(n)$ is an $O(F(n))$ function."

If not used with some care, big-O expressions can grossly misrepresent the true running time of an algorithm. For example, if an algorithm runs in $O(n)$ time, then we could also say that it runs in $O(n^2)$ time (since any function that is below a constant times n will also be below the same constant times n^2). But of course, it would be silly to say that an algorithm runs in $O(n^2)$ time, when we know that it runs in $O(n)$ time. When a programmer gives a big-O time, he or she usually means that it is a "good" big-O expression.

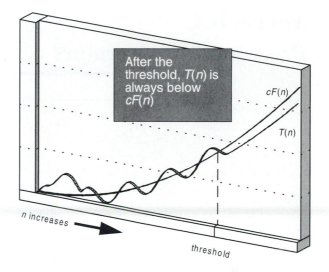

What Big-O Expressions Indicate

Big-O expressions are admittedly crude, but they do contain some information. A big-O analysis will not distinguish between a running time of $4n+3$ and a running time of $100n+50$, but it will let us distinguish between some running times and determine that some algorithms are faster than others. Look at the graphs of the four functions to the right. Notice that all three $O(n)$ functions eventually fall below the $O(n^2)$ function. This leads us to the following important big-O principle:

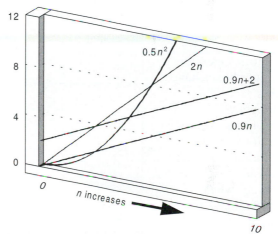

Big-O Comparison of Algorithms

Suppose that two different algorithms perform the same task with different big-O times. With a sufficiently large input, the algorithm with the better big-O analysis will perform faster.

What exactly does it mean when we say "with a sufficiently large input"? Does this mean that an input size of $n=100$ will result in a faster time from the algorithm with the better big-O? Or does it require $n=1000$, or maybe even $n=1,000,000$? Unfortunately, a big-O analysis does not tell us *how big* the input needs to be in order for the better big-O time to result in a faster algorithm. All that is known is that larger and larger inputs will *eventually* result in a faster time for the algorithm with the better big-O time.

Appendix C
Precedence of Operators

High Precedence

This table gives the precedence of C++ operators. Operators in higher boxes have higher precedence than operators in lower boxes. Unary operators and the assignment operator are done in right-to-left order when operators have the same precedence. For example, x = y = z means x = (y = z). Other operators that have the same precedence are done in left-to-right order. For example, x - y - z means (x - y) - z.

Low Precedence

Operators		Description
: :		Scope resolution operator
. [ ] ++	-> ( ) --	Member selection operators Array indexing and function call Postfix increment/decrement
++ ! ~ unary + * & *new* *sizeof*	-- unary - *delete*	Prefix increment/decrement Not Bitwise not Unary plus and minus Dereferencing operator Address of Memory allocation/deallocation Size in bytes
->*	.*	Member pointer selection
* %	/	Multiplication and division Remainder upon division
+	-	Binary addition and subtraction
<<	>>	Shift operators
< >	<= >=	Less than; less than or equal Greater than; greater than or equal
==	!=	Equal and not equal
&		Bitwise and
^		Bitwise exclusive or
|		Bitwise or
&&		Boolean and
||		Boolean or
? :		Conditional operator
= += -= *= /= %= <<= >>= &= |= ^=		Assignment operators
,		Comma operator

Appendix D
Command Line Compiling and Linking

Many C++ compilers provide an easy-to-use interface, including an editor (allowing you to create or edit programs) with simple buttons that you click to compile and run your programs. Other C++ compilers provide a "command line" mode. With a command line compiler, you use your favorite editor program to create or edit programs, and after a program is created you type one or more commands to compile, link, and run the program.

This appendix provides the details of compiling, linking, and running programs for two popular command line compilers:

- **The GNU Project C++ Compiler**, produced by Free Software Foundation, Inc., and widely available on Unix®, Linux®, and Microsoft Windows® machines. Appendix K provides instructions for obtaining the GNU compiler for Windows machines.

- The **Borland® C++ Compiler**, produced by Inprise, Inc., for IBM-compatible PCs running DOS or Windows. With this compiler, you may prefer to use the interactive interface, but you may also use it as a command line compiler, typing your command at the DOS prompt.

Compiling

Both command line compilers can compile any ".cxx" file on their own. The act of compiling creates an **object file**, which contains low-level machine instructions corresponding to your C++ code. By the way, these machine instructions are usually specific for a given type of machine. For example, you cannot create an object file for an IBM-compatible PC and expect the object file to work on a Sun workstation.

Anyway, the general command to compile a ".cxx" file with the GNU and Borland command line compilers are shown here:

Compiling with GNU

```
g++ -Wall -c filename.cxx
```

Compiling with Borland

```
bcc -w -c -P filename.cxx
```

In both commands, the `filename.cxx` may be any ".cxx" file that you want to compile. The minus signs in the commands provide various options. For example, -Wall (in GNU) and -w (in Borland) ask the compiler to provide all possible warning messages. The -c option specifies "compilation only" (rather than combining compiling and linking). In the Borland command, the -P option indicates that the file contains C++ code (rather than mere C code). For the Borland compiler, a file extension of ".cpp" is assumed to have C++ code, but other extensions, such as ".cxx", require the -P option.

The GNU command will compile `filename.cxx`, creating an object file named `filename.o`. The Borland command will compile `filename.cxx`, creating an object file named `filename.obj`.

A program that is split between several ".cxx" files can be compiled with a single command, placing all the file names at the end of the command line. Or, you may give separate commands to compile each piece of the program. For example, consider the demonstration program demo2.cxx from Figure 2.8 on page 61. This program makes use of throttle.cxx, so we must create two object files with the commands shown here:

<table>
<tr><td>**Compiling with GNU**</td><td>**Compiling with Borland**</td></tr>
</table>

```
g++  -Wall  -c  throttle.cxx        bcc  -w  -c  -P  throttle.cxx
g++  -Wall  -c  demo2.cxx           bcc  -w  -c  -P  demo2.cxx
```

If you are using an older compiler that does not support the *bool* data type, then these command lines need a modification. We'll discuss this modification in detail in Appendix E; for now you should know that these highlighted options must be added in order to provide simple boolean values:

Compiling with GNU compilers that do not have the bool type

```
g++  -Wall  -c  -Dbool=int  -Dfalse=0  -Dtrue=1  throttle.cxx
g++  -Wall  -c  -Dbool=int  -Dfalse=0  -Dtrue=1  demo2.cxx
```

Compiling with Borland compilers that do not have the bool type

```
bcc  -w  -c  -P  -Dbool=int  -Dfalse=0  -Dtrue=1  throttle.cxx
bcc  -w  -c  -P  -Dbool=int  -Dfalse=0  -Dtrue=1  demo2.cxx
```

With the GNU compiler, these commands produce two object files, throttle.o and demo2.o. The Borland compiler produces object files throttle.obj and demo2.obj. Once the object files are present, you can move to the next step: linking the pieces together.

Linking

Before you can run a program, you must link the different object files together. The general form of the linking commands for GNU and Borland are shown here with an example:

Linking object files with GNU

```
g++  file1.o file2.o  ...  -o  filename
```

Example:
```
g++  demo2.o  throttle.o  -o  demo2
```

Linking object files with Borland

```
bcc  file1.obj file2.obj  ...
```

Example:
```
bcc  demo2.obj  throttle.obj
```

The result of these commands is an executable file that can be run on your machine. In the case of the GNU compiler, the name of the executable file is explicitly given by the -o filename option at the end of the command. In the example, we have called the executable file demo2, so after the GNU linking step you would find a file named demo2 (with no file extension). If you forget the -o option, then GNU places the executable in a file with the peculiar name "a.out".

The name of the executable file does not need to be specified for the Borland compiler. This compiler automatically uses the name of the first object file, changing the file extension to ".exe". In the example given on the previous page, the executable file created by the Borland compiler will be demo2.exe.

Running a Program

Once the executable file has been created, it can be run by typing the file name (without any extension). In both of the examples shown above, you can run the demo2 program by typing the command:

```
demo2
```

This will run the demo2 program with standard input from the keyboard and standard output to the monitor.

You can also run a program with standard input taken from a file (rather than the keyboard) or run the program with standard output sent to a file (rather than the monitor). To **redirect input**, use the option "< infile" when you run the program (where infile is the name of the file that provides the input). To **redirect output**, use the option "> outfile" when you run the program (where outfile is the name of the file where you want the output sent). For example, to run the demo2 program with input from a file called data and output to a file called results, you would give the command:

```
demo2   <data   >results
```

Linking with the math.h Library

If you use the math.h library (or <cmath>), some versions of the GNU compiler require -lm to be listed during the link step, after all the object files. For example, if the demo2 program used the math library, then we would link with the following example command:

Linking object files with GNU (math library needed)
```
g++   file1.o file2.o ...    -lm   -o   filename
```

Example if the demo2 program used the math library
```
g++   demo2.o   throttle.o   -lm -o   demo2
```

The -lm option stands for "link math" (so make sure that you use the letter "l" rather than the digit one "1").

Specifying an Include Directory

Both the GNU and Borland compilers allow you to specify a particular directory where #include files can be found. The option is specified by -Idirectory . For example, we keep many of our header files in a directory named c:\source\headers, so with the Borland compiler we have:

```
bcc -Ic:\source\headers -w -c -P demo2.cxx
```

Appendix E
Dealing with Older Compilers

For additional information on older versions of Microsoft Visual C++, please see www.cs.colorado.edu/~main/vccode.html

The boolean data type, static member constants, namespaces, the new C++ header file names, the *typename* keyword, and new Standard Library features (such as iterators) are not supported by older compilers. This appendix has suggestions for handling these features in older C++ compilers.

If Your Compiler Does Not Have the bool Data Type

The *int* data type can simulate the new *bool* data type. The simulation is most easily carried out by placing these three definitions in your own header file called bool.h:

```
#define bool int
#define false 0
#define true 1
```

Any program that uses the *bool* type should include your bool.h. If you are using a command line compiler, such as the GNU compiler or the Borland® compiler described in Appendix D, then you may incorporate the three definitions directly in your compilation command. For example, using the GNU compiler to compile throttle.cxx, you would use the highlighted definitions shown here:

```
g++  -Wall  -c  -Dbool=int  -Dfalse=0  -Dtrue=1  throttle.cxx
```

If Your Compiler Does Not Have Static Member Constants

We have made extensive use of static member constants, particularly in container classes. For example, our first bag from Chapter 3 had the static member constant CAPACITY to determine the maximum number of elements that can be placed in a bag:

```
class bag
{
public:
    // TYPEDEF and MEMBER CONSTANTS
    static const size_type CAPACITY = 30;
    ...
```

The complete rules for writing static member constants are given on page 103. But what should you do if your compiler does not permit static member constants? There are two common solutions:

1. You may use an ordinary constant declaration, prior to the class definition. In the case of the bag we would write:

    ```
    const size_t BAG_CAPACITY = 30;
    class bag
    {
        ...
    ```

2. For integer values, you may use an *enum* definition within a class definition. An *enum* definition is allowed to assign integer values to a whole set of identifiers, but you can use it to create a name for just a single integer value. In our bag example, we would write:

```
class bag
{
public:
    enum { CAPACITY = 30 };
    ...
```

The keyword *enum* appears before the list of values that you want to define, and the list itself is enclosed in curly brackets. After this definition, the name `bag::CAPACITY` is defined to have the integer value 30. Although this is not the intended use of an *enum* definition, the result is the same as using a static member constant.

Namespaces

Older compilers do not support namespaces. We don't know of any good solutions to this problem, apart from not putting your classes into a namespace if your work is likely to be used on an older compiler. In addition, you will need to choose names of your classes and functions carefully so that conflicts are not created between your names and names chosen by others.

Include File Names

On page 11, we describe the differences between older header file names (such as `iostream.h` and `stdlib.h`) and newer names (such as `iostream` and `cstdlib`). Newer compilers may also use the older names (but in that case, the items in the header files are not part of the `std` namespace).

The Typename Keyword

Sometimes a template class defines auxilliary types such as `bag<Item>::size_type` which is part of the `bag<Item>` template class. Some compilers don't recognize an expression such as `bag<Item>::size_type` as a data type. These compilers require the keyword *typename* to appear before such expressions. The keyword is needed only when the `Item` is uninstantiated (for example, we can write `bag<int>::size_type` with no problems). More examples appear on page 291.

Older compilers won't recognize the keyword *typename*. For these compilers, write only the data type (such as `bag<Item>::size_type`) without the *typename* keyword.

The std::iterator Class

Building your own iterators was not a big part of this text, although we did show two examples in Chapter 6, both of which made use of the `std::iterator` class. The precise format of the `std::iterator` class was one of the last things finalized in the C++ Standard, so many compilers do not support the standard form of `std::iterator`. The GNU 2.95.2 compiler supports the standard iterator, but requires a bug fix to work properly.

Our latest information about writing your own iterators (with or without `std::iterator`) is provided online at `www.cs.colorado.edu/~main/iterators.html`.

Appendix F
Input and Output in C++

This appendix is primarily for students with a background in C programming, but with little or no C++ programming experience. In this appendix we provide details of the C++ approach to reading from standard input, writing to standard output, and reading/writing files. Throughout the appendix, we assume that your programs have a using directive `using namespace std;` for the standard namespace (otherwise you must write longer names such as `std::cout` rather than just `cout`).

Writing to Standard Output

The **insertion operator** (written <<) is used to write a value to an output stream such as the standard output device (usually the monitor screen). For example, if `i` is an integer variable, then the following statement writes its value to the standard output:

```
cout << i;
```

In this statement, `cout` stands for the "console output," and is defined as part of the header file `<iostream>`. You may write several items at once by chaining together a sequence of insertion operators. For example, if `i`, `j`, and `k` are integer variables, then the following statement first writes `i`, then `j`, and finally `k` to the standard output:

```
cout << i << j << k;
```

Writing the End of a Line

There are two ways to write the end of a line to an output stream. You may simply write the newline character `'\n'`, or you may write the special object called `endl` (which is part of `<iostream>`). For example:

```
cout << '\n';
cout << endl;
```

What's the difference between these two statements? The main difference deals with the fact that output is often written to a special place called a **buffer**, rather than to the actual output device. When the buffer becomes full, the output is "flushed" from the buffer to the actual output device. Such buffering can cause problems if a program crashes before the buffer is flushed. The buffer may contain some output that never shows up on the output device. To avoid this problem, whenever you write the `endl` object, the output buffer is automatically flushed. However, simply writing the newline character does not automatically flush the output buffer.

Setting the Field Width of an Output Item

The **field width** of an output item is the preferred number of output characters to be used when the item is printed. For example, if you print the number 123 with a field width of eight, the result will be five blank spaces followed by the digits 123 for a total of eight characters. If the output item won't fit in the specified field width, then more characters may be used. For example, if you print the number 123 with a field width of only two, then the entire number 123 is still printed (even though this requires three characters rather than just two). If you define the field width to be zero, the item will be printed using the minimum possible number of characters.

How do you define the field width for an output item? One method is to use a special "manipulator" named `setw`, which is part of `<iomanip>`. The `setw` manipulator is called like a function, with one argument that is the desired field width. This manipulator is placed in the output statement just before the item to be printed. For example, to print the number 123 with a field width of eight, you may write the statement:

```
cout << setw(8) << 123;        ──────uses setw from iomanip
```

The `setw` function may be used with the standard output device (`cout`), or with other output devices that you will use later. Keep in mind that `setw` affects the field width of only the next item to be printed.

Justification of the Output and Showing Plus Signs on Positive Numbers

When output occurs with a wide field width, each output item is padded with spaces to bring the total number of characters up to the required field width. For example, when the number 123 is printed with a field width of eight, the complete output will consist of five spaces followed by the three digits of 123. If you don't specify otherwise, the item is printed on the far right of the field width, with any padding spaces before the item. You can control the placement of the item by calling the `setf` function to set the control flags of an output device such as `cout`. This function is called with the syntax shown in these three examples:

```
cout.setf(ios::right,    ios::adjustfield); // Item appears on right side of field
cout.setf(ios::left,     ios::adjustfield); // Item appears on left side of field
cout.setf(ios::internal, ios::adjustfield); // "Internal" spaces (described below)
```

Once the justification is set with the `setf` function, it remains in effect for all subsequent outputs until it is reset to some other value. The `ios::internal` setting causes numbers to be printed with the + or – sign as the first output character, but the remainder of the number appears on the right side of the field width. (To force a number to be printed with a + sign, you will have to call `cout.setf(ios::showpos)`; when you no longer want the + signs to print, you may call `cout.unsetf(ios::showpos)`.)

By the way, you can see that `setf` and `unsetf` are both member functions of the `cout` output stream. They are defined in `<iostream>` and may be used with any output stream. The arguments, such as `ios::left`, are also defined in the header file `<iostream>`.

Format of Float and Double Numbers

The format for printing *float* and *double* numbers is also controlled by the setf functions. Here are three examples:

```
cout.setf(ios::fixed,        ios::floatfield);
cout.setf(ios::scientific, ios::floatfield);
cout.setf(0,                  ios::floatfield);
```

Fixed-point notation. The first example, using ios::fixed, causes numbers to be printed in *fixed-point notation,* which is the common way of writing numbers with a decimal point. For example, the number 19¼ will be printed as 19.25.

Scientific notation. The second example, using ios::scientific, causes numbers to be printed in *scientific notation,* consisting of a number times some power of 10. For example, the large number 1.8×10^{16} will be printed as 1.8e16. The letter e indicates the exponent.

Automatic notation. The third form, using the number 0 as the argument, causes C++ to select the format that it thinks is best for a number (either fixed-point or scientific notation).

If you don't specify one of the three formats, then C++ uses the automatic format. Once a format is set, it remains in place for all subsequent outputs.

Precision of Float and Double Numbers

Output streams have a precision function with one integer argument to determine how many digits are printed for each number. For example, this statement sets the precision to 12:

```
cout.precision(12);
```

(An alternative is cout << setprecision(12);, which uses setprecision from <iomanip>.) With a precision of 12, the fixed-point and scientific notations will both have 12 digits of accuracy after the decimal point. The automatic notation will have a total of 12 significant digits. Once you set the precision, it stays in effect for all subsequent outputs.

When the automatic notation is used, trailing zeros and the decimal point are not always printed. For example, the *double* number 123.0 will be printed as 123 (with no decimal point). With a precision of 12, the number 19¼ will be printed with no trailing zeros, resulting in 19.25 (rather than 19.250000000000). You may force the decimal point and trailing zeros for fixed-point numbers with the function call cout.setf(ios::showpoint). You may revert to the usual method of automatic notation with the function call cout.unsetf(ios::showpoint). As usual, these functions may be used with any output stream (not just with cout).

Reading from Standard Input

The **extraction operator** (written >>) is used to read a value from an input stream such as the standard input device (usually the keyboard). For example, if i is an integer variable, then the following statement reads an integer value from the standard input and stores the result in i:

```
cin >> i;
```

In this statement, `cin` stands for the "console input," and is defined as part of the header file `<iostream>`. You may read several items at once by chaining together a sequence of extraction operators. For example, if `i`, `j`, and `k` are integer variables, then the following statement first reads `i`, then `j`, and finally `k` from the standard input:

```
cin >> i >> j >> k;
```

There are several details that you should be aware of regarding the extraction operator:

1. If the standard input device is a keyboard, then usually nothing is read until the user presses the return key. This gives the user a chance to use the backspace key to correct mistakes before pressing the return key.

2. When the extraction operator reads a data value, it starts by skipping any whitespace that occurs in the input. This whitespace consists of any blanks, tabs, and newline characters. Skipping the whitespace occurs even if you are reading a character value, which means that the extraction operator cannot be used to read a character if the value that you want to read might be a blank or other whitespace.

3. The extraction operator reads the input until the end of the input value is reached. The end of the value occurs by reaching any character that is not part of the input value. This ending character is called the **delimiter**, and the delimiter is not actually read. For example, suppose that `i` is an integer variable, `c` is a character variable, and we execute the statement:

    ```
    cin >> i >> c;
    ```

    The program's user might type the following input (followed by the return key):

    42xyz

    With this input, the number 42 will be assigned to `i`, and the character `'x'` is assigned to `c`. The characters `'y'` and `'z'` remain in the input, perhaps to be read at a later time.

Reading a Null-Terminated String or a C++ String

You may use the extraction operator to read a null-terminated string. For example:

```
char message[100];
cin >> message;
```

In this case, the extraction operator skips any initial whitespace and reads characters into `message` until more whitespace is encountered. For example, suppose that the program's user types the following input line (followed by the return key):

The quick brown fox jumps over the lazy dog.

The statement cin >> message will skip any initial whitespace and read the characters **The**—ending when the blank is encountered after the **e**. The blank itself is not read. The three characters that were read are placed in message, with a null terminator after the third character. There is no checking to ensure that the array is large enough to hold the characters that were read.

C++ strings (from the <string> header file) can be read in the same manner as null-terminated strings, but there is also a getline function that will read an entire line into a string variable. For example:

```
string message;

// Reads one input line into message, including whitespace. The end-of-line is read, but not
// added to the end of the message string:
getline(cin, message);
```

Failed Input

Sometimes a user provides illegal data for an input operation. For example, the program might be reading an integer, but the user types the word **quick**. Whenever illegal data is encountered, the input stream is marked as **failed**. Once the input stream has failed, any subsequent attempts to read from the input stream will *have no effect*! Nothing is read; no variable values are assigned.

You may use the name of an input stream as a boolean expression to test whether the stream has failed. A failed stream results in a false expression; a device that is still good results in a true expression. For example:

```
if (cin)
    cout << "Input is still good." << endl;
else
    cout << "Input is bad." << endl;
```

The failure can occur for many reasons, but the most common failure is encountering the wrong type of data in the input stream. If an incorrect data type is the cause of the problem, you may reset the input stream and try to read the data again using a variable of a different type. The member function to reset a failed input stream is clear( ). For example, cin.clear( ) will reset the console input, allowing you to try to read the data again.

Three More Functions: get, ignore, and peek

Many other input functions are part of <iostream>. We'll describe three of the most useful functions. The first function, called get, has several forms, including a form that simply reads the next input character. For example, suppose that c is a character variable. The following statement reads the next character from the standard input, and assigns the read value to c:

```
cin.get(c);
```

Notice that get is called as a member function of the cin object. How does cin.get(c); differ from cin >> c;? The answer is that get always reads the next character without skipping whitespace; on the other hand, the >> operator skips whitespace before reading the next character.

Another member function, called `ignore`, allows you to read and discard the next input character. With `cin`, the function is called as shown here:

```
cin.ignore( ); // Read the next character from cin, and discard this character.
```

Another member function, called `peek`, allows you to look at the next available character without actually reading it. For example, the following code checks to see whether the next character is the letter `'X'`:

```
if (cin.peek( ) == 'X')
    cout << "I am about to read an X from the standard input." << endl;
```

The peek function always returns the next input character without skipping whitespace. As another example, this code will read and discard characters until the input stream fails, or a newline character is reached:

```
while (cin && (cin.peek( ) != '\n'))
    cin.ignore( );
```

Here is one more example of a function that reads and discards characters until the input stream fails or a non-whitespace character is reached. The function makes use of a boolean function, called `isspace`, to determine whether a character is whitespace:

```
void eat_white( )
// Postcondition: Characters have been read from standard input until the input stream
//   becomes bad, or a non-whitespace character is reached.
// Library facilities used: cctype (provides isspace)
{
    while (cin && isspace(cin.peek( )))
        cin.ignore( );
}
```

Detecting the End of a File

It is possible for the standard input to be connected to a file of characters. In this case, a program must be able to detect when the end of the input file has been reached. When the last actual character of the file has been read, the peek function returns a special constant named EOF (which is part of `<iostream>`). For example:

```
if (cin.peek( ) == EOF)
    cout << "There is nothing more to read." << endl;
```

One warning: The peek function does not return the EOF constant until all characters of the file have been read—including any blanks or newline characters that may appear after the last piece of actual data. For example, suppose that the standard input is a file of integers. We want to read and add up all these integers until the end of file is reached. The correct way to process the input file is shown here (using the `eat_white` function, written earlier):

```
int sum = 0;    // The sum of all the numbers that we read
int next;       // The next number that we read

eat_white( ); // Skip any whitespace at the front of the file.
while (cin  &&  (cin.peek( ) != EOF))
{
    cin >> next;
    eat_white( );
    sum += next;
}

cout << "The total of all numbers is: " << sum << endl;
```

The special EOF character at the end of a file can be read by the usual get function. After this character is read, a member function cin.eof( ) will return true.

Writing or Reading a Text File

So far, we have shown output and input using the standard streams cout and cin. A program can also create its own streams, connecting these streams to files. Such a program should include both <iostream> and <fstream>, and proceed as follows.

Opening a file. For writing, a program should declare a variable of type ofstream. For reading, a program should declare a variable of type ifstream. Once the variable is declared, it can be connected to an actual file with the open member function, as shown here:

Opening an Output File:

```
#include <iostream>
#include <fstream>

ofstream outfile;

outfile.open("results");
```

Opening an Input File:

```
#include <iostream>
#include <fstream>

ifstream infile;

infile.open("data");
```

The argument to the open function is the name of the file that you wish to write. In our output example, this argument is the constant string "results", so we will be writing a file named results. Our input example is reading text from a file named data. The argument to the open function may also be a string variable, or any other string expression.

Checking for failure. Sometimes, when you open a file, the open operation fails. For example, opening a file for writing can fail if the computer's disk is already full. Opening a file for input will fail if the specified file cannot be found. If the open operation fails, then the stream will be marked as failed. You may use the name of a stream as a boolean expression to test whether the stream is bad. A failed stream results in a false expression; a device that is still good results in a true expression. Thus, after opening a file, you should check for possible failure. A simple approach uses the assert function (from `cassert`), as shown here:

Check for Failure of an Output File:	**Check for Failure of an Input File:**

```
#include <iostream>
#include <fstream>
#include <cassert>

ofstream outfile;

outfile.open("results");
assert(outfile);
```

```
#include <iostream>
#include <fstream>
#include <cassert>

ifstream infile;

infile.open("data");
assert(infile);
```

Using the ofstream or ifstream. Once an `ofstream` is open, you may use it in the same way that you have used cout. For example, using `outfile` (opened as shown above), you may write:

```
outfile << "This sentence will be written to the file." << endl;
```

Once an `ifstream` is open, you may use it in the same way that you have used cin. For example, suppose that `infile` (opened above) contains lines of digits. You can read the next integer in the input file, storing the result in an integer variable i, as shown here:

```
infile >> i;
```

Closing a file. When you are done writing or reading a file, you should activate the `close` member function of the `ofstream` or `ifstream`. This function has no arguments, as shown here:

Closing an Output File:	**Closing an Input File:**

```
#include <iostream>
#include <fstream>
#include <cassert>

ofstream outfile;

outfile.open("results");
assert(outfile);
```

```
#include <iostream>
#include <fstream>
#include <cassert>

ifstream infile;

infile.open("data");
assert(infile);
```

. . .Statements that use outfile...

. . .Statements that use infile...

```
outfile.close( );
```

```
infile.close( );
```

Closing a file releases any resources that the file implementation uses. If output buffering is used, then closing an output file also flushes the output buffer.

Appendix G
Selected Library Functions

The <cassert> Facility

The assert facility from <cassert> can be used by writing a statement of the form:

```
assert(expression);
```

Notice that assert is not part of the std namespace (the name is simply assert, rather than std::assert). If the expression is true, then the assertion does no action. If the expression is false, then the assertion prints an error message that includes the text of the expression and stops the program. For example, consider this assertion:

```
assert(i > 0);
```

If i is positive, then the assertion does nothing. If i is non-positive, then the assertion will print a message such as "Assertion failed on line 42: i > 0". The primary purpose of using such assertions is to aid a programmer in finding errors at the earliest possible moment.

Once a program is no longer undergoing testing, a programmer can turn off all assertions by placing the following at the top of each file:

```
#define NDEBUG
```

Functions from <cctype> to Manipulate Characters

```
isalpha(c);  // Returns true if c is a letter from 'A' to 'Z' or from 'a' to 'z'.
isalnum(c);  // Returns true if c is a letter from 'A' to 'Z' or 'a' to 'z', or a digit from '0' to '9'.
isdigit(c);  // Returns true if c is a digit  from  '0'  to  '9'.
isspace(c);  // Returns true if c is a blank, tab, newline, or carriage return.
tolower(c);  // If c is an uppercase letter, then the function returns the equivalent
             // lowercase letter. Otherwise c is returned unchanged.
toupper(c);  // If c is a lowercase letter, then the function returns the equivalent
             // uppercase letter. Otherwise c is returned unchanged.
```

Random Number Facility from <cstdlib>

```
int rand( );                      // Successive calls to rand( ) return a sequence of
                                  // pseudorandom numbers in the range 0 to RAND_MAX.
void srand(unsigned int seed);    // The seed for the pseudorandom number generator
                                  // has been set to the specified value.
const int RAND_MAX;               // The largest return value from the rand function
```

String Conversions from <cstdlib>

```
int atoi(const char[ ] s);
    // The name stands for "ascii to integer." The parameter s is a null-terminated string. The
    // function inteprets the string as if it were typed from the keyboard and read into an
    // integer. For example, the return value of atoi("42") is the integer 42.
    // The function may also be used with a C++ string s, such as atoi(s.c_str( ));
    // In this example, s activates c_str( ), which returns an equivalent null terminated string.

double atof(const char[ ] s);
    // The name stands for "ascii to float," although the return value is actually a double
    // number rather than a float. The parameter s is a null-terminated string. The function
    // inteprets the string as if it were typed from the keyboard and read into a double
    // variable. For example, the return value of atoi("42.2") is the double number 42.2.
```

Standard Library Sorting Functions
(See Section 13.4 for Details)

```
void sort(Iterator begin, Iterator end);
void qsort(
    void* base,
    size_t number_of_elements,
    size_t element_size,
    int compare(const void*, const void*)
);
```

Functions from <cstring> to Manipulate Null-Terminated Strings

```
char* strcat(char target[ ], const char source[ ]);
    // A copy of the null-terminated string source is copied to the end of the null-terminated
    // string target. The function returns a pointer to the first character of target.
int strcmp(const char s1[ ], const char s2[ ]);
    // Compares two null-terminated strings. A negative return value indicates s1 < s2; a zero
    // return value indicates that s1 == s2; a positive return value indicates s1 > s2.
char* strcpy(char target[ ], const char source[ ]);
    // Copies the null-terminated string source to the null-terminated string target. The function
    // returns a pointer to the first character of target.
size_t strlen(const char s[ ]);
    // The return value is the length of s (a null-terminated string).
char* strchr(const char s[ ], char c);
    // The return value is a pointer to the first occurrence of c in the null-terminated string s (or
    // the NULL pointer if c does not appear in s).
int strpos(const char s[ ], char c);
    // The return value is the first index i such that s[i] = c (or – 1 if c does not appear in the
    // null-terminated string s).
char* strstr(const char s[ ], const char sub[ ])
    // Returns a pointer to the first occurrence of the substring sub in the string null-terminated
    // string s (or the NULL pointer if sub does not appear in s).
```

The Swap Function from <algorithm>

```
template <class Item>
void swap(Item& a, Item&b)
   // The value of a has been interchanged with the value of b.
```

Selected Functions from <algorithm> for Manipulating Arrays

In general, the "location" arguments are iterators of various kinds. But a useful way to begin using these functions is to have each argument be a "location" in an array. These locations may be the name of an entire array. Or, for an array a and an integer i, a location a+i indicates the spot beginning at a[i].

```
copy(<beginning location>, <ending location>, <destination location>)
   // The function starts at the specified beginning location and copies an item to the destination.
   // It continues beyond the beginning location, copying more and more items to the next spot of
   // the destination, until we are about to copy the ending location. The ending location is not copied.

fill(<destination begin location>, <destination end location>, <value>)
   // The function puts copies of the value into the destination, starting at the begin location,
   // then the spot after that, and so on up to (but not including) the end location.

fill_n(<destination begin location>, <n>, <value>)
   // The function puts a copy of the value into the begin location of the destination, then
   // another copy into the next spot, and so on until n copies have been placed.
```

Appendix H
Brief Reference for the Standard Template Classes

This brief introduction can't cover all details of the Standard Template Classes. For more detailed information, we suggest The C++ Standard Library by Nicolai M. Josuttis or an online guide such as P.J. Plauger's www.dinkumware.com.

Parameters Used in this Reference

```
begin and end          // Two iterators that specify a range of items starting at the
                       // begin iterator's item and going up to (but not including) the
                       // item of the end iterator
comp                   // The name of a function that takes two items as arguments
                       // and returns true if the first item is less than the second
pos                    // An iterator from the actual container that activated the
                       // member function
m, m1, m2              // A map or multimap
r, r1, r2              // A set or multiset
s, s1, s2              // A string
t, t1, t2              // A stack, queue, or priority queue
w, w1, w2              // A vector or list
```

Sets and Multisets from <set>

The set<Item> template class provides a collection of items. Any given item may appear in the set only once. The multiset<Item> class is like a set, but a given item may appear more than once in a multiset. For both sets and multisets, the items are typically stored in a balanced binary search tree, so that the Item type must have a less-than operator forming a strict weak ordering (see Figure 6.4 on page 302).

CONSTRUCTORS:
In these examples, **set<...>** may be any instantiated set or multiset (such as set<double> or multiset<int>).

```
set<...> r                     // Create an empty set or multiset.
set<...> r1(r2)                // Copy constructor
set<...> r(comp)               // Create an empty set or multiset using the specified comp
                               // function to determine when an item is less than another.
set<...> r(begin, end)         // Create a new set or multiset that initially contains the
                               // range of items from [begin...end).
set<...> r(begin, end, comp)   // Just like the previous constructor, but it will use the
                               // comp function to determine when an item is less than
                               // another
```

CONSTANT MEMBER FUNCTIONS:
```
r.count(target)                // Returns the number of times that target occurs in r
```

```
r.empty( )                  // Returns true if r has no items.
r.max_size( )               // Returns the maximum number of items that r can hold.
r.size( )                   // Returns the number of items currently in r.
r1 == r2 and r1 != r2       // Boolean tests to see whether two sets are equal or unequal.
r1 < r2 and r1 > r2         // Tests for lexicographical ordering of sets.
r1 <= r2 and r1 >= r2
```

FUNCTIONS THAT RETURN BIDIRECTIONAL ITERATORS:

```
r.begin( )               // Returns an iterator that is positioned at the start of r.
r.end( )                 // Returns an end iterator (just beyond the last item of r).
r.equal_range(target)    // Returns a pair of iterators:
                         // r.equal_range(x).first is equal to r.lower_bound(x),
                         // r.equal_range(x).second is equal to r.upper_bound(x)
r.find(target)           // Returns an iterator that is positioned at the first occurrence of
                         // the target (or an end iterator if target does not occur).
r.lower_bound(target)    // Returns an iterator that is positioned at the first item that is
                         // greater than or equal to the target (or an end iterator if there is
                         // no such item).
r.rbegin( )              // Returns a reverse iterator that is positioned at the last item of r.
r.rend( )                // Returns a reverse end iterator (just before the first item of r).
r.upper_bound(target)    // Returns an iterator that is positioned at the first item that is
                         // greater than the target (or an end iterator if there is
                         // no such item).
```

MODIFICATION MEMBER FUNCTIONS:

All of the erase functions return the number of items removed. Most of the insert functions return an iterator that is positioned at the new element. However, for a set m, the return value of r.insert(element) is a pair where r.insert(element).first is the usual iterator and r.insert(element).second is a boolean value (true if the element was newly inserted, and false if the element was previously in the set).

```
r.clear( )               // Removes all elements from r.
r.erase(element)         // Removes all copies of the specified element .
r.erase(pos)             // Removes the one element of the position iterator.
r.erase(begin, end)      // Removes all elements from the range [begin...end).
r.insert(element)        // Puts the specified element into the set.
r.insert(pos, element)   // Same as r.insert(element), but uses the iterator pos as a hint
                         // about where to put the new element. A good hint will improve
                         // the speed of the function.
r.insert(begin, end)     // Inserts all elements in the range [begin...end).
```

Stacks, Queues, and Priority Queues from <stack> and <queue>

The stack<Item>, queue<Item>, and priority_queue<Item> template classes provide a collection of items organized as a stack, a queue, or a priority queue. For the priority queue, the Item type must have a less-than operator forming a strict weak ordering (see Figure 6.4 on page 302).

CONSTRUCTORS:

The stack, queue, and priority queue each have a default constructor (to create an empty container) and a copy constructor. There are additional constructors, especially for the priority queue.

CONSTANT MEMBER FUNCTIONS:
```
t.empty( )              // Returns true if t has no items.
t.size( )               // Returns the number of items currently in t.
t1 == t2 and t1 != t2   // Boolean tests to see whether t1 and t2 are equal or unequal.
t1 < t2 and t1 > t2     // Tests for lexicographical ordering of t1 and t2.
t1 <= t2 and t1 >= t2
```

FUNCTIONS THAT GIVE ACCESS TO ITEMS:

All versions of the `top`, `front`, and `back` functions return a reference to the next item. When `t` is not a const object, this return value can be used to change the item (see Section 8.5).

```
// Return the next item of a stack or const stack:
Item& t.top( )
const Item& t.top( ) const
```

```
// Return the next item of a queue, const queue, priority queue, or const priority queue. For a
// queue or const queue, this is the first item that was added. For a priority queue or
// const priority queue, this is the highest priority item. If a priority queue has several items
// items with equally high priority, the Standard does not specify which is accessed first.
Item& t.front( )
const Item& t.front( ) const
```

```
// For a queue or const queue, these return a reference to the most recently added item.
Item& t.back( )
const Item& t.back( ) const
```

FUNCTIONS THAT ADD OR REMOVE ITEMS:
```
t.pop( )                // Remove the next item from the container.
t.push(element)         // Add the specified item to the container.
```

Strings from <string>

The simplest `string` class allows easy creation and manipulation of sequences of characters. Our list of string functions is not complete, but it contains the functions that we have found most useful. Many of these functions have a string as an argument and can take the string in a variety of forms. In our list of functions, we will use these names to specify the various formats of arguments:

1. *const* `string&` `str`
   The sequence of all characters in `str`.
2. *const* `string&` `str`, `size_type` `index`, `size_type` `n`
   The sequence of up to n characters from `str`, starting at `str[index]`.
3. *char* `c`
   The string that contains just the one character `c`.
4. `size_type` `n`, *char* `c`
   The string that contains n consecutive copies of the character `c`.
5. *const char* `carray[ ]`
   The string that contains characters from the start of the array until the null terminator character occurs.
6. *const char* `carray[ ]`, `size_type` `n`
   The string that contains characters from `carray[0]` through `carray[n-1]`.

7. `iterator begin, iterator end`
   The string that contains characters from *begin up to (but not including) *end, which is [begin...end).

CONSTRUCTORS AND ASSIGNMENT:
   Note that there is no constructor that takes a single character as its parameter. Each of the assign functions assigns a new value to s using the seven forms of arguments listed previously.

```
string s( )
string s(str)
string s(str, index, n)
string s(n, c)
string s(carray)
string s(carray, n)
string s(begin, end)
s.assign(str) or s = str
s.assign(str, index, n)
s.assign(c) or s = c
s.assign(n, c)
s.assign(carray) or s = carray
s.assign(carray, n)
```

CONSTANT MEMBER FUNCTIONS:

```
s.capacity( )           // Returns the maximum number of characters that could
                        // be put in s without having to add more memory.
s.c_str( )              // Returns a const array of characters that contains a null-
                        // terminated string with the same characters as s.
s.data( )               // Same as s.c_str( ) but without the null terminator
s.empty( )              // Returns true if s has no characters.
s.length( )             // Returns the current number of characters in s.
s.max_size( )           // Returns the maximum number of characters that s
                        // could ever have.
s.size( )               // Same as s.length( )
s1 == s2 and s1 != s2   // Boolean tests of whether two strings are equal or unequal
s1 < s2 and s1 > s2     // Tests for lexicographical ordering of strings
s1 <= s2 and s1 >= s2
```

FUNCTIONS THAT GIVE ACCESS TO THE CHARACTERS OF THE STRING:
   For an index in the range 0 to s.length( )-1, the notation s[index] or s.at(index) returns the character at the specified index. Both of these functions return a reference to a character. When the string is not const, then this reference can be used to change a character, such as s[2] = 'x'. The at version causes an exception when the index is out of range, but the s[index] behavior is undefined in this case.

CONCATENATION:
   The expression s1 + s2 is a new string containing the characters of s1 followed by those of s2.

APPEND FUNCTIONS:
   These add the specified characters to the end of what's already in the string, using one of the forms of arguments shown above.
   ```
   s.append(str) or s += str
   s.append(str, index, n)
   s.append(c) or s += c
   s.append(n, c)
   s.append(carray) or s += carray
   s.append(carray, n)
   s.append(begin, end)
   ```

INSERT FUNCTIONS:
   These insert new characters, specified using one of the forms of arguments shown above. These characters are inserted beginning at s[i]. The value of i must be less than or equal to s.size( ). Any characters that were already at s[i] or beyond are shifted rightward to make room for the new characters.
   ```
   s.insert(i, str)
   s.insert(i, str, index, n)
   s.insert(i, n, c)
   s.insert(i, carray)
   s.insert(i, carray, n)
   ```

REPLACE FUNCTIONS:
   These function replaces len characters of s starting at s[i]. The value of i must be less than or equal to s.size( ), and if there are fewer than len characters starting at this spot, then all characters to the end of the string are replaced. The new characters are specified using one of the forms of arguments shown above.
   ```
   s.replace(i, len, str)
   s.replace(i, len, str, index, n)
   s.replace(i, len, n, c)
   s.replace(i, len, carray)
   s.replace(i, len, carray, n)
   ```

FUNCTIONS TO FIND A POSITION IN A STRING:
   These functions return a value of type string::size_type. The return value is the constant string::npos if the character is not found.
   ```
   s.find(c)         // Returns index of first occurrence of the character c in s
   s.find(c, i)      // Returns index of first occurrence of c that is at or after s[i]
   s.rfind(c)        // Returns index of final occurrence of the character c in s
   s.rfind(c, i)     // Returns index of final occurrence of c that is at or before s[i]
   s.find(str)       // Returns index of first occurrence of the substring str within s
   s.find(str, i)    // Returns index of first occurrence of str that is at or after s[i]
   s.rfind(str)      // Returns index of final occurrence of the substr str within s
   s.rfind(str, i)   // Returns index of final occurrence of str that is at or before s[i]
   ```

FUNCTIONS THAT RETURN A SUBSTRING:
   ```
   s.substr(i)       // Returns a string containing characters from s[i] to the end of s
   s.substr(i, n)    // Returns a string containing up to n characters, starting at s[i]
   ```

OTHER MODIFICATION MEMBER FUNCTIONS:
```
s.clear( )          // Removes all characters from s.
s.erase( )          // Removes all characters from s.
s.erase(i)          // Removes all characters from s[i] to the end of s.
s.erase(i, len)     // Removes up to len characters starting at s[i].
s.reserve(amount)   // Requests that the capacity of s be changed to the specified amount
                    // (which may be smaller than the current capacity). However, the
                    // changed capacity will never be smaller than the current string size.
s.resize(n, c)      // Changes the length of s to n (if this increases the length, new
                    // characters are the character c).
s.resize(n)         // Same as s.resize(n, '\0')
```

INPUT AND OUTPUT:
```
cout << s            // Print all of s to cout.
cin >> s             // Skip whitespace and then read characters into s until whitespace is
                     // encountered. The terminating whitespace is not read.
getline(cin, s, c)   // Read characters from cin into s until c is encountered.
                     // The terminating c is read but not added to the end of s.
getline(cin, s)      // Same as getline(cin, s, '\n')
```

Vectors from <vector> and Lists from <list>

The vector<Item> template class provides a sequence of items, similar to the way that a string provides a sequence of characters. Although not required by the C++ Standard, the typical vector implementation stores the items in a dynamic array.

The list<Item> template class also provides a sequence of items, similar to our sequence class in Chapters 3 through 5. Insertions and deletions at any point that is marked by an iterator are more efficient with lists because they are typically implemented with a linked list.

CONSTRUCTORS AND ASSIGNMENT:
Vectors and lists have a default constructor (creates an empty sequence), a copy constructor, and an assignment operator. The function w.assign(n, element) changes w to a sequence that contains n copies of the specified element.

CONSTANT MEMBER FUNCTIONS:
```
w.capacity( )              // (Vector only) Returns the maximum number of items
                           // that could be put in w without adding more memory.
w.empty( )                 // Returns true if w has no items.
w.size( )                  // Returns the current number of items in w.
w.max_size( )              // Returns the maximum number of elements that w could
                           // ever have.
w1 == w2 and w1 != w2      // Boolean tests of whether two vectors are equal or unequal
w1 < w2 and w1 > w2        // Tests for lexicographical ordering of vectors.
w1 <= w2 and w1 >= w2
```

FUNCTIONS THAT GIVE RANDOM ACCESS TO THE ITEMS OF THE VECTOR (BUT NOT A LIST):
For an index in the range of 0 to v.size( )-1, the notation v[index] or v.at(index) returns the item at the specified index. Both of these functions return a reference to the item. When the

vector is not const, then this reference can be used to change an item such as `v[2]` = `'x';`. The at version causes an exception when the index is out of range, but the `v[index]` behavior is undefined in this case.

INSERT FUNCTIONS:

Each insert function has a parameter pos that is an iterator for the vector. The new element is inserted at this position. Any items that were already at or beyond this position are shifted rightward to make room for the new items.

```
w.insert(pos, element)       // Inserts new element at specified position.
w.insert(pos, n, element)    // Inserts n copies of new element at specified position.
w.insert(pos, begin, end)    // Inserts elements [begin...end) into the vector at the
                             // specified position.
```

OTHER MODIFICATION MEMBER FUNCTIONS:

```
w.clear( )              // Removes all elements from v.
w.erase(pos)            // Pos is an iterator for the vector; this function removes the item at
                        // this position.
w.erase(begin, end)     // Removes all elements from *begin up to (but not including) *end;
                        // i.e., the left-inclusive interval [begin...end).
w.erase(i, len)         // (Vector only) Removes up to len elements starting at w[i].
w.front( )              // Returns a reference to the first element of the sequence.
w.back( )               // Returns a reference to the last element of the sequence.
w.pop_back( )           // Removes the final element of w.
w.push_back(element)    // Appends the specified element to the end of w.
w.pop_front( )          // Removes the first element of w.
w.push_front(element)   // Inserts the specified element to the front of w.
w.reserve(amount)       // (Vector only) Requests that the capacity of w be increased to the
                        // amount. (Unlike the string, this will never reduce the capacity.)
w.resize(n, element)    // Changes the length of w to n (if this increases the
                        // length, new items are the specified element).
w.resize(n)             // Changes the length of w to n (if this increases the length, new
                        // items are the default value of the Item type).
```

FUNCTIONS THAT RETURN ITERATORS:

```
w.begin( )      // Returns an iterator that is positioned at the start of w.
w.end( )        // Returns an end iterator (just beyond the last item of w).
w.rbegin( )     // Returns a reverse iterator that is positioned at the last item of w.
w.rend( )       // Returns a reverse end iterator (just before the first item of w).
```

Maps and Multimaps from <map>

The `map<Key, Item>` and `multimap<Key, Item>` template classes from <map> allow a programmer to store a collection of items in which each item has an associated key, similar to the hash tables of Chapter 12 (but stored in a different manner that depends on the keys being ordered by a less-than operator). The map is limited to having at most one distinct item for any given key, whereas the multimap allows many different items with the same key. The map and multimap have a variety of the member functions similar to the set, but they also allow unique map operations described here:

INSERTING AN ITEM WITH A PARTICULAR KEY:

To insert an item e with a key into a map m, write `cout << m[k];` . For a multimap, the syntax is more complex: `m.insert(multimap<xxx,yyy>::value_type(k,e));`, where xxx is the type of the key and yyy is the type of the items.

RETRIEVING AN ITEM WITH A PARTICULAR KEY:

The item associated with key k can be retrieved from a map with the `m[k]` notation, for example: `cout << m[k];`. For a multimap, the sequence of items that all have a specified key k can be obtained in several ways. One approach used by Lippmann and Lajoie is to use the `count` and `find` functions, as shown here (where it is an iterator for the multimap m):

```
int i;
int many = m.count(k);
it = m.find(k);
for (i = 0; i < many; ++i, ++it)
    // Do something with *it
```

Operations for Bidirectional Iterators

In these operations, p is a bidirectional iterator (such as provided by the all the classes of this appendix).

```
*p          // Returns a reference to the current item of p.
++p         // Move p to the next item (and return a reference to the new iterator).
p++         // Move p to the next item (and return a copy of the iterator before the move).
--p         // Move p to the previous item (and return a reference to the new iterator).
p--         // Move p to the previous item (and return a copy of the iterator before the move).
```

Operations of Random Access Iterators

In these operations, p is a random access iterator (such as provided by a vector, but not the other classes in this appendix) and i is an integral value.

```
p[i]        // Returns a reference to the item that is i spots forward from p's current item.
p += i      // Moves p forward i spots.
p -= i      // Moves p backward i spots.
p + i       // This expression is an iterator that is i spots beyond p (but p itself doesn't change).
p - i       // This expression is an iterator that is i spots before p (but p itself doesn't change).
```

Appendix I
A Toolkit of Useful Functions

Header File

```
// FILE: useful.h
// PROVIDES: Five useful functions for random numbers and displays. These functions are
// in the global namespace.
//
// FUNCTIONS PROVIDED:
//    double random_fraction( )
//       Postcondition: The return value is a random real number in the closed interval [0..1]
//       (including the endpoints).
//
//    double random_real(double low, double high)
//       Precondition: low <= high.
//       Postcondition: The return value is a random real number in the closed interval [low..high]
//       (including the endpoints).
//
//    void display(double x)
//       Postcondition: The function has written one line of output to the standard output, with a
//       vertical bar in the middle. If x is positive, then approximately x stars are printed to the
//       right of the vertical bar. If x is negative, then approximately -x stars are printed to the
//       left of the vertical bar. If the absolute value of x is more than 39, then only 39 stars
//       are printed. Examples:
//       display(8) prints:                              |********
//       display(-4) prints:                         ****|
//
//    void eat_line( )
//       Postcondition: Up to next newline has been read and discarded from cin.
//
//    bool inquire(const char query[ ])
//       Precondition: query is a null-terminated string of characters.
//       Postcondition: query has been printed, and a one-line response read from the user.
//       The function returns true if the user's response begins with 'Y' or 'y', and returns false if
//       the user's response begins with 'N' or 'n'. (If the response begins with some other letter,
//       then the query is repeated.)

#ifndef USEFUL_H
#define USEFUL_H

    double random_fraction( );
    double random_real(double low, double high);
    void display(double x);
    void eat_line( );
    bool inquire(const char query[ ]);

#endif
```

Implementation File

```
// FILE: useful.cxx
// IMPLEMENTS: Five useful functions (see useful.h for documentation)
// These functions are in the global namespace.

#include <cassert>      // Provides assert
#include <cctype>       // Provides toupper
#include <iostream>     // Provides cout, cin, get
#include <cstdlib>      // Provides rand, RAND_MAX
#include "useful.h"
using namespace std;

void display(double x)
// Library facilities used: iostream
{
    const char STAR = '*';
    const char BLANK = ' ';
    const char VERTICAL_BAR = '|';
    const int  LIMIT = 39;
    int i;

    if (x < -LIMIT)
        x = -LIMIT;
    else if (x > LIMIT)
        x = LIMIT;

    for (i = -LIMIT; i < 0; i++)
    {
        if (i >= x)
            cout << STAR;
        else
            cout << BLANK;
    }
    cout << VERTICAL_BAR;
    for (i = 1; i <= LIMIT; i++)
    {
        if (i <= x)
            cout << STAR;
        else
            cout << BLANK;
    }
    cout << endl;
}
```

(continued)

```
double random_fraction( )
// Library facilities used: cstdlib
{
    return rand( ) / double(RAND_MAX);
}

double random_real(double low, double high)
// Library facilities used: cassert
{
    assert(low <= high);
    return low + random_fraction( ) * (high - low);
}

void eat_line( )
// Library facilities used: iostream
//
{
    char next;

    do
        cin.get(next);
    while (next != '\n');
}

bool inquire(const char query[ ])
// Library facilities used: cctype, iostream
{
    char answer;

    do
    {
        cout << query << " [Yes or No]" << endl;
        cin >> answer;
        answer = toupper(answer);
        eat_line( );
    }
    while ((answer != 'Y') && (answer != 'N'));
    return (answer == 'Y');
}
```

www.cs.colorado.edu/~main/appendix/useful.h and useful.cxx   **WWW**

Appendix J
Fundamental Style Guide

This appendix outlines three of our fundamental style guidelines.

Specifications with Preconditions and Postconditions

Each of our function's *behavior is specified with a precondition/postcondition contract.*

- For a function that is provided as part of a collection of functions, the contract appears in a comment at the top of the toolkit's header file.
- For a member function of a class that is provided with a header file and implementation file, the contract appears in a comment at the top of the class's header file.
- For a function that is implemented and used only in a ".cxx" file, the contract appears with the function's implementation in the ".cxx" file.

Capitalization

Variable names and *function names* are written with all lowercase letters. If the name consists of several words, then these words are separated by an underscore (such as eat_white).

Declared constants and member constants of a class are written with all uppercase letters. If the name consists of several words, then these words are separated by an underscore (such as MANY_COLUMNS). However, constant function parameters are written with lowercase letters (just like any other parameter).

New class names are written in lowercase, preferably as a noun. This differs from our first edition of the text (where we used an initial capital letter). The reason for the change is to better match the Standard Template Library, where class names are lowercase letters and the name of a template parameter (such as Item) has an initial capital.

Indentation

- Any statements grouped between brackets ('{' and '}') are indented four spaces. The brackets themselves appear on separate lines with no extra indentation. The only exceptions are the keywords *public*, *private*, or *protected* (in a class definition), which appear on lines by themselves with the same indentation as the brackets.
- In a loop or conditional statement with a one-line body (i.e., no brackets), the one line appears on a line by itself with four spaces of indentation beyond the loop or conditional statement.
- The statements that follow a case label of a switch statement are written with at least four spaces of indentation beyond the case label.

Appendix K
Downloading the GNU Compiler and Software

Many of our classes have used the GNU g++ compiler and related software from the Free Software Foundation. Although the compiler lacks a graphical interface, it does work well in combination with the emacs editor and the gdb debugger. In addition, our students can download the software to run on a typical Microsoft Windows® machine, and later find virtually the same programming environment on a Unix® or Linux® machine.

Our current version of the software comes primarily from the mingw32 GNU Windows tools, initially written by Colin Peters with significant modifications by Jan-Jaap van der Heijden and Mimit Khan. Other authors of our current tools include Geoff Voelker and Andrew Innes (ntemacs), Binu Jose Philip (dlgopen), Jean-loup Gailly (gunzip and tar), Steve Kirkendall (elvis), and Konstantine Knizhnik (winbgi). Overall, the tools include

- The g++ compiler for C++
- The GNU gdb debugger
- The GNU make facility
- NT emacs editor
- Elvis editor
- Winbgim graphics library for the GNU compiler

To download and install the software, please follow the directions at:

    www.cs.colorado.edu/~main/cs1300/README.html

Although we cannot provide technical support for this software, we have used it with over 1000 students with relatively few problems. The www.cs.colorado.edu/~main/cs1300/README.html page also contains links to some lab exercises that we use to introduce students to the compiler and related software.

Appendix L
Exception Handling

Using exception handling in C++ programs creates robust programs with error recovery. This allows programs to be safely reused as components in other programs, a key goal in object-oriented programming. When an exception occurs, there is considerable overhead in the run-time environment. Therefore, exception handling should be done with care, so as not to impact run-time speed under normal circumstances.

Throwing an Exception

Throughout the book, we have used the C assert facility to verify that arguments to a function were valid. When an invalid argument was detected, an assertion would fail and the program would print an appropriate error message before ending. An alternative is to "throw an exception" whenever an invalid argument is detected. Here's an example to show the syntax of throwing a particular kind of exception called domain_error, which is part of <stdexcept>. You can compare this example to our earlier version in Figure 1.1 on page 9.

```
#include <stdexcept>
using namespace std;

double celsius_to_fahrenheit(double c)
// Precondition: c is a Celsius temperature no less than absolute zero (-273.15).
// Postcondition: The return value is the temperature c converted to Fahrenheit degrees.
{
    const double MINIMUM_CELSIUS = -273.15; // Absolute zero in Celsius degrees

    if (c < MINIMUM_CELSIUS)
        throw new invalid_argument("Fahrenheit temperature is too small.");
    return (9.0 / 5.0) * c + 32;
}
```

The highlighted line is is an example of *throwing an exception*. The syntax consists of the keyword throw followed by an expression that creates some kind of exception object. The object that we have created is a new domain_error exception with a message that indicates what went wrong. There are a handful of other exception types, but domain_error is the type that is well suited to violations of a precondition.

Catching an Exception

Our new celsius_to_fahrenheit function may be used just like the original version. For example:

```
cout << "Enter a Fahrenheit temperature: ";
cin >> value;
f_value = celsius_to_fahrenheit(value);
```

With this code, if the user types a value that is below MINIMUM_CELSIUS, then the celsius_to_fahrenheit function will throw the exception. This will cause the program to halt with an appropriate error message. However, as the programmer who uses the exception-throwing celsius_to_fahrenheit function, we can take control, catch the exception and take some error-correcting action. The general form for taking this control involves two steps:

- The call to the function that might throw the exception is put inside a block with the keyword *try* at the front.
- After the *try* block, a new block of code (called the *catch* block) is inserted containing the code that will handle the error situation.

Here's an example that shows the format of the *catch* block:

```
bool valid;
double value, f_value;

do
{
    cout << "Enter a Fahrenheit temperature: ";
    cin >> value;
    try
    {
        f_value = celsius_to_fahrenheit(value);
        valid = true;
    }
    catch (domain_error)
    {   // Write an error message to cerr, which is the standard error output device.
        cerr << "Illegal input value. Please try again." << endl;
        valid = false;
    }
}
while (!valid);
```

If there are several kinds of exceptions that might be thrown, then the *try* block can be followed by several different *catch* blocks. You may create a *catch* block that catches any type of exception by using ellipses in the argument list: catch (...). This catch-all block should be placed at the end of the catch sequence so that it will not catch exceptions that are intended for more specific type parameters.

An exception that is caught can be given a name to use in the catch block. By giving the exception a name, you can then activate various member functions that are associated with the exception. The most useful member function is a function called what( ), which returns the string that was attached to the exception when it was created. With this in mind, we can rewrite our sample code as shown on the top of the next page. In the rewriting, we have also handled the possibility that the user has typed non-numeric input (using the technique for failed input shown on page 784).

```
bool valid;
double value, f_value;
string error_input;
```

```
do
{
    cout << "Enter a Fahrenheit temperature: ";
    cin >> value;
    if (!cin)
    {   // The user did not type a number:
        cin.clear( );                    // Fix the input stream.
        getline(cin, error_input); // Get the illegal line, so it isn't read again.
        cerr << "Please type a number." << endl;
        valid = false;
    }
    else
    {
        try
        {
            f_value = celsius_to_fahrenheit(value);
            valid = true;
        }
        catch (domain_error e)
        {
            cerr << e.what( ) << endl;
            valid = false;
        }
    }
}
while (!valid);
```

Exception Specification

It is good programming practice to inform the person using your function what exceptions you might throw. This is accomplished by writing an *exception specification* (also called a *throw list*), which appears after the argument list of the function header. For example:

```
double celsius_to_fahrenheit(double c)
throw (domain_error)
```

If more than one possible exception can be thrown in the function, the exceptions are listed, separated by commas. For example, suppose that our function could also throw an overflow_error when the resulting Fahrenheit temperature is beyond the legal range of double numbers. Then the heading would be:

```
double celsius_to_fahrenheit(double c)
throw (domain_error, overflow_error)
```

If a function has no exception specification, any type of exception can be thrown inside the body. If you want to specify that a function cannot possibly throw an exception, then put an empty list in the exception specification:

```
double supersafe(double c)
throw ( )
```

Uncaught Exceptions

An exception that is thrown in a function but is not caught has two possible cases. If there is an exception specification and the exception is not listed, then a function `unexpected( )` is called. On the other hand, if the exception is listed in the exception specification, the function `terminate( )` is called. The default behavior of `unexpected( )` is to call `terminate( )`, and the default behavior of `terminate( )` is to end the program. You may override the default behavior of these functions.

Standard Exceptions

The C++ Library provides a set of exceptions in the `<stdexcept>` facility. You can also define your own classes for exceptions, but it is often more efficient to use the standard exceptions. Here is a list of some of the standard exceptions arranged by class hierarchy:

```
exception
  logic_error
    domain_error (violation of a precondition)
    invalid_argument (invalid argument to a function)
    length_error (a length value has been requested larget than the maximum allowed)
    out_of_range (an index or similar value is outside the range for an array or similar object)
    bad_cast (an invalid dynamic type cast has occurred)
  runtime_error
    range_error (when a function returned, its postcondition was unexpectedly invalid)
            This can be used, for example, when a function interfaces with a physical device for
            measurements such as temperature or pressure, and the return value of the function
            is outside the physical realm of possibility. Don't confuse the range_error with
            out_of_range (although some early implementations of the STL vector made
            exactly this confusion).
    overflow_error (arithmetic overflow)
    bad_alloc (failure to allocate dynamic storage, usually by the new operator)
```

In the following example, the ranges of a vector are checked with an `out_of_range` exception:

```
vector <int> v(20);
int index, item;

cout << "Enter an index:\n";
cin >> index;
try
{
    item = v.at(index);
}
catch (out_of_range e)
{
    cerr << e.what() << endl;
}
```

We'll leave it to you to put this code inside of a loop that also checks for possible non-numeric input.

Index

Symbols

A

B